Coke.
The Royal Commission on the Losses and Services of American Loyalists, 1783-85.

Date Due

| | | | |
|---|---|---|---|
| | | | |
| | | | |
| | | | |
| | | | |
| | | | |
| | | | |
| | | | |
| | | | |
| | | | |
| | | | |
| | | | |

# MASS VIOLENCE IN AMERICA

MASS VIOLENCE IN AMERICA

[Coke, Daniel Parker]

# THE ROYAL COMMISSION ON THE LOSSES AND SERVICES OF AMERICAN LOYALISTS 1783 to 1785

*Edited by Hugh Edward Egerton*

ARNO PRESS & THE NEW YORK TIMES
*New York • 1969*

Reprinted from a copy in
The University of Chicago Library

*



*

Library of Congress Catalog Card No. 79–90166

*

Manufactured in the United States of America

# Editorial Note

NATIONS, LIKE MEN, ARE SOMETIMES INTERESTED IN BURYING THE PAST.

In early 1968, after more than five years marked by political assassinations, racial uprisings, campus disorders, mass demonstrations and the violent suppression of protest, *The New York Times Magazine* asked a group of distinguished scholars to reply to the question, "Is America by nature a violent society?" In answer, University of Chicago anthropologist Clifford Geertz wrote:

> "We do not know very well what kind of society we live in, what kind of history we have had, what kind of people we are. We are just now beginning to find out, the hard way . . ."

The proposition was astonishing but correct: what was least understood about domestic political violence was its role in American history. It was common knowledge that the United States had had a Revolution, a Civil War, some trouble with the Indians and a period of labor-management conflict. But one could search the shelves of the nation's great libraries without discovering more than a handful of works on the subject of violence in American history, and these hopelessly out of date.

Historians had generally ignored or soft-pedaled the history of farmer uprisings, native vigilantism, labor-management struggles, ethnic conflicts and race riots; comparative work in the history of social conflict was particularly weak. Sociologists and political scientists in the grip of "consensus" theory tended to treat episodes of mass violence in America as insignificant or aberrational—temporary exceptions to the norm of peaceful progress. Psychologists and behavioral scientists discussed "mob violence" in terms which suggested that riots, revolts, insurrections and official violence were the products of individual or group pathology. All such interpretations had the effect not only of minimizing group violence in America, but of depriving it of political content—hence, of relevance to the present.

As a result, as late as 1968, the rich, multifarious and often terrifying history of domestic political violence was still largely *terra incognita.* So long as most Americans wished to keep certain skeletons locked away in their closets, few scholars would attempt to open doors. Conversely, once the American people, frightened yet emboldened by the sudden reappearance of intense social conflict, began to ask new questions about the past, so did the scholars.

Our purpose in helping Arno Press and *The New York Times* select and publish significant documents in the history of political violence has not been to compound past errors by overemphasizing the role of conflict in American history. On the contrary, our aim has been to provide materials which will aid in the search for an accurate perspective on the present. MASS VIOLENCE IN AMERICA includes eyewitness reports, government documents and other descriptive and analytic material relating to mass political violence in the United States. These documents not only provide information—they give the "feel" or "flavor" of past eras of civil disorder by evoking the emotional and political context in which revolts took place. Most of them have long been out of print and are obtainable, if at all, only in the nation's largest libraries.

The scope of this series is wide, ranging from accounts of Indian warfare to descriptions of labor-management violence, from narratives of colonial insurrections to reports on modern racial uprisings. It is not, however, limitless, nor were the constituent volumes carelessly selected. The principle of coherence which guided the selections is implicit in the phrase "mass political violence." "Mass" denotes activity engaged in by large groups rather than individuals acting alone; "political" suggests a relationship between such activity and competition among domestic groups for power, property and prestige; and "violence" is narrowly construed as resulting in physical damage to persons or property. In short, the materials reproduced herein are intended to illuminate the resort to violence by American groups seeking to change or to preserve the status quo. Although historical, they are of interest to any who wishes to understand the causes, nature and direction of domestic political violence, whether they be social scientists, historians or just interested Americans.

Of course, we are particularly hopeful that these volumes will prove useful to those now engaged in curriculum-revision and the teaching of high school and college courses in the area of American studies. What Christopher Jencks and David Reisman term "the Academic Revolution" has made difficult demands on all educators, not the least of which is the demand for courses which are both relevant to the condition of modern America and of the highest academic quality. These volumes are meant to provide raw material for such courses—primary source matter which will help both instructors and students to deepen and enrich their views of the American experience.

Most important, the editors and publisher recognize that these volumes appear during a national crisis which is also a crisis of the spirit, a time in which the public response to various manifestations of civil disorder is increasingly governed by anger, fear and hysteria. In such an atmosphere it is important to recognize that one is not alone in time—that such events have taken place before in America and, unless fundamental changes in our social and political life take place, will probably recur in the future. Our fondest hope is that this work, and others like it, will help to keep alive, in a time of growing unreason, the spirit of reasoned inquiry.

RICHARD E. RUBENSTEIN
*The Adlai Stevenson Institute*
*Chicago, Illinois*

ROBERT M. FOGELSON
*Harvard-MIT Joint Center for Urban Studies*
*Cambridge, Massachusetts*

# THE ROYAL COMMISSION ON THE LOSSES AND SERVICES OF AMERICAN LOYALISTS

## 1783 to 1785

Painted by B. West P.R.A.

Drawn & Engraved by H. Moses.

RECEPTION OF THE AMERICAN LOYALISTS BY GREAT BRITAIN,

IN THE YEAR 1783.

# THE ROYAL COMMISSION ON THE LOSSES AND SERVICES OF AMERICAN LOYALISTS 1783 TO 1785

BEING THE

NOTES OF Mr. DANIEL PARKER COKE, M.P.

ONE OF THE COMMISSIONERS DURING THAT PERIOD

EDITED BY

HUGH EDWARD EGERTON

BEIT PROFESSOR OF COLONIAL HISTORY IN THE UNIVERSITY OF OXFORD

OXFORD

PRINTED FOR PRESENTATION TO THE MEMBERS OF

The Roxburghe Club

MDCCCCXV

DEDICATED AND PRESENTED

TO

THE PRESIDENT AND MEMBERS

OF

The Roxburghe Club

IN MEMORY OF

HIS EXCELLENCY THE

HON. WHITELAW REID

# The Roxburghe Club

M DCCCC XV

THE EARL OF ROSEBERY, K.G., K.T.

PRESIDENT

DUKE OF DEVONSHIRE, G.C.V.O.
DUKE OF PORTLAND, K.G., G.C.V.O.
DUKE OF NORTHUMBERLAND, K.G.
DUKE OF ROXBURGHE, K.T., M.V.O.
MARQUESS OF SALISBURY, G.C.V.O.
MARQUESS OF BATH.
MARQUESS OF CREWE, K.G.
EARL OF ILCHESTER.
EARL OF POWIS.
EARL BEAUCHAMP, K.G.
EARL BROWNLOW.
EARL OF PLYMOUTH.
VISCOUNT COKE.
LORD ALEXANDER THYNNE, M.P.
LORD C. FREDERICK BRUDENELL-BRUCE.
LORD ALDENHAM, *Vice-President.*
HON. JOHN FORTESCUE, M.V.O.
RIGHT HON. ARTHUR JAMES BALFOUR, M.P.
SIR JOHN STIRLING MAXWELL, BART.
SIR MARK SYKES, BART., M.P.
SIR WILLIAM OSLER, BART., M.D., F.R.S.
SIR EDWARD MAUNDE THOMPSON, G.C.B.
SIR FREDERIC KENYON, K.C.B.
LT.-COL. SIR GEORGE LINDSAY HOLFORD, K.C.V.O.
SIR GEORGE FREDERIC WARNER.
JOHN MURRAY, ESQ., C.V.O. *Treasurer.*
SYDNEY RICHARDSON CHRISTIE-MILLER, ESQ.
GEORGE EDWARD BRISCOE EYRE, ESQ.
CHARLES HARRY ST. JOHN HORNBY, ESQ.
MONTAGUE RHODES JAMES, ESQ. (*Provost of King's Coll., Cambridge*).
CHARLES W. DYSON PERRINS, ESQ.
CAPTAIN ARCHIBALD STIRLING OF KEIR.
HENRY YATES THOMPSON, ESQ.
MICHAEL TOMKINSON, ESQ.
VICTOR WILLIAM BATES VAN DE WEYER, ESQ.

*Mrs. Whitelaw Reid, widow of the lamented Ambassador of the United States, who left so delightful and abiding impression on this country, was anxious to present a book to the Roxburghe Club on behalf and in memory of her husband, who was not spared to do this himself. She therefore commissioned Lord Rosebery to act for her, and he found these manuscript volumes in the possession of Mr. Quaritch. He thought them suitable to the occasion, as not merely furnishing a congenial book for the Club, but also precious documents which might well be lodged in the United States under the care of Mrs. Reid.*

## DESCRIPTION OF FRONTISPIECE

The description of the Picture is as follows:

'Religion and Justice are represented extending the mantle of Britannia, whilst she herself is holding out her arm and shield to receive the Loyalists. Under the shield is the crown of Great Britain, surrounded by Loyalists. This group of figures consists of various characters, representing the Law, the Church, and the Government, with other inhabitants of North America; and, as a marked characteristic of that quarter of the Globe, an Indian chief extending one hand to Britannia, and pointing the other to a widow and orphans, rendered so by the Civil War; also a Negro and children looking up to Britannia in grateful remembrance of their emancipation from slavery. In a cloud, on which Religion and Justice rest, are seen in an opening glory the Genii of Great Britain and of America binding up the broken fasces of the two countries as emblematical of the treaty of peace and friendship between them. At the head of the group of Loyalists are likenesses of Sir William Pepperell, Bart., one of the Chairmen of their Agents to the Crown and Parliament of Great Britain, and William Franklin, Esq., son of Dr. Benjamin Franklin, who, having His Majesty's Commission as Governor of New Jersey, preserved his fidelity and loyalty to his sovereign from the commencement to the conclusion of the contest, notwithstanding powerful incitements to the contrary. He was arrested by order of Congress, and confined for two years, when he was finally exchanged. The two figures on the right are the painter, Mr. West, the President of the Royal Academy, and his lady, both natives of Pennsylvania.'

# PREFACE

The Coke Papers formed part of that very miscellaneous collection, the Phillipps MSS., and at its dispersion came into the possession of Mrs. Whitelaw Reid, the widow of the late American Ambassador. Of their history before forming part of the Phillipps MSS. I have been unable to find any trace. Their character is apparent on the surface. They are the first-hand notes by a trained lawyer of the evidence given before the Royal Commission of 1783 on the claims of the American loyalists, during the time that Mr. Daniel Parker Coke remained a Commissioner. If further proof is required, it is supplied by a note on p. 1159 of the *Ontario Bureau of Archives Second Report*, 1904, wherein Colonel Thomas Dundas, a colleague of Coke, states that the evidence in twelve cases, which were examined, while he was away in Scotland, reducing the 80th Regiment and attending the General Election, 1784, were 'copied from Mr. Parker Coke's Book, September, 1784'.

The few scholars, in the British Empire and the United States, who are interested in the story of the American loyalists, will assuredly not doubt the wisdom of publishing these Papers. Both the Books and Bundles, at the Public Record Office, dealing with the same cases, are, many of them, in such a state of decay that they cannot be used, and it is hopeless to look to that quarter for future publication.

On the other hand, the few interested in the subject may object that it is a pity that the Papers have not been published in their entirety. The answer to this is that it was necessary to compress the material published within the limits of a single volume; so that the choice lay between publishing in full the evidence relating to only a portion of the cases, or selecting the material portion of the evidence. In every case the *ipsissima verba* of the witness have been given, and nothing has, I think, been suppressed which deals with the general aspects of the history. What has been omitted concerns details of property, often meaningless without a knowledge, at the present time impossible, of local conditions. Nevertheless, where the evidence seemed to throw light on social and economic history, with regard to the price of land or of slaves, professional earnings, or otherwise, it has been included.

Some space might, indeed, have been secured by omitting the fifty-eight cases which have been already dealt with in the *Ontario Report*, mentioned above. Inasmuch, however, as some of these cases were of historical importance ; as the *Ontario Report* contained no explanatory notes ; and as, finally, these cases appear to have been included by an oversight in a bulky volume of 1436 pages, dealing with the cases inquired into in British North America, it seemed advisable to include them in one volume.

Where an obvious word has been omitted, or where a word has been repeated inadvertently, the necessary correction has been made. In matters of doubt a note has been appended. An introduction and general notes have been added for those unfamiliar with the details of the history.

The present publication is due to the generosity of Mrs. Whitelaw Reid, and to the historical insight of Lord Rosebery. I have to acknowledge with sincere gratitude advice given by Dr. A. G. Doughty, the Canadian Dominion Archivist, and Dr. J. Franklin Jameson, the Director of the Historical Department of the Carnegie Institution of Research at Washington. I have also to express my thanks to that indefatigable student of the history of the American loyalists, Professor Wilbur H. Siebert, of the Ohio State University, who first called my attention to the invaluable *Winslow Papers*, and who has furnished me with his own learned and suggestive papers on different phases of the subject.

H. E. EGERTON.

*October*, 1914.

# INTRODUCTION

THE time is past when it was necessary to speak with bated breath on behalf of the American loyalists. There has been a great change in the tone of American writers since Sabine first dared hesitatingly and half-heartedly to act as *advocatus diaboli*. Amongst serious thinkers the luminous judgement of Tyler in his *Literary History of the American Revolution* carried conviction; and the modern school of American historians occupy, as a matter of course, the position which he so valiantly won. None the less are our thanks especially due to Mr. Van Tyne and Mr. Flick for their singularly luminous and impartial researches in this field. Moreover the war between the North and South, if it did nothing else, brought home to thoughtful Americans the dangers of a Constitution in the ambiguities of which there was room for a divided allegiance; and, when a distinguished American historian, the direct descendant of one of the protagonists of the American Revolution, could tell an English audience that, in similar circumstances, he might have acted as acted General Robert Lee, the most patriotic American must recognize that at the earlier date it by no means followed that every honest man must have adhered to the American cause. For present purposes, however, this general question hardly concerns us; because the great majority of the cases dealt with in the following pages were the cases of British subjects who had only emigrated to America at a comparatively recent date. Many of these had actually served in the British Army; so that they were not likely to transfer their allegiance. There were cases, indeed, of men, such as Gates, Montgomery, and Charles Lee, who, having served under the Crown, became American officers; but such cases were naturally rare; and it is not uncharitable to suppose that in some of them, at any rate, ambition was the dominating motive. It is not, indeed, right to draw from the figures of the claims before the Commissioners the general conclusion that 'the active Tory of the American Revolution was such, in a majority of cases, because he had not become a thorough American', inasmuch as great numbers of the Tory democracy, of whom Mr. Van Tyne elsewhere speaks, did not possess property for which they could claim compensation. It is obviously dangerous to take the three thousand and odd claimants before the Commissioners as representative of the many thousands who became the founders of New Brunswick and Upper Canada; whilst, as these Papers prove, many even of these belonged to the poorer classes.

In order to understand the state of things recorded in these Papers it is necessary to form some idea of the relative strength of the two parties that stood confronted in the War of Independence. That the loyalists, whatever their numbers, showed themselves singularly incapable of influencing the course of events, must indeed be admitted ; and it is therefore natural to minimize their importance.

Their failure to influence the course of events was due to various causes. Being by nature conservative, they were naturally slow to act, and thus found themselves forestalled by their more active opponents. It was the belief of British officials such as Lord Dunmore that the extreme measures of the Committees would inevitably lead to reaction and disgust. 'The Associations', he wrote to Lord Dartmouth on December 24, 1774, 'first in part entered into by the Colony and adopted by the Continental Congress are now enforcing throughout the country with great rigour. A Committee is chosen in every county to carry the Association of the Congress into execution. They inspect the trade and correspondence of any merchant, watch the conduct of any inhabitant, may send for, catechise and stigmatise him if he does not appear to follow the laws of their Congress. Every city besides is arming an independent Company to protect their Committees and to be employed against Government should occasion require. As to the power of Government . . . it is entirely disregarded, if not wholly overturned. Not a Justice of the Peace acts except as a committee-man. Abolishing the Courts of Justice was the first step taken. The General Court is much the same ; for the lawyers refuse to attend, nor would the people allow them. Interposition of Government, in its present feeble state, would only suffer the disgrace of a disappointment.' So far the prospect is gloomy enough ; but then comes the consolation : 'Every step taken by these infatuated people must defeat its own purpose. The non-importation and non-exportation agreements cannot fail in time to produce a scarcity which will ruin thousands of families ; and, as to manufactures here, the people are not naturally industrious. The arbitrary proceedings of the Committees cannot likewise fail of raising quarrels and dissensions which will create partisans of Government. He is persuaded that this colony by its own acts and deeds must be brought to see the necessity of dependence on the Mother Country and of embracing its authority.'[1] It is obvious how great an influence considerations such as these may have had in leading Loyalists to put off from day to day open opposition to the measures of the majority. When the familiar argument about giving plenty of rope, so that the man might hang himself, seemed to appeal to a governor who was by no means conciliatory, it is obvious what weight it would carry in the minds of peaceable, opportunist citizens. Moreover, at first they had such complete trust in the invincibility of Great Britain that they did not deem action on their own part necessary. Again the British authorities, for a long time, showed themselves singularly incompetent

[1] *Hist. MSS. Comm.*, 14th Report, App., part x, *The Dartmouth MSS.*, vol. ii, 'Am. Papers,' p. 243.

for the work of organizing the loyalists ; Cornwallis being the first British general who understood their management. Edward Winslow, who as Master-Muster-General of the provincial forces spoke with especial authority on the subject, wrote to a correspondent in 1779 : 'The original design in the institution of the Provincial Corps was to employ as beneficially as possible such of the Americans . . . as inclined to serve in a military line, that those who were of consequence in the country might exert their influence in procuring recruits for the service of Government. In this light the plan was viewed by the King's friends assembled at Boston . . . and I have not forgotten with what alacrity the idea was adopted by many of the most respectable characters among the refugees. Such, however, was the situation of the British Army, their distress for provisions and other perplexing circumstances, that an effort to raise recruits then would have been impolitic and must have proved ineffectual. . . . The first provincial recruits that joined the army were a party called the New York Volunteers. They were collected about the North River before the troops appeared in that quarter. After some months they were forwarded to Halifax, where they arrived a few days before the embarkation of the troops. Here they were reviewed and formed into two companies, and Grant and Campbell were appointed captains. At that time it was urged that no provision was made or fund established from which these unfortunate men could be cloathed or accoutred, and they embarked with the troops with only the wretched remnant of the apparel in which they had escaped from the rebels six or eight months before. In this distress they landed at Staaten Island. A few small articles were bestowed on them while there, but nothing to relieve them essentially. On the famous August 27, 1776, when the rebels were subdued on this island, the two companies served together and distinguished themselves in such a manner as to extort the most particular compliments from the Commander-in-chief. Almost naked and extremely feeble from a long series of fatigues, they absolutely did not murmur, but appeared to realise that the rebels of that country were the original causes of all their misfortunes, and this consideration whetted their resentment to a great degree of keenness. But the inattention to this meritorious little party (altho' it had not the effect which might naturally have been expected on the members who composed it), was matter of serious concern to others. Sensible men who were zealots in the King's cause had anticipated the most cordial welcome and ample support to such as should join the troops. They were exceedingly disconcerted at the treatment of these Volunteers. It was not credible that a general whose command was so extensive could possibly want the power to furnish necessaries for 200 men, if his disposition towards them was favourable.' [1]

[1] *Winslow Papers*, edited by W. O. Raymond for the New Brunswick Hist. Soc., 1901, pp. 42-4.

Such was the state of things under Howe; nor were matters mended by the accession to power of Sir Henry Clinton. Edward Winslow wrote to Governor Wentworth in 1781: 'Having long since established in your mind . . . the propriety and expediency of employing the gentlemen of this country, I readily declared my resolution to engage in the provincial service. Till the present time I have seen no fair opening. The anticipations of impediments in the recruiting business, had it not been for the discouraging partiality shown to particular regiments, would never have discouraged me, but the necessity of contact with men whose ideas of service were different from my own was the obstacle that weighed most in my mind; for till lately there have been to all the Provincial Regiments recommendations of officers which were next to positive orders from the Commander-in-chief. . . . In one instance a plan as well digested as ever a recruiting officer formed failed merely from the difficulty of obtaining a pass from head-quarters to bring off the recruits, and 18 men who could have been doing duty as dragoons . . . are now suffering punishment in Simsbury Mines' (Connecticut). Again: 'In short it was evident that the General (Ruggles) had from the unpardonable inattention to him and from other causes contracted such a disgust to present men and measures here that he could neither negotiate with confidence nor serve with alacrity.'[1]

There was doubtless malice as well as exaggeration in the account given by the Americans of the contemptuous treatment accorded to the loyalists by their British comrades in arms; but considering the attitude generally taken up by the British officers towards the Americans in the Seven Years' War, and the natural contempt of the professional for the amateur, it is pretty certain that loyalists must have found very often their patience sorely tried.[2]

Whilst excellent work was done by loyalist leaders, many of whose cases will be found in the following papers, the system under which enlistment went on no doubt encouraged the enlistment of deserters and men unworthy of confidence. We find complaints of the licence given to enlist men through the prison bars, who could thus be released on easy terms without regard to their principles or character.[3] No wonder that Major Gray declared that he had been thirty years a soldier but had never had so much trouble as with these fellows.[4] 'The true spirit of a refugee loyalist', wrote Haldimand, 'driven from his country by persecution, is to carry arms, but there is no end to it if every man that comes in is to be considered and paid as an officer.'[5] Infinitely more harm, it was recog-

[1] *Winslow Papers*, p. 69.

[2] On the 'illegal and cruel treatment of Loyalists by the British military during the war' see *Hist. of New York during the Revolutionary War*, by T. Jones (vol. ii, ch. v), but, as is elsewhere emphasized, Jones must be read with caution.

[3] Brymner, *Can. Archives*, 1888, 'Haldimand Coll.', vol. ii, p. 653.

[4] Ibid., p. 641.

[5] Ibid., p 665

nized, had been sustained by friends of Government through recruiting parties than their services could ever atone for.[1]

A further cause of loyalist weakness was the uncertainty in which men stood with regard to their neighbours' opinions. Beverley Robinson, one of the most active and able of the loyalists, wrote to Ethan Allen in March 1780 that the reason for the long continuance of the war was that those who wished for an equitable connexion with Great Britain did not communicate their sentiments to each other ;[2] but his choice of a confidant shows the dangers of such communication. When to these causes are added the strange and unprecedented methods of carrying on the war employed by Great Britain—successive evacuations which of necessity shattered confidence ; hesitation and delays when a bold stroke could hardly have met with failure ; cruelty and repressive measures when conciliation was indispensable—we shall not be surprised if, in spite of their numbers, the loyalists found themselves at a hopeless disadvantage. Moreover, when the British authorities showed some energy, as in the case of Lord Dunmore and Governor Tryon, it took so questionable a shape as to shock the conservative instincts of many of the loyalists. Lord Dunmore having ravaged without result the portion of Virginia which touched the sea coast, and having made an ineffectual attempt to burn the town of Hampton, adopted a measure which the British military historian of the war recognized to have been so far from politic that it stimulated the minds of the Virginians almost to a degree of frenzy. He issued a Proclamation declaring martial law to be in force throughout the colony. He erected the royal standard to which he commanded His Majesty's subjects to repair, and he emancipated all the slaves who should take up arms in defence of the British cause. By these means he obtained a considerable accession of strength, but far below the force which he had expected. The British being in possession of the country between Norfolk and the sea, the Americans determined to put a stop to his proceedings. In November 1775 a detachment of about 1,000 men marched from Western Virginia to Norfolk, in the neighbourhood of which they arrived in December. The river Elizabeth running between them and the town, they were under the necessity of making a ten miles circuit to a village called the Great Bridge, where the river was fordable. Previously, however, to their arrival the bridge had been destroyed, and some works thrown up to prevent their passage by a body of loyalists, provincials and negroes. In these circumstances the Americans contented themselves with entrenching on the opposite side of the river. Lord Dunmore was impetuous and impatient. Accordingly he adopted a measure which was both doubtful and dangerous. An attack was made upon the American intrenchments which the Americans, having been forwarned, repelled with ease.

[1] Ibid., p. 729. [2] Ibid., p. 741.

The British were obliged to abandon not only their post on the Elizabeth but also Norfolk itself, the Americans taking possession of the town. The loyalists were now in the most pitiable condition. Provisions were scarce, and boats sent on shore to obtain fresh supplies were exposed to the fire of the Americans from the wharves. In consequence these wharves were, on January 1, 1776, set on fire. The Americans retaliated by burning the rest of the town; Norfolk being thus levelled to the dust. The damage done by its destruction was reckoned at some £400,000.[1] It is obvious how little these proceedings could have enured to the credit and popularity among the Virginians of the cause of Great Britain.

Not less unfortunate, though more deserving of success, was another project which obtained the approval of Lord Dunmore. This plan originated with Colonel Connolly, whose case is dealt with on a subsequent page. The plan was to invade Virginia and the southern colonies 'on their back and inland parts where it was known that the people were strongly attached to the British Government'. 'The projector, Mr. Connolly, was peculiarly fitted for the conduct of such an enterprise. He was active, enterprising, patient of fatigue, and he possessed that which is the soul of enterprise, unconquerable perseverance.' Notwithstanding the difficulties and dangers in the way, Connolly crossed the province of Virginia from Chesapeake Bay to the Ohio, a journey of between three and four hundred miles, negotiated a treaty with the Indians on that river, and brought over to his purpose the white people situated in those distant settlements. The intention was that Connolly in the spring of 1776 should collect at Pittsburg a British force. He was then to cross the Alleghanies and penetrate into Virginia. Leaving a strong garrison at Fort Cumberland, he was to sail down the Potomac and seize upon the town of Alexandria, where Dunmore was to join him with as many ships as possible. It was hoped by these means to cut off all communication between the northern and southern colonies, divided from each other by the Potomac.[2]

The whole scheme, however, came to nothing through the recognition of Connolly by an American whose suspicions were aroused. In consequence he was seized, thrown into prison, and though his papers were destroyed, his designs were already known to Congress, through the treachery of a friend entrusted with them. Connolly was sent a prisoner to Philadelphia, where he was put in irons and treated, as we shall see, with the utmost rigour. Once more a meditated blow on behalf of Great Britain had proved a veritable *coup manqué*. Once more to the people of Virginia the danger had been shown of following the fortunes of a Government which had on its side neither good management nor good luck.

Hardly more encouraging to British sympathizers was the conduct of Tryon,

[1] *Hist. of the American War*, by C. Stedman, 1794, vol. i, pp. 146–9.

[2] Stedman, op. cit., p. 150; *Col. John Connolly*, by F. R. Diffenderffer, Lancaster County (Pa.) Hist. Soc. Papers, vol. vii, no. 6, p. 121.

the Governor of New York. Tryon was an active and well-meaning public servant, who had, at the time, seen the true significance of the Boston tea-party.[1] But when war was once on foot he expressed the most bloodthirsty view in favour of employing the Indians against the Americans,[2] and the following pages will show that unless the witnesses seriously maligned him, he was not too scrupulous in his methods of assisting Great Britain. He seems to have encouraged loyalists to disguise their sentiments, so as to obtain influence over those with whom they came in contact; and he was almost certainly in the thick of plots such as that to assassinate Washington, which assuredly did not strengthen the cause of Great Britain in the sympathies of moderate men. It is probable that Tryon's expedition against Danbury in Connecticut in 1777, though from a military point of view it met with success, did more harm than good to the cause by the bitterness aroused by the destruction of property.

In North Carolina the fault lay not with the Governor but with the premature action of the loyalists themselves. In February 1776 a body of Scottish Highlanders and American Regulators, i.e. up-country residents, who had been refused fair treatment by the dominant majority, marched to Cross Creek. An American force under Colonel R. Caswell attacked them at Widow Moore's Creek Bridge on February 27 and put them to rout.[3] The depression caused by this failure and the stern measures taken by the Americans to stamp out disaffection cowed the people into submission; and, even when, at a later period of the war, the British seemed to have secured the ascendancy in the Carolinas, the note of confidence in the loyalists was still lacking. Governor Martin considered that egregious misconduct had contributed to the loyalist failure and that they might have made good their way, even with their small force, if they had been led with a little more prudence.[4]

In South Carolina the loyalists were very strong in the back country, and it is the opinion of Mr. McCrady, the patriotic historian of that province, that 'had Lord William Campbell (the Governor) at this time boldly gone up among the people of this section, had thrown himself upon Fletchall (the colonel of the militia who had declared for the King), collected his men around him and acted with promptness and efficiency, the whole proceedings of the Provincial Congress would have been overthrown.'[5] 'Had Lord William grasped the situation and appealed openly and boldly to the Upper Country, there is little reason to doubt but that the merchants in Charlestown and the planters on the coast would have risen with them and have overthrown the Council of Safety and their Government. For wiser purposes, however (says one), Providence had not so directed his actions, but left him in Charlestown to experience the daily loss of his executive powers

[1] *New York Col. Docs.*, vol. viii, p. 408.
[2] Ibid., vol. viii, p. 707.
[3] *N. Carolina Records*, vol. x, p. 482.
[4] Ibid., p. 735.
[5] *The Hist. of S. Car. in the Revolution, 1775–80*, by E. McCrady, 1901, p. 39.

and the little consideration in which he was holden as well by the public authorities as by the citizens at large.'[1] The treaty or *modus vivendi* drawn up between the loyalists and continentals at Ninety Six on September 16, 1775, though it shocked the loyal feelings of the more stalwart Tories, showed at any rate how much the loyalist strength had impressed its adversaries. The failure of the expedition of 1776 under Admiral Parker and Sir H. Clinton against Charlestown did not improve the loyalist position. 'The expedition which so confidently set out to crush and subjugate the southern colonies was utterly defeated, and these colonies were relieved for three years from invasion, to remain a source of strength and supply to their friends at the North;'[2] but with what consequence to those who had put their faith in the strength and ubiquity of the British power can easily be imagined. Nor were the Cherokee Indians, who, with the approval of the British authorities, brought destruction and death upon the American settlements in the back country, likely to inquire too curiously whether the victims of their raids were or were not American insurgents. No doubt 'the Indian uprising was injurious to His Majesty's cause in Carolina. The fact that these savages had been instigated by the agents of the royal Government to rise up on the people of the frontier, and indiscriminately to massacre the king's friends as well as his enemies, roused great indignation and resentment, and turned many a supporter of the royal cause to the new Government'.[3] Moreover, the complete success of the Americans against the Indians was an object-lesson in the strength of the new Government. According to Mr. Van Tyne, in Georgia, where the loyalists were strong, it was the sending of a British squadron to Savannah which changed the situation. 'The insult ruined the work of Wright (the prudent governor); the Whigs seized the governor and such of the Crown officers as had not fled, and, at once, in February 1776, assembled a provincial congress.'[4] Not a little affecting was Wright's speech to the Assembly on January 18, 1775: 'I have lived and presided over you upwards of fourteen years. . . . I have a real and affectionate regard for the people and it grieves me that a province I have been so long in and which I have seen nurtured by the crown . . . should by the imprudence and rashness of some inconsiderate people be plunged into a state of distress and ruin.'[5]

In considering the history we note that although the actual power of the British governor, without the command of the public purse, was doubtless small, indirectly his influence was still considerable. The violence with which the provinces entered into the revolutionary war depended in no small degree upon the terms upon which they had stood with their respective governors. Thus

[1] *The Hist. of S. Car. in the Revolution, 1775–80*, by E. McCrady, 1901, p. 40. [2] Ibid., p. 161.
[3] Ibid., p. 199. [4] *The Loyalists in the Am. Revolution*, by C. H. Van Tyne, 1902, pp. 97–8.
[5] G. White, *Hist. Collections of Georgia*, p. 51.

Maryland, where Sir Robert Eden's conduct of affairs had been a model of tact and discretion, excited the scorn of its sister provinces for the half-hearted manner in which it dealt with the Crown authorities. Had Lieutenant-Governor Bull been Governor of South Carolina and had Governor Martin in North Carolina met with a little more luck, the Carolinas might possibly have been for some time saved for the Crown; and considering the strength of the loyalists in New York, who can doubt but that an adroit and popular governor might have kept it attached to the British interest? Similarly the character and conduct of Dunmore played no little part in deciding the uncompromising attitude taken up by the oldest and the most English of the American provinces.

Unfortunately there is more to be said. The excesses and depredations of the British and Hessian troops disgusted men of all parties.[1] These troops made no distinction between the property of rebels and of loyalists; indeed, inasmuch as the former had often hidden their goods, the latter in fact seem to have suffered the most. According to contemporary accounts, the progress of the British and Hessian troops through New Jersey was attended with such scenes of desolation and outrage as would disgrace the most barbarous nations; though these men at any rate did not claim to be apostles of culture. 'Jersey', an American wrote, 'will be the most whiggish colony on the continent. The very Quakers declare for taking up arms. You cannot imagine the distress of the country. They have stripped everybody almost without distinction even of all their clothes and have beat and abused men, women, and children in the most cruel manner ever heard of.'[2]

It may help readers who, like the present writer, are of necessity ignorant of the economic conditions prevailing in the southern districts of which we hear so much in the following Papers, to quote the account given in Professor U. B. Phillips's Introduction to volumes i and ii of *Plantation and Frontier Documents, 1649–1863*.

'1. The Chesapeake Lowlands and the eastern part of the neighbouring hill country were the seat of the tobacco industry, then yielding what was still the most important staple on the continent. By far the most of the output was produced by the plantation system and by far the most of the labourers were negro slaves.

[1] *Am. Archives*, 5th ser., vol. ii, p. 1188. It should be noted that Mr. Fortescue throws doubts on the charges of misbehaviour by the British troops on the ground (1) that they were denied by Howe; (2) that Stedman's support of them rested mainly on the evidence of a 'renegade', J. Galloway; and (3) that affidavits are 'cheap in times of revolution'. But Howe's laxity of administration was too notorious to make his denial of real value, and if a renegade is one who advocates moderate reforms and then, when these are refused, prefers the *status quo* to disruption, it is perhaps a pity that there were not more 'renegades'. I presume that American, like other affidavits, differ in weight and quality. The overwhelming argument in favour of the general truth of the accusations is the complete change in the sympathies of the inhabitants after the passage of the troops, a change which seems well attested.

[2] Ibid., p. 1487.

The units of plantation industry were relatively small, ranging usually below twenty and often below ten field hands to the plantation. There was a large number also of free farmers and an appreciable number of indented servants, especially in Maryland. The lands in the older parts of the districts were by this time largely exhausted and industry somewhat depressed. Eastern Virginia on the whole had begun to pass the zenith of her prosperity. The tobacco staple was a resource of decreasing value, and many people were finding it necessary to resort instead to the production of food-stuffs for market. A readjustment was beginning which involved the decline of the plantation system in that district. There was a striking dearth of towns and of manufacturing. The trade of most planters with London was inconveniently remote. The towns of Baltimore, Annapolis, Norfolk, and Richmond were rising to some little consequence; but the Virginia-Maryland community on the whole was overwhelmingly rural. Across the North Carolina boundary the district about Albemarle Sound was merely a subprovince of the Chesapeake region. By this time it had receiyed some slave-holding immigrants, from Virginia, and thus added to its small farming population a certain number of tobacco planters.

2. The Shenandoah Valley and most of the Piedmont country from Maryland to Eastern Georgia was now occupied by a large but thinly scattered population of backwoods farmers, whose area of occupation touched the plantation district in Virginia, but was widely separated from it in the Carolinas and Georgia by the intervening pine-barrens. The western portion of these settlements were made of the frontier complexion. The main advance guard of the pioneers, however, had now reached the 'western waters' in what we now call Eastern Tennessee, and the most adventurous of them had recently crossed the barrier of the Cumberland range and staked out claims in central Kentucky and the Nashville district.

'3. The South Carolina-Georgia lowlands were a segregated area occupied by plantations of a large average size and with but few non-slaveholding farmers. Most of the unattached working men who by chance entered this district either took employment in the commercial towns or pushed across the pine-barrens to join the backwoodsmen of the Piedmont.'[1]

Such being in rough outline the character of the country, it is at first sight somewhat surprising to find that it was in the second of these three southern districts that the strength of loyalism lay. The frontiersman is almost inevitably a radical, and it was this class which largely decided, some ninety years later, the issue of the American Civil War. But there were special circumstances which, at the time of the War of Independence, made the frontiersman less zealous on behalf of the American claims. To begin with, a considerable immigrant population had hardly had time to become good Americans. Especially, the numerous body of Scottish Highlanders had little understanding of, or sympathy with, American political ideals. Moreover, the western frontiersman saw himself denied civic equality by the jealousy and cunning of the eastern districts; and between the known injustice of the colonial

[1] pp. 83–4.

Assembly and the unknown, and to him largely hypothetical, injustice of Great Britain, might well prefer the less acute and definite of the two evils. The Scottish-Irish Presbyterian immigrants to South Carolina from Pennsylvania found on their arrival a state of things prevailing profoundly jarring to their deepest convictions. 'The system of government was based here, as it had been in the old country which he had left, upon the Church of England. He could only be represented in the Assembly by having the lands which he and his people had taken up made into a township and then into a parish.' [1]

The existence of the Regulators in South Carolina, a kind of law and order league, organized for the purpose of inflicting summary punishment on criminals, through the neglect of the colonial authority to provide local courts, was a dangerous symptom of disunion, though it may be true that the responsibility for refusing its sanction to a remedy lay with the home Government which disallowed the South Carolina Act of April 1768 for establishing courts.[2] Still, whether rightly or not, the western districts of the Carolinas were in little sympathy with the eastern at the time of the beginning of the troubles. 'These newcomers', in Mr. McCrady's words, 'were reluctantly to enter the contest with the royal Government inaugurated upon the coast.' It is perhaps the deepest disgrace to British statesmanship and strategy amongst the melancholy records of this time of shame that the words which follow seem equally true. 'But, goaded into it by the folly and cruelty of the British army, were to turn upon the invaders and by their stubborn resistance and heroic conduct were to wrest from them the fruits of their success in the low country.' [3]

Great stress has been laid upon the calculations of John Adams and Thomas McKean as to the numbers of the loyalists, made in after years. But for practical purposes it is more important to note how the question presented itself to the men of the time. In a confidential letter to Silas Deane, dated October 1, 1776, the Committee of Safety wrote: 'The only source of uneasiness amongst us arises from the number of Tories we find in every state. They are more numerous than formerly and speak more openly; but Tories are now of various kinds and various principles. Some are so from real attachment to Great Britain; some from interested views; many, very many, from fear of the British forces; some because they are dissatisfied with the general measures of Congress; more because they disapprove of the men in power and the measures in their respective states.' [4] Similarly Washington wrote to his brother in the same month: 'Between you and me I think our affairs are in a very bad condition; not so much from the apprehension of General Howe's army as from the defection of New York, New Jersey,

[1] McCrady, *Hist. of S. Car. under the Royal Gov., 1719–76*, pp. 314–15.
[2] *Acts of the Privy Council, Colonial Series, 1766–83*, pp. 166–71.
[3] McCrady, op. cit., p. 320.
[4] Force, *Am. Archives*, 5th ser., vol. ii, p. 821.

and Pennsylvania. In short the conduct of the Jerseys has been infamous. Instead of turning out to defend their country and affording aid to our army, they are making submissions as fast as they can.' [1] How strong was the position of loyalism in Pennsylvania may be gauged from the fact that we find a list of no less than 495 names of persons proclaimed traitors during the war.[2] We are thus able to explain the extraordinary bitterness which characterized the relations between the republicans and the loyalists. Though a bully is not necessarily a coward, still fear begets cruelty ; and in this unhappy contest both sides were afraid of each other. Familiar as we have become with the details of many cases of cruel persecution, we are apt, at least on this side of the Atlantic, to regard the loyalists as so many harmless victims, the easy prey of their powerful persecutors. But, in fact, tarring and feathering and the like were a game which both sides, when the opportunity occurred, could carry on. Thus, in March 1775, a deponent swore that he had been tarred and feathered by a party of English soldiers with the knowledge and approval of their colonel.[3] In Dutchess County, New York, the Whigs believed that they were in so much danger from the disaffected that strong measures were necessary.[4] It was fear that led to an act of retaliation such as the following : 'James Smith, Esq., a judge of the Court of Common Pleas for that county, was very handsomely tarred and feathered for acting in open contempt of the Resolves of the County Committee. . . . The Judge undertook to sue for and recover the arms taken from the Tories, by order of the said Committee ; and actually committed one of the committee, who assisted at disarming the Tories. Which enraged the people so much that they rose and rescued the prisoner, and poured out their resentment on the villanous retailer of the law.' [5] Tarring and feathering were a rough-and-ready method of dealing with offenders whose cases were not deemed worthy of more serious treatment. Thus on December 6, 1775, in New Jersey one T. Randolph, a cooper, 'being judged a person of not consequence enough for severer punishment, was ordered to be stripped naked, well coated with tar and feathers and carried in a wagon publicly round the town. As he soon became duly sensible of his offence, he was released. . . . The whole was conducted with that regularity and decorum that ought to be observed at all public punishments.' [6] There were complaints from Westchester County that the Tories were getting the upper hand and threatening these people daily. They were equipped and constantly in arms, walking about at night six, eight, or ten at a time.[7] Some of the counties treated the Provincial Congress as non-existent. Washington himself was seriously alarmed at the condition of affairs. He recommended more drastic measures against the Tories. 'Why should persons

[1] Force, *Am. Archives*, 5th ser., vol. iii, p. 1275.
[2] *Penns. Archives*, 4th ser., vol. iii, pp. 937–45.
[3] *Am. Archives*, 4th ser., vol. ii, p. 94.
[4] Ibid., vol. iii, p. 467.
[5] Ibid., p. 823.
[6] Ibid., vol. iv, p. 203.
[7] Ibid., p. 1321.

who are preying upon the vitals of their country be suffered to stalk at large ? '[1] In July 1776 a plot was discovered at Albany to set the town on fire in different places and to blow up the magazine. In the absence of soldiers the citizens took turns in guarding the jail and magazine.[2] In this state of things men nervously complained that the Declaration of Independence must be followed by a Declaration of High Treason.[3] The state could not exist without the extermination of traitors. ' It it amazingly wonderful ', an American wrote on July 17, ' that having no capital punishment for our intestine enemies we have not been utterly ruined before now.' [4] In a later letter the same correspondent insisted that the people were clamouring that some of the big Tories must be hung. Unless strong measures were taken it would be impossible to resist this cry.[5]

We have complaints from the Manor of Livingston of outrages committed by the Tories.[6] An American officer wrote to General Heath on November 25, 1776 : ' Every man and I was going to say every woman within a large circle of this place (Camp Ramapaugh) who stand for Whigs, and are, for aught I know, are constantly distressing me with their fears and apprehensions of the Tories.' [7] The behaviour of some of the militias caused Washington to apprehend the presence of treason in the ranks.[8] From Orangetown, New York, we hear of the Tories making great havoc, and insulting and abusing the Whigs in a manner not to be borne.[9] The Tories, not content with joining the enemy, insulted and disarmed the Whigs, stripping them of their cattle, effects, &c.[10] It was the presence of this active, dominant fear which led to the enunciation of doctrines such as that ' every Tory is a coward ; a man under such influence, though he might be cruel, could never be brave '.[11] It is only fair when we read the treatment accorded to a Francis Green, mobbed and hustled merely because he had signed a loyal address,[12] or a James Murray, bullied and persecuted for remaining faithful to the Crown,[13] or an Israel Williams nearly burnt alive by a brutal mob,[14] to remember that there was another side to the shield, and that Tories, when they got the upper hand, were not above using the methods of their Whig antagonists.

But it may be said, granting that fear accounts for much of the extreme bitterness which characterized, during the war, the mutual relations of Whig and Tory, how came it that, when the struggle was over, and the Republicans had gained once and for all the day, the bitterness still continued, indeed, if

[1] Ibid., p. 1389. [2] Ibid., p. 1563. [3] Ibid., 5th ser., vol. i, p. 357.
[4] Ibid., p. 403. [5] Ibid., p. 700. [6] Ibid., vol. iii, p. 242. [7] Ibid., p. 840.
[8] Ibid., p. 1232. [9] Ibid., p. 1123. [10] Ibid., p. 1169.
[11] Ibid., p. 1292, quoted from ' The American Crisis ', Phil., No. 1.
[12] See *Nova Scotia Hist. Soc. Collections*, xiii, ' The Life and Times of the Rev. J. Wiswell ', by E. M. Saunders, p. 12.
[13] *The Letters of James Murray, Loyalist*, ed. by N. M. Tiffany, Boston, 1901.
[14] Rivington's *New York Gazetteer*, March 9, 1775.

anything grew in intensity and volume? The answer to this question lies, I think, in the fact that a new fear had taken the place of the old. The American Revolution was not in its origin or intention a social revolution, its aims and ideals having been purely political; nevertheless a revolution must of necessity have social consequences; and the effect of the American Revolution had been to give economic, as well as political, power to the *nouvelles couches sociales* which the revolution had evoked. To take a single instance: consider the social effect of the distribution of James de Lancey's landed property among some two hundred and seventy-five owners. The Tory view was that, at the time of the Stamp Act agitation, the better classes had allowed the mob to get the upper hand; and, ever afterwards, found it impossible to regain the control. Whatever there may have been of prejudice in this view, it is, I think, impossible to deny that the revolution involved a forward movement, all along the line, in the direction of democracy, which the restoration of the Tories to their property and civic rights would have done much to arrest.[1] Even as things were, we know how strong were the conservatives, represented by men like Washington, Hamilton, and John Adams, and how it took some twenty years for Jeffersonian radicalism to win its way. To those who believe that the conservative forces of society are an indispensable element to the well-being of a political community the action of the Americans, in deliberately weakening such forces, will seem a blunder, bound to be big with future mischief; but, apart from grounds of expediency, from their point of view, leaving aside the undertakings of the Treaty, there was not a little to be said for the course adopted by the Americans. The loyalists had deliberately denied the right of the Americans to found a new nation; largely through their exertions the task of founding such nation had been costly in blood and treasure; was it unnatural to look upon them with distrust as future citizens and to maintain that their property had been justly forfeited by their past conduct? It is impossible here to deal in detail with the action of the various states with regard to the property of loyalists. As an example we may take the leading state of Massachusetts. Here two bills had been passed in the April of 1779, the one directed against the estates of Mandamus Councillors, Commissioners of Customs, and certain other royal office holders, the other against the estates of refugees in general. By the former the estates of the persons therein named were confiscated without hearing. In the general Confiscation Act there were detailed provisions regarding the mode of trial where such estates were in question. Under the fifth article of the Treaty

[1] Since the above was written, President Hadley, of Yale University, in lecturing at Oxford, has laid great stress on the fact that democracy did not really prevail in the United States till after 1820; but everything is a question of degree, and it cannot, I think, be denied that the Revolution did involve a distinct step forward, in the direction of democracy, though the ultimate goal might still be far off.

of Paris, 1783, it will be remembered that Congress earnestly recommended to the several states that the estates, rights, and properties of loyalists should be restored to them, they refunding to any persons who might be in possession the bona fide price which such persons might have paid on purchasing such lands or properties since their confiscation. In what manner, then, did the leading state of Massachusetts deal with this recommendation ? (It is of course clear that the American Peace Commissioners had no power to bind the respective states in this matter.) 'The first step taken by the Legislature', writes an American historian, 'after it was furnished with the knowledge of these recommendations, was to put forth efforts to close up the estates of absentees. . . . The first Act passed in which the obligations of the Treaty were distinctly recognized was the Act for repealing the laws of this state and for asserting the right of this free and sovereign commonwealth to expel such aliens as may be dangerous to the peace and good order of government.' Absentees were pronounced to be aliens. Acts against absentees were formally repealed, but absentees mentioned in the Confiscation Act, or who had borne arms against the country in the late war who should return with the intent to reside, were to be reported upon by Justices of the Peace to the Government; and if they did not immediately depart from the state, when so directed, were to be committed to jail.[1]

Such then was the object-lesson in the 'spirit of conciliation' given by the most experienced and capable of the American legislatures; let us glance for a moment at the public opinion of which such legislation was the inevitable outcome. In May 1783 S. Jarvis, a lieutenant in the South Carolina Royalists, ventured to pay his father a visit at Danbury, Connecticut, the scene of Tryon's exploits. Forthwith he was visited by the populace and informed that he must immediately retire; at present they did not intend to hurt him, but if he was seen within thirty miles of Danbury after sunset, he must stand the consequences, for they would not answer for his safety. In vain he presented his permit from the authority and select men of Danbury to visit his father. They damned the authority that would allow such a person as he was to come into the country. 'Several other people', Jarvis wrote, 'have been punished very severely, carried on a rail and then mounted on horseback without a saddle, with their face to the horse's tail, their coat turned, and a wooden sword by their side; then drove back and forth to the great joy and satisfaction of the spectators.'[2] One T. Hassard wrote in July 1783 that on his way to 'git' his property so that he might go to 'Noviscosia' he put into 'Rhodyisland' and went on shore to see his family. 'Was seased upon

[1] A full account is given of this subject in chapter iii of *The Confiscation of John Chandler's Estate*, by A. McFarland Davis, Boston, 1903.

[2] *Hist. MSS. Comm., Am. MSS. in R. Inst.*, vol. iv, p. 155. See also on Stephen Jarvis, *Can. Mag.*, vol. xxvi, p. 366.

and was put to prison and kep five days in prison, and my vessel seased upon and broken open and plundered and my chest broke open and plundered and abused. Threatned to take my life and made me pay them the most exstravagant charges for it and then sent me here (New York) by a warent from the governor; never to return upon the pane of death. And I thort it was proper to inform your Excelencey of it; and if the frends of government is to be treated in this manner and no notis taken of it, I should be glad to know how to conduct myself for the futer.'[1] In September 1783 one D. Bonnet had a writ served against him for what he knew not; but afterwards learnt it was on a pretext of enticing away a slave in 1776. The sum claimed was £200. He was ordered to quit the country on pain of being tied to a tree and receiving five hundred lashes.[2] From a New York loyalist we have a graphic account of the state of things prevailing. With a wife and eleven children he knows no quarter in the city where any loyal subject could hope for protection, or the benefit of the provisional articles. 'The country in general is under the dominion of Committees, and there can be no confidence even in the new erected Government, which the Committees despise. Mr. Clinton (the Governor of New York state) indeed talks favourably to those who are oppressed and against the usurped power of committeemen, but they find no relief. The language of the Committees is that none shall rule but the majority of the people, and that the Committees represent the majority—that the acts and agreements of the Congress, the legislatures, governors, and rulers are all to be subject to the will of the people expressed by the committees; and upon this principle they hold the provisional articles to be not binding, for that the Congress had no authority to give to the Commissioners but what shall be controllable by the Committees, as the representatives of the majority of the people.' An exchange had been made of a farm in Dutchess County for one on Long Island, with Governor Clinton's knowledge and approval, and yet after the removal of the Long Island proprietor to Dutchess County he was abused by the local committee, whipped thirty-nine lashes, and a resolution made to repeat the whipping if he remained twenty-four hours in the precincts and to give the same punishment to such as harboured or assisted him. The transaction had been reported to Governor Clinton, but it was followed with no remedy.[3] It is evident that public opinion was too strong for the authorities, weak as they were, to act in defiance of it. We have a suggestive affidavit from one Peter Stout in September. He had been confined in a New Jersey jail in 1782 for some four months and released on giving bond for £1,000 not to leave the country. After the peace repeated applications to be released were refused. He then asked his security to surrender him and he

[1] *Hist. MSS. Comm., Am. MSS. in R. Inst.*, vol. iv, p. 242.
[2] Ibid., p. 353.
[3] Ibid., pp. 359–60.

was confined in a dungeon in irons till his 'antient mother' conveyed to one John Burrows her life interest in the deponent's confiscated estate, upon which he was at once released.[1] A refugee who returned to Rhode Island after the peace was taken up on a charge of joining the British and returning to the colony. He was thrown into jail, then brought before the Assembly and banished. In this case the property had been already sold, so there was less motive for the cruelty.[2] More instructive is the statement of Cavalier Jouet, one of our claimants.

'Some little time after the publication of an armistice between the belligerent Powers, I thought it might prove of use to myself and family to pass into the Jerseys, and speculate on the spirit and temper of the times there, in order to determine whether it would be feasible to replace my wife and children in the Township where they formerly resided, for the purpose of a more easy maintenance of them and to be in the way, with the assistance of their friends, of finally recovering their property; and accordingly I pitched upon the neighbourhood of Woodbridge to make my entrance, where I had been subject for near three years past in the capacity of a prisoner of war on my parole given to General Washington, in consequence of a parole of a like nature given by a certain John Hampton to his Excellency Sir H. Clinton. . . . In this place where I had received much civility, for a course of time, as well from the particular party, who captured me, as from the inhabitants in general, between whom and myself had passed a reciprocation of good offices, they frequently granting me real indulgences that were not common to every one in a like predicament with myself, and I embracing every opportunity to make all possible acknowledgements consistent with my avowal of the strictest loyalty and fidelity to the cause of my rightful sovereign, I say in this place I received the most outrageous insults, and narrowly escaped the most shameful and degrading abuse. A number of fellows came about me with sticks and whips (the most of whom had *formerly* treated me with *great courtesy*) telling me the case was altered now; that when a prisoner of war, they thought it incumbent to be civil to me, but the peace had dissolved all paroles, and I had no right or title to come there, and they were determined to give me (as they insultingly termed it) a *continental jacket*. I expostulated with them whether I had ever injured any of *them* or others they had heard of in their properties; or had so much as in the slightest manner affronted their persons; in answer to which they told me that I had proved a traitor to my country and joined the enemy and they were determined that no such damned rascals should ever enjoy the benefits of the country again; and had with the approbation of the magistrates of the township entered into an association for the purpose of expelling every rascal that attempted to come into it in like form as they meant to treat me, by whipping them out again. Near or at this juncture came General Heard, of their militia, and appeared to aggravate the spirit of the mob very much by pointedly asking them what they meant to do with that *damned rascal*? And a justice Freeman coming up shortly after called out aloud, *Hang him up, hang him up*. A justice Bloomfield, too, who finally showed a disposition to appease the spirit that had arisen in the people

[1] Ibid., p. 368. [2] Ibid., p. 451.

first told me it was a crime to come there, and on my enquiring whether their conduct was authorised by the magistracy, he said so far as that they had entered into an Association *with the knowledge of the magistrates* to treat persons coming as I had done in such sort, and believed they would find no redress. In short it was with infinite difficulty I escaped their clutches with all the assistance I could get from a certain Thomas Edgar who pleaded that he had received favours from one of my sons when a prisoner under his charge, and held himself under obligations to the family; and from the benevolent interposition of their clergyman, Mr. Rowe, who in every instance and respect behaved very much like a Christian and a gentleman.

'I could mention many other circumstances expressive of a most intolerant spirit prevailing amongst them, but I have been already too prolix.' [1]

Such being the temper of the Americans we can understand something of the panic and despair which took hold of the loyalists when they at last realized that peace was to be made with their enemies. A striking picture of their feelings is given in a letter of Benjamin Thompson to Lord Sackville, dated August 6, 1782.

'You cannot conceive nor can any language describe the distress that all ranks of people here (New York) have been thrown into by the intelligence of the independence of America being acknowledged by Great Britain, and the loyalists being given up to the mercy of their enemies. The militia, who for some weeks have done the whole of the garrison duty in this city, have refused to serve any longer, and the general has been obliged to relieve them by bringing regular troops into town. The loyalists at Lloyds Nek and the other posts are in a state of anarchy and confusion, little short of actual rebellion. Papers have been stuck up about town, inviting Sir G. Carleton to take the command of the army here and to oppose by force the measures of the new administration, and promising thousands to assist him. In short a universal despair and phrenzy prevails within these lines, and I should not be very surprised if very alarming consequences were to follow from the temper people are in. They seem to be as void of prudence as they are destitute of hope, and a kind of language is now spoken publicly in the streets that is enough to make us tremble for what is to follow from these convulsions. The provincial corps will disband of themselves, or what is infinitely more to be dreaded, they will take arms in opposition to these measures. They feel themselves deeply injured.' [2]

Confronted by this attitude, it is obvious what a wall of prejudice and suspicion the Commissioners on their claims had to surmount in entering upon their labours. Here and there indeed a more cool-headed loyalist looked on matters in another light. Peter van Schaack wrote to his brother on March 4, 1783: 'Are there no descriptions of loyalists but such whose estates have been confiscated? are none relieved by the Treaty such as it is? . . . Is it nothing that

[1] Letter of Cavalier Jouet, May 4, 1783, *Hist. MSS. Comm., Am. MSS.* in *R. Inst.*, vol. iv, pp. 69–70.
[2] *Hist. MSS. Comm., Stopford-Sackville MSS.*, vol. ii, 'Papers Relating to the Am. War,' pp. 252–3.

the numbers who have little or no property and can get their bread in America and who would otherwise have been compelled to quit it are now enabled to remain there?'[1] But van Schaack's attitude was exceptional; and the almost universal feeling was one of deep resentment against a great betrayal. Upon this point Samuel Curwen, representing the left wing of the loyalist party, was at one with Dr. Peter Oliver, who belonged to the extreme right. 'Expectation is on tiptoe,' wrote Curwen in February 1783 respecting the result of the commissioners Wilmot and Coke. 'Think you that while this spirit lasts we useless, burdensome aliens shall escape untouched? that we dogs shall be longer suffered to take the bread out of the children's mouths? I trow not.'[2] Peter Oliver wrote in July 1784: 'We are obliged to put up with every insult from this ungrateful people the English without any redress—as witness the cruel neglect from those who had publicly declared in our favour. What are commissioners chose for? Not to make good our losses. What are all the promises of protection and retribution? but to mortify, insult, and disappoint . . . and I have the best authority to say we are well off if our small pittance is not taken from us. Blessed are ye, who expecteth . . . nothing for ye then will not be disappointed.'[3] 'This huge, unwieldy town', wrote J. H. Cruger from London on March 28, 1784, 'swarms with Americans grumbling and discontented; in two or three years it is said we may know what Government will or will not allow us for the loss of property, for services, &c.'[4] The feelings of these men can be understood and excused, living as they were in exile, having lost most of their property, compelled to jostle among strangers, sometimes ill mannered, and at the best not too liberally endowed with social tact. Still, so far as was within the power of Great Britain, the loyalists were treated with justice and generosity; and it is not a little disappointing to find a distinguished Canadian historian, Dr. Kingsford, refurbishing the old weapons. 'The bill (appointing Commissioners) was passed', he writes, 'at the end of June. Notwithstanding the urgent circumstances under which the Committee had been appointed, there was no meeting of the Commissioners until September, and it is not a pleasant fact to record. The investigations were carried on from year to year until 1788. During this inexcusable delay bitter disappointment and suffering were felt on the part of those interested, and this culpable dilatoriness on the part of the Commissioners is a painful passage in the history of these times, for admitting that great difficulty in the adjustment of these claims presented itself, five years taken to the consideration of them was an unwarrantable period . . . . Such was the endeavour of the Imperial Government to relieve the sufferings of those who had

[1] *The Life of Peter van Schaack*, by H. C. van Schaack, New York, 1842, p. 322.
[2] Sam. Curwen's *Journal and Letters . . . from 1775 to 1784*, ed. by G. A. Ward, 1842.
[3] T. Hutchinson's *Diary and Letters*, ed. by P. O. Hutchinson, 1886, vol. ii, pp. 408–9.
[4] Raymond, *Winslow Papers*, p. 174.

lost all in her cause. The great ground of complaint is that it was not put forth more energetically and rapidly. As we read the clauses of the treaty affecting the loyalists and the proceedings which followed in the United States to stay the enforcement of them the words of Livy must rise to our minds: "Nimis callidi exsolvendi iurisiurandi interpretes." '[1] Far more judicial was the tone of Colonel Beverley Robinson, himself one of the claimants, who wrote on April 29, 1784: 'The affair of the loyalists goes on but slowly; these troublesome elections have taken up the time and attention of the Commissioners for some time, but they are going on again: they seem to take great pains and pay attention to our unhappy situation, but they have a troublesome and difficult task to get thro'. Many very extraordinary claims are put in such as you would be astonished to see. . . . As the matter is like to be so very tedious, the Commissioners have recommended, I believe, most that have applied for a temporary support from £40 to £200 a year which is the highest they can go.'[2]

Mr. Wilmot afterwards explained that why the Commissioners did not meet till September was that one of them could not sooner return from Ireland, but preliminary work was done which facilitated their subsequent inquiries. In reading Kingsford's remarks, no one would gather that the great majority of these claimants were already receiving a subsistence allowance from the Treasury, and that however hard their general position, there was no need for extreme urgency in the decision of their claims. In July 1782 Lord Shelbourne had appointed Wilmot and Coke to inquire into the cases of the American sufferers, both of those who were already in receipt of public assistance and of those who were claiming it. They undertook this 'arduous and invidious' task on the express condition that they should not receive any payment for it. Hitherto they had both been those *rarae aves* in an eighteenth-century Parliament, independent members, and they did not wish to expose themselves to the charge of being parties to a ministerial job, or of being under ministerial influence. Both of them had generally opposed, on independent lines, the Government's American policy. Of the three hundred and fifteen persons in the Treasury list, the allowance of fifty-six was suspended, from want of appearance; though most of them appeared and received an allowance at a later date. Twenty-five claimants either did not come within the description of American loyalists or appeared to have no just claim to relief from Parliament. In most cases the allowance was somewhat reduced, but in ten cases it was adjudged too small and was accordingly raised. Some four hundred and twenty-eight new cases were added to the list, so that when the Commission began its work an annual sum of £43,245 was being distributed amongst American loyalists. The title of the Act was altered so as to make

[1] *The Hist. of Canada*, by W. Kingsford, vol. vii, pp. 216–17.
[2] Raymond, *Winslow Papers*, p. 198.

loyalty the corner-stone, the ground-work of the whole. Commissioners were to be appointed 'to enquire into the losses and services of all such persons who have suffered in their rights, properties, and professions during the late unhappy dissensions in America in consequence of their loyalty to his Majesty and attachment to the British Government'. In this state of things the point of inquiry, in Wilmot's words, 'was the loyalty and conduct of the claimant . . . Though, in general, the Commissioners found the loyalty of the party uniform and unequivocal, yet there were some who had not been early in the part they had taken, and others who had at first taken part with the Americans; and, as the Commissioners thought it was their duty to place them in separate classes, not knowing whether Government or Parliament might or might not make any distinction in this respect, it became a necessary but an invidious and arduous part of the enquiry in some of these claims'.[1]

As a comment on Kingsford's charge of dilatoriness we may note Wilmot's statement that the evenings were devoted to inquiring into cases requiring immediate relief. In July 1784 the Commissioners found that they had, notwithstanding their utmost assiduity, been able to hear and determine the cases of persons claiming property only to the amount of £534,705, whereas the amount claimed by the whole number of claimants at that date was £7,046,278. It was of course easy to complain of the careful manner in which the Commissioners went to work. Stress has been laid on the fact that there were only twelve fraudulent claims amongst the whole number. But, considering the character of the fraudulent claims which were made during the first months of the Commission, it is more than probable that, had not the Commissioners shown, by the exhaustiveness of their inquiries, how difficult it would be to overreach them, their subsequent experience might have been very different. Assuredly the Ministry were singularly fortunate in their choice of Commissioners. No better tribunal could be found than one consisting of keen lawyers, who were also men of the world, and soldiers, who had had practical knowledge of American affairs. Wilmot was the son of a distinguished judge, whose biography he wrote. He was at first intended for the Church, but finally chose the Bar, becoming a Master in Chancery. He seems to have been a man of exceptional highmindedness; and it is impossible to read his apologia of the Commission without recognizing the dignity and zeal with which he carried through his task. The verdict of history has upon the whole made good his claim that whatever may be said of this unfortunate war, all the world has been unanimous in applauding the justice and humanity of Great Britain in rewarding the services and in compensating with a liberal hand the

[1] *Hist. View of the Commission for inquiring into the losses, services, and the claims of the Am. Loyalists at the close of the War . . . in 1783: with an account of the compensation granted to them by Parliament in 1785 and 1788*, by J. Eardley-Wilmot, 1815, p. 11.

losses of those who suffered so much for their firm and faithful adherence to the British Government. It was only fair that one who had recognized the expediency and necessity of the peace should have been the chief instrument to make its consequences less disastrous to those who had suffered for their loyalty to the British connexion.

No less fitted for the work was the Commissioner to whose industry we owe the transcripts of the evidence here published. Mr. Daniel Parker Coke may have been less devoted to the work, in that, after two years, he resigned his position as Commissioner. But, while he remained a Commissioner, no one could have been more active and zealous. When at last in 1788 Pitt explained his plan of dealing with the claims of the loyalists, Coke maintained that the loyalists who had been resident in America when the war broke out should be paid in full; whilst Wilmot explained that he had always expected that the full amount reported to be due by the Commissioners was to be paid to the claimants.[1] The Tory who could say, 'Had I been in Birmingham when Dr. Priestly's property was attacked, I would have lost my life in his defence', was assuredly no mere party hack; as was further evidenced by Coke's suggestion 'to impose a tax upon the stalls of deans and prebendaries, and upon pews appropriated to private persons'. His opposition to the formation of volunteer corps, without the sanction of Parliament, and his bold defence of the right of landlords to exercise influence over their tenants smacked of the same sturdy independence. 'Judged by the standard of the time', we are told, 'his public career was marked by independence, moderation, and sober feeling.' But these qualities, coupled with a legal training and the judicial faculty of weighing evidence, were precisely the qualities essential for an inquiry of this character.

Curiously enough, both Colonel Kingston and Colonel Dundas had been connected, indirectly, with the two great British tragedies of the American War. It was Major Kingston, then adjutant-general, who was sent by Burgoyne to the American camp with the offer of entering into negotiations for surrender; and his repudiation of the terms at first offered may have led Gates to recognize the danger of driving the British army to desperation; though no doubt Gates's main motive in conceding more favourable terms was an exaggerated fear of Clinton's resources. Colonel Dundas had been, along with Major Ross, the messenger by whom Cornwallis had conveyed to Washington his determination to capitulate. He had been a doubtless unwilling party to the tenth article of that Capitulation, by which the loyalists who had joined the army were delivered over to be treated at the discretion of the American civil power. It is true that the serious consequences of this article had been evaded, through the loyalists being smuggled away in the

[1] *Hans.*, vol. xxvii, p. 615.

sloop of war which Cornwallis was allowed to dispatch to head-quarters. Nevertheless the apparent treachery and disgrace of the article must have been revolting to the generous feelings of a brave officer. He may well have looked upon his work upon the Commission as in the nature of reparation for this gloomy episode. Otherwise Dundas's record in the war was glorious enough. Being given the command of a brigade, under Cornwallis, he especially distinguished himself at the engagement at James City Island. 'The brunt of the action fell', wrote George Damer to Lord George Germain, 'on this Brigade, and particularly upon the two young regiments, who did themselves great credit, having by their coolness and attention to their officers completely routed the three lines opposed to them with two pieces of cannon which they took in little more than an hour. Colonel Dundas distinguished himself very particularly and invited the approbation of my Lord Cornwallis given to him in the handsomest terms and manner.' [1] It is noteworthy that Cornwallis, when Governor-General of India afterwards, in 1788, wrote to the home authorities: 'I doubt your being able to persevere in the military line in your choice of governors. . . . I have before mentioned the names of some others and particularly of Colonel Thomas Dundas.' [2]

More than once in the inquiry these officers were able to bring their personal knowledge of men and places to bear upon the cases before them; and it is evident from Colonel Dundas's proceedings in British North America that he was eminently fitted for the purpose in hand.

Of the other civilian Commissioner I have sought in vain to obtain knowledge. Inasmuch as Wilmot says that the beginning of the Commissioners' proceedings was delayed by one of their number being in Ireland, and I have found in the Treasury Minute Book (April 1783 to January 1784) a direction that Mr. Marsh, Navy Agent at Cork, should be at once summoned to London, the inference is natural that he was summoned for the purpose of acting as Commissioner. In this case he was probably the Mr. John Marsh who died as Chairman of the Victualling Board in 1817.

With regard to the Commission generally, it has proved very difficult to find contemporary notices. I have looked in vain through the newspaper files of the year 1783 in the British Museum, and researches in the Manuscript Room and at the Record Office have been equally fruitless. If there are such notices, and they have been overlooked, it is not from want of searching for them.

Such being the personnel of the Commission, it is necessary to say a word as to the manner of their procedure. It must be remembered that they were not enacting the part of final arbiters, awarding compensation as they saw fit. They

[1] *Hist. MSS. Com., Stopford-Sackville MSS.*, vol. ii; *Papers relating to the Am. War*, p. 210.
[2] *Correspondence of Charles, first Marquess Cornwallis*, ed. by C. Ross, 3 vols., 1859, vol. i, p. 377.

were merely a Court of Advice, recommending cases to the Government and Parliament, with whom would afterwards rest the final settlement. In this state of things it was necessary to arrange the claimants in certain defined classes. The first was of those who had performed exceptional services on behalf of Great Britain. The second class was of those who had borne arms against the Revolution. The third was of uniform loyalists. The fourth, of loyalists resident in Great Britain. The fifth, of those who took the oath of allegiance to the Americans but afterwards joined the British. The last consisted of those who bore arms for the Americans, but afterwards joined the British forces. It proved quite impossible to maintain a hard-and-fast barrier between these different classes and to arrange them in marks of comparative merit. For instance, Joseph Galloway might have been described as at first adhering to the cause of the Americans ; but he had done far more service to Great Britain than many who had been out-and-out Tories from the first. In their attempt to weigh motives the Commissioners were confronted with psychological problems incapable of solution. It is clear from several of these cases that, at one time, the general opinion in the Middle and Southern colonies was that the cause of Great Britain must in the end prevail. What merit, then, attached to men who at first had adhered to the Americans, had then transferred their favours to what they thought was the winning power, and had found themselves unable afterwards to suit their politics to the course of events ? The answer could only be that, if they had finished as loyalists, and, as such, had suffered losses, it was impossible to inquire too curiously into their moral merits. At first Pitt intended that those who had borne arms or been of service should receive 40 per cent. of their claim against 30 per cent. received by the other classes, but it proved impossible to maintain this distinction or indeed to make any difference in the treatment of the classes most widely separated.

The Act of 1783 expired in 1785, and, on its renewal in that year, the Government asked Parliament to distribute on account the sum of £150,000, in part payment of the claims already examined and adjudicated upon. No doubt the ignorance in which the claimants stood of the grounds and principles on which the Commissioners had proceeded, in arriving at awards which largely reduced the amount claimed, called forth a feeling of uncertainty and fear which added to the not unnatural discontent. At the same time the Commissioners were clearly of opinion that they could not give this information, without the authority of Ministers and of Parliament, and for the time being it was thought that their Reports should remain secret documents. On the suggestion being made in Parliament, in June 1785, that some publicity should be given to the Reports of the Commissioners, Wilmot remarked that they consisted of 246 large folio volumes, so that it would be impossible to lay their substance before the House. Dealing in this manner merely with the names of the claimants could be productive of no good, and might do much harm by incensing friend against friend and brother against brother.[1] Nevertheless, the secrecy, combined with the long delay, gave rise to natural ill-feeling. A correspondent wrote to the *Morning Chronicle* on May 30, 1785: 'Notwithstanding the great assiduity of the Commissioners for two years, no more than four hundred claims out of two thousands and upwards have been yet examined. At this rate and in the present mode it will require five or six years to go through all the claims; and, if the loyalists are kept in their present state of suspense and no compensation is made to any of them for five or six years to come, then I aver that it will be an act of mercy in Government to order them, with their wives and children, to be instantly shot or strangled.'[2] In fact, the rules and principles on which the Commissioners acted were simple enough. In the first place, they disallowed all claims for uncultivated lands, where the conditions of the grants had not been complied with; and only allowed the purchase-money actually given, when such lands had been the objects of sale, and the fees of patenting and surveying, when they had not. This rule seems obvious, but, as we shall see in the papers, in the easy-going, slovenly public opinion of the eighteenth century, the matter did not seem clear even to distinguished governors and lieutenant-governors, and the Commissioners thought it necessary to fortify their position by the considered opinion of the Attorney-General. Next, the Commissioners invariably disallowed purchases after the beginning of the troubles; except where they were made in parts in full possession of the British authorities, or where there was some urgent necessity of investing moneys in land. This rule again seems fairly self-evident. A man could hardly be called a loyal subject who gambled in lands under American occupation. Further the Commissioners disallowed all rents and profits of estates and all estimated profits of offices, professions, and trades which accrued during the duration of the troubles. These they regarded as not peculiar to loyalists, and as met by the grants of temporary support.

Claims upon the Government for work done, money expended on, or goods furnished to the army or navy, were obviously not 'losses in consequence of loyalty'. Neither were such incidents of war as losses occasioned by the action of the rival armies. Similarly losses resulting for a depreciated paper currency were felt by all the inhabitants and were not a special consequence of loyalty. The Commissioners held it to be outside their province to advise compensation for debts due to the claimants from Americans. These could not technically be treated as losses, the Treaty of Paris having provided that creditors, on either side, should

[1] *Gentleman's Mag.*, vol. lv, part ii, p. 871.

[2] *Morning Chronicle*, June 3, 1785.

meet with no lawful impediment in the recovery of the full value of such debts in lawful money. They, however, judged it proper to receive an account of such debts, as stated by the claimants, for the information of Government; and the result was a subsequent Commission, intended as a Joint Commission, consisting of British and American members; the final outcome of which was that the British and loyalist creditors obtained, years after, a very partial and inadequate satisfaction of their claims. With this very confused chapter of the history we need not, however, for present purposes concern ourselves.

In their first Report dated August 10, 1784, the Commissioners wrote:

'The following descriptions of claims (which have likewise been subject-matter of doubt) we have considered as falling within the extent of our inquiry.

1. Losses of property in the United States, sustained by persons of undoubted loyalty, who have resided in England or elsewhere, out of the limits of the United States, before or during the troubles; and which losses have been sustained in consequence of their loyalty and adherence to the British Government.

2. Losses of offices for life, or during the pleasure of the Crown, possessed before the breaking out of the disturbances.

3. Losses of professional income which the party was accustomed to acquire before the commencement of the troubles.

4. Claims of real and personal representatives for losses sustained by deceased loyalists, such claimants proving the loyalty of themselves as well as of the persons they represent.'

'The principle', they added, 'which has directed our mode of conducting the inquiry, has been that of requiring the very best evidence which the nature and circumstances of each case will admit: we have in no case, hitherto, thought fit to dispense with the personal appearance and examination of the claimant, conceiving that the inquiry would be extremely imperfect, and insecure against fraud and misrepresentation, if we had not the advantage of cross-examining the party himself as well as his witnesses; nor have we for the same reason allowed much weight to any testimony that has not been delivered on oath before ourselves. We have investigated with great strictness the titles to real property, wherever the necessary documents could be exhibited to us, and when they have not been produced we have required satisfactory evidence of their loss, or of the inability of the claimant to procure them.'

But, in spite of strict rules and careful practice, there was a block in the path that no strictness or care could surmount. Their principal and most obvious difficulty, inseparable from the nature of the inquiry, was the ascertainment of the value of the property proved to be lost. 'In the investigation of matters of fact', they ruefully wrote, 'the judgement is only in danger of being misled by wilful, false testimony; but the estimate of value is the subject-matter of opinion, in which the most upright must ever be liable to differ even concerning ordinary objects; and with respect to landed property in America, they will perhaps rarely concur, because it is reducible to no fixed standard or mode of estimate; but the value of such estate is so distinctly dependent upon its peculiar circumstances, in respect of local situation and state of cultivation or improvement, that, in general, it will not afford a rule whereby to measure that of the estate next adjacent. These difficulties are not a little augmented by our distance from the spot, and scanty means of information drawn in great measure from the memories of persons not unconcerned in the issue of the inquiry. Aware of the extent of this difficulty at the outset, and sensible of the influences of interest and prejudice upon the testimony likely to be offered in the cases of individuals, we employed a considerable part of our time in applying ourselves to every source we could discover from whence general information might be drawn, as to the value of the different species of property, real and personal, in the different provinces; we examined the most intelligent and most respectable characters from each province, and by comparison of their several accounts with each other, and with the other evidence we were able to procure, we endeavoured to acquire such knowledge of the subject as might in some degree shield us from fallacy and imposition. But, after every precaution we were able to adopt, it is almost needless for us to confess that we have found ourselves in many instances of landed property at a remote distance from certainty. In most cases we have been obliged to depend for information upon such witnesses as the claimant produced to us, but whenever we could find out any persons of character possessing knowledge of the subject-matter, we have on our authority sent for and examined them.' At a later date a great improvement was made by the sending of a new Commissioner, Mr. John Anstey, to America to inquire upon the spot with regard to values; but it must be confessed that, for the period with which alone we are here concerned, this part of the inquiry leaves on one an impression of extreme vagueness, reminding the present editor of the remark of a kindly clergyman at his old home who, when it was suggested to him that he was being cheated by the local coal merchant, replied with regard to the coal that there seemed a good lot of it. We all know what a difficult matter it is, even in the most favourable circumstances, to arrive at any general agreement in matters of valuation. What wonder was it when the lands were situated upon the other side of the Atlantic, when the witnesses were for the most part more or less prejudiced, being largely past or future claimants, when the state of things inquired into belonged to a dead past, buried under the cataclysm of a political and social revolution, that this branch of the Commissioners' work proved wellnigh insoluble?

In brief the plan proposed by Pitt and approved by Parliament was to pay the full amount of their losses in the case of loyalists whose losses did not exceed the sum of £10,000, making deductions upon an increasing scale when the losses exceeded that amount after payment of the first £10,000.[1]

In the case of loyalists who had lost the benefit of either offices or of professional incomes, the plan was to put such persons upon half pay when the income lost amounted to not more than £400 per annum. Those whose losses were greater were to be paid 40 per cent. for every £100 of such income, about £400 when the value did not exceed £1,500 altogether. Where it did exceed £1,500, the proportion was to be reduced to 30 per cent. Although there had been indignant letters in the newspapers denouncing the injustice of not paying the claims in full, the conclusion reached seems to have fairly met the equities of the case.

The twelfth and final Report of the Commissioners belongs to a date (May 15, 1789) of course much later than the cases here dealt with, but it may be interesting to inspect the general statement of claims made by and losses liquidated of American loyalists as appended to the Report set out on the next page.

The general result in 1790, according to Wilmot, was that the number of claims preferred in England and British North America had been 3,225.

| | | |
|---|---|---|
| Of these were examined . . . | | 2,291 |
| Disallowed . . . . | 343 | |
| Withdrawn . . . . | 38 | |
| Not presented . . . . | 553 | |
| | — | 934 |
| | | 3,225 |

The total amount of claims preferred had been £10,358,413. The total amount of claims examined had been £8,216,126. The amount awarded on such claims was £3,033,091.

The amount of pension paid to two hundred and four loyalists on account of losses of office or profession was £25,785 per annum, besides annual allowances to five hundred and eighty-eight persons, chiefly widows, orphans, or merchants who had no means of livelihood, though they had lost no real or personal estate.

[1] There is a careful *résumé* of Pitt's speech of June 8, 1788, in the *Annual Register* of 1788, pp. 136–9.

## LOSSES OF PROPERTY CLAIMS UNDER THE ACTS OF 1783 AND 1785

| | *No. of Claims.* | *Amount of Claims.* £ | s. | *Losses Allowed.* £ | s. |
|---|---|---|---|---|---|
| 1. Loyalists who have rendered services to Great Britain . . . . . . | 176 | 1,904,632 | 4 | 640,090 | 19 |
| 2. Loyalists who bore arms in the service of Great Britain . . . . | 252 | 1,040,506 | 6 | 263,135 | 6 |
| 3. Loyalists zealous and uniform . . | 414 | 1,744,429 | 18 | 531,616 | 4 |
| 4. Loyal British subjects resident in Great Britain . . . . . . . | 31 | 342,139 | 4 | 140,927 | 0 |
| 5. Loyalists who took oaths to the American States, but afterwards joined the British . . . . . . . | 22 | 137,718 | 3 | 36,530 | 0 |
| 6. Loyalists who bore arms for the American States, but afterwards joined the British . . . . . . . | 13 | 103,362 | 19 | 26,738 | 1 |
| 7. Loyalists sustaining losses under the Prohibitory Act, 21 (N.B. of the 21, 15 are included in other classes) . . | 6 | 31,427 | 1 | 14,412 | 13 |
| 8. Loyal British proprietors . . . . | 2 | 537,854 | 0 | 290,000 | 0 |
| 9. Loyalists now subjects or settled inhabitants of the United States, some of whom are persons of great merit and have met with peculiar hardships . | 21 | 51,578 | 0 | 20,077 | 0 |
| 10. Claims disallowed and withdrawn: | | | | | |
| (i) Disallowed for want of proof of loyalty . . . . . 5 | | | | | |
| (ii) Disallowed for want of satisfactory proof of loss . . 189 | | | | | |
| (iii) Disallowed, being fraudulent . 9 | 243 | | | | |
| (iv) Disallowed, being for debts only . . . . . . 16 | | | | | |
| (v) Withdrawn . . . . . 24 | | | | | |
| 11. Loyal British subjects who appear to have relief provided for them by the Treaty of Peace, but state the utter impossibility of procuring it . . | 2 | | | 13,270 | 0 |
| 12. Claims presented but not prosecuted . | 448 | 959,387 | 19 | | |
| | 1,630 | £6,857,035 | 14 | £1,976,797 | 3 |

## LOSSES OF INCOME

| | *No. of Claims.* | *Amount of Claims.* £ | *Losses Allowed.* £ |
|---|---|---|---|
| Claims for losses of income which have been allowed . . . . . . . | 252 | 92,388 | 75,234 |
| Claims for a person not a subject or inhabitant of the United States . . . | 1 | 600 | 500 |
| Claims where the parties have died since their claims were examined . . . | 15 | 4,683 | 3,838 |
| Claims which have been disallowed . . | 30 | 9,685 | |
| | 298 | £107,356 | £79,572 |

LOSSES OF PROPERTY UNDER THE ACTS OF 1783 AND 1785 OF CLAIMANTS IN BRITISH NORTH AMERICA

| | *No. of Claims.* | *Amount of Claims.* | | | *Losses Allowed.* | | |
|---|---|---|---|---|---|---|---|
| | | £ | *s.* | *d.* | £ | *s.* | *d.* |
| 1. Loyalists who have rendered services to Great Britain . . . . . . | 74 | | | | 99,765 | 7 | 6 |
| 2. Loyalists who bore arms in the service of Great Britain . . . . . . | 857 | | | | 125,146 | 0 | 0 |
| 3. Loyalists zealous and uniform . . . | 293 | | | | 88,676 | 14 | 0 |
| 4. Loyalist British subjects resident in Great Britain . . . . . . . | 1 | | | | 700 | 0 | 0 |
| 5. Loyalists who took oaths to the American States, but afterwards joined the British | 12 | | | | 1,635 | 0 | 0 |
| 6. Loyalists who bore arms for the American States, but afterwards joined the British . | 7 | | | | 4,484 | 15 | 0 |
| 7. Loyalists sustaining loss under the Prohibitory Act . . . . . | 3 | | | | 1,554 | 0 | 0 |
| | 1,247 | £919,322 | 9 | 5 | £321,961 | 16 | 6 |

It should be noted that the above Lists do not include the claims under an Act of 1788, the chief claimants under which were the two Penns, who received £500,000 against a claim of £944,817; but I confess that I cannot altogether reconcile the different figures given in the Commissioners' Report and in Wilmot's book.

(The Reports are set out in the *Second Report of the Bureau of Archives for the Province of Ontario* by A. Fraser, provincial Archivist. Toronto, 1905.)

It remains to say a few words upon the character of these claimants. The best general evidence as to this is the impression they left upon the minds of the Commissioners. These men spent long hours in private conference with them and their witnesses, and saw them as it is seldom given to us to see other men. What then was the testimony of Messrs Coke and Wilmot? In a debate in the House of Commons on June 26, 1786, on the motion for the House to go into a Committee upon the Appropriation Bill, which contained a grant of £175,500 for the relief of the American loyalists, Mr. Coke 'observed that when he entered upon the execution of his duty as a Commissioner to investigate the cases of these unfortunate sufferers, he was far from having a predilection in their favour; but that, in the course of his inquiries, he had discovered such merit and sufferings, and such fidelity and attachment to the Government that he now entertained the warmest sentiments in their favour, that he always considered the House pledged to grant the full amount of the losses, as they were liquidated, and, under that idea, he had been intent to pass them down and reject them unless they were proved in the most satisfactory manner. That he was surprised after the House had been called upon to grant £700,000 for the purpose of erecting useless fortifications, there could be any hesitation to comply with a demand so evidently founded on the principles of justice and humanity.' [1]

'Mr. Wilmot began with observing that when he entered upon his duty as a Commissioner, the conduct and the situation of the loyalists had raised in his mind a predilection in their favour, which continually increased as he proceeded in the business. That for near four years past his daily and almost his hourly labour had been employed in that service, and, during the course of it, he had received such proofs of fidelity and attachment and sufferings and distress as in his opinion justly entitled them to every mark of favour and attention which the Government could confer. . . . It was his earnest wish the House could replace them in situations equal to what they had lost in America. But that was not possible; double the sum liquidated by the Commissioners would not indemnify them; and, besides, most of them had to lament the loss of a husband, father, son, or brother, who fell in defence of the cause of his country.' [2]

In turning to the individual cases, the first thing that strikes one is their very miscellaneous character. In this crowd the peer and ex-colonial governor are found side by side with the liberated slave. The aristocracy of New England and New York receive no more careful treatment than the British immigrant tradesman or mechanic. In reading the history, one fails to realize the extent of the immigration that took place to America from the British Isles, amongst those who were not merely the victims of British economic oppression. A large proportion of this immigration consisted, it is true, of soldiers retired from the service. Still, there were many civilians of humble rank. But, in spite of its miscellaneous character, this assemblage divides itself, under close scrutiny, into certain distinct classes. To begin with, in order to be done with an unsavoury subject, mention must be made of the fraudulent claimants. Stress has been laid upon the fewness of their numbers. But, considering the proportion of fraudulent claimants amongst those appearing in the first months of the Commission, the inference is probable that it was only the drastic and salutary treatment they received at the hands of the Commissioners which frightened off impostors. Human nature is so complex in character that it by no means follows that, because a man is a brave soldier, he may not also be a consummate scoundrel. The present writer has been told of a man who left, at the time of the South African War, a calling too infamous to be named amongst honest men, to behave as a soldier with conspicuous gallantry, and then returned, unblushing and without hesitation, to his life of shame. Thus it need not surprise us that the most conspicuous figure among the fraudulent here exposed seems to have been no fraud in the field of action. In tracing the pretensions of Ferdinand Smyth (p. 127), who afterwards added the name of Stuart, his claim being that he was the great-grandson of Charles II, admirers of George

[1] *Ontario Bureau of Archives Report*, 1904, p. 1316.

[2] Ibid., p. 1317.

Meredith will recall the immortal memory of Roy Richmond. It is the advantage of the novelist over the historian that the former can keep his pleasant scoundrel in an environment where he need not be tempted more than he is able. Hardly less interesting in his way is the busybody Samuel Hake (p. 155), the tradesman who becomes bankrupt in spite of, perhaps because of, a particular kind of ability; the type of man whom an honest soldier recognized as good company for General Arnold.[1] It does not speak very highly for the critical judgement of the Board of Trade that one George Boyd, chosen by them to be a councillor (p. 348), was declared by several witnesses to be in fact not a loyalist, the Commissioners pronouncing his claim to be fraudulent. It is, however, needless to go seriatim through our Black List. It is enough to note that such a class had a very definite existence.

Turning to more reputable company we note the great number of Scottish Highlanders amongst our claimants. Out of sixty names beginning with the letter M amongst the claimants here dealt with, no less than thirty-seven have the prefix Mac; and other Scottish names such as Murray, Menzies, and Munro tell the same tale. We find somewhat querulous complaints that the Scottish Highlanders had been treated with great kindness on their arrival by the American people and had then turned against their benefactors. But all this was nothing to the point. The fact was that these Highlanders were still in the feudal stage of civilization; and that personal services to a Macdonald or whoever might be the chief counted for much more than recognition of a political organization which was beyond their understanding. Be this as it may, the claims of the poor but still canny Scotsmen are a leading feature of this volume.

Again, there is a long procession of officials, from those who were a power in the land to the humble tide-waiter and lowest custom-house official. The interests of all these were inextricably bound up with the past system of government, and it was inevitable that they should feel the first shock of the earthquake. Ranged with these were the representatives of the colonial aristocracy, who, no more than in England, thought it shame to add to their patrimony by the loaves and fishes of fees pertaining to office. Still, the members of the colonial-born aristocracy stand on a different footing from the official classes. To the New England representatives dealt with in the following pages we may apply the words of Tyler: 'To any one at all familiar with the history of colonial New England that list of men denounced to exile and loss of property on account of their opinions, will read almost like the beadroll of the oldest and noblest families concerned in the founding and upbuilding of New England civilisation.' Names such as Winslow, Sewall, Hutchinson, Chandler, Vassall, Loring, Hatch, had been closely identified

[1] Letter of Lieutenant Hugh Mackay Gordon to Edward Winslow, November 20, 1785, *Winslow Papers*, p. 321.

with all that was most essential in New England life. Whatever New England loyalism was it was not an imported exotic. To some extent the same truth holds good of New York; though here money played a more leading part; and the division of parties already foreshadowed a struggle between rich and poor. Still the de Lanceys and Crugers could claim to be an aristocracy on the ground that they proved their own fitness in most difficult circumstances. Among the heroes of the war none more conspicuously distinguished himself than John Harris Cruger, whose case will be found below (p. 376). Still the New York of the middle of the eighteenth century was already threatened with the danger of a plutocracy; and it gives one pause to note that two bearers of a distinguished name, themselves, like their illustrious French namesake, *sans peur* if not *sans reproche*, thought it not unseemly to claim compensation for lost property when the one brother was proved to have made at least £24,000 in New York currency or £13,500 in sterling money, and the other to have made at least £16,000 by official privileges during the continuance of the war (p. 322 and p. 325). That men of position like Dunmore should have pressed their claims is symptomatic of a certain want of delicacy in the eighteenth-century character, but the case of the two Bayards points the moral with a vengeance. It is a curious and not a little surprising fact that, so far as these Papers go, there is little evidence of a colonial-born aristocracy in the southern colonies in active sympathy with the cause of Great Britain. The families of the country gentlemen in Virginia and the Carolinas who took part with the British, to judge from this evidence, were in almost all cases comparatively recent arrivals from Great Britain.

Another important class of claimants consisted of the members of the learned professions, clergymen, lawyers, doctors, and teachers, 'a clear majority of whom', in Tyler's words, 'seem to have been set against the ultimate measure of the Revolution'. Here again our list is singularly representative of all that was best in these classes. In it we find Seabury, who knew how to combine loyalty with American patriotism and who finally returned to his native soil as the first bishop of the American episcopal church (p. 203); we find Joseph Galloway, the distinguished barrister, who was also the one statesman of moderate views whose plan of a quasi-federal union might, under happier auspices, have untied the knot of the constitutional deadlock (p. 82). We find in it a blameless doctor like Sylvester Gardiner, 'a public spirited man of great zeal and energy', 'respected by all classes' (p. 218). It adds not a little to the interest of these claims from members of the professions that they throw welcome light on the earnings of the professional men of the America of the middle of the eighteenth century. A further division is of those who did yeoman service in the war; though here there is some duplication of parts, inasmuch as distinguished lawyers like Cortland Skinner showed themselves as conspicuous in the field of battle (p. 113). Mention has already been made of John Harris Cruger, a civilian who proved himself a heaven-born leader of men. No figure in the war was more romantic than that of James Moody, according to the Americans, 'guilty of atrocious offences', such as 'robberies, thefts, and other felonies'; [1] according to the English so gallant an undertaker of risks that in his case a special exception was made to the practice of the rules governing the Commissioners (p. 133).

Little need be said of the merchants and traders, of whom we meet with a considerable number; because in their cases the losses occasioned by their loyalty were for the most part a disagreeable incident in their mercantile career rather than a matter of life and death.

But behind and besides these various classes there is a numerous procession of humbler, less clearly defined folk who in many cases swam with the stream, and then in some cases found that the current had changed too late for them to avail themselves of it. It was such cases that presented a psychological problem of no little difficulty. It was common ground that only loyalists were to be rewarded. Yes; but who was a loyalist? It was impossible to resist the moral of the parable of the lord and the workers in the vineyard, and to deny to the later adherents the reward that others had earned in the heat and toil of the midday. But was the change of mind really genuine? There were many who confessed that they considered the hold of Great Britain over at least the middle and southern colonies to be irrevocable; and who, therefore, in recognizing British sovereignty, were merely doing homage to accomplished facts. Upon the whole, not without some mental doubts and misgivings, the Commissioners seem to have arrived at the conclusion that it was impossible to inquire too curiously into motives; and that a man whose action was correct must be given the benefit of the doubt.

But the matter was further complicated because many who had sworn allegiance to the American authorities boldly took the line that in so acting they had not been false to their loyalty. The rebel Government having no foundation in right, oaths made to it were, it was contended, like the repetition of some Abracadabra, devoid of meaning. Placed in a difficult corner the average man clings with touching fidelity to time-worn sophistries; and it need not surprise us to hear in a new world the old excuse:

Ἡ γλῶσσ' ὀμώμοχ', ἡ δὲ φρὴν ἀνώμοτος.

Others maintained:

The imposer of the oath 'tis breaks it
Not he who for convenience takes it.[2]

[1] Proclamation of Governor Livingston quoted in Moore's *Diary of the Am. Rev.*, vol. ii, p. 466.
[2] Force, *Am. Archives*, 4th ser., vol. i, p. 720.

But such conduct might not be the offspring of weakness. There is evidence in these Papers to suggest that Tyron, at least, encouraged loyalists to become *soi-disant* rebels so as to act as spies upon their nominal associates; a dangerous game which was not likely, if discovered, to promote kindly feelings. Still the work of a spy requires considerable nerves; and the impression left on the mind, after the perusal of these cases, is that not many of them were men of this exceptional character. Assuredly most readers will rise from a perusal of these papers with a strong agreement with the wisdom of Mr. Van Tyne's statement that the American loyalists have been either unduly depreciated or unduly extolled. They were, the bulk of them, just ordinary people, exposed to extraordinary circumstances which required for their management that they should be more than average men. But in every generation, the mass are average men and should thank God that they live in times when it requires no special faculties to adjust themselves to their environment. In times of stress things are otherwise; and the lightning flash reveals the lack of character. Take the case of Harrison Gray, jun., the son of a distinguished father. His own plea was that he left America for reasons of ill health, but the stout-hearted John Chandler more brutally put it: 'Does not know that he was much out of order and believes that nothing ailed him; says he believes he came away for fear of being killed' (p. 234). Neither does one Colin Clark cut a very heroic figure. 'He was always a loyalist. It is not certain whether he took an oath to them or not. Prevaricates a great deal about it and admits that he did take an oath but says that it was about delivering up his arms. Afterwards says he does not know what was in the oath.' At the same time, 'he quitted the province N. Carolina because he would not take the oath of allegiance and abjuration. He took arms with the British at Savannah in 1779', as a militiaman. Still this doughty champion of British interests seems to have carried on his trade under a flag of truce, permission for which he alleged was given by Colonel Balfour. The Board, however, held that the flag of truce was contrary to all rules; whilst his family appeared to be in peaceful possession of his property (p. 385). Similarly one Hugh Fraser, a British half-pay officer, admitted that he applied in the year 1775 to the Committee of Safety at New York for leave to remain in a state of neutrality, and was told by them that he might depend upon remaining in a state of quiet whilst he continued to give them no molestation (p. 31). As a good instance of the material with which the British authorities had to work, we may cite the case of John Davies. Here was a man of sufficient reputation to be appointed upon the taking of Savannah one of the referees for reporting on the condition and characters of such persons as applied to be admitted as British subjects. But what was his own past record? 'Says he took the oath of allegiance to the rebel states upon the first tendering of that oath long before the King's troops arrived there. He did it on compulsion. An option was given to him to quit the country and his property within a limited time or take the oath and he preferred the latter. Was not imprisoned before he took it.' It is fair to mention that he underwent imprisonment sooner than take up arms against the Crown. But his admission that he had valued his property at double its real value upon the advice of a friend does not suggest a very high moral standard (p. 10).

But though this is one side of the shield, and though it is necessary to remember that men do not always rise to the occasion in great emergencies, it is equally true how much heroism became apparent amongst ordinary commonplace folk who assuredly did not seem to their neighbours to be heroes. More than one case is found of men who spent months and even years in waste places in great misery and want because of their loyalty. Most striking is the testimony of James Moody, himself a desperate man, that though there was a price upon his head and though the people amongst whom he moved were in sore straits, no one dreamed of securing a reward by his betrayal. The old fiction, to which even Sir George Trevelyan, in his earlier volumes, seems almost to lend the weight of his authority, that the loyalists were a mere pack of office-holders and politicians on the make is even more ludicrously false than the opposite view that one and all were prospective martyrs on behalf of King and Empire. From this, as from every other chapter of history, we can only draw the familiar, but none the less necessary, moral, *Res duplex*. It needs something more than the Guildenstern of the ordinary historian to read the riddle of the Hamlet of world movements.

Apart, however, from the light thrown upon the workings of human character in extraordinary circumstances, these papers are not without interest as illustrating ways and methods which worked in no small measure to the undoing of the old eighteenth-century colonial system. We find here a boy of fifteen years of age in a position of some importance under the Navigation Act. Stephen Haven deposes (p. 141) that 'he was fixed at Savannah when the troubles broke out. He was fifteen years of age. He was naval officer of Georgia and produces an appointment dated the 17th of August 1775. The duty of this office is to sign all Papers that the Collector, Comptroller and Searcher sign. There was no salary but the emoluments arose from the fees. His mother received the emoluments and therefore he cannot say what they were. He charges the loss of the office for eight years at £300 a year; but he admits that he received about £250 when the Province of Georgia was last in possession of the British troops'. An interesting method by which the sword could be turned into a ploughshare is revealed by the evidence of Thomas Goldthwaite (p. 264). He was commandant of Fort Pownall. 'His own pay was £3 sterling per month. He was allowed £9 per month for six servants.

He values the loss of the whole office at £530 a year. He had rations for all his servants. By employing the soldiers on the farm he gained £200 a year. There was an annual payment of rum and sugar which he estimates at £30 a year.' Again, what light does the evidence of Abijah Willard throw on the waste and jobbery that threatened to bring the whole state to bankruptcy? In the stress and hurry of wartime it is inevitable that the financial vultures will gather for their prey; and British experiences in South Africa forbid the assumption of too Pharisaic an attitude. Still the system of men fattening at the expense of their country went on in the eighteenth century systematically and as a matter of course; whereas it now skulks in dark places. Abijah Willard was that *rara avis* in eighteenth-century life, a contractor with a conscience. 'After the battle of Bunker's Hill he at the request of General Gage undertook to supply the King's troops with fresh provisions, which he did at the head of a hundred refugees. He conceived it to be a service of danger. He had no reward for this, but he received the thanks of the Commander-in-chief. . . . When he came to New York he had likewise a company of loyalists under his command. He was immediately appointed by Sir W. Howe as Assistant-Commissary and remained so till the evacuation of the place. He had a salary of 10*s*. a day.' . . . 'Being asked whether he had done any services to Government not mentioned in his memorial, he says he saved a great deal of money to Government in the Commissary's line. He might easily have made £20,000, and he could have made £10,000 in one article. Being asked to explain this article, he says he believes that hides and tallow are usually perquisites—and Col. Kingston confirms him in it—and he says he paid every shilling of this into Government and has the receipts to produce; and if he had taken this fair perquisite he should have put £10,000 into his pocket' (p. 138). But what is to be said for a system in which such things were a matter of course?

Allusion has already been made to the Bayard brothers, but in this connexion it is worth while to append the particulars of their case. William Bayard 'had an allowance of £200 a year which was given to him in 1779 and had been continued ever since. Upon his return to New York in that year he was appointed agent for prizes by Several Captains. He was sole agent for particular Captains. He had 5 p.c. for this. Says he did not get £10,000 by it. He acted as agent for the Contractors of Provisions. He never got in the whole more than £200 or £250. He was employed in this situation for nearly two years. He was not concerned in any contract with the Quarter-Master General's Department. He had two waggons which he was paid for at the common price and a "petty ancre",[1] the profit of these was more than £1,000 a year. A witness, Mr. Henry White, was

[1] *Sic* in text. I presume a right is meant of taking anchorage dues from boats landing.

of opinion that Mr. Bayard must have made full £10,000 currency by his agency for prizes during the war. Being asked what was the general opinion at New York concerning Mr. Bayard's profits during the war he says he does not think that he made so much as his brother Robert (£20,000 s.).' Mr. Coke's final note is : 'It appears that Mr. Bayard must have made during the war 24,000 currency at least which is £13,500 sterling' (p. 325).

Robert Bayard 'after the landing of the troops at New York was appointed by Governor Tryon a judge of the Vice-Admiralty Court. No salary was annexed thereto. He had one half and the Registrar and Marshall the other half of the fees. Says that during the war he made by his office between £15,000 and £16,000 sterling but his expenses and living were considerable. He held no other office but the one mentioned.' The same Mr. White 'thinks he must have made £20,000' as judge of the Vice-Admiralty Court. 'He lived in a very genteel and handsome manner.' The note is : 'Gained during the war by his office £16,000 sterling as appears by his own evidence. White thinks full £20,000 sterling' (p. 326). There was surely something radically wrong in the public opinion of the time when men of character and reputation thought it no shame to appear in these circumstances before a Commission the main business of which was the relief of those who had lost their all through their loyalty to the British connexion. It is after reading such claims that we notice the force of Rodney's remarks, which are quoted in the notes, that the extinction of the rebellion was being retarded 'to make the fortunes of a long train of leeches, who seek the blood of the State, and whose interest prompts them to promote the continuance of the war, such as quartermasters and their deputies, *ad infinitum* ; barrack-masters and their deputies, *ad infinitum* ; commissaries and their deputies, *ad infinitum* ; all of which make princely fortunes, and laugh in their sleeves at the generals who permit it, and by every means in their power continue to discountenance every active measure, and instead of having an idea of speedily concluding this unhappy war their common discourse turns upon what may happen in two or three ensuing campaigns.'[1] Well might Benjamin Thompson write to Lord Sackville (August 6, 1782) : 'You remember the scheme for a commission of accounts in this country ; believe me it is *absolutely* necessary. It is impossible to form any idea of the manner in which the business is done without being on the spot. I see enough to make a man less anxious and less severe than myself, half mad. I *know* more than I ever could have been persuaded to believe had I not come to America. But I dare not, at present, trust myself upon this subject. The first good opportunity I will write fully.'[2]

[1] *Hist. MSS. Comm.*, *Stopford-Sackville MSS.*, vol. ii, *Am. Papers*, p. 191.

[2] *Hist. MSS. Comm.*, *Stopford-Sackville MSS.*, vol. ii, 'Letters to and from Lieutenant-Colonel B. Thompson,' p. 251.

In this connexion we may note the sledge-hammer blows which Judge Jones, a New York loyalist who had good means of knowing what went on, directs against 'the base transactions of commissaries, quartermasters, barrackmasters, and engineers in America'.[1]

In other ways light is thrown by these Papers on the life of the time. We find in them valuable material regarding the professional incomes of lawyers, doctors, and clergymen in the America of the eighteenth century. Upon the whole, considering the simpler standard of living and current prices, the earnings of medical men and of lawyers seem to be fairly high. Thus Dr. Nathaniel Perkins (p. 258) claimed for the loss of his profession only. 'He chooses to rate his practice low and he states the profits of his profession at £600 a year in the town of Boston. He had likewise the practice in the neighbouring places and puts it at £100 a year.' Dr. Jefferies 'knew Dr. Perkins. He practiced as a physician only. He looked upon him to be the first physician of the place and he always thought that he made £600 or £700 a year. The witness practiced physic himself and the fee for a visit to a patient was 3*s.*; and if another was called in then the fee was 6*s.*; and he says that Dr. Perkins had a great deal of that sort of business. He says that Dr. Perkins did not practice surgery but that he sold medicines'.

John Watson (p. 81) went from Scotland in 1767 and settled as a surgeon at Newcastle on the Delaware. He had a very extensive practice there and it was a sickly country. The clear profit of his business was worth £1,000 a year in 1773, 1774, and 1775.

Brigadier-General Skinner, who had been Attorney-General of New Jersey, stated that the salary of Attorney-General when he came to the office was only £30. It was afterwards augmented to £60. He put the emoluments of his profession and office at from £900 to £1,000 per annum currency (p. 114). Thomas Phepoe, a lawyer at Charleston, said (p. 119) that he got from £1,000 to £2,000 a year from his profession in 1773, 1774, and 1775. He made at least £900 a year. The Rev. W. Edmiston (p. 109), a clergyman in Maryland, said that the value of his living was worth *communibus annis* £300 sterling exclusive of the surplice fees which amounted to about £15 sterling more per annum, says that the latter were always increasing. According to the Rev. Jacob Duché (p. 199) the emoluments of the united churches of Christ Church and St. Peter's at Philadelphia were about £600 a year. (The salary was £300, the glebe £100, and the surplice fees £200.)

Incidentally these Papers will be found to contain matter of interest. Thus, considering the past relations of the two men, it comes as a shock to find Howe giving evidence as to the character of Joseph Galloway (p. 89). It must regretfully

[1] Jones, op. cit., vol. i, ch. xvi.

be admitted that the gallant general showed no great generosity in his grudging admissions with regard to the loyalty of his former adversary. Through the claim of G. D. Ludlow (p. 180) we touch the fringe of what was nearly being a great tragedy, the threatened execution of Captain Asgill. On this melancholy subject enough is said in a note; but I would venture again to emphasize that one may recognize that Washington combined in himself more perhaps than any other individual in the annals of political history the qualities of moral and intellectual greatness, and yet admit that, being human, he had also the defects of his qualities.

The events hereafter referred to relate to a time when feeling between England and America and between those Americans who had adhered to Great Britain and their successful fellow countrymen was as bitter as can well be imagined. And yet when, in his last years, Wilmot wrote the history of the Commission, in which he had played so creditable a part, he was able to write, fresh from the disillusion and disappointment of another war, itself unnecessary and indecisive,

'In amicitiam coeant et foedera iungant
Perpetua.'

True it is that the hundred years of peace between the two English-speaking races have been not such a peace as good men desired. If there has been an absence of actual warfare, too often this has been due to causes other than genuine friendship. The Maine and Oregon boundary questions and the Alabama claims are only the most prominent of the rocks which have threatened to wreck the cause of peace. No one can follow dispassionately the course of British public opinion during the American Civil War without recognizing that the majority of such persons as had any interest in world-politics desired the victory of the South, on the simple ground that a strong American union might mean a sword ready to be thrown into the scale on behalf of the enemies of Great Britain. The democracy, however, which was beginning to feel its future strength, thought otherwise; and, with the growth of democracy in Great Britain, the road became easier for the development of better relations with the United States. Other causes, into which it is unnecessary to enter here, have contributed to the same result; and in this good work none has been more zealous than the younger school of American historians. If there is truth in the old saying 'tout comprendre est tout pardonner', perhaps a more intimate knowledge of these loyalists' circumstances may lead to a better understanding of the cause for which they suffered much, and for which, in many cases, they were willing to give their lives.

H. E. EGERTON.

# BIBLIOGRAPHY

The following works have been used for the purposes of this volume :

Public Record Office. Audit Office, 12 and 13 (Memorials in Books and Bundles).
Ontario Bureau of Archives, 2nd Report, 1904. Toronto, 1905.
WILMOT, J. EARDLEY. Historical View of the Commission for Enquiring into the Losses, Services, and Claims of the American Loyalists at the Close of the War between England and her Colonies in 1783 with an Account of the Compensation granted to them by Parliament in 1785 and 1788. 1815.
HISTORICAL MSS. COMMISSION. American MSS. in the Royal Institution of Great Britain. 4 vols.
—— Various Collections. Vol. v : The Knox MSS.
—— Stopford-Sackville MSS. Vol. ii.
—— 14th Report, Appendix, Part X, Dartmouth MSS. Vol. ii.
FORCE, P. American Archives. 4th series, 6 vols.
—— Ibid. 5th series, 3 vols.
O'CALLAGHAN, E. B. Documents relating to the Colonial History of New York. Vol. viii.
WHITEHEAD, W. A. New Jersey Archives. 1st series, vol. x.
SAUNDERS, W. L. North Carolina Records. Vols. ix–xi.
HAZARD, S. Pennsylvania Archives. 1st series, vols. iv–vii.
—— Ibid. 4th series, vol. iii.
WHITE, G. Historical Collections of Georgia. 3rd edition, 1855.
RIVINGTON. New York Gazetteer, 1773–5.
Annual Register.
COBBETT. Parliamentary History.
Morning Chronicle. 1783–5.
JONES, T. History of New York during the Revolutionary War. 2 vols. Written about 1790, first printed 1879.
HUTCHINSON, P. O. Diary and Letters of Thomas Hutchinson. 2 vols, 1883–6.
WARD, G. A. Journal and Letters of Samuel Curwen. 1842.
VAN SCHAACK, H. C. The Life of Peter van Schaack. 1842.
RAYMOND, O. V. The Winslow Papers. New Brunswick Historical Society Publications. 1901.
TIFFANY, N. M. Letters of James Murray, Loyalist. 1901.
LIEUTENANT JAMES MOODY. Narrative of his Exertions and Sufferings in the Cause of Government since 1776. 2nd edition, 1783.
SMYTH, J. F. D. Tour in the United States of America. 2 vols. 1784.
—— The Case of Ferdinand Smyth Stuart with his Memorials to the King, &c. 1807.
CONNOLLY, J. Narrative of the Transactions, Imprisonment, and Sufferings of John Connolly, an American Loyalist and Lieutenant-Colonel in his Majesty's Service. 1783. (Reprinted in Pennsylvania Magazine of History and Biography, vol. xii, pp. 310–24, 407–20 ; vol. xiii, pp. 61–70, 153–67, 281–91.)

GALLOWAY, J. The Examination of before the House of Commons, in a Committee on the American Papers. 1779.
—— Letters to a Nobleman on the Conduct of the War in the Middle Colonies. 3rd edition, 1780.
HOWE, SIR W. Narrative of in a Committee of House of Commons, 29th April, 1779. 2nd edition, 1780.
BURGOYNE, J. A state of the Expedition from Canada. 1780.
DAVIS, A. MCFARLAND. The Confiscation of John Chandler's Estate. 1903.
Nova Scotia Historical Collections. Vols. ii, vi, and xiii; the latter contains: 'The Life and Times of the Rev. J. Wiswell.' By E. M. Saunders.
Canadian Magazine. Vol. xxvi: 'Colonel Stephen Jarvis.'
BRYMNER, D. Report on Canadian Archives. 1887, 1888. Haldimand Collection. Vols. i and ii.
DOUGHTY, A. G. Report on Canadian Archives. 1912.
MOORE, F. Diary of the American Revolution. 2 vols, 1860.
—— Correspondence of H. Laurens. Edited for Zengler Club. 1861.
Journals of the Continental Congress, 1774–89. In progress.
PALTSITS, V. H. The Minutes of the Commissioners for Detecting and Defeating Conspiracies in the State of New York. Albany County Sessions, 1778–81. 3 vols., 1909.
MUNRO, J. Acts of the Privy Council, Colonial Series, 1766–83.
JAMESON, J. FRANKLIN. Report of the Historical MSS. Commission of the American Historical Association. 1897. (Introduction to Letters of Phineas Bond.)
ELLIS, G. E. Memoir of Benjamin Thompson, Count Rumford. n.d.
GILPIN, T. Exiles in Virginia. 1848.
DRAYTON, T. Memoirs of the American Revolution as relating to South Carolina. 2 vols., 1821.
ROSS, C. Correspondence of Charles, first Marquess Cornwallis. Vol. i, 1859.
GRAHAM, J. J. Memoir of General S. Graham. 1862. (Privately printed.)
MACKENZIE, R. Strictures on Lieutenant-Colonel Tarleton's History. 1787.
STEDMAN, C. History of the Origin, Progress, and Termination of the American War. 2 vols., 1794.
Pennsylvania Magazine of History and Biography. Vols. vii, ix, xii, and xiii.
Acadiensis. Vol. vi.
SABINE, L. The American Loyalists. 2nd edition, 2 vols., 1864.
STARK, J. H. The Loyalists of Massachusetts. 1910.
RYERSON, EGERTON. The Loyalists of America and their times. 2 vols., 1860.
SIEBERT, W. H. The Flight of American Loyalists to the British Isles. 1911.
—— The Colony of Massachusetts Loyalists at Bristol, England. (Reprinted from the Proceedings of the Massachusetts Historical Society for 1912.)
—— The Legacy of the American Revolution to the British West Indies and Bahamas. Ohio State University Bulletin, vol. xvii, no. 27, 1913.
—— The Exodus of Loyalists from Penobscot to Passamaquoddy. Ibid. vol. xviii, no. 26, 1914.
—— The American Loyalists in the Eastern Seigniories and Townships of the Province of Quebec, Ottawa, 1913.

The Dispersion of the American Tories. Reprinted from the Mississippi Valley Historical Review. 1914.

SMITH, J. Toryism in Worcester County during the War for Independence. Massachusetts Historical Society Proceedings. October, 1914.

DIFFENDERFFER, F. R. Colonel John Connolly, Loyalist. 1903.

VAN TYNE, C. H. The Loyalists in the American Revolution. 1902.

FLICK, A. C. Loyalism in New York during the American Revolution. 1901.

BANCROFT, G. History of the United States. New edition in seven volumes. n.d.

CHANNING, E. History of the United States. Vol. iii, 1912.

WINSOR, J. Narrative and Critical History of America. Vols. vii and viii, 1889.

TYLER, M. C. The Literary History of the American Revolution, 1763–83. 2 vols. 1897.

—— Patrick Henry. American Statesmen Series. 1887.

PHILLIPS, U. B. Plantation and Frontier Documents, 1649–1863. Introduction to vol. i, 1909.

WEEDEN, W. B. Economic and Social History of New England, 1620–1789. Vol. ii, 1890.

FORTESCUE, HON. JOHN W. History of the British Army. Vol. iii, 1902.

TREVELYAN, SIR GEORGE O. The American Revolution. Part III, 1907.

—— George III and Charles Fox, the Concluding Part of the American Revolution. 2 vols. 1912 and 1914.

MCCRADY, E. The History of South Carolina under Royal Government, 1719–76. 1899.

—— The History of South Carolina in the Revolution, 1775–80. 1901.

—— Ibid. 1780–3. 1902.

SMITH, W. ROY. South Carolina as a Royal Province, 1719–76. 1903.

RAPER, C. L. North Carolina. 1904.

LINGLEY, C. R. The Transition in Virginia from Colony to Commonwealth. 1910.

FISHER, E. J. New Jersey as a Royal Province, 1738–76. 1911.

BATES, F. G. Rhode Island, the Formation of the Union. 1898.

BECKER, C. L. The History of Political Parties in the Province of New York, 1760–76. 1909.

STEINER, B. C. Life and Administration of Sir Robert Eden. 1898.

BALDWIN, E. H. Joseph Galloway. 1902.

MORISON, S. E. Life of Harrison Gray Otis. Vol. i, 1913.

CROSS, A. L. The Anglican Episcopate and the American Colonies. (Harvard Historical Studies, no. ix.) 1902.

ANDERSON, J. S. M. The History of the Church of England in the Colonies . . . of the British Empire. Vol. iii, 1856.

# BOOK I

*This is the first Book containing the Evidence & Decisions upon such Cases as come before us under an Act of Parl pass'd in July 1783 entitled an Act for appointing Commissioners to enquire into the Losses & Services of all such persons who have suffer'd in their Rights Properties & Professions in America in consequence of their Loyalty &c.*

Commissioners named in the Act of Part
John Wilmot
Danl Parker Coke
Coll Robt Kingston
Coll Thos Dundas
John Marsh.

Septr the 18th 1783.

**Memorial of Wm Knox Esq in respect of his Estate in Georgia**

Determin'd the 12th of Novr 1783.

Memorial read.

Willm Knox [1] Esq—the Claimant—sworn.

Swears to the truth of his Memorial. Has not been in America since 1761. He was Under Secretary of State to the American Department when the Troubles broke out. In all his Correspondences with the first people in America he excited them to support Govt as far as he could.

A Loyalist & Servt of the Crown. Has been in Engd during the whole War. Did not bear Arms.

Loyalty undoubted.

The mode of granting Lands in Georgia was in proportion to the size of the family—100 Acres to the head of a family & 50 Acres more for every Individual of that family black or white. Mr Knox had 126 Negroes & was entitled to Lands in proportion to that number.

Mr Knox is personally attainted & his Estates confiscated by a special Act of the Legislature of Georgia—to which he refers.

Proof of Confiscation.

Septr the 22d 1783.

John Graham Esq late Lieutt Govr of Georgia—sworn.

Knows Mr Knox & speaks to his Loyalty. He was well acquainted with Mr Knox's property being one of his Attornies. About 200 Acres were cultivated with Rice besides high Lands for the purpose of raising provisions for the Negroes & Lands which produced Lumber which was a very profitable Article. The situation of the plantation being near the River made it rather precarious on acct of its being frequently overflowed. In one or two Years from this Circumstance the Crops were entirely lost. The last Year there was but little Rice planted & the Negroes were principally employed in cutting Lumber which he says was equally profitable. He has heard Mr Hall (Mr Knox's Manager) say that the last Year he expected to have remitted to Mr Knox above £2000. He values Rice at 40*s*. per Barrel & says that each Acre would produce about 2 Barrells.

The Board allow for the Estate at Knoxborough &c. including all those which are not disallowed £3000.

[1] See Additional Notes, p. 75.

He believes that M^r Knox's Plantation was worth £4000 & thinks that it would have sold before the troubles for more than that. He believes it was valued at more. M^r Graham knows that these Plantations have been sold under the Rebel Gov^t. M^r Graham after he went out to his Gov^t in 1779 wrote to M^r Knox advising him to sell his plantations & in that Letter he gave him his Idea of the Value—that Letter has not been produced. He has heard the Estate at Knoxborough (which was the name of M^r Knox's plantations) valued at £6000 Sterling but he should not have valued them himself so high.

Being asked whether Lands granted upon Condition that a certain Number of Acres should be cultivated are consider'd as forfeited He says that it was always consider'd as a Compliance with the terms of the particular Grant if the stipulated Quantity had been cultivated in any part of the Grantee's Estates in the same province And he does not think that the Circumstance of the Conditions of the Grant not having been complied with would make any difference in the Sale of such Lands.[1] Says there were Offices for the Registering of Estates in Georgia & makes no doubt that M^r Knox's Estates were register'd. But he thinks it would be difficult to get Extracts from these Offices. He is very clear that there were no Mortgages on M^r Knox's Estate. He estimates the Value of good Rice Ground at ten Guineas per Acre. He says M^r Knox had more than 100 Negroes on the Estate & speaks of the Value of Negroes in the Provinces of South Carolina & Georgia being from £50 to £60 sterling per Head. He says he knew that M^r Knox's Overseer turned Rebel & carried off some of M^r Knox's Negroes & he believes they were sold for the use of the State Gov^t. Graham being asked more particularly to the Value of M^r Knox's Estate He admits that he would not give more than £3000 for it.

Sept^r 23^d 1783.

Lieut^t Gov^r Graham's subsequent Examination—sworn.

Says he values the whole of the two Plantations at Knoxborough by way of Appraisement (which he produces) at £7056 12*s.* 6*d.* But as far as he recollects he advised M^r Knox to take £4000 for it. M^r Graham proves the Signature to the Valuation dated 7^th May 1776 to be the Handwriting of the Parties by whom it appears to be signed. Confirms what he said before that notwithstanding the Valuation he has made by way of Appraisement he would not himself have given above £3000 for it nor advised any Friend who had applied to him to give above £4000.

Sept^r 24^th 1783.

Sir James Wright Bar^t—sworn.

He knew M^r Knox's Plantations & speaks very much of it in the same manner with Lieut^t Gov^r Graham. He conjectures the Value of the Plantation at Knoxborough to be about £6000 tho' he admits that he would not have bought it

[1] It is strange to find able officials like Graham and Wright (see pp. 3 and 15) aiding and abetting a clear violation of the law. The Commissioners, however, were able to entrench themselves behind the opinion of the Attorney-General, Lloyd Kenyon, that uncultivated lands held under grants from the Crown containing a clause of forfeiture for the non-performance of certain conditions in respect of cultivation, &c., being forfeited to the Crown, could not support a claim for compensation. Parties who had no title could not claim for the loss of lands.

on any Acc[t] it being so precarious on Acc[t] of the floods &c. He likewise confirms the Acc[t] of M[r] Knox's Negroes & says they were worth about £50 per head.

Being asked his Opinion about the Clause of forfeiture in Grants He says it was generally understood that where a Man had several different Grants each of which had a Clause of forfeiture for non-cultivation of a certain Quantity if the Grantee cultivated a sufficient Quantity to cover the whole tho' it was all on one Plantation it was esteem'd to be equal to a Compliance with the Clause in the several Grants. He never knew an Instance of any Grant being resumed Nor did he ever receive any Instructions from home for that purpose during the 22 Years that he was Gov[r] of the Province. He says M[r] Knox's Grant was free from Quitrents for ten years & that the Expence of taking out the Grant was very trifling.

Sept[r] the 18[th] 1783.

**Memorial of W[m] Knox Esq in respect of his Office of Secretary of the Province of New York**

W[m] Knox Esq—the Claimant—sworn.

Letters Patent dated 8[th] Aug[t] 1772 granting to W[m] Knox Esq the Office of Secretary of the Province of New York from & immediately after the Death Surrender &c of George Clarke Esq—produced & read. M[r] Knox paid M[r] Clarke £3000 for resigning the said Office.

Disallowed being amply compensated by the Pension.

He appointed M[r] Bayard his Deputy who rented the Office of him at £1000 a Year & which was paid to M[r] Knox only two Years.

Bond dated 26[th] Jan[y] 1774 from Sam[l] Bayard John Blackburn & W[m] Neat in the penalty of £5000 condition'd for the due performance of his Duty—read.

M[r] Knox believes he may have got about £600 from his Office of Secretary since the King's forces have been in New York—viz—for Marriage Licences & searching records.

A Pension of 1200 a Year has been granted to M[r] Knox as a Compensation for the Loss of his American Office. But he has rec[d] no Compensation for the Loss of his Post of Under Secretary of State as the other Officers did & thinks he should have had a Pension of £750 a Y[r] if it had not been for his former pension. The only thing like a Compensation that he has rec[d] for the latter has been that in the Original Grant of the Pension of £1200 a Year (which Grant was drawn by himself) it was therein expressed to be as a Compensation for the Loss of his American Office. And he has since obtain'd a new Grant whereby the Pension is divided between him & M[rs] Knox giving to each £600 a Year. And in this new Grant it is not express'd on what Consideration it is granted.

**Memorial of Jaheel Brenton[1] Capt[n] in the British Navy**

Determin'd the 1[st] of Dec[r] 1783.

Capt[n] Brenton—the Claimant—sworn. Sept[r] the 19[th] 1783.

Memorial read.

Produces a Paper which is sworn to be a Copy of a printed Paper & an

[1] Jahleel Brenton, *b.* 1729, *d.* 1802. There is a full account of him in Sabine, *The Amer. Loyalists*, 2nd ed., vol. i, pp. 251–2. He is not to be confused with his brother Benjamin, who was a contractor for the royal forces. Captain Brenton's son of the same name was a British admiral of some distinction.

Extract of an Act of the Gen$^{l}$ Assembly of Rhode Island confiscating the Estate of Capt$^{n}$ Brenton & declaring him a Traitor to the Liberties of America.

A Loyalist. Bore Arms.

A Certificate from Gen$^{l}$ Gage to the Character of Capt$^{n}$ Brenton produced & read.

Capt$^{n}$ Brenton Says he lived upon his own Estate about 3 Miles from the Town of Newport at Brenton's Point in Rhode Island.

Bounty £100 a Y$^{r}$.

N.B. Capt$^{n}$ Brenton had an Allowance of £50 a Y$^{r}$ which was augmented to £100 a Y$^{r}$ upon his being reduced to Half Pay which he now receives.

Sept$^{r}$ the 28$^{th}$ 1783.

Determin'd y$^{e}$ 12$^{th}$ of Nov$^{r}$ 1783.

## Case of Capt$^{n}$ John Orde of the British Navy

Memorial read.

Capt$^{n}$ John Orde—the Claimant—sworn.

British Subject & served in the Army. Bore Arms.

He married Miss Stevens in 1781. Miss Stevens was an Orphan in 1781 & had none but distant Relations. M$^{r}$ Reeve the surviving Executor of M$^{r}$ Stevens her father dying in 1775 M$^{r}$ Barnwell M$^{r}$ Carson & M$^{r}$ Gibbes as Executors to M$^{r}$ Reeve took possession of the property papers & everything respecting the Estate. Miss Stevens not satisfied with this consulted M$^{r}$ Dunning how far she had it in her power to displace them & he being of Opinion that she might nominate her own Guardian She appointed M$^{r}$ Boone of the Customs her Guardian with a view to take the Estate out of the hands of M$^{r}$ Barnwell & M$^{r}$ Carson. M$^{r}$ Boone appointed a M$^{r}$ Joiner & this M$^{r}$ Barnwell jointly her Attorneys. The whole of this M$^{r}$ Orde speaks to from information & not of his own knowledge. Upon those Powers being sent out to America M$^{r}$ Barnwell refused to act under them & would not have suffer'd M$^{r}$ Joyner to do so alledging that Miss Stevens had no power to send such Authorities that he was empower'd to act under M$^{r}$ Reeve's will & should act under that Authority alone. These powers were sent out in 1775 soon after the death of M$^{r}$ Reeve. Has understood that M$^{r}$ Joiner had taken a decided part on the side of the Americans.

Determin'd the 27$^{th}$ of Jan$^{y}$ 1784.

## Memorial of Thomas Skelton [1]

Oct$^{r}$ the 6$^{th}$ 1783.

Thomas Skelton—the Claimant—sworn.

Upon the Consideration of the whole of this Case The Board were of Opinion that the Claim was a fraudulent one & so reported it to the Treasury.

Says he never held any Office under the American States or served in their Militia or Army during the Rebellion. The first Act of Loyalty was delivering the Message mention'd in the Memorial. The Message was from his father in Law to Gen$^{l}$ Cortland Skynner to be thro' him convey'd to the Commander in Chief.

Produces a Pass sign'd Will$^{m}$ Livingston mention'd in the Memorial.

Says his father in Law M$^{r}$ Tho$^{s}$ Lowry adhered to the Americans was a Col$^{l}$ in their Militia & a Commissary. He never has been consider'd by them a Loyalist.

Never had any reward for the Message he carried or any other service than for his Labor as a Clerk. Capt$^{n}$ Laird gave him the Appointment from personal Acquaintance.

[1] In 1781 Thomas Skelton was serving in the Quartermaster-General's Department under Captain Chad (*Hist. MSS. Comm.*, *Am. MSS. in R. Inst.*, vol. ii, pp. 316, 329).

Says he came to New York in Augt 1771 & brought with him £3310 Sterling. Says he owed no Money at the time of his Arrival.

Courtland Skynner Esq—of New Jersey Brigadier Genl in the British Service—sworn.

Knows Thos Skelton & has known him since 1772 or 1773. Confirms the Acct Mr Skelton gave of the Message convey'd by Genl Skynner to the Commander in Chief. He says the information he gave was material to the British Army and believes his Motives for giving it were those of Loyalty. That he has continued loyal & zealous ever since. Believes he was not paid for his service but says he would have been if he had applied.

David White—late of the County of Somerset in New Jersey Farmer—sworn.

Knows the Claimant. Recd a Letter from him acquainting him that his property was confiscated. Believes & is well satisfied that Mr Skelton is a loyal Subject & attached to the Govt of Great Britain.

Nathan Combes—late of Amwell in Hunterdon Co Merchant—sworn.

Knows Thos Skelton—always understood him to be a Loyal Subject. Knows he left his Plantation with his Stock & effects thereon in 1776—that his family remain'd upon it. Knows he was advertised in the Papers to appear & shew Cause or he would be attainted of high Treason & his Property confiscated. Mr Lowry his father in Law informed him the Property was confiscated & sold & was told this by Lowry at Elizabeth Town in 1779 & 1780 & since at New York 1783. Did not mention for how much it sold. Did not say who purchased it. Mr Skelton did not come into the British Lines till 1780. A Mr Wood was in possession of it this Year—he came into New York to settle there. He told the Witness he resided on ye Estate.

Lowry said that he hoped that the Witness & Mr Skelton might come over & reside in America but not then he has since recd a letter from Mr Lowry dated in July last informing him he could not safely go over & advising him to stay here. Witness left Amwell in 1778. No part of the Estate was then seiz'd to his knowledge but the last time he was at the House Mrs Skelton lived there he believes she lived there in February 1778.

Claimant produces no Act of the State or other Evidence of the Confiscation.

Capn Laird of the British Navy says

He never heard Mr Skelton say what Money he left in his father's hands. He says he does not know but he believes not much. He says he knows that Mr Skelton may go to America whenever he pleases for Nathan Combes is now in town & shipping off a Cargo for America. He believes that Skelton will get every farthing due to him from the partnership. He says he is worth at least £5000 in this Country & he told him that he ought to be ashamed to come here to make any Claim. He says his Clerk has told the Witness that Mr Skelton expects nothing from this board & that he wishes that he had never applied. Captn Laird being asked whether he came originally into New York from motives of Loyalty or for his own Interest. He says that he generally consulted his own

Interest & seems to insinuate that that was his Motive. Capt$^{n}$ Laird says that to his knowledge M$^{r}$ Skelton has better'd his Circumstances by the War & instead of losing by the War he has gain'd considerably & more than trebled his fortune. And that he ought to be ashamed of making any Claim for Compensation.

N.B. The Board at present are of Opinion to report the Case of M$^{r}$ Skelton as coming within the Clause in the Act which relates to persons who shall deliver in fraudulent Claims.

### Memorial of David White

Determin'd the 14$^{th}$ of Oct$^{r}$ 1783

Memorial read. Oct$^{r}$ the 7$^{th}$ 1783.

David White—the Claimant—sworn.

Lived in the County of Somerset in New Jersey when the Rebellion broke out. Came there in 1774 & lived there from that time till he was taken Prisoner. As soon as the Symptoms of Rebellion appear'd in April & May 1775 He avowed his Loyalty. Resided from that time till the latter end of Nov$^{r}$ 1776 at his own House when he went to Trenton. It was early in the Morning on the 8$^{th}$ of Dec$^{r}$ that having made his way to this place he join'd the British Army. This was the Day that the Army enter'd the Town.

A Loyalist.

Produces Gen$^{l}$ Howe's Pass dated Dec$^{r}$ 9$^{th}$ 1776.

Staid with the Army till Jan$^{y}$ 1777 When by the direction of Lord Cornwallis & Gen$^{l}$ Grant [1] on the 14$^{th}$ of that Month He went out to reconnoitre the Enemy's Army & to bring in Men for Gov$^{t}$. Produces a Pass signed by Gen$^{l}$ Grant dated 14$^{th}$ Jan$^{y}$ 1777 which he says was given to him on that Occasion.

The Board are of Opinion that the Claimant has grossly prevaricated in his Examination & that he deserves no Credit And of course disallow the whole of the Claim.

Was taken Prisoner on the 16$^{th}$ & kept Prisoner 6 Days when he was released on his parole. He then returned to his own House where he staid ten Days & afterwards went to New York where he continued till Dec$^{r}$ 1777 when he departed for Jamaica. He was appointed under Gen$^{l}$ Howe by Gen$^{l}$ Skynner's recommendation to be Lieut$^{t}$ Col$^{l}$ of a Batt$^{n}$ of 500 Men could he have raised them. Produces a Pass from Gen$^{l}$ Washington's Aid de Camp dated 22$^{d}$ Jan$^{y}$ 1777 (vide the Pass) continued at Jamaica till Dec$^{r}$ last & arrived here in February.

Does not know from his own knowledge of the Confiscation but has been told of it.

Married Miss Eliz$^{th}$ Gould Tucker in 1775 received £2000 Sterling as her fortune. Did not receive the whole of the Principal till two Years after. His Wife was also entitled to an House & Garden in Trenton mentioned in his Memorial which was the Estate of her father deceas'd And it was taken out of the Claimant's possession & made an Hospital for the American Army in 1776. Purchased his Plantation in March 1776 of Cornelius Lowe who was formerly a Merch$^{t}$. It consisted of 600 Acres left his title Deeds with M$^{r}$ Skelton when he left New York in 1777—& M$^{r}$ Skelton has informed him that he sent them to his father in Law M$^{r}$ Lowry in Jersey. He paid £4000 New Jersey Money for it as the Consideration for the Purchase. He paid M$^{r}$ Lowe £2500 down & gave him a Bond for £1500 payable at 12 Months Date. After this he gave a long & complicated Acc$^{t}$ of many Bills drawn by him upon other persons & by others on him which seems not to be very material.

[1] James Grant of Ballindalloch. He is in the *Dict. of Nat. Biography*.

Thos Skelton—sworn. Octr the 8th 1783.

Knows David White—does not know whether he brought any Substance with him to America. White had no settled abode till he purchased his Plantation which was early in 1776. He bought it of Cornelius Lowe was present when he made the bargain with Lowe. Don't know the extent of the Plantation. The Bargain was for £4000 but does not know whether it was New York or New Jersey Money the difference is as *7s. 6d.* to *8s.* Can't recollect anything more of the transaction than that he agreed to give £4000 for it. Does not remember when or how the Money was to be paid. Has heard the Claimant got money with his Wife 2 or £3000. Heard the Claimant had in right of his Wife one or two Houses in Trenton. Has heard Mr White say he owed a considerable part of the purchase Money for his plantation. Did not think things were desperate in 1776. Has heard the Plantation was confiscated & sold & that the Purchaser was one Thos Irwin heard it sold for 28000 Congress Money & believes it was in 1779.

Arthur Wadman—was a Captn in ye 26th Regt & was quarter'd near 16 Years in the Jerseys & New York Govt.

Knows perfectly David White—believes he was a loyal Subject. He must have been a Man of Substance by his buying a Farm. Did not know him till he purchased it. Knew that Mr Lowe was a cautious Man believes the Plantation was paid for & thinks that Mr Lowe would not have permitted him to have the farm without paying for it thinks the Price was about £4000.

David White—again sworn.

Says his Purchase Deed was recorded in the Province of New Jersey is sure he left his Marriage Settt with Mr Skelton at New York. He deliver'd that Deed & the Purchase Deed at the same time. He told Mr Skelton he had given Mr Lowry a power of Attorney but never directed him to send the Deeds to him. Will send the Settlement the letter of Mr Hawker & Mr Morris (respecting several Bills which were drawn by him & them) & the Extracts from the Account Books.

Mr Lowe offer'd to take his Bond for half the Money. The Estate was mortgaged for £1500 & a Bond was given as a Colll Security. Paid the Purchase Money part in Congress Money & part in Proclamation Money. The £4000 was New York Money.

Mr Worrall at Bristol prepared the last Settlement which he lately made on his Wife & wherein the former Settlement is recited.

The Original Mortgage to Delpratt was made for 6050 Curr. of Jamaica.

## Arthur Savage's [1] Memorial

Determin'd 14th of Octr 1783.

Arthur Savage—the Claimant—sworn. Octr the 10th 1783.

A Loyalist & did his Duty as an Officer of the Crown.

States no particular Acts of Loyalty but says he did his Duty as a Custom House Officer. Produces Certificates from Govr Hutchinson & Govr Wentworth of his good Conduct as an Officer of the Customs.

[1] *b.* 1731, *d.* 1801. He was appointed Controller of the Customs at Falmouth, Mass., in 1755. In 1771 he was mobbed and soon afterwards retired to Boston. He accompanied the British army to Halifax at the evacuation of Boston. He was proscribed and banished by the Act of 1778 (Sabine, op. cit., vol. ii, p. 258; J. H. Stark, *The Loyalists of Mass.*, 1910, pp. 133, 139).

Did not bear Arms.

Was entitled to an undivided share of a tract of Land situate at North Yarmouth in Mass. Bay consisting of 3400 Acres granted 30 Y$^{rs}$ ago or upwards to one Timothy Prout. Claimant's father purchased 600 Acres part thereof of M$^{r}$ Prout but does not know what he gave for it. It was a piece of Woodland uncultivated with only a Grist Mill upon it & never has been productive. Don't suppose that his father gave £50 Sterling for it. His father died 46 Y$^{rs}$ ago & devised it by Will between him & his Brother.

Disallowed for want of Evidence.

Produces an Appointment of Dan$^{l}$ Chamier dated 5$^{th}$ of July 1772 as Deputy Surveyor & Searcher for the Port of Boston.

Disallowed.

Bounty £60 a Y$^{r}$.

From Jan$^{y}$ 1777 in addition to his Salary The Treasury have allowed M$^{r}$ Savage £30 a Y$^{r}$. Since the Abolition of his Office Gov$^{t}$ has allowed £60 a Year in the whole which he now continues to receive.

Thinks M$^{r}$ Savage's Salary & Fees as Comptroller at Falmouth worth £183 per Ann. Sterling. In the Office of Deputy Searcher M$^{r}$ Savage was removeable at the pleasure of his Principal.

Determin'd the 7$^{th}$ of Nov$^{r}$ 1783.

## Mr. John Savage's Memorial

Oct$^{r}$ the 16$^{th}$ 1783.

John Savage [1]—the Claimant—sworn.

Went to Charles Town from Bermudas (where he was born) in 1729 & continued there except at short intervals till the 24$^{th}$ of May 1775. The reason of his leaving it was his dislike of the temper of the times the troubles had then broke out. Was President of the Chamber of Commerce at Charlestown. Avow'd his Sentiments in favor of the British Gov$^{t}$. Did not leave it on acc$^{t}$ of any personal ill treatment. Left the Place before any Association was formed or Oaths tender'd. His principal Object then was to reside in Eng$^{d}$ on acc$^{t}$ of his Son.

A Loyalist.

Did not bear Arms.

Governor Bull [2]—sworn.

Has known M$^{r}$ Savage 40 Y$^{rs}$. Knew him when the troubles broke out in S$^{o}$ Carolina. Knows he conducted himself as a loyal Subject. Is not a Man of active Life. In the Meeting of the Chamber of Commerce knows he frequently express'd his disapprobation of the Conduct of the Promoters of the Innovation. He knows that he was personally included in the Confiscation Act. Being asked to M$^{r}$ Savage's Property he says he has known him for many Years in possession of two Lots in Charlestown.

John Simpson—of Threadneedle Street Merch$^{t}$—sworn.

He formerly lived in Charlestown and knew M$^{r}$ Savage there in 1774 or 1775. Knows his property very well was his Attorney. He had three Houses in Charles Town two of them in Thraddle Street & one in Meet's House Street. Being asked to the Value of the Houses in Thraddle Street He says he thinks they let for about £600 Currency. Does not know what they were worth in 1775 but says they were then in good repair And he believes that the House in which M$^{r}$ Savage lived would have let for about £500 Currency.

[1] This John Savage escaped the vigilance of Sabine.

[2] See Additional Notes, p. 76.

Mr Hopton—of Cecil Street Strand Mercht—sworn.

He was formerly a Mercht in Charlestown & knew Mr Savage there in 1775. Being ask'd whether he knew his Property He says he did & that he was in treaty with him for the two houses in Thraddle Street. He likewise knew the House that Mr Savage lived in And he would have given for the three Houses before the fire £3000 Sterling & that he had the Money ready. Since the fire he would give £2000 if Mr Savage could recover them. Being asked what reasons he has to think that Mr Savage can ever recover them He says that he has a good right under the Provisional Articles as a British Subject.

### Memorial of Mr Robt Parker [1] late an Officer in the Customs in the Port of Boston

Determin'd the 7th of Novr 1783.

Robt Parker—the Claimant—sworn. Octr the 16th 1783.

In July 1772 he was appointed Surveyor in the Port of Boston with a Salary of £80 a Year.

When the Rebellion broke out he fled to Boston & enter'd into an Association with other Inhabitants for the Defence of the Town agt the Rebels. Three Months before the Troops left Boston (they left it in March 1776) He was reduced by a severe fit of illness & was obliged to leave that Town & embark for England. His Income in that Year amounted to £250 Sterling.

A Loyalist & did his Duty as an Officer of the Crown. Did not bear Arms.

He is a Native of America. Has not his Appointment with him but can prove it. He recd several Fees besides his Salary but did not keep an exact Acct. But he never recd less than £200 a Year.

Office £80 a Yr. Abolished in Octr 1782.

Since the 5th of Jany last He has recd from the Treasury a Pension of £50 a Year. He has no other Losses to claim he lost nothing but his office.

Bounty £50 a Yr.

Charles Paxton Esq—sworn.

He was a Commissioner of the Customs at Boston & knew Mr Robt Parker. He was appointed Surveyor soon after his Arrival in 1771 or 1772. The Salary was £80 a Year but he does not know what the Perquisites were. He says his Line was such that there were no fees his Perquisites arose from Seizures. Being asked whether he can form any Judgment of the whole value of the Office communibus annis He says he cannot but says it was looked upon to be a support for a Gentleman. He says Mr Parker always exerted himself zealously & was active in difficult services & always acquitted himself with great propriety.

### Mr Arody Thayer's Memorial

Determin'd the 7th of Novr 1753.

Arody Thayer [2]—the Claimant—sworn. Octr the 16th 1783.

He was resident at Boston in 1775—left Philadelphia in Octr 1773—was Marshal & Serjt at Mace of the Vice Admiralty Court of Appeals of Philadelphia

A Loyalist And did his Duty in the Execution of his Offices.

[1] *b.* 1750. He settled in Nova Scotia in 1783 and was afterwards appointed Storekeeper of the Ordnance and Controller of the Customs for the port of St. John, New Brunswick. He died there in 1823 (Sabine, op. cit., vol. ii, p. 149). According to George Leonard, an active member of the New Brunswick Council, Robert Parker, in after years, connived at the illegal American trade. 'Wanton and Parker,' he wrote (December 14, 1805), 'are afraid of the illegal transactions at Porto Bello making their appearance' (Raymond, *The Winslow Papers*, p. 545). (There is a misprint in Raymond, ibid., p. 544, note, where Robert Parker the loyalist is stated to have 'died in 1852, aged 84 years'.)

[2] His name is contained in the Massachusetts Banishment Act of 1778.

under an Appointment dated 30th Septr 1769 (produces the Appointment from the Court of Admiralty here). No Salary was annex'd to it. The Profit arose from fees & the produce from the 30th of Septr 1769 to 1772 was little or nothing—in 1773 the business increased delivers a Book containing an Acct of fees amounting to £108 18*s.* 0*d.* Currency or £65 7*s.* 0*d.* Sterling. He never recd any other profit from the Office. He appointed a Deputy when he left Philadelphia who never accounted to him. Was Marshal & Serjt at Mace for Mass. New Hampshire Rhode Island &c produces the Appointment dated the 6th of July 1769. He executed his Office at Rhode Island by Deputy—the clear Profit he believes to be about £50 Sterling per Ann. & not less—after paying his Deputy who had half the fees.

Did not bear Arms.

No Loss but that of Office.

He was appointed in Feby 1771 by the Commrs of the Customs at Boston Tide Surveyor at the Port of Philadelphia at the Salary of £80 a Yr Sterling—enter'd on his Office the 1st of April 1771. No perquisites or fees—continued in Office at Philadelphia till 1779 & recd ye Salary to the 30th of Septr 1782.

Office £80 a Yr.

Charles Paxton Esq—one of the Commrs of the Customs in America—sworn.

Says that in 1766 he got Mr Thayer appointed a Marshal of the Court of Vice Admiralty for the four New Engd Govts in 1769. When the four High Courts of Admiralty were established he was appointed Marshal of the Court of Philadelphia. Was appointed Tide Surveyor of the Customs at Philadelphia about 1771—his Salary as Surveyor was £80 a Year.

£40 a Yr.

Says he never knew a Man of more fidelity and that he ever distinguish'd himself for his Loyalty & zeal in the Support of Government.

## Mr John Davies's Memorial

Determin'd the 14th of Novr 1783.

Octr the 17th 1783.

John Davies [1]—the Claimant—sworn.

Says he took the Oath of Allegiance to the Rebel States upon the first tendering of that Oath long before the King's Troops arrived there. He did it on Compulsion. An Option was given him to quit the Country & his Property within a limited time or take the Oath And he preferr'd the latter. Was not imprison'd before he took it. Never took the Oaths to the King nor was ever desired to do it As evidence of his Loyalty. Says he retired to his own House in 1779 when Genl Prevost [2] landed And did not take up arms to defend the Garrison. He was order'd by the Coll or Lieutt Coll of the Rebel Militia to go into Garrison & defend the Place but refused in consequence whereof he was seis'd by a Party of the American Troops carried on board a Prison Ship where he remain'd in the common Gaol 17 Weeks. He then had permission to return to his own House where he continued till Sir Henry Clinton landed (being about 7 or 8 Weeks) & was then order'd back into the Garrison where he went to (& was order'd to remain in) his own House. During the whole of the siege he never did any Act agt the King's Army few or none of the Inhabitants of the town took

A Loyalist. But took the Oath of Allegiance to the State of South Carolina & admits that he did it to preserve his property.

Did not bear Arms.

[1] Sabine (op. cit., vol. i, p. 360) remarks that he probably went to England after 1782, which is here made certain.

[2] Colonel Augustine was made Brigadier-General in April 1777. He commanded in East and West Florida, and had bitter altercations with Governor Tonyn. He became Major-General in 1779. Prevost distinguished himself by his successful defence of Savannah in the same year. He was intimate with Haldimand and there are numerous references to him in the latter's *Diary* (Brymner, *Can. Archives*, 1889).

the Oaths of Allegiance they only sign'd a Declaration of their Allegiance. He sign'd the Declaration of Allegiance some time after the arrival of Sir Henry Clinton. This he did voluntarily but says that if his character had not been known & he had declined to sign the Declaration he would have been obliged to quit the Town. He was consider'd as a loyal Subject & was therefore not called upon to sign it. It was long after the Capture when he sign'd it.

He was appointed soon after the Capture of the town one of the Referrees for reporting on the conduct & Characters of such persons as applied to be admitted British Subjects. The town was taken the 12th of May he sign'd the declaration of Allegiance either in July Augt or Septr. It was before he was appointed a Referree. He sign'd with other Inhabitants an Address to the Commrs Sir Henry Clinton & Admiral Arbuthnot expressive of their Loyalty in June 1780. This was the first Address to any Officer under the Crown of Great Britain. He was urgently pressed to accept the office of Referree by Coll Balfour.[1]

His property was confiscated in consequence of his signing an Address to the Commander Lord Cornwallis for embodying the Militia. His property is not sold to his knowledge. Mrs Davies (his wife) now resides in the House. She was born in America but educated in England. She lives in Charlestown. Does not know whether she pays rent for it or not. She has a Brother (Mr Kennan) a violent American. Has two Children who are with his Wife. He was not on good terms with his brother in Law. He believes the whole of his Property is confiscated & that neither himself or family will ever have any benefit from it & that it will not be in the power of his Brother in Law to procure the restoration of his property. Proof of Confiscation.

N.B. The Claimant in his Schedule values the Stock at double the real value & admits that he does so & says that he was advised to do it & supposed that the Commrs would moderate it. Being asked who advised him to do it He refuses to tell & says he cannot recollect it. Personal Estate allowed £100.

Says the furniture taken & destroy'd during the siege were worth £300 Sterling.

Speaks to a Coach 3 Chairs Coach Horses &c & swears they were worth £200 Sterling.

That he lost Charlestown Bank Notes to the amt of £150 & in lawful Paper Money £80 which were taken with his Cloaths total £230. Disallowed.

That 3 Negroes were Seduced during his Confinement in the Prison Ship & were well worth £60 per head £180 Sterling. Disallowed.

That 5 were taken by the Army during the siege which he lost & they were well worth £300 Sterg. Disallowed.

Waves the protested Bills of Exchange mentd in the Memorial & the Bonds of Wm Moultrie & Benjn Guerard. Believes the other Debts are good.

Has heard several Gentn say that he ought to put his Cattle &c at the full Value as it would be reduced by the Commrs. This advice was given at Charlestown. Since he came to Engd he was advised to put his Negroes at their full

[1] General Nisbet Balfour, *b.* 1743, *d.* 1823. He is in the *Dict. of Nat. Biography.* He was commandant of Charlestown and Lieutenant-Colonel of the 23rd Regiment. Clinton wrote in December 1781 that he could not be allowed to go home as his services were essentially necessary (*Hist. MSS. Comm., Am. MSS. in R. Inst.*, vol. ii, p. 367).

value. Can't tell when or where this Advice was given him but thinks it was in a public Company—can't recollect one person present.

Gov^r Bull—sworn.

Has known the Claimant about 20 Years. He was in trade & a Man of credit. When the troubles grew violent the Claim^t frequently in conversation express'd his disapprobation of them. He always appear'd averse to the Proceedings of the Rebels. The Claimant was confined 17 Weeks by the Rebels for what reason he knows not. Gov^r Bull employ'd him as his own Secretary after his return to Carolina on the Recapture of Charlestown & entrusted him confidentially to write his Letters to the Secretary of State. The Witness did not know that he took the Oath of Allegiance to the American State. If he had known it the Circumstance would not have shaken his Opinion of his Loyalty as he was probably overawed by the Ruling Powers.

Rob^t W^m Powell [1]—Col^l of the Charlestown M^a—sworn.

Says he was not much acquainted with the Claimant but he was reputed a Loyalist. Col^l Powell did not take the Oath to the Rebels but left the Country. He did not know that the Claimant took the Oath but has no doubt he did otherwise he could not have remain'd in the Country. At the time of the siege he & those in the King's army who knew the Claimant's Character consider'd him as a Loyalist. Thinks M^r Davies was one of the first who sign'd the Declaration of Allegiance. He recommended him & press'd him to take the Office of Sheriff of the Police. The Office was given on Acc^t of his Losses on the Neck by way of producing something to him for present Support. The Witness consider'd him as a Loyal Subject & still thinks him such.

Determin'd 7^th of Nov^r 1783.

### Memorial of Nath^l Hatch [2] Esq

Oct^r the 17^th 1783.

Nathaniel Hatch Esq—the Claimant—sworn.

He was in 1773 (as he thinks) appointed one of the Mandamus Council of the Province of Massachusets Bay.[3]

Has given the most satisfactory proofs of Loyalty.

Did not bear Arms.

At the time the Mob assembled in Boston to compel the Consignees of the India Company to resign their employments The Memorialist as a Justice of the Peace appear'd to quell it & remain'd with the Consignees till the Mob was dispers'd. He was obliged to quit his House in 1775 after the Affair at Lexington & fly to Boston with his Wife & Children. Staid at Boston till it was evacuated & then went to Halifax where he staid till the winding up of the business of the Admiralty Court. Was very ill treated by the Mob at Boston when he compell'd the Boston Mob to disperse.

The three Offices which he held were

[1] *d.* 1835. See Sabine, op. cit., vol. ii, p. 200. There is a memorial from him to Carleton on behalf of the Committee of South Carolina loyalists, dated August 13, 1782, in *Hist. MSS. Comm., Am. MSS. in R. Inst.*, vol. iii, p. 68.

[2] Son of Colonel E. Hatch, one of the heroes of the Louisbourg expedition (Stark, op. cit., p. 430). Mr. Stark erroneously states that he died in 1780. In fact, Nathaniel Hatch 'About a fortnight ago cut his throat at Pangbourne soon after a cheerful dinner' (Letter of Dr. Peter Oliver (July 27, 1784) in *Diary and Letters of Thomas Hutchinson*, vol. ii, p. 409).

[3] His name does not appear in the list given by Stark, op. cit., p. 136.

Office of Clerk to the Court & Justice of the Common Pleas—valued at £40 a year. — Office £40 a Yr.

Deputy Judge of the Court of Vice Admiralty established at Boston—valued at £100 a Yr. — Disallowed.

One of the two Clerks of the Superior Court of Judicature Court of Assize & general Gaol Delivery for the Province of Massachusets Bay—the value of this Employment £135 a Yr. — Office £135 a Yr.

Admits that he [1] £100 from Genl Gage at Boston to support him there And when he came to Engd He had £200 given to him immediately upon his Arrival & an Allowance of £200 a Yr which Allowance commenced in the Year 1777 & has been continued to him ever since. — Bounty £200 a Yr.

N.B. No Evidence given of Confiscation & Sale but from Mr Hatch's Situation it must inevitably be so.[2] — Presumptive Proof of Confiscation.

### Memorial of Mr Joshua Loring [3]

Determin'd Novr the 8th 1783.

Joshua Loring—the Claimant—sworn. Octr the 18th 1783.

Was Sheriff of the County of Suffolk. He held a Commission of Lieutt in the 15th Regt of foot & served many Years in the last War. He gave very sufficient proof of his Loyalty. He was born at Boston & resided there till the commencement of the troubles. On the 19th of April 1775 He was obliged to abandon his House with his Wife & Children & fly for refuge to Boston. He resided at Dorchester 4 Miles from Boston. He was Sheriff of the County of Suffolk & Deputy Surveyor of the King's Woods in North America. He had £100 a Yr Salary as Surveyor of the Woods & 6*s*. 8*d*. a Day for traveling Expences when employ'd—this Office ceas'd in Decr 1777. He had an House in Dorchester with 13 Acres of Land situated 4 Miles from Boston. This he values at £750. — A Loyalist. Did not bear Arms.

Office of Sheriff.

Produces the Appointment which was during pleasure under Genl Gage. There was no Salary annex'd to it but it arose from fees And he values it at £300 a Yr. He gave £500 to the Person who held it before to resign it. — Office. No annual Loss the Office having been granted in 1775 But a Loss of £500 in the whole.

Office of Deputy Surveyor.

Produces the Commission or Deputation from Govr Wentworth [4] in March 1767 Salary £100 a Yr The traveling Charges about £100 a Yr. He never recd any benefit from it after Decr 1777. — Disallowed.

In 1776 he was appointed Commissary of Prisoners at New York at 20*s*. a Day. He continued to receive this Allowance to June 1783 when it ceased. When at New York he was allow'd an House Coals & Candles a ration for himself & one for his Servt.

He never actually bore Arms against the Americans but he has been in such active situations as to justify their considering him to have done it.

[1] *Sic* ? received.

[2] His name was in the Conspiracy Act of 1779. There seems a misprint in Stark, who speaks of the landed property belonging to Hatch being purchased for £18,000 and afterwards offered to Hancock for £45,000. The sums should be, I presume, £1,800 and £4,500.

[3] See Additional Notes, p. 77.

[4] Sir John Wentworth, *b.* 1737, *d.* 1820. He was Governor of New Hampshire from 1766 to 1776, and of Nova Scotia from 1792 to 1808. He is in *Dict. of Nat. Biography*.

Determin'd the 6$^{th}$ of July 1785.

## Memorial of W$^{m}$ M$^{c}$Gilliwray

18$^{th}$ Oct$^{r}$ 1783.

W$^{m}$ M$^{c}$Gilliwray—the Claimant—sworn.

A Loyalist. Did not bear Arms.

Since Dead.

He is a Capt$^{n}$ in his Majesty's Invalid forces. He was reduced after the peace in 1762. He upon all occasions discouraged & discountenanced the Disturbers of Gov$^{t}$. In the Year 1776 He was confined & afterwards banished & his Estate confiscated. The reason of his being imprison'd was that he refused to take the Oaths to the Rebels & a Party was sent to make him Prisoner in consequence of which he was banished in the Year 1777 & was obliged to leave all his property behind him. He was only permitted to take two Servants with him. He was detain'd a Year in Charlestown before they would give him a passage.

Determin'd the 7$^{th}$ of Nov$^{r}$ 1783.

## Memorial of M$^{rs}$ Gibbes

21$^{st}$ Oct$^{r}$ 1783.

The Board are of Opinion that the Claimant's late Husband John Gibbes was inimical to the Cause of Great Britain & that his Property has not been confiscated and therefore the whole of the Claim is disallowed.

Mary Ann Gibbes—the Claimant—sworn.

She never in any shape gave any Assistance to the Rebels. Being asked whether her Husband took any part in the Dispute She says he never did that she knew of And in fact that his State of health would not permit him to do it being at that time a very infirm Man. Her Husband is dead. She does not know that the Estate is confiscated. Her Husband's Brother upon his death administer'd to his Effects & sold all the Negroes off the Plantation. She says she has lost considerably by the misconduct of the Administrator but she admits that she has a remedy ag$^{t}$ him & does not claim for that Loss. She says her Husband's Brother took no part in the dispute & that he was not molested by either side. She admits that she is entitled to Dower upon the Estate but it has never been assign'd to her. The House on the Plantation call'd the Grove was accidentally set on fire & the Loss about £700. She claims a Compensation for this. Col$^{l}$ Balfour for two Years allow'd her £50 a Y$^{r}$ for the Use of her Plantation. Afterwards upon her Complaining that it was too little He & Gen$^{l}$ Leslie [1] allow'd her £160 a Year untill the Evacuation.

James Carson—Witness—sworn.

Knows M$^{rs}$ Gibbes knew her Husband. Believes there was no Will. Being asked to the principles of the two M$^{r}$ Gibbes's he says they were easily sway'd according to the Company they were in. M$^{rs}$ Gibbes was uniformly loyal. He looked upon her Husband's Brother to be rather ag$^{t}$ the British Gov$^{t}$ And being press'd upon the Subject He says that upon the whole he thinks that M$^{rs}$ Gibbes's Husband was rather inclined to the American Cause.

Determin'd the 20$^{th}$ of Oct$^{r}$ 1783.

## Memorial of Sir James Wright [2] Bar$^{t}$

20$^{th}$ Oct$^{r}$ 1783.

Sir James Wright—the Claimant—sworn.

A very meritorious Loyalist.

He was appointed Governor of the Province of Georgia in the Year 1761 And was Lieut$^{t}$ Gov$^{r}$ the Year before. He continued Gov$^{r}$ untill the Evacuation in 1782. He resided there from Oct$^{r}$ 1760 to July 1771. He then came home

[1] Alexander Leslie became Brigadier-General in 1776, Major-General in 1779, and Lieutenant-General in 1781. He took the command at Charlestown in December 1780.

[2] See Additional Notes, p. 77.

with the King's leave of Absence & never meant to go back. He meant to settle in this Country but the King's Ministers desired him to go out again & he accordingly left Falmouth in Dec^r 1772 & landed in Georgia in Feb^y 1773. He staid till March 1776 when he was driven away & he came to Eng^d in June 1776 where he remain'd till April 1779. The Province was retaken by Col^l Campbell in Dec^r 1778. He was ordered out again by Lord Sackville in April 1779 & staid there till the Evacuation. Bore Arms & render'd essential Services to the British Gov^t.

To prove his Loyalty (of which there was no doubt) He produces a Letter from Lord Mansfield & refers to an extract from a Letter written by Lord Sackville dated the 19^th of January 1780 published in a Pamphlet which he produces & the Original of which he promises to send to the Office. This Letter speaks in the highest terms of Sir James Wright's conduct.

Property.

He speaks first to the three Savannah Plantations And produces many Deeds (having preserved them all) to support his title to them. Foreseeing the Storm He had all his Lands apprais'd in 1776 with a view to prove the Value when the Rebellion should be quell'd & to recover it from the Rebels as he had not the smallest [1] but that this Country would prevail.

The extent of the three Savannah Plantations are 780 Acres. Produces a Plan of it taken by the Surveyor Gen^l. He values these Lands at £8400 & would not have taken that Sum for them. When he bought these Lands they were uncultivated. He cultivated them & they are now the highest cultivated Lands in the Province. One of the Men who valued his Lands is now here & the other in Georgia. He really thinks that they would have sold for £8400. He means if they had been sold upon Credit. He was possess'd of this Estate in fee Simple & there were no Incumbrances upon it. He had made no Settlement of it or conveyance of any sort. £5000.

Estate at Conuché.

He produces the title Deeds belonging to it. He purchased it in 1769. At that time a good deal of the Land was clear'd. It consisted of 500 Acres & the Purchase Money was £714 2*s.* 8*d.* It was a very compact Estate & 14 Miles & ½ from the Town of Savannah. This Plantation was valued by the same Gent^n at the same time & for the same purpose. This Estate was employ'd in making Rice. Thinks it was worth £2100. Can't say what this Estate produced. £600.

Estate at Mount Laurel.

This was his own Plantation (the reason for saying this is that he had given several of his Estates to his Children which he agreed to strike out of this Memorial). This was the first Land which he purchased.

Values the Lands at Wrightsborough at least at 10*s.* an Acre. He contends that Lands granted & not cultivated ought not to be rejected. However he says he wishes the Commissioners would examine with great strictness & wishes they would totally reject Lands in that predicament. He has 1600 Acres of Land which he purchased in Wrightsborough which he values at 10*s.* an Acre—2000 another part of the 5200 Acres He values at 30*s.* an Acre tho' not cultivated. He bought them of his Brother & gave £1000 for them. He has lost the Interest

[1] *Sic.* ? doubt.

upon the Money since that time but he has taken no steps to cultivate them. 1000 Acres another part of this purchase he bought of Mr Moody & he values them at 10s. an Acre.

Disallowed. He had 19.354 Acres of Land in different Tracts. He values them all at 10s. an Acre. 6804 parcel of these were in Wrightsborough. He has seen them & values them at 10s. an Acre. The other part he has not seen but he believes it is of equal Value.

Disallowed. He mentions some Dwelling Houses which he purchased in the Town of Savannah in the Year 1781 & gave about £300 for them. These with two Lots of Land containing 45 Acres each he values at £900. He says they were at least worth £700. His title to these Houses was under an Execution in which 500 Acres of Land were included. He had six Lots in the Township of Brunswick which were uncultivated. He values these at £20 each. These Grants cost him only the fees of Office they were made to him in 1772. Being asked as to the Expence of his Grants he says in general they cost him about £8 each. £48.

Here ends Sir Jas Wright's Landed Property.

Negroes.

£9000. He lost originally 523 Negroes when the British Govt was first subverted & when he returned to his Govt in Georgia He recover'd at different times 323 which leaves the Number of Negroes lost exactly 200. He values them at £52 15s. each. 523 were deliver'd to the Rebel Commissioners in 1778 And the 200 are totally lost to him to all intents & purposes. Being asked to their value He says upon his Oath that they were at least worth that Money upon an average. He admits that he recover'd back most of the valuable Negroes. He confines his Value to his own Gang of Negroes & not as a general Value all over the Province. Being asked to the Average Value of Negroes in the Province of Georgia He says he should estimate them from £40 to £45. As he admits that he got back most of the valuable Negroes the Average upon those lost must certainly be less & upon considering the matter again he consents to average his own Negroes the whole 200 at £50 each which makes exactly £10000—Sterling.

Disallowed. Besides this he makes a Charge for 43 Negroes killed & taken at different times by the Americans which he values at £52 15s. each. These were a part of the Negroes which he recover'd & they were some of the most valuable of his Negroes. They shot his best Carpenter. Has some memorandums respecting this business & promises to deliver them to the Commrs. He says these Minutes were made at the time. Respecting the Insurance of the Negroes which cost him near £1000 He says he was obliged to send them away & he thought it prudent to make the insurance because if they had been lost in their Passage he should have thought he had a right to apply to Govt for the Loss. No allowance having been made for death Sir James being asked how many upon an Average die in each Year He says about 3 in each £100.

Rice.

The first Article respecting the Rice is 4596 Barrels of merchantable Rice on the several Plantations & which were deliver'd over to the Rebel Commrs by his Attornies in Jany 1777. He estimates these at £2 10s. per barrel. He values clean Rice at 50s. per barrel. He admits that Govr Graham perfectly

Clean Rice £5124
rough Rice £925 10s.

understood the Value of Rice (and he had valued Rice upon Mr Knox's Estate at only 40*s.* per barrel). But it appears by the Evidence that Mr Knox's barrels were only 500 weight & Sir James Wrights 550. Sir James Wright produces an Inventory by which it appears that there were only 4307 Barrels which is 289 short of the number mention'd by Sir Jas Wright. The Inventory is sign'd by the Rebel Commrs & attested by Sir James's own Attornies. He endeavours to acct for the 289 Barrels & gives some Acct of 136 Barrels taken by the Rebels prior to the seizure by the Commrs but he gives no Acct of the remainder only by Conjecture that as the Rebels from time to time used to take his Rice they must probably have taken at least to that amount.

Plantation Tools £500.
Coach Phaetons £150.
Crop of Rice left at the Evacuation £1200.

Indian Corn.

He estimates the Loss of Indian Corn at 1020 Bushels. It appears by the Inventory that so much was deliver'd to the Rebel Commrs & Sir James estimated it at 3*s.* per Bushel. £102.

N.B. Many persons at different times have been asked as to the Value of this Article & they have generally put it at about 2*s.* per bushel And Mr Simpson in another Case said that from the Year 1770 to 1775 he had known it sell from 1*s.* 6*d.* to 2*s.* But he thinks if the Corn was good the fair Average Value would be about 2*s.*

Stock & Tools.

He says his Plantations were very well stocked & that he values this head of Loss at the time it was deliver'd to the Rebel Commrs at £1604 9*s.* 3*d.* The Cattle he estimates between 8 & £900 the Tools he says were worth between £7 & £800. Cattle £546 10*s.*

Sir James Wright being asked to his Salary from Govt He admits that he receiv'd his Salary from Govt during the Years 1777 & 1778 which Salary was £1000 a Yr without any Deduction. His Salary is now stopp'd & he seem'd to think that he was now receiving nothing from Govt. However he was informed He had an Allowance of £500 a Yr from the Treasury to commence from the time that this Salary as Govr ceased.

Proof of Confiscation.
Bounty £500 a Yr.

John Jameson—sworn. 23d Octr 1783.

He was employ'd by Sir James Wright in 1776 to appraise his Negroes. He did it as an Act of friendship & was not paid for it. He is no common Appraiser. The paper of Appraisement is produced to him but he says it is not his writing. He has sign'd it but he sign'd it since he came to Town. He says the Negroes were some good & some bad they were like other people's Negroes but not better.

He appraised all Sir James's Plantations soon after he apprais'd the Negroes by the Desire of some of Sir James's Attorneys. He was not upon all the Plantations. Admits it to be impossible to make a very correct Valuation of Land without being upon it. Being asked how much he valued the real & personal property of Sir James Wright He says he thinks he never valued anything but Lands & Negroes & he thinks he valued them together at between 60 & £70.000 Sterling. He thinks the Rice Ground worth £15 an Acre because he thinks it would produce 4 barrels an Acre which would be worth £10—if it would only produce two Barrels an Acre (which is the Average Quantity) he would only give half that Sum. The Lands at Ogeeche he says (tho' in themselves as good Lands) He does not value at more than one half of the other Lands because they were not half so highly cultivated. Being asked whether the Barns were included in the Valuation he says he will not speak positively but he thinks they were included. He says the net proceeds of the three Savannah Estates were near £2000 a Year. He speaks of some uncultivated Land which he himself purchased at 10*s.* an Acre.

Lieut^t Gov^r Graham—sworn.

Knows Sir James Wright's Plantations they were very highly cultivated. There were three Plantations at Savannah—there were 330 Acres of Rice Land & he recollects that in one Year he made above 1100 barrels thinks it was in 1770 or 1771. He has seen a Paper of Sir James's Overseer by which it appears that 1100 Barrels were made in the Year 1776. The Lands were very valuable & Sir James always managed his Estate very well. He has seen a Valuation of £8000 & upwards. He thinks it a very high Valuation but Sir James's Estates were in such high estimation & so near the Town that he thinks they would have sold for so much if they had sold upon credit. He thinks the Rice Land worth £15 an Acre. Thinks the high Land worth £3 an Acre separate from the Rice Land but taking the Rice Land & high Land together (as they cannot be sold separately) He thinks the Estates worth £8000 & that the Estates in high Land as attached to the Rice Land were worth £4 an Acre. Thinks the cultivated Rice Lands at Ogeeche worth £10 an Acre & the high Lands adjoining 20*s.* an Acre. Being asked to the Price of Rice he says 8*s.* for Hundredweights. He does not say anything very material respecting the other Estates.

Gov^r Graham being asked whether he can speak to any particular Acts of Sir James Wright's zeal for Gov^t—Says—he was zealous in his Exertions about the Stamp Act & that he was at all times very strenuous both in Council & War for the British Gov^t. He adds that he did very material Service in the defence of Savannah.

Being asked what he thinks might be the produce of Sir James's Estates upon the whole He says he cannot say but has frequently heard that it amounted to £6000 a Y^r. In the Year 1776 Rice sold for 50*s.* a barrel but thinks 45*s.* a fair Average price taking it for ten Years together.

Office £1000 a Y^r.

Rates the Emolument of his Office at 1000 per Ann. Ster^g.

**To the Memorial of Sir Ja^s Wright Bar^t**

17^th Nov^r 1783.

Colonel James Moncrief [1]—sworn.

Says that on the day the French summon'd the Town of Savannah to surrender which was the 16^th of Sept^r 1779 in the Afternoon Sir Ja^s Wright being one of the Members of the Council of War a Reflection was thrown out by a Member of the Council that he was prejudiced in favor of the Defence of the Place as he had great property in the Province. Sir James declared that so far from having any prejudice of that kind if the Town surrendered upon

[1] Commanding Engineer to the south district during the last years of the war.

terms he was sure of getting his property as he was convinced the French would give the Garrison any terms to obtain possession of the Place And that he had rather see his whole Property torn to pieces than so shameful a thing should be done as to surrender the Town without fighting. Says that he is of Opinion that the conduct & behaviour of Sir James Wright was of material importance & that in the first Instance he was very instrumental towards the saving of the Place & that his Behaviour tended materially to confirm the minds of the wavering. He was a Member of the Council of War as being the Gov^r of the Province & had no Military command. Says he considers Sir James Wright as the first Loyalist he has met with And has been Witness to many instances of his Exertions in favor of the British Gov^t.

**The Memorial of Thomas [1] and Elisha [2] Hutchinson Sons of Gov^r Hutchinson**

Determin'd Nov^r the 18^th 1783.

27^th Oct^r 1783.

The Cases of these Gent^n were put into the same Memorial as they were very much the same & they came together. They were Consignees of the Tea & Sons of Gov^r Hutchinson. They took a decided part in favor of Gov^t & in consequence of that they were proscribed & banished. They took refuge in Castle William untill Gen^l Gage came to Boston with the Troops—the Act of Confiscation read & it contains the names of these two Gent^n. A Letter produced & read from Lord Dartmouth to Gov^r Hutchinson highly commending his Loyalty &c. They were appointed Consignees of the Tea by the East India Company. The Tea was sent to Boston in 1773 & thrown into the Sea. They produce the Probate of their father's Will by which they are appointed Joint Executors. Their Cases were enter'd into separately.

Both Loyalists.

Confiscation proved.

Did not bear Arms.

Thomas Hutchinson—the eldest Son—sworn.

Tho^s the present Claimant is the eldest Son & Heir at Law. This Gent^n is entitled to two 4^th parts of the Gov^r's property under the Will. His Brother is entitled to another 4^th part & his Sister to the other 4^th part. She is dead but she survived her father & married M^r Oliver & has left 4 Children.

Receives an Allowance of £150 a Y^r from the Treasury.

Office of Justice of the Court of Common Pleas.

He was appointed to that Office in Dec^r 1772. He produces the Appointment sign'd by his father the Gov^r. There was no Salary but it produced to him in fees &c about £45 a Year. He held it to the Year 1776. The Appointment was during pleasure but it was always understood to be for Life.

This Gent^n is Heir at Law to the father & entitled to the Estate part in fee Tail & part in fee Simple. This goes to all the Land except the Warehouse which was given by the father to the two Brothers but w^ch being convey'd to y^e eldest Bro^r belongs to him.

Bounty £150 a Y^r. Disallowed.

Elisha Hutchinson—the Brother—sworn.

Was likewise one of the Consignees of the Tea. Being asked as to the Debts He says he thinks they were all good Debts & recoverable before the troubles. He receives an Allowance of £150 a Y^r from the Treasury.

Did not bear Arms.
Bounty £150 a Y^r.

[1] See Additional Notes, p. 77.

[2] *b.* 1745, *d.* 1824. He accompanied his father to England in 1774, leaving his wife in America.

## The Memorial of Mr Walter Barrell [1]

Determin'd Novr the 6th 1783.

29th of Octr 1783.

Walter Barrell—the Claimant—sworn.

A Loyalist & did his Duty as an Officer of the Crown. Did not bear Arms. Bounty £50 a Yr.

Swears that he was appointed Clerk in the Office of Inspector of Imposts by the Commissioners of the Customs at Boston. The Salary was £60 a Year. It not being usual to turn the Clerks out of their Places unless on acct of ill Conduct he consider'd it as an Appointment for Life. He was one of the Association at Boston. He has £50 a Year recommended by Mr Wilmot & Mr Coke. Has also £60 a Year (as a Pension) from his former Situation as a Clerk in Lord Sackville's Office.

Disallowed.

He came from Boston in 1776 at the time of the Evacuation. He lost some furniture at the time but cannot put any Value upon it. He at this time has £50 a Yr for doing business in Lord North's Office but this is temporary.

Office £60 a Yr. Abolished in Octr 1782.

His Salary as a Custom House Officer was paid up to the 18th of Octr 1782 When it was discontinued since which time Mr Barrell has recd an Allowance of £50 a Yr & now continues to receive it.

Sir Willm Pepperell Bart—Witness—sworn.

Knows that Mr Barrell was one of the Association for patroling the Streets of Boston during the Blockade. He says the King has not a more loyal Subject than Mr Barrell.

## Memorial of George Walker [2]

Determin'd the 29th of March 1784.

29th Octr 1783.

George Walker—the Claimant—sworn.

He was born in Engd And was appointed Gunner of fort Johnson near Charlestown. The Salary was £28 a Yr & the Advantages made it up to £300 a Year.

A Loyalist & Did his Duty at the Fort where he was wounded & lost his Effects. Bore Arms.

In 1775 He went on board a Brig in Charles Town to clear a Ship when a very treasonable Toast was proposed to him which he resolutely refused & went on Shore. The same Day he was seiz'd by a Mob of above 500 Men who put him under a Mock Tryal as a Tory & Enemy to that Country & sentenced to be stripp'd naked tarred & feather'd carted thro' the Town & pelted with Stones for 5 Hours together & then pumped upon him for an Hour & thrown into the River off the Wharf. He swears that he had recd many violent wounds had two Ribs broke & from these Assaults one of the Men who guarded him was so near kill'd that he has heard that the Man never recover'd. In

[1] A paper in the handwriting of Walter Barrell, containing a list of the inhabitants of Boston who went in 1776 with the army to Halifax, describes him as 'Inspector-General'.

[2] 'A Mr. Walker, gunner of Fort Johnson, had a new suit of clothes yesterday without the assistance of a single taylor. His crime was nothing less than damning us all. During his circumcartation he was stopped at the doors of the principal non-associators and made to drink damnation to them all' (Letter in J. Drayton, *Memoirs of the Am. Rev. as relating to S. Carolina*, vol. ii, p. 17). See McCrady, *S. Car. in the Rev. 1775–1780*, pp. 66–7, for an account of the taking of Fort Johnson.

His memorial states that he was asked to drink damnation to King George; that he was sentenced to be put into a cart, stripped naked, tarred and feathered, pelted with mud. At the expiration of five hours to be put under a pump and pumped upon one hour, and finally to be thrown into the river. The whole of this sentence was punctually carried into execution (P.R.O., *Audit Office, Am. Loyalists*, vol. xlvi).

Addition to these Sufferings He mentions many more instances of spirited Loyalty.

Property lost.

He swears to the Loss of his Watch Cloathes & £39 16*s*. Sterling or £200 Currency. Also to the Loss of 5 Hogsheads of Rum Prime Cost £151 5*s*. Sterling. Quantity of Cheshire Cheese at prime Cost £39. Biscuit 1000 W^t prime Cost £15. 16 Loaves of Sugar—prime Cost—£13 8*s*. And other Articles to the Amount of £395 3*s*. 1*d*. Deduct £2 for an overcharge on Hogs & there remains £393 3*s*. 1*d*.

£22.

Disallowed.

The other Articles sworn to as lost &[1] make up a total Sum of £593 12*s*.

Disallowed.

In addition to this he mentions that he lost £122 10*s*. by disbursing Money at different times for Gov^t Dispatches by order of Lord W^m Campbell[2] & this has never been paid.

The Board do not decide upon this but say in their report to the Treasury that it ought to be paid.

George Rich^d Walker—Son of the Claimant—sworn.

Confirms the whole Schedule of Articles amounting to the £895. Reckons the Household furniture at above £100. Never was at New York. Does not speak to those Articles.

M^r George Walker the father called again And asked if he owed any Debts in America. He said he owed none.

Hugh Stewart—late of Philadelphia—sworn.

Said that with respect to M^r Walker's House & furniture he knew the former was burnt in 1778 as also the latter but cannot speak to the Value but the House was looked upon to be well furnish'd.

N.B. M^r Walker said that he had applied to the Treasury several times for payment of the Money which he disbursed by order of Gov^t & that the last time he was there M^r Pitt told him that if he could produce the original Certificates (which he is now able to do) he should be paid. He is therefore desired to go again to the Treasury upon a Supposition that they will pay him And in that Case this must be struck out of the Catalogue of his Losses.

## Memorial of Sam^l Sparhawk

Determin'd Nov^r the 7^th 1783.

Oct^r 29^th 1783.

Sam^l Sparhawk—the Claimant—sworn.

Produces an Appointment under the hands & Seals of Office of the Comm^rs of his Majesty's Customs in America dated y^e 10^th of June 1783 Whereby he is appointed Clerk in the Office of Inspector of Exports & Imports & Register of Shipping at Boston. Says he had a Salary of £50 a Y^r but no other fees from his Office. Says the Duty of his Office taking up very little of his time he was enabled to employ himself in Mercantile business which afforded him a comfortable Subsistance. Swears that he was one of the Persons who associated for the defence of the Town of Boston during the Blockade of the town & did Duty as a Common Soldier.

A Loyalist & did his Duty as an Officer of the Crown.

Office £50 a Y^r. Abolish'd in 1782.

Did not bear Arms.

Says he continued to receive his Salary of £50 a Y^r up to the 10^th of Oct^r

[1] *Sic.* ? omit 'and'.

[2] He was appointed Governor of South Carolina in 1773, but did not arrive at Charlestown till June 1775. He was mortally wounded at the battle of Fort Moultrie fought on June 28, 1776.

Former Bounty £100 a Yr. Present Bounty £800 a Yr.

No Evidence of Confiscation.

1782 & has recd £100 a Yr in addition thereto from the 5th of Jany 1778 to the sd 10th of Octr & has since recd £80 a Yr £20 a Year being deducted from the £100 & the £50 a Yr having been discontinued in consequence of the Investigation of Mr Wilmot & Mr Coke.

Sir Willm Pepperell Bart—sworn.

Says the Claimant was one of the Persons associated for the Defence of Boston. Has seen him in the Association Chamber where he could not have been if he had not been one of the Association. Believes him to be a very loyal Subject to his Majesty.

Determin'd ye 26th of Jany 1784.

## Memorial of Bernard Carey [1]

Bernard Carey—the Claimant—sworn. 30th Octr 1783.

A Loyalist.

Did not bear Arms.

Says he went to America in 1764 to Philadelphia & from thence to Virginia in 1766. He remain'd ten Years in Virginia. He was a Linen Draper in Williamsburgh. In the Year 1775 He says he was taken up for having in his Conversation opposed the Ideas of the Ruling powers & imprison'd for 4 Days & nights. Says he was afterwards brought to a trial before Coll Christie [2] a Rebel Coll & on a Charge of being a Tory He was found guilty but was pardon'd & set at Liberty. Says that in his Conversation he advised the people at Williamsburgh not to take up Arms agt Britain for that they were not strong enough to contend with her & that they would be more oppress'd with their own Taxes than any which would be laid on them by Gt Britain.

Says that nothing was taken from him nor did he lose any property at that time. Says he remain'd quiet in his own House for about 9 Months afterwards. Says he continued unmolested in his own House from the Month of Feby 1775 when he was tried till the Month of July following. Says Lord Dunmore was on board a Ship before he was tried. Says when he left Williamsburgh he had got together £1800 Currency which arose from the Sale of the Goods in his Shop & furniture. Says he was not interrupted in the Sale of his furniture. He left Williamsburgh in the Month of July with the £1800 in his Saddle Bags & was stopp'd by a Committee of Safety at Little York Town & this Money was taken from him by the Committee. Says after he lost his Money he came back to Williamsburgh to get a Character in order to get his Money restored.

He gives a very strange & inconsistent Acct of this business.

He says he carried the Character he recd from Mr Page & Mr Hubberd to Coll Nelson [3] who was a Rebel & a Member of the Congress. The Character

[1] As a specimen of style may be noted Carey's memorial, which runs: 'That your memorialist afterwards effected an elopement from among the rebels to that government he had at the risk of his life and fortune endeavoured to support from motives of the most ardent love thereof' (P.R.O., *Audit Office*, *Am. Loyalists*, vol. liv).

[2] He led the Virginia contingent in the expedition organized by South Carolina against the Indians in 1776 (McCrady, *S. Car. in the Rev., 1775–80*, p. 198).

[3] Thomas, *b.* 1738, *d.* 1789. He proposed a resolution in favour of independence at the Virginia Convention on May 15, 1776. He was a delegate from Virginia to the Continental Congress 1775–7 and was elected Governor of Virginia in 1781. In common with the majority of the Virginian political leaders he disapproved of the United States Constitution (Tyler, M. C., *Patrick Henry*, pp. 174, 254, 284; Ford, *Journals of the Continental Congress*, vols. ii–ix *passim*; Appleton, *Cyclopaedia of Amer. Biography*, vol. iv, p. 491).

was "that the Money he carried away with him was his own Money & that he owed no Debts" for he had been stopp'd on Suspicion & under pretence of his being carrying off the Money of the Country by leaving Debts behind him. At least this was the reason assigned by the Committee. Says that the whole of the Certificate given him by those Gent[n] Was that the Money was his own & that he was not indebted to anybody. It made no Mention of his trial or Character as a Subject. Thro' the Interest of Col[l] Nelson He obtain'd an Order from Congress to y[e] Committee of Safety for having this Money returned. Says the recommendation of the Congress to the Committee was to this effect that they sh[d] return the Money to him as they (the Congress) did not think it was an Object to take the Money of an Individual.

Says that after he got this Order he carried it to the Committee of Safety. He deliver'd it in the Evening & he was paid his Money the next morning. It was in the Month of Aug[t] When he deliver'd the Order. He says the Committee grumbled at having the Money to repay but said that as they had rec[d] Congress's Order they would not disoblige them & since they must pay it they would pay it in Paper Money. Says he afterwards sold this Paper Money for £335 Currency or thereabouts. After he got his Money he went to Philadelphia & in his Way he sold his paper Money. He went away peaceably & unmolested & after touching at Martinique & Dominique he came to Havre de Grace & afterwards to Ireland where he staid two Years.

Loss by the Paper Money £672 0*s.* 0*d.* Disallowed.

Admits that he took no active Step on behalf of the British Gov[t].

Swears that he lost by the late troubles in America by Bonds Notes & Book Debts £2000 Ster[g]. Being asked to produce the Bonds Notes & Books He says he has none of the Bonds Notes or Books for all his Papers were in a Trunk which was stol'n from him at Derby—out of his Room at M[r] Dawsons at the Castle & Falcon—this was in the Month of Dec[r] 1778. He receives £30 a Y[r] from Gov[t].

Debts £2000.

Bounty £30 a Y[r].

On being desired to name the persons from whom the £2000 Debts mentioned in his Schedule were due He names them.

Will[m] Fra[s] Bickerton—late of Williamsburgh—sworn.

Says he left Virginia in 1779. Says he knew a little of the Claimant was not intimate with him. He kept a Store in Williamsburgh. He was looked upon as a Middle Trader not one of the first rate. Says that after the troubles commenced those who were attached to the British Gov[t] were obliged to keep themselves very quiet—that the Claimant was taken up for some Expressions inimical to the ruling powers in Williamsburgh believes this was in 1775 or 1776. Heard that he had been tried & thinks it was by a Court Martial & that on his trial he made use of some Expressions which gave offence to the Court which tried him insomuch that they said he deserved to be hanged. The Claimant was pretty well respected & some of the Inhabitants petitioned in his favor & they got him off. Believes that having made himself obnoxious by these Expressions was the reason of his quitting Williamsburgh.

Says that he was afterwards himself sent up the Country as a Prisoner upon Parole as a Loyalist & he then met with a M[r] Benj[n] Day who had followed the Claimant when he left Williamsburgh & was told by M[r] Day that he had been employ'd by M[r] Ritchie to follow the Claimant under an Idea that he had carried away Money belonging to his Brother upon whom M^r Ritchie had a Claim. M^r Day told him that £1500 or £2000 in Specie was upon that Occasion taken from him by the Committee of Safety at York Town. He also told the Witness that the Money had been returned to him but in paper Money. Believes at this time there was not much difference between the Value of Paper Money & Specie but that the Paper Money was useless out of America. Says he knows nothing more of the Case of the Claimant but what he has said & what he has heard from the Claimant himself. Says he sh^d not think from M^r Carey's situation that he could have had so large a Sum as £2000 due to him besides the Effects in his Store.

John Randolph Esq [1]—late Att^y Gen^l of Virginia—called by the Board & sworn.

Knew the Claimant that he was a Resident in Williamsburgh & that he kept a Shop there. Knows nothing of his property or Loyalty. M^r Randolph was Chairman of a Gen^l Meeting of the American Loyalists out of whom a Committee was formed for the purpose of enquiring into the Claims of the Loyalists from that Province And of which Committee Major Grimes was one. Says he never heard of any landed property possessed by the Claimant. Being asked to the Depreciation of Money M^r Randolph says that in 1775 or 1776 He is of opinion it could not be equal to what is stated by the Claimant in the Memorial presented to the Board.

John Randolph Grymes [2] Esq—sworn—called by the Board.

Says he never saw the Claimant till his arrival in Eng^d. Major Grymes was a Member of the Committee above mention'd by M^r Randolph. The Claimant put in a Claim before the Committee for £2000 in Debts only. That he did mention some lands to Major Grymes but they lying in another Province the Committee took no Notice of them. Says the Claimant did mention something to him respecting the Loss of the £1800 but the Witness conceiv'd it to be included in the Sum of £2000 which was the whole extent of the Claim before the Committee.

Rob^t Gilmour Esq—sworn.

Knew nothing of the Claimant in Virginia. Speaks generally to the Claimant having put in a Claim for £2000 only & that for Debts only. Speaks of this having passed before the Committee mention'd by M^r Randolph & M^r Grymes & of which M^r Gilmour was a Member.

N.B. This Man having given a very strange & inconsistent Acc^t of himself & having greatly prevaricated in his testimony M^r Coke (knowing that he could detect him if he had sworn falsely respecting the Trunk which he says he lost

[1] John Randolph, a Virginia loyalist, was said to have been the author of a spurious collection of letters (*Letters from G. Washington to several of his friends in the year 1776*) ascribed to Washington (J. Winsor, *Narrative and Critical Hist. of Am.*, vol. viii, p. 416). He was the only officer of Government in Virginia who gave Dunmore any support (Lingley, C. R., *The Transition in Virginia from Colony to Commonwealth*, p. 118, quoting Dunmore's own language).

[2] In *Hist. MSS. Comm., Am. MSS. in R. Inst.*, vol ii, p. 338, is a note from Lord G. Germain to Sir H. Clinton, dated October 3, 1781, recommending to him Mr. Grymes of Virginia. Grymes was described by Dunmore as of the first family of Virginia, a gentleman of fortune, of amiable character, and of strict honour. He died in Virginia (Sabine, op. cit., vol. i, p. 502).

at Derby) wrote to M$^{r}$ John Harrison who is a Surgeon at Derby to enquire into the fact In consequence of which M$^{r}$ Coke rec$^{d}$ the following Answer from M$^{r}$ Harrison.

Copy of M$^{r}$ Harrison's Letter

D$^{r}$ Sir

M$^{r}$ Dawson is now with me & assures me no such person as Barnard Carey was ever at his House to his knowledge & he is certain no person whatever ever lost a Trunk at his House & says if such a thing had happen'd he must have known it & remember'd it. The Man mistakes the sign in your Letter. He calls it the Castle & Falcon but the Sign is the Elephant & Castle. I am afraid you have too many such Impostors. I am Dear Sir

in haste

Yours most sincerely

John Harrison.

Derby

Nov$^{r}$ the 1$^{st}$ 1783.

### Memorial of Jonathan Dowse [1]

Jonathan Dowse—the Claimant—sworn. Nov$^{r}$ 1$^{st}$ 1783.

Says he is a Native of Boston—was appointed extra Surveyor & Searcher of the Customs in June 1774 His Duty in that capacity at Salem & Marblehead from that time till the fall of 1775. He remain'd at Salem afterwards till the fall of the Year 1776. Says he then got from thence by way of Boston in an English Vessel which was suffer'd to come away to Eng$^{d}$ with some English Prisoners. Says his Salary was £50 a Y$^{r}$. He had no fees. Says his father was Surveyor & Searcher of the Customs & that he is still in America. Says he understands his father was not well used at first but he has latterly been permitted to reside quietly. Says he (Claimant) had no property in America And that he was the first person who was appointed extra Surveyor which Office was render'd necessary by the great increase of business owing to the Prohibitory Acts.

Determin'd Nov$^{r}$ y$^{e}$ 6$^{th}$ 1783.

A Loyalist & did his Duty as an Officer of the Crown.

Did not bear Arms.

Office £50 per Ann. Abolished in Oct$^{r}$ 1782.

Claimant produces his Appointment sign'd by the Comm$^{rs}$ of the Customs & under the official Seal whereby he is appointed Searcher of the Port of Salem & Marblehead.

John Fisher Esq—sworn.

Says he was Collector of the Customs at Salem—knew the Claimant & says he was a loyal Subject to the King. Says he was extra Surveyor & Searcher of the Customs. Says he thinks his Salary was £50 a Y$^{r}$ with no fees. Says he was appointed extra Surveyor for the purpose of doing Duty chiefly at Marblehead The Port of Salem which comprized that of Marblehead being very extensive. Says the business of the Office principally ceased after the Affair at Lexington but Witness remain'd there (tho' not constantly) till about the Month of Sep$^{r}$ following. He continued there with very little Molestation. Says he thinks the Claimant might be allowed to remain at Salem till the fall of 1776 without being imprison'd but subject to ill Usage. Says he thinks if the Port of Boston had been open the Office of an Extra Surveyor would have been

[1] The father, Joseph Dowse, signed the address presented to Gage on his arrival at Salem in June 1774.

*continued.* Says he believes the original Appointment was made on acc[t] of the extra business arising at Marblehead from the Operation of the Boston Port Bill.

Peter Frye [1]—late of Salem in Massachusets Bay—sworn.

Says he was a Justice of the Court of Common Pleas in Massachusets Bay. Says the Claimant was his Neighbour—that he was some time in the Year 1774 in the Custom House. That he always conducted himself as a faithful Subject & Servant of the Crown in his Office. That some time before the Affair of Lexington he made a considerable Seizure by means whereof he render'd himself obnoxious to the people of the Country—but does not know of any particular Act of ill treatment he suffer'd therefrom. Says that herein he acted only in the execution of his Duty.

Bounty £40 a Y[r].

N.B. The Claimant receives an Allowance of £40 a Y[r] from the Treasury which he has rec[d] since 1776.

**Memorial of Tho[s] Danforth [2] Esq**

1[st] Nov[r] 1783.

Tho[s] Danforth Esq—the Claimant—sworn.

Determin'd Nov[r] the 6[th] 1783.
A Loyalist.
Did not bear Arms.

Says that his father [3] was Judge of the Probate Court of Wills & first Justice of the Court of Common Pleas in the province of Mass. Bay. He lost his Appointments in consequence of his Attachment to the British Gov[t].

Profession £100 a Y[r].

Office Disallowed.

The Claimant before the War broke out was a Barrister & lived at Charlestown near Boston. Says that the Income of his Profession was about £100 a Y[r]. That during the Blockade of Boston he was appointed by Lieut[t] Gov[r] Oliver to the Office of Register *pro tempore* of the Vice Admiralty Court of Appeals for the 4 New Eng[d] Colonies vacant by the former Deputy having joined the Rebels without Application. Says that the Gov[r] appointed him from a knowledge of his Loyalty & Abilities as also from a Desire to serve him having been intimately connected with his family. Produces the Commission signed by Gov[r] Oliver.

Left Boston with the Army. Was never in a Situation to be necessitated to take any Oath of Allegiance to the Americans—was proscribed by them & his Name included in the Act. He bore Arms at Boston arrived there in June 1776 & did Duty under Gen[l] Gage such as patroling the Street. Had a Commission of Lieut[t] from the Gen[l]. He brought a great many Records with him to Eng[d] which had been lodged in the Office of the Vice Admiralty Court of Appeals. Swears that the Statement in his Memorial of the produce of his practice at the Bar is a just one. From Jan[y] 1777 he has been allow'd by the Treasury £100 a Y[r] which is continued to him by M[r] Wilmot & M[r] Coke's decision.

Bounty £100 a Y[r].

James Putnam Esq—late Attorney Gen[l] in the Massachuset's Bay—sworn.

Knew M[r] Danforth. Has not the least Doubt of his Loyalty. He had not been above four Years in the practice of the Law before the troubles commenced. Thinks he might have made £100 a Y[r] by his profession And being shewn the way in which M[r] Danforth estimates his Profits in his Memorial the

[1] *b.* 1723, *d.* 1820. His daughter married Dr. Peter Oliver (Sabine, op. cit., vol. i, p. 449).

[2] *d.* 1825. Sabine, op. cit., vol. i, pp. 358–9.

[3] Judge Samuel Danforth (*b.* 1696, *d.* 1777) was appointed a Mandamus Councillor in 1774, but never took the oath of office and was coerced by a revolutionary mob into resigning (Stark, op. cit., p. 187).

Witness says it is a very fair Acc[t]. He believes that the Claimant was in the Boston Association.

### Memorial of John Murray [1] Esq

Determined the 23[d] of March 1784.

John Murray Esq—the Claimant—sworn. 3[d] Nov[r] 1783.

He went to America in the Year 1735. And soon after he got to America He bought property in the County of Rutland & in 1751 He was elected Member of the Gen[l] Assembly for the County of Rutland & continued so till 1774. He was appointed in 1775 to buy provisions for the Provincial Army & in the Year after for the King's Army as well as the Provincial Corps. He produces several Commissions to shew Offices which he held amongst which is a Commission sign'd by Gen[l] Gage in 1774 appointing him one of the Judges of the Common Pleas. He was a Col[l] of Militia in 1761. He was made one of the Mandamus Council in 1774. He always exhorted the people to be peaceable & has often been insulted for so doing & had Stones thrown at him. He went to Boston the 25[th] of Aug[t] 1774. He took the Oaths at Salem the 16[th] of Aug[t] 1774 as one of the New Council. He continued at Boston till the Evacuation & took an Active part. Was one of the Associated Loyalists for the Defence of the Town. He came from Boston to Halifax & from Halifax to Eng[d]. He says his property is confiscated & refers to the Act in which M[r] Murray's name is mention'd & he is stiled one of the notorious Conspirators. He produces a Copy of the Act publish'd in a Newspaper.

A Zealous & Meritorious Loyalist.

Did not bear Arms.

Proof of Confiscation.

Sir W[m] Pepperell attending & being only to speak to M[r] Murray's Character & Loyalty he is called in.

Sir W[m] Pepperell Bar[t]—sworn.

Was first intimate with M[r] Murray in 1774 & knew no person in America who was more loyal. He was one of the Associators & very active. He was upon the Patrole with him. He always believed him to be a warm friend of Gov[t] even before these troubles.

He claims for the Loss of the Office of Justice of the Court of Common Pleas £30 a Y[r] Sterling. M[r] Murray admits that he rec[d] £100 before he left Boston & since he came to Eng[d] he has rec[d] £200 a Y[r] from the Treasury up to the time that M[r] Wilmot & M[r] Coke enquired into the List of American Pensions since which time he has rec[d] an Allowance of £250 a Year.

former Bounty £200 a Y[r].
present Bounty £250 a Y[r].

### Memorial of Will[m] Fortune [2]

Determin'd the 19[th] of Nov[r] 1783.

Will[m] Fortune—the Claimant—sworn. 4[th] Nov[r] 1783.

Says he is an Irishman. He went over with his father to America in 1766. Says he was settled on a Plantation of his own when the troubles broke out.

An Active & Zealous Loyalist.

[1] *d.* 1794. He was a Colonel of the Militia, and, for many years, a member of the General Court. He was never sworn into the office of Mandamus Councillor. After the Revolution he became a leading resident of St. John, New Brunswick. There is a portrait of him by Copley. 'The manner in which Colonel Murray kept his books and papers shows that he was a calculating, careful, and exact man in his transactions. Method is seen in everything' (Sabine, op. cit., vol. ii, pp. 115–16; see also Raymond, *Winslow Papers*, p. 209).

[2] In his memorial he states that he was taken prisoner eight different times, and that he spent three years in hiding, often seeing no one till compelled by starvation.

He purchased his Plantation in 1772. It was in Camden District. He has not got the Deed. All his papers were lost. He purchased it of his Brother. The Quantity he bought was 100 Acres. He paid for it in Horses which he thinks were worth £40 S. There were about 5 Acres clear'd. He purchased Land Warrants for 300 Acres more which he survey'd & added to it. Thinks he gave about £80 S. for this 300 acres. This was about two Years after his purchase of his Brother. It was unimproved. He built a small Dwelling House & another new House which was not finished with Corn Houses &c. He did the chief of the work himself but if he had hired people to do it it would have cost him above 100 Gas. He purchased besides this Warrants for 500 Acres more. He bought them just about the beginning of the troubles. Can't say what he gave for them—they were all unclear'd when he bought them. Says that these Lands would have sold for 6*s*. S. an Acre upon an Average. Says he is sure he gave more than £150 for the last mention'd 500 Acres. Says his father died in 1776. He died possess'd of 650 Acres upon Jackson's Creek in Camden District. About 40 or 50 Acres were clear'd. He had been possess'd of them about ten Years it was Bounty land there was a good House upon the Plantation. Thinks this Tract on an Average worth about 6*s*. an Acre. His father died without a Will & he is the eldest Son. Produces an Aff[t] sworn before one of the Intend[ts] of the Police at Charlestown whereby two persons swear to having been present at the funeral of John Fortune. Says he succeeded to 100 Acres on Jackson's Creek on the death of his Brother who died in 1768 this he values at £40 or £50 S. Says he inherited 200 Acres upon the Wateree River from another Brother who died in 1782 it was all Wood land & unclear'd. His brother did not become possess'd of it till 1777 or 1778.

Bore Arms & render'd Services. £100. £100. £35. Disallowed.

Says his Name is not down in the Confiscation Act but he apprehends himself to be banished from the State.

No proof of Confiscation.

Says in the Year 1777 He was obliged to absent himself from his Plantation & not to appear in public. This was on Acc[t] of his Attachment to the British Gov[t]. He had about 40 head of Cattle on his farm. Says he values these at 30*s*. S. a Head but admits it was the Custom in selling a large Stock to sell them for 20*s*. S. a head round. He had 8 or 9 Horses at this time on the Plantation. He values these about £4 or £5 S.

Says he had 100 Head of Hogs worth 10*s*. S. each. Values his Household furniture tools &c 30 Guineas.

Stock £95 Furniture £31 10*s*. Other Effects £25. Horses £30.

He values his own Plantation (without that of his fathers & Brothers) together with the Stock & other things upon it at £1000.

He lost 45 p[r] of Shoes valued at £12 Books valued at £12 Rum at £31 S. Says he was plunder'd by the Rebels of £80 S. in their March thro' the Country.

Disallowed.

Produces an Instrum[t] under the hand of Sir Egerton Leigh Surveyor Gen[l] of the Province whereby he is appointed to be a Deputy Surveyor for the Province.

Disallowed.

He first join'd the British Troops at Camden when they first arrived there under Lord Cornwallis it was about two Months before the battle. He did not take the Oaths. His Character was so good that it was not required. He was employ'd by the Army to look out for Corn & Cattle & had a Dollar a Day for it. He was then appointed a Captⁿ in the Militia for which he rec^d 9*s.* 4*d.* a Day besides the Dollar. He was not at the first Action at Camden. He was afterwards in several Actions.

Says he never took out the Grants upon the Warrants which he had purchased.

James Barber—Quarter Master of the Camden M^a—sworn.

First knew the Claimant after the battle of Camden about 1781. He appear'd always zealous & very forward. He was employ'd in conveying Expresses. He commanded the greatest part of the Camden M^a at the battle of Eutaws [1] where he exerted himself much his Mare was killed under him. Believes he was never paid for his Mare.

Sam^l Grakex—Waggon Master under Lord Rawdon—sworn.

Knew the Claimant first in the Year 1780. About July he was Captⁿ in the M^a. He commanded the flanking Party up to Ninety Six. Knew that he bought a Mare at Ninety Six & gave for her & a two Year old Foal £24 or £25 S. He says he distinguished himself at the Battles of the Eutaws & was made a Col^l in consequence. He was always active was much entrusted by Lord Rawdon. He was consider'd as a Man of landed Property.

Rob^t Cooper—sworn.

Witness was a private in the M^a. Knew the Claimant in 1780. Witness was out with him on an Expedition to collect Horses—they got 20 or 30. He was always a zealous Loyalist. He was in his House in the Year 1781. It was a good Country House & well furnished his Wife & family was there & in peaceable possession there was plenty of Stock about it.

### Memorial of Bartholomew Havers

Determin'd the 8^th of Nov^r 1783.

Bartholomew Havers—the Claimant—sworn. 8^th Nov^r 1783.

Produces a Certificate from Sir Will^m Pepperell to his Loyalty.

Swears that at the beginning of the troubles he render'd himself obnoxious to the Insurgents so that he was subject to great Insult.

A Loyalist.

Produces an Act of the State of New Hampshire whereby he is banished by name from that State.

Says he was Post Rider between Boston & Portsmouth was nominated thereto but had no Appointment in writing understood it to be a place during good behaviour. He consider'd himself as subject to be turned out. Has known many turned out. Consider'd it as a thing from which he might be removed.

Did not bear Arms.

Says the Salary was £40 a Y^r S. And by the advantage of carrying Money backwards & forwards he made in the whole £60 a Y^r more. Says of this he made £30 or £40 a Y^r by the Employment of the Merch^ts in carrying their Money. Says this employment of the Merch^ts arises from the Situation of Post Rider. He was employ'd in the same manner by the Comm^rs of the Customs. He was obliged to keep two Horses which cost him 40 a Year.

Disallowed.

Says he has a Wife & three Children his Wife & two of his Children are in

[1] The battle of Eutaw Springs, fought on September 8, 1781, was claimed by both sides as a victory. There is a careful account of it in McCrady, *S. Car. in the Rev. 1780–3*, pp. 441–63.

America. His furniture was partly destroyed but he cannot put any value upon it. Says he was obliged to quit his House in Nov^r 1774. Says the reason he quitted his House so soon was he had been obnoxious ever since the Stamp Act. He was appointed Post Rider about the Year 1761.

Claimant—again examined.

Says he had leave to come to Eng^d in 1771 And during his Absence the Commiss^rs of the Post Office put in another & he never had it again nor did he afterwards receive his Salary.

Says when he quitted America he kept a little Shop & had a concern in a Trade. Confesses the Loss of his Employment had no concern with the Troubles.

Sam^l Hale—late of Portsmouth New Hampshire—sworn.

Says he wrote the Claimant's Memorial. Says he was led into the Mistake of stating him as Post Rider from his own representation. Believes him to be an honest Man & a thoroughly loyal Subject. That he was a Partizan of Great Britain. Says that he himself knew the Claimant not to have been Post Rider at the time of his quitting America but the Claimant applied to him to draw up his Memorial whilst he was engaged with other Persons. And in his hurry it did not occur to him Otherwise he would not have stated it in the manner that he has done in the Memorial.

Bounty £40 a Y^r.

N.B. The Claimant receives an Allowance of £40 a Year from the Treasury.

Determin'd the 24^th of Nov^r 1785.

**Memorial of Janet Russell** 11^th Nov^r 1783.

Widow of David Russell settled in Georgia who bore arms.

Stephen Haven—late of Savannah in Georgia Naval Officer—sworn.

Says he has seen David Russell & knew that he belonged to the Irish Settlement at Queensborough. Says he understood that he was a reputable Farmer there & possess'd of Land. He always understood the Claimant to be his Wife. Says that most of the people in that Settlement went into Rebellion & David Russell was one of the very few who preserved his Loyalty.

The Settlement was upon Briar Creek about 70 or 80 Miles from Savannah.

Bounty £40 a Y^r.

N.B. She receives an Allowance from the Treasury of 40 a Year.

Determin'd the 24^th of Nov^r 1783.

**Memorial of Eliz^th Thompson** 11^th Nov^r 1783.

Eliz^th Thompson—the Claimant—sworn.

The Claim^t & her Husband Loyalists.

Says she is an Englishwoman. She went to Charlestown about 1768 or 1769 & was a Mantua maker. She afterwards kept a Shop. Says her Husband quitted Charlestown in 1776 & came to Eng^d. Says that the Council of Safety applied to her Husband to take the Oaths to the Rebel States which he refused & therefore quitted the Country. He never went to America afterwards. She continued there unmolested after her Husband's Departure except that the Rebels took her Negroes from her & they threatened her.

House in which she had a life Estate in Charlestown £350.

Says she assisted the British Prisoners at Charlestown but never got into any trouble on that Acc^t. She does not know that they had any Suspicion of her. The Letters she convey'd were private ones. She employ'd a Negro in carrying Letters from the British Officers in Charlestown (particularly a Captn Ferguson) to the British Army. Says that she supported 7 British Officers in her House near four Months when they were Prisoners. They were Provincial Officers. She made it a rule to enquire what Prisoners were brought in & she always assisted them.

James More—late of Charlestown Storekeeper—sworn.

Says he was acquainted with the Claimant & that she kept a Store in Charlestown. She had a good House there which he has heard was her own. Knows no particulars of her property. Says she was a Loyalist & very serviceable to the British Prisoners. When he was Prisoner himself has known several Bottles of Rum & other things sent to several of the Prisoners in Distress which he understood came from the Claimant. Says she was in a good Way of business & was esteem'd to be worth a good deal of Money.

### Memorial of Lieut Hugh Fraser [1]

Determin'd the 28th of Novr 1783.

Lieut Genl Richd Prescot [2]—sworn. Novr 1783.

Says the Claimant was driven from his property on Acct of his Loyalty & came to the British Lines at Rhode Island. Believes this was in 1775 or 1776. Says he served under him at Rhode Island as under Commissary of Provisions. He undertook the baking for the Troops & furnished them with one Pd of bread per Man a Week more than the Commissary did at the same Price. Says his Loyalty is unquestionable And he found him full of resource & zeal for his Majesty's service & he gave a great deal of useful Intelligence for which he has never recd a reward. Believes his Pay was a Dollar a Day. Says he had a farm at Bennington or near it but is ignorant of its value.

A Zealous Loyalist.

Did not bear Arms.

Lieut Hugh Fraser—the Claimant—sworn.

Says he was a Lieut in the latter part of the War before the last. He was reduced to half pay on the Peace & made a purchase at Mapleton near Albany in the Province of New York where he settled. Says in the Year 1775 He applied to the Committee of Safety at New York for leave to remain in a State of Neutrality & was told by them that he might depend upon remaining in a State of Quiet whilst he continued to give them no Molestation.

Says in June 1778 he was made a Prisoner by the County Committee of Albany. Says he was carried by a Captn's Guard before the Committee at Albany And was by them permitted to return home on promise not to go out of the County.

Says in the Octr following when Genl Carleton came over the Lakes he was again made Prisoner & confined to the Town of Albany from whence he made his Escape to the British Army in the Jersey whom he join'd in Novr. Says

[1] The following paragraph may refer to this Hugh Fraser: 'Oct. 30, 1778, Hugh Fraser, who was some time ago brought down from Harperfield and confined, was brought before the Board; and he, having produced a number of certificates in his favour from a number of persons well attached to the American cause, and no special charges being alleged as against him, . . . discharged . . . on his entering into recognisances.' (*Minutes of Commissioners for Conspiracies, Albany Board*, vol. i, p. 268.)

[2] General Prescott was twice taken prisoner in the war. According to Sir G. Trevelyan (*The Am. Rev.*, part iii, p. 363, note), 'Prescott is remembered as a tyrannical, violent-tempered man,—a terror to the revolted colonists everywhere, except in battle'.

his Motives for making his Escape were that he expected Ruin by being kept Prisoner during the whole War & he was attached to the British Gov^t^.

Says that in a Conversation between him & a M^r^ Duane [1] a Member of the Congress at Albany M^r^ Duane offer'd to put him at the Head of a Reg^t^ if he would accept anything in the service of the Congress. This he refused. He left his father his Wife & his family at this time at his House in the Country. Says that after Col^l^ Baume's Action [2] his family were stripp'd of every thing by Gen^l^ Gates's Army.

Says that immediately upon his joining the British he was recommended from Gen^l^ Howe's former knowledge of him to M^r^ Chamier [3] the Commissary under whom he was employ'd as Under Commissary with the pay of 5*s*. a Day & went with the Expedition to Rhode Island. Says he continued about 8 or 9 Months at the Pay of 5*s*. a Day When he made a Proposal to the commanding Officers of the different Corps at Rhode Island to supply the Troops with 8 Pound of bread per week for 7 P^d^ of flour which Proposal was accepted & he continued to perform the Contract till the Evac^n^ of Rhode Island.[4]

Says upon this Contract being made with him he was dismiss'd from his Employment by Major Morryson the Principal Commissary at Rhode Island who furnished the troops with bread before them & who had given the troops only 7 P^d^ of bread for 7 P^d^ of flour. Says he never rec^d^ anything during the furnishing the troops with bread but the profit he made of the Contract.[5]

## Memorial of James Barber

Determin'd the 19th of Nov^r^ 1783.

13th Nov^r^ 1783.

James Barber—the Claimant—sworn.

Produces several Certificates to his Loyalty from Lord Cornwallis & others—read.

A Loyalist.

Says he is an Irishman. He went to America in the beginning of 1775. He was about 16 when he went away from Ireland.

Did not bear Arms.

He first settled in Pensylvania as a Labourer & left the Country on his being called upon to take the State Oath & to serve in the M^a^ rather than comply with this requisition. He went from hence to South Carolina where he employ'd

[1] James Duane, *b.* 1733, *d.* 1797, represented the Conservative wing of the revolutionary party in New York. As late as May 1776 he wrote: 'There seems no reason why our Colony should be too precipitate in changing the present mode of government. . . . Let us see the conduct of the middle colonies before we come to a decision. It cannot injure us to wait a few weeks' (C. L. Becker, *The Hist. of Political Parties in the Province of New York, 1760–76*, Madison, Wisconsin, 1909, p. 266; for biography see Appleton, op. cit., vol. ii, p. 235).

[2] The ill-fated Bennington expedition of August 1777 is vividly described in a French account in *Hist. MSS. Comm., Stopford-Sackville MSS.*, vol. ii, *Am. Papers*, pp. 76–7; and see Trevelyan, op. cit., pp. 140–50.

[3] Grave charges with regard to his conduct as commissary were made by Judge Jones (*Hist. of New York during the Rev. War*, vol. i, pp. 116–18). Jones, however, cannot be accepted as an unprejudiced witness.

[4] There is a spirited account of the operations at Rhode Island in Trevelyan, *George III and Charles Fox*, vol. i, pp. 129–41.

[5] In this connexion note the scathing denunciation, dated December 22, 1780, by Rodney of this vicious system in *Hist. MSS. Comm., Stopford-Sackville MSS.*, vol. ii, *Am. Papers*, p. 191; and by Jones, op. cit., vol. i, pp. 330–52. But see note [3] above.

himself in farming till the Arrival of the King's Troops at Camden after the reduction of Charlestown. He join'd Col$^{l}$ Rugely's [1] Corps as a Militia man at the hanging Rocks.[2] He was appointed a Serj$^{t}$ in the Reg$^{t}$ & did Duty as such till he was appointed Quarter Master. In this latter Capacity he continued till the Year 1781 when he got leave to quit the Reg$^{t}$ & come to Ireland.

Says in 1778 he took possession of 100 Acres of Land under a borrowed Warrant—which was survey'd to him. He paid for the Survey & Expences in Continental Money—which he was paid in Pensylvania when he should have been paid hard Money. It did not cost him much. Believes the whole Expence was about £20 S. He cultivated part of it.

Disallowed.

Says he had a little knowledge of Tanning & he was employ'd to tan Leather. He had one side for tanning the other. Swears he had 18 sides of tann'd Leather. He can't speak to the Value but has been informed that 10*s.* per Side is a fair price.

Says he has an Allowance of £20 a Year from Gov$^{t}$.

Bounty £20 a Year.

N.B. No Evidence of Confiscation or Sale. But it is immaterial as the Lands to which alone it can apply are disallowed by the Board for Want of title.

### Memorial of George Derbage

Determin'd the 18$^{th}$ of Nov$^{r}$ 1783.

George Derbage—the Claimant—sworn. 18$^{th}$ Nov$^{r}$ 1783.

He is an Englishman went first to America in 1760. He went to his friends there. He went from School.

In 1767 He was first appointed Deputy Surveyor of North America. The Appointment produced & read it is dated in Dec$^{r}$ 1766. He was Deputy to M$^{r}$ Holland who was the Surveyor. He had 5*s.* a Day & continued in that Appointment till 1775 when the troubles interrupted & put an end to the Office. It appears by the Warrant that he was removeable at the pleasure of M$^{r}$ Holland. M$^{r}$ Derbage admits that Gov$^{t}$ have paid this Salary for six Years after the Office ceas'd. This was the only Office which he held prior to the troubles.

A Loyalist.

The Office of Deputy Surveyor being an Appointment held during the pleasure of an Individual held by the Board not to be an Object of our Enquiry. The whole of this Claim therefore is to be allowed.

In 1778 He was appointed Sole Assistant to the Secretary of the Commission under Lord Carlisle Gov$^{r}$ Johnson & M$^{r}$ Eden it was by the recommendation of M$^{r}$ Eden & he was paid for it. In July 1779 He was appointed Secretary Register of Deeds &c of the province of Georgia. Col$^{l}$ Thompson [3] was the Patentee & M$^{r}$ Derbage was his Deputy. He produces the Agreement between him & Col$^{l}$ Thompson by which it appear'd that he was to have a Moiety of the fees exclusive of the Salary. He rec$^{d}$ from this Office whilst he held it £580 & he says the Province are indebted to him in the Sum of £217. He was likewise Deputy Clerk to the Council & Upper House of Assembly. He acted in this

[1] Rowland Rugely, who was a member of the South Carolina Congress in 1775, became a Colonel in the South Carolina Militia. His surrender without firing a shot to a party of cavalry destroyed his prospects of becoming a Brigadier-General (McCrady, *S. Car. in the Rev. 1780–3*, p. 12). Rugely was the recipient of a letter from Lord Rawdon, which excited the indignation of Washington (Spark's *Washington*, vol. vii, p. 554).

[2] Hanging Rock, near the Catawba River, was the scene of a battle in which Sumter, the American partisan leader, defeated the British on August 6, 1780.

[3] The famous Count Rumford.

Situation from 1799 to 1782. He says upon being asked to the profit of these several Situations under Coll Thompson He says he has recd £200 for his share from 1779 to 1782. He says there was due to his share in 1782 about £108.

About the Year 1780 He was appointed by Sir James Wright Master Register & Examiner of the Court of Chancery. He had a Salary of £30 a Year granted by the Province to him on his particular Acct. He recd including the Salary about £100 in the whole. There was due to him £50 or £60 for fees in this Office.

He had no real property in America.

Sir James Wright Bart—sworn.

He never saw Mr Derbage till ye Yr 1779. When he was going out to his Govt & found that Mr Thompson was appointed to the Offices above mention'd & that he could not attend them as he was going out in a Military Line. He said he must have some Man of understanding appointed Deputy to Mr Thompson Upon which Mr Cumberland recommended Mr Derbage & vouched for his fidelity &c Upon which Sir Jas consented that he might go out as Deputy Secretary. He went out in the same Ship & Sir Jas says he found him to answer the Character which Mr Cumberland had given of him. These Offices being trifling he made him a Master in Chancery. He did this at the Request of some professional Man but he referr'd nothing to him because he knew him not to be fit for the Office & so he took the trouble to determine everything himself. Sir James being asked whether he thinks he would have filled any one of the Offices which he held in Georgia if the troubles had not happen'd He says he does not know it is impossible to say.

Govr Franklyn—sworn.

Speaks to Mr Derbage's Wife being made a Prisoner & says she was a very confidential person & used to carry Letters from Mrs Skynner to Genl Skynner. She was looked upon as a Loyalist & an active woman. Genl Skynner had fled at that time from Amboy & got on board a Vessel. Mrs Derbage being suspected of carrying intelligence & being very loyal she was ill treated. She was an American Woman. She was not paid for carrying these Letters &c. She did it from a true spirit of Loyalty & to serve Great Britain.

Mr Derbage being repeatedly asked whether (if the troubles had not happen'd) he thinks he should have held any one of the Offices which he happen'd to hold He says it was possible he might but he does not choose to speak positively. However it is not very difficult to guess what the Answer would have been if he had given a positive Answer.

## Memorial of the Revd Alexr Cruden

Determin'd the 19th of Novr 1783.

19th Novr 1783.

Revd Alexander Cruden—the Claimant—sworn.

He is a Native of Aberdeen & went to Virginia in 1750. He was ordain'd in 1749. Upon his Arrival he was elected to the Living of South Farnham & held it for 26 Years before he was molested. First molested in June 1776.

A meritorious Loyalist.

The people would not allow him to read the prayer for his Majesty & insisted on his reading a prayer for the Commonwealth—this was a Law of the province.

Did not bear Arms.

He refused to do it & that was the reason of his being turned out of his Parish.

He obtain'd leave from the Vestry who are the leading Men in the parish to live in the Glebe House as a favor. He lived here till the Dec^r following. The Vestry are the Patrons of all the Churches in Virginia. He left it in Dec^r & went to the County of Midd^x but he never officiated after July. He continued 17 Months in America & then he came to S^t Eustatia & from thence to this Country.

The Value of the Living he estimates at £150 a Year. It consisted of a Salary of 16000 pounds of Tobacco. The Tobacco was worth £8 for a Thousand Pounds which made £128. Besides this He had 250 Acres of Land besides a Dwelling House. The House & buildings he values at £25 a Y^r exclusive of the Land. He sets very little value upon the Land notwithstanding great part of the Land was cultivated. He values the Land at £12 a Year. He thinks the Land worth about £300. The Vestry were once offer'd 300 Guineas for it when they thought of exchanging the Glebe for other Land. £150 a Y^r.

He left nine Negroes with an Attorney to sell for him & believes they were sold for £375 S. He makes no Claim for this. He left furniture &c in the same situation with the same person to sell &c & part of this consisted of Debts which his Attorney was to recover for him this He values at £425 but he makes no Claim for this. The furniture Stock &c were sold to divers persons. Waved.

He says his Attorney (M^r James Mills) took a Valuation of his Negroes when they were left behind which makes £32 15*s*. for each Negro but it is under the Mark & they sold for £100 more than they were valued at. And he produces a Bond given at the same time by Ja^s Mills that he would sell all these Articles for him & remit the Money to him.

Major Grymes—sworn.

Knew M^r Cruden & that he was in possession of a Living which he thinks was worth £200 a Year Ster^g. He makes it out by valuing the Tobacco & Glebe higher than M^r Cruden. He was consider'd as a Man of substance & was a very respectable Man & a loyal Subject.

Jack Power Esq—sworn.

He knew M^r Cruden very well he lived in the same Parish. Knew him to be the Minister & that he lost the Living by his Loyalty. Being asked to the value of the Living He says he can't exactly say but says it was at least worth £150 a Y^r.

## Memorial of Will^m Keeling

Determin'd the 28^th of Nov^r 1783.

Will^m Keeling—the Claimant—sworn. 20^th Nov^r 1783.

Resided in Charlestown from 1774 till the War broke out—is an Irishman. He kept a Shop there & a Punch House. He remain'd there untill the Oath [1] was tender'd the Rebels wanted him to go with them to Florida but he refused & left the Town. The Oath was never tender'd to him. He join'd Gen^l Prevost at Nelson's ferry. He staid with him till he was taken Prisoner which was better A Loyalist. Bore Arms.

[1] In February 1777 the South Carolina Assembly passed an ordinance establishing an oath of abjuration of the King and allegiance to the State. The oath was intended to be administered to persons suspected of holding principles injurious to the rights of the State. Any persons refusing to take the oath were to be deported; and, if they returned, were to be adjudged guilty of treason, and, upon conviction, were to suffer death as traitors.

than two Months. He was more than three Months a Prisoner. He was releas'd by bail. He wanted to make himself a Prisoner of War but they would not permit him as an Inhabit[t] of the Town. He join'd the British Army again upon Charlestown Neck. He admits that the Oath was generally tender'd to everybody but persists in it's being never tender'd to him. After the taking of Charlestown He was supported as a Loyalist by Rations &c. He staid at Charlestown only three or four Months & then went to New York where he enter'd on board the Royal Oak as a Volunteer. He was in the Engagement off the Chesapeak & came home in the Roebuck with Admiral Arbuthnot.[1] He had no Land. When he left Charlestown they took his property. He took with him 7 or 800 Continental Dollars. He left all the property in his House. Says he had more than 200 Gallons of Rum. He values the Rum at 5*s.* per Gallon. He gave that for it. He could have sold it for 9*s.* He left 15 Barrels of Rice clean besides Rice in Bags. The Barrel weigh'd about 450 pound. He valued them for £1 8*s.* a Barrel. He gave that for them. This is the common price—it was cheaper before the troubles this was a great price. He used to give £4 10*s.* or £5 a Barrel Currency which is 14*s.* 6*d.* Ster[g] & the Barrels weigh'd 450 W[t]. He left 450 Bushels of Corn. He is positive as to the Quantity. Before the troubles he has bought Rum for 12*s.* 6*d.* Currency. He gave 5*s.* a Bushel for the Corn in Sterling Money. He says it was Continental Money & he paid for all the Articles in his Memorial in Continental Money. This was Indian Corn Bacon & Ham he says he had 220 P[d] & charges it at 8*s.* a P[d]. He paid that Money for it. Q[r] of Hundred w[t] of Indigo which he values at 3*s.* 6*d.* a P[d] two Hundred & ½ of Sugar valued at 8*d.* a P[d] 30 P[d] of Coffee 8*d.* a P[d] 30 P[r] of Men's Shoes—he used to sell them—values them at 3*s.* 6*d.* a P[r] 4 Horses & Cow valued at £5 apiece. He had a Stallion. He gave 350 Continental Dollars for this Horse. He was at least worth £15. Being asked how much he carried with him to America he says he had £7 or £8. He had a Chair for which he gave £5. He values his Household furniture at £25. He had 3 Beds besides tables Chairs &c. Beds cost £5 each.

All his Property £94 18*s.* 4*d.*

John Pearson—sworn.

Knew W[m] Keeling had known him for five Years he lived there then & it was a little time before Gen[l] Prevost came but does not know what Year. The Witness had been in America from 1774. He lived some time in the back Country & came to Charlestown in 1776. Being asked whether he ever took the Oaths to the Rebels he says he did not but he obtain'd a Certificate from a Justice of the Peace *that he had taken the Oaths to the Rebels* which enabled him to be quiet being asked whether M[r] Keeling could have staid without that He says he does not think he could. M[r] Keeling is called in again & says he never had such a Certificate but M[r] Pearson persists in saying that he thinks M[r] Keeling must have had such a Certificate. The Certificate was sign'd by M[r] Car Michel who was an Irishman & was then well inclined to the Rebels. He afterwards join'd the British & after that he join'd the Americans. He says Keeling was

[1] Admiral Marriot Arbuthnot, *b.* 1711 ?, *d.* 1794, is in *Dict. of Nat. Biography.* For description of encounter between the French and British fleets off the Chesapeake see Mahan, *Influence of Sea-power upon History, 1660–1783*, p. 186.

put into the Guard House more than once. The Witness had made an Aff[t] before M[r] Justice Wilmot at Shoreditch to the Property & Loyalty of M[r] Keeling. Being asked about M[r] Keeling's rum He says he has known him have some Hogsheads by him at a time. Keeling traded in the same way after Charlestown was taken.

James Moore—sworn.

Was settled at Charlestown. Kept a Store there. Knows M[r] Keeling a little but has very little Acquaintance. He has no Acquaintance with him now but he saw him in prison. He knows nothing of his keeping a shop there or being in any business but says he might have been & he not known it. Saw him the Day he came out of prison but never was in his Company since. The Witness knows all the Streets in Charlestown & being asked whether he knew that Keeling lived in King Street (which is the Street in w[ch] Keeling says he lived) he says he does not know it but it might be. However he thinks he could not be in a considerable Way of business. Being asked whether Keeling could have remain'd there without taking an Oath or signing some test He says he thinks he could not. He never knew any false Certificate given. He knows M[r] Car Michel & he was a Justice. He has heard from M[rs] Thompson that Car Michel gave one to his Partner. He says Rum was worth about 4*s.* 6*d.* a Gallon Rice about 9*s.* per Hundred. Speaks of the time before the troubles as to the Rice. He considers him as a Loyalist & has heard that he suffer'd for his Loyalty. The Witness has himself taken the Oath to the Rebels & says he is sure M[r] Keeling could not have lived in the Province so long as he did if he had not taken the Oath or had some paper or Certificate to shew.

Will[m] Keeling—the Claimant—called in again.

He is asked to clear up the business of the Oath & to account for this Circumstance How he could stay in the Province without taking an Oath to the Rebels. He swears positively that he never did take any Oath to the Rebels or give them any Assurance of his Attachment to the American Cause. The Witness's House was in the same Street with M[r] Moore's & about as far distant from it as one side of Lincolns Inn fields. He never pretended to be a friend to the Rebel Cause in order to remain quiet. He admits that in Conversation he was often advised to take the Oath but he always said he would not & cursed them for it. Being asked how he got the 7 or 800 Dollars He says it was in the Course of trade & being asked what he did with them He says he spent them & they served him for support.

He is a Roman Catholic by persuasion & being desired to cross himself & give an Answer to the Question whether he ever took any Oath to the Rebels He swears in the most solemn manner that he never did.

He has an Allowance of £15 a Year from the Treasury.

### Memorial of George Platt

Determin'd the 28[th] of Nov[r] 1783.

20[th] Nov[r] 1783.

George Platt—the Claimant—sworn.

He produces several Certificates to Loyalty one from Col[l] Balfour. He lived upon the Catabaw river in S[o] Carolina. He had several Grants of Land but they

A very meritorious Loyalist & he & his family have suffer'd much for their Loyalty.
Did not bear Arms.

are all lost. The lands lay round him. He had Grants from Gov^r Bull & Lord Charles Montague. He speaks of a Grant of 300 Acres granted to him in 1760. It was then uncultivated but he cultivated about 50 Acres of it. This was from Gov^r Bull. He had another from Lord Cha^s Montague the first Year that he came to be Gov^r. This contain'd 200 Acres & was near to the other Land it lay in the same County Craven County. He agreed with a Man to clear it for him & he was to give him 20 an Acre for it. He meant it for his Son. Only three Acres were clear'd before the Rebellion. He had an House & Mill upon the first 300 Acres where he lived. His House cost him nothing but his Labour & the labour of his Negroes. He had 4 Negroes. He says he was offer'd £3000 Currency for these 300 Acres. A Man who lived near him offer'd it to him. He has rais'd 4 Hogsheads of Tobacco in a Y^r. He values the Tobacco at £10 per Hogshead. The farm produced about 200 or 250 Bushels of Corn besides Potatoes Pease &c. He admits that by the terms of the Grant he ought to have cultivated it & he intended to do it. He had possession of this Island for 16 or 17 Years. He quitted his property when Lord Cornwallis came to Camden. He was not forced away. He came away because he would not take the Oath & lay in the Woods for some time. He does not know whether his property is confiscated or not. He left behind him Children & Grand Children 21. The Rebels executed two of his Sons. None of his family are in possession of the Estate. He had 4 Negroes. He values them at £100 Ster^g. They were taken from him by the Rebels.

£400.

No proof of Confiscation.

Negroes £100.
Bounty £25 a Y^r.

Determin'd the 29^th of Nov^r 1783.

### Memorial of George Chalmers[1] Esq

21^st Nov^r 1783.

George Chalmers Esq—the Claimant—sworn.

A Decided & Zealous Loyalist.
Did not bear Arms.

Says he went to settle in Maryland in Aug^t 1763 & says that in no one instance has he ever swerved from his Loyalty & that his whole Conduct from May 1774 has been one continued exertion on the behalf of Great Britain. With the view of assisting this Country he furnished the Loyalists with arguments to enable them to suppcrt the Cause of Britain as they used to apply to him when they were at a Difficulty to answer the arguments of their Opponents. He not only furnished them with Arguments but shew'd them by his own example that they ought not to yield any obedience to the usurped powers or to sign any Association against this Country.

At the first great meeting of Baltimore County in May 1774 (when he dates the commencement of the troubles in y^e province of Maryland) He attended in concert with the principal friends of the British Gov^t in order to act as the principal Speaker in favor of the Gov^t in opposition to the endeavours of the rebels. When he went to this Meeting he found the leaders of the Opposition

[1] *b.* 1742, *d.* 1825. He is in *Dict. of Nat. Biography.* He is well known as the author of *Political Annals of the United Colonies*, vol. i, to 1688, 1780 (three chapters of a second volume were published by the New York Hist. Soc. in 1868), and an *Introduction to the History of the Revolt of the Amer. Colonies*, 1782. These works, though written under a strong Tory bias, anticipated modern methods in being written from first-hand material at the Record Office.

In 1786 Chalmers became Chief Clerk to the Committee of the Privy Council.

A good account of the beginning of the Revolution in Maryland will be found in B. C. Steiner, *Life and Administration of Sir Robert Eden*, Johns Hopkins Univ. Studies in Hist., &c., xvi. 7–9.

had brought the principal Lawyers from Anapolis to support them as they were apprehensive their own Numbers & Talents would be insufficient to carry the point they aim'd at. There were several inflammatory Speeches made by a M$^{r}$ Alexander. Says that he retired to his own House which was near the Meeting in order to refresh himself it being very hot. On his return thither he met M$^{r}$ Thompson who was bloody & dishevel'd & was by him informed that on his speaking in Opposition to M$^{r}$ Alexander & his friends a Tumult had arisen & they had attempted to throw him out of the Window or over the Stair Case. In consequence of this Information Claimant abstain'd from going again to the Meeting which he says was very fortunate for him as he afterwards learned that there had been a Plot concerted to throw him out of the Court House Window in case he should make a Speech there And from the Violence he observed at the Meeting & their treatment of M$^{r}$ Thompson he entertains no Doubt they would have carried their intentions into execution. From this time neither himself nor any of the friends of Gov$^{t}$ attended any Meeting As they had tried alone what could be done & found great Danger & no benefit from it. Says that in consequence of the above tumult Challenges pass'd between the Parties & he himself carried one of the Challenges. From this time he thought it necessary whenever he went out to carry Pistols for his Defence & likewise to have them by his bed side at Night As he consider'd his Life to be in Danger from the violence of the Opposers of the British Gov$^{t}$ owing to the decided part he had taken in its favor.

When he found the antient Gov$^{t}$ was overturned he endeavour'd to promote at Baltimore Town an Association among the friends of Gov$^{t}$ for their mutual protection. It was a part of this plan which he concerted with M$^{r}$ Christie to bring about a Change in the Commission of the peace As the then Justices were of the most inflammatory part of the people. By an application to the Gov$^{r}$ this matter was brought about & better and abler Men were substituted in their Room. This made so great a Noise in the province that the Claimant is of Opinion had it been discover'd before he quitted the Province that he was the principal Promoter of the Plan he should have been massacred. This measure of changing the Comm$^{n}$ of the peace was not meant merely to change the Men but as part of a plan whereby it was intended that the Associators should act as the posse comitatus in dispersing by force any Mob when they were called upon by the High Sheriff (who was a loyal Subject) so to do. He therefore was deputed to apply to the Gov$^{r}$ for some stands of the Province Arms. The Gov$^{r}$ highly approved of the Plan & furnish'd the Arms—but they were never sent—as he believes the Gov$^{r}$ on considering the Matter more coolly was of opinion that if it should be discover'd that he had furnished the friends of Gov$^{t}$ with Arms it would render him very unpopular throughout the Province. This was in the beginning of the Year 1775.[1]

Says he considers himself as having been put to considerable Risque by giving his Advice to the Rev$^{d}$ M$^{r}$ Edmiston when he was brought to Baltimore Town by the Committee for his Opposition to the British Gov$^{t}$. And he likewise

[1] At the end of April 1775 the Governor in fact agreed to surrender the provincial arms, powder, and stores to the colonels of the militia (Steiner, op. cit., p. 90).

visited M$^{r}$ Christie [1] who was under the Custody of a Serj$^{t's}$ Guard on acc$^{t}$ of his having written a Letter (which was intercepted) which offended the Committee.

Says he acted as a Lawyer in the usual mode of practice in America in the
£350 a Y$^{r}$. double Capacity of an Attorney & Counsellor in the diff$^{t}$ Courts & says that in the Year 1773 the emoluments of his profession were £354 Ster$^{g}$ And doubts not he would have made as much or more in the successive Years had not the Troubles broke out.

Says he left Maryland in Sept$^{r}$ & arrived in Eng$^{d}$ in Nov$^{r}$ 1775 & in y$^{e}$ Year
Bounty £100 a Y$^{r}$. 1774 he rec$^{d}$ from the Treasury an Annuity of £100 a Year (with a retrospect for one Year) which he still continues to receive. The Claimant requests that his Services may be compensated by an Annuity of £300 a Year but does not ask of Gov$^{t}$ any other Compensation. He waves all other Claim for Losses but from his Loss of Profession.

The Rev$^{d}$ Will$^{m}$ Edmiston—late of Baltimore County in Maryland—sworn.

Says he was very intimately acquainted with the Claimant & lived in the same County with him. Says the Claimant was a Man of distinguish'd Loyalty throughout the whole of the troubles And he apprehends he was of material Use to this Country by his exertions. He acted with great personal fairness & is of Opinion that his person was thereby endanger'd.

Says he remembers M$^{r}$ Chalmers practising in the Commissary's Court. He remembers a Conversation he once had with M$^{r}$ Dulany the Head of that Court who said M$^{r}$ Chalmers came before him better prepared than any other Lawyer who attended the Court. And the Witness is of Opinion he was in a very rising Situation in his profession.

He says he is of Opinion that had not the troubles arisen the Claimant would have been one of the first Lawyers in the Province & has had frequent Conversations with the first people of the Province who all concurred in the same Sentiment. Witness says he has known the Claimant from 1769 & from that time has never known him do anything but what was perfectly honorable & just. He was a Man of excellent Character.

Witness says he was called before the Committee of Baltimore County who gave him two Hours to consider of the Answer he was to give to the Questions they had put to him. He sent on this Occasion to M$^{r}$ Chalmers to advise with him as a friend but doubted whether he would come to him owing to the violence of the people. The Claimant however did come to him & he considers by so doing that he ran a great personal risque.

Says he has been informed by M$^{r}$ Lawson with whom he had conversed on the Subject of the Claimant's professional Claims—that his Tobacco fees were about 60000 Weight of Tobacco And adds that his profession produced him a sufficient Income to maintain him in a very genteel Situation.

Being asked whether M$^{r}$ Chalmers lived at the rate of £350 a Y$^{r}$ in Maryland He says certainly not that he could not spend so much. The Expences of living in Maryland were so very reasonable.

[1] Perhaps the Mr. Christie whom Lord G. Germain recommended to General Howe (April 27, 1776) as a man of merit and a great sufferer in his fortune by the unhappy disputes (*Hist. MSS. Comm., Am. MSS. in R. Inst.*, vol. i, p. 36).

## Memorial of John Pearson

John Pearson—the Claimant—sworn. 21st of Novr 1783. Determin'd the 29th of Novr 1783.

Says he went to America in 1774. He is an Irishman by Birth. He went to Charlestown. He knew nothing of the troubles till he arrived there. He carried the Value of 100 Guineas in Linen Cloth out with him. He arrived there about Christmas 1774. He went to the back Country & staid there two Years & in 1776 came to settle in Charlestown. He took an House there when he came back to Charlestown. Says he was obliged to leave the back Country or join the Rebels. He came to Charles Town in order that he might not be obliged to go agt the Indians. Says he continued in Charlestown upwards of a Year before he was applied to to take the Oath to the usurped Govt. There were then public Proclamations for all persons to take the Oath or quit the Province within a limited time. This was in 1778. He then applied to a Mr Carmicheel who gave him a Certificate that he *had* taken the Oaths to the Rebel Powers tho' in fact he had never taken them. For some time after he obtain'd this Certificate he remain'd unmolested. When Genl Prevost came agt Charlestown he was order'd to join a Company & go upon the Lines. But refusing so to do he was tried by a Court Martial & fined £50 for his Neglect. Some time after when Sir Henry Clinton came agt the Town the Insurgents took him out of his Bed put a Gun into his Hand & would have had him join them but he refused so to do & was consequently imprison'd. He was tried for not bearing Arms agt the British Army & was let go on condition of joining a Company of Rebels but not doing so he was imprison'd & continued in Prison till a Day or two before the Town was taken when the Prisons were open'd & the Prisoners set free. After the town was taken he join'd a Company of Ma under Captn Greenwood & went on an Expedition to escort Prisoners from Camden to Charlestown. Never did any other actual Service.

A Loyalist.

Did not bear Arms.

Says he left America about a Yr before the Evacuation in 1781 in order to visit his friends in Ireland And during the time he staid after the Town was taken till he left the Place He dealt in the way of business he had been in before it was taken. He intended to return to America but recd a Letter which prevented him & which Letter he produced.

Says he was possess'd of 300 Acres of Land situate in Amelia Township 60 Miles from Charlestown. He bought it in 1777 or 1778 after he came to Charlestown. Swears he paid for it £350 S. in liquors Sugar & Continental Money. There were 12 Acres cultivated when he bought it. He never cultivated any part of it.

Disallowed.

He has an Allowance from the Treasury of £25 a Yr from Midsummer 1783.

Bounty £25 a Yr.

Colonel John Philips [1]—sworn. 22d Novr 1783.

The Witness was a Coll of Ma in Charlestown but before the troubles he was a Planter & resided on Jackson's Creek. Knew Mr Pearson in Charlestown. He always bore the Character of an honest Man. Knew him from 1776 when

[1] McCrady (*S. Car. in the Rev., 1780–3*, p. 586) comments on the fact that his name, like those of other up-country loyalists, is not found in the list of those whose estates were confiscated.

he first knew him he lived in Charlestown. At that time he kept a Grocery Store & dealt principally in liquors. He had a large store about one year before the taking of Charlestown he thinks Mr Pearson went & resided in the back Country two Years.

Believes him to have always been loyal & that he heard of his doing many Acts of kindness to our Prisoners. Says that he knew Mr Carmicheel & being asked to Mr Carmicheel's Character says that his Character was not the best & that he thinks it very probable that he might give the sort of Certificate which Mr Pearson represents. Being asked if he thinks if any person could have resided from 1776 to 1780 without being obliged to take the Oaths to the American States says he thinks not but that some people had a mode of conducting themselves which answer'd the same effect.

Determin'd the 6th of Decr 1783.

### Memorial of Torquil M Leod

25th of Novr 1783.

Torquil McLeod—the Claimant—sworn.

A Loyalist.

The Property lost appearing to have been taken to America as Merchandize The Board are of Opinion that such Loss does not fall within the meaning of the Act. Therefore the Claim is disallowed altogether.

He went from Jamaica 1775 & arrived in America in June. He went with a Cargo of Rum & meant to settle there & to buy a Plantation. He took 700 Gallons. It was in Casks 5 Puncheons & 2 Quarter Casks. He lost it all by joining with the Loyalists at Cross Creek.[1] He lost nothing else. He sold some of the Rum & bought two Horses with the Money that he sold his Rum for. He follow'd the Army during the whole War. He did not sell 100 Gallons. Being asked what he gave for the Rum He says 4*s*. Jamaica Currency or about 2*s*. 8*d*. Sterling. Six hundred Gallons at 2*s*. 8*d*. were worth about £80. He sold the 100 Gallons of Rum for 10*s*. Currency. He recd nothing from the Army but rations. He admits that if he had paid for the rations they would have cost him as much as the price of his rum. He never did Duty with any Corps. He drew his rations with the 71st Regt. He says he lost a Chest of Cloathes worth £25 Sterg.

John McLeod—sworn.

Witness lived in Anson County in North Carolina. He was a Planter there & was afterwards a Lieut in a Body of Men rais'd by Col Martin called the No Carolina Highlanders. He produces Govr Martin's appointment. He is first Cousin to the Claimant & knew him well. He came to America in 1775 & in 1776.

Determin'd the 6th of Dec. 1783.

### Memorial of Willm McLeod

25th Novr 1783.

Willm McLeod—the Claimant—sworn.

A Loyalist. Bore Arms.

He was appointed Ensign in Govr Martin's Corps in 1776. He went to America in 1772. He cannot produce the Appointment. He lived in Cumberland County. He was not in the Action at Moors bridge[2] but was then employ'd in guarding the Prisoners. He was afterwards taken Prisoner in March 1776 at Smith's Ferry. He made his escape in about a week And from this time to

[1] A premature rising of loyalists was completely suppressed on February 27, 1776. A good account of the proceedings is in *N. Car. Records*, vol. x, p. 482.

[2] Moore's Creek Bridge was about twenty miles above Wilmington.

the Year 1780 He was in danger of his Life & then he join'd the British at Camden. The Militia was rais'd soon after & he was made a Captⁿ in the Militia. He was appointed by Lord Cornwallis But he has no Commission to produce. He had one from Major Craig but he was obliged to hide it in America. He was taken Prisoner in Oct^r 1781 & carried to Salisbury. He served with Col^l Fanning[1] & went with him to Wilmington in July 1781 from Chatham Cumberland & Guilford. They were armed at Wilmington & returned to the back Country. He was taken sick in his return And left behind & taken prisoner by the Americans & carried to Salisbury where he was very ill treated. He was at this time kept in Irons for four Months. He never rec^d Pay excepting one Sum of £25 which he rec^d at Charlestown in 1782.

### Memorial of M^rs Ann M^cLeod

Determin'd the 6th of Dec^r 1783.

Ann M^cLeod—the Claimant—sworn. 26th Nov^r 1783.

Her Husband died 1st of March last. He was Captⁿ in Gov^r Martin's Corps. He served ag^t the Rebels & was taken Prisoner & kept 4 Years Prisoner. He died in Jamaica where he went upon the Evacuation of Charlestown & he had half pay from Sir Henry Clinton. She knows that her Husband's Estate was confiscated his Name was in one of the Acts & the Rebel Commissioners took an Acc^t of all the Effects Stock &c.

She & her Husband Loyalists.

Her Husband bought the Estate in Question the first Year they went. Does not exactly know what he gave for it. There was no House upon it when they came there. There were four fields clear'd they grew Wheat & Rye & Corn upon it.

### Memorial of Thomas Mackaness

Determin'd the 8th of Dec^r 1783.

Thomas Mackaness—the Claimant—sworn. 27th Nov^r 1783.

Is an Englishman & went to America about the Year 1767 or 1768. Was settled at Philadelphia. He kept a Store there. He left Philadelphia because he should otherwise have been obliged to take an active part ag^t G^t Britain. He left it purely for this reason & a Rebel Gen^l attends who can prove it. When he heard that Philadelphia was in our possession he went out again & found Gen^l Howe & the Troops quitting the place. He went from thence to New York where he staid three Years & then he went to Charlestown. He served at New York in an Association & likewise he served at Charlestown in another Association. His Property has been confiscated & it appears by an American Newspaper that he is mention'd by name in one of their Acts.

A firm & determin'd Loyalist.

Did not bear Arms.

John Thornton Esq—of Lothbury Merch^t—sworn.

He knows M^r Makaness's loyalty has known him from the time he first went over to America. He knows that Orders were given for killing him because he had spoken his Sentiments very freely in favor of G^t Britain. He says he certainly

[1] David Fanning, *b.* 1755, *d.* 1825. See Sabine, op. cit., vol. i, pp. 417–18. For an account of his adventures after the Peace see Siebert, *The Legacy of the Am. Rev. to the Brit. West Indies*, pp. 22–4. He seems to have been a stormy petrel throughout his life. He must not be confounded with Colonel Edward Fanning, who became in 1786 Lieutenant-Governor of Prince Edward Island.

quitted America on acc[t] of his Loyalty. He knows that he might have been permitted to stay if he would have remain'd Neuter but he refused to do it. When he came away it was very inconvenient to him on Acc[t] of his Wife who was then with Child & died on her passage. He speaks in the highest terms of his general Character & says we may rely on any Acc[t] which he shall give of his property.

Determin'd the 8[th] of Dec[r] 1783.

### Memorial of M[r] David Lorimer

27[th] of Nov[r] 1783.

David Lorimer—the Claimant—sworn.

A Loyalist.

He is an Irishman & went to America in 1774. He went first to Charlestown. He produces two Certificates to his Loyalty from Lord Cornwallis & Col[l] Cruger. Lord Cornwallis in addition to Loyalty says he believes the Contents of his Memorial to be true. He had a Capt[n's] Comm[n] in a Company of Loyal M[a]. He went to Ninety Six in 1774. He was wounded in the Service & has lost the use of his Arm. He join'd Col[l] Balfour [1] at Ninety Six[2] in the Year 1780. He took no part before for Great Britain. But he never took the Oaths to the Rebel Gov[t]. He was taken up in the Year 1779 & imprison'd because he would not take up Arms for the Rebel Gov[t]. He was frequently obliged to abscond & was always suspected.

Bore Arms in the M[a] & was wounded.

Determin'd y[e] 29[th] of March 1784.

### Memorial of Philip Henry Esq

2[d] Dec[r] 1783.

Philip Henry Esq—the Claimant—sworn.

He went from Eng[d] to America in 1768 & settled in Charlestown. At first he resided for 18 Months with a Merch[t]. He was to have been in Partnership with this Gent[n] if he had lived but he dying in 18 Months M[r] Henry went into trade for himself.

A Loyalist.

There are two sorts of Oaths which were tender'd. He refused both. They were first tendered to him in 1776. In consequence of this he could not stay in the town & was obliged to retire into the Country & quit his trade. He was pelted in the Streets & when in the Country he was insulted by the Mob who threaten'd to burn his House & him in it. He was called upon in March 1778 to take the Oath of Allegiance to the Rebels the refusal of which was death after 60 Days. He embarked within the 60 Days for Rotterdam. He was taken in his passage & carried into New York. He suffer'd much hardship & expence in consequence of it.

He says all his property is confiscated. He produces an Act by which he is banished &c. but the words are general. He is not included by name.

[1] See note on p. 11.

[2] So called because it was ninety-six miles from Keewie, the chief village of the Cherokee Indians. It consisted entirely of wooden houses within a stockade. Lord Cornwallis wrote to Lord George Germain, August 20, 1780, that in the district of Ninety-Six, by far the most populous and powerful of the province, he had formed seven battalions of militia (*Cornwallis Correspondence*, ed. by C. Ross, 1859, vol. i, p. 489).

## Memorial of Zacharias Gibbes [1]

Determin'd the 13th of Decr 1783.

Zacharias Gibbes—the Claimant—sworn. 4th Decr 1783.

An Active & meritorious Loyalist.

Bore Arms in the Ma & render'd Services to the British Govt.

He is a Native of America was born in Virginia. Has lived 20 Years in South Carolina. He took a very active part from the first. He sign'd a Protest in June 1775 agt a requisition made by Congress at that time that they would take up Arms agt the British Govt. They refused & he was the second Man who sign'd the Protest against it. In Septr 1775 they marched a force agt them. Mr Gibbes & his friends kept themselves embodied for a fortnight—they sent three Hostages into the Camp where Col1 Gibbes & friends were but they would not accept them. However they came upon the terms of a 14 Days peace. Lord Wm Campbell was driven on board a Ship between June & Novr—provided the 14 Days truce was broken they were to be tried condemn'd &c. There was a battle in Novr 1775 [2] between these people & the Rebels at Ninety Six which ended in Col1 Gibbes & Co taking the fort. After this a Cessation of Hostilities was agreed upon for 20 Days at the end of the 20 Days Col1 Gibbes's people broke into small parties & took to the Mountains & the Rebels were augmented to about 8000. He went into the obscure parts of Virginia & remain'd there 4 or 5 Months. He then returned & soon after that he was pursued & taken by Col1 Brannan [3] in the Spring 1776 who tender'd a Death Warrant to them which he & his Party sign'd consenting that if they ever took up arms again agt the Cause of America they should be put to death. After this time he remain'd in a very unpleasant Situation tho' they permitted him to go home they suspected him & watch'd him &c. He remain'd tolerably quiet untill the State Oath was tender'd which was in 1776 this was the Oath of Abjuration. It was tender'd to him the Oath of Allegiance which he refused. His Situation was made then more unpleasant. However he still staid on his farm. He was taken Prisoner in July 1776 by the Americans upon the Indians breaking into the Province & they thought he had been instrumental in stirring up the Indians & he was carried into the Indian Nation. He was only kept for a fortnight. He then made his escape. He returned home but absconded at different times till the Year 1779. The 1st of Jany 1779 Gen1 Prevost & Col1 Campbell took Savannah this Intelligence was sent to him & he took Steps to embody his Neighbours & raised 600 Men in two Days he was principally instrumental in this. On the 7th of Feby 1779 He marched with these Men. About 350 of them got to Savannah. They had two battles in their way. They repulsed the

[1] McCrady, *S. Car. in the Rev., 1780–3*, points out (p. 586) that the estates of Zachariah Gibbes, as well as those of other leading up-country Tories, were never confiscated by the South Carolina Legislature.

[2] The attack by the loyalists upon the Americans under Major Williamson at Ninety-Six caused the first bloodshed in South Carolina during the Revolution. In this attack the loyalists were without a leader capable of directing them by influence or authority; 'and every captain considered himself as having a right to take a lead in affairs, and as nearly on a footing with Major Robinson, the Commander-in-Chief. . . . Failing in this respect and their provisions and ammunition fast decreasing, they lost what little confidence they had in their officers, and confusion of course ensued' (Drayton, op. cit., vol. ii, p. 121). During the twenty days' truce the heterogeneous forces of the loyalists fell to pieces. Gibbes seems somewhat to have exaggerated his own importance.

[3] ? Brandon, Colonel of Militia in Picken's Brigade.

Rebels on the first Attack they took 13 Prisoners. Three Days after this they had another Engagement at Kettle Creek where Col^l Gibbes was taken prisoner. 20 were killed on each side but Col^l Gibbes's Party were defeated. He was marched down the River about 40 Miles & then he was put into Irons he was afterwards march'd 50 Miles further when he was brought before a C^t of Enquiry near Augusta. They asked him how he came to go out at the head of such a Banditti he said it was to join the British Army & to support the British Gov^t. They made a Minute of this & recorded it as a Confession And then he was taken to Ninety Six & tried. He lay about 30 Days in Gaol & then he was tried. He was one of 22 who were condemn'd without mercy. Of the 22 five were hanged. He was one of the 5 pointed out to be robbed but he was let off & his Brother in Law was hanged. On the 17^th of April there came a Habeas Corpus from the Gov^r to remove them 90 Miles to Orangebourg. A fortnight after this the 5 were sent back to Ninety Six & were hanged. Then the Gov^r gave out an order that the remainder should be let off upon giving security for their good behaviour & that they would never return to Ninety Six. He gave three Securities to y^e Am^t of £15000 Currency that he should comply with this. For near 30 Days his Gallows & his Grave was in his Sight & he thought he really should have been executed. He went out of Gaol the 3^d Day of April & went into Camden District where he remain'd untill June 1780 when Lord Cornwallis came there. He joined the Army & Lord Cornwallis & Col^l Balfour both gave him Commissions. The Commissions are produced. Lord Cornwallis's is that of a Major & Col^l Balfour's is the same. He was sent by them to raise a number of Loyalists in Ninety Six & he was to have the Command. He rais'd 500 Men. He went in the front of Lord Cornwallis's Army at the head of a body of Loyalists. Major Ferguson[1] sent him to raise 200 Men more. He went & did raise them & was bringing them back when he rec^d an Express from Major Ferguson not to join him which he produces. After he rec^d these Dispatches he went to Col^l Cruger at Ninety Six from this time to the Evacuation of Charlestown he served in the Militia & had in the meantime the Commission of Colonel given to him by Lieut Col^l Balfour. He rec^d the pay of a Dollar a Day which was the Pay of a Capt^n & a Colonel had no more. Several very strong Certificates produced & read from Lord Cornwallis Col^l Balfour Gen^l Leslie Col^l Moncrief Col^l Cruger Capt^n Douglas Col^l Vernon Col^l Campbell Major Cha^s Frazer & other Officers to the Loyalty & Services of Colonel Gibbes. They all speak of him & his Conduct in the highest terms. Col^l Balfour is desired to attend at a future Day to speak to his Services.

Colonel Cruger—sworn.

He believes Col^l Gibbes to have been a Man of Property but knows nothing of it but from hearsay. As to Loyalty he was frequently under Col^l Cruger's command in different excursions & he executed all his Orders faithfully & as a good Officer. He believes him to be a very meritorious & decided Loyalist.

Colonel Balfour—sworn. 6^th Dec^r 1783.

He was desired by the Board to speak to the Character & Loyalty of Col^l

[1] Patrick Ferguson, *b.* 1744, *d.* 1780, is in *Dict. of Nat. Biography*. He was perhaps the most brilliant leader in guerrilla warfare on the British side.

Gibbes. He speaks in the highest terms of Col[l] Gibbes. He says that in the Month of June 1780 He was brought to the British Army with the strongest recommendation from all the persons in the Neighborhood saying that from his property & Loyalty he was a very proper person to be entrusted with a Command. In consequence of this he was sent into the District of Ninety Six in order to raise & embody the Militia there. He did do so & in about a Month he rais'd 600 Men. He afterwards had the Commission of Lieut[t] Col[l] Commandant & tho' as Col[l] Balfour says not a very good Soldier he is one of the truest Loyalists & an excellent Man. He says he must have been a Man of Property because if he had not He never would have been recommended to a Command. Col[l] Balfour does not know anything of his former Services excepting from hearsay but he believes them. Upon the whole Col[l] Balfour's Character of this Man added to his own testimony &c gives us the highest impression of his Loyalty & meritorious Conduct.

N.B. The Allowance was afterwards divided between Col[l] Gibbes & his Wife & £40 a Y[r] given to each.

### Memorial of John Hardy

Determin'd the 21[st] of Jan[y] 1784.

John Hardy—the Claimant—sworn. 9[th] Dec[r] 1783.

He is an Englishman & went to America in 1761. He went sometimes to Sea otherwise he resided in America till the troubles. His first Act of Loyalty was to join Lord Dunmore at the great Bridge[1] in 1775. He was in that Action & continued with Lord Dunmore & the British Army & fleet during the whole War. He was taken Prisoner in 1776 in Lord Dunmore's Vessel & carried into Philadelphia & kept 9 Months in Prison. They then let him out to go to work & he went to Bermuda where he found his Wife & Children. He came back immediately to New York & settled there where he got his Living by his Industry. He was afterwards taken Prisoner at the Capes of Virginia & carried to Richmond where he was kept in Irons ten Days. He was taken again at Sea & carried into New London. He was likewise taken Prisoner at his own Plantation. The last time he was taken Prisoner was in Virginia. Has £20 a Y[r] from Gov[t].

A Loyalist. Bore Arms.

Bounty £20 a Y[r].

Colonel Ellegood—sworn.

Knows the Claimant. He was with the Army at Great Bridge & very active. He remembers his Houses being burnt does not know the exact Number but says there were several.

### Memorial of M[rs] Margaret Reynolds

Determin'd y[e] 21[st] of Jan[y] 1784.

Margaret Reynolds—the Claimant—sworn. 9[th] Dec[r] 1783.

Her Husband died in Charlestown in Feb[y] 1781. Before that he lived in Ninety Six District but he was obliged to quit his property. His Property lay upon Long Cane Creek. Her Husband was a Planter & afterwards Capt[n] of M[a] in Col[l] King's Reg[t]. He was appointed a Capt[n] in the M[a] after the British

Her Husband & herself Loyalists.

[1] On operations at Great Bridge in December 1775 see C. Stedman, *Hist. of the Am. War*, vol. i, pp. 147–8.

took Ninety Six. She says he never took the Oath to the Rebels they offer'd it to him but he refused it they did not molest them they only threaten'd him. He lived upon the farm till Ninety Six was taken.

Bounty £20 a Y^r.

M^rs Reynolds has an Allowance of £20 a Year from the Treasury.

Determin'd the 6th of July 1785.

**Memorial of Colonel John Philips** [1]

10th Dec^r 1783.

Colonel John Philips—the Claimant—sworn.

A most active zealous & meritorious Loyalist.

Bore Arms & render'd Services very essential to Gov^t.

He was born in Ireland & went to America in 1770. He settled on Jacksons Creek in South Carolina near Winsbourn. He first declared his Sentiments in July 1775—the principal people there at that time began to associate ag^t Gov^t & proposed resolutions to every person to sign & proposed it to the Claimant & he refused to sign it in the public Meeting House which prevented all (excepting two persons) from signing it. This first drew the Vengeance of the Rebels upon him. In Nov^r he was first fined for not going out to do Duty for them. He had then two Sons who were able to do Duty but they refused. There was no Oath tender'd to him untill 1778. In 1777 He run a risque of his Life by swearing Allegiance to the King & by inducing others to take the same Oath & He was tried for this Offence in 1778. In 1775 the Rebels offer'd him a Lieut^t Col^s Commission if he would join them. In the Month of April or May they tender'd the Oath of Allegiance & Abjuration to him. He refused it. They in general gave 60 Days but they only allowed him 4 Days to go to Charlestown. He performed it within the time. He was afterwards deliver'd Prisoner to Gen^l Williamsburgh [2] a Rebel Gen^l at Augusta. He was detain'd a Prisoner for two Months. The 3^d Day of December following he was tried & condemn'd to be hanged. They kept him for 15 Days with the Gallows before the Window & during the whole of that time He was fully persuaded that he should suffer. At this time one of his Sons died in Gaol at Orangebourg in consequence of their Cruelty. Col^l Philips says the reason that he was not executed was that Col^l Campbell had at that time taken Savannah & issued a Proclamation. In consequence of which near 100 of the people petition'd to save his Life upon an Apprehension that two of his Brothers who were with Col^l Campbell would retaliate. He then went home & staid tolerably quietly untill Charlestown was taken. He then came & joined the British Army at Camden in June 1780. He took 50 Loyalists with him when he first went & afterwards between 5 & 600 Men. In June 1780 Lord Cornwallis appointed him a Colonel in M^a. He cannot produce the Comm^n the Rebels took it from him from this time he served constantly with Lord Cornwallis untill he went to North Carolina. He never rec^d Pay untill Lord Cornwallis went to North Carolina from Jan^y 1781. He had the Pay of a Colonel which was 20*s*. Ster^g a Day. He rec^d this Pay untill Charlestown was evacuated. Lord Cornwallis gave him for his Services at one time 50 Gãs & at another 100 Dollars. He was very useful in transmitting provisions to the Army from Winsborough to Rocky Creek. He was in two or three Engagements. He was again taken Prisoner the 21^st day of January 1781

[1] McCrady, op. cit., points out (p. 586) that Lieutenant-Colonel Philips's property was not confiscated.

[2] Presumably General Andrew Williamson, who was in command of the militia at Augusta.

& carried into N° Carolina & very inhumanly treated. He was prisoner about six weeks. Col[l] Philips's Son was taken by Colonel Hampton in Aug[t] 1781 & most inhumanly murder'd. About this time they drove his Wife & family off from their Plantation & they came in great Distress to Charlestown.

Several Certificates produced & read from the following persons Lord Cornwallis Lord Rawdon Several Officers of distinction & rank in that Army Colonel Balfour &c.

Colonel Balfour called—& sworn.

First knew Col[l] Philips in 1780 at Winsborough. He knows that Lord Cornwallis placed very great Confidence in Col[l] Philips & that he employed him to procure intelligence of the Enemy's movements & many other matters of importance. He trusted to this Man to discriminate between the friends of Gov[t] & those who were not to be trusted & he relied entirely upon him. It is within Col[l] Balfour's knowledge that he came to Charlestown in 1781 as Col[l] of M[a] that Col[l] Balfour relying perfectly upon his Integrity confided the whole of the District of Camden to his Direction. He considers him as an Active & Zealous Loyalist & a most honest & upright Man. He knew he had an Estate having been upon it but does not know the Value of it. He says there cannot be a better Man in America than Colonel Philips.

**Memoiral of Capt[n] Alexander Chesney**

Determin'd the 19[th] of Jan[y] 1784.

Alexander Chesney—the Claimant—sworn. 11[th] Dec[r] 1783.

He went from Ireland in 1772 & settled on Pacolet River in the district of Ninety Six in 1773. He lived with his father when the rebellion broke out. He was press'd to enter into the association in the Summer of 1775—but he refused it & went to Jackson's Creek to join the Loyalists under the Command of Capt[n] Philips Brother to Col[l] Philips. He brought these Loyalists to his father's House where they staid about a fortnight. Soon after this in the beginning of 1776 He was made Prisoner by a Party of Rebels under Col[l] Steen.[1] He was kept in prison about ten Days & then he was bail'd out. In the Summer following he was again taken Prisoner And he had the option of going to Gaol or going with them to Charlestown. He chose the latter & joined them & bore Arms for them. He was in Charlestown about three Months During which time he made an Attempt to get away with another Loyalist to join Sir Henry Clinton but fail'd. After this they marched ag[t] the Indians. He staid with them till June 1777 when he got clear of them then the Corps in which he served was discharged & he came home. When the State Oath was made general in 1778 He agreed with a Party to go to Florida to avoid it but they could not accomplish it & so he staid at home till 1780 when Charlestown was taken. He says they never tender'd the State Oath to him. He join'd Gen[l] Williamson a Rebel Gen[l] with a view to join the British Army & staid two Months with him. He had leave to return home at that time. He & the other Loyalists who meant to desert from Gen[l] Williamson's Army sent a Man to reconnoitre the British Army & he never returned. After Charlestown was taken in the Year 1780 He

A Loyalist.

Bore Arms.

But first served with the Rebels at the beginning of the War.

Bounty £50 a Y[r].

[1] Presumably James Stein, who distinguished himself under Sumter in various engagements.

embodied with several Loyalists in Sugar Creek & he was one of the foremost. He afterwards join'd Col$^{l}$ Balfour & afterwards Major Ferguson took the Command of them. He was constantly with Major Ferguson till he was defeated y$^{e}$ 7$^{th}$ of Oct$^{r}$ 1780.[1] He wishes to mention some particular Services At a time when Major Ferguson apprehended he should be attacked he sent the Claimant with written & private Instructions to Capt$^{n}$ Moore which he deliver'd. He afterwards gave material Evidence to Major Ferguson in consequence of which he intercepted 500 of y$^{e}$ Rebels at the Iron works & defeated them.[2] He never rec$^{d}$ any Compensation for his services. Major Ferguson gave him his thanks in writing he might have been paid but refused it. He was afterwards appointed Adjutant of many different Battalions & rec$^{d}$ pay for it. He says he has undertaken many very hazardous services. He was taken Prisoner when [with] Major Ferguson And was offer'd by the Rebels that if he would serve one Month with them he should have all his possessions again. He refused it at the risque of his Life because they threaten'd him with death. They marched him about 150 Miles to Moravian Town he made his Escape from hence & went home where he remain'd very privately till he join'd Col$^{l}$ Tarleton.[3] He raised a Company in Dec$^{r}$ 1780 & obtain'd a Capt$^{n's}$ Commission from Col$^{l}$ Balfour which is produced. He was in an Action with Col$^{l}$ Tarleton in 1781. He soon afterwards went to Charlestown.

Several Certificates are produced & read from Lord Cornwallis Lord Rawdon Col$^{l}$ Balfour Col$^{l}$ Tarleton Major Doyle I. Cruden Commissary of sequester'd Estates &c &c to determined Loyalty & good Conduct.

Colonel Philips—sworn.

Knew Capt$^{n}$ Chesney from his Infancy. Knew his father's plantation on Pacolet river. He confirms him in the Acc$^{t}$ he gave of the first act of his Loyalty in bringing the Loyalists to his father's House. He says he believes him to have been loyal from the first notwithstanding he knows he bore Arms for some time with them. But Col$^{l}$ Philips had an Opportunity when he was Prisoner of conversing with M$^{r}$ Chesney & he knows that at that moment he was a true Loyalist & wished to serve the Cause of Great Britain. After Charlestown was taken he says he was particularly active & he knows he ran risques in carrying intelligence frequently. He believes he was paid for some of these services but not for others. He does not think the worse of him because he served in the Rebel Army many good Men were obliged to do it.

Colonel Zacharias Gibbes—sworn.

Knows Capt$^{n}$ Chesney & has known him many Years. He was an Adherent to Gov$^{t}$ from the beginning of the troubles. In 1776 when he was obliged to conceal himself he took refuge in old M$^{r}$ Chesney's House & he thought himself safer there than anywhere on Acc$^{t}$ of the loyalty of the family. He admits that

1 This was the battle of King's Mountain, in which the Loyalists were defeated and Ferguson was killed (Draper, *King's Mountain and its Heroes*, p. 205; and McCrady, *S. Car. in the Rev. 1775–80*, pp. 776–805).

2 Presumably this alludes to the action of Old Iron Works, fought on August 8, 1780.

3 *b.* 1754, *d.* 1833, is in *Dict. of Nat. Biography*. His *Hist. of the Campaigns of 1780 and 1781* gives a very exaggerated view of his own merits.

Chesney did serve in the Rebel Army. He says he would not have done it himself but Chesney was a young Man & he imputes it to his Youth. He was a very active zealous Officer when under the Command of Major Ferguson. He says he believes that Chesney & several others whose Names are mention'd to him & who enter'd into the Rebel Service under Genl Williamson made & enter'd into a Combination at the time to desert the first Opportunity to the British Army & he believes them all to have been determined Loyalists. He says he does not know any Man for whom he can say more than he can for this Young Man.

### Memorial of James Miller [1]

Determin'd the 21st of Jany 1784.

James Miller—the Claimant—sworn. 12th Decr 1783.

He left Ireland in the Year 1774 & went to America early in the Year 1775. He then immediately purchased a Plantation from Mr James Philips on Jackson's Creek. He gave for it £225 Currency & paid it in Gold & Silver. The Province when he first went into it was at peace & he bought the Estate before April. His first Act of Loyalty was going to the Attack of Ninety Six in Novr 1775 when they defeated the Rebels. He was obliged to lay in the Woods all that Winter. He returned to his plantation with many others in the Spring 1776 in consequence of a proclamation by the Rebels. They broke their faith however & took them all Prisoners. They were all tried by a Committee for being in Arms against them. They then offer'd him his Liberty if he would swear to be true to them he refused And they threaten'd to carry him to Charlestown but they did not do it & let him go home. Afterwards they offer'd the State Oath to him in 1778 & he would not take it & endeavour'd to go to St. Augustine. But he was taken in his way there & carried to Orangebourg Gaol & put in Irons. He was kept there 19 or 20 weeks. They then sued out a Habeas Corpus & obtain'd it & he was tried & acquitted never having sign'd any Allegiance to the Rebel States. He afterwards lived occasionally at his own plantation till 1780 when he took the first Opportunity of joining the British & he join'd them at Camden & was employed in taking up disaffected people. He was soon after appointed Lieutt in the Ma. He was always with Coll Turnbull [2] during the whole War with the New York Volunteers untill the Evacuation of Charlestown. He was afterwards appointed Captn of Ma by Coll Turnbull. His Commission is dated Augt 4th 1780 & is produced & read. He recd Pay as Captn of Ma for six Months & temporary Subsistence whilst he was at Charlestown.

An Active & Zealous Loyalist.

Bore Arms.

Bounty £40 a Yr.

Colonel Philips—sworn.

Has known James Miller from a Child. He is a very deserving Man & there cannot be a better Loyalist or a better Man. He was much persecuted for his Loyalty & he bore it very firmly & would never sign any paper or take any Oath. He joined the British Troops the same day that Coll Philips did.

[1] This James Miller is not to be confused with the James Miller of whom the Carolina County (Virginia) Committee of Safety wrote with extreme bitterness in September 1776 (Force, *Amer. Arch.*, 5th ser., vol. ii, p. 104).

[2] George Turnbull, Lieutenant-Colonel commanding the 3rd American Regiment of New York Volunteers.

Capt^n Chesney—sworn.

Believes that James Miller is an exceeding Loyal Man knows him very well. He is one of those whom he pilotted up to his father's House. He has always understood that he suffer'd greatly before the Year 1780. But since that time he has known him very well & says he always bore the Character of a very honest Man.

## Memorial of John Gordon

Determin'd the 23^d of Jan^y 1784.

12^th Dec^r 1783.

John Gordon—the Claimant—sworn.

A Zealous Loyalist.

He was of Camden District & went to America between 40 & 50 Years ago. He settled in Camden District in 1767. He was in the Commission of the Peace untill America declared for Independence. He never took any Oath to the Rebels or sign'd any Paper the Oath was tender'd to him but he refused it. He is 70 Years of Age & therefore was excused from military service. But old as he was he could not stay in the Country & be quiet & in the Y^r 1780 he was much persecuted ill treated & knock'd down &c. He was obliged to fly for refuge to the British Camp. He often express'd his Sentiments in the favor of y^e British Gov^t. He has been informed that his property has been confiscated but does not know it.

Bounty £30 a Y^r.

Colonel Gibbes—sworn.

Knows M^r Gordon has known him 14 or 15 Years. Before the War He was one of the most leading Men in the Country & a Magistrate. He made the first opposition to the rebellion. He fled from Camden District to Ninety Six where he signed the Protest ag^t the Association. He afterwards went home again. He was driven from his property in 1780 on Acc^t of his Loyalty. He knows his property better than he knows his own. It lay on fishing Creek. Confirms the Acc^t of the purchase given by M^r Gordon. He gave a considerable price for it. He has improved it very much. The Buildings are the best in that Country. He thinks the Buildings might fairly be estimated. He values the whole at 30*s*. an Acre Ster^g & thinks it as well worth that as his own Plantation which he has in that Neighbourhood is worth 10*s*. which is the Sum that he values his own at. Says it is doubtful whether his family are not in possession of the Property. Confirms the Acc^t of his personal property.

John Gordon—called in again.

Bounty £30 a Y^r.

He has £30 a Y^r from the Treasury. He is desired to obtain a Certificate to the present situation of his family.

## Memorial of James Walker

Determin'd the 19^th of Jan^y 1784.

15^th Dec^r 1783.

James Walker—the Claimant—sworn.

A Loyalist.

Is a Native of Ireland & went to America in 1767. He went to Charlestown where he procured Land Warrants & went up to Ninety Six. His first Act of Loyalty was joining the Party of Loyalists at Ninety Six in 1775. He afterwards remain'd at home till 1780 when the British came again into that Neighborhood. He never took any Oath to the Rebels & they never tender'd any Oath to him because he was sick. After the British Army came into the Province he was generally with the M^a & after the Evacuation of Ninety Six He came to Charlestown & staid till the Evacuation of that place. After he went to Charlestown he was made Quarter Master to a Party of Refugees.

James Walker the Claimant applied to the Treasury about the Month of April last & rec^d 20 Gās in full to carry him & his family to Ireland.

He now says that he is in great Distress & does not know how he shall return to his family unless he receives something from the Treasury. He is told that that is not the Object of this Enquiry. But some little Money was given to him to assist his Necessities & carry him to his family in Ireland.

### Memorial of Samuel M^cKee

Determin'd the 20^th of Jan^y 1784.

15^th Dec^r 1783.

Samuel M^cKee—the Claimant—sworn.

He is an Irishman & went to America in 1772. He followed the business of a Weaver for some time. He fix'd on Broad river in Camden District. He was for the King from the beginning. He was at the battle of Camden. He never fought for the Rebels they took him prisoner in 1775 & he was afterwards taken Prisoner again. They did tender the Oath to him in 1777 & he told them that he never would. At that time he had no other property but one Horse & Saddle & Cloaths & a bed. He had about 700 Dollars at that time paper Money. He join'd the British Troops under Lord Cornwallis in 1780 & continued afterwards as a M^a Man till the evacuation of Charlestown. He was three times taken prisoner.

A Loyalist.

Did not bear Arms except in the Militia.

Bounty £20 in full.

### Memorial of James Murphy

Determin'd the 20^th of Jan^y 1784.

15^th Dec^r 1783.

James Murphy—the Claimant—sworn.

He is a Native of Ireland & went to America in 1771. He went to New York. He followed the weaving business. He continued in that situation till the Year 1773. He proceeded to S^o Carolina in the latter end of 1773. He carried 4 suits of very good Cloaths & 3 Doz^n & ½ of Shirts. He carried a young Woman with him a 3 Years Serv^t & he sold her service for £17 New York Money. He went to Ninety Six District in 1773 & began to teach school. He kept it two Years. About the end of 1775 He removed to another Settlement & taught School there two Years. Then he removed into the town of Ninety Six & engaged to keep a Stall or Shop for D^r Derbry [*sic*]. He was in this situation for 9 Months & then he went to join the British Troops as a Volunteer in Georgia. He was under Capt^n Anderson. In Jan^y following he was taken Prisoner & kept till the reduction of Charlestown by Sir Henry Clinton. The Oaths were tender'd to him by the Americans in the Y^r 1778 but he refused to take it & never sign'd any paper or took Arms for them. After the reduction of Charlestown he served in the M^a till the Evacuation.

A Loyalist & bore Arms.

Bounty £10 10*s*. in full.

### Memorial of M^rs Jane Gibbs

Determin'd the 20^th of Jan^y 1784.

15^th Dec^r 1783.

Jane Gibbs—the Claimant—sworn.

She was formerly the Wife of Major W^m Downes of the Province of So Carolina & is now the Wife of Col^l Gibbes.

The Claim[t] & all her Husbands Loyal.

Her first Husband was M[r] Lindsey. He & she went to America in 1763. He was a farmer they settled in Georgestown & M[r] Lindsey lived till 1772.

Major Downes her Second Husband went to S. Carolina 14 Years ago. She married him in the Year 1773. He was in the mercantile Line. He kept a blacksmiths & Turners Shop &c. The first Act of his Loyalty was refusing a Commission from the Americans in 1775. The next time they applied to him to be a private Man & he refused it. He next refused to hire a Substitute. They then seiz'd on his Effects to pay the fines. He was afterwards killed at Camden in 1781. He first joined the British Army at Charlestown in 1780 & he was appointed Major of M[a] by Lord Rawdon. Major Downes made no Will. He left two Daughters.

On the 15[th] of April 1781 A Rebel Officer came to the Door & asked for Major Downes & asked him to surrender. There was a party of 163 Rebels. He refused to surrender. He fired 24 rounds at the Rebels & he & his Overseer were killed.

Alexander Burnside—sworn.

He knew Major Downes. He went with him to America in 1765. He was as good & as loyal a Subject as any that could be found. He lived very comfortably well. He knows the land on Hanging rock believes there were about 900 Acres he has frequently been upon it. There was a large Plantation cultivated & thinks it must have been 60 or 70 Acres. He can't tell on which tract the Cultivation was. There was a good House with Indigo Oaks &c. He thinks the 900 Acres all together were worth 25*s.* an Acre. He says that Land was increasing in value every [year] before the troubles.

George Platt—sworn.

He knew Major Downes at Camden. He was a very grand Loyalist. He knew his plantation which he had of the rebels. He lived well. The Crop was in its Minority. The Crop & fencing he thinks would have cost about £20 S. provided there were 100 Acres. He kept a Waggon & rode very good Horses. Values a Waggon at £12 from Pensylvania. He can't value the Blacksmith's Tools. He remembers Major Downes's death & was at his funeral. He says he was greatly esteem'd & regretted by the British Army.

Disallowed.

Confiscation not proved.

100 Acres on White Oak Creek granted to Hugh Brown in 1764. He bought it of him the same Year. He gave him to the value of £73 S. for it. He gave it to him in Money except an Horse which he valued at £18 S. The Conveyances are left with his other papers. He never cultivated this himself but he gave a Man £20 S. to build an House & he hired a Man to clear 3 Acres of y[e] Land.

Disallowed.

400 Acres situate on Holstein's river N[o] Carolina which he bought from John Lenn. John Lenn's title to it was taking it up as King's Land & cultivating it. He says he knew that Lenn had no title to the Land. He gave him 1900 Continental Dollars & a Rifle Gun for it. He bought it in 1778. Part of it was improved perhaps 5 or 6 Acres. He never cultivated any part of it himself. He values it at 20*s.* an Acre & thinks it was very well worth it. He thinks the 1900 Continental Dollars at that time worth about £40 S. He owes nothing

in America. He had one very good Negro. He gave £75 for him in the Exchange when he sold his Estate & Mill. He was taken away from him. He values him at £70 S.

Crop on the Ground he values at £40. There was nothing but Indian Corn. Nine Acres were in Cultivation. He says Indian Corn is worth 2s. a bushel. He says he has had 50 bushels from an Acre but from 30 to 40 is the Common run.

### Memorial of James McCulloch

Determin'd the 21st of Jany 1784.

James McCulloch—the Claimant—sworn. 16th Decr 1783.

He went to America in 1761. He went to Charlestown from Ireland. He hired himself Servt to Mr Williamson. He staid six Months & then was made his Overseer. Soon after he dealt in Horses in No Carolina. In 1774 he was a Miller. They tender'd him the Oath in 1775 & he refused it. Then they order'd him to turn out to do regular Duty. He did not choose this & he sold his Land & Mill & left the Country & went to Holstein river. His first plantation was on Beaver Creek. He returned after a few weeks to So Carolina. He first join'd Coll Turnbull & the British Troops ye 13th of June 1780 & went to rocky Mount. He was made a Captn of Ma by Coll Turnbull but has lost his papers. He was soon after taken Prisoner & kept at Salisbury untill Lord Cornwallis came there. He went again to the English Troops & continued with them till the Evacuation of Charlestown.

An Active & Zealous Loyalist. Bore Arms.

Bounty £30 a Yr.

### Memorial of John Robinson

Determin'd the 22d of Jany 1784.

John Robinson—the Claimant—sworn. 17th Decr 1783.

He went from Ireland to Charlestown in 1771. He settled about 35 Miles from Camden. He first shew'd his Loyalty by refusing to take the Oath. He never took that Oath afterwards. He was a Carpenter. He was frequently drafted but it did not fall to his Lot to go. In 1778 he was drafted & the Lot fell upon him & he went for the Americans about two Months. He explains this away by saying that he took that Opportunity of endeavouring to get to the British Lines but he was prevented. After that he came home & staid at home till Septr or Octr 1779. He attended a race which was made for the purpose of collecting together the Loyalists. In consequence of this he was sent to prison with 70 others for meeting after the race in Arms they meant to take the rebel Magazine at Camden. In March the Rebels sent a Party to warn them out & go to Charlestown this was in 1780. In consequence of this refusal they tried him & took him to Camden & from thence to Charlestown they came to him in the night. He went home again in June 1780 & afterwards served with the British under Coll Webster [1] & other officers. He raised 30 Men

A Loyalist & bore Arms.

Served a short time in the American Army.

Bounty £25 a Yr.

[1] Colonel Webster commanded the right brigade at the battle of Camden. Cornwallis wrote to Lord G. Germain: 'I directed Lieutenant-Colonel Webster to begin the attack, which was done with great vigour. . . . I was particularly indebted to Colonel Lord Rawdon and to Lieutenant-Colonel Webster for the distinguished courage and ability with which they conducted their respective divisions' (*Hist. MSS. Comm.*, *Stopford-Sackville MSS.*, vol. ii, *Am. Papers*, pp. 180–7). He was wounded at the fiercely contested battle of Guildford (March 15, 1781) and died of his wounds. Fortescue, *Hist. of the British Arms*, vol. iii, p. 404, describes him as an excellent officer.

by an Authority from Lord Rawdon. He was then soon after wounded in the thigh at Beaver Creek about 20 Miles from Camden.

Alexander Burnside—sworn.

He has known Robinson many years. He believes there never was a Man more loyal in the 3 kingdoms. In 1775 & 1776 He was of the same Class with him & he says he was uniformly loyal. He never knew that he served with the Americans or was drafted. The evidence given by Robinson being read to him he appears surprized & says he must have gone very unwillingly. After this time he was very active.

James M$^{c}$Culloch—sworn.

First knew M$^{r}$ Robinson in y$^{e}$ Year 1780. He knew nothing of him till this time of his Loyalty &c from this time he conducted himself remarkably well. He never heard of the Circumstance of his serving with the Americans. He says before he would have done this they should have sacrificed him. He always behaved very well after he knew him.

He knows nothing of his property. He never was at his House or place. He was a Capt$^{n}$ at Camden & when he returned he was called a Major. He says he rais'd a Company of Men.

Colonel Fortune—sworn.

Has known M$^{r}$ Robinson from the Year 1781. He always conducted himself extremely well & was greatly beloved by his Men. He looks upon him to be a very good Loyalist & always ready to do his Duty. He has heard of his being with the Americans but that does not alter his Opinion.

Determin'd the 22$^{d}$ of Jan$^{y}$ 1784.

## Memorial of Alexander Burnside

17$^{th}$ Dec$^{r}$ 1783.

Alexander Burnside—the Claimant—sworn.

A Loyalist & bore Arms.

Bounty £50 a Y$^{r}$.

He went to America from Ireland in 1765. He went to Charlestown & went over at the time of the bounty. He settled within a few Miles of Camden & he was there when the rebellion broke out. He was molested in 1775 or 1776 & they tender'd the Oath to him at that time the Oath of Abjuration. He refused it. They frequently harrass'd them about this time & carried him before a Magistrate. Nothing else material happen'd to him before the Year 1780. He had no Opportunity of taking up Arms before the British came to Camden which he did immediately & was in Col$^{l}$ Rugely's Reg$^{t}$. He went after y$^{e}$ Evacuation of Camden to Charlestown with Lord Rawdon.

Determin'd the 22$^{d}$ of Jan$^{y}$ 1784.

## Memorial of Will$^{m}$ Gist

18$^{th}$ Dec$^{r}$ 1783.

Will$^{m}$ Gist—the Claimant—sworn.

A Loyalist.

Took the Oath to the Americans.

He is an American & lived in Ninety Six in the beginning of troubles. He first set out to sign a Protest in 1775 but was taken sick. He first shew'd his principles in Dec$^{r}$ 1775. He took arms to protect some Loyalists who had taken a Magazine of Powder which was sent by the Rebels to the Indians. He afterwards endeavour'd to raise some Men & was taken prisoner in the same Month & was sent to Charlestown gaol & kept there for more than six Months.

He then went home after six Months imprisonment. Just before he was let out of Custody they tender'd him an Oath which he took or they would have confined him longer. He then went home & encouraged the Loyalists for which he was again sent to Prison but at last committed to Gaol. In Jan^y 1777 Major M^cCleod [1] came to his House where a number of Loyalists met. He came from Florida. He was betray'd to the Rebels for holding a Correspondence with him. In consequence of which 25 Men came to take him & were carrying him to Gaol but having a good Horse he made his Escape. He kept in the Woods ten Months. In Oct^r 1777 Colonel Thomas [2] proposed to him to take the State Oath or to take his tryal. He refused to take the Oath & was tried. The Grand Jury found the Bill but thinking that he should be hanged he gave 5000 Continental Dollars to the Witness to absent himself—5000 Dollars worth about £60 or £70 S. He was therefore discharged. He was kept bound till Nov^r 1779 when his recognizance was discharged. After the surrender of Charlestown was known in their neighborhood Many of the Loyalists met on the 6^th of June 1780 about 300 of them. They attack'd Col^l Brannam [3] the next morning & defeated him. They increas'd very fast until they had near 1000 Men. He was a Magistrate from the Year 1768 & when the Rebels came into them at this time he administer'd an Oath to them & they laid down their Arms. On the 1^st of July 1780 Major Ferguson joined them & took the Command. M^r Gist was with him afterwards in several Engagements. He staid with him till his death & was then made Prisoner & march'd near Virginia. He was kept in Prison about a Month & then made his escape & got to the British Lines at Ninety Six in Sept^r or Oct^r 1780. He afterwards acted as Assistant Commissary untill 1781. He had 5*s*. a Day for it & continued to act in that Capacity for 14 Months. He then came to Charlestown & went to Johns Island to act as Commissary under Colonel Cruger. He was kept in Pay till June 1782 & after that he staid at Charlestown till the Evacuation & rec^d the Pay of Capt^n till the time that he came to Eng^d which was the 1^st of January last.

Bounty £60 a Y^r.

He receives £60 a Year from the Treasury & has rec^d it from January last. He has a Wife & 5 Children in America.

Bounty £60 a Y^r.

Benjamin Booth Boote—sworn.

The Witness was in prison with M^r Gist in Feb^y 1776. He was then consider'd as a Loyalist And he behaved with great firmness. He went out in July 1776. He does not know the terms that he was let out upon And thinks that any Oath tender'd to him or them at that time was short of Abjuration. He looks upon M^r Gist as a very loyal Man.

Col^l Gibbes—sworn.

He has known M^r Gist about 17 Years. He was a Magistrate there & took part with Great Britain from the first. The first Act of his Loyalty was in 1775

[1] Presumably Major Alexander Macleod of the North Carolina Loyalists. 'After reverses and living six weeks in the swamps escaped to Sir H. Clinton' (*Hist. MSS. Comm., Am. MSS. in R. Inst.*, vol. ii, p. 7).

[2] Colonel John Thomas, a native of Wales, became Colonel of Militia in the place of Colonel Fletchall (McCrady, *S. Car. in the Rev., 1775–80*, p. 608).

[3] ? Colonel Brandon who belonged to the Ninety-Six district.

& he was taken to Charlestown Gaol. He looks upon him to be a true & steady Loyalist. He remembers the Circumstance of M^r^ Gist & several others coming out of prison upon condition that they took the State Oath being asked whether this was the Oath of Abjuration or the Oath of Allegiance He says the Latter. He shew'd his Loyalty soon after & he thinks he was imprudent in doing so. He never heard any other Circumstance to impeach his Loyalty & believes him to have been as good a Loyalist as any in the Country. He does not know whether he was in a bad State of health at that time.

Colonel Fortune—sworn.

He has known M$^{r}$ Gist 17 Y$^{rs}$. He lived 80 Miles from him. He has only heard of his former Loyalty but he remembers him as Assistant Commissary in 1781. He always seem'd to be very active & did his Duty frequently at great risque. He says if he had not been so active the Army would have been in great Distress for provisions. He was a Surveyor at first when he knew him. He was not then a Man of Substance but 12 Years ago He was a Man of substance & since that time he has heard that he had great landed property. He thinks he was one of the first people in the back Parts & very few People lived better than he did in that Country.

Determin'd the 4$^{th}$ of June 1784.

### Memorial of Lieut$^{t}$ Gov$^{r}$ Graham[1]

19$^{th}$ Dec$^{r}$ 1783.

Lieut$^{t}$ Gov$^{r}$ John Graham—the Claimant—sworn.

A Zealous & active Loyalist bore Arms & render'd Services to the British Gov$^{t}$.

Bounty £400 a Y$^{r}$.

Has been in Georgia since y$^{e}$ Year 1753. He went out with a view to succeed to the fortune of a relation there but did not succeed to it. He then went into trade but he left off business & began planting some Years before the troubles. Previous to the Rebellion he was one of the Council & Receiver of the Moneys arising from the Sale of the ceded Lands. In Aug$^{t}$ 1775 He had first an Opportunity of shewing his Loyalty by opposing the sending Delegates to Congress. This was the first commencement of the troubles in Georgia. They succeeded in defeating it at this time. Soon afterwards they carried the matter ag$^{t}$ the Loyalists. In the latter end of 1775 He was appointed Lieut$^{t}$ Governor. In Jan$^{y}$ 1776 they were surrounded by an armed force & all the Council present were taken Prisoners. He did not get the Commission till March 1776 & of course could not act as Lieut$^{t}$ Gov$^{r}$ before that time. There never was a Lieut$^{t}$ Gov$^{r}$ before that time but cannot absolutely say that such an Appointment was made necessary by the troubles but perhaps it might. After being taken Prisoner they were let out on parole the next Day. When the Scarborough Man of War came soon after off the Coast of Georgia He thinking they were come with Troops to protect the Province went on board but finding it to be otherwise

[1] In July 1788 Graham again memorialized the Commissioners, explaining that the amount he had received was not much more than five years' purchase of the annual income which the properties brought in. He had omitted to mention the loss of his office as receiver of all moneys arising from the sale of lands ceded by the Creek and Cherokee Indians. These lands amounted to two and a half million acres; and a commission of 10 per cent. on £200,000 would have fallen to him (P. R. O., *Audit Office, Am. Loyalists*, vol. iv). In *Acts of the Privy Council, Col. Ser. Unbound Papers*, No. 1301, there is a petition from Lieutenant-Governor Graham and the sons of Sir J. Wright for lands in St. Vincent. He acted as Inspector of Refugees in Georgia (*Hist. MSS. Comm., Am. MSS. in R. Inst.*, vol. ii, p. 252).

he remain'd there for some time till they sail'd again & then he went on shore to bring his family to Savannah. He came to Eng^d in May 1776 & staid till April 1779. He arrived at Savannah in July 1779 & staid there till the Evacuation which was in July 1782. In 1781 He went to quiet the back Settlements & they effected it with about 300 Men.

Lieut^t Gov^r Graham—call'd again & sworn. 20^th Dec^r 1783.

Being asked how much his Income would be from all his Plantations He says they do not compute in that way in that Country but as well as he can conjecture the gross produce of the three plantations was about £2700 S. For the Deductions to be made he refers to a paper given in by himself some time ago in the Case of Sir James Wright. Gov^r Graham's valuation is £10000 higher than that of the Appraisers & he thinks his property was worth it. However he is willing to abide by their Appraisement. He does not pretend to say that his property would have sold for what he puts upon it but he says he would not have taken it for it. He says being asked as to the comparative value of his property & Sir James Wrights that he thinks Sir James Wright's property was worth double the Money that his was in every respect. He had double the Number of Negroes & more than double the Quantity of Land. In 1776 He made a Settlement upon his Wife & family with a view to save the Confiscation of his Estate. He had mortgaged his American Estate to Mess^rs Clark & Millagan for some Money which he owed to them but when the troubles grew more desperate they were dissatisfied with the Security & restored the Mortgage Deed.

Sir James Wright—Bar^t—sworn.

Has known Lieut^t Gov^r Graham from the Year 1760. He was then in trade. He was afterwards appointed one of the Council by the recommendation of Sir James Wright. He appear'd to be a Man of property. He was an extensive Planter. He took a very early part in favor of Great Britain & recites several active services & principally those which have been before mention'd by Lieut^t Gov^r Graham. He was appointed Lieut^t Gov^r in 1775 & continued so during the War to the time of the Evacuation. He behaved extremely well in Council at Savannah when it was besieged & upon all Occasions but being in a civil Situation He was not much exposed to personal Hazard. Sir James is very well acquainted with his plantations. The Rice lands on the Mulberry Plantation were worth £12 an Acre. He values the whole of it at £1700 S. more than Gov^r Graham does.

The 2^d Plantation containing 847 Acres. That part which is call'd River Swamp is worth £6 an Acre & he values the other land from 45*s*. to 50*s*. He values the high Land tho' not clear'd.

Sir James Wright being asked to the Estimate which he had given of the Expences of banking &c & to which Gov^r Graham refers confirms it.

With respect to the Land on Alatamaha river He confirms the Acc^t which Gov^r Graham [gave] & thinks they were worth in 1775 about 30*s*. an Acre.

Simon Monro—sworn.

He is called to speak to the value of the 1500 Acres on the Alatamaha River. He does not know any other part of his property sufficiently to speak to the Value.

They were not at all cultivated but upon recollection he has heard the Gent[n] say who owned it before M[r] Graham that a part of it was cultivated. Gov[r] Graham had possess'd it several Years but he does not know what he gave for it. He likewise knows that he lost all his Papers. He saw the remains of some of the Deeds. He says that Gov[r] Graham had the largest property in the Province excepting Sir Ja[s] Wright. He never heard him mention'd as being worth any particular Sum. He knew Gov[r] Graham in the Year 1761. He was then a Man in great business. A Man in that Country at that time would have been esteem'd a Man of great fortune if he had £5000 in his [1]. He says it was a very cheap Country to live in but not so cheap he believes as those parts of America which had been longer established. Georgia Money was Sterling with the difference only of 8 per Cent.

22[d] Dec[r] 1783.

Lieut[t] Gov[r] Graham—sworn.

This Memorial respects the Offices which he held of Superintendant of Indian Affairs [2] & Lieut[t] Gov[r] of the Province. He has rec[d] notification of the Loss of his Salary as Lieut[t] Gov[r] of the Province & expects soon to receive the same Notice with respect to the other Office of Superintend[t] of Indian Affairs. No Salary was at first annex'd to the Office of Lieut[t] Gov[r] but soon after the Memorialist came to Eng[d] the King annex'd a Salary of £300 a Y[r] to him as Lieut[t] Gov[r].

His Commission as Lieut[t] Gov[r] dated in 1775 produced & read. He had no Salary when first appointed or Perquisites. When he came to Eng[d] in 1776 the Salary was given to him but not with a retrospect. It was given in consequence of his Application.

A Letter from M[r] Great [3] Elliott dated in June last produced & read by which it appears that the Salary would be discontinued from Midsummer last.

This Office was given to him totally without solicitation. He never applied for it. He says in 1775 He certainly thought that the British Gov[t] in America would prevail. A subsequent Commission produced & read dated in Jan[y] 1780 when the Province was restored to the Peace of this Country & he was re-appointed.

His Commission as Superintend[t] of Indian Affairs is left with his Deputy at S[t] Augustine. He cannot produce it. It was signed by M[r] Ellis [4] & must have been dated in 1782. He believes it was sign'd in March 1782. A Certificate produced from M[r] Nepean [5] one of the Under Secretaries of State by which

[1] *sic.* ? possession.

[2] In January 1782 Benjamin Thompson wrote from South Carolina to Lord G. Germain : 'Lieutenant [*sic*] (Lieutenant-Governor) Graham is here from Georgia. General Leslie has appointed him to succeed Cameron as Superintendent of Indian Affairs, and I have pledged myself for your approbation. I have told Graham very explicitly that if he does not contrive to diminish the expenses of the department very considerably, notwithstanding his being at the head of it, I shall certainly give my opinion for its being abolished altogether. The expenditure of late has been enormous, and the advantages derived from the Indians perfectly trifling. The fact is, very little is to be expected from them as friends, and as foes they would not by any means be formidable' (*Hist. MSS. Comm.*, *Stopford-Sackville MSS.*, vol. ii, *Am. Papers*, p. 251).

[3] Presumably Grey Elliot, who was a member of the Board of Trade.

[4] Welbore Ellis, *b.* 1713, *d.* 1802, first Baron Mendip, was Secretary of State for America in 1782.

[5] *b.* 1751, *d.* 1822. He became Sir Evan Nepean in 1802.

it appears that he held that Office & that the Salary was 500 a Y[r] with an allowance of £80 for House & Store rent & £30 for Stationary Wares &c. The Perquisites were casual but he believes they would have been about £500 a Y[r] more. He did not stay in the Country 3 Months after he was appointed. It was an old establish'd office. He succeeded M[r] Cameron who succeeded M[r] Stewart. He looks upon this as lost. He says that he has been informed that Half Pay has been given to persons holding such Offices upon many Occasions but he has never made any Application to the Treasury for it. This Commission does not extend to any other Province. He was recommended by Gen[l] Leslie & Sir Henry Clinton but he was appointed by the Crown. This was not an Office for Life but he was removeable at the pleasure of the Crown from both of his Offices.

He mentions the Loss of two Negroes killed by the Enemy.

### Memorial of James Hamilton

Determin'd the 22[d] of Jan[y] 1784.

22[d] Dec[r] 1783.

James Hamilton—the Claimant—sworn.

He went from Ireland when he was 8 Years old & believes he is now about 30. He went first to Pensylvania. His Mother was married & settled in Maryland at this time. His Situation at the Commencement of the troubles was that he was married & settled upon a Plantation. He bought this Plantation above eleven Years ago. He bought it of his father in Law. He never had any other Plantation but this. His first Act of Loyalty was refusing to sign an Association & he thinks it was in the Year 1778. This was the first Opportunity of shewing his principles. The next thing he did was to refuse the State Oath. About 3 Months afterwards he was cited to Court but he did not attend for some time. And upon some Conversation which he had with several persons He was taken up for speaking respectfully of the King. They were going to send him to prison but they took Bail from him And soon afterwards with the consent of his Bailsman he went & join'd the British Army y[e] 29[th] of March 1780 at the Neck of Charlestown. He was afterwards employed by Major André to circulate Manifestos in the back Country. But not being able to get there he returned to the lines & remain'd with them till Charlestown was taken. He was afterwards at the battle of the Hanging rock [1] & at the battle of Gates's Defeat [2] & at the battle of Guilford [3] upon the Baggage Guard. He was made a Capt[n] of M[a] by vote of a Party of Men after the battle at Camden whose Capt[n] was wounded. He had no Pay for this. He left Charlestown by the Consent of Gen[l] Leslie & came to Ireland.

An Active & Zealous Loyalist.

### Memorial of James Robertson Esq [4]

Determin'd the 31[st] of Jan[y] 1784.

23[d] Dec[r] 1783.

James Robertson Esq—the Claimant—sworn.

He went from this Country to America in 1767. He went to Georgia

[1] There were two engagements of that name, fought on August 1 and on August 6, 1780.

[2] August 16, 1780.

[3] March 15, 1781, in which Cornwallis defeated the Americans under Greene. Cornwallis's account of the battle is set out in Moore, op. cit., vol. ii, pp. 403–8.

[4] See Siebert, *The Legacy of the Am. Rev. to the W. Indies and Bahamas*, p. 48.

A Loyalist & bore Arms as Col$^{l}$ of the Militia.

Before took the Oath to the State of Georgia.

Bounty £50 a Y$^{r}$.

where he has always resided. He served his Clerkship there for five Years. He was admitted to the Bar in 1772 & followed the Profession untill the Commencement of the present troubles. His first Act of Loyalty was in 1774 by signing a Protest ag$^{t}$ all the improper Proceedings of the violent people on the other side. He bore his part in many other loyal resolutions which kept that Province a long time from entering into the Confederacy. He retired in the Year 1776 into the Country when Sir James Wright was obliged to go on board the Ship. In 1775 He was chosen a Delegate to the Congress of the Province but refused it. When he retired up into the Country He acted as an Overseer to M$^{r}$ Hume. He produces the Copy of a Warrant by which he was Seiz'd by order of the Rebel State in June 1776. This was at the time that Sir Peter Parker & Sir Henry Clinton lay off Charlestown. He was then told that he should remain in Confinement untill he should take a part with them. At last they brought to them an Oath to be true & faithful to the Cause of America & that he had not secreted any Arms. He found after the repulse of Charlestown that he should still be confined if he did not take the Oath. Notwithstanding he had refused it at first. He then took it & thinks it justifiable. He does not think that this Oath involves in it an Abjuration of the King of Great Britain. On his being set at Liberty He returned into the Country again & to his former Situation of retirement. He continued here till Oct$^{r}$ 1777 taking no part either with or ag$^{t}$ Great Britain. In Oct$^{r}$ 1777 He was called upon to take an Oath of Allegiance to the American States & to abjure their Allegiance to Great Britain. This Oath was not tender'd to all but only to suspected persons. Produces a Summons to attend them for that purpose & produces an Order by which it appears that he had been there & having refused to take the Oath he was order'd to depart the province in 40 Days. Accordingly he did depart tho' not within the 40 Days yet he took his Passage within the limited time. He embarked for New Providence one of the Bahama Islands. Produces a Permit from the Rebel Gov$^{r}$ of the Province dated Savannah 10$^{th}$ Dec$^{r}$ 1777. A Power was then given to persons to leave a power of Attorney to sell one half of the property & the other was to remain as a Pledge. He was admitted to the Bar there & staid about 3 Months & in March 1778 He went to S$^{t}$ Augustine & continued there till the reduction of Georgia. Upon Col$^{l}$ Campbell's establishing Civil Gov$^{t}$ in Georgia having before held the Office of Attorney General in that province He was applied to to return & to act in several other Departments. He returned immediately & continued there as Att$^{y}$ Gen$^{l}$ & Advocate Gen$^{l}$ till the return of Sir James Wright in 1779. Upon his return the Council was new model'd & M$^{r}$ Robertson was left out of the Council in order that he might be more serviceable in the House of Assembly. Soon afterwards He was chosen Member for Savannah & remain'd so for more than a Year. He then went into the Council & continued till the Evacuation of Savannah. He served as Lieut$^{t}$ Col$^{l}$ of the Militia from May 1779 & was afterwards a Col$^{l}$. Upon the Evacuation He went to New York. He never rec$^{d}$ Pay but rations when on actual Service. He staid at New York 3 Months & arrived in London Nov$^{r}$ 1782. He then applied to the Treasury & receives an Allowance from Jan$^{y}$ 1782 of £50 a Year. He is now appointed Chief Justice of the Virgin Islands with a Salary of £200 a Yr from this Country. Does not know what the emoluments will be exclusive of the Salary. The profits of his profession he considers about £200 a Year. He is a single Man. He understands that his £50 a Yr as an American Sufferer is to cease. But he wishes to apply to the Treasury for a Sum of Money to carry him out.

He states the Loss of the Office of Attorney Genl at £125 a Year.
He states the Loss of the Office of Advocate Genl at 125 a Yr.

**Further testimony to the Memorial of James Robertson**

Jany the 27th 1784.

The Claimant himself was examin'd the 23d of Decr 1783 & the following persons are call'd as Witnesses to his Case.

Sir James Wright—Bart—sworn.

Has known Mr Robertson 12 or 14 Years ago. He was then Clerk to the Atty Genl. He was then admitted to practise for himself. Before the troubles he appointed him Lieutt in the Ma. He was a practising Atty at the time of the commencement of the troubles. He afterwards appointed him Attorney Genl in 1776. Mr Hume the former Atty Genl was driven away which was the Occasion of his being appointed. He was Lieutt Coll during the siege. As to Loyalty Sir James says he thinks him a truly loyal & deserving Subject & that he acted from Principle. He never heard of his taking an Oath to the Rebel States & thinks it must have proceeded from Necessity. Knows nothing of his property. Believes he had no settled Plantations but knows he had an House which he purchased in the town of Savannah.

Lieutt Govr Graham—sworn.

Was very well acquainted with Mr Robertson. He considers him as a zealous & firm friend to the Cause of Great Britain. He was chosen a Delegate to go to Congress in 1775—but he refused to serve. He has understood that he took an Oath of Neutrality to the American States. Does not know much of his property but knows that he had some lands. Does not know what he gain'd by his profession but says he was in good business & in partnership with Mr Hume but does not know what share of the profits Mr Robertson had. Between the Years 1779 & 1782 He exerted himself as much as anybody & he was very active in the siege of Savannah.

John Jameson—sworn.

Has known Mr Robertson many Years. He looks upon him as a very active & loyal Subject. Never heard of the Circumstance of his taking an Oath to the rebel States. Believes he was banished for not doing it. Says about the time that the Americans declared for independence they tender'd an oath of Neutrality to many persons. Being asked to the Substance & purport of this Oath He says the terms of the Oath were that the persons should take no active part agt the Americans & that they should not detain or secrete any Arms.

## Memorial of John Simpson

Determin'd the 28th of Aug^t 1784.

James Robertson Esq—sworn. 23^d Dec^r 1783.

This Gent^n is appointed Chief Justice of the Virgin Islands & being under a Necessity of going soon M^r Simpson applies that he may be now heard to certain facts in his Case.

He held the Offices of Clerk of y^e Crown & Prothonotary of the General Court. Being ask'd to the value of the Office of Clerk of the Crown He thinks the Value of the two Offices about £600 a Year including the business which he did for the Public Office of Clerk of the Crown he thinks worth from 130 to 150 the other Office from £450 to £500. He enter'd upon the Execution of these two Offices in May or June 1779 to the evacuation. He can't say whether he thinks he would ever have had these Appointments if the troubles had not happen'd. He says he can't tell but seems to admit that he probably would not & that he is not fit for the Office not being a professional Man.

## Memorial of Peter Dean

Determin'd the 29th of March 1784.

28th Jan^y 1784.

Peter Dean—the Claimant—sworn.

An Active & Zealous Loyalist & bore Arms.

He went to America in 1774. Before he landed he heard of the troubles to the North from the Pilot. He landed at Charlestown in Jan^y 1774. The troubles began in that province in 1775 & the Gov^t was Subverted in 1776. He then took an active part for the British Gov^t. His first Act of Loyalty was the joining in a protest ag^t the proceedings of the Rebels. In 1776 the disaffected people spiked the Guns of the fort that they might not be fired on the Kings Birthday. He assisted in restoring them. The next transaction was turning out under Arms with about 100 others & protecting the Gov^r's House. Next he turned out under arms to prevent several persons being tarr'd & feather'd. When the Gov^r made his Escape he went into the Country to conceal himself from the resentment of the people. Soon after that he attempted to make his escape in the night & he was seized & imprison'd for 14 Days & they condemn'd the Indigo he had with him & sold it but the Indigo was not his own. Soon after that he was brought before a Rebel Committee they then tender'd him an Oath of Abjuration & Allegiance to them which he refused to take in consequence of which he was order'd to depart the State in 40 Days it was afterwards enlarged to 60 Days & he left it in that time. He was banished the State in Oct^r 1777 & they permitted him to sell the half of his property & retain'd the other half as a Security that he should not bear arms ag^t them. After he had left the province in March 1778 He was declared guilty of high treason ag^t America. The half of his property which was detained as a Security was sold and confiscated. He then went to reside in the West Indies & staid there till the British Gov^t was restored. He came back to Savannah in June 1779. He was present at the siege & took an active part. He was in the hottest part of the engagement when D'estaing[1] was repulsed. He then acted as Lieut^t of the Militia but he had

Presumptive Proof of Confiscation.

[1] The French admiral who, at the age of thirty, had been transferred from the army to the navy with the rank of rear-admiral.

neither Commission nor Pay. He was afterwards elected a Member of Assembly & served in that Capacity & did everything in his power to reestablish the British Gov[t]. He remain'd at Savannah till the Evacuation which happen'd the 11[th] of July 1782. He was then in May 1782 by an Act of their Assembly banish'd & his property confiscated. He is mention'd by name in that Act. He then went to Charlestown to settle some business & he remain'd there after the Evacuation till the peace. He then returned to Georgia after the peace with a View to settle there. But he was refused Admission & produces some papers to prove it.

### Memorial of Justice Walker

Determin'd the 29[th] of Jan[y] 1784.

Justice Walker—the Claimant—sworn. Jan[y] the 29[th] 1784.

He was settled in Philadelphia & went out from London in 1775. He took only £15 with him. He hired himself as a Serv[t] to a Sugar Baker for £36 a Year. His Wife followed him to America soon afterwards & brought £80 with her. Within a Month or two after he arrived in America the Rebels beat up for Volunteers & they called upon him to sign the Association which he refused & he was in consequence of it turned out of his place. He join'd the British Troops in New York he was in the Militia. He went with the Army from Philadelphia at the Evacuation. About the Year 1780 he enter'd into the Militia & carried Arms. He says what he left behind him at Philadelphia was worth £100. It consisted of furniture two barrels of Beer & 15 Gallons of rum. He had wood in the Cellar which cost him £17 Currency. He thinks his furniture was worth £50 Currency. He applied to the Treasury & rec[d] £10 in full.

A Loyalist.

Bounty £10 in full.

### Memorial of John Lovell [1]

Determin'd 29[th] of Jan[y] 1784.

John Lovell—the Claimant—sworn. Jan[y] the 29[th] 1784.

He was born at Boston in New England & resided there at the time the troubles broke out. When Gen[l] Gage came to Boston he was sent to by him to do some private services this he did because his principles were known as he had always taken part with Gov[t]. He frequently attended Meetings at Boston & whenever Measures were proposed hostile to Gov[t] He always opposed them. Gen[l] Gage wanted to procure some papers which were in the possession of some of the Rebel Committees. He did procure them & deliver'd them to the Gen[l] himself. This was attended with an Expence which has never been repaid to him & he likewise did it at the risque of being tarr'd & feather'd. He took up arms under Gen[l] Gage & Gen[l] Howe as an Associator & continued to do Duty till the Evacuation of Boston. He has no Witnesses to prove this but he says that Gen[l] Gage & Gen[l] Howe can prove it. He is therefore desired to send Certificates from those two Gent[n]. As to the property lost—He says he can't look upon his property to be lost so long as the King & Par[t] have offer'd to

A Loyalist.

Did not bear Arms.

[1] John Lovel, sen., is in the list of those who went from Boston with the troops to Halifax. He is not otherwise mentioned by Mr. Stark. His son James adhered to the Americans and was a prisoner at Halifax at the same time that the father was there as a refugee. See Sabine, op. cit., vol. ii, p. 30, who erroneously states that John Lovel died at Halifax in 1778.

negotiate for it. And when he has stated it He shall go over to America to make his Claim.

Determin'd the 5th of July 1784.

## Memorial of Mrs Hamilton

Jany the 30th 1784.

Mary Hamilton—the Claimant—sworn.

Her Husband a Loyalist.

All the Claim rejected.

Her Husband died in July 1780. He was a Native of Scotland & went to America about 9 Years ago. He went to New York to settle as a Surgeon. She was married to Mr Hamilton before he went to America. She never was in America. When he had been in America about 5 Years he returned to Engd. He took out with him in Money & Medicines more than £200. She knows nothing of Mr Hamilton's Losses in America. When he came over from America in 1779 or 1780 He told her that he had lost everything & said he had lost about £1000 S. He died on board the Centaur about 3 Years ago. She says he never bought anything in land but he had Horses furniture &c. America was in rebellion when he went there. She says he was used ill by the Americans on acct of his zeal for his Majesty's Govt. Her Husband left a Will with a power to his Agent to receive any Money for him.

Determin'd the 17th of Feby 1784.

## Memorial of Willm Moorhead

Jany the 30th 1784.

Willm Moorhead—the Claimant—sworn.

A Loyalist.

He went from Ireland to Philadelphia in 1773 & took his family with him viz. a Wife & two Children. He carried out more than £100 in Cash & Cloaths. He sold a Lease which he held under Lord Mountcashel. In 1774 He purchas'd 180 or 190 Acres of Land about 100 Miles from Philadelphia he paid near £100 S. for the Land. When he bought it about 18 Acres were cultivated. He continued in possession more than four Years. Then he was driven away by the Inhabitants of the Country because he would not take up arms agt the Crown. They seiz'd him & everything he had. He made his Escape & fled down to the English Lines. He would have taken arms for the British if his health had permitted but he remain'd sick for six Months & then came to Ireland. He left Philadelphia in April 1778 & has been in Ireland ever since. He does not know whether his property is confiscated or not as he has never enquired after it since.

Determin'd the 3d of Feby 1784.

## Memorial of John Lightenstone

30th Jany 1784.

John Lightenstone—the Claimant—sworn.

A Zealous & active Loyalist.

Bore Arms.

He was born at Petersburgh of English Parents. He went to America in 1755. He followed the Sea & was then Mate of a Vessel. He soon afterwards commanded a Vessel out of New York. At the Commencement of the troubles he was settled in Georgia & commanded the Scout Boat which is by Commission from Govt & paid by Govt. He produces the Commission sign'd by Sir Jas Wright in 1768. She was then taken from him in 1776 by the Rebels out of the Dock at Savannah. The Rebels offer'd to continue Mr Lightenstone in the Command of her if he would follow their measures which he refused. He apprehends it was an Appointment for Life & thinks he clear'd £200 a Yr by it. After Sir Jas Wright went away the Claimant went to the Island of Skidaway

& was very cautious of shewing himself. He went to Halifax & from thence to New York. He continued with the British Army till 1782. He was appointed by Sir Ja[s] Wright after the restoration of the Province to a troop of Dragoons. He produces the Commission which is read. He rec[d] the Pay of 15*s.* 6*d.* a Day & continued in this Command till the Evacuation. He was at the taking of Savannah by the British & was then Assistant Quarter Master Gen[l] for which he rec[d] Pay. He was present at the taking of most of the Towns in America. Bounty £60 a Y[r].

Certificates produced from Sir James Wright & Capt[n] Berkley to his Loyalty & Services & Sir Ja[s] Wright speaks of his name being in the Confiscation Act.

Property.

381 Acres purchased at different times & contain'd in many Conveyances the title Deeds to which are produced. They were principally cultivated. He did not give quite 20*s.* an Acre for them but he has improved them much. He made the Buildings & Indigo Vats himself. He was offer'd £500 for a part of it 320 Acres but he refused it. He values them at 40*s.* per Acre. £550 0*s.* 0*d.*

150 Acres of Land in Wrightsborough. No part whereof is cultivated. It was his property by Grant from Gov[t] dated in 1774. He meant to have cultivated it if the troubles had not happen'd. The Expence of taking it out was about £10. He values this tract at 20*s.* per Acre. £30 0*s.* 0*d.*

Crop of 40 Acres left in June 1782 valued by M[r] Lightenstone at £100—480 bushels of Corn valued at 2*s.* 6*d.* per bushel 200 bushels of Pease at 2*s.* 6*d.* 3 Acres of Potatoes at £10 Corn left in the Store £5. £50 0*s.* 0*d.*

Horses Cattle Hogs &c valued at £100 18 Head of Cattle at 40*s.* 8 Sheep at 15*s.* 30 Hogs at 10*s.* 1 Horse at the Siege £11 two Horses on y[e] Plantation £10 one Dragoon Horse £22. He swears that they were all taken from him by the Rebels. £50 0*s.* 0*d.*

## Memorial of Lieut[t] Col[l] Conolly [1]

Determin'd the 24[th] of May 1784.

John Conolly—the Claimant—sworn. Feb[y] 2[d] 1784.

Is an American born & was settled in Virginia from the Year 1770. He was in the Military Line some time during the last War & served ag[t] the Indians. He had a patrimonial Estate originally in Pensylvania which he sold & purchased lands in Virginia. At the commencement of the rebellion he commanded the Militia in Augusta County. His first Act in the course of this rebellion was to join Lord Dunmore which he did when he was on board a Ship. He join'd him in July 1775. He was then dispatched by Lord Dunmore to Boston. He went accordingly & got to Boston. Immediately on his return from Boston he was appointed Lieut[t] Col[l] Commandant on the 5[th] of Nov[r] 1775 & appointed to command an Expedition. He was taken Prisoner the 19[th] of the same Month when he had just enter'd on his Expedition. He remain'd Prisoner in Maryland about six weeks when he was removed by order of Congress to Philadelphia. He remain'd a Prisoner with them for five Years. He was not particularly ill treated. His Exchange was effected in Oct[r] 1780. He then went to New York. He was taken prisoner again in Sept[r] 1781 in the vicinity of York Town. A Zealous & active Loyalist & render'd essential Service to Gov[t].

[1] See Additional Notes, p. 78.

He was continued a Prisoner till March 1782. He was confined in Gaol from Jan^y to March 1782. He then was let out on parole on Condition that he would come to Eng^d which he did accordingly. He mentions a Circumstance of loyalty by which he did some service early in the rebellion by inducing four persons of Consequence in America to take part with Gov^t which they did but the Congress afterwards got them over to their Cause. He was frequently offer'd a Command by the Rebels. The Congress offer'd him to command the 2^d Virginia Reg^t. He has rec^d whole pay to the 24^th of October last but does not know whether he is to receive half Pay or not. Gen^l Washington made him offers if he would have come into their Service. He was intimate with Gen^l Washington before the War. Col^l Conolly has made several Applications to the Treasury for temporary Support but there being a Doubt whether he is to receive half pay or not no Report has yet been made.

Earl of Dunmore—sworn.

Knew Lieut^t Col^l Conolly in Virginia. He commanded the Militia of Augusta County before the rebellion & was concerned ag^t the Indians & Lord Dunmore employ'd him in making a Treaty with the Indians. He did this business well & was of great use. He looks upon Col^l Conolly as well attached to the British Gov^t. He appointed him Lieut^t Col^l Commandant in 1775. Knows he was confined for several Years. Lord Dunmore confirms him in the Acc^t he gave of the grant of 4000 Acres. Lord Dunmore being asked as to the Demand which Col^l Conolly had upon the Province He says he thinks part of it is just & that he ought to have been paid & he believes that it never was paid. He can't speak to the Sums. He says he certainly would have receiv'd it if it had not been for the rebellion.

Major Stockton—sworn.

Has known Col^l Conolly since 1776. He was in prison with him at York Town & in Philadelphia. He believes him to be a very loyal Subject. He was in prison with him when two persons offer'd to buy part of his Land they appear'd to be serious & offer'd to pay for it in Gold & Silver & believes the Sum was 1100 Pistoles.

**To the Memorial of Lieut^t Col^l Conolly**

6^th Feb^y 1784.

Joseph Galloway Esq—sworn—call'd by the Board to satisfy them as to a Custom which Col^l Conolly said existed in Pensylvania respecting the title to Lands by pre-occupancy.

He says the Proprietors hold their title by Patent from the Crown. They establish'd a Land Office in order to dispose of their Lands to whom persons wishing to purchase must apply. Upon their Application to the office they rec^d a Warrant to the Surveyor to survey & locate latterly they sent only a Copy of the Application & not the Warrant. Upon a return of the Survey the title to the Purchasor is reckon'd so far compleat that he has a right to take out a Patent of Confirmation upon paying the residue of the purchase Money whenever he pleases. He says the Warrant & Survey was always pleaded in their

Courts & was held to give a legal title. There have been many instances of persons sitting down to clear a small number of Acres & building a little House upon it without a Warrant & Survey & that these persons have always had a right of preemption but there have been instances to the contrary. Mr Galloway says that the title of Mr Conolly is better than the title of those persons employ'd by him.

### Memorial of Joseph Hooper [1]

Determin'd 4th of March 1784.

3d Feby 1784.

Joseph Hooper—the Claimant—sworn.

He was born in America. As soon as the restraining Act was pass'd he sign'd a Protest & induced others to sign it contrary to the resolutions of the town & constantly opposed them in their Town meetings at Marblehead where he lived. He followed the business of a Rope maker as well as Merchandize. His House was called Tory Hall from his known adherence to Govt. He was obliged to go armed for some time before he left America after the troops left Marblehead they left Marblehead a short time before the battle of Lexington. He constantly lived with the Officers of the British Army. Immediately after the battle of Lexington Captn Bishop in the Ship Lively lay off the Port of Marblehead & blocked up the Port the Town chose Mr Hooper as a friend to the British Govt to mediate for them. After this he was constantly attacked & insulted & frequently put in danger of his Life three Attempts were made to burn his House in the night & he killed one Man in the Attempt. On May 1st a Town Meeting was held at Marblehead & all the Adherents to the British Cause were order'd to renounce their Allegiance & he was the only person in the town who refused to make a temporary submission. They immediately drew up a form of recantation which a friend of his who was in that Committee told him he must be obliged to sign the Friday following or his Life would be the forfeit. He took the Opportunity of going in a Ship of his fathers & went to Bilboa in Spain & he lay 42 Nights on some dried fish. He came from Spain to France & thro france to Engd since which time he has never been in America.

A zealous & steady Loyalist.
Did not bear Arms.

Bounty £80 a Yr.

Saml Curwen [2] Esq—sworn.

Knew Mr Hooper very well from his Infancy. He lived at Salem himself which is 4 Miles from Marblehead. The Hooper family were always esteem'd loyal. He does not himself know any Acts of Loyalty. He knew he carried on the Rope business & he always consider'd him as the Owner of the Rope Walk. He cannot put any Value upon his Rope Walk his Mansion House or any part of his property. He knows the Woman he married believes her father was a Loyalist but does not know what he had with her father had fail'd in business

[1] The address of the inhabitants of Marblehead to Governor Hutchinson of May 25, 1774, was signed by no less than five members of the Hooper family. Joseph was the son of Robert, known as 'King', who rose from poverty to great wealth. Joseph became a paper manufacturer at Bungay in Suffolk, where he died in 1812. The Marblehead Revolutionary Committee recorded on May 8, 1781, that 'they believed he had voluntarily gone over to our enemies', and proceeded to administer his affairs (Stark, op. cit., p. 224).

[2] S. Curwen records (*Journal and Letters, 1842*, p. 396) under February 3, 1784: 'Joseph Hooper called on me to accompany him to the American Commissioner's office in Lincoln's Inn Fields, which I did, and gave a relation on oath which proved my unacquaintedness with his affairs, of no advantage to his cause.'

some years before. The Witness came away before Mr Hooper & has heard nothing of Mr Hooper's conduct by which he displeas'd the Rebels. He says that Mr Coombes could give the Board some Information but he is at present absent. He says he knows nothing more of Mr Hooper's Case. In short he knows nothing of it And Mr Monro is desired to inform Mr Hooper that the Board will expect some further Evidence to corroborate Mr Hooper's testimony.

### To the Memorial of Joseph Hooper

24th Feby 1784.

Peter Frye Esq—sworn.

He lived at Salem & Hooper at Marblehead. Hooper was a Rope maker & he believes the Rope Walk belonged to Mr Hooper Junr. He knows the rope Walk it was a considerable Expence to make it into a rope Walk it was at the End of the town & the Ground was not valuable for any other purpose. He thinks it might have let for £100 a Yr. He would not have given £2500 but he thinks he could have bought & built the whole for £2000 lawful Money. He had the principal business. He always consider'd the father & the Son as very loyal Subjects. He knows the Mansion House in which he lived it was a large House & one of the best Houses in the Town. He thinks it would have cost about £2500 S. with all the Outbuildings &c & he was at great Expence in clearing the ground which was a Rock. It might have been built for £2000. If he had been to buy the House he should have thought 2000 a great price for it. If it had been to have been sold at public Auction He thinks it would not have taken more than £1500 S. & he would not have given more himself. It was a well furnished House. He thinks the furniture Plate &c might be worth £350. He has heard that Mr Hooper had a Concern in another Rope Walk. He has seen the House at Newbury Port it came by his Wife. He has rode round it & says supposing the Outhouses to be good it might be worth 7 or 800. He can't speak at all to the furniture &c never having been in the House. He knows he had Negro Servts but does not know the Number. He had two or three Carriages. Being asked to the price of Carriage Horses he says £10 a piece was a great price. He cannot form an Opinion of what he might get by his Rope Walk but he says he thinks he might make £500 a Yr & some Years more. He does not know whether Mr Hoopers property is confiscated And he doubts whether their proscriptive Laws go so far as to prevent persons attainted in their own persons from inheriting property. He says He never knew an Instance of property coming to a Man in right of his Wife when the Wife remain'd in the Country being confiscated. This goes to the Estate at Newbury Port & the Principle which he lays down respecting the inheritance of Property applies to the estate in reversion to come to him at the Death of his father.

### Memorial of Jacob Ellegood[1] Esq. Lieutt Coll

Determin'd the 5th of Feby 1784.

4th Feby 1784.

Jacob Ellegood Esq—the Claimant—sworn.

Is a Native of America of the Province of Virginia. Lord Dunmore when he first issued his Proclamation sent Letters to Coll Ellegood who was then

[1] See Additional Notes, p. 79.

Col[l] of the Militia of his County. In consequence of which he brought him in 600 Men in Nov[r] 1775. They were all in Arms. Part of these people had before attacked Lord Dunmore. They then took the Oaths to the Gov[t] owing to the influence of Col[l] Ellegood with them. Lord Dunmore then proposed to Col[l] Ellegood to command a Reg[t] which he was to raise to support the town of Norfolk. He rais'd the Reg[t] accordingly & had a Commission from Lord Dunmore to command it the name of the Reg[t] was the Queens Royal Virginia Reg[t]. And he commanded this Reg[t] at the battle of the Great Bridge where the English were defeated. After this defeat it was found necessary to abandon Norfolk & he had a Commission from Lord Dunmore to conduct some Women &c to the eastern Shore. He was taken Prisoner on this Expedition. He was kept Prisoner at Northampton for 4 weeks & afterwards in close Confinement at Williamsburgh & other places. He was upon the whole detain'd a Prisoner with them for 5 Years & 4 Months. Frequent applications were made for his Exchange but they never would exchange him. He came into the British Lines upon Parole in the Month of May 1781. He still remain'd under parole during the whole of the War. Sir Henry Clinton wished to carry him out with him & endeavour'd to get him exchanged for that purpose but it could not be done. His Services were interrupted by his being a Prisoner. But he did all that he could untill he was made Prisoner.

A Zealous & active Loyalist.
Bore Arms & render'd material Services to Gov[t].

Bounty £200 a Y[r].

M[rs] Ellegood has always been treated with great Civility & attention but she is so highly taxed that he is obliged to remit Money to her from time to time. He remitted some last Week. The Property now stands thus as Colonel Ellegood believes. By an Act of the State of Virginia passed about 1778 the Property of Loyalists who had join'd the Kings Army when they had Wives & Children was directed to go immediately to the Wife & Children if upon the Spot & was vested in them one third to the Wife &c as if the father was dead And he conceives his family to be in possession of his Estate under this Act. And he is at present prohibited from ever returning into that Country as a Subject but he means to go to settle in Nova Scotia.

Tho[s] Macknight Esq—sworn.

Knows Col[l] Ellegood very well. He was settled in Virginia when the troubles broke out. He inherited the Estate from his father. He was Col[l] of the Militia of his County. His father was County Lieut[t] there which seems to be similar to a Lord Lieut[t] of a County in Eng[d]. The Plantation where he lived was very extensive. Speaks of Lord Dunmore writing to Col[l] Ellegood to request him to take part with the British Gov[t] in consequence of which in two or three Days he came in at the head of 600 Men who were the Militia of the County. He was afterwards made Lieut[t] Col[l] Commandant of a Reg[t] & was at the battle of the great Bridge. He rais'd several Men for the Reg[t] the Command of which was given to him. Has always understood that he had the Command of that Reg[t]. He was a Man in whom Lord Dunmore placed great Confidence. The Witness has known some spirited exertions made by Col[l] Ellegood.

## Memorial of the Rev^d John Doty[1]

Determin'd the 16th of Feby 1784.

The Rev^d John Doty—the Claimant—sworn. 6th Feby 1784.

A Loyalist.
Did not bear Arms.

Is a Native of Albany but was always brought up in New York. He consider'd himself bound by the Oath of Allegiance which he had taken several times to the King of Great Britain to adhere to Gov^t which he did do. At the commencement of the troubles He was Rector of St. George's Church in Schenectady. In the Year 1775 He did both in the pulpit & out of it exhort his Parishioners to good Gov^t this soon drew upon him the resentment of the opposite faction. They did not molest him personally till after the declaration of Independence when his Church was shut up. Soon after that he was brought before the Committee & charged by two young Men with plotting ag^t the State this was in the Summer 1776. He denied the Charge of plotting but admitted that he was & would be loyal. They threaten'd to send him to prison to Albany however he was discharged & remain'd unmolested for a few weeks when he was again taken. He was taken in his bed by two armed Men. They hurried him & some others off in a Waggon & sent them away to Albany. When they came to Albany They proposed an Oath to him (he believes it to have been an Oath of Neutrality) but he refused to take it. He believes the others who were with him did take it. Notwithstanding he refused to take the Oath they releas'd him & let him go back to Schenectady where he remain'd till Gen^l Burgoyne's defeat when despairing of any succour or future happiness he obtain'd leave from Gen^l Gates to go into Canada by the means of his friends at Albany. Gen^l Gates offer'd him a Living of £200 a Year if he would stay. He went to Canada & was appointed by Sir Guy Carleton to be Chaplain to the 1^st Batt^n of Sir John Johnson's Reg^t. He continued in this situation till he & his Wife came to Eng^d in 1781. He came to Eng^d on acc^t of his health & was permitted to appoint a Deputy to the Reg^t in his Absence. He has now half pay but that is mortgaged for a Year to come to a Gent^n at Montreal who advanced him some Money. He was appointed a Missionary in 1773 & has remain'd so ever since the emolument of that is £40 a Y^r. But he is going again to Canada with an additional Appointment of £10 a Y^r. So that he has now £50 a Y^r from that Society. He has 40 a Y^r from the Treasury. He produces a Commission from Sir Guy Carleton appointing him Chaplain & a letter from D^r Morice Secretary to the Society for propagating the Gospel speaking very highly of M^r Doty & saying that the Society had appointed him to go again to Canada which he intends to do next Month. His Land is not confiscated.

Half Pay £60 a Y^r.

Missionary £50 a Y^r.
Bounty £40 a Y^r.

## Memorial of Peter Rose

Determin'd the 5th of March 1784.

Peter Rose—the Claimant—sworn. 6th Feby 1784.

Is not an American. He is a Swede & went to America in 1766 to Boston. He was by trade a Shoemaker. At the commencement of the troubles He

[1] In Brymner, *Can. Arch. 1888, Haldimand Coll.*, vol. ii, p. 656, under date October 19, 1781, it is reported that the Rev. J. Doty, instead of wanting leave to the 1st of July next, wished to remain permanently in England, retaining his position as Chaplain in the army, having arranged with a deputy to perform his duties. He was in charge of the English church at Sorel in Canada in 1784, when he applied for the use of a Government building in which to hold services (Siebert, *The Am. Loyalists in the Eastern Seigniories and Townships of the Province of Quebec*, p. 41).

associated for the defence of the Town as appears by a Certificate of Sir W$^{m}$ Pepperell. Upon the Evacuation of Boston He went with the troops to Halifax & came to Eng$^{d}$ in the latter end of 1777 or beginning of 1778. He was obliged to leave behind him at Boston some little matters or articles of furniture which are enumerated in a Schedule annex'd to his Memorial & amount to £15 2*s.* 2*d.*

A Loyalist.
Did not bear Arms.
£15 0*s.* 0*d.*

He makes a Charge for the Loss of three Apprentices of £50. One ran away to the Rebels one to the West Indies & he left the other behind.

Certificates read from Lieut$^{t}$ Gov$^{r}$ Oliver Sir W$^{m}$ Pepperell Col$^{l}$ Cleaveland Rob$^{t}$ Achmutz Esq. But these all go to Loyalty only.

He says losing his Situation in trade was his principal Loss. He now works journey work occasionally & gets about 10*s.* or 11*s.* a week.

John Barnard—sworn.

He is a Furrier. He knows M$^{r}$ Rose & knew him in Boston. He was a Shoemaker & kept a great number of Workmen. He had the best business in the Town. He believes him to be a Loyalist. He worked for all the Army. He believes he join'd an Association at Boston. He knew him first in London. He went to America about 7 Years before the Witness & he carried all that he had out with him but he does not know what it amounted to.

N.B. This Mans Allowance from the Treasury is £20 a Y$^{r}$ & it commenced from Christmas 1782 & he states the first payment made to him to be on the 14$^{th}$ of April & that to be all the Assistance which he has rec$^{d}$ from Gov$^{t}$.

Bounty £20 a Y$^{r}$.

## Memorial of John Saltmarsh

Determin'd the 16$^{th}$ of Feb$^{y}$ 1784.

John Saltmarsh—the Claimant—sworn. 7$^{th}$ Feb$^{y}$ 1784.

He is an Englishman & went to America in 1768. He was settled at Norwich in 1774 & 1775 in Connecticut. He followed the trade of a Breeches maker Glover & Dyer. In 1775 He was applied to teach the Americans the use of Arms. He refused to do it tho' they offer'd to pay him for it & they offer'd to make him a Capt$^{n}$ if he would & to give him 10*s.* a Day. In consequence of this they abused him & would not employ him. He left the place in June 1775 & went to New York. He was employ'd by Gen$^{l}$ Tryon & Capt$^{n}$ Vandeput to get intelligence of the Enemy for five Months. He was apprehended in Oct$^{r}$ 1776. He lay near three Months in prison during which time he was ill treated. They made him many offers to espouse their side. He did not get clear out of Bondage till March 1777. In 1777 He took an Oath which he says was that he had no writings so as to give any intelligence to the British Army. On this he was permitted to depart & join'd the British fleet in April 1777. He has been twice wounded in passing the lines of the Enemy which has affected his health. He came to Ireland in March 1779. He never rec$^{d}$ anything for his services but £10. He came to Eng$^{d}$ in May 1779 & has been here ever since.

A Loyalist.

Before he went to America He was a Gunner at Hythe the emolument of which is £18 5*s.* 0*d.* When he returned to Eng$^{d}$ there were ten Years Arrears due & Lord Townshend order'd them to be paid & he receiv'd for his Arrears £190 or upwards. He had about the Year 1780 an Allowance of £80 a Y$^{r}$ from the Treasury which was reduced by M$^{r}$ Wilmot & M$^{r}$ Coke to £30 a Y$^{r}$.

Salary as a Gunner £18 5*s.* 0*d.* a Y$^{r}$.
former Bounty from Gov$^{t}$ £80 a Y$^{r}$.
present Bounty £30 a Y$^{r}$.

## Memorial of Duncan Stewart

Determin'd the 20th of Feby 1784.

7th of Feby 1784.

Duncan Stewart Esq—the Claimant—sworn.

A Loyalist & Did his Duty as an Officer of the Crown.

He claims for no Property real or personal but only for the Loss of his Office. In 1764 He obtain'd the Office of Collector of the Customs in New London [1] & went to America in consequence of it. The Appointment is produced & read it is dated the 12th of April 1764. He came back to Engd in 1771 & staid about a Year & ½. When the troubles broke out in 1774 & 1775 He was at New London in the Execution of his Office. He was frequently molested before but he was always able to quell it till the Yr 1777. He staid as long as he could in the Country in hopes that Govt would be reestablish'd. He came away in July 1777 & it was impossible for him to stay any longer. They never offer'd him any Oath but they frequently offer'd him employments in their service but he constantly refused.

Bounty £150 a Yr.

Salary of Office £80 0*s.* 0*d.* Perquisites £450 0*s.* 0*d.* Former Bounty £200 a Yr. Present Bounty £150 a Yr.

The Salary of his Office was £80 a Year & the Perquisites & fees about £500 a Yr besides. The Salary was continued till Octr 1782 & the fees & Perquisites gradually decreas'd & finally ceas'd for some time before he left America from 1777 to Octr 1782. He recd the Salary & £120 as an Allowance in Addition since which time the Salary was discontinued in consequence of the Report made by Mr Wilmot & Mr Coke & he now receives an Allowance from the Treasury of £150 a Yr but no Salary. He has seven Children.

## Memorial of Colonel Billup [2]

Determin'd the 26th of May 1784.

9th Feby 1784.

Genl Stirling—sworn.

He has known him from 1776 & 1777. He was then a Coll of Militia & a Loyalist. When the Witness commanded at Staten Island in 1779 & 1780 Coll Billup served under him with activity & zeal. During his Command there Lord Sterling invaded the Island & upon that Occasion Coll Billup lost a part of his property which was returned to the Witness but it is amongst his papers in Scotland. He thinks the Loss upon that Occasion to Coll Billup was from 6 to £900 New York Currency. When things went ill He says that Coll Billup said he would take £3000 for it but the Genl says he has frequently heard that his property was worth about £5000 New York Currency.

An Active Loyalist & a very spirited Magistrate. Bore Arms & render'd Services to Govt.

Coll Christopher Billup—the Claimant—sworn.

He was born in Staten Island. He lived upon his own Estate in Staten Island when the troubles broke out. He was Representative in the Genl Assembly of New York & opposed all the measures of the Rebels & prevented

Bounty £80 a Yr.

[1] Connecticut.

[2] Christopher Billup, *b.* 1737, *d.* 1827, a prominent inhabitant of Staten Island, was a member of the Committee of Grievances of the New York Assembly which reported that it was the right of Englishmen that no tax should be levied saving by consent given personally or through representatives in Assembly, and that certain Acts were subversive of the rights of the Colonists (Becker, op. cit., p. 177). He came to St. John after the Peace, and in 1785 was elected a member of the first New Brunswick Assembly. In 1792 he was appointed a member of the Council. In 1823, on the death of the Governor, he claimed the position of administrator as senior member of the Council; but before he had made good his claim a new Governor had arrived (Raymond, *Winslow Papers*, p. 423, note). (There is a full account of him in Sabine, op. cit., vol. i, pp. 229–30.)

the County which he represented from joining in their Measures. In the Year 1775 the Assembly refused to send Delegates to Congress & he was very instrumental in carrying that point. He tried by all means in his power to keep the people on the Island quiet till the British Army arrived on the Island which was in 1776. He effected this. And when Gen^l Howe came on the Island He did everything in his power to assist him. He was a Col^l of the Militia of his own County before the Rebellion & continued so during the whole of the Rebellion. He was in one Engagement in the course of the War & produces an American Newspaper which contains a Paragraph much to the Honor of Col^l Billup. He never had any Pay.

Gen^l Robertson—sworn.

Knew Col^l Billup when he was a Member of Assembly & he did everything in his civil Capacity to prevent the Rebellion & when it did happen he put himself at the head of the British Troops on Staten Island & by his Spirit & knowledge of the Country was very useful in driving them off. Some time after he fell into their hands & they imprison'd him & treated him with great Cruelty. When he was Gov^r He appointed him to act as a Judge & he acted with great uprightness. He has a very large family is a very good Man & had great property. He had a very good Estate there & it suffer'd much by both Armies but he does not know the value of it.

Colonel Billup—called again.

He was imprison'd 7 or 8 weeks during which time he was chain'd to the floor & kept upon bread & water. During the whole of the War he was Prisoner about 8 Months. He refused great offers from the Rebels.

The Board are of Opinion that the Losses stated by the Claimant do not come within the meaning of the Act.

## Memorial of Redmund Burke

Determin'd y^e 24^th of Sept^r 1783.

24^th of Sept^r 1785.[1]

N.B. This Case came on third in order of time but when the Memorial came to be looked at it appear'd not to be a Case within the Act of Par^t & therefore it was dismiss'd without being examined into.

Evidence upon it

which was principally taken from the Memorial as the Claimant was not sworn.

The Memorialist residing in America when the unhappy Dispute commenced with the Mother Country to avoid taking a more active part & for the purpose of extending his professionary knowledge enter'd the American Service as a Surgeon's Mate & rose gradually to be Surgeon Major in the Southern Department with the pay of Col^l but when the Dispute changed from redress of Grievances to the Avowal of Independence & he perceiv'd from the Interference of other European powers that serious evil Consequences were likely to ensue to his Native Country & perhaps to America he thought he could no longer consistently with Honor & Conscience hold his Commission especially as he intended to make some strenuous efforts to bring others who had influence to his way of thinking he therefore resign'd sacrificing to the Love of his Country very flattering prospects of promotion having already distinguished himself in

[1] Obviously a slip for 1783.

the Line of his profession & having a Brother [1] then a Member of Congress who is now Gov^r of North Carolina. Memorialist still avoided taking any active part on his Country's side lest it should be a Bar to his Endeavours & in fact wishing well to both Countries. Shortly after his resignation his House near Combakee ferry happening unluckily to be in the line of March of Gen^l Prevost's Army to Charlestown was by that Army burnt & the principal part of his Stock furniture &c taken away or destroy'd being then at Beaufort to avail himself of the Kings protection & never after returning to the place of his residence he cannot specify the particulars of his Loss but the chief Injury to him arises from being obliged to abandon his possessions & prospects in that Country.

The Memorialist unwilling to trouble Gov^t endeavour'd to provide for himself in the Danish West Indies but the Climate not agreeing with him he return'd to Europe thinking to recover some paternal Claims he had in Ireland but found himself precluded by the Stat. of Limitation & being now in danger of falling into Despondency & Indigence submits the premises to the Cons^n of the Board.

[1] Thomas Burke (*b.* 1747, *d.* 1783) was appointed a North Carolina delegate to Congress in 1777. He became Governor of North Carolina in 1781. In a prefatory note to *N. Carolina Records*, vol. xi, p. xx, it is said that Dr. T. Burke's letters show him to have been one of the foremost men of his day.

## ADDITIONAL NOTES

### William Knox (page 1)

*b.* 1723, *d.* 1810. He went out to Georgia as Provost-Marshal in 1756. His salary was £100 a year, and the fees of the office amounted to about £50. 'This is all I am allowed to live on as a member of council in a country where every imported commodity sells at an advance of 75 per cent., and every necessary of life is proportionately expensive. This you must suppose when I tell you that day labourers will not work under 2/-' (*Hist. MSS. Com. Report on MSS. in Various Collections, The MSS. of Capt. H. V. Knox*, 1909, p. 84). The Legislature appointed Knox their agent in England in 1762. The salary was only £50; but he farmed his office of Provost-Marshal for £60, exclusive of the salary, and let his plantation and negroes for £130 per annum. In 1770 he became joint Under-Secretary with John Pownall for the Colonial department and remained in that office till the abolition of the Secretary of State for America in 1782. Knox considered himself very badly treated after the report on his case by the Commissioners. Although they reported strongly in his favour, 'he has been laid aside', he declared in May 1787, 'by the Treasury as a neutral person and has received nothing whatever'. He prayed 'for a place in the list of such loyalists as have rendered services in opposing the rebellion' (ibid., p. 197). He had been hung in effigy at Boston for his publications, and the State of Georgia had passed an Act for the sole purpose of confiscating his estate and attainting his person on the ground that he had shown himself inimical to the liberties of America. It would have been ludicrous to regard an active public servant like Knox in the light of a neutral; but the Treasury may well have considered that, inasmuch as he had a pension of £1,200 a year and, according to his own statement, in November 1783, was in a position to support the dignity of a baronetage, he was in no urgent need of money.

A further grievance was that his pension had been granted in consideration of the loss of his office as Secretary of New York; but notwithstanding the express terms of the grant, it was treated in 1782 as including compensation for the loss of his office as Under-Secretary; and although every clerk in that office had their full salaries allowed them, he was discharged without any compensation at all. He had seen three Under-Secretaries raised to the peerage, and two more of his colleagues appointed Commissioners of the Customs and retaining all their patent offices and pensions; and the Secretary of the Board of Trade, who was suppressed along with him, allowed his full salary; while he, who had served much longer than any of them, was denied common justice for no reason but because he had dared to avow himself attached to His Majesty and not to his Ministers (ibid., p. 197). Knox was appointed in 1784 agent to the new province of New Brunswick and showed himself, as in his other posts, active and able. In 1801 he became also agent for Prince Edward Island.

There is a list of his writings in the *Dict. of Nat. Biography*.

### Governor Bull (page 8)

*d.* 1791 in England. As Speaker of the Commons, Member of Council, General of Militia, and Lieutenant-Governor, Bull remained in the public service for thirty-five years. He acted as Governor, at various intervals, for nearly nine years. 'He had had', writes Mr. McCrady, 'a most difficult part to perform, but so strictly had he adhered to the line of his duty to his King and to his Country, as he conceived it, that not in all those troublesome times had he incurred the enmity of any class of his fellow-citizens. So beloved was he that tradition has brought down to us the opinion entertained at the time that, had the government of the province been left entirely and untrammelled in his hands, . . . he might possibly have successfully resisted the revolutionary movement in South Carolina. . . . This . . . could scarcely have been possible; but it is a great encomium upon his character that such an opinion should have been entertained, and that in all the bitterness of that time tradition has brought down to us no unkind word of him who stood so long in the position most exposed to the virulence of party feeling' (*S. Carolina under the Royal Gov., 1719–1776*, 1899, pp. 794–5).

### Joshua Loring (page 13)

*b.* 1737, *d.* 1789. He was the son of Commodore Joshua Loring,[1] who on the morning of the battle of Lexington made the reply, 'I have always eaten the King's bread and always intend to'.

Joshua jun. signed the addresses to Governors Hutchinson and Gage; and the latter made him sole vendue master and auctioneer (Stark, op. cit., pp. 424–5).

He incurred great odium for his conduct as commissary of prisoners. He was alleged to have become rich 'by feeding the dead' (i.e. charging for the provisions of dead prisoners) 'and starving the living' (Moore, *Diary of the Am. Rev., 1860*, vol. ii, p. 110). Upon the other hand, according to his own statement, the United States Commissary after visiting the prisoners at New York was well satisfied with their treatment (*Hist. MSS. Comm., Am. MSS. in R. Inst.*, vol. i, p. 191); but his constant study to be as frugal as possible (June 29, 1780) may have had its sinister side (ibid., vol. ii, p. 144). The scandal of the day associated the name of his wife with that of the Commander-in-Chief, Sir William Howe (T. Jones, *Loyalist Hist. of New York during the Revolutionary War*, vol. i, p. 351). Jones shows considerable animus against Loring. Mr. E. Floyd de Lancey, however, who edited the history for the New York Historical Society, quotes from a letter from an American prisoner, General S. Silliman, which puts Loring's behaviour in a very favourable light (ibid., vol. ii, pp. 425 and 565).

### Sir James Wright (page 14)

*b.* 1716, *d.* 1785, is in *Dict. of Nat. Biography*. He was the son of Robert Wright, Chief Justice of South Carolina, who was himself the son of Robert Wright, Chief Justice of the King's Bench at the time of the trial of the seven bishops. James Wright was successively Attorney-General, Chief Justice, Lieutenant-Governor, and Governor of Georgia. McCrady (*S. Car. under Royal Gov., 1719–1776*, p. 108) recognizes him to have been 'a man of marked ability and character'. Wright wrote to Gage, June 27, 1775: 'I have neither men nor money; and the Governors had much better be in England than remain in America and have the mortification to see their power executed by committees and mobs. I am really amazed that these southern provinces should be left in the situation they are, and the Governors and king's officers and friends to Government naked and exposed to the resentment of an enraged people' (Force, *Amer. Archives*, 4th ser., vol. ii, p. 1109). (See Introduction, p. xx, for his speech to the Assembly of June 18, 1775.) In May 1782 Wright wrote to Carleton: 'Upon hearing of your Excellency's arrival with full powers to treat and settle terms of peace with the Congress . . . the loyalists have applied to me to request that your Excellency will be pleased to advert to their situation—men who have been firm in their allegiance throughout from the beginning; men who have suffered every kind of distress for their loyalty, and men the *remains* of whose property have been lately confiscated by the rebel powers and is now under orders for being sold at public auction.

[1] On Joshua Loring, senior, see note at p. 479 of Doughty, Knox's *Hist. Journal of the Campaigns in North America*, vol. i (Champlain Society Publications, viii).

'But, Sir, I trust that your Excellency well knows they have not only justice and equity on their side, but also an undoubted claim to the interference and protection of Government, you will be pleased to stipulate that their property shall be restored to them.

'The king's officers in the civil government here are in the same predicament and have suffered greatly. I myself have had my property to the amount of £40,000 sterling *already* carried away and destroyed from time to time by them; and the remainder of my property, as well as that of the other gentlemen, is now under confiscation and orders for sale' (*Hist. MSS. Comm., Am. MSS. in R. Inst.*, vol. ii, pp. 505–6).

Wright was very indignant at the abandonment of Georgia 'when a reinforcement of some four or five hundred men would have effectually held the country; and when the last letters I received from his Majesty's Secretary of State authorised me to declare to the people that his Majesty's loyal and faithful subjects in Georgia might rely on his Majesty's protection and support' (ibid., vol. iii, p. 11).

(There is a biographical notice of Sir J. Wright in G. White, *Hist. Collections of Georgia*, pp. 188–96.)

### Thomas Hutchinson (page 19)

*b.* 1740, *d.* 1811 in England. He was the eldest son of Governor Hutchinson and was the 'Tommy' of the *Diary*. The day before he set sail for England in 1774 his wife was delivered of a boy, who had not a drop of milk during the whole voyage.

He wrote to his brother Elisha:

Brompton, August 31, 1785.

Dear brother,

As they began paying at the Treasury the grants of 30 and 40 per cent., I called to-day to enquire for myself when they gave me the memorandum as below. . . . It seems they consider me as heir to all the real estate by the law of England, and that they had no power to proceed otherwise than by the law, the will [of the Governor] being deficient to convey real estate.

| | |
|---|---|
| Order to pay Thos. Hutchinson | £1,860 |
| T. and Elisha, as Executors | £150 |
| Elisha | £60 |

(Hutchinson, op. cit., vol. ii, p. 421.)

### Lieut.-Colonel Connolly (page 67)

John Connolly, *b.* 1743 (?), published in 1783 in London a sketch of his career (*Pennsylvania Magazine of Hist. and Biog.*, xii. 310–24, 407–20, and xiii. 61–70, 153–67, and 281–91), of which good use has been made in a Paper written by Mr. Driffenderfer (*Lancaster County, Pa., Hist. Soc. Papers*, vol. vii, No. 6). Mr. Driffenderfer writes in a very different style from that to which we are accustomed in the younger school of American historians; but epithets such as 'land grabber', 'subservient political intriguer', culled from Bancroft, do not obscure our vision of an active, capable man, who may have been quite honest up to his own lights. Bred for medicine, Connolly preferred the life of a soldier and served as volunteer first in the Martinique expedition and then on the Western Virginian frontier, when he 'explored our newly-acquired territory, visited the various tribes of native Americans, studied their different manners and customs, undertook the most toilsome marches with them through the extensive wilds of Canada, and depended upon the precarious chase for very subsistence for months successively'. Meeting Lord Dunmore at Pittsburg, he became his active ally first in his attempt to secure for Virginia what was recognized as belonging to Pennsylvania, and afterwards in the attempt to organize from the West an attack upon Eastern Virginia. Indignant protests against Connolly's behaviour at Pittsburg from Governor Penn of Pennsylvania will be found in *Penns. Archives*, 4th ser., vol. iii, pp. 454, 464, 478, and 480. 'He seizes upon the property of the people without reason and treats the persons of the magistrates with the utmost insolence and disrespect, and with menaces not only of imprisoning them but even of pulling down their houses; and it is said he has sent out or is to send out parties against the Indians with orders to destroy all they meet with, whether friend or foe.'

In the course of his efforts he was several times arrested but succeeded in escaping. In November 1775 he started for Detroit armed with a commission as Lieutenant-Colonel, with full power to raise a battalion of men and as many independent companies as he could. Being, however, recognized by an old acquaintance, he was on November 19 arrested on the Virginian frontier. He remained a prisoner till October 1780. He complained bitterly of his treatment; the contention of Congress being that, inasmuch as he had not been taken in actual warfare, he could not of right claim to be treated as a prisoner of war; but was amenable to martial law as a spy and emissary from the British army.

After his release he was placed in command of the Virginia and North Carolina Loyalists for operations on the peninsula formed by the James River and Chesapeake Bay. Once more taken prisoner, he was suffered to live on parole in the back country, where he remained till the capture of Yorktown. He was in London in February 1783, and on March 1 of that year was found soliciting the government of Niagara or Detroit (*Hist. MSS. Comm., Am. MSS. in R. Inst.*, vol. iii, p. 380).

There are letters from Connolly in *Am. Archives*, 4th ser., vol. iv, p. 617.

When Lord Dunmore left Virginia, he carried the Queen's Loyal Virginia Regiment to New York, where it was incorporated with the Queen's Rangers, then raising there (P. R. O., *Audit Office, Amer. Loyalists*, vol. liv).

### Jacob Ellegood (page 70)

After the Peace Ellegood settled first at Fredericton (New Brunswick) and then at Dumfries. A correspondent in January 1793 comments on the smallness of Ellegood's house and the largeness of his family (Raymond, *Winslow Papers*, p. 398). In 1795 he was elected a member of the House of Assembly. He was an active magistrate and took a leading part in local government. The Rev. Canon Ellegood of Montreal is his grandson (ibid., p. 397, note).

In *Hist. MSS. Comm., Am. MSS. in R. Inst.*, vol. iii, p. 95, is a warrant dated August 27, 1782, New York, to pay to Lieutenant-Colonel Ellegood of the Virginian Loyalists the sum of £300 to enable him to go to England for the purpose of soliciting money, &c.

Carleton wrote on September 13 to the Secretary of State (ibid., p. 116) that Ellegood had informed him that he had received a commission as Lieutenant-Colonel of Provincials in 1776, was taken prisoner soon after, and on arriving at New York he requested his pay; but this was not granted as Clinton was undecided in the matter. £300 was paid him in consideration of his distresses and the question of his claims left for decision in England. His property was only confiscated for life and his family was still in possession of it.

# BOOK II

## Memorial of Owen Richards[1]

Determin'd the 21st of feby 1784.

9th of Feby 1784.

Owen Richards—the Claimant—sworn.

He was born in Wales & went to America in 1744. He was bred a Seaman. In 1774 He was a Custom House Officer settled at Boston as a Tidesman. Produces the Appointment & Deputation dated 8th of April 1768. His Salary was £25 a Yr & 1s. 6d. a Day when upon Duty. This 1s. 6d. amounted to about £20 a Yr. He was sent from Boston to Marblehead when the Port was shut up. He was unable to do any Duty from the time of the Battle of Bunker's Hill. He always acted as a Loyal Subject & did his Duty & therefore they pointed at him & treated him more severely. Staid at Marblehead near a Year. He left Boston at the Evacuation & from thence he went to Halifax & came to Engd in Augt 1777. When he came to Engd he applied to the Treasury & obtain'd £30 a Yr from the Treasury which was confirmed by Mr Wilmot & Mr Coke & he still receives it. He has never recd any Salary since he left America.

Cust. Ho. Officer Salary £25 a Yr.

A Loyalist & Did his Duty as an Officer of the Crown.

Did not bear Arms.

William Murray—sworn.

He has known Owen Richards since 1773. He lived in Boston at that time & was a Tidewaiter. He lived at the North End of the Town & he believes in his own House. When the troubles broke out He took part with the British & was one of the Associators for the Defence of the Town. The Witness is likewise a Tidewaiter. The place was worth 45 a Year. They were both paid off at Halifax in May 1776 & the Witness has never recd any pay since. He did his Duty as a good Subject And he was so obnoxious to the Rebels that he believes he was tarr'd & feather'd before the Year 1773. Speaks to the House he lived in. It was a good House. It was an old House & he had done some little repairs to it. Being asked how much he had laid out He says he heard him say about £60. It was well furnished. But he does not know how to value it.

Owen Richards—called in again.

He was tarr'd & feather'd in 1770 on Acct of a Seizure which he had made. Being asked whether he did not tell Mr Murray that he had laid out £60 He says that Murray was either present when he paid the last Bill or heard him speak of it but he never told him that he had laid out only £60 And he is positive that he has laid out £140.

## Memorial of Hugh Warden

Determin'd ye 20th of Feby 1784.

10th Feby 1784.

Hugh Warden—the Claimant—sworn.

He went to America in June 1775. He had been in America before from 1763 to 1770. He went to Virginia to recover his Debts which were about

[1] Owen Richards is described as coxswain in the list of the inhabitants of Boston who removed in March 1776 to Halifax with the army. In the Banishment Act he is described as tide waiter.

£2000 S. He recover'd only £200. No Man was more active in Conversation than he was. He was in several Engagements as a Volunteer & recd no Pay. He was at Kemps Landing. He did Duty in the Lines at Norfolk & Great Bridge. He then went on board a Ship & remain'd there 4 Months & then went to Boston & the Troops having left it He went on to Halifax where he arrived the 15th of April 1776. He took Goods with him on Speculation to sell Rums Sugars Wines &c. He arrived in Engd in Novr 1776. He went from London to New York in 1777. He went with a Cargo of Merchandize. He had no landed property & makes no Claim for any nor for any personal property excepting what was lost by the fire at New York. Believes all the Money due to him in Virginia was due to him from responsible people. He lost Merchandize by the fire in New York to the amount of £3500 S. He says he thinks it was set on fire by Design & that the Committee who sat to enquire into the Cause of it were of that Opinion. He saved £2000. He had better than £5000 in his Store.

An Active Loyalist & bore Arms.

Debts £737 0s. 0d.

He formerly recd £80 a Yr from the Treasury but was reduced by Mr Wilmot & Mr Coke to £50 a Year which he now continues to receive.

Bounty former Bounty £80 a Yr present Bounty £50 a Yr.

## Memorial of John Watson

Determin'd ye 20th of Feby 1784.

John Watson—the Claimant—sworn. 10th of Feby 1784.

He went from Scotland in 1767 & settled as a Surgeon at Newcastle on the Delaware. In 1777 He took an active part with the British Govt. He was then settled at Newcastle. He remain'd quiet & unmolested till that time. Says he had publickly express'd his Sentiments in favor of the British Govt upon which in 1777 He was insulted as a Tory. When Sir Wm Howe landed at the head of Elk He was obliged to go out as Surgeon to a Provincial Regt. This he was obliged to do or go to prison. When he went out he told a friend of his that he hated the Rebels & meant to make his Escape to the British. He accordingly did escape & join'd the British Army at the head of Elk the 24th of Augt 1777. He remain'd with the British during the remainder of the War. He never recd pay from the Rebel Army nor from the British till he was obliged to do it. He was made Mate of the Hospital & had 5s. a Day. He conducted Major Ferguson into the Enemy's Country in two Expeditions. In Conjunction with another Gentn He fitted out a Galley to harrass the Rebels & he lost her by Captn Laird but he was paid for her by Captn Laird & Sir Henry Clinton. In the Year 1780 He was promoted to be Apothecary to the Hospital & receiv'd 10s. a Day as Pay. This Appointment was made at New York. He has recd this 10s. a Day up to the 24th of Decr last. He does not know whether he is to receive any more pay or not. He has no Certificates but he says he can procure them.

A zealous & active Loyalist.

Did not bear Arms.

## Memorial of Lieutt Coll James Chalmers [1]

Determind ye 21st of Feby 1784.

Lieutt Coll James Chalmers—the Claimant—sworn. 11th Feby 1784.

He was born in Scotland & went to the West Indies about 13 Yrs of Age & after having staid some time in the West Indies he went to America in 1759 or 1760 And he took with him about £10000. He soon afterwards married

An active & zealous Loyalist.

[1] See Additional Notes, p. 142.

Did bear Arms.

Miss Jekyll by whom he got 3 fourths of the Lands enumerated in his Schedule. He settled first in Pensylvania & then went to Maryland. He states some Circumstances which prove that he was possess'd in fee of his Lands. In the beginning of the troubles He was offer'd a Reg^t to command in the service of the Rebels in Pensylvania. He did everything in his power to keep his Neighbours to their Allegiance. He was frequently summon'd to attend their Committees & armed his family to repel force by force. He lived then on his own Plantation within 4 Miles of Chester. He was first molested in the Summer of 1776. He was insulted & much bruis'd by the populace. This was in consequence of his Loyalty. He was never imprison'd by the Rebels. He pass'd his time at home till 1777 when he join'd the Royal Army at New York. He says he might have staid at home when he went to New York but he conceiv'd that he might be of use to Sir W^m Howe. After he got to New York he attended Sir W^m Howe to the Chesapeak. He had given intelligence on paper to the British Army of the weakness of the Enemy. He went with the fleet & went to Philadelphia. When he came there Sir W^m Howe on acc^t of his Services appointed Col^l Chalmers to raise a provincial Corps without his Solicitation. He did raise the Corps in consequence of this. He was Lieut^t Col^l Commandant & had Lieut^t Colonel's Pay. He rais'd nearly 400 Men. In the retreat thro' the Jerseys with Sir Henry Clinton His Reg^t flanked the Army & in Florida a detachment of his Reg^t behaved with great spirit & suffer'd greatly but he was not present. He was sent to Rhode Island & afterwards was embarked for Pensacola but he was detain'd at Jamaica in consequence of which several of his Reg^t died of the small Pox. He was at the taking of Charlestown & returned with Sir Henry Clinton to New York where he remain'd till the Provincial Reg^ts were disbanded. He arrived in Eng^d in October last. He has rec^d full pay up to the 24^th of Oct^r last from which time he expects to receive half pay.

Determin'd 5^th of June 1784.

### Memorial of Joseph Galloway [1] Esq.

12^th Feb^y 1784.

Joseph Galloway Esq—the Claimant—sworn.

Is a Native of America. In the Year 1774 He was Speaker of the Assembly of Pensylvania. He had given up the profession of the Law three Years before 1774. He had been Speaker of that Assembly 13 or 14 Years. The Congress met in Oct^r 1774 early in which Year he was solicited to accept a Delegation to the Congress.[2] So early as the Stamp Act M^r Galloway saw a Disposition to resist the Gov^t of Great Britain in the Americans & wrote a Pamphlet [3] ag^t it which he produces. To shew his good disposition to the power of the Crown He join'd in a petition to the Gov^t of this Country to take the Gov^t of this

[1] *b.* 1731, *d.* 1803. There is a biography of him by E. H. Baldwin, reprinted from the *Pennsylvania Magazine of History and Biography*, 1902. He died in England.

[2] The Pennsylvania Assembly resolved *n. d. c.* on July 22, 1774, 'that there is an absolute necessity that a Congress of Deputies from the several colonies be held . . . for establishing that union and harmony between Great Britain and the colonies which is indispensably necessary to the welfare and happiness of both' (*Journals of the Continental Congress, 1774–89*, vol. i, p. 20).

[3] The pamphlet on the Stamp Act was published in 1765 under the signature of 'Americanus' This is omitted in Mr. Baldwin's list of Galloway's more important publications (op. cit., pp. 104–9).

Province of Pensylvania into their hands [1] on acct of the weakness of the Proprietary Govt making a Compensation to the Proprietors but after being consider'd here for some time it was adjourned sine die & no Answer was given. He was the Mover of this proposition assisted by Dr Franklyn. He was always a friend to Monarchy. He agreed to go into a Congress appointed by the lawful Assemblies at the solicitation of the province of Pensylvania.[2] It was thought better to appoint a Congress from the General Assemblies than to permit it to be done by the Convention which they saw would be the Case. The Assembly agreed to send Delegates to this Congress. He expected to have met Delegates of this description. The Govr took no part in this business. Most of the Govrs objected but some suffer'd their Assemblies to appoint. The Province of New Jersey Pensylvania & some other Provinces did send Delegates but the Majority of the Delegates were sent by Conventions in the particular Provinces. He is clearly of Opinion that if the Assemblies had appointed Delegates there would have been no rebellion. The Province of Pensylvania appointed him & four [3] others to go to the Congress. He agreed to it upon Condition that he might draw his own Instructions. He has not a Copy of these Instructions but they are published in a Pamphlet out of which they are extracted & make a part of his printed Case. The Instructions were very short. They then wished to be represented in the British Part. He regulated his Conduct entirely by his instructions to the best of his Judgment. He sign'd the Association for a Non importation Agreement in the first Congress notwithstanding he endeavor'd to prevent it when the Matter was debated in Congress. He was supported by the Delegates for New York & some others. He was told by his friends out of Doors that it would not be safe to refuse to sign it. He proposed himself in the Congress a Plan for an Union between Great Britain & her Colonies [4] a Copy of which is contain'd in the Pamphlet alluded to. Mr Galloway afterwards laid this Plan before the House of Commons in 1779. This Plan was enter'd into the Minutes of the Congress & carried for further Consideration by one Vote. The Congress afterwards set it aside & order'd it to be erased from their Minutes. Upon this he protested agt it & he offer'd his protest in writing but they refused to receive it. A Letter from Govr Colden [5] to Lord Dartmouth dated 7 Decr 1774 produced & read in which he mentions the Plan alluded to in the Pamphlet written by himself intitled a candid Examination into the American Claims written by Mr Galloway. Upon all occasions he opposed every violent measure proposed by the Congress. He frequently communicated his opinions at the

Resolved That the Claimt appears to the Board to have been a Member of the first Congress but the Commrs are of Opinion that during that time he endeavor'd to promote the constitutional Dependence of the Colonies on Great Britain & that he has since conducted himself as a zealous Loyalist & render'd Services to the British Govt.

Bounty £500 a Yr.

[1] Galloway's speech in favour of the Crown taking over the government, delivered in the Assembly May 24, 1764, was published as a pamphlet. Mr. Root (*The Relations of Pennsylvania with the British Government, 1696–1765*, p. 375) has pointed out that in seeking a change of government the members of the Assembly, under the leadership of Franklin and J. Galloway, were not actuated by motives of zeal for the royal prerogative or imperial interests, but by the hope that royal government would free them from the evils of proprietary rule.

[2] See note 2, p. 82.

[3] There were *five* others: S. Rhoades, T. Mifflin, C. Humphreys, J. Morton, and L. Biddle.

[4] On Galloway's plan, and speech introducing it, see ibid., pp. 44–51 and note on p. 51. J. Duane seconded his proposal. See also J. Adams, *Works*, vol. ii, p. 387.

[5] Colden's letter is in *New York Colonial Documents*, vol. viii, p. 513.

time to Gov$^{r}$ Franklyn & several persons out of Doors. Letter from Gov$^{r}$ Franklyn [1] produced & read & likewise one from M$^{r}$ Galloway to Gov$^{r}$ Franklyn dated the 9$^{th}$ of Dec$^{r}$ 1774. He sat in the first Congress during the whole time that they sat. He did not concur in the first petition [2] sent by the Congress but there was no Division upon it. He wished it to be more full & disliked many things in it. However he believes he sign'd it because it was signed by all the other Delegates. This petition contain'd many grievances which in his Opinion did not exist. When he returned to the Assembly he communicated what was done in the Congress. He was unanimously elected Speaker after his return from the Congress but he declined it thinking he could be of more use upon the floor. He was in hopes that he could have prevailed on the Assembly to reject the measures of Congress & for that purpose he made several Motions. He carried two of them & lost a third by a report which was then circulated from Eng$^{d}$ that the King had been insulted Lord North's House pulled down &c. Immediately after he published the Pamphlet [3] alluded to early in 1775. This book charges the Congress with a direct view to Independence. Upon his being supposed to be the Author of this Pamphlet He rec$^{d}$ a Box with an halter in it & persons open'd a Policy of insurance to insure his Life for ten Days. In the Box were these words " they desired him to hang himself or they would do it for him ". This had no effect upon his Conduct. A Letter from Gov$^{r}$ Franklyn dated 12$^{th}$ March 1775 to M$^{r}$ Galloway produced & read. He always deliver'd his Sentiments in the Congress in favor of the Supremacy of Par$^{t}$ And he wrote that Par$^{t}$ from his Notes taken in the Congress. Several other Letters from persons of distinction in America produced & read. An Answer was written by M$^{r}$ Dickenson to M$^{r}$ Galloway's Pamphlet to which he made a reply which is subjoin'd to the original Pamphlet. Immediately after this in April 1775 He was obliged to quit the Town of Philadelphia & retire to his Country Seat. He did not resign his Seat in the Assembly but continued a Member till Oct$^{r}$ 1775. Before he quitted the Assembly in his Absence they appointed him a Delegate to the 2$^{d}$ Congress but he requested in the Assembly that they would erase his name & he absolutely refused to go. They appointed after some time another person in his room. He continued at his own House from April 1775 to Dec$^{r}$ 1776 when Sir W$^{m}$ Howe came to Philadelphia. He consider'd himself in great danger & was to a Degree imprison'd in his own House. Two or three Mobs came to his House with a view to tarr & feather him but were diverted by his friends. And the last mob consisted of 13 Dutchmen who becoming

[1] There is some interesting correspondence between Galloway and Governor Franklin in *New Jersey Archives*, 1st ser., vol. x. Franklin writes in 1775 (p. 578): 'The more I have thought on the subject, the more I am convinced that the most eligible Scheme . . . will be the sending members to the British Parliament; I know this is likewise your [Galloway's] opinion.' Galloway wrote on March 26 (p. 584): 'I intimated before that I had met with insults during my stay in the city. . . . A box was left at my lodgings nailed and directed to me. Upon opening it next morning I found in it a halter with a threatening letter. I read the letter and nailed up the box. . . . From the clue so far as I have traced it, it comes from two members of Association, a discarded Association officer and a head of the White Oaks.'

[2] The petition to the King is set forth in *Journals of the Continental Congress, 1774*, pp. 115–21.

[3] *A Candid Examination of the Mutual Claims of Great Britain and the Colonies, with a Plan of Accommodation on Constitutional Principles*, 1775.

On Galloway's literary output see Tyler, *The Literary History of the Am. Rev.*, vol. i, pp. 369–83.

intoxicated quarrel'd whether they should tarr & feather him or hang him & the Innkeeper gave him Notice of it. This Mob was instigated by M^r^ Adams. Having advice of this Plot he left his House that night & did not sleep at home. He could not join the British before Sir W^m^ Howe came to Philadelphia. In Dec^r^ 1776 He join'd the Army at New Brunswick. When Sir W^m^ Howe came to Philadelphia the executive Gov^t^ issued an order to apprehend him but he eluded it. He came in with 5 or 6 friends all people of Consequence. He immediately gave all the Information he could to Gen^l^ Vaughan. He continued with the Army till they left the Jerseys & went to New York before the Army. He staid at New York till he accompanied the Gen^l^ to the Chesapeak in June 1777. He was not then in any military Capacity. When the Army came into Pensylvania He was employ'd to procure Horses for the Army & Charts of the roads. He sent out upwards of 80 Spies. He informed them of 1500 Horses but his Plan was imperfectly executed & they got only between 3 & 400 Horses. He accompanied Lord Cornwallis to Philadelphia. He was soon after of great use in erecting the Batteries ag^t^ Mud Island & finish'd the business in six Days. During the whole of his residence at Philadelphia he was confidentially employ'd in procuring intelligence of the movements of the Enemy &c all of which he communicated to the Gen^l^ or his Aid du Camps. From his knowledge of the Country He made whilst he was at Philadelphia a general Chart of all the roads which he was enabled to do from his general knowledge of the Country. He was likewise employ'd in numbering the Inhabitants & distinguishing the Loyal from the disaffected. He likewise was desired to fix the price of forage & wood by which he saved a great deal of Money to the Public. He was about this time appointed Superintendant of the Police (produces the Commission) it is dated in Dec^r^ 1777. He was also Superintend^t^ of the Port & prohibited Articles. This concludes all the Civil Services.

A Letter dated the 18^th^ of May 1778 produced from Sir W^m^ Howe to M^r^ Galloway speaking of him in the highest possible terms.

Commission dated 1^st^ of July 1777 by Sir W^m^ Howe appointing him Colonel of the Troops to be raised in Pensylvania merely to give him rank in the Army. As soon as he got to Philadelphia he offer'd to raise a Reg^t^ of Horse. Upon this the Gen^l^ sent him a Warrant to raise a Troop. He did it accordingly. He afterwards raised two Companies of loyal refugees who were farmers Sons &c & served without Pay. These Men did very essential service & took a great number of prisoners. He promoted an Association of the Loyalists in the Neighborhood amounting to 13000.[1] Colonel Rankin who was one of them proposed thro' M^r^ Galloway to Sir W^m^ Howe to bring the whole Congress Prisoners to Philadelphia. The Associators were then about 600. The Congress were then sitting at York Town under a guard of a very few Invalids 30 or 40 & these Associators proposed to seize them in the night & carry them on board a Ship. M^r^ Galloway being asked whether he thinks it was a practicable Scheme He says he thinks it was because Washington's Army was at a great distance & there was no Militia in the Country thro' which they were to pass. No answer was given to it. He did not mention it to him only to his Aid de Camp because

[1] ? 1300.

Mr Galloway upon reconsidering this matter wishes that this may be taken out of the Evidence because indirectly it conveys a Charge agt the Commander in Chief.

he had once before made a similar offer to him to bring in the Govrs & all the Magistrates of New Jersey Prisoners[1] & he rejected it. He says he could have done it with great Ease & yet it was more difficult than the proposal to bring the Congress prisoners. He never recd any pay for his Military services. He never recd any reward for his intelligence or services.

In Consequence of these services the State of Pensylvania passed a Law in 1778 attainting his person which is produced & confiscating all his Estates. He came to Engd in Decr 1778 from New York from which time he has recd an Allowance of £500 a Yr from the Treasury & still continues to receive it. Before he left New York he open'd a Communication for intelligence from New York the whole of which he laid before his Majesty's Ministers & never recd asked or wished any Satisfaction for it.

Joseph Galloway Esq—called again & sworn. 13th of Feby 1784.

Refers to a printed Copy of the Proceedings of Congress held at Philadelphia the 5th of Septr 1774. He produces a printed Copy of the Book publish'd at Philadelphia. This Book is produced to explain the Instructions given to Mr Galloway when he was deputed to attend the General Congress. Produces a Copy of a Memorial presented by the Associated Loyalists to Welbore Ellis Esq with several attendant Letters in order to shew that Mr Galloway had been very instrumental in promoting this Association. Produces likewise a book containing several original & very important Letters recd by Mr Galloway from time to time & communicated by him to his Majesty's Ministers. He has two or three more Volumes of the same sort.

An Act of the State of Pensylvania produced & read which was passed in the Year 1778 by which his person was attainted & his property confiscated.

He mentions as the only Incumbrances affecting his Property the Ground Rent which he paid for his House & the Quit rents payable out of his Estates to the Proprietors.

rejected.

He submits whether he has not a right to charge the Loss of his profession as he might have returned to it & should have returned to it if he had the power as he has lost his Estate. The Emoluments of his Office as Speaker of the Assembly were £200 a Yr. His professional Gains were about £2000 a Yr Currency. He had no other Office. He began to decline the practice of the Law in 1769 & finally quitted it in 1771.

General Vaughan[2]—sworn. Feby the 17th 1784.

In Decr 1776 Lord Cornwallis & Genl Vaughan were detach'd in pursuit of Genl Washington towards Brunswick. When he came to Brunswick the Rebels had left the place & were on their march towards Philadelphia. When he had been there a short time he had information that two Gentn were come to surrender themselves. Mr Galloway was one of these two Gentn & said he was

[1] In a note at pp. 81–2 of *The Examination of Joseph Galloway . . . before the House of Commons in a Committee on the Amer. Papers, 1779*, it is said: 'He also laid a plan for the seizing of the rebel Governor Livingston, his Council and Assembly at Trentown. His intelligence was so good and his scheme so well concerted that there could be no doubt of success; but he was not permitted to carry the design into execution.'

[2] General John Vaughan, *b.* 1748, *d.* 1795, became K.B. in 1792. He is in the *Dict. of Nat. Biography*.

well affected to Gov$^{t}$ & wished to take that Opportunity of surrendering himself. M$^{r}$ Galloway staid with him all night & then he believes he went to Lord Cornwallis. He communicated at that time some Intelligence but not very material information. He thought from his Discourse that he was a well wisher to Gov$^{t}$. He was a good deal with the Gen$^{l}$ afterwards & he found him a sensible zealous & steady Man. He believes he was a very useful Man in Philadelphia. He never had any reason to suspect his Loyalty during the whole time that he was under his Eye.

Gen. Roberdean—sworn.

He was particularly acquainted with the Sepicken estate. He had an estate adjoining to it, but M$^{r}$ Galloway's land was better than his. It was equal in quantity to his and he believes about twenty nine acres.

It was extremely valuable from it's situation & he has known 3 Tons produced from an Acre in the first mowing. He thinks M$^{r}$ Galloway's account of the produce moderate. Being asked as to the Market price He thinks it worth £50 an Acre. He has let his for £3 an Acre & Interest being at Six per Cent. He therefore thinks it worth £50 an Acre & M$^{r}$ Galloway's was better than his. He is not so well acquainted with the tract of Boon's Island but believes it was similar. He has never been on the Tinickum Estate but has been on the adjoining Lands. The Lands are as good in quality but not so valuable being at a greater Distance (9 Miles) from Philadelphia. He does not know the Hog Island Estate but has sail'd round it. He believes it to be the same sort of Land. He knew his House in Market Street which is now appropriated for the residence of the Gov$^{r}$ but he does not know the Value. It is an elegant House. He knows all the Valuers & says they are Men of Character the Valuation is shewn to him & he knows the handwriting of two of them. He says they are very competent to put a value on Estates & says all the Valuers are Men of Credit & reputation.

Gen$^{l}$ Gage—sworn.

He went over Gov$^{r}$ of Massachusets in 1774. He never saw M$^{r}$ Galloway but once in his Life. When he wanted to enforce a Mutiny Act He went to Philadelphia & called on M$^{r}$ Galloway & notwithstanding he was of an Opposite Party he told the Gen$^{l}$ that he would do all that he could to get the Troops quarter'd &c & he believes that he did. He knows nothing of M$^{r}$ Galloway since the Commencement of the troubles but from report The Gen$^{l}$ arrived in Eng$^{d}$ in Nov$^{r}$ 1775. He did not promote sending Delegates to the Congress but did all that he could to prevent it as he understood it was a leading Step to rebellion.

Lord Cornwallis—sworn.

He recollects perfectly M$^{r}$ Galloway's joining the Army. He cannot immediately recollect the particular intelligence which he gave. He appear'd perfectly zealous & attached to the British Gov$^{t}$. He was always esteem'd as well affected & he believes he was not suspected by any person for want of sincerity on acc$^{t}$ of his connections with the Congress. When Lord Cornwallis took possession of Philadelphia M$^{r}$ Galloway was sent with him to assist &c. He attended him at all times gave every Assistance in his power & appear'd to be a very zealous Loyalist. He never had the smallest Suspicion of him. He gave very material Intelligence at that time & was of great Use. He thinks he was of great use in the taking Mud Island. He render'd in his Lordship's Opinion very essential Service to the Cause of Great Britain. His Lordship thinks that Mr Galloway took the side of the British Govt from Principle & believes him to be a true & zealous Loyalist.

18th Feby 1784.

Govr Franklyn—sworn.

He came over with his father in 1757 to request the King to take the Govt of Pensylvania into his hands & Mr Galloway as Speaker of the Assembly had been very active in promoting that Measure & Dr Franklyn relied upon Mr Galloways assistance in the Assembly to preserve the same Disposition in the Assembly. Remembers Mr Galloway publishing a paper called Americanus about this time in support of the British Govt which made him very obnoxious & he went by the nick Name of Americanus for some time by way of reproach & they used to abuse him as a Ministerial Hireling. He has known Mr Galloway from a Boy they were particularly intimate. He has every proof that the Nature of the Case will admit that he was from the commencement of the troubles a friend to the British Govt over the Colonies. He has frequently recd Letters from him & conversed with him upon the Subject. He always found him a staunch friend of Govt & that he uniformly endeavour'd to give more weight to the Crown in America thinking it would be for the benefit of the people. He says that Mr Galloway told him before he went into the Congress that he would not go into it unless the Assembly would permit him to draw up his own Instructions & believes they did permit him to do so. He understood the purport of those Instructions to form an Union between the two Countries. Is sure that Mr Galloway would not have accepted the Delegation upon any other terms than preserving an Union between the two Countries. He knows that he did promote a Plan of Union in the Congress. He sent it over to Govr Franklyn who sent it to Lord Dartmouth & that Plan was founded on a Constitutional dependance upon Great Britain. This Plan was frustrated in Congress & Mr Galloway became unpopular for having proposed this plan. Govr Franklyn says he approved of Mr Galloway going into the Congress & he never opposed his Assembly sending Delegates because as he was convinced that a Congress would be held. He thought it an Object that that Congress should consist of respectable Men. Mr Galloway being abused for his Conduct published a Pamphlet in his own defence which has been before stated & was called a Candid Examination &c. He thinks he ran great hazards in publishing his Sentiments at such a time. He was soon afterwards obliged to leave his Country House & fly to the British Arms. Dr. Franklyn & Mr Galloway a short time before this had an interview & Dr Franklyn pressed him to go again into Congress. Mr Galloway said he had a great Opinion of Dr Franklyn but that he thought his person not safe & that he did not approve of the Measures of the Congress. Dr Franklyn would have given security for his personal safety but he would not do it & Dr Franklyn accused his Son of having poison'd Mr Galloway's sentiments. Upon the whole he believes Mr Galloways conduct to have been uniformly loyal

& he has given the most unequivocal proofs of it. He is not acquainted with any of the Services which he did after he join'd the British Troops because he was then a Prisoner. He believes that he join'd the King's Troops from Principle only. Because tho' he might have been personally afraid of Danger yet he knows that M^r Galloway might have made his peace at any time with the Rebels.

He is not sufficiently acquainted with M^r Galloway's property to speak to the value of it but he knows that he had a very considerable Estate. Gov^r Franklyn says that his Loyalty & Attachment to this Country is so undoubted that when Congress was sitting He frequently used to communicate secret Intelligence which the Gov^r sent at different times to the Ministers here. The Americans suspected him of doing this & it was frequently made Matter of Accusation ag^t him. The Declaration of Independence was made in July 1776.

Sir Will^m Howe—sworn.

M^r Galloway join'd the Army in 1776. He communicated intelligence at different times but not very material Intelligence. He consider'd him at *that time* as attached to the British Gov^t. He conducted himself as a Loyalist from the time he came in & upon several Occasions was of material service. He was employ'd in a confidential Situation. He found him zealous in the Cause of Gov^t. He can't say upon his Oath that he ever communicated any material Intelligence. He was for some time employ'd by Sir W^m Howe in the Channel of giving intelligence by means of Spies but soon after altering his Opinion of him he removed him from that Situation. He remembers his Brother consulting him about the navigation of the Delaware & he gave some Intelligence respecting it but Lord Howe did not follow it. He went with him & Lord Howe upon that Expedition at their request. He remembers his making a proposition to bring the Gov^r & all the Magistrates of New Jersey Prisoners to Philadelphia & he should have been very glad to have adopted it if it had been practicable but he did not think it practicable. He does not recollect his giving material Intelligence the night before the Battle of Brandywine. M^r Galloway had said that his intelligence was so material that the Battle of Brandywine was undertaken in consequence of it. Sir W^m Howe says he does not remember the Intelligence & is sure that he did not act upon it for it was determined long before that Night to attack them the next Morning. He was appointed Superintend^t of the Police &c which he discharged very well & for which Sir W^m gave him his thanks in writing. All his Emoluments at Philadelphia were about £600 a Y^r S. He never paid him any Bill or incidental Charges for secret services. He says he was not anxious for rewards. He made proposals to Sir W^m in 1778 to raise a Troop of Horse from the County of Bucks & he consented to it thinking it would be some Emolument to him but upon examining into the Troop it was found to consist chiefly of Deserters. He has no Doubt about his Loyalty or his wishes to promote the King's service so far as he can judge from his Actions but does not believe his Heart was materially concern'd in it.

## To the Memorial of M^r Galloway

20th of Feb^y 1784.

Colonel Montresor [1]—called by the Board & sworn.

He was Aid de Camp to Sir W^m Howe in 1776 & afterwards chief Engineer. He remembers M^r Galloway joining the Army & believes he did communicate Intelligence thro' him to the Commander in Chief but cannot recollect what it was. He accompanied the Army to Philadelphia & went in Col^l Montresor's Vessel. He frequently gave intelligence thro' the Witness to the Commander in chief it was always meant to be important & sometimes was so. He was active in procuring it. Remembers his making a proposition to drain the waters of the Delaware & he suggested a person who was to execute it. M^r Galloways information was very material & he admits that tho' it might have been done without him it would not have been done so expeditiously or so well. Upon the whole he had reason to think that M^r Galloway was a zealous Loyalist & he always endeavour'd to promote the Success of the British Arms & meant to render Service to Gov^t. But the Witness cannot say whether he really did service or not as the Commander in chief must be the best Judge of that.

Determin'd 20th of Feb^y 1784.

## Memorial of Phineas Atherton [2]

20th Feb^y 1784.

Phineas Atherton—the Claimant—sworn.

A Loyalist & bore Arms.

He was born in America and lived in Lancaster in Massachusets Bay. He was in London when the troubles broke out & lived in Spring Gardens. He went to America in 1775 to Montreal & join'd Sir John Johnson.[3] He had been in America great part of the late War & served under Lord Amherst. When he join'd at Montreal He soon after got a Lieutenancy. He served with the Army till the Army surrender'd at Saratoga when he was included in the Convention. He had Lieut^t's Pay. He went to look after his Estate when he was a Prisoner & lived at Cambridge. He lived in Eng^d between 1770 & 1775 & he lent his Estate to a friend who paid no rent when explain'd it turns out to be his Mother. His Mother was alive & then living in the House. He does not know what is become of the House or whether his Mother is alive. He saw her last in the Year 1778. His title is by Deed from his father made as he thinks in 1758. His father died in 1760. He built an House upon it at the time his father gave it to him. His Mother lived upon it from 1760 to 1778 but has never paid him a farthing for it. He swears that it is his property but cannot say whether it is lost or confiscated.

The Land consisted of 100 Acres 20 of which were cultivated. He built an House but can't tell what it cost him. When he was at Lancaster the Rebels told him that he should not live upon it because he had taken Arms against them.

[1] *b.* 1736, *d.* 1788 (?). Is in *Dict. of Nat. Biography*.

[2] The name of Phineas Atherton has escaped the vigilance of Mr. Stark. His estates do not seem to have been confiscated.

[3] There seems a mistake here. Sir John Johnson did not arrive at Montreal till the end of April 1776, a week after its re-occupation by the British. The fact is established by several witnesses before Commissioner Dundas in America (Siebert, *The Amer. Loyalists in the Eastern Seigniories and Townships of the Prov. of Quebec*, p. 4, quoting from the *Second Report of the Bureau of Archives of the Province of Ontario*, 1904, *passim*).

He has applied lately to Whitehall for support but obtain'd nothing. Col^l Kingston knows him & confirms him in saying that he was Provost Marshall to the Northern Army with 5*s*. a Day & that he behaved very well.

### Memorial of Sir James Wallace [1]

Determin'd y^e 5^th of March 1784.

21^st Feb^y 1784.

Sir James Wallace—the Claimant—sworn.

He was on board several of his Majesty's Ships on different Stations in America from the Year 1762 to the Conclusion of the late War & after that during the present troubles until the Evacuation of Philadelphia. He married the Daughter of Sir James Wright in 1778 or 1779 in Georgia by whom he got the Plantation which he claims. His Loyalty & Conduct so well known that no Acc^t of it necessary to be given.

A Loyalist. Bore Arms as a Capt^n in the Navy.

### Memorial of Thomas Dare

Determin'd y^e 26^th of Feb^y 1784.

23^d Feb^y 1784.

Tho^s Dare—the Claimant—sworn.

He is a Native of Eng^d & went to America in 1768 or 1769. In 1769 He was appointed by the Comm^rs of the Board of Customs at Boston Weigher & Gauger & afterwards Tide Surveyor both in the port of London.[2] He continued in that Situation untill he was obliged to leave America in 1776. He never bore Arms but he refused a Commission from them. He continued as long as he could. He came away in March 1776 came to Halifax & from thence to Eng^d where he arrived in May. He was mobb'd & was obliged to go out of Town in the night for several Nights. The Duties of his Office had been at a Stand for some time. The Collector staid longer than he did. The Collector had more influence than he had with the people. He admits however that he might have staid longer if he could have afforded it. He was in no danger of Personal safety. He has a Wife & one Child.

A Loyalist & did his Duty as a Custom House Officer. Did not bear Arms.

Bounty £40 a Y^r.

The Salary of his Office was £40 a Y^r which was continued till Oct^r 1784. The Emoluments were very trifling But thinks the Office with the Emoluments worth £60 a Y^r. He had no Allowance from the Treasury before his Salary was stopp'd when he applied to M^r Wilmot & M^r Coke who reported an Allowance of £40 a Y^r to him from the time that his Salary ceased which he still continues to receive. He has been Ensign & Lieut^t in the North Devon Militia for five Years. He rec^d the pay of Lieut^t up to the time of the Peace.

Duncan Stewart Esq—sworn.

Witness was Collector of the Port of New London. Knew M^r Dare he was a Tide Surveyor previous to the troubles. Remembers his being mobbed & ill treated & that he was obliged to secrete himself. He left New London before the Witness but [3] having no Money. He did his Duty very well. His Salary was 40 a Year. He might have been removed by the Commissioners. He remembers one Man being removed by the Comm^rs.

[1] *b.* 1731, *d.* 1803. Is in *Dict. of Nat. Biography*.
[2] New London, Connecticut.
[3] The meaning is doubtful. ? *Through* having no money.

Determin'd ye 3d of March 1784.

## Memorial of Thos Broadhead

24th Feby 1784.

Thomas Broadhead—the Claimant—sworn.

A Loyalist.
Did not bear Arms.

He is an Englishman & went to America in 1766. He settled in So Carolina in 1774 or 1775. He went first to Pensylvania. He lived in Ninety Six [1] at the beginning of the troubles & was not disturbed till the Year 1781. He never took Arms for the Rebels or took any Oath. They did tender such an Oath but he put it off from time to time & at last they forgot it. He is unable to bear Arms being a Cripple in one of his feet. At the siege of Ninety six Genl Green wanted him to join the Rebel Army but he refused & lay out during the night to conceal himself. He says they offer'd to make him a Lieutt if he would join. As soon as Ninety Six was evacuated he join'd the British. He was employ'd as a Labourer in the Armoury & recd rations & £4 a Month. He was discharged by the Army in April 1782 & he came away in the August of that Year. He applied to the Treasury after he came to Engd for assistance & receives £10 a Year.

Bounty £10 a Yr.

Produces a Certificate from Genl Cunningham which proved that he was employ'd by the British Army & a pass from the Mayor of Falmouth to shew when he landed.

Determin'd the 3d of March 1784.

## Memorial of Robert McLelland

24th Feby 1784.

Robert McLelland—the Claimant—sworn.

A Loyalist & bore Arms.
But took an Oath of Allegiance to the American State.

He is a Native of Ireland & went to America in 1767. He settled in Craven County So Carolina. He resided there when the rebellion broke out & lived upon his own land. After Lord Cornwallis took Charlestown in 1781 He join'd Coll Turnbull. He had done nothing before this time but he had taken the Oath & was compell'd to do it. He could not live in the Province without doing it. He has muster'd with the Rebels but never took Arms agt the British. After he join'd the Army he continued with them till he lost his Eyes which he did by the Explosion of some Gunpowder. He was a Lieutt in the So Carolina Rangers under Major Doyle.[2] He never recd Pay excepting £15.

He lost his Eyesight by the Explosion of some Gunpowder when he was making Cartridges for the Army. He acted as a Commissary in driving in Cattle. He recd a Dollar a Day for it.

Determin'd the 4th of March 1784.

## Memorial of Mary Rothery

25th Feby 1784.

Mary Rothery—the Claimant—sworn.

A Loyalist.

She is a Native of Virginia & married Mr Rothery at Norfolk in Virginia about 20 Years ago. She was a Widow living at Norfolk at the Commencement of the troubles. She came away to Engd in Augt 1774 on acct of the Storm which she saw coming on. The Tea had been thrown into the Sea before she came & the town of Norfolk was in great Divisions & many families would not suffer Tea to be drank in their Houses. She has often blamed the Americans

[1] See note at p. 44.

[2] Writing to General Leslie on February 24, 1782, Benjamin Thompson called attention to the gallantry displayed by the South Carolina Militia under Major Doyle (*Hist. MSS. Comm., Am. MSS. in R. Inst.*, vol. ii, p. 404).

in Conversation. She was not driven away she might then have remain'd with great personal Safety. As she has been absent during the whole War She says she has been informed that her Estate is not confiscated on acc[t] of the Minority of her Son. She claims for it in her Memorial because she then did not know the fact but now she only claims for the Injury done to the Estate. Bounty £40 a Y[r].

Will[m] Farrer—sworn.

He lived at Norfolk in Virginia. He knew M[rs] Rothery in 1774 & she appear'd to him to be well affected to Gov[t]. Being asked what was her reason for coming to Eng[d] He says she had not so much respect shewn to her on acc[t] of the Loyalty of her father & he believes she came on that Acc[t]. He came from Norfolk in Nov[r] last. The troubles were not very high in Norfolk in Aug[t] 1774. He knows there were some Negroes left but does not know what is become of them. M[rs] Rothery's Husband was consider'd a Man of considerable Substance & property.

Bartlet Goodrick—sworn.

Lived at Baltimore & knew M[rs] Rothery. She came away before the rebellion. He knew her father M[r] Orange. He lived then at Liverpool. He [1] was one of the Gent[n] appointed to investigate the Claims of the Loyalists for Virginia. He is desired to look at the Schedule & to say whether she claim'd before that Committee for the same property which she now claims. He says she did. He knew one of the Houses perfectly. When the Claim was given in it was thought a moderate one provided she came within the Description. He says their Committee thought no persons entitled to claim excepting those who had been active or who had been driven away. This Gent[n] accounts for M[rs] Rothery's saying that she could not stay on acc[t] of the Divisions. He says there was a great division in that Neighbourhood on acc[t] of Inoculation [2] & her father had taken an active part in this business & he was made very unpopular & he believes this made M[rs] Rothery's Situation uncomfortable but it had no connection with the present troubles. Nothing was done in Virginia untill the blockade of Boston. The Committee of which he was a Member did not reject her Claim but it appear'd to be very vague & doubtful.

M[rs] Rothery—called again.

Being asked to the Cause of the Division at that time She says it arose in part from the Dispute occasion'd by the Inoculation & in part from the Dispute between the two Countries & persists in it.

Robert Gilmour Esq—sworn.

He knew M[rs] Rothery at Norfolk in 1774. She left it in the Summer of 1774. There was at that time no Appearance of rebellion but there was a Dispute about Inoculation & several Mobs assembled about it. There were no political Disputes at that time & there was no Disturbance at Norfolk till 1775. M[r] Orange her father had taken a strong part in this Inoculation business & had made himself very unpopular.

[1] i.e. Mr. Goodrick.

[2] There was the same trouble over inoculation in South Carolina. See McCrady, *S. Carolina under Royal Government, 1719–75*, pp. 424–8.

Henry Fleming thinks her reason for leaving Norfolk at that time was foreseeing the troubles which have since divided the two Countries. He says the Committees met in June 1774 & in Aug[t] 1774 the Town was under the Direction of these Committees. He doubts whether it was 1774 or 1775. Explain'd to mean 1775 because it was after the Engagement of Bunker's Hill. He says the Tea was thrown into the Sea in the beginning of 1774 & thought the Committees sat immediately after but upon the different Dates being explain'd to him He says that he must have been mistaken in the Year & that it must be the Year 1775.

Determin'd the 3[d] of March 1784.

## Memorial of Lynn Martin

25[th] Feb[y] 1784.

General Prescot—sworn.

He knew the Claimant to be a very active & zealous Loyalist & a very useful Man. He was in decent Circumstances & had been Master of a Merch[t] Ship. He carried Arms at Rhode Island & was very Active & did his Duty unexceptionably. He was made Capt[n] of the Port & had a Dollar a Day. He had property but cannot tell how much. He never knew a better Man in his life.

Lynn Martin—the Claimant—sworn.

An Active & zealous Loyalist & bore Arms.

He is an American & lived at Newport in Rhode Island that was his Home when he was not at Sea he was a Master of a Merch[t] Ship. When the troubles broke out he was at Sea. When he came home the Island was under the Rebel Gov[t]. He arrived at Rhode Island in Oct[r] 1775 & wished to be quiet or at least to take no part with them. They offer'd him a Command of a Battery if he would have taken part with them but he refused it. He continued quiet till the British Troops came to Rhode Island which was the 8[th] day of Dec[r] 1776. He join'd them immediately. The Rebels offer'd an Oath to M[r] Martin but he refused to take it. They threaten'd him & sent some Soldiers to carry him to prison but being known to the Officer they did not do it. When he join'd the British Sir Henry Clinton appointed him to the Command of a Schooner. He had 40*s.* a Month for it. In 1778 He was appointed by Sir R. Pigot [1] Capt[n] of the Port of Rhode Island & had 5*s.* a Day for it. He continued in that Situation till the place was evacuated in 1779. He went with the troops to New York where he remain'd till the 25[th] of June last when he sail'd with his family to Quebec where they now are.

Determin'd the 4[th] of March 1784.

## Memorial of Edward Thorp

26[th] Feb[y] 1784.

Edw[d] Thorp—the Claimant—sworn.

Zealous & active Loyalist.

He was born in America & lived at Stamford in Connecticut. He kept a Store & traded by Sea. He had two Vessels one third of which belonged to him. He traded with these Vessels to Jamaica. He always declared his Opinion in favor of Great Britain & was imprison'd several times in the Y[r] 1775. He had the Oath frequently tender'd to him. He was committed to prison first on a Charge of having given intelligence to Capt[n] Vandeput [2] of the Asia. He was kept in prison five Days. In the same Y[r] he was obliged to give a Bond

[1] *b.* 1720, *d.* 1796. He is in *Dict. of Nat. Biography.* [2] *d.* 1800. He is in *Dict. of Nat. Biography.*

of £1000 that he would not act agt the Americans. Another who join'd with him in it is likewise a Loyalist & they are both come away. In 1776 they agreed not to deal with him & he was obliged to come away in Consequence of it. He removed to New York.

The Revd Mr Peters—sworn.

Lived at Hebron in Connecticut about 90 Miles from Stamford. Has known Mr Thorp for above 20 Years. He always looked upon him to be a very loyal Subject. The Witness was driven away in 1774. He has had Letters from New York from which it appears that Mr Thorp was driven away afterwards & lost his property on acct of Loyalty. He has been at Mr Thorp's House. He lived very well & his House was very well furnished. He was always looked upon as a Man of Substance & has frequently heard the Neighbours say that they looked upon him to be worth between 3 & £4000 of the Money of the Province. Thinks the House & Lot where he lived would have sold for more than £500.

## Memorial of Willm Pennington

Determin'd the 3d of March 1784.

Willm Pennington—the Claimant—sworn. 27th Feby 1784.

He is a Native of Engd & went to America in 1764 to the Port of Brunswick.[1] He went as Comptroller of the Port & was appointed by the Lords of the Treasury the Salary of the Office was 40 a Yr. He continued at Brunswick till Feby 1776. He never was molested personally. In Septr 1775 the Emoluments of his Office ceas'd & a Stop put to all business at the Custom House. He went in Feby 1776 on board the Scorpion & went to wait on Govr Martin & Genl Clinton. He was then put on board the Cruiser Sloop of War where he remain'd on board that & the Thetis Sloop till Augt when he arrived at New York having first been to Charlestown. On the 20th of Augt 1776 He sail'd for Cork & he arrived at Cork on the 27th of Septr & then came to Engd where he has remain'd ever since. He does not pretend any Act of Service. He says he never had any Opportunity of doing any service to his Country. The fees of his Office upon an Average amounted to £110 or thereabouts making his Office in the whole about £150 a Yr. He recd the Salary up to Octr 1782 when it was discontinued & likewise he recd £60 a Yr from the Treasury from the 5th of April 1777 to Jany 1784 & He still continues to receive £60 a Year.

A Loyalist & did his Duty as a Custom House Officer.

Did not bear Arms.

Salary £40 a Yr. Emoluments £100 a Yr. Salary discontinued from Octr 1782. Bounty £60 a Yr.

Property.

He had an House at Brunswick which belonged to Genl Tryon. He went into it in 1771 & Genl Tryon then said that Mr Pennington was very welcome to that House as long as he staid in America. And he then did not understand that he meant to give the perpetuity of it. But he claims it as an absolute Gift & produces a Certificate from Genl Tryon.

rejected.

There is likewise a Certificate from Mrs Lobb that her Husband recd 100 Gās from Govr Tryon for this House. He values the furniture which he lost in that House at £50.

Furniture £50 *os. od.*

Govr Martin Govr of No Carolina—sworn.

He remembers that this Gentn was reported to him as holding the Office

[1] North Carolina.

of Comptroller & believes he was so. He was an unexceptionable Man & respected by all his Acquaintance And he is perfectly satisfied with the Loyalty of Mr Pennington. Mr Pennington is desired to produce his Deputation from the Commrs of the Customs to prove that he held the Office. He produces it accordingly.

Determin'd the 8th of July 1785.

## Memorial of Zephaniah Kingsley

27th Feby 1784.

Zephaniah Kingsley—the Claimant—called upon his Affirmation being a Quaker.[1]

A zealous Loyalist.

Did not bear Arms.

He is a Native of Engd & went to Charlestown in 1770. He carried over a Cargo of goods with an Intention to establish himself there. When the troubles came on He did everything in his power to oppose the rebellion & he suffer'd much persecution in consequence of it & was imprison'd three times. They often applied to him to bear Arms but he always refused. He admits that the Principles of his religion exclude him from bearing Arms. In the Year 1778 He sign'd a Paper purporting to be a Test Oath & it was to be true & faithful to their State. He conceives it bound him to take a part with them but he never did. When Genl Prevost was coming to Charlestown they took away 300 Barrels of Rice & some Hogsheads of Tobacco but they paid him for the rice in depreciated Paper. At the time of the Siege He was made Overseer of the Negroes which was the only Service that he ever did for the Americans. He is desired to explain his signing the Test. He says they insisted upon his affirming that he would be true &c but that he always refused & would have left the Province sooner than do it. But it was done by a friend of his in this Way. He desired him simply to sign his Name & then he gave him a Certificate that he had affirmed &c. He did not consider it under these Circumstances as at all binding upon him. After the reduction of the town He subscribed 100 Gās towards raising a Corps of Horse. He continued till the Evacuation. He does not know when his property was confiscated but knows it has been so & that a part of it has been sold & apprehends that he shall not be permitted to return.

Sign'd a Test to the Americans.

Bounty £100 a Yr.

Mr Kingsley receives from the Treasury £100 a Year. He has recd it from the 5th of Jany 1783 & still continues to receive it.

Disallowed.

He claims £1911 10*s.* 6*d.* for Paper Currency made under the King's Govt which thinking as secure as Bank Paper he kept. He admits that after he recd this Paper he might have paid it away without Loss. But having no Doubt of it He chose to keep it. He gave this Money to Govr Bull about a Year ago thinking that Govt would make some Allowance for it.

Debts due to him there £6500. Due from him £12000 Cur & in Eng £10000.

He has Debts due to him in America to the Amount of £6500 or thereabouts And he admits that he owes about £12000 Currency in America & 10000 S. here.

He had several Negroes but at present makes no Claim for them as they are not taken away. Some are in Jamaica & the rest are in Charlestown in the

[1] There were not many Quakers in Charleston. Fothergill wrote from there in 1755: 'I am here amongst a poor handful of professors' (R. M. Jones, *The Quakers in the Amer. Colonies*, 1911, p. 300).

hands of his Agent. He believes they permit his Agent to keep the Negroes under an Idea that they belong to his Children & indeed he did make a Deed of Gift of them to his Children before he came away.

Waved. Presumptive Proof of Confiscation.

Doct^r^ Garden—sworn. 28th Feb^y^ 1784.

He has known M^r^ Kingsley about 15 Years & believes him to be perfectly attached to the British Gov^t^ from the beginning. He has never heard that he sign'd any paper acknowledging Allegiance to the Rebel State. He is sure the Oath of Abjuration was never tender'd to him. He looks upon him to be a very steady Loyalist & was very kind to the Loyal Prisoners. That Conduct render'd him very obnoxious to the Rebels. He knows that he subscribed to raise a Corps for the use of Gov^t^ in the Year 1781 or 1782.

## Memorial of Henry Peronneau [1] Esq

Determin'd the 5th of March 1784.

Henry Peronneau, Esq—the Claimant—sworn. 28th of Feb^y^ 1784.

Is a Native of South Carolina & at the Commencement of the troubles He was Joint public Treasurer. In 1770 He was appointed sole public & in 1771 Another person was join'd with him in the Appointment. He produces his Appointment by the Gov^r^ & Council which is read. Benj^n^ Dart is join'd with him in that appointment & it is dated in 1771. He produces a Paper dated the 6th of March 1776 by which he is prohibited from issuing any further Money out of the Treasury. About ten Days before this time a Member of the Congress called upon him & intimated that such an Order would come & asked him whether he would obey any Orders from the Congress & he answer'd that he would not on any Acc^t^. And he accordingly paid no Attention to it. And on the 26th of March he was dispossess'd of the Office. And he soon after paid the balance to the Rebel Gov^r^ M^r^ Routledge.[2] He produces an Order imposing the Oath of Allegiance & Abjuration & a Copy of the above Oath. This Ordinance was issued on the 13th of feb^y^ 1777. All his friends prior to this time requested him to take part with them but he constantly refused & he said he would sooner forfeit his Life & property. He was banished in Consequence of this & he was immediately put in prison for refusing. He was often threaten'd but did not receive any personal Insult till he was banished. His Connections were

A zealous & meritorious Loyalist. Did not bear Arms.

[1] He was acting Public Treasurer during the latter part of the dispute between the South Carolina Assembly and the Home Government over the constitutional rights of the former, which is dealt with in Monro, *Acts of the Privy Council, Col. Series, 1766–83*, pp. 229–35 (see also W. R. Smith, *S. Carolina as a Royal Province*, pp. 369–87).

For refusing to comply with an order of the Assembly which had been made without the concurrence of the Legislative Council, Peronneau and his colleague were declared guilty of contempt and committed to the common gaol (McCrady, *S. Car. under the Royal Government, 1719–76*, p. 694).

[2] John Rutledge, *b.* 1739, *d.* 1800, was a delegate from South Carolina to the Continental Congress, 1774–6. He resigned his seat on February 15, 1776 (*Journals of the Cont. Congress*, vol. iv, p. 306, note 1). He was chosen President under the new régime in March 1776, and in that capacity organized the resistance to the British fleet at Fort Moultrie. In spite of his hesitating attitude towards the new State Constitution he was elected Governor under it in January 1779. After the expiration of his term he was again chosen delegate to the Continental Congress. He was afterwards an important member of the Convention which framed the American Constitution (see McCrady, *S. Car. in the Rev., 1776–80*; Max Farrand, *The Records of the Federal Convention, passim*; and Appleton, op. cit., vol. v, pp. 355–6).

considerable & they prevented the Mob attacking him. He was banished in April 1777 when he went to Holland & came from Holland here. As soon as he came here he applied to the Treasury & they gave him £200 a Y$^{r}$ which he rec$^{d}$ from the 1$^{st}$ of Jan$^{y}$ 1778. On the reduction of Charlestown he was order'd out again & rec$^{d}$ a Year's Allowance in advance & Passage Money. He arrived there the 3$^{d}$ of June 1781 & continued there till the place was evacuated. He had a little office there for which he rec$^{d}$ 10*s*. a Day & it continued only till he rec$^{d}$ £107 & he never rec$^{d}$ any more Money whilst he was there. When he returned he applied again to the Treasury & his Case was heard by M$^{r}$ Wilmot & M$^{r}$ Coke who reported the same Allowance that he had before which commenced from the 1$^{st}$ of Jan$^{y}$ 1783 & which he now continues to receive.

Bounty £200 a Y$^{r}$.

Office £400 a Y$^{r}$.

The Loss of Office he states to be to his Share £800 a Y$^{r}$. It was worth £1600 a Y$^{r}$ to both. The profits of the Office arose from 2½ per Cent on all Monies paid in & issued out of the Treasury. This Office was not restored to him upon the Capture of Charlestown Civil Gov$^{t}$ never being restored. M$^{r}$ Peronneau says that he believes there never was any other Oath tender'd in America but the two Oaths which have been produced. Being told that the Comm$^{rs}$ had heard of an Oath of Neutrality He says there never was any such Oath.

John Hopton Esq—sworn.

Knew M$^{r}$ Peronneau very well. He was Joint Treasurer. It was consider'd as a very lucrative Office superior to the Gov$^{r}$ but he had only the half of it. It was in his Opinion about £2000 a Y$^{r}$. Knows M$^{r}$ Peronneaus Dwelling House &c. He thinks it worth upwards of £2000 St. M$^{r}$ Peronneau lived in it ever since he knew him. He knew his Negroes but does not know the exact Number. He remembers the black Mother with two Mulatto daughters. He values them at 100 or 120 Gās a piece. The three were worth at least 300 Gās.

John Savage Esq—sworn.

He lived at Charlestown & knew M$^{r}$ Peronneau very well. Knew that he was Joint Treasurer & thinks the Office was worth to him upon an Average about £450 a Y$^{r}$ it was about £900 a Y$^{r}$ to both exclusive of the Money left in their hands. The other Advantages about £600 a Y$^{r}$. He always looked upon M$^{r}$ Peronneau as a very honest Man & he believes he was very loyal because he refused to conform to their Gov$^{t}$. Being asked whether he considers the Money arising from Interest to be one of the fair Emoluments of Office He says it was always consider'd fair till very lately when they had thoughts of reforming it.

His Estate appearsto have been confiscated by an Act pass'd in 1782. But it is taken off by an Act pass'd in 1784. Therefore no part of his property will be Lost.

Henry Peronneau Esq—sworn.

Being desired to give an Acc$^{t}$ of the Emoluments of his Office He mentions first 2½ per Cent on all Monies rec$^{d}$ & paid in the Office. To the best of his recollection tho' he can't be positive there was no Commission on the Taxes He estimates this at 500 a Y$^{r}$—5*s*. for making Entries & 20*s*. for clearing all Ships The produce arising from the Interest of Money in their Hands he believes was £8000 [1] or £1100 S. He is sure that it was £1000 a Y$^{r}$ at least. He believes the Commission Money was about £500 a Y$^{r}$ & the Clearance upon Ships about

1 Currency.

£400 a Y^r^. He says he is sure He can say that independent of the Interest the Emoluments of the Office in the whole were £800 a Y^r^. At the time he refused the Orders of the Assembly Many people came to him & told him that if he would obey their orders they would permit him to retain the Money in his hands but if not they would make him pay & account for the Interest. This was in 1771 & was occasion'd by a Dispute between the Gov^r^ & the Assembly.[1] And it happen'd during the King's Gov^t^. But no reform was actually made.

### Memorial of Rich^d^ Wilson

Determin'd the 4^th^ of March 1784.

Rich^d^ Wilson—the Claimant—sworn. 2^d^ March 1784.

He was born in Ireland. He served all the last War as a Noncommission'd Officer in the 22^d^ Reg^t^. In 1775 & 1776 He was Lieut^t^ of Fort Johnson in Carolina. Produces his Commission sign'd by Gov^r^ Martin 4^th^ of May 1773. In the Year 1775 He rec^d^ an Order from Gov^r^ Martin to dismantle. It was done accordingly. In 1775 He had a Commission given to him by Gen^l^ Gage appointing him Lieut^t^ of the Royal Fencibles. He produces the Commission. He continued so till July 1782. He settled as a Planter in America after the last War & continued so till 1771 when on the troubles then breaking out he join'd Gen^l^ Tryon & in 1773 He was made Lieut^t^ of Fort Johnson. He produces a Warrant dated July 1772 from Major Brace ordering him to raise a Company of Loyal Americans And afterwards was made Capt^n^ of it after he had raised it as appears by a Commission which he produces sign'd by Gen^l^ Carleton in Aug^t^ 1783 appointing him Capt^n^ of this Company. He expects to receive half Pay but yet has rec^d^ none. The Reg^t^ was reduced the 24^th^ of October last.

A Loyalist & bore Arms.

### Memorial of Francis Green[2] Esq.

Determin'd the 17^th^ of March 1784.

Francis Green Esq—the Claimant—sworn. 2^d^ March 1784.

The Memorial being read which is a very long one M^r^ Green is sworn generally to the truth of it & swears that he wrote it under the solemn sense of an Oath. Reference is therefore had to the Memorial instead of stating it over again & He proceeds to produce his Vouchers to prove it. First he produces

An Active & zealous Loyalist. Did not bear Arms.

A Letter from Gen^l^ Gage to the Gov^r^ of Connecticut Gov^r^ Trumbull stating that in consequence of his Loyalty he had been violently attacked & ill treated to which an evasive Answer was rec^d^.

A Boston Gazette dated 14^th^ July 1774 from which several Extracts are read to prove that the Americans consider'd him as an Enemy to the State & that they treated him very ill the particulars of which are recited.

[1] See note [1], p. 97.

[2] *b.* 1742, *d.* 1809. There is a full account of him in Sabine, op. cit., vol. i, pp. 492–6. '"Out with him! out with him!" shouted the mob as they rushed at Francis Green in a Norwich Inn. His crime was that he had signed an address to Governor Hutchinson' (*Nova Scotia Hist. Soc. Collections*, vol. xiii, p. 12, 'The life and times of the Rev. J. Wiswell', by the Rev. E. M. Saunders). Green became Sheriff of Halifax, and we find Penelope Winslow writing in April 1785: 'The High Sheriff enjoys all the pomp of this pompous town, and you would by the style and state he takes upon himself swear he was a born Halifaxian' (Raymond, *Winslow Papers*, p. 288). Nevertheless, Green returned in 1799 to the land, of his birth, where he died.

A Certificate from Sir Wth Howe speaking strongly of Mr Green's Character & Loyalty & to property from report dated in 1782.

A Commission from Sir Wm Howe dated in 1775 by which he appoints Mr Green Captn in an associated body of Loyalists. Produces likewise orders from Sir Willm Howe in 1775 to Mr Green to take charge of particular Districts &c & to order Arms &c.

Certificate from Genl Gage Governor Wentworth &c to the Loyalty & services of Mr Green.

Do from Lieutt Coll Hamilton who commanded the 59th Regt at Boston in 1774 or 1775 to shew that Mr Green served in the Army during the late War & behaved very well.

Do from the Commander in chief in Nova Scotia dated 9th Septr 1776 that Mr Green was appointed a Magistrate in Halifax.

Proclamation dated 24th Septr 1778 by Govr Tryon by which Letters of Marque were granted to Loyal Subjects.

Certificate of Govr Franklyn dated 26th Octr 1782 to his zealous & active Loyalty.

Do from Coll Balfour & Mr Fisher late Under Secretary of State to the same point.

He never recd any Pay nor any other Advantage from Govt excepting a few bushels of Coals &c. He had no Office or Emolument during the rebellion.

He fitted out a Vessel in 1778 under letters of Marque which was of great use to the British Army by giving material intelligence of the french fleet &c.

Former Bounty £100 a Yr. Present Bounty £150 a Yr.

Mr Green recd an Allowance of £100 a Yr from the Treasury from the Year 1780 Which was afterwards examin'd by Mr Wilmot & Mr Coke & they were so sensible of his Loyalty & Losses that they augmented it to £150 a Yr which he now continues to receive.

His property has been confiscated & his Name has been in several Acts.

He has frequently served as a Volunteer upon many Occasions & has served this Country with his Pen as well as his person. These two Circumstances are not mention'd in his Memorial.

The Revd Mr Peters.

He knew Mr Green first in 1774. He knew all his family before. He speaks of the Execution & says he sold the Land for Mr Green but he never got the Money for it & the reason assign'd was that he had sign'd an Address to Govr Hutchinson. They siez'd him & all his papers & treated him very ill. And he had Conversation afterwards with the Rebel Govr who said that the people had treated him very properly. This violence prevented his receiving the £100 so that he lost it by his Attachment to this Country. He found him a Loyalist & an Outlaw when he came to Boston the September following. He does not know any other Land belonging to him. The Note was £100 & there was some Money due upon it for Interest. When the Witness was at Boston which was only three weeks Mr Green was very active. He believes he was in the Association & likewise in the Militia. He has heard that the House in which Mr Green was a Partner was an House in great business & good Credit.

## Memorial of Thos Rogers

Determin'd the 6th of March 1784.

Thos Rogers—the Claimant—sworn. 6th March 1784.

Is an Irishman & went in 1772 to Maryland. In 1774 He went to South Carolina & was settled in Craven County when the troubles commenced. He carried 150 of Linen Cloth with him. He took Arms at first for his Majesty in the Year 1775. He associated under Coll Fletcher [1] with many other Loyalists & soon after this in the same Year he fought the Rebels at Ninety six. He was taken Prisoner at Linley's fort [2] in 1776. He was brought to trial in the fall of the Year & was sentenced to death. Two or three were hanged & he was repriev'd. He never took their Oath. He went after this & lived with his Brother & remain'd quiet till Charlestown was taken & then he join'd Major Ferguson.[3] He remain'd in his Majesty's Service with the Army till the Year 1781 when he came home. He never was more than a Serjt in the Army & he never recd any pay. He receives £20 a Year from the Treasury.

An Active & zealous Loyalist & bore Arms.

Bounty £20 a Yr.

Colonel Gibbs—sworn.

Has known Thos Rogers from the Year 1774. He then lived in Ninety six District. He says he thinks he is a very true & good Loyalty as far as his Understanding goes. He first took up Arms with Coll Gibbs & persever'd with him during the whole War. He was in many Actions & was an excellent Soldier. He has heard that he was taken Prisoner. He was acquainted with two of his plantations. He says he always understood that he did purchase a Plantation from Andrew Thompson it was within 4 Miles of Mr Gibbs's mother. It was good Land but not cultivated. He values it at 20*s*. an Acre S. Thinks in 1774 these Lands would have sold for 15*s*. an Acre. He thinks he could not have bought it for 17*s*. Currency. He believes Mr Rogers to be a very honest Man. He knows the 150 Acres. He was possess'd of it before the War began & he believes it was his Land. He thinks this worth per Acre 15*s*. S. He does not know that the Land is confiscated but is satisfied that he will never be able to return to it. He knows he had some Horses & some Cattle but cant tell the Number. Being asked what he thinks he was worth at the beginning of the troubles He says he should think that in the Year 1774 he was worth £300 or £400 Sterling.

Samuel Greatorex—sworn.

The Witness lived in the province of Virginia. He knew Thos Rogers in 1780 he had seen him before but did not know him till 1780. He knows him to be well attached to the British Govt. Has known him to be in several Engagements. He has been in two Engagements with him under Coll Tarleton. Rogers behaved very well in those Actions. He knows nothing himself of his property excepting one very valuable Horse. He has often heard in America that he had two plantations [and] some Stock. He thinks the Horse was worth about £15 S. He heard that his Land was Cane break & that it was very valuable. He has heard several people say that it was worth 20*s*. an Acre. He should

[1] ? Colonel Fletchall who was in command of the Militia.

[2] July 15, 1776 (see McCrady, *S. Car. in the Rev., 1775–80*, p. 194).

[3] For particulars as to Major Ferguson's Riflemen see *Acadiensis*, vol. vi, p. 237, article by Mr. J. How.

imagine they meant Currency [1] as people generally speak in the Money of their own Province. Being asked what led to the Conversation He says in the Camp they generally used to talk with each other about the property which they had left behind. He does not know that he lost the Horse but he knows that he had him.

Thos Rogers called in again.

He adheres to the Acct which he first gave of the 17s. being Sterling Money.

Determin'd the 24th of May 1784.

**Memorial of Alexander Stenhouse**

6th March 1784.

Alexander Stenhouse— the Claimant—sworn.

A Zealous Loyalist. Did not bear Arms.

Dr Stenhouse went to America from Scotland in 1756 & settled on his own Acct in 1759 in 1764 He came to the town of Baltimore from this time to April 1776 He remain'd in Baltimore in the practice of Physic. He always supported the King's Cause. He could not take an active part being so constantly employ'd in business. He was called upon to bear Arms by the Rebels & desired by his Customers to take that part & he constantly refused in consequence of which he was deprived of the exercise of his profession & he was treated with Contempt by his former friends. In April 1776 He left Baltimore & went to Philadelphia with a view to go to New York but not being able to go to New York He came in a Vessel to Lisbon & landed in Engd in July 1776. He never was imprison'd. He lost some property when he lost his Situation in that Country. But he makes no Claim for that. However he is advised by the Board to make a Claim for all his Losses of every sort. And being at this moment not ready to prosecute such a Claim He is indulged with being heard at a future time & in the mean time is to send in a more extensive Schedule of Losses.

Determin'd 1st of Novr 1784.

**Memorial of Thos Miller**

8th March 1784.

Thos Miller—the Claimant—sworn.

Zealous & active Loyalist & render'd Services to Govt. Did not bear Arms.

Is a Native of New Jersey. In the Summer of 1775 while he was a Resident at New York as a Mercht he was called upon to sign the Association which he refused & being apprehensive of receiving similar ill treatment to what others had done for the like Conduct went to Long Island where he exerted himself in influencing the Councils of the County to his Majesty's Service & succeeded so well that both the Kings Ships & Troops benefited greatly thereby in getting Supplies of Provisions exclusive of his giving very useful Intelligence from time to time to Govr Tryon who was then on board an armed Ship in the Bay of New York. In 1776 about July the Committees recd information by some Deserters from Long Island of the Claimant's zealous Attachment to the British Govt when he was proscribed and advertised. Says that one of the Advertisements was sent to him. He thought it prudent to conceal himself in Queen's County in unfrequented Swamps at times until the Arrival of Genl Howe. In Augt Genl Howe appointed him to conduct the two Brigades under Majr Genl Grant.

[1] The Paper Currency in South Carolina retained its value undiminished from June 1775 to January 1777. Then began a most ruinous depreciation (see Table at p. 227 of McCrady, *S. Car. in the Rev., 1775–80*).

In Oct^r of the same Year his health grew very bad when he came to Eng^d & returned in Dec^r 1777 to Long Island where he was employ'd by Gen^l Tryon to settle the differences between the Refugees who were put upon the Rebel Estates & the families who were left behind in them. He came to Eng^d in 1780 & was allowed £80 per Ann. from the Treasury.

Former Bounty £80 a Y^r. Present Bounty £60 a Y^r.

John Blackburn—Merch^t in London—sworn.

Was acquainted with the Claimant many Years ago in Eng^d. Knew him in 1768 & 1774 when he commanded a Merch^t Ship & was consign'd always to his Address. The Claimant went out to New York with Gen^l Tryon in 1775 with an intention of fixing there. He had kept a Store at New York during the time he traded to London in the afs^d Ship. Knows nothing of the Claimant's being possess'd of any landed property.

Will^m Davis—sworn.

Has known M^r Miller upwards of 20 Y^rs both as a Merch^t & Mast^r of a Ship. He knew M^r Miller at New York in 1762 or 1763. He then kept a Store. In 1776 the Claim^t came to Eng^d & went out again he believes with Gen^l Tryon. Believes that the Claimant was always very much attached to the Cause of Great Britain. Knows nothing of his having any landed property in America. Heard of his having some in Florida.

The Rev^d Sam^l Seabury—sworn.

Late of the province of New York. Speaks to the Six Rights of Land does not know how the Claim^t became possess'd of them. Says that to the best of his recollection the Rights granted by Gov^r Wentworth consisted of 330 Acres. Has known M^r Miller upwards of 30 Y^rs was always looked upon as a very staunch Loyalist. Cannot say anything with respect to their value.

## Memorial of Robert Cooper

Determin'd the 17^th of March 1784.

Rob^t Cooper—the Claimant—sworn. 8^th March 1784.

Is a Native of America born in Prince Frederic's Parish George Town S^o Carolina. On the Commencement of the troubles in 1775 He was at School & in 1777 He came into possession of a property left to him by his father who died in 1774. In 1779 towards the latter end of the Year He went to the House of a Loyalist (a M^r Coulson) in N^o Carolina. It was on acc^t of the Americans wanting to make him do Duty in their Militia that he left his own Plantation. Says that he was under the Necessity of serving with them for 2 Months. Never was desired to take the Oaths. Served with them out of fear they obliged him to do so but he avail'd himself of the first favorable Opportunity after of getting away from them & going into N^o Carolina. In June 1780 he join'd a Detachment of the British Troops under Major M^cArthur [1] at Cherause in S^o Carolina & continued as a M^a Man to the time of the evacuation of Charlestown. Served in the Engineers Department at Charlestown for 10 Months in the Quality of a Clerk to one of the Foremen of the Corps of Engineers & produces a Certificate

A Loyalist after the Year 1780 before which time he served in the American Army. Did not bear Arms.

[1] Lieutenant-Colonel Archibald McArthur commanded the troops in East Florida at the close of the war (*Hist. MSS. Comm., Am. MSS. in R. Inst.*, vol. iii, p. 199).

of the same from Col[l] Moncrief.[1] Also a Certificate to his Loyalty from Lord Cornwallis Col[l] Gibbs & others.

Colonel Gibbs—sworn.

Knew M[r] Cooper in 1781 at Charlestown. He was then in the Engineer's Department & had Negroes under his Care. Says that he heard Claimant say he had been with the Americans before the British took Charlestown. Imagines that he had been in Action ag[t] the British. Claimant's Sister was married to a Loyalist (M[r] Coulson in N[o] Carolina) And Col[l] Gibbs thinks that M[r] Coulson advised the Claimant to leave the American Army & join the British Troops near Camden. Claimant's father died in 1773. Says that he saw a Copy of the Will in the Office in 1782 by which the Claimant was left 550 Acres of Land on Blackming's Swamp besides some Stock for his Life. Does not know the Land but has heard in Eng[d] that there were Indigo Vats on the Land. Knows that the Claim[t] had Negroes at Charlestown has known him to have 8 exclusive of one that was seduced away from C. Town by a Rebel. Has heard that he had Stock on his Plantation. Says that he thinks the Claim[t] has not valued his Lands at the price he ought for that he believes Lands in such a Situation as those of the Claimant were worth 40*s.* an Acre instead of 25*s.* Does not know if the Claimant's property has been confiscated. Believes it has not.

Colonel Fortune—sworn.

Has known M[r] Cooper since 1781 at the Congarees. At that time he was with the British Troops as a Volunteer. Heard at that time that he had come from George Town S[o] Carolina of his being a young Man & who had a property. Also knew him at Charlestown when he was employ'd in the Engineer's department as an Overseer. Has heard since he came to Eng[d] of the Claimant having served with the Rebels before he join'd the British Troops in 1781. Says that the Claimant's own Brother was always a Rebel & who press'd him as he has heard to return but he refused. Believes that the Claimant during the time he was with the British Troops was well attached to the Cause of Great Britain. That he has heard Colonel Gibbs say that the Claimant had not half valued his Landed Property. Believes that the Claimant when he was with the American Troops served in his Brother's Company.

Determin'd the 10[th] of March 1784.

## Memorial of Gray Harrison[2] Esq.

Harrison Gray Esq—the Claimant—sworn. 9[th] March 1784.

One of his Majesty's Council & late Treasurer of the Province of Mass. Bay in New England.

Was born at Boston—lived there the most part of his Life. Was a Merch[t] there a great many Years ago. Treasurer of the Province since 1753. As soon as the Tea was destroy'd he endeavour'd to prevail on the people to make

[1] See note at p. 18.

[2] Harrison Gray, *b.* 1711, *d.* 1794. There is a good account of him in Stark, op. cit., pp. 334–6. It is regrettable that John Adams stooped to make wholly false insinuations against his financial probity. In fact, so far from leaving Massachusetts a debtor, he had many private debts owing to him. From his chief debtor, John Hancock, he received no better treatment than did Harvard College. Gray was satirized under the name of Scribblerius Fribble in Mercy Warren's play *The Group*, 1775.

Compensation for it. When Gen^l Gage arrived he accepted the office of one of the New Council this in June 1774. Staid at Boston in the execution of this business till Gen^l Howe quitted. Went from Boston to Halifax & came from thence to Eng^d in 1776. In the latter end of 1774 he published a Pamphlet entitled *the two Congresses cut up*.

A Zealous & active Loyalist.
Did not bear Arms.

Receives from the Treasury £200 per Ann. from 1776. Had £200 given to him in advance on his Arrival in Eng^d in July 1776.

Bounty £200 a Y^r.

Colonel John Chandler—sworn. 10^th of March 1784.

Knew the Claimant first in 1752. Always esteem'd him a Loyalist. Never heard of any Circumstance regarding his Conduct to be of a different Opinion. That he was very zealous in endeavoring to prevail on the people to pay for the Tea. Speaks of the Pamphlet which M^r Gray published. That in every matter he shew'd the greatest Attachment to Great Britain. The office of Treasurer he thinks was worth as follows Annual Allowance from £200 to £250 Cur. Extraordinaries 100 to £150. House & fireing £66. Advantages by Money £600 per Ann.

## Memorial of Sam^l Greatorex

Determin'd the 17^th of March 1784.

Samuel Greatorex—the Claimant—sworn. 11^th March 1784.

A Native of England. Went to America in 1769. Was in Rockingham [1] County in 1770 where he settled & continued till the Commencement of the troubles. Kept a Store there & dealt in sundry Articles.

A zealous & active Loyalist & bore Arms.

In 1775 He was one of 400 who enter'd into an Association & a M^r John Davis was afterwards appointed by Sir Henry Clinton to command them. He continued with them till 1780 during which time they were not employ'd. When some of the Men informed a M^r Smith (an American Colonel) of their having enter'd into an Association for the defence of the British Gov^t eleven of them were taken up & 4 were hanged. In Oct^r 1780 he was informed that the Rebel Constable had orders to take him up & that they meant to hang him at his own Door. It was from the Constable's Sister he rec^d this Information in consequence of which he immediately fled & went to Ninety Six S^o Carolina. He had been three times examin'd by M^r Smith before the Association was known to have been set on foot & is sure he says that he should have been hanged had he not made his Escape. Join'd Colonel Tarlton 1^st Jan^y 1781. And was with the Kings Troops about a fortnight after at the battle of the Cowpens.[2] Served as Private with a great number of Loyalists. Went with the Troops & join'd Lord Cornwallis the next Day. Continued to bear Arms & was at the battle of Guilford. Was frequently employ'd by Lord Cornwallis in Dispatches & as a Spy. After the battle of Guilford [3] he & a M^r Lancaster an Englishman were intrusted with Lord Cornwallis's Dispatches for Lord Rawdon at Camden. They were afterwards sent by Lord Rawdon with Dispatches to Col^l Balfour at Charlestown. Remain'd at Charlestown till the Evacuation. Produces

[1] North Carolina.

[2] Fought on January 17, 1781. The British under Tarleton were defeated.

[3] Fought on March 15, 1781. The British under Cornwallis defeated the Americans under Greene; but the victory was dearly purchased.

Confiscation immaterial.

Certificates from Lord Rawdon Col[l] Cruger & a Copy of one from Lord Cornwallis (the original at Whitehall) to M[r] Greatorix's Loyalty & Col[l] Cruger's mentions his having lost his property. Was Waggon Master in the Barrack Master Gen[l's] department for 3 Months & had a Dollar a Day during that time. When he & a M[r] Sharpless went to America they carried out £500 between them in goods. M[r] Sharpless died soon after they arrived & left him what property he had in Goods.

Determin'd the 24[th] of March 1784.

## Memorial of John Brooks [1]

March the 15[th] 1784.

John Brooks—the Claimant—sworn.

An Active & Zealous Loyalist render'd services to the Bri. Gov[t] & suffer'd two Years Imprisonment thereby & render'd Services to the Brit. Gov[t].

Is a Native of England went to Quebec in 1774 as a private Agent to Gov[r] Skene [2] who was then in Eng[d] but he had a large landed property in the province of New York at a place called Skenesborough. He arrived there in June or July 1774 & continued in the execution of his business till May 1775. Says that the Gov[r's] Son Major Skene lived in the House with him that he the Claimant had frequently declared his disapprobation of the Measures going on to a M[r] Dan[l] Tucker who used to visit at the House & who he has reason to think was a Spy that on the 8[th] of May he & the Major were taken Prisoners by a Party of Americans from New England also the Governor's two Daughters & their Aunt. The Ladies were conducted to Salisbury New Eng[d] about 100 Miles from Skenesborough where they were left under the Care of a Gent[n] & Claimant carried to Hartford in Connecticut remain'd there on Parole with the Major about a fortnight when he went to Salisbury & had leave to go back with the Ladies to Skenesborough under the care of two American Officers Capt[n] Biddilo & Sheridan—remain'd there till Sept[r] 1775 during which time he was under constant Apprehensions from the dislike the people had against him & was obliged to go to Philadelphia & apply to M[r] Jay to get some Order from Congress to prevent his being any more molested but notwithstanding this he still continued to be insulted & then from Skenesborough he went in quest of intelligence to Albany then went to Philadelphia & formed a friendly Connection with a Doct[r] Kearsley [3] a Zealous Loyalist. Was taken Prisoner in Philadelphia the 5[th] of Oct[r] 1775 in consequence of he & Doct[r] Kearsley being suspected of giving information. Committed to Lancaster Gaol & kept therein 728 Days. Doct[r] Kearsley was also taken up & kept a much longer time in Goal this Gent[n] died at Carlisle the Day after he was permitted to come out on Acc[t] of his ill state of health. The Claimant was able to effect his Escape on the 3[d] of Oct[r] 1777. Says that during his Confinement he was treated in a most rigorous manner not suffer'd the use of Pens Ink or Paper or to have any Conversation with any person whatever. After making his Escape he went to Philadelphia then in poss[n] of the British Troops & presented himself to Sir Will[m] Howe who after hearing his Story asked

[1] In *Hist. MSS. Comm.*, *Am. MSS. in R. Inst.*, vol. iii, p. 258, there is a memorial dated December 11, 1782, from J. Brooks that he was late Captain in Lieutenant-Colonel Emmerick's Light Dragoons. The 5*s*. a day not being sufficient to support his family, he solicits for a passage to England and six months' advance pay.

[2] See Additional Notes, p. 142.

[3] See Additional Notes, p. 143.

him if he could raise a Company which he said he could not for want of Money. Sir Wm Howe then order'd him to be paid 10 Gās. He staid at Philadelphia till the 10th of Decr when he obtain'd Sir Wm's Pass to go to New York in a Ship. Got to New York the 22d of Decr where on his arrival he found himself in great distress but fortunately he recd great Assistance from a Mr Chamier[1] the Commissary who knew his family & Connections. The 3d of May 1778 He got a Warrant as Captn from Coll Emerick[2] at New York to raise his 2d troop of Light Dragoons & went to Philadelphia to recruit got 14 Men but the Evacuation happening at that time returned with the Army at New York after having put his Men on board a Transport. He deliver'd them on his Arrival at New York to the Agent where he rais'd 5 more but was order'd not to raise any more Says that he did not receive anything for raising these Men remain'd in an inactive State till the 20th of Novr 1778 when he embarked for Engd. He recd under the Denomination of pay as Captn £9 7*s*. S. Says that it was only the pay of 2 Months & that he did not receive more as the Troop was not compleated. Arrived in London the 8th of feby 1779 & presented a Memorial to the Treasury stating his Sufferings & obtain'd a Letter from Mr Robinson to the Commr in chief at New York. The Treasury order'd him £50 for Passage Money the 3d of Septr 1779. On his applying for a greater Assistance He got £100 more in August 1780 & then went to New York where he arrived in June 1781 & deliver'd the Letter to Sir Henry Clinton. Says that he was detain'd from Septr 1779 to Augt 1780 soliciting the additional Sum afsd of £100 the first £50 not having proved sufficient to pay his Debts. The Letter from the Treasury which he took out with him was to recommend him to a Commn in the Army or in the Provincial Troops. Did not succeed in this but was appointed to receive 5*s*. a Day from the 25th of July 1781 on the Refugee List which he continued to receive till Decr 1782 when he embarked for Engd & had 6 Months advance paid to him by order of Sir Guy Carlton.

Governor Franklyn—sworn. 16th March 1784.

Knew the Claimant in 1778 brought the Witness a Letter from Govr Skene recommending the Claimant to him as a Loyalist & as a Man who had suffer'd in the King's Cause for any assistance he might stand in need of. The Witness recommended him to Sir Henry Clinton does not know whether Sir Henry did anything for him then that he soon came to Engd & Govr Franklyn says that the Claimant carried out with him a Letter of recommendation from the Treasury to Sir Henry & had 5*s*. a Day as a Loyalist but don't know how long he recd this Allowance.

Joseph Galloway Esq—sworn.

Was not acquainted with the Claimant till after he got out of Gaol which was in 1778. Heard of his being concerned with Doctr Kearsley in writing Letters respecting the State of the Country to persons in Engd. Believes him to be an exceeding zealous Loyalist. Says that in 1778 or the beginning of 1779

[1] See note 3 on p. 32.

[2] Emmerick made several proposals with respect to the raising of troops (*Hist. MSS. Comm., Am. MSS. in R. Inst.*, vol. i, p. 104; vol. ii, p. 528; vol. iii, p. 255). Vol. iv, p. 199, contains a memorial from him to Carleton asking for subsistence money in advance to pay some accounts before he embarks.

the Claimant applied to him for a recommendation to Lord North & thinks that it was £150 in the whole which was given to him on an Assurance that he would not be more troublesome to Gov$^{t}$ but then M$^{r}$ Galloway observes he expected to have been provided for in the Military Line in consequence of the Letter given to him by the Treasury to Sir Henry Clinton & which he did not succeed in.

Andrew Allen[1] Esq—sworn.

Late Attorney Gen$^{l}$ of Philadelphia & a Member of the Committee of Safety. Says that he never knew the Claimant till he was apprehended in 1775 by a Set of People called the Committee of Inspection of Correspondence & fearing that he might from the enraged State of the Mob be very ill treated he the Witness got him brought before the Committee of safety to examine him & thereby the resentment of the Multitude was lessen'd. Says that M$^{r}$ Brooks was apprehended on acc$^{t}$ of his being concern'd with others in holding a Correspondence with people in Eng$^{d}$. Says that he is satisfied M$^{r}$ Brookes was only committed for his Loyalty to his King. That it was at Lancaster he was confined & is satisfied that he must have suffer'd a great deal of hard Usage during the time he was kept in Goal. Thinks he might have been confined upwards of two Years.

Miles Snowdon—sworn.

Late of Philadelphia a Brewer. He has known M$^{r}$ Brooks since 1775. Knew him at Philadelphia for about a Month & as an Agent to Gov$^{r}$ Skene. Says that he was apprehended in consequence of some Letters which were given to him the Witness address'd to a M$^{rs}$ M$^{c}$Cawley which inclosed others for M$^{r}$ Charles Jenkinson. Knows they were for him & that their being put under Cover to M$^{rs}$ Macaulay was only to prevent suspicion. Says that the Claimant was a very long time confined & has heard of his being very ill treated & suffering very hard Usage in the Gaol.

Governor Skene—sworn.

Late Gov$^{r}$ of Ticonderoga. Says that in 1774 when he was in Eng$^{d}$ & wanting a person to act as his Agent in taking care of his landed property in America agreed with M$^{r}$ Brookes of whom he had heard a very good Character. Gov$^{r}$ Skene having got the Appointment of Inspector of all Lands not claim'd as private property within the Province of Quebec as also of the Woods in 1764 appointed M$^{r}$ Brookes verbally his Deputy & meant to have allowed him £100 per Ann. as his private Agent & Deputy Inspector. Thinks he would well have deserved £50 per Ann. as his Deputy Inspector. Speaks very highly of M$^{r}$ Brooks's great zeal & attachment to the Cause of Great Britain. Gave his promise to M$^{r}$ Brooks of appointing him Deputy in 1764 before he left Eng$^{d}$. The troubles prevented him from giving M$^{r}$ Brooks a formal Deputation. Gov$^{r}$ Skene speaks very highly of M$^{r}$ Brooks's Loyalty. It was sometime in 1774 that M$^{r}$ Brooks was settled on the Witnesses Estate. In July 1775 when Gov$^{r}$ Skene was a Prisoner M$^{r}$ Brooks at the risque of his Life went to him to give an Acc$^{t}$ of the Gov$^{rs}$ Daughters & family which had been driven away from his House & offer'd his Assistance to him. Says that it was at his desire M$^{r}$ Brooks

[1] He was a delegate from Pennsylvania to the Continental Congress in 1775 and 1776.

employed himself in procuring information which he knows he transmitted to Sir Will[m] Howe & General Gage. Knows of his having been taken up at Philadelphia on acc[t] of his being concern'd with Doct[r] Kearsley in transmitting Intelligence from Philadelphia. Says that it was at his Desire M[r] Brooks went to Philadelphia. Can't speak particularly to what Articles M[r] Brookes lost at Skenesborough of Cloaths but says that he was very well supplied & accustomed to dress very genteelly.

George M[c]Kay—sworn—formerly Serj[t] in the 42[d] Reg[t].

Knew the Claimant in Lancaster Gaol in 1777. Was in Gaol all the time he was a Prisoner there which was seven Months. Says that he heard the Gaoler say something about the Claimant being confined for taking part with the British. He never had an opportunity of speaking to him because he says that M[r] Brookes was very closely confined.

### Memorial of George Thomson

Determin'd the 26[th] of March 1784.

George Thomson—the Claimant—sworn. 16[th] March 1784.

Was born in Scotland. Went to Charlestown in 1772. Was there in 1775 on the Commencement of the troubles as a Merch[t]. Was desired to sign the Association but refused doing so. They left him quiet till 1777. Says that a Man of his name having signed the Association he in order to avoid the better getting clear of the Americans when they press'd him to sign the Association pointed out his Namesake's name in a printed List by which means he evaded the signing of it. That afterwards when he was press'd to take the Oaths he positively refused & told them he would rather lose his Life than do so. Went from Charlestown to Cape Francois then to Jamaica & came to Eng[d] in Oct[r] 1777. Rec[d] £100 per Ann. for temporary Support till he went out again in Nov[r] 1780 to Charlestown & remain'd there till Dec[r] 1782 when it was evacuated. Came to Eng[d] in Jan[y] 1783 & is allowed £50 per Ann. by the Treasury produces Certificates to his Loyalty from Lord Will[m] Campbell & Col[l] Balfour.

A Loyalist.
Did not bear Arms.

### Memorial of the Rev[d] W[m] Edmiston [1]

Determin'd the 27[th] of March 1784.

Will[m] Edmiston—the Claimant—sworn. 17[th] March 1784.

Is a Native of Eng[d]. Rector of the Parish of S[t] Thomas's prior to the troubles. Says that on the Commencement of them & when subscriptions were made for collecting Arms & Ammunition (early in 1774) he exhorted his Parishioners to continue to their Allegiance to the British Gov[t] & circulated Pamphlets among them which had been written for the purpose of shewing them the Evils intended by those who promoted violent Measures in Dec[r] 1774 or Jan[y] 1775 he was brought before the Committee & charged with having in his exhortations to the people told them that by taking the Oaths to the Insurgents they were guilty of treason to the King. Says that they required him to sign a recantation of all he had said which he refused to do but the paper being alter'd by some of his Acquaintance who wished to prevent any ill Usage being offer'd to him on acc[t]

A Zealous Loyalist.

[1] See evidence in case of George Chalmers at p. 39.

of his Attachment & it's only going to his desisting from holding the Language he had before done he signed it. In Sept^r 1775 when the Association paper was going about a friend asked him if he meant to sign it & if he did not that his House would certainly be pulled down whereupon he left the place & his wife & family & embark'd for Eng^d & arrived in Nov^r 1775.

Witnesses.

George Chalmers Esq—sworn.

Was well acquainted with M^r Edmiston. Confirms his being the Rector & says that he was very active in persuading his Parishioners to remain quiet particularly against associating & deliver'd his Sentiments on some Occasions from the Pulpit & believes that he went so far as to have refused administering the Sacrament to many who had taken part against us. He persever'd in his Loyalty till he was obliged to leave the province in Sept^r 1775.

His Living of S^t Thomas was worth about £300 per Ann. Sterling—including Surplice fees.

Rob^t Alexander—sworn.

Knew the Claimant. Confirms what he said respecting his being brought before the Committee. Was very much respected. Speaks highly of his Loyalty. The Living about £270 per Ann. Ster^g the Surplice fees from £50 to £80 Currency. Witness was a Member of the Committee who examin'd him in Dec^r or January 1775.

M^r Stenhouse—sworn.

Was well acquainted with the Claimant. Has heard him go as far in the Pulpit as he could well do to inculcate a principle of Allegiance amongst his Parishioners. Knows he had Lands. Can't speak positively about the Value of the Living. Thinks between 4 & £500 Currency.

Bounty £100 a Y^r.

He receives an Allowance of £100 a Y^r from the Treasury.

## Memorial of Tho^s Alexander

Determin'd the 27^th of March 1784.

19^th March 1784.

Tho^s Alexander—the Claimant—sworn.

Was born in Scotland. Went to Boston in 1761. Followed the Hosiery business & kept a Store at Boston in 1774. When the troubles broke out was appointed a Lieut^t in the Associated Company rais'd at Boston in July 1775 by Sir W^m Howe. When it was evacuated he went with the Company to Halifax & from thence to New York in Sept^r 1776 with the King's Army. At New York he remain'd in a trading Line & tho' not belonging to any Corps frequently bore Arms & was wounded at the battle of Brandywine.[1] He was then with the Queen's Rangers. Came to Eng^d in 1779 returned in 1780 & in feb^y 1781 went to Virginia where he was appointed Port & Harbour Master of the Ports of Portsmouth & Norfolk by Gen^l Leslie. Continued in this Situation till the Ports afs^d were evacuated by Gen^l O'Hara then went to York Town where he was appointed to his former Station for the Ports of York Town & Gloucester by Lord Cornwallis & was taken prisoner with his Lordship. Was allowed 10*s*. S.

A Loyalist & bore Arms in the Service of Great Britain.

[1] Fought September 10, 1777. There is a good account of the battle in Trevelyan, *The Am. Rev.*, part iii, pp. 244–52.

a Day during the time he held this employment & was paid up to the time of the Surrender. Is allowed £50 per Ann. by the Treasury from the 5th of January 1783.

Bounty £50 a Yr.

### Memorial of Mrs Penelope D'Endé

Determin'd the 29th of March 1784.

Penelope D'Endé—the Claimant—sworn. 20th March 1784.

She is a Widow & was the Wife of Wm Forsayth a Native of Scotland. Went to Norfolk 2 or 3 Years before the troubles. She married in 1775 when her Husband kept a Shoemaker's Shop. That in 1775 her Husband join'd an Association & quitted his residence when Lord Dunmore & the Troops left it. Continued with the Army till Augt 1776 but did not bear Arms on acct of his bad health. He died on his passage to the West Indies. She has no Children. She is a Native of Virginia came to Engd 2 Months ago from New York. Her Husband's property was on board a Schooner belonging to him it was put on board at the time Lord Dunmore came away & burnt she says by British Sailors.

Claimant a Loyalist and her deceas'd Husband a Zealous one & bore Arms.

### Memorial of the Revd Robt Cooper

Determin'd the 29th of May 1784.

Revd Robt Cooper—the Claimant—sworn. 20th of March 1784.

Is a Native of Engd. Went to America to Charlestown in 1758. Got a Living that Year in Prince Willm's Parish. On the Commencement of the troubles he was Rector of St Michæls Church at Charlestown And says that on his being required to observe a Fast which he refused it was in feby 1775 the Committee of the State then consider'd whether he ought not to be deprived of his Living. The Majority were in his favor. In June he was applied to to sign the Association which was to renounce his Allegiance to the King. He signed it with a reserve of his Allegiance but about 3 Months afterwards a Committee of 3 Gentn waited on him & told him that if he did not sign it erasing the Condition which was annex'd to his Name before that he would be consider'd as an Enemy & the Consequences might be very disagreeable to him. He then struck out the Conditions & his name remain'd on the List as a Subscriber. Continued after this in the Execution of the functions of his Office without any Molestation taking care to avoid giving any Cause of Complaint by the Language he held till the beginning of June 1776 when on Sir Peter Parker's appearing he was called upon repeatedly to attend the Musters which he declined. At this time an Oath was tender'd to the Inhabitants for the Defence of the place but was not regularly tender'd to the Claimant but was proposed to him by the Captn of the Company in which he was inrolled but he refused to take it. The Claimant continued to pray for the King at public Prayers & the day of the Attack made by Sir Peter Parker (28th of June 1776) having done so he was the Sunday following Dismiss'd from the Vestry. He remain'd in Chas Town till April 1777 without receiving any Injury but being obliged to quit his Parsonage House. In April 1777 He was called upon to take the Oath of Allegiance to the State & Abjuration to the King. He refused to take it & in consequence was obliged to quit the place in 60 Days & went to Holland from whence he came to Engd where he arriv'd in June 1777. He applied to the

Claimant a Loyalist.

The Claimt was among those whose Property was confiscated. But by an Act passed in 1784 that Confiscation is taken off.

Treasury on his Arrival & rec$^{d}$ an Allowance of £100 a Y$^{r}$ untill the reduction of Charles Town. In 1781 he returned to Charlestown & was on his Arrival appointed to the Church of S$^{t}$ Philip by the Vestry of the Parish & continued there till the Evacuation when he came to Eng$^{d}$. He had about £130 given him by the Treasury for his passage out to Charlestown. He has a pension of £60 a Year from y$^{e}$ 5$^{th}$ of Jan$^{y}$ 1783.

Bounty £60 a Y$^{r}$.

Determin'd the 28$^{th}$ of May 1784.

## Memorial of James Green

March 24$^{th}$ 1784.

James Green—the Claimant—sworn.

Is an Englishman & went to America in 1763. He settled soon after his Arrival at Newbern in N$^{o}$ Carolina. He was first employ'd as Master of a Vessel. Says he refused to join the Insurgents in their resolves or sign their Association. They made him take an Oath in Nov$^{r}$ 1775 That He would not give any information or assistance to the British Gov$^{t}$ whilst he staid in the province. If he had not taken this Oath he would have been sent to prison. Early in 1776 he left Newbern & went to Cape Fear having obtain'd a clearance for that place from the King's Collector. But says that at this time an Ordinance had been pass'd in the province that no Vessel sh$^{d}$ be permitted to sail unless they undertook to bring back warlike Stores. Says upon sailing from Newbern He clear'd out for Cape Fear & gave a Bond in the Penalty of £295 that he would deliver his Cargo at Cape Fear. He never did deliver that Cargo there nor ever meant it. He intended to apply to the Gov$^{r}$ & to go out of the Country. He was obliged to leave Effects in the hands of a friend who was Security for him to the amount of £295. Upon his arrival at Cape Fear he did deliver Gov$^{r}$ Martin's furniture & Baggage & went with his own Vessel to Antigua & had passes from Gov$^{r}$ Martin. He first intended to go to London & afterwards alter'd his mind. By this means the bond became forfeited & the Rebels took & seized upon the Effects left in y$^{e}$ hands of his friend. He left besides other Effects behind him to the Amount of £408. He went to Antigua thinking himself perfectly safe with this pass & when he came into the Harbor he was immediately seiz'd by Capt$^{n}$ Keeler who took the Ship & libel'd him in the Admiralty Court but he could not appear there because he was obliged to give Security & he could not do it. He made a Claim upon the Treasury for this above 4 Years ago. Sir Guy Cooper [1] said it was a very hard Case & that he should have an Answer but he never has had any. The Vessel & Cargo was his sole property & they were worth about £1400 S. No person speaks to the Value but himself.

A Loyalist.

£390 to be reported under the Prohibitory Act. Disallow for the forfeiture of the Bond.

Gov$^{r}$ Martin—sworn.

The Claimant he believes clear'd out as he states & he believes him to be very well attached to the British Gov$^{t}$. He apprehends that the letter which he gave to him was to secure him from the Clearance. He is not sure whether he knew of the Prohibitory Act [2] at the time but he rather thinks not & that he gave him this to protect him from the want of a Clearance. He can't form any judgment of the value of the Vessel. He would have been liable to be seiz'd

[1] ? Sir Grey Cooper, who was Secretary of the Treasury, 1765–82.

[2] This was the Act 16 George III, c. 5, prohibiting all trade and intercourse with the colonies.

not having a Clearance from Cape Fear & Gov^r Martin gave him this to supply the want of that if he had proceeded to deliver his Cargo at Cape Fear he would have been seiz'd by the Ships there.

### Memorial of Brig^r Gen^l Skynner [1]

Brig^r Gen^l Skynner—the Claimant—sworn. 25^th of March 1784

Determin'd the 27^th of May 1784.

Was Attorney Gen^l of the Province & Speaker of the House of Assembly when the troubles broke out. Was appointed in 1754. Is a Native of New Jersey. In April 1775 soon after the Battle of Lexington he was insulted in the Execution of his Office & in the Sept^r following at Morristown he was called upon before the Town Committee & found guilty of being inimical to the liberties of America but on his declaring himself generally a friend to Liberty & this Country his friends on the Committee took advantage of these general Expressions & obtain'd his Discharge for him. From this time to the 7^th of Jan^y 1776 He met with various obstructions in the Execution of his Office.

An Active & Zealous Loyalist bore Arms as a Brig^r Gen^l & render'd the most essential service to the British Gov^t.

In Aug^t 1775 He had an offer made him of the Command of the provincial Troops by the provincial Congress with what rank in the province he chose which he refused.

In Jan^y 1776 Upon the Discovery of some papers which the Claimant had copied for Gov^r Franklyn concerning the Proceedings of Congress he was obliged to quit the Province & went to New York. His Wife & family retired to Amboy but were in the Course of 3 Months forced to quit by an order of the Provincial Congress. The 4^th of Sept^r 1776 He rec^d a Commission from Sir W^m Howe of Brig^r Gen^l of all the provincial Troops. Continued as such till the arrival of Sir Guy Carleton when he was order'd to Paulus Hook & then to Long Island. He arrived the latter end of May or beginning of June 1782. He was in an engagement on Staten Island on the first of Aug^t 1777 with Gen^l Sullivan under the Command of Gen^l Campbell. He had previously been in a Cannonade at Trenton in Dec^r 1776 & in two at Brunswick [2] early in 1776.

Says that in 1777 when he enter'd Jersey he found six Battalions were raising. He was very instrumental in getting them collected. The Battalions were to be of 500 Men each. In 1778 they were reduced to four & these were nearly compleated to 400 each. Gen^l Howe commission'd the Officers principally by his Advice. Says that the first Year he was at £100 S. expence in raising his own Company which consisted of 56 rank & file. It cost him from 30 to 40 Gās a Y^r for raising Men over & above the Royal Bounty from 1777 to 1781. That he constantly furnished Lord Cornwallis & the Commander in chief with intel-

[1] 'An influential member of the Council of East Jersey Proprietors, Attorney-General of the province for many years until the Revolution, and an eminent lawyer, Skinner was a man of authority in the colony' (E. J. Fisher, 'N. Jersey as a Royal Province', *Columbia Univ. Studies in History*, &c., vol. xli, p. 91). He acted as Speaker from 1765, with the exception of a short interval, till the overthrow of the royal rule. 'His early opposition to British oppression changed as the Revolution broke out and he supported the British cause' (ibid., p. 271). Skinner was appointed in 1776 Colonel and Brigadier-General of the New Jersey volunteers, consisting of some fifteen hundred men, and proved himself an active and able leader. He was termed in a Pennsylvania newspaper the most ungrateful man in the world, and instances of his cruelties were adduced (Moore, *Diary of the Am. Rev.*, vol. i, pp. 396 and 421).

[2] New Brunswick, N.J.

ligence & says that Lord Cornwallis will speak particularly thereon. Was always paid for the Expences he was at in procuring information by the Commanders in chief. Rec$^{d}$ full pay as Brig$^{r}$ Gen$^{l}$ from the 4$^{th}$ of Sept$^{r}$ 1776 till Oct$^{r}$ 1783 but as Colonel only from April or June 1781 till Oct$^{r}$ 1783. Does not know yet whether he is to receive half pay from that time. From last fall he has rec$^{d}$ at the rate of £200 per Ann. from the Treasury & gave a Rec$^{t}$ up to July 1784.

£200 0*s*. 0*d*.
Salary £36 a Y$^{r}$.
Profession
£500 a Y$^{r}$.

Library of Books 482 Vol. Values them at 500 Cur.

The Salary of Att$^{y}$ Gen$^{l}$ when he came to the Office was only £30 per Ann. It was afterwards augmented to £60. The Emoluments of his Profession & Office from £900 to £1000 per Ann. Cur. Produces a Copy of the Order under which M$^{rs}$ Skinner was turned out from Home which he says he believes to be a true Copy.

Lord Cornwallis—sworn. 26$^{th}$ March 1784.

Says that his first personal knowledge of the Claimant was in Nov$^{r}$ 1776. At that time he join'd his Lordship in the Jerseys & had the rank of Brig$^{r}$ Gen$^{l}$ Says that he went thro' all the hardships of the service with the utmost chearfulness & that he was of the utmost Assistance to him that he was entrusted in matters of the most confidential nature by his Lordship & that he always found him to be a most Zealous Man. In Dec$^{r}$ 1776 as soon as they got poss$^{n}$ of the Country the Claim$^{t}$ began to raise Men & Lord Cornwallis says that on one Day 100 Men join'd him that he had nearly rais'd the Complement of 6 Batt$^{ns}$. Does not think that he ever met a Man who had so perfect a knowledge of the Country as the Claim$^{t}$. Lord Cornwallis says that he does not think it possible that any Man could shew more real zeal & attachment towards Great Britain than the Claim$^{t}$. That he had from him once a week a perfect Acc$^{t}$ of the real State of Washington's Army.

Brig$^{r}$ Gen$^{l}$ Skynner—again sworn.

In Aug$^{t}$ 1775 He was called upon by a M$^{r}$ Dickenson[1] who was a Major Gen$^{l}$ in the American Service. He asked him to dine with him which the Claim$^{t}$ refused fearing that some Conversation might be held at the table by persons who were to be there disagreeable to him but that he dined with him alone the next Day. Says that before he did so the Secretary to the Provincial Congress M$^{r}$ Carter & two other Gent$^{n}$ M$^{r}$ Ellis & M$^{r}$ Stewart deputed by that body acquainted him with their being authorized to offer him the rank of Major Gen$^{l}$ which should be confirmed by the Gen$^{l}$ Congress or if he prefer'd it the Gov$^{t}$ of the Province or any Station within it upon such terms as he should point out. That he has seen the Minute of Congress ordering the Deputation to wait upon him. This he refused to accept of. In June 1776 he rec$^{d}$ a Commission from Gov$^{r}$ Franklin (after he was taken Prisoner) appointing him Major Gen$^{l}$ of the Militia of the Province & delegating to him all the Military powers granted to him under the Great Seal of Great Britain. Says when he went into the Jerseys after the arrival of Sir W$^{m}$ Howe he did endeavour to put the Comm$^{n}$ in force

[1] John Dickinson, the author of *Letters of a Pennsylvania Farmer to the Inhabitants of the British Colonies*, 1767. He opposed the adoption of the Declaration of Independence, but enlisted as a private in the continental army to prove his patriotism. In October 1777 he was commissioned as a Brigadier-General (Appleton, *Cyclopaedia of Am. Biography*, vol. ii, p. 173).

& with some effect but the Evacuation of the Province render'd it afterwards useless.

Governor Franklin—sworn.

Says that the Claim[t] was Att[y] Gen[l] & Speaker of the Assembly of the province when the troubles broke out in 1775 in which Situation he had been for several Years previous to the rebellion. He says that the Conduct of the Claim[t] on all occasions was such as to deserve his fullest confidence that from time to time he rec[d] the most material Information from him before he resolved to leave the Province. Confirms what the Claim[t] has just said relative to his giving him a Commission to act as Maj[r] Gen[l]. Says that he was an active Zealous Subject & that he did everything in his power to render Services to the British Gov[t].

Isaac Ogden Esq—sworn.

Was acquainted with the Claim[t] in 1775 & many Years before. Says that he heard in 1775 from some Members of the provincial Congress that they wished him (Witness) to serve therein which he refused & that they then told him that M[r] Skinner would be offer'd the post of Maj[r] Gen[l] & used that as an Argum[t] to induce him to serve as a Member of Congress. Witness believes that Gen[l] Skynner's practice was worth £500 S. per Ann. Would have given the Claim[t] £300 S. per ann. for the Att[y] Generalship. This Office led the Claim[t] into great practice.

David Ogden Esq—sworn.

Has known Gen[l] Skynner from his Infancy. Was Att[y] Gen[l] & Speaker of the Assembly when the troubles broke out. Says that Claim[t] was most sincerely attached to the British Gov[t].

Sir Henry Clinton—K.B.—sworn. 12[th] May 1784.

Says that Gen[l] Skynner conducted himself with great Zeal during the War. He has frequently receiv'd material Information from him & found great Use from his Extensive knowledge of the Country & the Characters of the Americans. He says that upon the whole Gen[l] Skynner was particularly zealous & active in the Cause of Great Britain.

## Memorial of Jermyn Wright[1] Esq.

Determined the 18[th] of Dec[r] 1784.

Jermyn Wright Esq—the Claim[t]—sworn. 27[th] April 1784.

An Active Zealous & meritorious Loyalist.
Did not bear Arms.
Bounty £200 a Y[r].

He was born in Eng[d] & went to America in 1758. He was a Planter & traded as a Merch[t]. He swears that the Contents of his Memorial are true *to the best of his knowledge*. He bore Arms first, in feb[y] 1776. He had about 100 Men under his Command. He left Georgia in April 1782. And he has from the 10[th] of Oct[r] 1782 rec[d] an Allowance from the Treasury of £200 a Y[r].

[1] Brother of Sir James Wright. 'In 1776 he was in command of a fort on the St. Mary's river which became a general rendezvous for the Tories of that section. The fort was assailed, but the Whigs were defeated' (Sabine, op. cit., vol. ii, p. 460).

## Memorial of Gen[l] Delancey [1]

3[d] May 1784.

Began to be determin'd the 23[d] of Dec[r] 1784. A Zealous Active & meritorious Loyalist.

Bore Arms & render'd Services.

Oliver Delancey—the Claimant—sworn.

Swears to the whole of his Memorial being true.

Says he was employ'd by Sir W[m] Howe to command on Long Island. He had a civic as well as a military Command.

In 1775 he lived at Greenwich on New York Island & in consequence of his avowing principles of Loyalty he was frequently mobbed.

Says he underwent great fatigues hardships & Dangers in the Course of the rebellion & materially injured his health by his exertions in favor of the British Cause. Gen[l] Delancey has at present the half pay of a Col[l] which is 12*s.* a Day & an Allowance from the Treasury in the name of M[rs] Delancey of £200 a Y[r] & £100 in the name of Miss Delancey. Says he did raise one Batt[n] which he commanded himself part of the War & it was afterwards detached to the Southward under the Command of Col[l] Cruger.

Bounty £300 a Y[r].

Property.

He esteems his property in America to be worth more than £100000 St[g].

The Expence of patenting Lands in New York was £25 for every 1000 Acres.

General Robertson—sworn.

Has known Gen[l] Delancey many years before the rebellion. He was one of the first in point of fortune & situation. He had great merit in stepping forward to raise provincial Troops & his example had great influence. He was amongst the first fortunes in the province. He says that American Estates are very difficult to be estimated. He bought a great deal of Land in New Jersey. He believes the burning of his House was a mark of their Enmity. He was consider'd as a Man of great integrity & Honor. He kept a very good table & lived with great splendor. Being asked as to the fire He says the fire was well contrived. He first thought it was the Enemy But he now rather thinks it was accidental. He enquired a great deal into it but he never could find any reason to think that it was by design.

General Stirling—sworn.

Has known General Delancey many Years. He was a Colonel in the War before the last & was always well attached to this Gov[t]. Gen[l] Stirling went to America in 1776 & he found him at that time very active. Upon Sir W[m] Howe's arrival at New York He offer'd to raise three or four Battalions & he was the first that did raise a Corps. These Provincial Corps were not much employ'd they were kept at New York. Knows little of his property but he was understood to be a Man of great property & lived very well. He was in New York when the fire happen'd & thinks it was by design. Some persons were caught with Combustibles which he looks upon as evidence of the design it broke out in three or four places at once.

[1] Oliver de Lancey was born in 1717. In 1756 and 1758 he commanded the New York Provincials in the military operations at Lake George. He became a member of the New York Assembly in 1759 and of the Council in 1760. He died in England in October 1785 (Biog. Notice in *N. York Col. Docs.*, op. cit., vol. viii, p. 788). In 1776 he was appointed Brigadier-General to raise fifteen hundred men for the defence of Long Island (ibid., p. 687).

Knew his House at Bloomendale. It was a new House & a large one. He thinks it was worth about 16 or £1800 & the furniture about £2000 or perhaps not quite so much.

Does not know whether he ever made any Application to Gov$^{t}$ to be paid for this & if he had he believes it would not have been paid.

Brig$^{r}$ Gen$^{l}$ Skynner—sworn.

Gen$^{l}$ Delancey in 1776 came on board the Dutchess Man of War & told General Skynner that he was going to take an active part & the next time he saw him he was a Brig$^{r}$ Gen$^{l}$ but he never served with him. He always consider'd him as a very active Loyalist & he thinks it very possible that he may have hurt his Health by it. He looks upon him as an active & zealous Loyalist & that he took his part from principle.

The Gen$^{l}$ had large rights in Jersey. He purchased of the Heirs of one Dockera more than two 24$^{th}$ Shares of the whole province.[1] These rights were granted by Charles 2$^{d}$ to the Duke of York & by him to the first two Proprietors Lord Berkley & Lord Carteret. Gen$^{l}$ Delancey had not taken out his share of Warrants when the Committee of the Council of the proprietors examin'd into it & it was determin'd that he might issue more. He did issue some & he sold others.

12$^{th}$ May 1784.

Sir Henry Clinton K.B.—sworn.

Speaks in general terms of the Loyalty of Gen$^{l}$ Delancey & speaks of him with great respect.

## Memorial of James Johnson[2] Esq.

Determin'd the 12$^{th}$ of May 1784.

7$^{th}$ May 1784.

James Johnson Esq—the Claimant—sworn.

Is a Native of Great Britain. Went to America in 1764 to So. Carolina. He went as Clerk to a Prothonotary there. He was compell'd to leave the Country in 1777. He was a Civil Officer at the time the rebellion broke out. He was Clerk of the Crown. He had 60 Days to quit the Province. He went to Bourdeaux & from thence to Eng$^{d}$. He returned to Carolina in 1781 in consequence of orders given here to return. At the end of that year he was appointed Att$^{y}$ Gen$^{l}$ upon the death of Sir Egerton Leigh. Does not produce his Commissions but promises to do it. The value of his office of Clerk of the Crown £350 S. It was for life. He bought it of M$^{r}$ Cumberland whose life was in the patent. He got about £750 a Year by his profession the Year before he left the Country.

A Zealous & meritorious Loyalist. Did not bear Arms.

Bounty £120 a Y$^{r}$.

M$^{r}$ Johnson receives £120 a Y$^{r}$ from the Treasury & now continues to receive it.

He makes no charge or Demand for anything but the loss of his profession.

8$^{th}$ May 1784.

Governor Bull—sworn.

Has known M$^{r}$ Johnson 10 or 11 Y$^{rs}$ ever since he grew up. He was then

[1] See on 'The Proprietory System and the Land Troubles' in the Jerseys, Fisher, op. cit., pp. 171–209

[2] He acted in 1782 as British Commissioner in negotiations with a view to check plunder on both sides (McCrady, *S. Car. in the Rev., 1780–3*, p. 658).

Value of his Offices £350 a Yr. Got by his Profession £700 a Yr.

Clerk to the Clerk of the Pleas & Clerk of the Crown. When the times were critical he lived a good deal with Govr Bull at his House in the Country. He was a very Zealous & steady Loyalist & took his part upon principle & he believes on that Acct he was obnoxious to the rebels. He went out again with Govr Bull & he appointed him Atty Genl sometime in the Year 1782. He likewise made him Clerk of the Crown which was 3 or £400 a Yr S. The Clerk of the Pleas was about £900 a Year. He had the office of Clerk of the Crown & Peace at the time of the Rebellion as appears by a Commission given to him in 1770. The Atty Genl's office was no profit to him. He was very diligent & a very rising Man; & he was in very good practice. He thinks he might in the Year 1774 get 7 or £800 a Yr by his profession. The Office of Clerk of the Crown & Pleas was a Patent Office & not removeable but for misbehaviour.

Thos Knox Gordon [1] Esq—sworn.

Late Chief Justice of the province. Has been acquainted with Mr Johnson since 1771 when he first went as chief Justice. He found Mr Johnson then acting as Prothonotary of the Com. Pleas & he was then Clerk of the Crown. Clerk of the Pleas was about 8 or 900 a Yr but he does not know the value of the Clerk of the Crown. Mr Johnson was in good practice & thinks he might have made 7 or £800 a Year. Fees were very high then.

Edward Savage Esq—sworn.

Knew Mr Johnson very well. He was 2d Judge & went Circuits with him. He says he was rising extremely fast & had a great deal of business & he has no doubt but he would have made a great fortune if the troubles had not happen'd. Being asked to the profits of his profession in 1774 He says from £600 to £800 a Year.

James Trail Esq—sworn.

Was well acquainted with Mr Johnson from the beginning of 1772. He was intimate with him in 1774. He was at the Bar & was in great practice. He was Clerk of the Crown. He was perfectly loyal & was banished by an Act of the Legislature but his banishment was subsequence to Mr Trail's leaving the province. The value of the Office of Clerk of the Crown near 400 a Yr. Mr Johnson by his practice in 1774 made at least £700 a Year & he thinks it would have increased. He knows that Mr Johnson had Debts owing to him about £5000 S. before the troubles. He was called to the Bar in 1772 & he accounts for his being worth so much Money by his having held a lucrative Office & practised under the Bar which enabled him to save so much Money & was likewise the reason of his coming so immediately into Business it being like Pleading under the Bar in this Country.

[1] He was a Dublin lawyer appointed Chief Justice of South Carolina by Lord Hillsborough in 1770. Taking him as example, McCrady (*S. Car. under Royal Government, 1719–76*, p. 469) laments the use of the Bench as a place of reward for partisan services in England, and describes his appointment as that of ' a vulgar, ignorant bully ', ' for the gratification of the mistress of a Secretary '.

## Memorial of Tho$^{s}$ Phepoe Esq.

Tho$^{s}$ Phepoe Esq—the Claimant—sworn. 10$^{th}$ May 1784.

Determin'd the 28$^{th}$ of May 1784.

Is a Native of Ireland & went to Charlestown in 1771 with M$^{r}$ Knox Gordon & M$^{r}$ Savage. He practis'd the Law there at the time of the rebellion. He dates the commencement of the rebellion from the battle of Lexington. He continued at Charlestown & was a Member of the rebel Assembly by the advice of M$^{r}$ Knox Gordon. He was Member for Prince Frederic's Parish. He was requested by the whole Parish (who were all loyal) to represent them. He continued there under the rebel usurped Gov$^{t}$ till April 1782 when he join'd Lord Cornwallis. He did everything during the time that he lived under the rebel Gov$^{t}$ to promote the Cause of Great Britain. He was always employ'd by those who were tried for Sedition. No other Lawyer dared to plead for them. He remain'd at Charlestown till July 1782 when he embarked for Eng$^{d}$. When the British took the town Gen$^{l}$ Pattison [1] gave him his House & Lord Cornwallis in Sept$^{r}$ 1780 made him a Capt$^{n}$ of the Militia. He took the Oaths to the rebel Gov$^{t}$ one Oath of fidelity but he did not look upon it to be binding. He admits that he might have refused it with safety if he had quitted the province. He was put into prison in the Year 1779 for pleading for a particular person.

A Loyalist. But he took the Oath of fidelity to the State of So Carolina & served as a Member of the Assembly in 1778 & 1779.

Bounty £100 a Y$^{r}$.

Profession.

He says he got from £1000 to £2000 a Year in 1773 1774 & 1775. He made at least £900 a Y$^{r}$ by his profession. He had no Office.

£800 a Y$^{r}$.

In the Assembly he occasionally made Conciliatory propositions to promote an Union between the two Countries. He voted ag$^{t}$ the Banishment Act & spoke ag$^{t}$ it. He says that he was (whilst he was a Member of their Assembly) & ever shall be an Enemy to all their Councils & Measures.

Certificates read from Col$^{l}$ Philips to the loyalty of M$^{r}$ Phepoe who was Counsel for him. He obtain'd Col$^{l}$ Philips's pardon from the Gov$^{r}$. He says Col$^{l}$ Philips would have been hanged if it had not been for his interposition.

Knox Gordon Esq—sworn.

M$^{r}$ Phepoe went to America in the same Ship with him from London. Knew very little of him before that time. Believes he had spent his fortune before he went out. He was admitted to the Bar as soon as he arrived there. He got but little at first but before the King's Gov$^{t}$ was overturned he got as much business as anybody. He supposes that M$^{r}$ Phepoe made about £900 or £1000 a Y$^{r}$. The King's Courts were shut in 1775 but he continued to act in the rebel Courts. M$^{r}$ Phepoe mention'd to him that he had an offer to be sent to their Assembly & asked his Opinion about it. He says that some time before he had suspicions of M$^{r}$ Phepoe's loyalty & he wished to talk with him upon the Subject. But he found him Loyal. M$^{r}$ Phepoe sign'd the Association which he was sorry for. The King's Gov$^{t}$ had not left the Province in 1775 when M$^{r}$ Phepoe mention'd his Intention to him. He would not have advised him to become a Member of the rebel Assembly if he had thought it was necessary

[1] Major-General James Patteson was made Commandant of Charlestown on its capture by the British in 1780.

for him to take an Oath of fidelity to the States. He thinks he did not give him advice so late as 1777 to go into their Assembly And thinks in such a Situation as the Country was in in 1777 He should not have given him that Advice. He believes he was always consider'd as well inclined to the British Gov[t] by the Assembly.

Tho[s] Burke—sworn.

Lives at Charlestown. Has known M[r] Phepoe these ten Years their Acquaintance commenced at Charlestown. Does not choose to answer whether M[r] Phepoe took part with Great Britain or America. He believes M[r] Phepoe's property has been confiscated but wishes to avoid saying whether he thinks it will be enforced or not. No Answer. He left M[r] Burke his Attorney in 1782 in the Management of all his Concerns. He speaks to the House for which he gave £1500 & he sold it for £1100. M[r] Burke says he has a very good Opinion of M[r] Phepoe & believes he was a Loyalist at all times—afterwards corrects himself & says *after the reduction of Charlestown.* This Man is a Subject of the States of America.

Lauchlan Macintosh—sworn.

He lived at Charlestown & left it in 1778. He is a Lieut[t] on half pay. He knew M[r] Phepoe when he first came there. He does not recollect M[r] Phepoe being a Member of the Assembly. He sold some land to M[r] Phepoe in 1778. He paid him £1500 Cur. for it. Money was then depreciated. Being asked whether he sold his property to a Loyalist or a Rebel He says he thinks no Loyalist could buy his property. His opinion of M[r] Phepoe has alter'd. When he went there he thought him a Loyalist when he staid longer than he did he thought otherwise. He now thinks him loyal again.

Doct[r] Fife—sworn.

Has known M[r] Phepoe ever since he went to America. Looks upon him as a Loyalist. He did everything at the beginning of the troubles that he could. He did not know he had taken the Oaths to the American States at that time. He knew he was a Member of the Assembly. He told him that he went into the Assembly to serve Great Britain. He believes during the whole time that he was a Member of the Assembly he was a friend to the british Gov[t] And when he came over to the British Troops he believes he did it upon principle.

Edw[d] Savage Esq—sworn.

Knows M[r] Phepoe. He behaved very well after he join'd the British. Being asked what his opinion of M[r] Phepoe's loyalty is he says it is hard to form an Opinion of that. He believes if Interest had been out of the way that his wishes were for Great Britain. He believes M[r] Phepoe was the most obnoxious Man to the new State. With respect to his profession he says he is sure he made more than M[r] Johnson about 8 or £900.

Rev[d] James Stewart—sworn.

Has known M[r] Phepoe about ten Y[rs]. Knew him in 1775 1776 & 1777. Did not know he was a Member of the Rebel Assembly. He consider'd him as rather a friend to this Country than otherwise tho' he yielded. Believes he always wished that this Country might get the better. In 1777 The Witness was persecuted & he employ'd Mr Phepoe & he took neither fee nor reward And he believes he did it in general to Loyalists. He offer'd Money to Mr Phepoe for it but he refused it.

Mrs Fortune (Wife of Coll Fortune) sworn. 12th May 1784.

She knew Mr Phepoe at Charlestown in the Year 1777. Believes he was then a Member of the Assembly. Speaks of a piece of service that Mr Phepoe did to her when the Rebels took almost all she had. And this she says he did as she believes for no other reason but to befriend her & Coll Fortune because they were Loyalists. He was at this time called the *Tory* Lawyer. She desired him to give her his Advice in writing but he declined it saying that if he did it & was found out he should run a risque of being hanged.

Doctr Saffory—sworn.

Has known Mr Phepoe about 3 Years after the Capitulation of Charles Town. He took part with the British & was more active than most others were. He render'd every service in his power to the British Govt.

Lord Cornwallis—sworn. 22d May 1784.

He is called by the Board to speak to the Loyalty of Mr Phepoe.

Mr Phepoe was at Charlestown at the time of the Surrender. He believes he was favorable to the Loyalists but he acted under the Rebel Govt And after the time of surrendering himself he conducted himself very well. Says that the Proclamations issued by him & other Commanding Officers held out great encouragement to the Loyalists to come in & so much so that they distress'd him to know how to act when he was in the back Country.

## Memorial of the Revd Mr Clarke [1]

Determin'd the 12th of May 1785.

Revd Wm Clarke—the Claimant—sworn. 12th of May 1784.

He swears in general terms that to the best of his Judgment every word of his Memorial is true. He had the Living of Dedham which in the whole was worth £50 a Year. He had besides £20 a Yr from the Society for propagating the Gospel which still continues. His Living for life if the troubles had not happen'd.

A meritorious Loyalist.

N.B. The Memorial contains an Acct of very loyal & meritorious Conduct & great sufferings & persecution in Consequence of it. He has almost lost the use of his Speech by the very severe Confinement which he underwent.

He says that he lost in the whole of personal Estate about £200 S. part of

£120 0s. 0d.
Debts £70.

[1] The Rev. W. Clarke died in 1815. His memorial (P. R. O., A. O. 13, Bundle 73) states that 'he continued peaceably till May 1777, when on account of recommending a distressed loyalist (who had been almost murdered and drove out of the town of Dedham by a mob) to the humanity of a gentleman of another county, and at the same time harbouring another gentleman whom the mob had drove out of Boston, he became himself subject to that merciless rabble.' He was tried at Boston on June 9 and would have been acquitted had he been willing to renounce his allegiance. He was condemned to be transported as a felon to the West Indies and sent on board a guardship, where he was kept a year. The close confinement and the unhealthy surroundings affected his lungs so as almost to deprive him of speech; whilst a tendency to deafness was much aggravated by his treatment. On being released in 1778, he embarked upon a British transport.

Living £50 a Yr. this being a Bond. He is desired to say what he lost exclusive of the Bond & he says about £120 or £130 S.

His father died in 1768. Mr Clarke was driven away from America because he would not give his Consent to American Independence. He was tried & condemn'd to Transportation & was imprison'd closely for 10 Weeks. His treatment & persecution were the Occasion of his present Infirmities.

Bounty £60 a Yr. He receives £60 a Year from the Treasury from the 10th of Octr 1782 And now continues to receive it. He likewise receives £20 a Yr from the Society for propagating the Gospel. But he has no Authority for saying that this will continue.

Revd Mr Peters—sworn.

Has known Mr Clarke by Character from the time he went into Orders & personally from 1772. Knows that he had the Living of Dedham. He knows that Mr Clarke's Character was a very good one & has always heard that he was a staunch Loyalist. In 1772 he was deaf but was able to perform Duty extremely well but his Infirmities were not like what they are now. He has heard even from the Rebels themselves that he was very ill treated. He is a single Man now. He had one Child & a Wife but they are both dead. They died in Rhode Island. Believes the Living is moderately stated.

Revd George Bisset—sworn.

Lived at Rhode Island was Rector of Trinity Church. Has known Mr Clarke from 1771 or 1772. He was settled & had the Living of Dedham does not know the value of it but knows that he had £20 a Yr from the Society.

He believes he took the side of Govt remembers his being brought to Rhode Island to be transported. His voice was extremely good & strong when he first knew him but when he saw him in 1778 He had almost lost it & has always understood that he lost it in Consequence of ill treatment from the Rebels.

## Memorial of John Andrews

Determin'd the 13th of May 1784.

13th May 1784.

John Andrews—the Claimant—sworn.

Was born in New Jersey. In 1778 he carried an Express from Sir Robt Pigot [1] to Lord Howe & Sir Henry Clinton (produces a Certificate from Sir Robt Pigot & a Letter from Sir Henry Clinton which proves it). In consequence of this he was tried & banished. He has done other Services but Govt always paid him for them. He came 4 Months ago from New York. He believes he is to have £40 from the Treasury but he has not recd it & it appears to be so but the Report is not yet made to the Lords of the Treasury.

A Zealous & active Loyalist.

He literally has no Allowance at this moment from the Treasury but upon looking into the books &c from Whitehall It is found that £40 was intended to be recommended to him in full & instead of any Annual Allowance & for the purpose of carrying him out again to America.

Bounty £40 in full.

[1] See note 1 on p. 94.

## Memorial of Alexander Stenhouse

Determin'd the 24th of May 1784.

Alexander Stenhouse—the Claimant—sworn. 13th May 1784.

Is a Native of Scotland & went to America in 1756 & settled in 1759 as a Physician in Baltimore County & in Baltimore town in 1764. He remain'd there till 1776 when he was obliged to come away. He avow'd his principles from the earliest moment of the troubles. In that part of the Country all those who would not join the Insurgents were consider'd as Enemies & those who dealt with them before refused to continue to deal with them. He was abused as a Tory & sent to Coventry. He left Baltimore in April 1776 & came to Philadelphia for the purpose of embarking for Engd & he came to Lisbon in July 1776 & from thence to Engd. If he had held other principles he might have remain'd in good business.

A Zealous Loyalist.

Bounty £80 a Yr.

George Chalmers Esq—sworn.

Knew Mr Stenhouse at Baltimore Town in Maryland from 1768 or 1769. He was then established in business. The Witness lived in Baltimore Town at the Commencement of the troubles. He believes that Dr Stenhouse was uniformly loyal from the first & he applied to the Witness for arguments. Dr Stenhouse was much respected. He recd no Insults whilst the Witness staid. He believes he lost all his practice by the part which he took. He believes he took his part from principle & mentions a reason for thinking so. He does not know anything particular about the Lot but knew he had a Claim & states the Nature of the Claim. He says whenever Land escheats to the proprietors for want of heirs the first Discoverer has a sort of preference. Dr Stenhouse was in very handsome practice but can't say what he might gain by it. He thinks however that he might get in the whole by his business £600 Ster. a Yr. And he thinks his business would have continued. He was consider'd a very able Man in his profession.

## Memorial of Willm McQueen

Determin'd the 24th of May 1784.

Willm McQueen—the Claimant—sworn. May the 15th 1784.

He went from Scotland to America in 1773. When the troubles broke out He was on his own plantation in North Carolina. He first join'd the King's standard in Jany 1776 at Cross Creek. Swears in general to the truth of his memorial. He took up Arms & was in a Company of Volunteer Horse. Had no pay. Served about a Month. In Augt 1780 He got a Captn's Commission from Lord Cornwallis (the Commn lost with his other papers). He was in two or three Engagements & served in the ranks after the Year 1780. He was sent with dispatches from Genl Craig [1] to Lord Cornwallis was taken prisoner tried & condemn'd. He made his escape in the night. He came afterwards to Charlestown & staid till it was evacuated & then came round by Jamaica to Engd. He has an Allowance of £30 a Yr which he has recd from Mics last. He had about 8 Gās for carrying the Dispatches to Lord Cornwallis. He was Inspector of Refugees at Charlestown with a Salary of 5*s*. a Day which he recd for one Month.

An Active & Zealous Loyalist & bore Arms.

Bounty £30 a Yr.

[1] Sir James Craig, *b.* 1748, *d.* 1812. He is in *Dict. of Nat. Biography*. As Governor of Canada (1807–11) he took an active part against the French Canadians.

## Memorial of George Henry Blenkinhorn

Determin'd the 24th of May 1784.

George Henry Blenkinhorn—the Claimant—sworn. 15th May 1784.

A Loyalist.

Was born in Germany & came to America in 1762. He went then to Philadelphia. He went in 1768 to the Congarees & when the rebellion broke out he was in Charlestown. He took part with the British. He went with the rebels to take care of the Waggons when they went to Savannah. He never took the Oaths. When Sir Henry Clinton & Lord Cornwallis took Charlestown he join'd the British & served in Captn Phepoe's Company. They tender'd him the Oaths but he was sick & they excused him.

Bounty £40 a Yr.

## Memorial of Thos Ryan

Determin'd 28th of May 1784.

Thos Ryan—the Claimant—sworn. 15th May 1784.

A Loyalist.

He is an Irishman & went to America 14 Years before the troubles. He lived at New York when the troubles broke out. He was a Car Man. When the Rebellion broke out he refused to sign the Association & they threaten'd to take his Life &c. And he was obliged to absent himself for two Years untill the British Troops took the place. He came to Engd 5 Years ago last Michaelmas. He left New York on acct of his Health he never bore Arms.

## Memorial of Murdoch McDonald

Determin'd the 28th of May 1784.

Murdoch McDonald—the Claimant—sworn. May the 18th 1784.

A Loyalist & bore Arms.

Born in Scotland. Went to America to North Carolina in 1774. He found America in rebellion. He join'd the British in 1776 as a Volunteer & bore Arms. In about 20 Days after he join'd he was taken Prisoner at the Moor's Creek Bridge. He was kept Prisoner for one Day & then suffer'd to go home.

A Loyalist and bore Arms.

The Rebels tender'd him the Oaths but he never took them. He lived quietly in the province from 1776 to 1781. When Lord Cornwallis came again in 1781 He join'd him again at Cross Creek. Colonel Ray [1] who was a Coll in their County called upon him to join & he did & he recd pay as a private. He recd 18 Dollars in Charlestown for 6 Months pay. He staid at Charlestown till the Evacuation & did Duty as a Soldier. He was then order'd by Genl Leslie to come to Engd who gave him a passage home. He could not return to his plantation because the rebels had taken it. He believes the Plantation is confiscated. He carried out with him £400.

Bounty £20 a Yr.

He receives £20 a Yr from the Treasury from the 5th of Jany 1783.

## Memorial of Kenneth Hewart

Determin'd the 28th of May 1784.

Kenneth Hewart—the Claimant—sworn. May the 18th 1784.

He is a Native of Scotland & landed in America in Novr 1775. He landed at Cape Fear. He had heard of the rebellion & the battle of Bunkers Hill. The Govr of the Province could not remain in it (Govr Martin) when he got there

[1] In September 1781 Duncan Ray or Rae was appointed Colonel of the Loyal Militia of the Highland district of Anson County (*Hist. MSS. Comm., Am. MSS. in R. Inst.*, vol. ii, p. 332).

& he was then on board a Ship. He swore the Claimant & many others that they would take up Arms if wanted. He proposed the Oath to them & would not let them land unless they took the Oath. He went to settle in it. The Rebels never tender'd him any Oath. He settled in Bladen County. In the February following he took up Arms & went to the Moors Creek. He had a Lieut$^{ts}$ Comm$^{n}$ from Gov$^{r}$ Martin under Col$^{l}$ M$^{c}$Donald. He was a very few days in Arms but he was taken Prisoner 2$^{d}$ of March & confined for six Months. He was very ill treated. He has rec$^{d}$ half pay from feb$^{y}$ 1776 to Dec$^{r}$ 1778. He never served without pay from 1776 to 1780. He pass'd his time very uncomfortably hiding himself to prevent a Discovery & he never lay three nights in a place. He rec$^{d}$ the half pay of a Capt$^{n}$ from 1781 from Gen$^{l}$ Leslie & continued to receive it till the Evacuation of Charlestown. He then came to Eng$^{d}$ & applied to the Treasury & rec$^{d}$ £50 a Y$^{r}$ from the 5$^{th}$ of Jan$^{y}$ 1783. He rec$^{d}$ a Wound in his Head when he was under a flag of Truce.

A Loyalist and bore Arms.

Bounty £50 a Y$^{r}$.

### Memorial of Enoch Hawkesworth

Determin'd the 28$^{th}$ of May 1784.

Enoch Hawkesworth—the Claimant—sworn. 18$^{th}$ May 1784.

He is a Native of England & went to America in 1764 as a Schoolmaster & resided at Alexandria in Virginia.

He kept a Store & there he lived at the Commencement of the troubles. He constantly took the part of Gov$^{t}$. In 1776 he apprehended he should be molested & he sold up his Goods & went to Baltimore.

A Loyalist. Did not bear Arms.

Swears in general terms to the truth of his Memorial. He came to England in 1776 & applied to the Treasury & obtained the Sum of £20. He makes no Claim for any Loss but the Loss of his Situation. He can't tell how much he gain'd a Year but he was in a comfortable Situation. He thinks he may say he gain'd £50 a Year S.

Bounty £20 in full.

The Claim$^{t}$ does not appear to have lost any property. The whole Claim being for the Loss of his Situation in trade which he says brought him in £50 a Year.

A Certificate produced & read from the Rev$^{d}$ M$^{r}$ Boucher [1] to Loyalty & general Character in which he says that M$^{r}$ Hawkesworth was in tolerable good business & that he lived in the Country with reputation.

M$^{r}$ Hawkesworth calls no Witnesses.

### Memorial of Vincent Peerse Ashfield

Determin'd the 29$^{th}$ of May 1784.

Vincent Peerse Ashfield—the Claimant—sworn. May the 20$^{th}$ 1784.

Was born at New York & was a Merch$^{t}$ there at the Commencement of the troubles & took the part of Gov$^{t}$. He was first molested in May 1776 in consequence of his refusing to sign an Association. He was imprison'd & kept near 7 weeks. He was releas'd upon signing a paper not to take up Arms ag$^{t}$ them. He went to join the British soon after the British troops landed on Long Island & he went with them to New York. He did not bear Arms with them. When he got to New York he was in the Militia & produces a Commission of Capt$^{n}$ in an associated Corps sign'd by Gen$^{l}$ Pattison. He served from 1780 to 1783. He came to Scotland in June last.

A Zealous Loyalist.

[1] The Rev. Jonathan Boucher, most stalwart of Loyalist divines (see *Notes and Queries*, 3rd ser., ix; 5th ser., i, v, vi, and ix; and Tyler, op. cit., vol. i, pp. 316–28). Boucher was the author of *A View of the Causes and Consequences of the Am. Rev. in Thirteen Discourses preached in America, 1763–75*, 1797.

*Determin'd the 5$^{th}$ of June 1784.*

## Memorial of Colonel James Cotton [1]

21$^{st}$ May 1784.

Colonel James Cotton—the Claimant—sworn.

*A Loyalist & bore Arms.*

*But took an Oath that he would not oppose the American Gov$^{t}$.*

Is an American was born in New Eng$^{d}$ was settled in Anson County No. Carolina when the troubles broke out. He then held several Offices viz. Public Register Surveyor of Lands Deputy Collector of Quit rents Ranger of the Woods & Wastes & keeper of the land Office for the back Counties. Value of the Register's Office £40 S. a Y$^{r}$ Surveyor of lands £200 a Y$^{r}$ this was during pleasure. Collector of Quit rents for which he had 5 per Cent on the Money collected. Appointed by the Receiver Gen$^{l}$ during pleasure £50 a Y$^{r}$ Ranger of the Woods & Wastes by Comm$^{n}$ from the Gov$^{r}$. This was during pleasure. Values it as about £30. Keeper of the Land Office £60 a Y$^{r}$. Appointment from the Secretary of the province & during pleasure. He held all these offices together at the time of the rebellion.

In May 1775 He refused to sign the Association. He swears to the whole of the Narrative of his Sufferings. In Aug$^{t}$ 1775 He was releas'd out of prison upon taking an Oath to the Congress the purport of which Oath was that he would not oppose them. He never took any other Oath. He rais'd 500 Men in feb$^{y}$ 1776. He was secreted from Aug$^{t}$ to the feb$^{y}$ following. He has lost Everything. All his Lands have been confiscated & sold. He had a Civil Appointment at New York with a Salary of 5*s*. a Day. He gave it up the 10$^{th}$ of Dec$^{r}$ 1776 & came to Eng$^{d}$ in the spring of 1777.

*Former Bounty £200 a Y$^{r}$. Present Bounty £150 a Y$^{r}$.*

He has an Allowance from the Treasury. It was £200 a Y$^{r}$ till last Year & then it was reduced to £150 a Y$^{r}$ which he now receives.

He was Lieut$^{t}$ Col$^{l}$ of the Militia of Anson County before the troubles. After the troubles he acted as Lieut$^{t}$ Col$^{l}$ at Moor's Bridge. But he only rec$^{d}$ the pay of a Capt$^{n}$ & he rec$^{d}$ that for 320 Days.

*Determin'd the 29$^{th}$ of May 1784.*

## Memorial of Walter Cunningham

25$^{th}$ May 1784.

Walter Cunningham—the Claimant—sworn.

*rejected being removeable at pleasure.*

*A Zealous & meritorious Loyalist.*

*bore Arms & render'd Services to Gov$^{t}$.*

Is a Native of Ireland landed at Wilmington the latter end of 1772. He went out to follow the business of a Surveyor to which he was bred. In 1773 he was appointed Deputy Surveyor for Anson County to the Surveyor Gen$^{l}$. He had no Salary. He held this till 1775. He states this as a Loss of 100 a Year. He held this during M$^{r}$ Palmer's pleasure.

In July 1775 He carried an Express from the Loyalists to Gov$^{r}$ Martin. He was fix'd upon on Acc$^{t}$ of his Loyalty. He was taken on his return & they took Gov$^{r}$ Martin's answer from him. In feb$^{y}$ 1776 Gov$^{r}$ Martin appointed him to a Company in the associated Corps of Loyalists. Was in the Action at Moors Bridge. He was taken Prisoner after & was kept Prisoner for more than two Years. He produces a Commission sign'd by Lord Rawdon of an Ensign in which

[1] Governor Martin wrote to Lord G. Germain on September 15, 1777: 'A Mr. James Cotton who went from home some time ago will probably have waited on your Lordship. I therefore think it necessary to mention him as a person who had all the merit set forth in my certificate; which, in a man of rather vulgar life and character, and especially in a native of New England, I cannot but estimate very highly' (*N. Carolina Records*, vol. xi, p. 768).

he continued till feb$^{y}$ 1784 when it was reduced. He receives half pay but on acc$^{t}$ of his Distresses he has been obliged to sell his Commission.

## Memorial of John Ferdinand Dalziel Smith [1]

Determin'd the 21$^{st}$ of June 1784.

John Ferdinand Dalziel Smith—the Claimant—sworn. 31$^{st}$ May 1784.

Is a Native of this Country & went from Scotland to America in 1763 or 1764. He sail'd from London & went out with a view to settle in that Country. He went to Virginia. He did not carry out much property. He was bred to Physic & was at one of the Scotch Universities. He went out with the Intention of practising. He landed first in Virginia. He did not fix himself till the Year 1768. He lived in New Kent County in Virginia & practised Physic there. He remain'd there till 1769 1770 or 1771. He fix'd in Charles County & purchased an Estate at each place. When the troubles broke out he averages his gains in his profession about £600 S. Believes he can prove this. He practised so low as Williamsburg. Being asked as to the part he took to his Sufferings services & exertions He says as he might not be able to recollect the whole he refers to his own book (Smyths Tour thro' America &c) lately published Vol. 2 from Page 188 to the End & says it contains a true Acc$^{t}$ & Narrative of what happen'd to him. They never tender'd the Oaths to him. He came to Eng$^{d}$ in the beginning of the Year 1780. He came on Acc$^{t}$ of his Health. He rais'd a Corps of 185 Men or thereabouts in the Y$^{r}$ 1777 called the royal Hunters. He raised them at his own Expence. He gives a long Detail of his preferring a Charge ag$^{t}$ Colonel Simcoe.[2] In May 1779 he rec$^{d}$ a Letter from Sir Henry Clinton in which he dismiss'd him from y$^{e}$ Army. The Charges made by Capt$^{n}$ Smith upon Col$^{l}$ Simcoe were found by a Court Martial to be false. He claims for the bounty Money paid to 185 Men £971 5*s*. 0*d*. & says it ought to have been paid to him by Capt$^{n}$ Mackenzie. He was appointed a Capt$^{n}$ of the Queens rangers in 1777 by Sir W$^{m}$ Howe. He continued so till about May 1779. His dismission was by Letter which was not in general Orders but written to him by Colonel Rooke.[3] He repeatedly applied for a Court Martial to sit upon him but without obtaining it & then he came to Eng$^{d}$ but not till after he saw it was in vain to expect a Court Martial.

Determin'd to be a fraudulent Claim.

John Ferdinand Dalziel Smith—the Claimant—sworn. June the 1$^{st}$ 1784.

The Evidence of yesterday was read over to him & he confirms it with some little Alteration. He thinks the Value which he has put upon his Lands to be what they were worth to him but he does not presume to claim that Value from this Country. Being desired for certain reasons to answer this Question with great Caution whether he was really & bonâ fide the purchaser of the lands in Maryland or whether he was not only the Tenant to M$^{r}$ Balthrope M$^{r}$ Ratcliffe or M$^{r}$ Smoote He swears positively that he was *not the Tenant but the Purchaser*.

[1] See Additional Notes, p. 143.

[2] John Graves Simcoe, *b.* 1752, *d.* 1806. As first Lieutenant-Governor of Upper Canada he placed himself in opposition to Lord Dorchester. There is a Life of him in the 'Makers of Canada' series by Duncan C. Scott.

[3] Major Rooke was Deputy Inspector-General of Provincial Forces.

He says he was a Storekeeper & Physician at this time. Yet he says the profession of Physic is as liberal there as it is here.

N.B. Some very material Information having been given to the Board that M^r Smith had deceiv'd them & that the persons were ready to come to verify the Charges ag^t him He was very strictly interrogated to all those points & the following is the substance of his Examination in which he will be found substantially to contradict everything which he had before said.

He swears that he went to America in 1763 & admits that he went to Patrick Copland & that he was employ'd by him at a Salary of £25 a Year believes for 3 Years He did not pay for his passage. M^r Copland was to pay for his passage. He does not recollect the Note given for his passage Money. He admits that he was arrested & bail'd by Rob^t Nelson who must have paid the Debt. He left M^r Copland in a few Months & believes he left him because he fail'd. He was then in great Distress & he went to live with M^r Thompson. He lived with him & did business for him. Believes it was in the Year 1764. He lived a very short time with him. He went afterwards to live with D^r Schultzer. He assisted him in his business & was Tutor to his Children. He does not recollect how long he staid with him. He went afterwards to live with Mr. Black & was a sort of Superintend^t & managed all his business for a Compensation. He cannot say how long but he believes he managed his business till 1768. He then was not in great business as a Physician. He lived at Chaptico & boarded with M^r Mills. He had a Shop & Medicines at Chaptico. He quitted M^r Mills's House voluntarily. He swears that he never boarded with M^r Barber afterwards or had any dispute with him about Board. He was between 1770 & 1773 upon Potomack river & He was at Allan's fresh in 1771 or 1772.

Being asked upon his Oath (& desired to answer the Question with great Caution) whether he did really & bonâ fide purchase the Lands in Maryland of Balthrope & Smoot or whether he only rented them. And he was informed that the reason of the Question being put to him was that the Board had been informed that he only rented it & that many persons were ready to swear it. He astonished the Board by appearing unwilling to give a direct Answer to the Question & desired a few Days time to be given to him. The Board were surprized at the request & press'd him to answer it being a very plain Question. However upon his refusing to do it & wishing not to hurry him (as they apprehended it might be necessary to make a special report on this Case) they gave him a few Days & required him to attend again on Monday the 7^th of June.

John Ferdinand Dalziel Smyth—the Claimant—sworn. 7^th June 1784.

Before he was sworn he called me out into a private room & said he was extremely hurt with the Questions which had been put to him the last Day on which he attended & confess'd that he had been very disingenuous in the Acc^t he had given of his property & that he was willing to tell the truth but ashamed to appear again before the board. However he was made sensible of the necessity of immediately stating the real truth to the Board And he was accordingly called in again & swears as follows.

He explains the Acc^t which he had given of the Maryland property & admits that tho' he bought it of one Balthrope it was a disputed title & Balthrope was not in possession. He says he gave Balthrope a Bond for his Chance. But he admits that he then took a Lease from M^r Smoot who was in possession for 3 Years & that he was to pay M^r Smoot £100 a Y^r. And he did pay him £100 a Y^r for two of the tracts. Smoot was Trustee for a Minor & he says he did not mean to contest it till the Minor came of Age. This relates to Bowles's purchase & St. George's & the other Tract was under the same Circumstances & belonging to one Ratcliff & Smoot. He took a Lease of these two & paid a rent of £11 a Y^r to each.

He admits likewise that he misstated his property in Virginia. He says he had it by Deed of Gift from Jane Apperson whose Dau^r M^r Smith was going to marry. But the Dau^r was very angry with him soon afterwards & wrote to him to say that she heard he was connected with her Mother. He wrote back to the Dau^r to express his surprize at her making such a Charge when she knew he had been connected with herself. He shew'd this Letter before he sent it to some of his friends & the Dau^r proceeded ag^t him for a Libel & a Judgment was had ag^t him for £2500. He says he then gave back this Estate Stock &c to M^rs Apperson to avoid its being liable to the Judgment. The Deed of Gift by which he claims this Estate he believes was not register'd. He admits that he lived in the same House with M^rs Apperson & her Dau^r. He says he gave the Estate back to her when he came away & thinks it very probable that she may be in possession of it at this moment. In short he proved that the first Acc^t which he had given both of the Maryland & the Virginia property was perfectly false & that he was the Owner of neither of them. Being asked how much he thinks himself worth in America after all his Debts paid & the Judgment satisfied He says he cannot say.

Major Grymes—sworn. Witnesses for M^r Smith 3^d June 1784.

Has known M^r Smith some short time before the Evacuation of Philadelphia. He was attached to the Queens Rangers & brought more Men than the Reg^t consisted of. Major Grymes commanded the Reg^t. He did not do Duty in the Reg^t whilst he staid in America. He was on the recruiting service. The bounty Money was originally 8 Dollars & afterwards 5 Dollars. His Loyalty is undoubted & his Sufferings great. When he join'd the Queens rangers He had two very fine Horses worth 100 or 200 Gās. The Certificate given by Peyton Randolph is shewn to Major Grymes. He says it is the handwriting of his Uncle but yet he cannot account for the Certificate because he believes M^r Randolph never heard of M^r Smyth in America. Major Grymes lived from June 1766 to the time of the rebellion in Williamsburgh & notwithstanding he had at different times lived in various parts of Virginia he never heard of M^r Smyth till the Y^r 1776 And he thinks he knew almost all the people of property & consequence in the province. He says he never knew anything of M^r Smyth but what [was] to his Advantage. Major Grymes was one of the Committee who enquired into the property of the Claimants from the province of Virginia & he says that M^r Smyth never came before them to make any Claim.

Alex^r Leybourn—sworn.

He first knew Capt^n Smyth in 1773 but he had a very slight Acquaintance with him. He then lived on Potomack River. He was called D^r Smith. The Witness traded up & down the river & seeing a fine plantation he stopp'd & asked whose it was & was told it was D^r Smyth's but does not know that it was his own property. He did not know Smoot & Balthrope. He saw a few Horses & a good Stock of Wheat. He has heard that he was a Loyalist & that he was a Physician. He was in prison with him at Philadelphia but did not see him tho' he was in the same prison with him. He admits that he knew very little of him.

The Board having now heard the whole of M^r Smyth's Case thought it incumbent upon them to call the following Witnesses to contradict him.

John Anderson—sworn. 9^th June 1784.

He formerly lived in Maryland & was a Merch^t. He knew him first in 1774. He lived in Cha^t County Maryland & he practis'd Physic but he had no great business & he lost it all almost in 1775 or 1776 And thinks he did not lose it on Acc^t of Loyalty. He says he rented the plantation he had. He thinks he began to rent it about 1774. He gave Security for the Rent. M^r Philpot was one of the Securities. He left it in the end of 1775 or beginning of 1776. He believes the reason of his leaving it was on acc^t of his Circumstances & not on acc^t of the troubles. When Smyth went away Philpot went after him & got some Assignment or Security from him & was in the possession of the Land. He had no Negroes of his own. He rented some with the Land. He left on the plantation some Stock & young Horses. He began to raise Horses & he bought a fine old Stallion & thinks he might have had him for 30 Gãs. He was 25 Years old. He thinks that M^r Smyth's Horses could not be worth more (including smiling Tom) than £300. He believes M^r Philpot kept them as his own property. He never saw any paper or Assignment between M^r Smith & M^r Philpot. He was supposed to be a Man worth nothing. M^r Anderson should not think the Plantation could grow so much as he states in the Schedule N^o 6. He thinks M^r Philpot took possession of this as well as the Horses. Believes he had the whole. Thinks the rent might be £100 a Y^r. He did not know any person whose Name was Balthrope. Does not know of any Dispute about Smoot's title to the Land. He knew that there was a Lawsuit between him & M^r Barber who lived in S^t Mary's County about board. He was in Court when it was tried. He says his Character was such in the Country that he would not have trusted him for a Shilling. Believes he was uniformly loyal. He is a Merch^t in London. Lives in M^r Oswald's House & is his Nephew.

Robert Nelson—sworn.

Formerly of Halifax in N^o Carolina. He knew M^r Smith more than 20 Years ago. When he first came to America He was not grown up. He came to one Peter Copland as an Assistant in the Store. Believes he was bound by Indre. He did not stay more than two Years. When he went away He knows he gave Copland a Note (as he was his Security) for about £20 & as he understood it was to defray the Expence of his coming to America. He was arrested in his presence after he left Copland & he was Bail for him. The Witness paid about £10 of the Money And the rest remains unpaid. He went from Copland to Mr Thompson to live with him as an Assistant in his Store. He believes he did not stay more than ½ a Year. He went afterwards to Dr Schultzer who lived in Halifax as Tutor to his Children. He never practised Physic to his knowledge whilst he was with Dr Schultzer. He thinks he was not a Year with Dr Schultzer. He then went to live with Mr Black in Bute County[1] who was a Mercht. & Smyth was his Assistant Storekeeper. He heard about two Years after that he practis'd Physic & was commenced Doctor & it was a joke amongst the Neighbors. Being asked as to the Identity He says he is sure of it & that in a Conversation with him he admitted it. He thinks that Smyth was very ill used in the matter between Copland & him.

Uriah Forest—sworn.

Now an American Mercht in London but formerly of St Mary's County. He first knew Mr Smith in 1772 or 1773 when he first came into the County. He then took Lodgings at Chaptico. He came on Horseback & believes he had no property but his Horse & his Saddle bags unless he had Money. He understood that he came to practise Physic. He believes he did not get much by his Profession. He believes he did not stay long. He thinks he removed to Mr Barber's who lived a few miles from Mr Mills. He believes he lived about six or 12 Months with Mr Barber. They had disputes when they separated they both brought Actions agt each other. Barber brought an Action for board & Smith brought an Action for Medicines &c. It was determin'd agt Mr Smith. He believes Philpot & Hop were Bail for him upon some Occasion or other. There was a report that Hop one of the Bail pursued him into Virginia to get Money &c from him And the report was that he did get some Horses from him. Being asked whether he ran away He says he does not know what to call it. He believes & has heard that he went away without paying the Demands upon him. He says he was not looked upon as a Man of Substance. He speaks of Augt 1775 & says he could not be worth much Money. The Witness was appointed a Commissioner of the confiscated Estates & was in the Assembly of Maryland. He says he never confiscated any property belonging to Mr Smith & says if he had had any he must have known it. Has frequently heard that he rented a farm of Mr Smoot.

He thinks Smiling Tom (he knew the Horse) did belong to him. He was kept as a Stallion & cover'd for 3 Gās a Mare. He speaks clearly to the Loyalty of Mr Smith—this Gentn is a Subject of the American States.

Mr Forest is shewn the Advertisement & says he believes it relates to this Mr Smyth & that the Horse belonged to him.

Thinks Smiling Tom was an old Horse & that he could not be worth more than £50 or £60 Sterling.

The Claimant—sworn again. June the 14th.

He says that he has no further Evidence to produce at present—but leaves a Paper which he says contains an Acct of Debts which he has contracted since the Yr 1779 & says they are still owing. They amount to £99 18s. Sterg.

[1] Virginia. Bute County was not one of the twenty-nine existing in 1720.

Determination.

The Board upon considering this Case were of opinion that the Claim was a fraudulent Claim & that it fell within that Clause of the Act of Par$^{t}$ which takes from him all the benefit of the Act & precludes him from any Compensation.

The Board were likewise of Opinion that in his Evidence he had committed gross & wilful Perjury & reported accordingly to the Treasury.

Determin'd 11$^{th}$ of June 1784.

## Memorial of Benj$^{n}$ Whitcuff

8$^{th}$ June 1784.

Benj$^{n}$ Whitcuff—the Claimant—sworn.

A Loyalist.

Is a Black & was born on Long Island. At the commencement of the Troubles He was a Farmer. He was born a free Man & his father was free. The farm he lived on was his father's. His father join'd the Americans in 1776 & was a Serj$^{t}$ in one of their Regiments. Claim$^{t}$ refused to join them. Says he join'd the British Troops at Staten Island in 1776 or 1777. He was employ'd as a Spy for near two Years by Sir Henry Clinton & receiv'd at different times about 15 Guineas. He was made Prisoner & hanged at Cranbury in the Jerseys. He was hanging three Minutes when a Party of the 5$^{th}$ Reg$^{t}$ came up & cut him down.

Determin'd the 11$^{th}$ of June 1784.

## Memorial of Lieut$^{t}$ Cha$^{s}$ Prince

8$^{th}$ June 1784.

Lieut$^{t}$ Charles Prince—the Claimant—sworn.

A Loyalist & bore Arms as Comm$^{r}$ of Vessels.

Was born in England. Was settled at Charlestown in 1764. He resided there at the Commencement of the troubles as a private Gent$^{n}$ on his half pay as Lieut$^{t}$ of the Navy. Quitted the Country soon after the rebellion began. Was frequently called upon to take part with the Americans but they did not press him or treat him with any disrespect. He quitted Charlestown in the Summer of 1777 would have done so sooner but was prevented by ill health. Says he sold the Stock on his Land. Was taken Prisoner going from Charlestown to S$^{t}$ Augustine.

In 1779 He went to New York & offer'd his services to Sir George Collier.[1] Was appointed to the Command of the Scourge Galley in the May of that Year & taken at the time Sir Ja$^{s}$ Wallace was captured.

Bounty £60 a Y$^{r}$.

Had an appointment afterw$^{ds}$ at S$^{t}$ Augustine of Commissary of Naval Stores from Admiral Digby[2] & towards the Conclusion of the War He was appointed Commissary of Prisoners at New York.

Property.

Disallowed the Damage being done by the British Troops.

Says he was possess'd in right of his Wife of two Dwelling Houses & other Buildings on Lempriere's ferry & at Princes Point. He married a Dau$^{r}$ of M$^{r}$ Clement Lempriere[3] of Charlestown. Makes no Claim for the Land as it remains unmolested. But he does for the Houses & buildings to the amount

[1] *b.* 1738, *d.* 1795. Is in *Dict. of Nat. Biography*.

[2] Robert Digby, *b.* 1732, *d.* 1815, was Commander-in-chief in North America in 1781. He is in *Dict. of Nat. Biography*.

[3] Mr. Clement Lemprière had served in the British navy, but adhered to the American cause. After capturing the gunpowder off the bar of St. Augustine, he received the command of a ship (McCrady, *S. Car. in the Rev., 1775–80*, p. 82).

of £1500 S. which were destroy'd by the Kings Troops in 1782. See a Valuation which he produces. He married his Wife in 1763. His father in Law died in 1779. Claims the Loss of a ferry from Lempriere's plantation to Charlestown at the rate of £150 a Y^r^ from 1782 to the present time the Buildings were destroy'd in 1782.

Henry Reeves—sworn.

Late of Charlestown. Knew the Claim^t^ at the Commencement of the troubles. He then lived on the Plantation at Princes Point which he understood was the property of his Wife. He says there were two Dwelling Houses besides other Buildings. He was not there when they were destroy'd in the Year 1782 & does not know who destroy'd them. He thinks the Houses on the plantations exclusive of the Outbuildings might have been worth from 6 to 800 Ster^g^.

Major Manson—sworn.

Late of Charlestown. He has known the Claimant many Years & says he understood that the property claim'd by M^r^ Prince was given to him at the time he married his Wife by M^r^ Lempriere her father. He is not able to set any Value on the Buildings. He has heard & believes that they were destroy'd by the British Troops at the time mention'd. He speaks very well of the Character &c of M^r^ Prince but knows nothing more about his property.

## Memorial of James Moody [1]

8th June 1784.

Determin'd the 11th of June 1784.

James Moody—the Claimant—sworn.

He is a Native of New Jersey. He was settled in Sussex County New Jersey on the Commencement of the troubles. In April 1777 He quitted his property having refused to take the Oaths to the Americans which render'd him very obnoxious & he then flew to the British Lines taking with him 74 of his Neighbours & friends who all but four enter'd into the King's service. Refers to a printed Pamphlet [2] which he produces & swears that it contains a just & true Acc^t^ of his Loyalty & exertions in behalf of the British Gov^t^.

A most distinguish'd Loyalist & render'd essential Services to the British Gov^t^ frequently at the hazard of his Life.

General Robertson—sworn.

Knew M^r^ Moody at New York. Says that he gave frequent proofs of his sincere Attachment to this Country & in his Exertions ran eminent risque of his Life. The General mentions a variety of Circumstances relative to M^r^ Moody's zeal for the King's service. Has read his Pamphlet & believes that it contains a just Acc^t^ of his Loyalty & Services.

Governor Franklyn—sworn.

Knew M^r^ Moody at New York in 1778. He was then looked upon as a very meritorious Man & believes that during the War he exerted himself as much as any Man could do for the British Gov^t^. He has read M^r^ Moody's Pamphlet & believes everything therein to be truly stated.

James Moody—the Claimant—called in again.

Says he rais'd 182 Men entirely at his own Expence. The Men receiv'd the King's Bounty but he never rec^d^ any Compensation for the Expence he

[1] See Additional Notes, p. 144. [2] See note on James Moody, p. 144.

had been at except £170 & his Expences amounted to £1500. He expected to have had the appointment of Major in consequence of the Number of Men he rais'd but only had that of Lieut[t] in the New Jersey Brigade in which Situation he continued the whole War. He has now the half pay of a Lieutenant.

Bounty £100 a Y[r].

He has an Allowance from the Treasury of 100 a Y[r] which commenced at Midsummer 1782. He is desired to furnish us with the particulars of his Expences for the public Service.

He claims £1330 for Monies expended in raising Men & other Services.

(Decision of the Board upon this part of the Claim.)

The Board agree to allow the £1330 being satisfied that he expended the whole of his property in rendering material Services to the British Gov[t] & on this Acc[t] they are induced to break their resolution on this Head.

The Board are of Opinion (notwithstanding their Gen[l] resolution to the contrary) that on Acc[t] of his distinguish'd Services this Money ought to be allowed to him as a Loss.

James Moody—the Claimant—sworn. 9[th] of June 1784.

Produces a Statement of his Expenditures for the public Service amounting to £1413 12*s*. Ster[g]. He frequently made Excursions without the Lines.

Says that he means to go to Nova Scotia soon to settle there. Being asked what Quantity of Land he is entitled to He says he is entitled to 600 Acres on acc[t] of the Commission which he held in the Army.

N.B. He is desired by the Board to inform them when he goes in order that they may recommend him to the Gov[r].

Determin'd y[e] 12[th] of June 1784.

## Memorial of Abraham Cuyler[1] Esq.

Abraham Cuyler Esq—the Claimant—sworn. 10[th] June 1784.

A Zealous & active Loyalist bore Arms & render'd Services to the British Gov[t].

A Native of Albany. In Oct[r] 1775 when it was proposed there to send Members to Congress He attended the Meeting held for that purpose & publickly protested ag[t] the Measure. In June 1776 He was seiz'd by a Party of Soldiers & confin'd in the Fort of Albany from where he was removed to Hartford in Connecticut. Produces the order for his removal 14[th] June 1776. Says that he suffer'd himself to sign an Association the purport of which was to procure a redress of Grievances in a Constitutional Way. Was afterwards called upon by the Committee to take an Oath of fidelity to the Americans which he refused. At the commencement of the troubles He was Mayor of the City of Albany & Coroner of the City & County. This was an annual Appointment from the Gov[r] & the emoluments thereof arising from Perquisites were about £150 Cur.

[1] *b*. 1742, *d*. 1810 (Sabine, op. cit., vol. i, p. 355). The King's birthday on June 4, 1776, was ushered in at Albany with rejoicings 'not agreeable to the inhabitants, and in the evening a party assembled with Abraham C. Cuyler at their head and was found carousing and singing "God save the King". The citizens became exasperated, rushed in and seized several of the party and carried them off to gaol' (*New York Col. Docs*., vol. viii, p. 480).

Siebert (*The Amer. Loyalists in the Eastern Seigniories and Townships of the Province of Quebec*, p. 39) writes: 'The most notable of the Loyalist Associates of the Eastern townships was undoubtedly A. Cuyler . . . who, after serving as Inspector of Refugees loyalist in the province of Quebec, became the promoter of a loyalist movement to the island of Cape Breton. . . . He claimed a part of Montreal, but, as this was not available, he was given three thousand six hundred acres elsewhere, and, in addition, he and his two sons received grants as Associates of Farnham in 1798. However, there is reason for believing that the disposable Crown lands in this township were exhausted before Cuyler secured his claim.'

A. Cuyler died in Lower Canada in 1810.

per Ann. Was also Major of the 1st Battn of the Militia of Albany County. In feby or March 1776 He recd a Dispatch from Govr Tryon for Sir Guy Carlton at Quebec & as the Messenger was afraid to go on he got it convey'd to Sir Guy. Afterwards & before he came into New York He frequently sent out people at his own Expence & communicated the Intelligence he recd to the Commr in chief. When Operations were going on to relieve Genr Burgoyne he attended this expedition as a volunteer together with 27 Men likewise Volunteers & exerted himself to the utmost. Went frequently to Genl Tryon's Quarters informing him of the Necessity of a part of the Army moving forward to the Assistance of Genl Burgoyne for six weeks before the Expedition took place & which had it been done in time would probably have saved that Army.

Produces an order sign'd by Sir Henry Clinton dated in Octr 1779 directing the Claimt to raise a Corps of Refugees whereof he was to be Lieutt Coll Commandant. This Corps was not rais'd.

A Commission dated 28th Augt 1780 sign'd by Genl Robertson appointing the Claimt Colonel of the loyal Refugees to be embodied as Volunteer Militia.

In July 1780 A Party embodied by himself defended a Block House he had erected at his own Expence on the Jersey Shore which was attacked by the whole of Genl Wayne's [1] Army. He was not present himself but as the Commander of the Party recd the thanks of the Commr in chief for this Defence.

General Tryon—sworn.

Confirms what Mr Cuyler said respecting his conveying a Dispatch to Sir Guy Carlton & says that on the whole he considers the Claimt to have been exceedingly loyal & to have render'd Services to the British Govt.

## Memorial of Joshua Locke

Determin'd the 14th of June 1784.

Joshua Locke—the Claimant—sworn. 11th of June 1784.

Is a Native of America Mass. Bay. On the commencement of the troubles he lived at Philadelphia as a Tidesman. The latter end of April 1776 He was threaten'd to be imprison'd when he fled to New York & got on board the Phoenix Man of War. He was appointed to an Office in the Commissary Genl Department at New York with a Salary of 4*s.* 6*d.* per Day & continued therein till June 1779 when he recd a Warrant from Henry Rooke Depy Inspr Genl of the Provincial Troops for raising a Company of Men for his Majesty's service. Recruited 17 & had only 5 muster'd. Staid at New York till the Decr following & then came to Engd. Recd his Salary of £30 a Year as a Custom House Officer up to the 5th of April 1783 & on his Arrival in Engd the Treasury gave him £50.

A Loyalist.

## Memorial of James Humphreys [2]

Determin'd the 25th of June 1785.

James Humphreys—the Claimant—sworn. 15th of June 1784.

Was settled at Philadelphia on the Commencement of the Troubles as

[1] Anthony Wayne, perhaps the most gallant of Washington's brigadiers, afterwards crushed the Indian resistance in 1794.

[2] J. Humphreys was the son of a conveyancer. He began the publication of the *Pennsylvania*

a Book Printer. He was born there. In the beginning of the Year 1775 He open'd a Newspaper entitled the Pensylvania Ledger expressly on the part of Gov$^{t}$ & which he continued to publish till Nov$^{r}$ 1776. This made him very obnoxious. He was frequently called upon to sign the Association but refused. The Oaths were not tender'd to him. He was on different Occasions accused before the Committee & threaten'd. Quitted Philadelphia on Acc$^{t}$ of the Apprehensions he was under of being ill treated the latter end of Nov$^{r}$ 1776 & returned there with the British Troops. Remain'd until the Troops left it in 1778. He settled afterwards at New York as a Printer & staid there till the Evacuation.

A Loyalist. Did not bear Arms.

Produces Certificates from M$^{r}$ Galloway & Gov$^{r}$ Franklyn which speak fully of the Claimant's Loyalty & attachment to Great Britain.

Bounty £50 a Y$^{r}$.

He has an Allowance of £50 a Y$^{r}$ from the Treasury from the 5$^{th}$ of Jan$^{y}$ 1784.

David Sproat—sworn.

Knew the Claim$^{t}$ at Philadelphia before the rebellion. Says that he was always a Loyalist that he kept a Printer's Shop. Sold books & Stationary Wares. When the troops were in Philadelphia the Claimant kept a large Shop. The Witness knew nothing of his property before the Rebellion. Nor can he form any Judgment of what the Value of it was after the troubles commenced. Says that M$^{r}$ Humphreys had a great deal of Business & was esteem'd a Man of very fair Character.

James Humphreys—the Claimant—called in again.

Says he printed all his Books himself And that he has only charged them at the prices they cost him. Never printed any paper in favor of the American Cause he constantly refused to do it & was in Consequence thereof much persecuted.

Rev$^{d}$ Jacob Duché—sworn. 18$^{th}$ June 1784.

Remembers the Claim$^{t}$ at Philadelphia. He was very young in business when the Witness left it. Speaks of the Newspaper which the Claimant had began to publish at Philadelphia & which was entirely in favor of Government. As to his business the Witness is not able to form any Judgment thereon. He thinks however that M$^{r}$ Humphreys had very fair prospects. He recollects having heard of the Claim$^{t}$ being under some Contract for Latin & Greek Grammars.

Determin'd the 25$^{th}$ of June 1784.

## Memorial of John Potts [1] Esq.

John Potts Esq—the Claimant—sworn. 15$^{th}$ of June 1784.

Was born in Pensylvania. At the commencement of the troubles He was one of the Justices of the Peace for the County & one of the Judges of the C$^{t}$ of

*Ledger* in June 1775. In spite of his Tory opinions he had good friends among the Whigs. He went from England to Nova Scotia, but returned to Philadelphia in 1797, where he died in 1810 (Sabine, op. cit., vol. i, p. 554). See also *Nova Scotia Hist. So. Collections*, vol. vi.

[1] In *Hist. MSS. Comm., Am. MSS. in R. Inst.*, vol. iv, p. 454, there is a note from Carleton recommending Mr. Potts, 'a refugee from Pennsylvania, where he has lost a considerable estate, in consequence of his attachment to the British Government'.

Common Pleas for the City & Co. of Philadelphia. No Salary or Emolument. He held these Offices 3 Yrs before the rebellion came on.

In May 1775 when the Inhabitants were arming & that he had made himself obnoxious by disapproving of their Conduct he left Philadelphia & went to his Country place about 39 Miles from thence where he remain'd 2 Years. Never sign'd any Association or took any Oath. In Septr 1777 he join'd the British Troops at Phila after Sir Wm Howe took possession of that City & by whom he was appointed a Magistrate of the Police & continued as such while the Troops remain'd in that province. Says that he frequently acquired intelligence for the Commander in Chief Sir Wm Howe & communicated such thro' Coll Balfour to whom he refers for several particulars concerning his zeal in this business.

An Active Zealous & meritorious Loyalist render'd many essential Services to the British Govt by communicating Intelligence to the difft Commanders for which he refused any reward.

Produces very handsome testimonies of his Loyalty from Sir Wm Howe Genl Abercrombie Sir Henry Clinton & Coll Balfour.

He accompanied the Army from Philadela to New York where he also acquired information for Sir Henry Clinton & refers to him.

Colonel Balfour—sworn.

Says that the Claimt always shew'd a great desire to render every Service in his power to the British Govt. That he was one of the most confidential Men Sir Wm Howe employ'd. Gave very material Information from time to time to the Commr in Chief & says that such great dependence was placed on the Intelligence the Claimt gave that several Movements of the Army were made in Consequence thereof. Witness says that the Claimt was appointed a Magistrate of Police at Philadelphia by Sir Wm Howe & that he never would accept of any reward for ye great services he render'd. Witness knows that Sums of Money were frequently offer'd to him for services he render'd & he did himself offer to the Claimant £500 which he refused to accept.

### Memorial of Abijah Willard[1] Esq.

Determin'd the 25th of June 1784.

Abijah Willard Esq—the Claimant—sworn. 16th June 1784.

Swears in general to the truth of his Memorial. He is a Native of America & in 1774 & 1775 He took measures which made him obnoxious. He left his own House the 19th of April 1775 He had not heard of the battle of Lexington when he left his own House which he did for the purpose of going to see his farm at Salem. After he heard of the battle of Lexington he was afraid to return home & never did & he went to the Troops at Boston. He was frequently molested & insulted before this & in 1774 He was confined. In Augt 1774 He dates the Commencement of the troubles in America. He says the people were in Arms all thro' the Country at this time. The reason of his being confined

A Zealous active & meritorious Loyalist & as a Commissary behav'd with great honesty & disinterestedness. Bore Arms & render'd Services to Govt.

[1] Abijah Willard, *b.* 1722, *d.* 1789, was compelled to sign on leaving Connecticut, in August 1774, an abject apology for having consented to become a Mandamus Councillor. He settled in New Brunswick, and gave the name of Lancaster to the parish in which he resided, having belonged to Lancaster, Mass. He became a member of the first Council of New Brunswick (Sabine, op. cit. vol. ii, p. 429; *Winslow Papers*, p. 111, note).

Jones (op. cit., vol. i, p. 345) writes: 'The Commissary of forage and the Cattle Commissary (George Brindly and Abijah Willard) were both Bostonians, as cunning, artful, and hypocritical as the Devil himself'; but his statements are not to be accepted without corroboration.

was that he was esteem'd a Tory & it was about a Week after he had been sworn a Mandamus Counsellor .

Bounty £150 a Y^r.

After the battle of Bunker's Hill He at the request of Gen^l Gage undertook to supply the King's Troops with fresh provisions which he did at the head of 100 Refugees. He conceiv'd it to be a service of Danger. He had no reward for this but he rec^d the thanks of the Comm^r in Chief. He remain'd in Boston from this time till the taking of New York in 1776. He acted as a Volunteer. He had Commissions from Gen^l Gage & Gen^l Howe to command a Co. of these Loyalists.

He went from Boston with the Army to Halifax & from thence to New York. When he came to New York He had likewise a Company of Loyalists under his Command. He was immediately appointed by Sir W^m Howe as Assistant Commissary & remain'd so till the Evacuation of the Place. He had a Salary of 10*s*. a Day. He produces a Comm^n from Sir Guy Carleton dated the 13^th of May 1783 from which time he rec^d Batt Forage Money to the Evacuation from the 7^th of July 1781. He had 20*s*. a Day by the orders of the Treasury here as appears by a Letter which he produces sign'd by M^r Robinson Secretary to the Treasury directing the Commander to give him 20*s*. a Day in consequence of his Services & the great Use he was of in his Examination before the Commissioners of Accounts. He went after his Examination before the Comm^rs back to America & staid there till the Evacuation of New York.

Bounty £150 a Y^r. He receives an Allowance of £150 a Year from the Treasury from the 5^th of April last.

Being asked whether he has done any Services to Gov^t not mention'd in his memorial He says he saved a great deal of Money to Gov^t in the Commissary's Line. He says he might easily have made £20000 & he could have made £10000 in one Article. Being asked to explain this Article he says he believes the hides & Tallow are usually a perquisite & Col^l Kingston confirms him in it And he says he paid every Shilling of this into Gov^t & has the Receipts to produce. And if he had taken this fair Perquisite he should have put £10000 into his pocket.

John Chandler Esq.

Has known M^r Willard ever since he was a Boy. He lived 14 or 15 Miles from him. He is as firm a Loyalist as any Man in the world.

Being asked what property he had he says he always heard of him as a Man of Property but not of great property. He knows part of the Property of M^r Willard. He knows the farm on which he lived at Lancaster. The House was a tolerable good House but not an elegant House. Being asked to the Value of the Land in that Situation He says a Son in law of his bought some Lands adjoining to M^r Willard's & gave £10 S. per Acre. He says if it had been his He would not have taken £1000 for it but doubts whether it would have taken so much. Thinks it would have taken £850 or £900.

**Memorial of Col[l] James Delancey [1]**

Colonel James Delancey—the Claimant—sworn. 17[th] June 1784.

Determin'd the 22[d] of Dec[r] 1784.

Is a Native of America. Was high Sheriff of the County of Chester for sev[l] Years before the troubles. He was frequently called upon to sign the Associations which he refused. In 1777 he was appointed to the Command of the Militia of the County & rais'd a Volunteer Corps to serve for that Campaign. In 1780 he was appointed Col[l] of the West Chester Refugees. Rais'd the Corps with the Assistance of his Officers it consisted of 490 Men without any Expence to Gov[t]. Had many engagements with the Enemy. Captured a number of Prisoners & was enabled thereby to exchange a great many others. He was at great expence in raising this Corps & paying Surgeons for attending the wounded Men also in procuring intelligence of the movements of the Enemy. The office of Sheriff was £160 per Ann.

An Active & Zealous Loyalist bore Arms & render'd essential Services to the British Gov[t].

Produces Certificates to his Loyalty from Sir Henry Clinton Sir Guy Carleton & Gen[l] Tryon And also Copies of the gen[l] Orders wherein the thanks of the Commander in Chief were given to him for his spirited Conduct at Kings Bridge.[2] Has an Allowance from the Treasury of £200 per Ann. from the 5[th] of July 1783.

Bounty £200 a Y[r].

**Memorial of Tho[s] Robinson late of the County of Sussex [3] on the Delaware**

Tho[s] Robinson—the Claimant—sworn. 18[th] June 1784.

Determin'd the 1[st] of July 1784.

Is a Native of America—Sussex Co. Says that in 1774 he was in the Assembly & opposed the measure of sending a Member to Congress. Never signed an Association or took any Oaths to the Americans. Was settled in trade for some Years & towards the Commencement of the rebellion He had Concerns in the farming way.

An Active & Meritorious Loyalist & render'd Services to the British Gov[t].

On Sir W[m] Howe's Expedition to the head of Elk he offer'd his Services to raise Men in the lower Counties of the Delaware & accompanied the Gen[l] on that service. In 1778 he attended Col[l] Campbell in his Expedition ag[t] Georgia. In 1779 He was appointed by Sir Henry Clinton a Capt[n] of Safe Guards & went on the Expedition to Charlestown. He had an Allowance of 5*s*. a Day as Capt[n] of Safe Guards which he continued to receive till Oct[r] 1783.

He has an Allowance of £100 per Ann. from the Treasury from the 5[th] of Jan[y] 1784.

Bounty £100 a Y[r].

Jos[h] Galloway Esq—sworn.

Says he has known the Claimant ever since he was a Boy. Believes that

[1] He was the son of Peter de Lancey, the brother of the Chief Justice, and of a daughter of Cadwallader Colden. At the close of the war he retired to Nova Scotia, where he became member of the Council in 1794. He died in 1800 (Biog. Notice in *New York Col. Docs.*, vol. viii, p. 718). Carleton wrote to Lord North on June 2, 1783, recommending Colonel James Delancey, 'who has commanded the West Chester Refugees. He has served without pay and the losses by the confiscation of his estate are very great' (*Hist. MSS. Comm.*, *Am. MSS. in R. Inst.*, vol. iv, p. 121).

[2] In the winter of 1776 the refugees at Kingsbridge waylaid a large parcel of cattle, passing through the county of Westchester on their way to the American army, surprised and made prisoner the guard with the cattle, and brought the whole drove into the British lines (Jones, op. cit., vol. i, pp. 118–19).

[3] New Jersey.

he was uniformly loyal & that he exerted himself as much as any Man could do in endeavoring to quiet the minds of the people when the Disturbances commenced. That the Claimant was of the House of Assembly many Years & set up an Address ag$^{t}$ the Measure of Independence which was sign'd by upwards of 5000 persons. He was in consequence of this put into the Pillory & very ill used. It was either in May or June 1776 that this happen'd. M$^{r}$ Galloway further says that the Claim$^{t}$ was afterwards obliged to sign a Bond not to oppose any Measure whatever of the State. M$^{r}$ Galloway remembers that the Claimant was very useful in procuring Pilots for Lord Howe's fleet in the Delaware.

Believes that the Claimant was possess'd of very good property. He was much respected & as a Magistrate could not be more active & useful.

Tho$^{s}$ Robinson—the Claimant—sworn. 21$^{st}$ June 1784.

Admits that the person who valued his property was his Brother—Peter Robinson.

Determin'd the 5$^{th}$ of July 1784.

## Memorial of Henry Reeves

Henry Reeves—the Claimant—sworn 19$^{th}$ June 1784.

Born in England. Went to America to So. Carolina in 1762 as Master of a trading Ship. On the Commencement of the troubles he was settled as a Merch$^{t}$ in Charlestown & was concerned in farming. He refused to sign the Associations as he did to take the Oaths when tender'd to him in 1777. In July 1778 He was banished & only allowed 30 Days to remove his person & dispose of his property. On this Occasion he disposed of all his property except 3 tracts of Land about 40 Miles from Charlestown & embarked for the West Indies where he remain'd till the latter end of 1779 & then removed to North Carolina & from thence to Virginia where he join'd the British Troops at Osborne under the Command of Gen$^{l}$ Philips [1] who gave him the Command of an armed Ship called the Tempest of 20 Guns to bring up the rear of the fleet going down James River. He had the Command of her about 6 weeks. From Portsmouth he went to York Town with the Army & remain'd as a Volunteer till the Capitulation on board his Majesty's Ship Guadaloupe. From thence he came to New York in the Bonnetta Sloop & went afterwards to Charlestown where he remain'd till the Evacuation & then came to Eng$^{d}$.

A Loyalist.

Bounty £50 a Y$^{r}$.

He has £50 a Y$^{r}$ from the Treasury. It commenced from the 5$^{th}$ of Jan$^{y}$ 1783.

Produces Certificates from Capt$^{n}$ Robinson of the Guadaloupe of his having served as a Volunteer during the seige of York Town. Certificate from Gov$^{r}$ Bull by which it appears that the Claim$^{t}$ was Harbour Master at Charlestown & had been in that office about 2 Years Another from Gen$^{l}$ Arnold & one from M$^{r}$ Powell all which speak of M$^{r}$ Reeve's Loyalty.

The Salary of Harbour Master was about £200 S. per Ann. there were Emoluments annex'd to this to the amount of £50 S. per Ann.

Brig$^{r}$ General Arnold—sworn.

He knew the Claimant in Virginia in March 1781. He says that he applied

[1] Major-General William Phillips. There are numerous references to him in *Hist. MSS. Comm., Am. MSS. in R. Inst.*, vol. ii.

to him for protection for his personal property which he accordingly gave. The Witness says that he recollects Mr Reeves making an Application about some Tobacco which had been burnt by the British Troops.

He speaks of the Claimant having been given the Command of the Tempest armed Ship by Genl Philips & that he gave Genl Philips & him information on several occasions respecting the movements of the American Army.

Henry Reeves—the Claimant—called in again.

Says that when he was banished in July 1778 He went to St Eustatia from whence he went to Virginia & that after he returned to Charlestown (some time after the Evacuation) he made a Voyage to the West Indies to Jamaica for a Cargo of Rum for the use of the Garrison of Charlestown.

### Memorial of Mrs Isabella Logan

Determin'd the 1st of July 1784.

Isabella Logan—the Claimant—sworn. 23d June 1784.

She is the Widow of George Logan Esq of Princess Ann County Virginia Mercht. She says that her Husband was born in Scotland & went to Virginia at a very [early] time of Life where he was bound an Apprentice to a Mercht. When the troubles commenced he was settled in Princess Ann County as a Mercht. He took an early & decided part in favor of Govt. Says that what she has stated in her Memorial respecting her late Husbands loyalty is strictly true.

Board satisfied of the Loyalty of the Claimt & her Husband.

Produces her Husbands Will dated the 28th of Jany 1781 by which it appears that the whole of Mr Logan's property real & personal was left to the Claimant except £10 per Ann. to his Brother at Glasgow. Mr Logan left no family but he had some poor relations whom she is obliged to assist.

The Claimt Executrix & Devisee of her Husband.

The Earl of Dunmore—sworn.

Knew the Claimant's late Husband & says that no Man could be more loyal. He join'd Lord Dunmore but could not on acct of his Age bear Arms but he acted as a Magistrate & behaved very well. The Witness had not seen a better House in Virginia it was exceedingly well furnished. Is not able to say whether the Ship Logan was hired or not by Government but recollects that some Goods belonging to the Crown were on board of her.

### Memorial of Stephen Haven

Determin'd the 26th of June 1784.

Stephen Haven—the Claimant—sworn. 26th June 1784.

Swears to the truth of the Memorial in general terms & that it contains to the best of his Judgment a true Acct of his property the fees of office &c. He was fix'd at Savannah when the troubles broke out. He was born in Ireland & went to America in 1771. He was 15 Yrs of Age when the rebellion broke out. He lived with Mr Young who was a Loyalist. He took no part till the Year 1777. In the Month of feby He got on board the Otter Sloop of War & gave Captn Squire intelligence of a Rebel Galley & he burnt her He went to Florida soon after & remain'd there till the Cession of the province. He never took any Oath to the Rebels.

A Loyalist.

Produces a Certificate from Gov[r] Tonyn to Loyalty & good Conduct during the War.

He lost some property & an Office under Gov[t].

He was Naval Officer of Georgia & produces an Appointm[t] dated the 17[th] of Aug[t] 1775. The Comm[n] is sign'd by Sir Ja[s] Wright & bears the Seal of the province.

Office £300 a Y[r]. afterw[ds] alter'd to £200 a Y[r].

Disallowed.

The Duty of this Office is to sign all papers that the Collector Comptroller & Searcher sign &c. There was no Salary but the Emoluments arose from fees. His Mother receiv'd the Emoluments & therefore he cant say what they were but he refers to M[r] Thompson who was Collector of the Port of Savannah & who attends. He charges the Loss of the Office for 8 Years at £300 a Y[r] but he admits that he rec[d] about £250 when the province of Georgia was last in possession of the British Troops.

Being asked why he values it at 5*s*. per Acre he says he thought it was necessary to put some Value upon it & he understood that others had valued lands of this sort at the same price.

Bounty £50 a Y[r].

He arrived in Eng[d] in August last & he applied to Whitehall for a temporary support & he obtain'd an Allowance of £50 a Year from the 5[th] of July 1783 & he now continues to receive it

## ADDITIONAL NOTES

### Lieut.-Col. James Chalmers (page 81)

A note in *Hist. MSS. Comm., Am. MSS. in Royal Inst.*, vol. iv, p. 479, probably by Carleton, says: 'James Chalmers and William Allen served from the time of their appointment under General Howe in Pennsylvania and afterwards at New York; embarked with their corps for Pensacola in 1778, where they served some time. Their corps continued there till it was taken by the Spaniards.' Chalmers was a county gentleman of some distinction and was appointed Lieutenant-Colonel of the First Battalion of Maryland Loyal Volunteers.

Raymond, *Winslow Papers*, contains particulars with regard to the Maryland loyalists and their colonel. On September 12, 1783, Carleton wrote to Lieutenant-Colonel R. Hewlett to take command of the British and American troops (including the Maryland loyalists) who were to proceed to the river St. John in the Bay of Fundy (pp. 132–3).

A considerable number of Maryland loyalists were wrecked off the Seal Islands (pp. 136–7); but forty-three, with some women and children, were receiving the royal bounty of provisions at the mouth of the St. John River (p. 244) preparatory to taking up a block of land opposite Fredericton (p. 156).

On May 15, 1785, Lieutenant-Colonel Chalmers wrote to Winslow from Newcastle on the Delaware River that he was proceeding to England with vouchers for the sale of his estate, which, for that country, might be termed a 'noble' one. 'As I have had it much at heart', he went on, 'to settle in your Province (New Brunswick), I am very anxious to endeavour that the lands destined to the Maryland Corps may be placed on such footing that an impartial division may be made to all those interested. My address is No. 7 Fountain Court, Strand' (p. 303).

### P. Skene (page 106).

After doing good service in the Seven Years' War, P. Skene formed a settlement at Wood Creek and South Bay, at the head of Lake Champlain. In 1765 the tract of land at Wood Creek became a township under the name of Skenesborough. He erected there forges for smelting iron, and saw mills, and made a road to Bennington. He died in 1810 (Biog. notice in O'Callaghan, *New York Col. Docs.*, vol. viii, p. 415).

Skene arrived at Philadelphia in 1775 with a commission as Lieutenant-Governor of Crown Point and Ticonderoga and Inspector of Crown lands within the province of Quebec and that part of New York which lay near Lake Champlain. The rumour went that his mission was 'to influence the members of the Congress by arguments drawn on the Treasury over which he has unlimited power'. He was made prisoner upon his parole to keep within eight miles of the city and not to correspond with any one on political subjects (Force, *Am. Archives*, 4th ser., vol. ii, p. 974; see also *New Jersey Archives*, vol. x, p. 648).

General Schuyler wrote to Governor Trumbull of Connecticut on December 12 that it was reported that both the Skenes had broken their parole and fled (*Am. Arch.*, 4th ser., vol. iv, p. 248). But Governor Skene was in captivity in May 1776, when he refused to give his parole not to give intelligence to the British directly or indirectly, or not to act in opposition to the measures of the Americans (ibid., vol. vi, p. 601). Howe reported in September 1776 that Skene was about to be liberated in exchange for the New Englander Lovell taken by Gage (*Hist. MSS. Comm.*, *Stopford-Sackville MSS.*, p. 42).

According to a French account of the affair at Bennington, Skene was largely responsible for that disaster (ibid., pp. 76–7). He was described by H. Cruger, M.P., as 'a vain, weak man' (*Life of Peter van Schaack*, by H. C. van Schaack, 1842, p. 44).

### Dr. Kearsley (page 106).

'Dr. Kearsley was seized on Friday by order of the Committee of Observation for having wrote letters to England . . . and is now confined in jail with one Brooks, who was here with Governor Skene. You must know Kearsley to be a considerable time since marked out as a thorough-paced Tory; for which, together with his having insulted the people, he was . . . carted through the streets' (Force, op. cit., vol. iii, p. 985). See also Moore, *Diary of the Am. Rev.*, vol. i, p. 146, quoting from *Constitutional Gazette*, October 14, 1775: 'This so enrages the people . . . that if it had not been for the humanity of some gentlemen, who conducted him to gaol, he would possibly have been very roughly handled. He is as sulky as when exalted on the cart, glories in the mischief he still hopes to do his country, and refuses to give any satisfaction.

'This ungrateful son of Galen has acquired a considerable fortune by his practice in Philadelphia and in manufacturing Keyser's pills which are sold as genuine by a "certain Tory bibliopolist in a neighbouring province".'

### John Ferdinand Dalziel Smith (page 127).

This very plausible and able, as well as courageous, adventurer, published a book *A Tour in the United States of America*, &c., by J. F. D. Smyth, 2 vols., London, 1784. The book was published by subscription; and Messrs. Wilmot and Coke each subscribed for two copies.

Smith did not take his defeat lying down, and in 1807 returned to the charge with a publication, *The Case of Ferdinand Smyth Stuart, with his Memorials to the King*. The volume opens with some very indifferent poetry. We are then informed that 'the whole proceedings of the said Commissioners in regard to me were decidedly contrary to law, justice, and truth, and that they even violated their oaths and actually perjured themselves in order to injure me. No charge against me was ever communicated to me, nor could I ever learn the nature of the report of the Commissioners, notwithstanding every exertion I made to discover it from 1784 until April 27, 1807, when the substance of it was mentioned to me by the Marquess of Tullibardine'. His change of name is explained by the fact that his father was son to the Duke of Monmouth by Lady Henrietta Maria Wentworth, baroness of Netherstead. This royal scion had 'raised a fine corps of two hundred and thirty selected men, served my King and country in arms, and cheerfully shed my blood, having been placed in the post of honour'. He had been possessed of a good estate; had an extensive and profitable practice of physic and lived in the most abundant manner, having an increasing income of more than £1,700 a year. Captain in the Queen's Royal Regiment of Rangers, November 5, 1775; escaped on the 30th of December with dispatches of great importance (no less than the preservation of all Upper Canada), and travelled 300 miles on foot over the Alleghany Mountains, the most inaccessible and extensive perhaps in the world; encountered a series of dangers and hardships not to be paralleled, and fifty times worse than death, when no one else dared to undertake the desperate enterprise.'

It is a little disconcerting to turn from this Paladin of romance to the actual Smith or Smyth Stuart as he showed himself when a prisoner. The brutality of facts has preserved a petition from Philadelphia Jail dated April 29, 1776. ' Lamenting,' he writes, ' this unhappy and unnatural contest, and wishing to avoid being active on either side, I endeavoured to remove to my lands on the Mississippi from the disagreeable scene. . . . Unfortunately for me, some expression of moderation of mine to Lord Dunmore caused me to be accused of being a spy. . . . Being offered the Commission of surgeon to the new regiment on this intended expedition and persuaded by Colonel Conolly (whom I never knew before and conceived to be a regular officer), I very inconsiderately accompanied him, which I am now sorry for. . . . Nothing could have induced me to join either side except the impossibility of remaining neutral ' (Force, *Amer. Archives*, 4th ser., vol. v, p. 1119).

### James Moody (page 133).

J. Moody, *b.* 1744, *d.* 1809, was one of the most picturesque figures among the loyalists in the American War of Independence. He published in 1781 a book, *Lieut. James Moody's Narrative of his Exertions and Sufferings in the Cause of Government since the Year 1776*, which quickly went to a second edition. His hairbreadth escapes would be hardly credible were they not well attested. He seems to have been treated with especial harshness—there is sworn evidence that he was, apparently with the knowledge of Arnold, confined in handcuffs ragged on the inside next the wrist—the American contention being that he was a spy and not entitled to the treatment of an open enemy. His effective operations with small parties against the American mails lent colour to this view. He pays a glowing tribute to his brother loyalists. Often obliged to put his life into their hands, he never was disappointed or deceived by any of them. He was several times in hiding for months at a time ; but, though many of these people were in sore straits and knew that they would be generously rewarded for handing over so obnoxious a person, they were so far from betraying him that they often ran great hazards in giving him assistance.

He states that during the first year he served for nothing ; in the second, third, and fourth he received the pay of an ensign ; and in the fifth that of a lieutenant. Besides his pay he received rewards of £100 and £200 for the capture of mails. In enlisting and paying men for the public service he had expended most of what was saved from the wreck of his fortunes.

In a Proclamation offering a reward for his apprehension, Moody was declared by Governor Livingstone of New Jersey, guilty of atrocious offences, robberies, thefts, and other felonies (Moore, *Diary of the Am. Rev.*, vol. ii, p. 466). Moody retorted by a counter-proclamation. He went to Nova Scotia, where he died.

The note on him in Sabine, op. cit., vol. ii, pp. 92–7, is very full.

# BOOK III

## Memorial of Alexander Selkrig

Determin'd the 26th of June 1784.

Alexander Selkrig—the Claimant—sworn. 26th of June 1784.

Is a Native of Glasgow & went from Glasgow to America in 1765. He went to carry on trade. He was fix'd in business in partnership with his Brother at Boston when the troubles commenced. He & his Brother sold Dry Goods. He took the Gov^t side. He left Boston the 2^d of feb^y 1775 & came home to Glasgow. He staid in Great Britain 1776 & then went out to New York. His Brother was a Loyalist & was obliged to leave Boston at the Evacuation. His Brother is since dead—in Jan^y last.

A Loyalist.

Did not bear Arms.

He claims for nothing but Debts which as he says are about £5500 S. He does not know that the House owed £20. These consist of Notes of hand & Book Debts.

Debts £5500 0*s.* 0*d.*

He says he is a Bankrupt & has gone thro' the whole of his Examination & he disclosed this to the Commiss^rs. He says he is sensible that this belongs to the Creditors but the Assignees have appointed him to receive & collect these Debts & he apprehends there will be an Overplus. His Brother has left a Widow & 2 Sons.

A Bankrupt.

## Memorial of James Delancey[1] Esq.

Determin'd the 22^d of Dec^r 1784.

James Delancey Esq—the Claimant—sworn. 28th of June 1784.

Was born at New York & is the Son of Lieut^t Gov^r Delancey who was Lieut^t Gov^r of the Province. He was a Member of the Assembly at the Commencement of the troubles. He never bore Arms. But immediately after the battle of Lexington he proposed to some of the middling people at New York to make a resistance but they agreed that tho' they could probably quel any opposition in the town yet that they should be overpower'd by the people of Connecticut &c & so the scheme was dropp'd at that time. He soon after left New York & went to Canada after looking at some lands which he had at Fort Stanwix.[2] He never returned afterw^ds to New York having made himself very obnoxious by the part which he had taken in the Assembly. When it was proposed in the Assembly to send Members to the first Congress the Measure was overruled by the Committee of which M^r Delancey was a Member. The Mob afterwards sent Delegates. In the latter end of 1774 many steps were taken to make the Assembly approve of the Associations &c all of which were resisted & overruled. A Petition was then moved for & carried to the King which was likewise opposed by the same faction. In that Petition the Authority of this Country was acknowledged as supreme over America but they objected to taxation. He had a great hand in drawing the Petition. He inspected M^r Rivington's Press & struck out

A Zealous Loyalist.

Did not bear Arms.

[1] See Additional Notes, p. 211.

[2] See note 2 on p. 277, *infra*.

everything which he thought would injure the Cause of Gov$^{t}$. He came to Eng$^{d}$ in the latter end of 1775.

Bounty £200 a Y$^{r}$.

He has an Allowance of £200 a Year from the Treasury which he has rec$^{d}$ from the latter end of 1779 or 1780.

He produces no Certificates nor are there any annex'd to his Memorial at Whitehall his Character being so well known.

Agent for the Loyalists.

He was chosen by the Loyalists of the Province of New York as their Agent to act for them in this County & he is now acting in this Situation.

The valuation put upon this Lot was done by himself & not by another person

He says he valued the whole in the proportion that he sold off a little part in the Year 1781. He says that he values at £100 what he let for £4 a Year. And another mode he takes of estimating it is by putting 30 Years purchase upon the Ground rents. This applies to the £994 per Ann. He is to bring a particular Valuation tomorrow.

Thomas Jones Esq—sworn. 30$^{th}$ June 1784.

Knows the three Lots let to the Forbes's but he can't put any value upon them. He knows they were M$^{r}$ Delanceys & says the rent was about £50 a Y$^{r}$.

He was Agent to M$^{r}$ Delancey & rec$^{d}$ the rents for him. He says he knows the whole of his Estate in the Island of New York produced above £1200 a Y$^{r}$ he knows it from this Circumstance that the third which was set apart for M$^{rs}$ Delancey's Dower was more than £400 a Y$^{r}$. He thinks £430 a Y$^{r}$. He says it is a very valuable Estate part of it is bad Land. He thinks in quiet times it would have sold for 70 or 80,000 Cur. He never has seen Mr. Delancey's valuation. When he says this He means to include all his property at New York. He can't set any value upon the other property belonging to M$^{r}$ Delancey. Being desired to say what this Estate would have sold for in 1775 not valuing it in Lots He says about £50000. He saw this property last in 1781. He would have given £50000 if he had wished to buy it. He says the Partition Deed of the Minisinck patent was drawn in his office & he believes the property stated in that Deed to belong to M$^{r}$ Delancey was his. Believes it was all confiscated by an Act in the Year 1778. He has sold Lands for M$^{r}$ Delancey since the Confiscation to persons who knew of the Confiscation but were willing to run the risque & he rec$^{d}$ the Money for it. He sold one part for 2500 Gās & the other for £3250 Cur.

Determin'd the 5$^{th}$ of July 1784.

## The joint Memorial of William & James Carsan of Charlestown Merch$^{ts}$

Will$^{m}$ & James Carsan—the two Claimants—sworn. 2$^{d}$ July 1784.

They are both from Scotland. Will$^{m}$ left Scotland in 1764 & James in 1760 They are not related tho' their names are the same. The Claimants enter'd into partnership with one M$^{r}$ Currie in the Y$^{r}$ 1764 & remain'd so till 1768 & then the two M$^{r}$ Carsans carried on business from 1768 to the Commencement of the troubles they bought out M$^{r}$ Currie & gave him £1000 S. besides paying all his Expences for 3 Years. They were Partners in equal shares. They

Loyalty established.

continued in trade till 1777 when James Carsan was banished & Will[m] had liberty to remain behind for a few Months to settle the trade &c. They both swear that they were worth above £13000 S. after all their Debts paid in the Y[r] 1776. The Acc[t] is stated by them up to 1777 but they say that as much was due to them in 1776 because one of the Partners was put into prison in 1776 & the other was obliged to go into the Country. They refer to the Abstract & Schedule produced & both swear that to the best of their knowledge it contains a true State of their Debts & the balance in their favor. This Schedule was extracted from their books by a Person in Town who has sworn to the truth of it before the Lord Mayor.

### Separate Memorial of W[m] Carsan

Determin'd the 5[th] of July 1784.

James Simpson Esq—sworn. 2[d] July 1784.

He has know him many years (W[m] Carsan). He was always esteem'd to be well affected to Gov[t] & he has reason to know that he was. He underwent a great deal of persecution & was obliged to quit the Province on acc[t] of his Loyalty. He knows that the Oath was tender'd to him & that he refused it & on that Acc[t] was banished. He is confident that he was very loyal. Notwithstanding this He says that he believes the Claim[t] sign'd an Association [1] which almost everybody did at that [time] which bound those who signed it to be ready to oppose the English Gov[t]. The Witness did not sign this Association himself but he says he believes there were not 40 persons in the Town who refused to sign it.

A Loyalist.

James Trail Esq—sworn.

He knew the Claim[t] in Charlestown very well in 1775. Says he was universally known by everybody to be loyal. The Witness left the Country before the Claim[t]. He says he believes he sign'd the Association because he was compel'd to do it but his Loyalty was so well known that this Circumstance did not alter anybody's Opinion respecting his principles. He mentions a Circumstance to shew his Loyalty of sending provisions & intelligence to the British when Lord W[m] Campbell was on board a Ship & he says he must have done this at some personal risque.

Colonel Innes [2]—sworn.

He knew the Claim[t] very well & his Character. He can not only vouch for the Loyalty of this Gent[n] & his principles but he knew that he gave very material Intelligence at different times at great risque to himself & that he was very active. The Witness knows this well from having been in a public Situation in that Country. He was Secretary to Lord Will[m] Campbell.

[1] The South Carolina Association, formed after the arrival of the news of the battle of Lexington, involved practically the establishment of a Provisional Government. Its members solemnly engaged themselves to obey the Continental and Provincial Councils in the defence of their rights.

[2] Alexander Innes was appointed in 1777 Inspector-General of the Provincial Forces, and was given in 1779 the command of a regiment of South Carolina Royalists (*Hist. MSS. Comm., Am. MSS. in R. Inst.*, vols. i–iv, *passim*). The South Carolina Royalists received lands at Country Harbor, Guysborough, Nova Scotia, when they were disbanded in 1783 (*Winslow Papers*, p. 161, note).

Will$^{m}$ Carsan—the Claimant—sworn.

He says he very early fell under the displeasure of the Americans on acc$^{t}$ of his known Loyalty. He admits that he sign'd the Association but was almost the last Man who signed it. He was three Days in a Garret before he submitted to sign it & then he did it to avoid being tarr'd & feather'd & being sent to prison which would have been the Consequence. He says he thinks he saved Capt$^{n}$ Maitland's [1] life & Ship by some intelligence which he gave & which made him very obnoxious to the Rebels.

Determin'd the 8$^{th}$ of July 1784.

### The separate Memorial of James Carsan

3$^{d}$ July 1784.

James Carsan—the Claimant—sworn.

A Meritorious Loyalist & suffer'd imprisonment on Acc$^{t}$ of his Loyalty.

N.B. All the Evidence given by M$^{r}$ Simpson M$^{r}$ Trail & Col$^{l}$ Innes with respect to Loyalty &c applies equally to the Case of this Gent$^{n}$.

The Claimant is a Native of Scotland & went to Charlestown in 1760. He was thrown into Gaol the 15$^{th}$ of June 1776 on Acc$^{t}$ of his Attachment to this Country. He was kept a close Prisoner till March 1777 when he was banished. He never took any Oath & the reason of his persecution was that he refused to bear Arms for the Rebels. He sign'd the Association. The 14$^{th}$ of June 1776 He went to inform the Gov$^{r}$ that he would no longer bear Arms & he sent him to prison.

A meritorious Loyalist.

Determin'd the 5$^{th}$ of July 1784.

### Memorial of Miss Eliz$^{th}$ Gibbs Carsan an Infant of 9 Years of Age by her Guardian M$^{r}$ W$^{m}$ Carsan

3$^{d}$ July 1784.

Will$^{m}$ Carsan—the Guardian—sworn

A Loyalist. Cattle £75. Sheep £10.

The Child's father was his Brother & was strictly loyal. His Brother died in 1777 & left her under the Guardianship of her Uncle & in case of her Death he left the Estate to the Witness. The Estate was on John's Island & consisted of 3000 Acres. There were above 500 head of Cattle on the Estate when he left the place & they were many of them driven away. Some were taken by the British & others by the Rebels.

Disallowed.

He has every reason to believe the Number taken by the British in feb$^{y}$ 1780 was at least equal to what is charged in the Schedule. He values them at 247. No Certificates were given tho' the Witness frequently applied for Certificates & for payment but he never obtained payment.

He says the Cattle charged in the Schedule to be taken by the Rebels were taken in the Year 1782 at the time of the Evacuation.

M$^{r}$ Carsan is desired to make an Application to the Treasury as he says others in the same Situation have been paid in full.

Determin'd the 8$^{th}$ of July 1784.

### Memorial of D$^{r}$ Sam$^{l}$ Clossy

8$^{th}$ July 1784.

D$^{r}$ Sam$^{l}$ Clossy—the Claimant—sworn

He is a Native of Ireland & went to America in 1763 to New York with a view to get into the Hospital there. At the Commencem$^{t}$ of the troubles He was Professor of Anatomy & Natural Philosophy in the Kings College at

[1] See McCrady, *S. Carolina in the Rev., 1775–80*, pp. 19–20.

New York. He was so much employ'd in the business of his profession that he took no part In 1775 in consequence of the Action at Lexington the violent people came to seize D$^{r}$ Cooper [1] who was President of the College but D$^{r}$ Cooper having had Intimation of it escaped & went on board Capt$^{n}$ Montagu's [2] Ship. He remain'd a Year after this in College. He quitted New York in the Summer of 1776 when Gen$^{l}$ Washington took it & went into the Jerseys & returned to it when Sir W$^{m}$ Howe took possession of it. He remain'd there in the service of the Hospital till the Y$^{r}$ 1780. He was allow'd 5*s.* per Day whilst he was Mate to the Hospital & he gain'd besides about £80 a Y$^{r}$ by teaching Anatomy &c. As professor he had £100 a Y$^{r}$ Ster$^{g}$ upon the foundation it was an established sort of Fellowship. The other advantages to the professorship over & above the Salary were about £60 a Y$^{r}$.

A Loyalist.

Professorship £100 a Y$^{r}$.

A Certificate produced & read from D$^{r}$ Inglis to his Situation in the College & to his Character likewise the same from D$^{r}$ Chandler but being to facts they could not be read.

He got £60 a Y$^{r}$ or thereabouts by his practice independent of what he has before stated before the troubles. The Salary of £100 a Y$^{r}$ He might have held for his Life if the troubles had not happen'd. He has deliver'd in a Schedule of personal Losses amounting to £753 18*s.* 6*d.* S. exclusive of his office & his professional Situation. He says he thinks the different Articles are moderately valued.

Profits in his profession altogether £120 a Y$^{r}$.

Personalty Lost £135.

There is a charge of £180 Cu. for old American Money likewise for Bonds & Mortgages with Interest £406 the rem$^{r}$ for Personalty. The old American Money was stopp'd by an Act of the British Par$^{t}$ previous to the troubles.

rejected.

Debts £229 0*s.* 0*d.*

He Receives £80 a Y$^{r}$ from the Treasury & has rec$^{d}$ it about a Year.

Bounty £80 a Y$^{r}$.

He owes no Money in America.

### Memorial of the Rev$^{d}$ D$^{r}$ Halyburton [3]

Determin'd the 8$^{th}$ of July 1784.

Rev$^{d}$ D$^{r}$ Halyburton—the Claimant—sworn. 8$^{th}$ July 1784.

Is a Native of Scotland. He went to America in 1757 to New York as Chaplain to the first Reg$^{t}$ or the Royals. He returned with the Reg$^{t}$ at the end of the War & went again in 1766 & return'd in 1768 or 1769 & has never been

[1] *b.* 1735, *d.* 1785. He went to New York from England in 1762 as Professor of Moral Philosophy at the College of New York. He became President in 1763. He published in 1774 *The American Querist* and *A Friendly Address to all Reasonable Americans.* His strong Tory views excited the fury of the mob, whose intention was to seize him in his bed, cut off his ears, slit his nose, and strip him naked. He escaped, however, through the loyalty of a former pupil, and took refuge in an English ship of war, in which soon afterwards he sailed for England. He resided for some time at Oxford, but afterwards became clergyman of the first episcopal church in Edinburgh. He died suddenly. (Biog. notice in *New York Col. Docs.*, vol. viii, pp. 297–8.)

[2] George, *b.* 1750 *d.* 1829. Is in *Dict. of Nat. Biography.*

[3] He is not to be confused with the father of Thomas C. Haliburton, the Chief Justice of Nova Scotia, creator of *Sam Slick*, and historian of the colony.

In *Acts of the Privy Council, Col. Series, Unbound Papers*, p. 390, there is a petition of the Rev. W. Halyburton, Chaplain for eighteen years to the Second Battalion of the Royal Regiment of Foot. Halyburton 'claims some small share of the honour acquired by that battalion in the late war, as he failed not to mingle with other instructions the sound military doctrines of bravery and regard to discipline' (June 11, 1765).

there since. On quitting the Army he obtain'd a royal Patent for 5000 Acres in the province of New York. Produces a Warrant or Mandamus from the Privy Council here dated in 1766. He tender'd it in the end of the Year 1766 to Sir Henry Moore & the Grant pass'd immediately or very soon after. He never saw them nor took any steps towards Cultivation. He says it being a Mandamus Grant it could not be forfeited but it would not have been so if it had been a common Grant. He says it was very good Land. He says he was offer'd £500 Cur. for it when he got the grant. He values them at £291 13*s*. 4*d*. He charges 17 Gās for the fees of the Mandamus & £27 5*s*. for his passage to America in 1766.

A British Subject Not having been in America for many Y[rs] before the troubles.

rejected in toto.

Between the Year 1774 & the present time he has been at Sea & in Europe & has served on board a Ship as Chaplain. He is going to Nova Scotia.[1] He receives no Allowance from the Treasury.

## Memorial of the Earl of Dunmore [2]

Determin'd the 23[d] of July 1784.

9[th] of July 1784.

The Earl of Dunmore—the Claimant—sworn.

Went first to America in 1769 as Governor of New York was removed to the Gov[t] of Virginia in 1770 & continued there till Aug[t] 1776. The Disturbances commenced in April 1775 the People at that time armed & beset Lord Dunmore's House. His Lordship early in June following was obliged to retire on board his Majesty's Ship Fowey having from the Month of April been obliged to keep his Servants & family in Arms every night to protect his House.

Was Gov[r] of the Province. Acted with Zeal & Spirit & thereby render'd Services to the British Gov[t].

While on board the Fowey He carried on a Negotiation with the Inha[ts] for near two Months when he saw it would turn to no Acc[t] He went to Norfolk. He had 114 Men of the 14[th] Reg[t] on board & with this party he kept the province in constant Alarm & their whole force in constant employ. Part of Norfolk was burnt by his orders. Those who took part with the Americans were paid for the Losses they sustain'd by the State.

He rec[d] his Salary as Gov[r] till Sept[r] last. Says that he rais'd Men in Nov[r] 1775 bought a Number of Vessels & fitted them for service with which he proceeded to New York. The Salary was £2000. Lord North afterwards gave him £1000 per Ann. it commenced the beginning of 1777 & ceas'd with the original Salary of the Gov[r] in Sept[r] 1773. The last half Year (£1500) was paid to him by M[r] Remnant.

The Year after he came home the latter end of 1777 he rec[d] from Lord North 15000 S. on Acc[t] of his Losses. He gave a Voucher for the same which specified that this Sum was either in part or on Acc[t] (He does not recollect which of the terms were used) of his Losses.

2/20[th] Shares of 37—497—600 Acres of Land on the river Occabeche between the Ohio & the Missisippi. His Lordship saw some of them when he went to fight the Indians. Says that when he came to Eng[d] he made an offer to Lord Shelburne that if he would give him Men & Ammunition he & the others concerned would go & take possession of the tract & thereby relieve this Country

rejected.

[1] There is no mention of him in A. W. Eaton, *The Church of England in Nova Scotia*.

[2] See Additional Notes, p. 211.

from the Necessity of making any Compensation whatever to Loyalists. It was a purchase from the Indians in Oct$^{r}$ 1775. Produces a Copy of the Deed by which it appears that a Quantity of Goods were given to them in payment. Says that his Lordship's share of the Presents made from first to last was about £1000 S. He makes no Claim for this as he cannot set a Value upon it but thinks he is entitled to the Sum he laid out of £1000 S. afs$^{d}$. Relates several Circumstances about these Lands not material to make Minutes of but to prove they were good He says that he has been riding on Horseback within ten Yards of another Man & has not been able to see him as the Grass was so high. rejected. Confiscation proved.

Major Grymes—sworn.

Says that he was in Virg$^{a}$ in 1775 when the troubles broke out. Believes that Lord Dunmore did everything that Man could do for the defence of the province. That he rais'd a Corps of Negroes & another of Whips—it was in 1775 & 1776 that they were raised.

Speaks of the 579 Acres & says that it was notorious that his Lordship paid £3 Cur. per Acre for them. The Situation was a very good one but the land was indifferent. Does not think they would have sold for more than what he gave [1] that Lord Dunmore made great Improvements. In general it was not a fertile tract of Land. Can't say whether the Buildings were included in the £3 per Acre.

Speaks to the 2600 Acres knew them well. He was about purchasing them the Year before Lord Dunmore—a Valuable Tract. 700 Acres of it were very valuable. Not a great many buildings. Did not see them after Lord Dunmore got them the 700 Acres of plain Land he thinks were well worth £5 Cur. or even £5 S. per Acre. The other land was Mountain. The whole was valued by the Committee at 40*s*. an Acre he thought it very fully valued at 40*s*. Mills Major Grymes says are always valued separately. He is not able to speak to the value of Lord Dunmore's property.

Major Gen$^{l}$ Read—sworn.

Speaks to the 51000 Acres. Says that he has understood it was in Vermont. If the Vermontese establish their independence he thinks the Tract will be within their State. Believes there were Settlers thereon. Has heard from his own Surveyor a good deal about these Lands. Thinks if Lord Dunmore could have kept it it would have proved a very valuable Estate. His Surveyor was employed by Lord Dunmore in letting the Lands. Has not a Doubt but Lord Dunmore would soon have reaped benefit from this Estate that [2] some of the people who had settled without Lord Dunmore's permission had disposed of the good Will of what they had so taken from one to two Dollars per Acre between 1771 & 1774. Had it not been for the War Lord Dunmore would certainly have got full poss$^{n}$ of the whole. He says that tho' the Vermontese should gain their point he does not think that Lord Dunmore could claim this property as the Grant was under the great Seal of New York however desirous they may be of indulging the Subjects of Great Britain. He thinks that in 1774 the tract was worth upon the most moderate Computation 5*s*. an Acre.

[1] ? Insert 'or'. [2] ? Omit 'that', and begin new sentence with 'Some'.

## Memorial of James Minzies

Determin'd the 19th of July 1784.

James Minzies—the Claimant—sworn. 10th July 1784.

A Loyalist.

He is a Native of Scotland. Went to Virginia in 1763 & was employed by Mr Blair [1] the Deputy Auditor of the Revenue in auditing the Accounts of his Majesty's Revenue & new modeling the Rent Rolls of the Quit Rents continued in that Office till March 1772 when Lord Dunmore appointed him his private Secretary. He continued with Lord Dunmore during the whole of his Govt.

His emoluments as private Secretary were £250 per Ann. on an Average.

Salary & Fees as Superintendt of the Auditors Office £120 per Ann.

He was also Clerk to the Committee for encouraging of Arts & Manufactures. £40 per Ann. S.

Bounty £100 a Yr.

Came to Engd with Lord Dunmore & has been allowed £100 per Ann. by the Treasury since the 5th of Jany 1783. The aforementd Employments were during pleasure.

## Memorial of John Lewis

Determin'd the 31st of July 1784.

John Lewis—the Claimant—sworn. 10th of July 1784.

A Loyalist.

Is a Native of Great Britain. Went to America in 1749 & continued there till Octr 1783. Was an Inhabitant of New York at the Commencement of the troubles. Lived in an House of his own & kept Cows. In the latter end of the Year 1775 he was called upon to take the Oaths but on his refusal he was put into Gaol at Lancaster where he continued till the Arrival of the British Troops when he made his Escape & got into New York where he was embodied in the City Militia. Says that he was employed by a Mr Stephens to collect Straw for the Army at Boston & was allow'd 4s. per Day New York Currency for about 6 Weeks that he was so employed.

Bounty £20 a Yr.

Has been allow'd £20 per Ann. by the Treasury from the 5th of Jany 1784.

Produces Certificates from Genl Tryon Mr John Wetherhead Mr John Newstead & Mr Thos Hughes to his Loyalty & Property.

Property.

Disallowed.

Says he lost three Horses. One was shot at the battle of Brandywine. He kept a Waggon & it was employ'd by the Army.

John Newstead—sworn.

Knew the Claimant & says that he often check'd him for speaking his Mind too freely [2] that he was embodied in the Militia at New York.

## Memorial of Sir Wm Pepperell [3] Bart

Determin'd the 22d of July 1784.

Sir Willm Pepperell Bart—the Claimant—sworn. July the 12th 1784.

Is a Native of New Engd. Shew'd his Attachment to this Country on the destruction of the Tea. In 1774 He was appointed a Mandamus Counsellor.

[1] He was also Clerk to the Council.

[2] ? Insert 'and'.

[3] Sir W. Pepperell was the son of Nathaniel Sparhawk, who married the daughter of Sir William Pepperell, 'the hero of Louisbourg'. Under the terms of his grandfather's will William became heir on condition that he took the name of Pepperell. He was allowed to take the title of Sir William Pepperell, Baronet. His estate in Maine extended from Kittery to Saco on the coast and many miles

Very soon after this his Estate was sequester'd by a Resolve of the County of York in Nov^r 1774. Prior to this time Sir W^m who then resided on Jamaica Plains near Boston was obliged to retire into the Town for safety & to avoid the fury of the Mob who he was informed intended to attack his House with a view of forcing him to resign his Seat at the Council Board. He nevertheless kept his Seat till a Month previous to the Evacuation of Boston when from a Conversation with the Commander in Chief learning that the Council were of no longer use he came to Eng^d.

A Zealous Loyalist & by the early & decided part he took in favor of Gov^t he render'd material Service. Did not bear Arms.

Sir W^m was one of the first who signed the Association for the defence of the place & held himself ready to do Duty if called upon. Produces in evidence of his Loyalty a Letter from Lord Dartmouth & a Certificate from Lord Sackville. Says that he has derived no Advantage from his property from the time the resolves were pass'd by the County of York. Lord North in cons^n of his Services granted him an Allowance of £500 a Year from Nov^r 1774 which has continued to the present time. He rec^d a Bounty from the Treasury of £500 in consequence of his Distress consequent to the Dutch War he having an estate in Surinam. Derives his title to the principal part of his Estate in North America from his Grandfather Sir W^m Pepperell to whom he was residuary Legatee. Left America very young & on his return appointed M^r John Sparhawk (a Cousin of his) his Agent. His Affairs were scarcely put into his hands when the Troubles began And he is therefore himself but very little acquainted with them. He sent for M^r Sparhawk from America who has possession of his papers to give Evidence on his Memorial & produces Certificates to his Character from M^r Lutwyche Agent to the New Hampshire Loyalists & from M^r Sewell Judge of the Admiralty in Nova Scotia both dated in July 1784.

Bounty £500 a Y^r.

General Gage—sworn. 13^th July 1784.

Says that from the Commencement of the troubles Sir W^m Pepperell took a decided part in favor of the British Gov^t & that he was one of those who offer'd to enroll in an Association for the defence of Boston also that he obey'd the King's Mandamus appointing him one of the Council for the Province of Mass. at a time when it was well known he would by so doing make himself very obnoxious to the Americans. The Gen^l says that Sir W^m was generally esteem'd to possess a very considerable property.

Sir Will^m Pepperell—again—sworn.

Says he hopes we shall take into our Consideration the very early & decided part he took in favor of the British Gov^t & that his Property was one of the first that fell a Sacrifice in consequence of his Loyalty.

back from the seashore . . . and the water-power and mill-privileges rendered it even at the time of the sequestration a princely fortune (Sabine, op. cit., vol. ii, p. 170). Returning to England in 1775, Sir William took a leading part amongst the Loyalists. He became President of the Association formed in 1779. After that the Board of Agents was set on foot to prosecute the claims of loyalists to compensation for their losses by the war, and under the Confiscation Acts of the several States, Sir William, upon the death of Sir James Wright, became its President. Sir William died in London in 1816 (Stark, op. cit., pp. 207–14). Hutchinson notes (op. cit., vol. i, p. 21) under date March 28, 1776: 'Sir William is more discouraged about the event of American affairs than anybody. His spirits are very low from the loss of his lady' (on the voyage).

## Memorial of the Rev^d^ Will^m^ Walter[1]

Determin'd the 31^st^ of July 1784.

15^th^ July 1784.

The Rev^d^ Will^m^ Walter—the Claimant—sworn.

A Loyalist.

Did not bear Arms.

A Native of Roxborough Massachusets. At the Commencement of the troubles he was Rector of Trinity Church in Boston had been so from 1767. Says that when the Stamp papers were distributed by M^r^ Oliver the Distributor & that Disturbances followed He exhorted his Parishioners ag^t^ violent Measures & constantly used his utmost Efforts to quiet their Minds & induce them to be obedient to the Mandates of their Sovereign. In doing this he made himself very obnoxious to the Inha^ts^ & that he might not by his Example in remaining give any encouragement to the Revolters He left Boston & went with the Army to Halifax from whence he proceeded to New York where he acted as Chaplain to three Reg^ts^ with the pay of *7s. 6d.* a Day S. Continued in this Situation for about a Y^r^ & ½ when on the removal of the Reg^ts^ afs^d^ & being left destitute of support Sir Henry Clinton gave him the Chaplainship of the 2^d^ Batt^n^ of Gen^l^ Delancey's Brigade with an Allowance of *6s. 8d.* S. per Day. In this Situation he continued during the remainder of the War. Came to Eng^d^ in feb^y^ 1784.

Bounty £40 a Y^r^.

He has been recommended by us in our last Report for £40 per Ann.

Edward Lutwych—sworn.

Late of New Hampshire where he commanded a Reg^t^ of Militia. Says that in May 1775 the Claim^t^ was Rector of Trinity Church Boston. Believes that he was always very loyal. Always understood that the Claim^t's^ Living altogether might be about £300 S. Says that he heard from Claim^t's^ Successor that the Gifts from the people amounted to as much as the Salary. Knows the House that the Claim^t^ lived in believes it to have been his property but can't put any Value on it—it was handsomely furnished.

Peter Fry Esq—sworn.

Knew the Claim^t^ at Boston. Says that before he got the Living there he resided at Salem where he had an Appointment of Deputy Collector. That he came to Eng^d^ to obtain orders 15 or 16 Y^rs^ ago & on an invitation from the people at Boston went thither. Knows nothing of his Conduct himself as he lived out of Boston. Has heard something of a letter which was written by the Claim^t^ to Sir W^m^ Pepperell wherein he signified something of a Disapprobation of the Measures of Great Britain. He never saw the Letter himself. A M^r^ Sam Porter who is now in France (a Loyalist) talked to him some Months ago about this Letter which brought it to his mind. It was thought an odd Letter to be written by a Clergyman of his persuasion. There was an House in Boston said to be M^r^ Walter's. Can't speak to the Value of the House.

Samuel Hale—sworn.

Late of Portsmouth New Hampshire. He practis'd the Law. Says that the Claim^t^ was Rector of Trinity Church. Understood it was one of the best

[1] *b.* 1739, *d.* 1800. In 1767 he joined with the Clergy of Massachusetts and Rhode Island in petitioning for a bishop for America. He went to Shelburne, Nova Scotia, but in 1791 he returned to Boston. He remained Rector of Christ Church, Boston, till his death (Stark, op. cit., pp. 339–42).

of the Northern Colonies about £300 per Ann. lawful Money. Says that he believes M^r^ Walter was well attach'd & that many prejudices were entertain'd ag^t^ him on Acc^t^ of his Loyalty. Being asked if he ever heard anything said ag^t^ the Claim^t's^ loyalty Says that he has but firmly believes they were fabricated by the Presbyterian Ministers on acc^t^ of the Claim^t^ being of the Church of Eng^d^.

Can't speak to any part of Claim^t's^ property but his Library which he values at £50 S.

Sir W^m^ Pepperell Bar^t^—sworn. 16^th^ July 1784.

Knew the Claim^t^ & says he was Rector of Trinity Church. Supposes that M^r^ Walter's Situation was a very eligible one. Had a very good Salary & was very much beloved by the people. Believes him to have been always very loyal & has understood that he sign'd the Addresses to Gen^l^ Gage & Gov^r^ Hutchinson.

Rev^d^ Will^m^ Walter—the Claimant—sworn.

Says that while he was at New York he held a Correspondence with Gen^l^ Parsons & believes that what he repeatedly said to him respecting the Disputes with G. B. soften'd his Mind towards British Subjects. He had before been very violent.

Rev^d^ Will^m^ Walter—the Claimant—sworn. 2^d^ Aug^t^ 1784.

Says that when he went from New York to Port Roseway [1] he had an invitation from the people at the latter place to be their Minister. Nothing is yet fix'd. He is going there & with the Expectation of being their Minister.

### Memorial of Zachariah Hood Late Comptroller of his Majesty's Customs in Philadelphia

Determin'd the 18^th^ of Dec^r^ 1784.

Zachariah Hood—the Claimant—sworn. 16^th^ July 1784.

A Native of Maryland. At the Commencement of the troubles He was Comptroller of the Port of Philadelphia & had been appointed to this office two Years before the troubles began. Says that in consequence of his having express'd his opinion of D^r^ Franklyn's Conduct who was then in Eng^d^ he was beat by the Doct^r's^ Son in Law [2] & immediately after in May 1775 quitted Phil^a^ & came to Eng^d^ when Lord North gave him £200 S. & £100 a Y^r^. His Salary as Comptr^r^ was also continued to him (£80 a Y^r^) untill it was struck off about 2 Y^rs^ ago since which time he has rec^d^ £100 a Y^r^ from the Treasury as an American Loyalist. His Salary as Compt^r^ £80 a Y^r^ S. The emoluments £677 a Y^r^ C. Produces his Commission for the Comptrollership dated 7^th^ Jan^y^ 1773 from the Comm^rs^ at Boston. He was only obliged to keep a Clerk at a Salary of £75 C. per Ann. The fees were established.

A Loyalist.
Did not bear Arms.

Office Salary £80 a Y^r^.
Fees £360 a Y^r^.
Bounty £100 a Y^r^.

### Memorial of Sam^l^ Hake [3] Esq.

Determin'd the 24^th^ of Dec^r^ 1784.

Samuel Hake Esq—the Claimant—sworn. 19^th^ July 1784.

A Native of Eng^d^ went to New York as an wholesale Merch^t^ in 1766. Continued in that situation till the War commenced in 1775 & he left America

[1] Shelburne, Nova Scotia. [2] Richard Bache. [3] See Additional Notes, p. 211.

This Case was very minutely investigated & great Attention paid to it. And after the whole was closed the Board were unanimously of Opinion that the Claim was a fraudulent one & it was accordingly so reported to the Lords of the Treasury as the Act of Par$^{t}$ directs.

in feb$^{y}$ 1776. Was always attached to the British Cause. He was in the Jerseys in Jan$^{y}$ 1776 when he heard of some Dispatches being stopped that were going from Gen$^{l}$ Tryon to Gov$^{r}$ Franklyn who was then at Amboy. He informed himself of the Contents & immed$^{y}$ went to Gov$^{r}$ Franklyn to inform him thereof. In consequence of this Gen$^{l}$ Skynner in whose handwriting the Dispatches were made his Escape. Claim$^{t}$ procured the Boat for & assisted Gen$^{l}$ Skynner in making his Escape on board the Duchess of Gordon transport then lying off New York. He at the same time carried Dispatches from Gov$^{r}$ Franklyn & deliver'd them to Gov$^{r}$ Tryon who was on board the same Ship. A few Days after he went over to Newark to see his family where he was made Prisoner & tried for having assisted Gen$^{l}$ Skynner but acquitted. M$^{r}$ Isaac Ogden [1] Son of Judge Ogden was one of the Committee. He afterw$^{ds}$ went to Phila$^{a}$ in feb$^{y}$ 1776 & came to Eng$^{d}$. He owed Money here as a Merch$^{t}$ but his Creditors treated him with great lenity & made no Objections to his return to America which he did in May 1778. He had rec$^{d}$ a Pension from the latter end of 1776 of £200 a Y$^{r}$ & was promised a Continuance of it by Lord North & Lord Geo Germaine. Says he did not return sooner to New York on acc$^{t}$ of his not having till then seen any prospect of peace at that time he expected it would take place. On his passage out he was taken by 2 American Privateers & carried into New London & was detain'd as a Prisoner upwards of 3 Y$^{rs}$ before he made his Escape which he did in the fall of 1781. Says he married the Dau$^{r}$ of Rob$^{t}$ Gilbert Livingston in 1770. His father in Law is first Cousin to the American Gov$^{r}$ of this name.[2] That in 1778 soon after he was made Prisoner he formed a Plan with John Livingston a Merch$^{t}$ to open a Communication with the Comm$^{rs}$ under the colour of trade & for this purpose obtain'd a Passport from Gen$^{l}$ Washington & went into New York on his Parole. He obtain'd a Flag from Sir Henry Clinton & carried out goods to the value of £2000 Cur. from New York to trade with. His intention was to have carried them to Livingston's Manor. They were however seized by Sir Ja$^{s}$ Jay [3] & sold for the benefit of the States. Says that the Comm$^{rs}$ were privy to & approved of his taking out the goods & he had Sir Henry Clinton's permission for carrying out the Effects & refers to the Passport which he undertakes to produce tomorrow. Carried out with him the Comm$^{rs}$ Proclamations & distributed them.

The Oath to the States was proposed to him which he refused. Was paroled 4 Miles for 5 Months afterw$^{ds}$ 2 Miles for 6 Months. Then confined close in Gaol for 3 Months then paroled to a farm till he made his Escape in the fall of 1781. Says he had 2 Addresses from Loyalists one from the Manor of Livingston the other from Duchess [4] County signed by about 70 persons part of 2300 which he carried into New York at the risque of his life proposing to join the Kings

[1] Haldimand wrote of this Isaac Ogden in his Diary (Brymner, *Can. Archives*, 1889, p. 227): 'There is a certain Ogden, formerly of Jersey, a great rebel and very much the friend of Smith, who has obtained for him an office in Canada.' This Ogden became judge of the Admiralty Court, Montreal, and in 1796 was made a judge of the Superior Court.

[2] William Livingstone became Governor of New Jersey on August 31, 1776.

[3] *b.* 1732, *d.* 1815. He was a brother of John Jay. There is a biographical notice of him in *New York Col. Docs.*, vol. vii, p. 498.

[4] Dutchess.

Arms to dispossess the Rebels & to take possn of West point. Produces a Paper dated 10th Novr 1781 containing propositions which the Claimt was commission'd to offer to Sir Henry Clinton. The Plan was taken into Consn but never executed. A Man was sent out with a letter & was shot—refers for the particulars to Govr Franklyn. He was always ready to give his Assistance till the Preliminaries were sign'd. When he came in after his Imprisonment Sir Henry Clinton gave him £50. Had no Employment or Pay—it was 50 Gās. He continued to receive his Pension of 200 a Yr from Engd. Never recd any Money but the 50 Gās. Returned to Engd on the Evacuation of New York. Does not intend to return to America.

Produces Certificates from Govr Franklyn & Genl Skynner. Copy of Govr Franklyns report to Sir Henry Clinton dated 24th Novr 1781 as President of the Associated Loyalists on the Enquiry into the propositions brought in by Mr Hake. Produces Address from Charlotte Precinct Duchess County dated 3d Septr 1781 Do & from Livingston Manor.

A Letter from John Cooke to Mr Hake dated 20th Septr 1781 relating to the last Address.

A Deposition of Esaia Wild dated 26th April 1782 in which is a Deposition of Dr Teller dated 3 Novr 1781. A Letter to Sir Henry Clinton from sundry Loyalists dated 2d May 1782 at New York praying permission for him to go to Engd in an armed Vessel. Copy of an Address to Sir Henry Clinton dated 2d May 1782 signed by 221 persons in favor of Mr Hake & vouching his Loyalty &c.

Governor Franklyn—sworn.

Never knew the Claimt till he went to him to give the Intelligence which he stated in his Evidence yesterday. Believes he was actuated from principles of Loyalty & that he ran a very great risque of his Life in going to the Witness. Knows nothing of the Claimts property heard that he was a Mercht at New York & that he had been very unfortunate in his Concerns. Witness says that he was a good deal disliked at N. York but does not know on what Acct. Govr Franklyn says that he shewed a great deal of zeal when he went to inform him of Genl Tryon's dispatches being stopp'd.

Ebenezer Jessup—late of Albany—sworn.

Knew Mr Hake previous to the rebellion. Knew him first in 1772. Dont know anything of his Conduct respecting his Loyalty. Knows nothing of his Estates can speak to nothing but the Indian property. Says that Mr Hake was an Associate of Mr Jos Totton & Stephen Crossfield. Witness was concern'd in making purchases in the province of New York on the branches of Hudson's river with said Totton & Crossfield. He made the purchases in July 1772 produces the Grant from the Indians (800000 Acres) Consn Money £1135 C. Says it was only a nominal Sum. The original purchase Money with the Expences of surveying & locating amounted to £12 6*s*. C. for every 1000 Acres. Mr Hake had 22500 Acres in the Township No 2 & two other Shares & ½ in other Townships amounting in the whole to 82500 Acres for which Mr Hake paid him at the rate of £12 6*s*. per thousand Acres as aforementd & if he is not mistaken the Interest Money also. Don't think that anybody was concern'd with Mr Hake in this purchase. To the best of his remembrance the Indians got about 5000 Dollars the Expences in treating them with Victuals & Drink were great but he don't recollect how much Witness sold some of his but does not remember at what price the 1000 Acres. Says that he believes the Tracts on an Average were worth at the Commencement of the troubles 1*s*. S. per Acre & believes that the Proprietors would have obtain'd this price for their several Shares. Believes no part of M^r^ Hake's Townships were settled.

Benj^n^ Davis—sworn.

Says that he was one of the Surveyors or Attendant on the Surveyors that survey'd the lands bought from the Indians. Thinks that they were worth 2*s*. 6*d*. S. per Acre on an Average. Allows that there were some very bad as well as good.

Ivy Hare—sworn. 21^st^ July 1784.

Knew the Claim^t^ & says that he assisted him in comparing Extracts of the Acc^ts^ in his Books swears to the particulars stated in Claimant's Schedule to be true Copies of s^d^ Acc^ts^. These Extracts were compared by him in Nov^r^ 1783 & understood it was for the purpose of laying them before his Cred^rs^ & to enable him to state his Claim to this board. M^r^ Hake had a Clerk at this time (his name Rob^t^ Miller) who occasionally attended with the Witness at the examining of the afs^d^ Acc^ts^.

Thomas Hood—sworn. 26^th^ July 1784.

Knows nothing of Claim^t's^ Loyalty refers to Gen^l^ Robertson [1] Col^l^ Morris M^r^ Smith Brother of Judge Smith W^m^ Waddell late Alderman of New York. Heard from several persons that Hake has no real or personal property but what he has assign'd over to others. For this he refers to Gen^l^ Robertson W^m^ Waddell & Rob^t^ Barkley.

A few Days previous to the time limited by the Act for bringing in Claims he accidentally called at Hake's House & Hake told him that he did not like some of the Articles in his Claim & wished to change them & fill them up with some other Claim to the same Am^t^ to correspond with the Schedule. One of these Articles was the charge of a Debt from *Ludlow*. He understood they were deposited in Ludlow's hands by Livingston. He (Hake) propos'd to transcribe the whole Schedule on paper similar to the last Sheet & to annex it—& examin'd the marks at the Window. The Witness advised him to desist. He shew'd him the Schedule & it was the same now produced. He afterw^ds^ sent him a Letter advising him to desist & promises to produce the Letter if he has not lost it which he dont think he has.

M^r^ Smith—Sir Henry Clinton's Secretary—sworn.

Says that Sir Henry being unwell he comes to answer any Questions in his power. He does not know anything of M^r^ Hake or of his having had permission from Sir Henry to go up the North river with a Cargo of goods.

[1] In 1779 he was appointed Governor of New York to succeed Tryon. He died in 1788 (Biog. notice in *New York Col. Docs.*, vol. viii, p. 706). Anecdotes of him are recorded in Moore, op. cit., vol. ii, pp. 110, 232.

W^m^ Smith Esq [1]—late Chief Justice of New York—sworn. 30^th^ July 1784.

Says he has known the Claim^t^ many Y^rs^ prior to 1778. He knew nothing of Claim^t's^ political Character. In Aug^t^ of that Year he saw M^r^ Hake at New York who avow'd to him the Witness his Attachm^t^ to the British Cause. The Claim^t^ he says went up the North river into the Enemy's Country with some goods & had he believes permission for so doing from the Comm^rs^. He also understood that he was then employ'd in distributing the proclamations & that he suffer'd Inconveniences from the people suspecting that he was partial to G. B. That in 1780 or 1781 on his returning to New York the Witness told him of his intention to give some material Information to the Comm^r^ in chief which he was enabled to do from his having been about 3 Y^rs^ absent in the Enemy's Country. Believes that the Information was given but thinks that Gen^l^ Robertson did not pay much attention thereto on Acc^t^ of his entertaining some doubts of M^r^ Hake's conduct & disliking him on acc^t^ of his conceiving that he was a Man of bad private Character. On the whole M^r^ Hake's conduct *as a Loyalist* the Witness is of Opinion that he was always well attached to the British Gov^t^. He relates a long Story of the Claim^t^ having made unjust Charges ag^t^ Col^l^ Morris [2] who was one of the King's Council at New York in order to shew us that M^r^ Hake is a Man of a strange disposition. Has heard that the Claim^t^ made Assignments of some of his property to his father in law Rob^t^ Gilbert Livingston when the Claim^t^ was embarass'd in his Circumstances. This he understood was before the War. Says again that those Assignments were made in Consequence of M^r^ Livingston having assisted him at a time when the Claim^t^ was under great difficulties in his trading Concerns but he cant speak particularly to what part of the property was assigned.

Joshua Smyth Att^y^ at Law—sworn.

Brother of the Chief Justice. Says that he knew the Claim^t^ & the family he was connected with. Recollects his being very much embarass'd in 1773 or 1774 on acc^t^ of the Situation of his private affairs & of having heard from the Claim^t^ of his assigning some property to M^r^ Livingston who had lent him Money.

Will^m^ Waddell—sworn.

Was acquainted with the Claim^t^ both before & after the rebellion. Says that he recollects M^r^ Hake having fail'd before the troubles. Thinks that his Affairs were still deranged when the rebellion commenced & that he had assign'd his property over to his father in Law but can't speak particularly to these Points but he thinks M^r^ Hake was always well attached to the Cause of Great Britain.

General Robertson—sworn. 3^d^ Aug^t^ 1784.

Knew the Claim^t^ at New York. Says that he believes he was uniformly loyal—previous to the troubles he had been a Merch^t^ & had extensive Dealings—

[1] Smith became in 1786 Chief Justice of Canada, which office he held till his death in 1793. He proposed at the time of the Constitutional Act a notable scheme for the union of all the British North American Possessions (Egerton and Grant, *Can. Constitutional Development*, pp. 104–10).

[2] *b.* 1717, *d.* in England 1794. He served under Braddock at the battle of Monongahela, July 8, 1755. He retired from the army in 1764 and became a member of the New York Council. In December 1781 Hake, in a letter to the Adjutant-General, accused him of disloyalty. The charge, after investigation, was declared 'false, scandalous, and malicious' (Biog. notice in *New York Col. Docs.*, vol. viii, p. 590).

in 1775 the Gen[l] thinks the Claim[t] fail'd is not certain whether it was in 1774 or 1775 & cannot say if Claim[t] made any Assignm[t] of his property to M[r] Livingston. He owed the Gen[l] about £2000 York C. & gave him a joint bond with M[r] Livingston for y[e] payment. A part was paid thinks about half. Says that Claim[t] had under various pretences leave to carry Goods up the North river but he the Witness was not in the Country at that time.

David Matthews Esq—late Mayor of New York—sworn. 5[th] Aug[t] 1784.

Is shewn the Schedule deliver'd in by M[r] Hake. Says it is the same that was signed by him. Says it is not the same that was first brought to him & which he refused to sign. The persons who came to testify before him to the Schedule were brought by M[r] Hake. One was a Menial Serv[t] to Adm[l] Digby. The other a Man of very bad Character. It struck M[r] Matthews that he could get no others. M[r] Hake had brought a Certificate ready drawn out whereby M[r] Matthews was to have certified that the persons swearing were *well known to him & worthy of good Credit.* He asked M[r] Hake how he could think of Doing such a thing & asked who the people were. M[r] Hake took it away & then brought that which he has produced here but in that he had left a large Blank which he thought looked suspicious & therefore took care to fill it up in such a manner as to prevent anything further being inserted therein. Rob[t] Miller was one of those he refused to certify to. He says at the time it struck him that something fraudulent was intended from Hake bringing two such people before him. Says he knows M[r] Hake stopped payment a little time before the troubles & understood that an Assignment was made of all his Effects. Says that every person from New York was amazed at hearing of M[r] Hake having made any Claim here. Remembers M[r] Hake having obtain'd permission to carry some goods up the North river. Does not know to what Amount.

Says that he thinks M[r] Ivy Hare who is a Witness to M[r] Hake's Case was a Steward or Cook to Admiral Digby.

### Further Witnesses to the Memorial of Sam[l] Hake Esq.

John Chevalier Roome—sworn. 21[st] of Aug[t] 1784.

M[r] Roome was acquainted with M[r] Hake at New York. He was in the Year 1775 a Merch[t] & about that time (either in the latter end of 1774 or the beginning of 1775) he was in Goal as he heard from his Clerks. He understood that his father in Law had taken the whole of the real Estate in execution to indemnify him for the Security which he had given. The Clerk who told him so is dead & that the business was carried on by one Jones. Does not know whether there was any Assignment & heard of no other Creditors but M[r] Livingston. It was the general Idea of people there that M[r] Hake was a Bankrupt & ruin'd. It was owing to the mode of conducting his business. He gave very extensive Credit & gave it to any body. He left New York in 1775 & it was then thought that he went to settle with his Creditors. He came back to New York in 1778 & he applied to M[r] Roome who was Secretary to the Commandant of the Garrison for the Houses in Queen Street which had been his & M[r] Roome's

Answer was that the Houses belonged to his father in Law M^r Livingston & were returned so on the barrack books. Hake never denied or even affected to deny it.

In Oct^r 1778 He obtain'd permission to carry up a Quantity of Goods into the Jerseys under a flag. After this he was to return to his Parole in Duchess County where he was Prisoner at that time. M^r Roome says that there was no public ground for this but it was done merely to accommodate M^r Hake (Hake had pretended to have been sent out on this Expedition by the Gen^l for some private reasons).

He has no Doubt of M^r Hake's loyalty & confirms him in the Acc^t before given of saving Gen^l Skynner's life & says he must have done it at some risque. They were stopped with this flag by an advanced Post of the Enemy at a Distance up the river & he went to the Gov^r for permission to land the Goods. Gov^r Clinton refused him that permission & order'd him to return to New York. Some of the Americans came on board & drank his Wine & when he came down the river his Goods were seized under an Act of the State (which he promises to produce) & he says that the Seizure was fairly made. This he knows officially it was a Report made to him as Secretary to the Commandant. He never heard of his having any property at Rinebeck. Has been there & thinks he must have known it if he had. Knows that his father in Law had property there. He looks upon his father in Law to have been worth 8 or £10000 & has several Children. He knows of 5 Children & therefore does not suppose that he could have given much fortune to M^rs Hake.

Daniel Hammill—sworn.

Knew M^r Hake. His first knowledge of him was in 1777 & he knows nothing of his property but by report.

He knew of some Houses burnt at Rinebeck by Gen^l Vaughan in 1777. One House was said to be M^r Hake's & M^r Livingston told the Witness this—that one of the Houses was said to be his. He did hear that M^r Livingston had taken all his property in Execution the person who told the Witness this was Brother to M^rs Hake. He says he fail'd & was a broken Merch^t before the War therefore he could have no property but he might have Book Debts. He lived within 12 Miles of Rinebeck & never heard that he had property at Rinebeck excepting in the Conversation with M^r Livingston. Believes M^r Hake to have been a Loyalist. Is rather of Opinion that the true State of the Case is that the father in Law took the House which Hake had bought & paid the Money for it & took the Conveyance. He has heard that the father in Law paid many thousands for him. He says that Hake behaved very ill to his Wife & believes he killed her by his Cruelty. He has heard the Brother of M^rs Hake say frequently when his Children were present that those were the Children of that damn'd Scoundrel Hake who had broke his Sister's Heart.

Confirms M^r Roome as to the Manner of seizing the Goods. Says that Hake had really sold them to one Thomas who gave him an Obligation for them & they were taken from Thomas. He has seen the Bond.

Major Van Cortland—sworn. 24^th of Aug^t 1784.

Remembers M^r Hake in New York but had no Acquaintance with him. Knows nothing of his Circumstances or property. Knows Rinebeck but does not know whether he had any property there or not. He never heard that he had property there.

Joseph Chew [1]—sworn. 27th of Augt 1784.

He was Secretary of Indian Affairs under Sir Wm Johnson before the rebellion & resided in the County of Tryon about 40 Miles from Albany. He had some little knowledge of him as a Mercht [&] in the latter end of 1773 & 1774. He was in Company with him at Sir Wm Johnson's. Mr Hake had been a great Mercht & had then fail'd. He knew Mr Livingston. Knows nothing of any surrender of Property to Mr Livingston but heard Mr Hake's Attorney in the County where the Witness lived say that his Affairs were put into his hands to be settled. Does not think him worth in 1775 £40000. Thinks him to have been in a very bad Situation.

Expresses a surprize that Mr Hake should receive an Allowance from Govt as having done service & says that when it was known it was consider'd a laughable Matter in America.

Says that Mr Henry White Mr Alexr Wallace & Coll Beverly Robinson know much more of Mr Hake than he does.

N.B. The Board gave Directions accordingly to send to the above Gentn to attend.

Isaac Ogden Esq—sworn. 31st of Augt 1784.

Knows Mr Hake. He was a Mercht there. There was a report that he was embarrass'd in 1775 & that he had made an Assignmt to his father in Law & to Mr Ludlow another part of his property to satisfy his Creditors in Engd. Believes if he had paid all the Money he owed in 1775 he would not have been worth much. Knows he had an House & Tavern in the Jerseys it was rented out in Hake's name. Says if his Debts could all be collected in He thinks he would be worth a considerable Sum of Money. Before the troubles he never heard of Mr Hake having any landed property but the House at Newark. Does not suspect any fraud in the Assignment to Livingston believes it to have been a bonâ fidê transaction. If he was to pay his Debts in Engd as well as America He wd be worth nothing.

## Further Witnesses to the Memorial of Mr Hake

Coll Beverly Robinson—sworn. 31st of Augt 1784.

Had no personal Acquaintance with Mr Hake but knew he was a Mercht before the troubles. Thinks he fail'd a Year or two before the troubles. He understood that he was a broken Mercht it was the general Opinion at the time. Knows the District of Rinebeck about 60 Miles from the Witness. Never heard of his having any property there but he might have had property there & the Witness not know it. Thinks Mr Livingston had property at Rinebeck. Knows nothing of Mr Hake or his property but by Report.

[1] He was recommended for the appointment by Sir W. Johnson as 'a gentleman of a respectable family in Virginia, formerly an officer in the troops of that colony and afterwards a Captain in the levies of this province under my command in 1747, in which he behaved very well. He has since had many opportunities of being acquainted with the Indians' (*New York Col. Docs.*, vol. viii, p. 424). He was taken prisoner in Long Island in June, 1777 (ibid., p. 712).

Thomas Lynch—sworn.

Knew M^r Hake first in 1770 1771 or 1772. He was a large Importer of Goods had many Dealings with him & M^r Hake paid him very well. The Witness came to Eng^d in 1772 & went back in 1774. M^r Hake had then quitted Trade & he understood it to be on Acc^t of his Affairs being deranged on acc^t of his Debts here. Knew of no landed property that he had but an House at New York. During the War M^r Hake told the Witness that he was jointly bound with M^r Livingston to pay several Bonds &c for which he had given a Security to his father in Law. Knows nothing more of M^r Hake or his Property.

John Rane—sworn.

Knew M^r Hake a few Years before the troubles. First knew him in 1771. He was a Merch^t in New York in a very considerable Line of business. About this time he married M^r Livingston's Dau^r. He would have had a considerable fortune with her if he had pleas'd the family but believes he had only £2000 with her. He did not understand that he was a Man of property independent of his Wife's fortune. He went with M^rs Livingston to M^r Hake's in 1773 & he purchased Goods to the Amo^t of £130 & gave M^r Hake his Note for the Money & when he went to discharge the Note about a Y^r afterw^ds he found the Note in M^r Livingston's hands. He understood that his Affairs had been bad & that he had assign'd this Note to his father in Law as a Security. He has since understood that he had at the same time assign'd the greatest part of his property to M^r Livingston. Says he had an House at New York which he understood was likewise assign'd. Says M^r Livingston was obliged to pay more for him than the property amounted to. Knows Rinebeck. M^r Livingston had property there but never heard that Hake had property there. M^r Hake's brother in Law had an House burnt there. Knows Ja^s Smith from whom Hake said he bought the House that he had an House & lived at Rinebeck & believes he lived there till 1778 when he came into the British Lines.

### Further testimony to the Case of Sam^l Hake Esq.

Alexander Wallace Esq—sworn.

The Witness has been settled at New York since the Y^r 1777. He did not know much of M^r Hake but was very intimate in M^r Livingston's family. M^r Hake took a Store near M^r Livingston & thinks he married Miss Livingston in 1769 or 1770. When he married he thinks he was not worth a Shilling. When he married he is sure he did not get a Shilling. He gave out that he got 1500 but he is sure he did not. He has heard M^rs Livingston say that her Husband had never given any fortune to her. Says M^r Hake fail'd in 1773 or 1774 & he was in Gaol in 1774. The Witness went amongst the Creditors on behalf of Gen^l Robertson & it was currently said by the Creditors at the time that all the good Debts were made over to M^r Livingston & that what remain'd would not pay two Shillings in the Pound. He never heard that he had any Land it did not appear to the Creditors then assembled that there was any Land to pay the Creditors. Knows Reinbeck very well & knows that M^r Livingston had a great deal of Land at Reinbeck & that he built an House & gave some Land to his eldest Son. Never heard that M^r Hake had any Land there. He has often heard Livingston & Hake both say that the Assignment made to Livingston was to indemnify him ag$^{t}$ a Bond which he had sign'd to Gen$^{l}$ Robertson. He has heard Hake say that he had assign'd certain Debts to M$^{r}$ Livingston & he has heard M$^{r}$ Livingston say that he was secured. From what he has heard in the family he says he believes that no land was contain'd in the Assignment made to Livingston. He never heard that M$^{r}$ James Smith had any Land at Reinbeck but knew that the father of M$^{r}$ Smith had some property at Reinbeck but does not know he left it to James. He says that from what he knew of Hake & from what he knew of M$^{rs}$ Hake's family he is perfectly convinced in his own mind & it was the general Opinion that in the Spring of 1775 M$^{r}$ Hake was considerably worse than nothing. The Witness knows that the British Troops set fire to some Houses at Reinbeck & has frequently heard the names of those who suffer'd by the fire & has heard M$^{r}$ Livingston mention'd as one but never heard M$^{r}$ Hake's name mention'd. Has no doubt but Lord Stirling owed to M$^{r}$ Hake the Money which Hake has mention'd. The Acc$^{ts}$ given in at different times to the Board are shewn to M$^{r}$ Wallace & he looks them over & after inspecting them deliberately He says he thinks they are not fair Acc$^{ts}$ that he ought to shew his Books from which they were taken & that after looking over them he has not a better Opinion of his Solvency than he had before.

### Further testimony to the Memorial of Sam$^{l}$ Hake Esq.

Robert Barclay Esq—upon his Affirmation. 23$^{d}$ of Oct$^{r}$ 1784.

Has known him for many Y$^{rs}$ as a Correspondent. He has known him personally since 1773. He was then at New York. He is a Native of America. His House were Creditors of M$^{r}$ Hake at that time. He believes under £1000. He then press'd him for the Money. He could not pay it but he said he had Money enough to pay all his Debts. He then at the instigation of his Creditors assign'd certain Debts to M$^{r}$ Ludlow. His House had that opinion of M$^{r}$ Hake that they would not trust him till he had paid his Balances. He never heard of M$^{r}$ Hake's having any Land. M$^{r}$ Cruger [1] was likewise a Cred$^{r}$ & he was anxious to get his Money. He does not recollect to have heard of his having any Land & says to be sure if they could have got landed Security they would have got it. Says that M$^{r}$ Hake told him that he had made an Assignment to M$^{r}$ Livingston but he did not hear that in America.

A Certificate is produced signed by several persons One of whom is M$^{r}$ Barclay (not this Gent$^{n}$ but one of the House) they recommend him to Gov$^{t}$ & say that many of his Losses *may* be owing to the War. But M$^{r}$ Barclay says that this was upon the credit of M$^{r}$ Hake's assertion & he desires us to pay but little Credit to that Certificate. He says that M$^{r}$ Hake insinuated to the Witness that if he obtain'd Compensation under the Act of Par$^{t}$ they would be paid.

M$^{r}$ Hake in 1773 was in such Circumstances that both himself & M$^{r}$ Cruger the Member for Bristol thought it necessary to press him for the balances due from him. M$^{r}$ Barclay is asked if he then consider'd M$^{r}$ Hake as a Man in insolvent Circumstances. He says he does not think himself able to give a full

[1] Henry Cruger, M.P. for Bristol, was the author of the familiar saying, 'I say ditto to Mr. Burke'. There is a *Life* of him by H. C. van Schaack.

Answer to the Question as he did not know exactly what his Circumstances were but he certainly thought he was embarrass'd otherwise he should not have thought it necessary to have press'd him.

He is shewn the Acc^t Current with the Certificate subjoin'd dated 6^th Oct^r 1784 & says the Commissioners ought not to pay any Attention to that Certificate as what is there stated arises entirely from M^r Hake's own Information.

Says that when M^r Hake came round to his Creditors he stated to them that whatever he got from Gov^t would go amongst them & he has no doubt he said so with a View to influence his Creditors to sign his Certificate.

Says he must acknowledge his surprize at M^r Hake's having made a Claim for so large a Sum as £40000.

### Memorial of James Nixon

James Nixon—the Claimant—sworn 21^st July 1784. Determin'd the 21^st of July 1784.

He was born at Rhode Island. At the Commencement of the troubles he was a Master of a Vessel that traded to the West Indies.

In 1777 He enter'd into the Association at Rhode Island. After the battle of Lexington he remain'd on shore to take care of his family. In the fall of 1776 He was sent for by the General Assembly & reprimanded for having with others made representations ag^t the taking up of the Custom House Officers. The Oaths were never tender'd to him he never took any. Remain'd quietly till the British Troops took possession. In July 1777 He was appointed to superintend the Vessels that were employ'd to bring Fuel from Long Island to Rhode Island for which he had an Allowance of a Dollar per Day. He continued in this employ till the Evacuation in Oct^r 1779 when he went to Long Island & was there employ'd in the Barrack Master Gen^l's Departm^t untill July 1782. In 1783 he was allow'd £20 N. York C. per Qua^r by the Board established at N. York for the relief of American Refugees. Rec^d this till July 1783. He rec^d 3 Qu^rs. Produces Certificates to his Loyalty & good Conduct from Col^l Crosby & Gen^l Prescott. A Loyalist.

After the Preliminary Articles were sign'd he went to Rhode Island to make enquiries concerning his property. Says it was to recover payment of a Vessel which he had sold to one Horsted Hacker he recover'd the Money 800 Dollars but was imme^y seized & put into Goal where he was kept till he embarked for New York. He is proscribed by Name in the Act that was pass'd imme^y after the Evacuation of Rhode Island.

Came to Eng^d the latter end of Jan^y 1784 & has been paid £30 by the Treasury lately to defray his passage Expences to Nova Scotia. He has no Annual Allowance. Bounty £30 in full.

### Memorial of Alex^r & James Robertson [1]

James Robertson—one of the Claimants—sworn. 22^d July 1784. Determin'd the 4^th of Aug^t 1784.

He went to America 18 Years ago. Is a Native of Scotland. His Brother went out two Years afterwards. He is at present at Port Roseway. They had

[1] The brothers continued the printing of the *Royal American Gazette* at Shelburne. After the death of Alexander, James retired to Edinburgh with his nephew, James, jun. (Siebert, *The Flight of American Loyalists to the British Isles*, Columbus, Ohio, p. 18).

Loyalists & appear to have been in good business as Printers.

at the Commencement of the troubles Printing offices at Albany & at Norwich in Connecticut. Swears to the truth of all he has stated in his Memorial. Bore Arms at Charlestown & commanded a Co. of Militia. Produces Certificates from M^r^ Cuyler late Mayor of Albany M^r^ Matthews late Mayor of New York & from Col^l^ Edmiston to his & his Brother's Loyalty. He went with the Army up the North river under the command of Sir Henry Clinton & he had served also in the M^a^ at New York under Col^l^ Willard.

Property.

Says he lost a compleat printing Office valued at £311 S. it was at Albany swears that it would have sold for more.

£200.

Determin'd the 4th of Aug^t^ 1784.

**Memorial of David Ogden [1] Esq.**

David Ogden Esq—the Claimant—sworn 23^d^ July 1784.

A Zealous & meritorious Loyalist.

A Native of New Jersey. Was appointed in 1752 of his Majesty's Council & was several Years one of the Supreme Court of Judicature for s^d^ Colony in which Offices he continued till the Commencem^t^ of the rebellion. Says that in the beginning of 1776 he used his utmost Efforts to oppose the then Measures adopted by the Provincial Congress & in consequence thereof became very obnoxious to the Americans & fearful of being apprehended he abandon'd his property in New Jersey & went to New York that the Day after he left his House a Reg^t^ of Continental Troops as he has heard plunder'd the same & destroy'd a great part of his most valuable Effects. Remain'd at New York till Nov^r^ 1783 when he came to Eng^d^. He had an allowance there of £200 per Ann. for about 3 Years & ½ prior to the Evacuation. He at present receives the same Allowance from Gov^t^ which commenced from the 5th of Jan^y^ 1784. Sir Guy Carleton order'd him on two Occasions to be paid £125 S. exclusive of the Annual Allowance. Says he used his utmost endeavours when Gen^l^ Grant with the Kings Troops took up his Quarters at his House in persuading the people to come in & take the Oaths to the King & with so much Success that 26 people only in Newark did not take the Oaths.

Bounty £200 a Y^r^.

His Salary as one of the Justices of the Supreme Court of the Province of New Jersey was £150 per Ann. of New Jersey £90 S. The fees & Perquisites communibus Annis amounted to £120 C. £72 S.

Brig^r^ Gen^l^ Skynner—sworn.

Says that he is perfectly satisfied M^r^ Ogden did everything in his power at the Commencement of the Troubles for the Support of the British Gov^t^ that he made himself very obnoxious & was in Consequence thereof obliged to fly to New York & abandon his property. Says that he M^r^ Ogden was

[1] *b.* 1707, *d.* 1800. There is a full notice of him in Sabine, op. cit., vol. ii, pp. 123–5. 'Ogden was a distinguished lawyer, and, as one of the Council for the Proprietors in suits against the Elizabeth town associates, became unpopular with the people. A man of conspicuous ability and integrity, he was in 1772 appointed a judge of the Supreme Court, which position he filled until his opposition to open resistance against the mother country led him to seek safety within the British lines, where he became an active loyalist. He was looked upon as an oracle of the law, and his opinions had almost the weight of judicial decisions' (Fisher, *New Jersey as a Royal Province, 1738 to 1776*, Col. Univ. Studies in Hist., &c., xli, No. 107, p. 62).

possess'd of a large Mansion House at Newark. It was a very good Stone House & values the same at £2500 New York Currency.

Knows the small House adjoining the foregoing is not able to set a Value on it it was built of Stone.

Values the Lot of 8 Acres at Newark (N° 3) at £800 C. Heard an Inhab$^{t}$ of Newark say 10 Y$^{rs}$ ago that the Lot was worth from £800 to £1000 C. Values the Salt Meadows in New Jersey from £12 to £15 C. per Acre. These Meadows being frequently overflow'd by Rains He says the Grass was exceedingly good.

Speaks of the Tracts at Horseneck & says that the Claim$^{t}$ made great improvements by lowering the Course of the river. He says that these were good Lands. Supposing them to be 3/4$^{ths}$ low Lands He values them at £7 or £8 C. per Acre.

As to the Dispute betw$^{n}$ the Proprietors of E. Jersey & the Inha$^{ts}$ of Eliz$^{th}$ Town [1] Gen$^{l}$ Skynner says that the title of the people of the latter derived under Gov$^{r}$ Nicholls [2] was established as valid. The only remaining Dispute was respecting the Northern Boundary. The Dispute was whether the Line should be run from the Mouth of the Paysack River or from the Mouth of the Bound Creek & also whether it should be drawn westward according to the points of the Compass as they stood at the time of the original Disputes or according to the variation as it now stands. He is of opinion that the Dispute as to the Boundary would before this time have been determin'd in favor of the Proprietors had not the troubles happen'd. And M$^{r}$ Ogden would have been in quiet poss$^{n}$ of his Land purchased of Burdge as it was clearly without the rights of the people of Eliz$^{th}$ Town & Bakers Patent was likewise without the Line as drawn from Bound Creek & great part of it if the Line was drawn from Paysack. Says the Dispute did affect the Price of the Lands within the Disputed Bounds.

## Memorial of Tho$^{s}$ Yorke

Determin'd the 4$^{th}$ of Aug$^{t}$ 1784.

Thomas Yorke—the Claimant—sworn. 26$^{th}$ July 1784.

Born at Lancaster in Pensylvania at the Commencem$^{t}$ of the troubles he was concern'd with others in a Sail Loft. From the beginning of the Disputes in America he took part with G. B. Says that in 1774 at the time of the Non-exportation Agreem$^{t}$ he took particular pains in opposing their Measures. Never took any Oath to them or sign'd any Association. In Nov$^{r}$ 1776 he was obliged to fly from his House & go into the Country for a few Weeks. He then embarked for France & came to Eng$^{d}$. Produces Certificates to his Loyalty from Gov$^{r}$ Franklyn Adm$^{l}$ Digby & M$^{r}$ Galloway. Never rec$^{d}$ any Allowance from Gov$^{t}$ either in America or since he came to Eng$^{d}$.

A Loyalist. Did not bear Arms.

Sam$^{l}$ Shoemaker Esq—sworn. 31$^{st}$ Oct$^{r}$ 1784.

Says that he knows the Claim$^{t}$ that he had thought his Conduct at the beginning of the troubles was rather equivocal. That he carried on a Trade between America and the West Indies & Witness thinks that he traffick'd in those things which were of use to the Americans at the beginning of the troubles.

[1] Fisher (op. cit., pp. 176–207) gives an elaborate and careful account of this controversy.

[2] Richard Nicolls, *b.* 1624, *d.* 1672, the very capable commander of the English expedition against New Netherland and first Governor of New York. He is in *Dict. of Nat. Biography*.

Don't think that the Claimant's opposition to the non importation Agreem^t was from any other Cause than because it affected his own Interest. He thinks that the Claim^t had sold his Share of the Snow Proteus to M^r Gibbs & he believes to M^r Potts also.

M^r Shoemaker expresses his surprize at hearing that M^r Yorke has made a Claim for Loss of Property.

Determin'd the 25^th of Aug^t 1784.

## Memorial of David Matthews [1] Esq. Late Mayor of New York

David Matthews Esq—the Claimant—sworn. 5^th of Aug^t 1784.

A Zealous & active Loyalist & render'd Services to the British Gov^t at the risque of his Life.

Office of Clerk of y^e C^o of Orange £125 a Y^r. Profession £250 a Y^r.

A Native of New York. In the Year 1775 He practised the Law & held the Offices of Clerk of the Court of Com Pleas & Clerk of the Court of Sessions for the County of Orange. These were Patent Offices. No Salary to either but he says the Fees amounted to £200 C. per Ann. & that he made on an Average £600 a Y^r C. by his practise. He made himself very obnoxious early in 1776 & was in consequence thereof apprehended by orders of the New York Convention & sent to Gaol where he was kept 2 Months & then removed to Connecticut where he was confined till he effected his Escape the 21^st of Nov^r 1776. He had exerted himself on various Occasions at the Commencem^t of the troubles in acquiring Information concerning the Designs of the Insurgents which he communicated to Capt^n Vandeput & in doing so he ran the risque of losing his Life particularly when he attempted with the assistance of some of the Magistrates to prevent the people from seizing 500 Stand of Arms. In this however he fail'd notwithstanding the most vigorous Exertions. Says that in Feb^y 1776 he was appointed Mayor of New York by Gov^r Tryon. Says that M^r Hicks his Predecessor made £600 C. per Ann. by the Office. In Dec^r following he was appointed by Gov^r Tryon Register [2] to the Court of Vice Admiralty which was afterw^ds confirmed by the Lords of the Admiralty. Says that in peace it was an office which hardly produced any Income but that in War time it might on an Average be worth £1000 C. per Ann. tho' he did not reap any great Advantage from it as his Deputy (for he could not attend the business himself) was very negligent. Says that he had formed a Plan for the taking M^r Washington & his Guard Prisoners but which was not effected by an unfortunate Discovery that was made of a Letter. One of the persons who was concern'd in the business (a M^r Hicky) was seized & executed. He the Claim^t was also seized & confined as he has already stated. He had been at £150 C. expence in making his Escape & Gov^r Tryon made him a present of 50 Gās. Says again it was £150 S. that it cost him to make his Escape.

[1] In June 1776 a serious conspiracy was detected in New York, the object of which was to capture Washington and secure the colony for Great Britain. The plot was believed to emanate from Governor Tryon, and David Mathews, the Mayor of New York, was involved in it, and was arrested (Force, *Am. Archives*, 4th series, vol. vi, pp. 1054, 1158). A contemporary letter in Moore, op. cit., speaks of 'that merry man' D. Mathews; but the letters he wrote from prison regarding his wife and ten children, and his treatment, do not smack of merriment (Force, op. cit., p. 1215, and 5th ser., vol. i, p. 1549).

Jones *more suo* gives Mathews the worst of characters (op. cit., *passim*).

Mathews became President of the Council and Commander-in-chief of the island of Cape Breton (Sabine, op. cit., vol. ii, p. 52).

[2] *Sic.* ? Registrar.

He had an Allowance of £200 per Ann. from the 1st of Jany 1777 to the 31st of Decr 1783. This was by Warrant of Sir Wm Howe. Bounty £200 a Yr.

Produces Certificates from Genl Tryon & Admiral Digby which make very full mention of his Loyalty & Services.

He has an Allowance of £200 per Ann. from the Treasury from the 5th of Jany 1784.

**Memorial of Miles McInnes**

Determin'd the 25th of Augt 1784.

Miles McInnes—the Claimant—sworn. 7th of Augt 1784.

Is a Native of Scotland. Went to America in Decr 1774. Says that in the Yr following He made a purchase of a plantation & in 1780 join'd the British Troops he had never taken any Oath to the Americans. He went to America with his father & he took with him of his own 114 Gās & his father had about 50. Says that his father was a Cripple & that he resided with him (the Claimant) on the plantation. Was appointed a Lieut in the North Carolina Regt of Ma & continued as such during the remr of the War. The whole of the Pay he recd did not exceed £30. He was taken Prisoner in Octr 1780 & confined in Cross Creek Gaol for 3 Months. The £30 he recd was for ½ a Years pay. A Loyalist & bore Arms.

Produces Certificates to his Loyalty from sundry Officers. He has an Allowance from the Treasury of £20 per Ann. from 5th of July 1783. Bounty £20 a Yr.

Miles McInnes—the Claimant—again.

Says that he did take out with him 114 Gās. Says that he taught the Children of a Mr Scotis in Scotland to read the bible & Magazines. He had £12 per Ann. He was 11 Yrs old when he began to teach & he was 3 Yrs in that Situation. Afterwards he was concern'd in Whiskey with his Brother. He was sixteen when he embarked for America. Says again that he purchased the Plantation with his own Money.

Colonel Cotton—sworn. 10th of Augt 1784.

Knew the Claimt in No Carolina in 1775. Heard that he had a piece of Land never was on it. Recollects his bringing a Deed to the Office of the Witness to be register'd. Does not remember the No of Acres or whether the Purchase was in the Claimant's Name or not.

**Memorial of Captn John Bowen [1]**

Determin'd the 25th of Septr 1784.

Captn John Bowen—the Claimant—sworn. 7th Augt 1784.

Is a Native of Engd. Served in America the War before last. Came to Engd on the Peace & was put on half pay as Lieut of the 45th Regt. Went again to America in 1765 & purchas'd lands at Princetown. In Augt 1774 A Mob went to his House & threaten'd him on acct of their suspecting he meant to go to Genl Gage at Boston which he did & till April following he was constantly going about the Country to procure information & was allowed for himself & the maintenance of 2 Horses a Dollar a Day. Brought his family into Boston from his Estate in June 1775. Says that when his Wife left it a family of Boston went A Loyalist & bore Arms.

[1] The name of John Bowen is in the list of those who left Boston with the British army and in the Banishment Act of 1778.

there to reside & gave up their House at Boston to Claimant. The Gent[n] of the family died soon after & then they returned to Boston. Don't know who took possession of it afterwards has read in an American paper that it was sold.

In Oct[r] 1774 a Proposal was made to him by a Member of Congress (M[r] Gill) [1] in presence of M[r] Hancock to serve in their Army under Gen[l] Lee & to have the nomination of his rank & Appointments. His Answer was that he would go as the next Day to look at their Military Chest but he preferr'd doing his Duty to his Country by going to & informing Gen[l] Gage of their offer.

In April 1775 he was employ'd as a Guide for Earl Percy's Brigade had no other Allowance than the Dollar a Day aforemention'd.

In May 1776 He was appointed by Sir W[m] Howe Furrier to the Army & in 1777 He was appointed Capt[n] of a Company in the Prince of Wales's American Volunteers.

Bounty £20 a Y[r].

He has £20 per Ann. from the Treasury from the 5[th] of April 1784. He has half Pay as a Captain.

Colonel Willard—sworn.

Knew the Claim[t] in 1756. Says he has always been loyal & active as far as he ever saw. Knows he bought a tract of Land whereon there was but little improvement believes it was 100 Acres he bought first. He built a good House & barn. Says he was a very industrious Man that he had a N[o] of Cows & Cattle & that he clear'd & improved a great deal of Land.

Colonel Ferguson—sworn.

Knew the Claim[t] in New Eng[d] particularly on the Day of Lexington when he gave the Witness some Assistance as a Guide. Col[l] Ferguson thinks that the Claimant was very useful to the Army.

Determin'd the 10[th] of Aug[t] 1784.

**Memorial of Will[m] Wylly [2]**

10[th] of Aug[t] 1784.

Will[m] Wylly Esq—the Claimant—sworn.

A Loyalist & bore Arms.

Is a Native of Georgia. Was in Eng[d] when the troubles commenced studying the Law & returned to Georgia the latter end of the Year 1780 & practised the Law for about 10 Months when he formed a Company consisting of 30 Men which were attached to the Royal Artillery in doing this he was at an expence of about £150 S. He afterwards in Nov[r] 1781 rais'd another Company from among the Refugees consisting of 55 Men & then was appointed a Capt[n] in the Reg[t] of Kings rangers to which these Men were attached. Continued serving during the War. The Reg[t] was reduced at S[t] Augustine in Nov[r] last & he is now on half Pay. He produces Certificates to his Loyalty

[1] Moses Gill was a member of the Massachusetts Council.

[2] W. Wylly went to New Brunswick, where he was the first Crown Counsel and Registrar of the Court of Vice-Admiralty. He removed himself to the Bahamas in 1787, and was appointed in 1788 Solicitor-General. In 1804 he became Advocate-General of the Vice-Admiralty Court. By 1812 he was Chief Justice, but two years later exchanged offices with the Attorney-General. As Attorney-General he bore the leading part in a fierce quarrel with the Assembly over the question of the resolutions regarding slaves. In 1822 he became Chief Justice of St. Vincent (H. Siebert, *The Legacy of the Am. Rev. to the British West Indies and Bahamas*, pp. 49 and 31–3).

from Sir James Wright & Brig[r] Gen[l] Clarke. Has no Allowance from the Treasury.

Lieut[t] Gov[r] Graham—sworn.

Knew the Claim[t] in Georgia. Says that when he came from Eng[d] He was called to the Bar & practised about 6 Months. That he raised Men for the Artillery & was appointed a Capt[n] in the Kings Rangers. Says that he was very truly attached to the Bri. Gov[t]. Knows the Plantation in Christ Church & understood it was the property of the Claim[t]. The Land was not very valuable but as there was a public House thereon & it being a public road it was thereby valuable & thinks it was worth £150. Speaks of the fourth part of several Houses in y[e] town of Savannah & says it was notorious they were left by the Claim[t's] father to his Wife & 3 Children. Has heard the family say they rented for £300 a Y[r]. He is confident they would have sold for £1000 before the troubles. Says they were insured in Eng[d] in £1500.

Susannah Wylly—sworn.

She is the Mother of the Claim[t]. Says that the House & Tenements in Savannah were left by M[rs] Piagot who died in 1769 in the hands of Trustees for the benefit of her Son & in Case of his Death equally betw[n] herself & 3 Children. The Son died in 1774. Her Husband M[r] Wylly rec[d] all the rents during the life time of the Son who was an Ideot. Never had the Will. It was recorded & thinks it was lost with the Georgia records. Thinks M[r] Grey Elliott made the Will.

## Memorial of Susannah Wyly

Determin'd the 11[th] of July 1785.

Susannah Wyly—the Claimant—sworn. 11[th] of Aug[t] 1784.

She is the Widow of the late Alex[r] Wyly late of Georgia. He died in 1781. He was Speaker of the House of Assembly & Clerk of the Council in Georgia.

Produces the Will of her Husband dated 1[st] Dec[r] 1780 in which he leaves everything to M[rs] Wyly. At the Commencem[t] of the rebellion he took a very active part in favor of G. B. He left the province in a bad state of health in 1776 & lived in East Florida till Savannah was taken. He was obliged to leave the province for fear of being tarr'd & feather'd. He came back to Savannah in 1778 & staid till he died & served in the Militia there. Was a Capt[n] of M[a] during the siege. She apprehends his Death was hasten'd by the troubles.

Her Husband a Zealous Loyalist & bore Arms in the Militia.

By the Will she is entitled to all his property real & personal but by his Attainder She has lost it. She does not know that there is any prospect of the Attainder being taken off.

The Widow entitled to all the property under his Will.

Lieut[t] Gov[r] Graham—sworn.

Knew the Husband of M[rs] Wyly. He believes His affairs went ill & that he & his Partners made over all their Effects & lands to Greenwood & Higginson a considerable time before the rebellion. He did not consider him as a Man of Substance in 1775. He knew he was a Man involved. He was a very loyal Subject & extremely violent.

Knows the House that he bought of Burrington has frequently been in it.

Thinks with the Additions he made to it after he bought it it was worth £700 or £750. Knew M^rs^ Piaget & has always understood it was left to M^rs^ Wyly & the Children & not to be affected by the Debts of the Husband &c. Being asked whether he thinks that M^r^ Wyly in using the words *If I have* &c alluded to the troubles or to his own private Circumstances He says he does not know but he should rather think he must allude to his own private Circumstances.

Determin'd the 24th of Aug^t^ 1784.

**Memorial of Tho^s^ Badge**

12th of Aug^t^ 1784.

Thomas Badge—the Claimant—sworn.

A Native of Eng^d^ educated in Ireland. Went to America in 1767. Was settled as a Soap boiler & Tallow Chandler at Phil^a^ on the commenc^t^ of the troubles. Refused to take part with the Americans but says he followed their Camp.

A Loyalist.

In the Summer of 1777 he went to New York & gave intelligence to Col^l^ Sheriff [1] respecting the movement of the American Army. Says that Col^l^ Sheriff employ'd him to go & procure more information which he communicated afterw^ds^ to Sir W^m^ Howe Sir W^m^ Erskine & Col^l^ Sheriff. He served as a Guide to the British Army from the Head of Elk to the City of Phil^a^ & in this service he receiv'd a Musquet Ball in the right arm from the Enemy.

Capt^n^ Hugh Stewart—sworn.

Knew the Claimant. Says he was very loyal & believes that when he went with the Rebel Army to buy Tallow he took great pains to acquire information for the British Army. Speaks to the House in Philadelphia confirms what Claimant has said concerning the Lease but is not able to say what Expence the Claim^t^ was at in the Buildings he erected. He saw the Americans while the Claim^t^ was at New York take out of his House a great many Boxes of Candles & Soap. Values the Negro Man & the Woman at £120 Cur. at least. Says he would have given £100 S. for them. Knows that all the Claim^t's^ property was seized.

Will^m^ Cunningham—sworn.

Has known the Claim^t^ from the time the British Army was at the head of Elk. Says he was with the Army as a Guide & as a person to be employ'd on any confidential Service. That the Claim^t^ was allowed Rations but don't think he had any Pay. Knows that the Witness was wounded in the Arm the Day after the battle of Brandywine. He lodged in the Claim^t's^ House at Phil^a^. Says that he kept a Store & supplied the Army with Shoes Shirts & other Articles. Heard of the Claim^t^ having kept a Tallow Chandler's Shop but this was before he knew him. Says that he was like a great many others at the Commencem^t^ of the troubles with the Rebel Army but believes that he was very loyal after he join'd the British Troops.

Determin'd the 26th of Aug^t^ 1784.

**Memorial of Isaac Hubbard**

12th of Aug^t^ 1784.

Isaac Hubbard—the Claimant—sworn.

A Native of America born at Stamford [2] & was an Officer of the Custom

[1] Lieutenant-Colonel Sheriffe was Deputy Quartermaster-General till 1781.

[2] Connecticut.

House at that place when the troubles broke out. He held the offices of Deputy Collector & Preventive Officer with the former he had a Salary of £15 & with the latter £25 S. which was an Appointment from the Commissioners.

A Loyalist & bore Arms.

In 1775 he associated with many others for the Defence of the town. In 1776 He was obliged to go into the back Country where he remain'd at his own Expence till 1777. Says that he was tried by a Committee at Stamford who order'd him to quit the town & go into the back Country. It was in April of the Y$^{r}$ 1777. He escaped & went to Long Island where he joined the Loyalists. Never was in any Action. Continued there & at New York till Oct$^{r}$ 1783 when he came to Eng$^{d}$ without his family which remain'd at New York. Has an allowance of £30 a Year from the Treasury from the 5$^{th}$ of April 1784.

Office of Preventive Officer of the Customs £25 a Y$^{r}$.

Bounty £30 a Y$^{r}$.

### Memorial of John Caleff [1]

John Calef—the Claim$^{t}$—sworn. 13$^{th}$ Aug$^{t}$ 1784.

A Native of Ipswich.[2] Bred to Physic was settled there in his Profession. In 1779 after having rec$^{d}$ many insults at Ipswich on acc$^{t}$ of his Attachment to the Cause of G. B. & that he could not be of further use he fled to Penobscot. In feb$^{y}$ of that Year he set out for Nova Scotia & made known to his Majesty's Officers some Circumstances respecting Penobscot which he thought material. Says it was concerning a Post there which he thought would prove advantageous to the Crown & He accompanied the British Troops during their operations at Penobscot.

A Meritorious Loyalist.

Certificate to his Loyalty & good Conduct from Gen$^{l}$ Gage & Gov$^{r}$ Parr.

He came to Eng$^{d}$ in 1780 & was appointed Assist$^{t}$ Physician to the Hospital in Nova Scotia. He returned to Nova Scotia but his Commission having been sent in a Ship that was captured He was not employ'd as Assist$^{t}$ Physician & came to Eng$^{d}$ lately to make application thereon. Says that he has succeeded in getting another Commission & is going out. In 1780 he was appointed by the Inhabitants of Penobscot their Agent requesting that that part of the Province might be sever'd from the residue of Mass Bay & erected into a Province under the Kings Gov$^{t}$. He came to Eng$^{d}$ on this business.

N.B. Dr. Calef appearing in great Distress & being a very meritorious Man was advised by us to apply for some temporary support at Whitehall And we accordingly reported £50 to be given to him in full to pay his Debts here & to carry him out to America.

[1] Dr. J. Calef, *b.* 1725, *d.* 1812 at St. Andrew, New Brunswick. He was present at Penobscot during the abortive siege by the Americans in 1779, and wrote *The Siege of Penobscot by the Rebels*, 1781. He was sent to England by the Penobscot Associated Loyalists to urge the fixing of the boundary between the British provinces and the United States at the Penobscot River (*Winslow Papers*, p. 256, note). Colonel Skene wrote to him in March 1782 : ' If you think the following testimonial worthy acceptance, you may make use of it. To John Caleff, Esq., Russel Court, Drury Lane.' That he was a surgeon with the army in the late war, member of the General Assembly of Massachusetts Bay, delegate to England from the inhabitants of Penobscot, and firmly attached to the King's authority to the risk of his life and loss of his whole estate (*Hist. MSS. Comm., Am. MSS. in R. Inst.*, vol. ii, p. 420). According to Inglis, first Bishop of Nova Scotia, Dr. Calef, ' a physician from New England, a weak, " enthusiastical " man, who was offended because one of Lady Huntingdon's preachers was not ordained ', brought charges of immorality against him. ' Hake, who is supposed to be responsible, is a Commissary to the Garrison of St. John.' (Note that Hake, who had been reported as a fraudulent claimant in 1784, is still acting as Commissary in 1789.) (See p. 211.) The bishop afterwards accepted Dr. Calef's apology and forgave him (A. G. Doughty, *Report on the Canadian Archives*, 1912, pp. 230–1).

[2] Essex County, Massachusetts.

Profession £100 a Yr.

Has no Pension from Govt but has recd at different times from Lord Sydney £60.

Made 1000 Dollars a Year on an Average by his profession. Says that he had no Idea when he deliver'd in his Schedule of claiming any Compensation from Govt he only did so to shew his Losses in consequence of his Loyalty.

Captn Mowatt—of the Navy—sworn. 14th Augt 1784.

Has known the Claimt many Years. Says that he resided at Ipswich & followed his profession as a Physician & Surgeon that he was esteem'd a Man of good property. In 1779 when the Witness commanded at Anapolis he recd material information from the Claimt respecting the state of Penobscot. Says that no Man could be more attached to G. B. & that the people of New Engd are well acquainted with the zeal he always shew'd in every matter that concerned this Country.

Peter Fry Esq—sworn.

Knew the Claimt says he lived at Ipswich & was a Member of the House of Representatives that he made himself obnoxious to the people by voting to rescind a Circular Letter sent out to all the Provinces by a former House. That by doing so he lost a great deal of practice as a Physician & Surgeon.

Thos Goldthwaite Esq—sworn. 18th of Augt 1784.

Knew the Claimant. Says he was a Zealous Loyalist. Sold the Farm of 125 Acres to Claimant. It was valued to the Claimant at about £100 Lawful Money. Says that he might have made £100 per Ann. by his business.

What he has heard of the Ship was in Engd. His property at Ipswich is not confiscated.

Thinks uncultivated Lands of no Value.

Determin'd the 26th of Augt 1784.

**Memorial of Colin Campbell Esq.**

Colin Campbell—the Claimant—sworn. 14th of Augt 1784.

A Loyalist.

Born at Burlington in New Jersey. At the commencemt of the Troubles he was settled there as an Atty & had been such for 3 Years before they began. He also held the Office of Master in Chancery. Produces the Appointment dated in Octr 1774 besides which he had an Appointment of Commr for taking Bail & Affts within the County of Burlington. Says that in Octr he was called upon to do military Duty which he refused he was fined in consequence of his refusal the Americans continued calling upon him monthly & he always refused.

In Decr 1776 He join'd the British Troops in the same County the Detachment was under the Command of Coll Sterling.[1] Continued with them till their sudden retreat a few Days after. He then went into Pensylva. Staid there at a friend's House till April 1777 when he returned to Burlington to secure some of his papers. He was seized by orders of the Govr kept two Days. They tender'd the Oaths to him which he refused upon which he was bound over

[1] Lieutenant-Colonel Thomas, to whom was mainly due the speedy reduction of Fort Washington, November 16, 1776 (J. Fortescue, *Hist. of the Brit. Army*, vol. iii, p. 192).

under two Securities of £2000 to appear at the ensuing Court of Qua[r] Sess[ns]. He did so & was sentenced to pay the Charges of the Prosecution which amounted to about £2 10*s*. He then kept out of the way went back to Pensylv[a] & staid there till the Arrival of the British Troops in Philadelphia when he join'd them in April 1778 & communicated some intelligence to M[r] Galloway but says it was not very material. Came from Philadelphia to New York with the Army where he practised as an Attorney & in April 1783 he was appointed Secretary to a Board of Commissioners for settling & adjusting matters of Debts. The Appointment was from Sir Guy Carleton & he was allowed 10*s*. a Day. Came to England on the Evacuation & has an Allowance from the Treasury of £25 per Ann. from the 5[th] of April 1784. Bounty £25 a Y[r].

For three Years before the troubles his Income arising from his profession & the Offices aforemention'd was £120 per Ann. Office £100 a Y[r].

Was banished by an Act of the Legislature of the State of New Jersey in the Year 1778.

### Memorial of James Putnam[1] Esq.

Determin'd the 26[th] of Aug[t] 1784.

James Putnam Esq—the Claimant—sworn. 14[th] of Aug[t] 1784.

A Native of America County of Essex. In June 1774 he resided at Worcester as a Lawyer & Magistrate for the County. Says that at this time the people began to assemble in Mobs he protested ag[t] their Measures the Protest was recorded & afterw[ds] when he was at Boston hearing that the Court meant to insist on those peoples recanting who had made such protests he declined going back to Worcester. At Boston in July 1775 Gen[l] Gage gave him the Command of a Company of associated Loyalists & did Duty with them till the Gen[l] quitted Boston & in Oct[r] 1775 Sir W[m] Howe renew'd the Appointment. In Aug[t] 1775 he was appointed under a Commission from Gen[l] Gage Attorney Gen[l] of the Province. Went with the Troops to Halifax & to New York the latter end of Oct[r] 1776 where he did Duty in a military Capacity but without any Appointment till he went to Long Island in 1778 & came to Eng[d] in Dec[r] 1779. Has been in Eng[d] ever since & has had an Allowance from the Treasury of 150 a Y[r] from Sept[r] 1775 being the time he was appointed Attorney Gen[l]. This Allowance was recommended by M[r] Wilmot & M[r] Coke to be continued to M[r] Putnam as an American Sufferer when they were desired to inspect into the Allowances that had been given to persons from America. A Meritorious Loyalist. Bounty £150 a Y[r].

He was appointed lately one of the Assistant Judges of New Brunswick with a Salary of £300 per Ann. Says again that he is recommended by Gov[t] to Col[l] Carlton[2] who is going out to New Brunswick for this Employ & that he

[1] *b.* 1726, *d.* 1789 at St. John's, New Brunswick. He was the last Attorney-General of Massachusetts under the Crown. Some characteristic quotations from his correspondence are given by Stark, op. cit., pp. 380–1; and incidental mention of him is made in the *Winslow Papers, passim.*

John Adams, the future President of the United States, boarded for some years with Putnam's family whilst reading in his Chambers. He testified to Putnam's acuteness of mind, the extent of his practice, and his general eminence. Putnam was appointed in 1784 Judge of the Supreme Court of New Brunswick and a member of the Council.

[2] Lieutenant-Colonel Thomas Carleton, the first Lieutenant-Governor of New Brunswick. He was the nephew of Guy Carleton, Lord Dorchester, and also his brother-in-law. Hence he is often spoken of by contemporaries as the brother of the Governor-General.

understands the Salary is to be what he has stated but he is unable to form any Judgment whether the same is to commence from his leaving Eng^d^ or from the time of his Arrival in Nova Scotia.

Major Upham—sworn.

Says the Claim^t^ was very loyal & well attached to G. B. that he was in great practice as a Lawyer & believes that it was worth £800 a Y^r^ to him before the troubles for several Years. The Salary of Attorney Gen^l^ £150 per Ann. Says that [from] the active part the Claim^t^ took it would have been unsafe for him to have remain'd longer in the Country. Values the Dwelling House in the Town of Worcester at £900 S. Values the Dwelling House adjoining the one in which the Claim^t^ lived at £450 S. Values the Building Lots at £35 or £40 per Acre.

17^th^ Aug^t^ 1784.

Caleb Wheaton—sworn.

Knew the Claim^t^. Says he the Witness commanded a Brig out of Boston & that on his Passage from thence to Halifax he was taken & had on board some Trunks Boxes & Packages belonging to the Claim^t^ which he was to land at Halifax. The Vessel was carried into Piscatoway.

Daniel Murray—sworn.

Says that he lived in the Claim^t's^ family 3 Years. Can't say what the Claim^t^ made by his Practice or what his Library was worth. Knows that M^r^ Putnam was obliged to quit Boston on Acc^t^ of the part he took in favor of the British Gov^t^. That he did more business than any other Lawyer & supposes that his practice might have been worth to him 6 or £700 per Ann. Values the Dwelling House & buildings at 8 or £900 & the House adjoining where an Inn was kept at £500.

The 4 Acres for House Lots he values at £50 per Acre. Says that the Mill was valuable but is not able to say what it was worth.

Values the 60 Acres purchased of Starnes from £7 to £8 per Acre.

The 40 Acres bought of Ward he values at 7 to £8 per Acre.

The 43 Acres at £7. Can't value the Buildings.

The 25 Acres of Pine Meadow He values at £20 per Acre. Says that M^r^ Putnam was at a great expence in cultivating them.

Knows that M^r^ Putnam had a Farm of 140 Acres where Starnes lived. Can't value it.

Can't speak to the Value of the 28½ Acres nor to the 60 Acres purchased from the town of Worcester & Lovell.

To the unimproved Lands at Totmick Says that the Claim^t^ sold some at 36*s*. per Acre.

Good Pasture Land in Worcester but well fenced particularly at Talmick. He values it at £5 per Acre.

## Memorial of Joshua Upham [1] Esq.

Determin'd the 28th of Augt 1784.

Joshua Upham Esq—the Claimant—sworn. 17th Augt 1784.

Is a Native of the Province of Mass Bay. When the troubles broke out he lived in the Town of Brookfield in County of Worcester. He was then following the profession of the Law. He was a Magistrate at the time & in that Capacity. He always opposed the licentious Conduct of the people. He did it with moderation but he never suppress'd his Sentiments. In the Town Meeting which was the last meeting that he attended he spoke agt the Independence of America. He left the Town of Brookfield in April 1777 & went to Boston. He went because he could not enjoy his property quietly. Admits that he was obliged to temporize & produces a printed paper which he says he was obliged to sign. It was published in 1775. The Americans called it a recantation. He made it in consequence of a threatening Letter sent to him by a person under a feign'd name. They never tender'd an Oath but they pass'd a Law ordering every person to take an Oath within a limited time which was the Occasion of his leaving the province. In 1777 the Assembly made a Law that no person should practise in any of their Courts of Law unless they should take an Oath. If he had not published that paper he says he should have been imprison'd. After he got within the Lines & had quitted his profession he took to the military Line. He remain'd holding different military Commissions to the time of the Evacuation of New York. In Jany 1779 he was appointed Inspector of the Claims of Loyalists with 10*s.* a Day & soon after was appointed King's Advocate in Rhode Island soon after which the Island was evacuated. Soon after the Arrival of Sir Guy Carlton he was appointed Major of Dragoons [2] & likewise Aid de Camp to him And he remain'd in full Confidence with him in his own family.

A Loyalist & bore Arms.

He now receives the half pay of Major 8*s.* a Day & £50 a Yr from the Treasury.

Bounty £50 a Yr which he afterwards commuted for one Sum of £50.[3]

He is going out to Brunswick with a promise that he shall be appointed Assistant Judge but he has no Commission here. The Salary will be £300 a Yr & the moment that commences the half pay will cease.

He says before the troubles began he gain'd by the Practice of the Law £450 S. a Yr which he claims for 9 Years from April 1775 to April 1784.

Profession £400 a Yr.

The next Demand is for service & Expences in commanding the Post of

[1] The explanation (dated May 20, 1775) of which Upham speaks in his evidence was to the following effect: 'I . . . submit to what I find to be the . . . resolution of the majority of my countrymen and expect to bear an equal share and proportion of such public charge and expense as shall be deemed by such magistracy to be necessary to extricate the country out of its present alarming and critical situation' (Force, *Am. Arch.*, 4th ser., vol. ii, p. 852). Although the Brookfield Committee of Correspondence naturally found this explanation satisfactory, Upham afterwards incurred the displeasure of the Whigs. He suggested to E. Winslow in 1780 the raising of a Massachusetts Brigade (*Winslow Papers*, p. 63).
Upham, *b.* 1741, *d.* 1808 in England, settled in New Brunswick and became Judge of the Supreme Court and a member of the Council (ibid., p. 49, note).

[2] King's American Dragoons. Benjamin Thompson wrote to Lord Sackville (August 6, 1782), Carleton 'appointed my friend Upham, one of the finest fellows I ever knew, second major in my regiment and has since made him his aide-de-camp' (*Hist. MSS. Comm.*, *Stopford-Sackville MSS.*, vol. ii, 'Papers relating to the Am. War,' p. 253).

[3] *sic.* ? £500.

Disallowed.

Lloyd's Neck one Year *without pay or reward.* He went to that Post in 1781.

Disallowed.

During this time he held the same Office of Inspector of Refugees on Long Island with 10*s.* a Day.

He never made any Application to the Commander in Chief for pay.

When the Loyalists were embodied there was a general Agreement that they should undertake the defence of that Post without Pay. Some of them got Money by labor but none of them rec$^{d}$ any Pay.

Disallowed.

In the Year 1777 The Memorialist was reduced to sell his Estate. He sold it for the support of himself & family. He sold it before he went to Boston & rec$^{d}$ part of the Money in payment in Paper Currency. He sold it for £1275 S. The Sale of it was voluntary. He rec$^{d}$ the whole in paper Currency. The Money was then good & several people to whom he paid Money which he owed took it & every body was willing to take it. He thinks he lost £1000 in the whole by the Depreciation. He considers £1275 as the Value of his Estate. He paid £525 out of the £1275 & a Depreciation followed upon the £750 by which & the Depreciation upon other Articles which he sold he says he lost £1000 in the whole. He sold Horses & Cattle Books &c for £465 & Book Debts Notes &c were paid to the Amount of £200.

James Putnam Esq—sworn.

Knew Major Upham very well before the troubles. He came to the Bar several Y$^{rs}$ before the troubles about 7 Y$^{rs}$ before. He had great reputation in the Profession. He thinks he must have got above £400 a Y$^{r}$. He looks upon him to be a true & uniform Loyalist. He heard of his recantation frequently but never heard any person who was acquainted with him suspect his principles.

Rufus Chandler—sworn.

Knew Major Upham in America. He always opposed the Measures of Congress & was a Tory. He followed the Bar & got a great deal of business. He practised with him. He thinks he got more than £300 a Y$^{r}$ in one County. He knows Major Upham had an Estate before the troubles. Good House & barn but does not know the Value of it.

Major Murray—sworn.

Major Upham married his Sister & he knew him well. His Loyalty was uniform from the first. Has frequently heard that he was single in opposing & speaking ag$^{t}$ the measure of Independence. He was in good business. He sold his Estate to John Brown & he sold it because he was not able to live as his Business failed.

Determin'd the 28$^{th}$ of Aug$^{t}$ 1784.

## Memorial of Daniel Murray [1]

Daniel Murray—the Claimant—sworn. 17$^{th}$ of Aug$^{t}$ 1784.

He is a Native of America. The eldest Son of Col$^{l}$ Murray of Rutland. Col$^{l}$ Murray left the Estate & went to Boston in 1774. He remain'd upon the

[1] David was the son of Colonel John Murray, a wealthy Massachusetts loyalist. Daniel settled in New Brunswick, being in command of the King's American Dragoons when they disbanded at the St. John River in 1783. He left the province in embarrassed circumstances in 1803, and died at Portland,

Estate & occupied it till 1776 & then he became a Tenant to the Committee & remain'd upon it till April. In 1776 He was drafted & sent to Gaol sooner than pay the fine. He remain'd two Hours & then paid the fine. He never paid any rent. They tender'd the Oath in 1776 & he refused it. The Committee seized his father's property (who was a Mandamus Counsellor) in 1775. They suffer'd him to occupy it till 1776 & then having declared for independence the Committee made him pay rent. In 1777 He was obliged to take the Oath or quit & he left the Province & came to Rhode Island when the British Troops were there. The next Month at New York He went as a Volunteer with Many others who were embodied into a Company & he had the Command. They disclaim'd any Pay. After serving ten Months he had Pay being unable to support himself. He had 2 Dollars a Day. He remain'd during the whole War in the Army. He was made Major in 1781 in Col[l] Thompson's Dragoons & had 20*s.* 6*d.* per Day. He has since the peace the half pay of a Major. When the Reg[t] was disbanded He settled the Reg[t] in that province. He at the same time obtain'd 1000 Acres for himself & located his own land before he came away. Whilst in Nova Scotia he was arrested for Money spent in the King's Service in the Company of Volunteers where they bound themselves jointly & separately to pay the Money. He has been obliged to mortgage £100 a Y[r] of his half pay for £600 to pay this Money.

A very active & Meritorious Loyalist & bore Arms.

He has no Allowance from Gov[t].

He has made an Application to the Treasury for the Debts incurr'd but has rec[d] no Answer. He swears that the Memorial contains a just Acc[t] of the nature of the Claims.

James Putnam Esq—sworn. 18[th] of Aug[t] 1784.

Knew Major Murray. He was a Clerk with him. He had just finished his Clerkship. He knows he was a very Zealous Loyalist. In the year 1774 & before the rebellion he heard the father say that he had given up a farm to him. He believes he gave it to him by Deed but he never saw the Deed & as a part of his portion. He thinks £1500 la. Mo. was about the Value which is between 11 & 1200. He does not in this valuation include the Buildings. He believes the Buildings would cost £500. Thinks including the buildings it would have sold for £1500. Knows nothing of the Stock. M[r] Putnam made out the List of Law books for him & thinks they would cost about £50.

Joshua Upham Esq—sworn.

Knew Major Murray lived 15 Miles from Col[l] Murrays. He was very Active in the British Cause. A Brother of Major Murrays was made Prisoner at Lexington when Gen[l] Putnam obtain'd leave for him to be sent to the family Estate. Lived upon the Estate till 1777 from whence he came into the British

Maine, in 1832. 'He was an able and enterprising man, but unfortunate' (*Winslow Papers*, p. 30, note). Benjamin Thompson wrote to Carleton on July 6, 1783: 'I took the liberty of soliciting the rank of Colonel of the King's American Dragoons and that Major Murray might be promoted to the rank of Lieutenant-Colonel of the same' (*Hist. MSS. Comm.*, *Am. MSS. in R. Inst.*, vol. iv, p. 205). Carleton replied on October 10 (ibid., p. 405): 'As the minister has given me no instructions respecting Major Murray, you must be sensible that I cannot take it on myself to give him an appointment which will be considered as a grievance by all the older Majors in the Provincial line.'

Lines. He would have come sooner into the Lines but was dissuaded by his father & Gen^l^ Gage. He enter'd into the service as a Volunteer & rais'd a Company of Volunteers & he was put at the head of them. They had no Pay for some time about ten Months but afterw^ds^ they had. Major Murray did everything in his power to serve the British Gov^t^. Remembers M^r^ Gilbert who had supplied Major Murray with Money for himself & the other Volunteers & has heard M^r^ Gilbert say that they had given him a Note for it. Says that Major Murray was principally instrumental in raising the Kings American Dragoons commanded by Col^l^ Thompson of which he is Major. Believes this was a Considerable Expence to him.

Colonel Willard—sworn.

Knew Major Murray & all the family they lived 20 Miles from him. He always appear'd to be loyal & he believes he took a very active part. He has heard Col^l^ Murray say before the rebellion that he design'd the farm for his Son & had given it to him. He knows the Land & the buildings very well & values it at £2000. Thinks it would have sold for that before the troubles & says it would have rented for £80 or £90 per Ann.

### Memorial of George Duncan Ludlow[1] Esq.

Determin'd the 28th of Aug^t^ 1784.

18th of Aug^t^ 1784.

George Duncan Ludlow Esq—the Claimant—sworn.

An Active & Zealous Loyalist & has render'd material Services to Gov^t^.

Is a Native of America. In 1769 he was Judge of the Supreme Court of the Province of New York. The last Court he held was in feb^y^ 1776. Says that after having supported the Courts of Justice amidst repeated Commotions & exerting himself to no purpose in endeavouring to allay the ferment he retired into Queens County Long Island untill the arrival of the fleet & Army when he returned to New York & staid there till 1780 consider'd in his former Capacity but did not act. In July of that Year he was made Superintend^t^ Gen^l^ of the Police with an Allowance of 20*s*. per Day & continued as such till June 1783 when he came to Eng^d^. He had been one of the Directors of the Board of Refugees establish'd in 1781 he differ'd in opinion with that Board concerning what was done in the Case of Huddy[2] & says that he retired from it in consequence of his disapproving their Measures. Has £200 a Y^r^ from the Treasury from the 5th of July 1783. Says that he undertook to build Hutts for the Army when they were distress'd for Barracks & that he rec^d^ no Compensation for his trouble. These Hutts were erected in a short time & at very little Expence to Gov^t^.

Bounty £200 a Y^r^.

Confiscation proved.

He is going to New Brunswick with an Appointment of Chief Justice of the Province. Believes the Salary will be £500 per Ann. S.

[1] *b.* 1738, *d.* 1825. He began life as an apothecary. In spite of physical difficulties he was very successful at the Bar. The genial Jones affirms that, at New York, Ludlow perverted his own natural good sense and former amiable character so as to prostitute the laws of the land by giving illegal opinions, making arbitrary decisions, and distressing loyal subjects, to please the pecuniary purposes of the avaricious old Robertson (op. cit., vol. ii, p. 22). Having retired to New Brunswick, he was a member of the first Council of that colony and its first Chief Justice (Biog. notice in *New York Col. Docs.*, vol. viii, p. 248). Numerous references to him will be found in the *Winslow Papers*, *passim*.

[2] See Additional Notes, p. 212.

### Memorial of Thomas Hazard

Determin'd the 28$^{th}$ of Aug$^{t}$ 1784.

Thomas Hazard—the Claimant—sworn. 19$^{th}$ of Aug$^{t}$ 1784.

An Active Zealous & meritorious Loyalist.

Is a Native of America. In the Year 1775 He was on his farm in New Kingston Rhode Island. On the commencem$^{t}$ of the troubles he advised the Inha$^{ts}$ to be peaceable. He was taken Prisoner. The Oaths were tender'd to him but he refused to take them. Join'd the British Troops in 1779. While they were on Rhode Island he procured Provisions for them. He procured Intelligence for the British at very great risque.

He rais'd 110 Men at New York. Held a Post at S$^{t}$ George's Manor 70 Miles from New York. He ran very great hazard of his Life in endeavouring to bring off a Doct$^{r}$ Halyburton.

Produces Certificates from Lieut$^{t}$ Col$^{l}$ Delancey to Loyalty to raising Men & procuring Intelligence. He was banished & a Schooner of his taken to defray the Expences of the prosecution against him.

He receives an Allowance of £80 per Ann. from the Treasury from the 5$^{th}$ of April 1784.

Bounty £80 a Y$^{r}$.

### Memorial of John Simpson [1]

Determin'd the 28$^{th}$ of Aug$^{t}$ 1784.

John Simpson—the Claimant—sworn. 20$^{th}$ of Aug$^{t}$ 1784.

An Active Zealous & meritorious Loyalist. Did not bear Arms.

Is a Native of Edinburgh & went first to America in the Year 1760. His father was then living in America. He went out in 1753 or 1754. He lived with his father till 1763 when he removed to Georgia. Some time after the father was appointed Chief Justice of Georgia in 1767. He settled a plantation for himself on Scentilly river. The Plantation was given to him by his father. His father died in 1768. When the troubles broke out he opposed the provincial Congress & obtain'd a protest ag$^{t}$ it. He condemn'd the proceedings of Congress to his Constituents. He leaves a paper containing an Acc$^{t}$ of his Exertions &c.

Refers to Sir James Wright & other Gent$^{n}$ for a proof of the facts contain'd in that paper.

Reads the Protest alluded to published in the Georgia Gazette N$^{o}$ 570 & another paper published in the Georgia Gazette N$^{o}$ 573 being another protest ag$^{t}$ the proceedings of the Congress. Reads another paper published in the same Gazette N$^{o}$ 591. This respects instructions given to him by his Constituents which petition was presented by him to the legal House of Assembly recommending Submission to Gov$^{t}$. He says these instructions to himself were procured by himself. Likewise another Extract from the Gazette Page 614. This Paper contains resolutions of Loyalty & was deliver'd to Congress by him & M$^{r}$ Jameson. He apprehends that these proceedings in which he took so active a part supported the legal Gov$^{t}$ for a Y$^{r}$ longer than in any other province. He produces Sir James Wright's Pamphlet & refers to Page 9 from which an Extract is read which is part of the Secretary of State's Letter & expresses the Kings opinion of the Act which M$^{r}$ Simpson brought into the House of Assembly & which is before alluded to.

Confiscation proved.

[1] John Simpson was amongst those who signed a dissent from the resolutions passed by a meeting at Savannah, August 10, 1774 (G. White, *Hist. Collections of Georgia*, p. 49).

In 1779 tho' he might have been a Member of the Council he remain'd in the Commons Assembly till 1782 because the Gov^r thought he would be of more use to Gov^t in that Assembly than the other.

Produces a Letter from Sir James Wright written to him the 6^th of Aug^t 1781 in which the Gov^r speaks highly of his Conduct & appoints him to be one of the Council.

Determin'd the 30^th of Aug^t 1784.

### Memorial of Dan^l Hammill

21^st Aug^t 1784.

Daniel Hammill—the Claimant—sworn.

A Loyalist & bore Arms since the Y^r 1777. But before that time he serv'd in the American Army.

Was settled in Duchess[1] County. Was born in Ireland & went to America in 1769. He first settled in Duchess[1] County & lived there when the troubles broke out. He took part with the Americans till 1777. He never took any Oath or signed any Association owing to the Circumstance of his having been sent to Fort Montgomery. He was 18 or 19 Months in their Militia. When the Rebel Army retreated from Fort Montgomery he remain'd behind & join'd the British. He continued from that time with the British & dares not go back. He was employ'd in the British Army in the Barrack Master Gen^ls department. Had the offer of a Commission from Lord Rawdon.

Certificates read from Sir Henry Clinton Lord Rawdon Col^l Crossby Barrack Master Gen^l M^r Matthews Mayor of New York & M^r Chew to Loyalty &c.

Says that he did great service in piloting the Expedition to Æsopus.[2] He was confined for carrying out the conciliatory Propositions. He was sent out by Sir Henry Clinton on this business & because he had piloted the British fleet he was treated as a Spy & confined 18 Months When he broke Prison & was in great danger of his life. He got on board a Ship & got to New York in the Year 1779 & he remain'd in the barrack Master's department almost till the Evacuation. When he was employ'd he had *6s.* a Day.

The Claimant is going to Nova Scotia.

Determin'd the 30^th of Aug^t 1784.

### Memorial of Alexander Thompson

23^d of Aug^t 1784.

Alexander Thompson—the Claimant—sworn.

A Loyalist & Did not bear Arms.

Deputy Postmaster at Savannah £35 a Y^r.

Collector of the Customs.

Native of Scotland. Went to America in 1767 & settled at Savannah previous to the troubles. He was appointed to the Customs in 1772. He was made Postmaster in the same Year. He had both these Offices at the beginning of the troubles. Upon the first breaking out of the troubles He associated with many others & protested ag^t the measures of the Americans. He was frequently insulted & threaten'd & in 1775 after he had made a seizure they treated ill some persons whom he employ'd. He did not however leave the province for these insults but for ill health. He left it in July 1775. He did not apprehend Danger at the time. He returned to Georgia in Nov^r 1779 & arrived there in March 1780. He again resumed both those Offices & executed them till the Evacuation.

[1] Dutchess.

[2] In October 1777, in order to make a diversion in favour of Burgoyne, Clinton advanced from New York up the Hudson River and captured Forts Montgomery and Clinton and burnt Esopus (now Kingston).

He left the Province in 1775 with leave of the Gov^r^. He has rec^d^ his Salary up to Oct^r^ 1782 to which he rec^d^ an Addition of £150 in 1776. In 1777 he had an Allowance of £60 a Year which he rec^d^ for 3 Years & ½ & £50 for Passage Money. He now receives an Allowance of £60 a Y^r^ which he has rec^d^ from Jan^y^ 1783.

Salary £60 a Y^r^.
fees £290 a Y^r^.
Bounty £60 a Y^r^.

## Memorial of Joel Stone

Determin'd the 24th of Aug^t^ 1784.

Joel Stone—the Claimant—sworn. 24th of Aug^t^ 1784.

Born at the Town of Guildford in Connecticut. He was settled in the Y^r^ 1775 at Woodbury (now called Washington) as a Shopkeeper. He first declared his principles in 1776 & they were hostile to the Congress. He was not obliged to declare sooner. In consequence of this a Warrant was issued ag^t^ him in Jan^y^ 1777. Copy of it produced. He made his escape from the Warrant & they immediately sold all his furniture & goods. He came into New York in 1777 & served as a Volunteer 10 Months & then he rec^d^ a Warrant from Col^l^ Ludlow to raise a Co. He did not raise it because when he was recruiting he was taken Pris^r^ in Connecticut & kept 3 Months. He then broke prison & got to Long Island. When he came into New York Gov^r^ Tryon gave him 10 Gās. He was then ill 5 Months. Soon after he went on board a Privateer by which Adventure he made Money & has supported himself ever since. He married at New York & kept a Broker's Shop.

An Active & Zealous Loyalist & bore Arms.

Produces Certificates to Loyalty &c from M^r^ Matthews Gov^r^ Tryon & Col^l^ Ludlow.[1] Produces likewise a Copy of a Certificate from a Rebel Justice in which he sentences him to Imprisonment.

He has an Allowance from the Treasury of £30 a Y^r^ from the 1st of Jan^y^ 1784.

Bounty £30 a Y^r^.

Joshua Chalmer—of Connecticut—sworn.

Knew Joel Stone but not so well as he knew M^r^ Bacon. He was in trade with M^r^ Bacon. He took a decided part in favor of G. B. which was the reason of his leaving the Country. He has heard M^r^ Bacon speak of the 500 Acres which Stone bought & he express'd an uneasiness about the Deed but not from a suspicion of Stone. Says Bacon was a Loyalist. Knows that Stone was confined & tried for Loyalty & near being executed.

David Fell—Lieu^t^ of the Navy—sworn.

Knew Joel Stone. They were Pris^rs^ together. Stone was deem'd a Pris^r^ for high treason. The Acc^t^ in the prison was that the Gov^r^ refused to consider him as a Pris^r^ of War & said he sh^d^ be tried as a Traitor & hanged.

Knows Stone to be a loyal Subject. Has been on several Expeditions with him & has seen him behave gallantly.

[1] Gabriel G. Ludlow, *b.* 1736, *d.* 1808. There is a short biographical notice of him in *New York Col. Docs.*, vol. viii, p. 696. He became President of the New Brunswick Council and acted as administrator of the Government. He was also Judge of the Court of Vice-Admiralty and served as first Mayor of the city of St. John (see *Winslow Papers*, note on p. 539 and *passim*).

## Memorial of James Thompson

Determin'd the 25th of Augt 1784.

25th of Augt 1784.

James Thompson—the Claimant—sworn.

Is a Native of Ireland & went first to America in 1748. Came back & went again to America in 1751 where he resided till 1770 & he was in Europe from 1770 to 1776. His family were left in America & he had a Son & a Daughter at New York during the whole of that time. He meant to have returned to America sooner. He went back in 1776 as a Mercht to New York. The Town was then in our possession. He always took part with this Country. His Children went to the Island of Jamaica. His Daur married Mr Jacob Rickets in 1774 or 1775. He left all his property in America. He had always supported G. B. & when he returned in 1779 he had many Conversations with Lord Geo Germaine & Lord Walsingham. He went back immediately & staid till after the Evacuation. He proposed a mode of getting at some of the principal people of the Congress which he believes was follow'd by the Effects which he saw. He married the Daur of Mr Jacob Walton long before the rebellion in 1753. Upon the death of her father which happen'd in 1750 She became entitled to £3734 New York Cur. This was in the hands of Trustees at the time of the rebellion & the Interest to be paid to her settled upon the family. She got by her Uncle £500 which was directed to be placed out to her sole & separate Interest. By the will of her Grandmother 210*s.* was order'd to be placed out for her sole & separate Use. By the Will of Thos Walton her Bror £1000 in the same manner & lastly by the Will of her Mother £783 in the same manner. These Sums were vested principally in Bond. No Interest has been paid from the time of the troubles. In New Jersey they have directed principal & Interest to be paid in to the State. In New York they have prevented the payment of Intt & part of the Money has been paid in in Paper Cur. He nor his Wife have ever recd any benefit from the Estate since the troubles. Principal & Interest together £12303 5*s.* 10¾*d.* C. or £6920 12*s.* 0*d.* S.

A Loyalist.

Debts £6470 12*s.* 0*d.*

They all died before the troubles excepting his Wife's Mother who died in 1780. The other four died many Years ago

He explains & says that this Money produced to him an Income of £565 C. of £317 17*s.* 0*d.* S.

He was not an establish'd Mercht in America between 1770 & 1776 but before & after his business produced him £1500 a Yr. His business was that of a factor to many great Houses & he likewise did business on his own Account.

Disallowed.

In the Year 1777 He had an House assign'd to him by the Commander in Chief. It was given to him as Agent for the Victualling of the Army. He did not understand that he was to pay rent for it. He was obliged to pay £450 Cur. for the rent. He cannot charge it to his Employers or the Contractors. He thinks he has no right to call upon them or upon the Commr in Chief & does not mean to do it but thinks he ought to charge it to Govt as proceeding from his Loyalty.

Disallowed.

He never applied to Whitehall as he does not want that sort of Assistance.

## Memorial of Col[l] John Hamilton

Determin'd the 30th of Aug[t] 1784.

John Hamilton—the Claimant—sworn. 27th of Aug[t] 1784.

Was born in Ireland & went to America in 1767. Settled at New York in 1774. He lived in Charlestown. Had the management of W[m] Clarkson's Affairs & was likewise a Merch[t] on his own Acc[t]. In 1775 He went with a Cargo of Rice to New York & Gibraltar & was absent about 9 Months. He returned to Charlestown in 1776. He found business dull & went into the Country & settled upon the plantation which he had bought in 1774 & carried on business till 1778. In 1777 or 1778 they frequently called upon him to muster & he was muster'd. In 1778 He was call'd upon to take Arms but did not go & was twice fined & frequently called upon betw[n] 1778 & 1780 & once he was obliged to join them & go to Augusta. He remain'd with them about 5 weeks. He apprehended the fine would be heavy but he did not ask what the fine would have been before he went. He took the Oaths to them in 1778. Believes it was the Oath of fidelity. He was permitted to return home by Gen[l] Williamson when he had been at Augusta about 5 weeks. As soon as the reduction of Charlestown he & several other Loyalists took an active part in disarming the disaffected. In 1780 He served under Major Ferguson. He left him about a fortnight before he was defeated. He was taken Prisoner the Morning that Ninety Six was besieged. He was detain'd Pris[r] till July 1781 when a general Exchange took place. He came to Charlestown & remain'd till the Evacuation & was appointed Inspector of the Refugees from Ninety Six District for which he rec[d] a Dollar a Day.

A Loyalist since the reduction of Charlestown. But before that time he took the Oaths to the Americans & served six weeks in their Army.

Bore Arms.

Confiscation not proved.

Produces Certificates to his Loyalty from the Year 1780 from Col[l] Cruger Col[l] Allen & several other Officers & from Edw[d] Savage Esq Judge in S[o] Carolina.

## Memorial of Will[m] Murray

Determin'd the 27th of Aug[t] 1784.

William Murray—the Claimant—sworn. 27th of Aug[t] 1784.

Is an Irishman & went to Boston in 1771 or 1772. He was appointed a Tidewaiter there in 1773. He carried out nothing but his Cloathes. Produces his Appointment Salary £25 a Y[r] & 1*s.* 6*d.* a day when on Duty. Continued in this Situation till the Evacuation of Boston. Then went to Halifax where he was employ'd by the Collector of the Customs. He has born Arms at Boston & New York. Came to Eng[d] in 1778.

Did not bear Arms.[1]

Produces Certificates from M[r] Hallowell & M[r] Parker to Loyalty & good Conduct as an Officer of the Customs.

A Loyalist & Did his Duty in his office.

States his Loss of Office at £140 but in order to bring it to that Sum he includes the 1*s.* 6*d.* a Day. He has rec[d] his Salary up to April 1783 except one Quarter which he lost at Salem in 1775 which he rates at £11 5*s.* 0*d.*

Loss of Salary £25 a Y[r]. Arrears Disallowed.

He has no Allowance from the Treasury.

Owen Richards—sworn.

Knows W[m] Murray. He was a Tide Waiter at Boston. Believes him to be a Man of good Character. He was associated with the Co. of Royal Irish

[1] *sic* in text.

at Boston. Knows nothing of the Quarter's Salary not being paid to him but he heard him say so at the time at Salem & said he should lose it because he was afraid of the Rebels if he went to Salem to receive it.

Determin'd the 30th of Aug$^{t}$ 1784.

**Memorial of John Atkinson**

30th of Aug$^{t}$ 1784.

John Atkinson—the Claimant—sworn.

A Loyalist.

Is a Native of this Country. Went to Boston in 1775 & first to America in 1767. He was a Merch$^{t}$ in Co. with M$^{r}$ Smith. Remain'd in the Town of Boston during the blockade & bore Arms both then & at New York in the Mass. Bay Volunteers.

He went with Sir Will$^{m}$ Howe to Halifax & came to England in Sept$^{r}$ 1776 & returned to America to New York in Aug$^{t}$ 1777 as a Merch$^{t}$ where he staid till 1780 & then came to Eng$^{d}$. The Rebels never offer'd any Oaths to him.

Determin'd the 4th of Sept$^{r}$ 1784.

**Memorial of Daniel Leonard[1] Esq.**

31st of Aug$^{t}$ 1784.

Sir Will$^{m}$ Pepperell Bar$^{t}$—sworn.

A Zealous Loyalist & did great service to Gov$^{t}$ by his Writings.

Sir W$^{m}$ knew M$^{r}$ Leonard before the troubles. He has ever been a Loyalist. He was one of the Mandamus Counsellors for the Province of Massachu & wrote under the signature of Massachutensis papers which were very useful to Gov$^{t}$. It was esteem'd at Boston that he was of great use to Gov$^{t}$. He was a Native of America. He was likewise Inspector of the Customs which Office was given to him in the Y$^{r}$ 1775 or 1776. He was bred to the Bar. He was in good business as a Barrister but does not know how much he got. He staid till the Evacuation of Boston & was one of the Association. Nobody was more hearty in the Cause of Gov$^{t}$ or did more than M$^{r}$ Leonard.

Daniel Leonard Esq—the Claimant—sworn.

The Claimant says He is a Native of America of the Province of Mass. Bay. He was fix'd there in the Profession of the Law at the Commencement of the troubles. He was one of those fix'd upon to be a Mandamus Counsellor. He took every opportunity of supporting the Authority of G. B. in consequence of which he was much insulted. He lived at Taunton. He was first molested in Aug$^{t}$ 1774 by an armed Mob surrounding his House. They fired small Arms into the House. This was in the night. In the Day time several Hundreds had assembled & insisted upon his resigning his Office. He was absent at this time & hearing of this Outrage he was afraid to go to his House & came into the Lines at Boston in Aug$^{t}$ 1774. His family were soon obliged to follow him.

Between this time & the battle of Lexington he employ'd himself in writing. He published about this time a Pamphlet called Massachutensis which had a con-

[1] *b.* 1740, *d.* 1829. At first Leonard seemed inclined to take the popular side; but in 1774 he burnt his ships by signing the address to Governor Hutchinson. In his absence some members of an angry mob fired into the bedroom where his wife was confined in childbirth, with the result that the child was born an idiot. This tragedy may have embittered him, as whatever the merits of *Massachusettensis*, it certainly does not breathe a spirit of sweet reasonableness. The letters, sixteen in number, were issued from December 19, 1774, to April 3, 1775. They were at first ascribed to Sewall, the Attorney-General. Leonard visited Boston in 1799 and again in 1808. He died in London, where he lived after resigning his office as Chief Justice (Stark, op. cit., pp. 325–32). (The best account of *Massachusettensis* is in Tyler, op. cit., vol. i, pp. 356–8.)

siderable Effect in keeping the Province quiet. In consequence of this the Govt here gave Mr Leonard the Appointment of Solicitor to the Board of Customs with a Salary of £360 a Yr this was given in 1775.

Immediately after the battle of Lexington He with many others associated & bore Arms to defend the Town. He assisted as Counsel for the Crown in all the prosecutions. Renderd more obnoxious by this.

He staid at Boston till the Evacuation & went to Halifax in March 1776 & came to Engd with the Commrs of the Customs in July 1776.

Former Bounty £560 a Yr. Present Bounty £300 a Yr now stopp'd.

In 1779 or 1780 He obtain'd an Allowance of 200 a Yr as a Mandamus Counsellor. This he recd in addition to the Salary of his Office till Octr 1782 When all Offices in the Customs were abolished since which time Mr Leonard has recd £300 a Yr in the whole.

In 1780 He was appointed Chief Justice of Bermuda & returned in the Spring of 1783.

### Memorial of Willm Wanton [1] Esq.

Determin'd the 4th of Septr 1784.

William Wanton Esq—the Claimant—sworn. 1st of Septr 1784.

A Loyalist but in 1775 sign'd a test to preserve his Liberty & property. Did not bear Arms.[3]

Native of Rhode Island. His father was Govr of Rhode Island.[2] When the troubles commenced He was a Mercht in partnership with his Bror Joseph who is dead And he claims in this Memorial for the Children of his Bror as well as for himself. Says he took an Oath to the Americans in 1774. He explains the Matter & says it was not an Oath but a paper which he sign'd. When he sign'd it He publickly said it was not voluntary. Supposes it to be a Declaration of Allegiance but did not read it. Says this was in 1775.[4] The Kings Troops came there in the Decr of the Year following. He was not obliged in the interim to suppress his Sentiments. In 1775 the Legal Govr was superseded. Upon the King's Troops coming there he immediately join'd them. He has continued with the Army ever since. Sir Robt Pigott appointed him Captn of an Associated Co. Upon the Evacuation of Rhode Island he went with the Army to New York & gave every Assistance to the King's Troops. Upon the Evacuation of Rhode Island He was obliged to leave all his property behind him excepting

[1] William Wanton, *b.* 1734, *d.* 1816, was appointed by Carleton in April 1783 a member of a Board of Commissioners for settling questions of debts of the value of £10 and upwards contracted in New York since November 1776 (*Hist. MSS. Comm., Am. MSS. in R. Inst.*, vol. iv, p. 36). He was for thirty years collector of Customs at St. John. It was stated in 1805 that he was interested in an illegal trade with American subjects (*Winslow Papers*, p. 545).

[2] 'Sprung from a family of colonial governors, and having in his veins the best blood of New England, he was alive to the wrongs of his country, but he shrank from rebellion. He came into office just at the time of the firing of the revenue vessel *Liberty*.' In the dispute regarding this, he vigorously championed his colony's interests; but he afterwards most solemnly protested against the raising of an army of observation. He believed that the happiness and prosperity of the colonies was founded on their connexion with Great Britain. In this state of things he was, of course, not re-elected Governor; but he was allowed to pass the rest of his life in retirement without persecution (F. G. Bates, *Rhode Island and the Formation of the Union*, Col. Univ. Studies in Hist., &c., x, 2, pp. 59–60).

[3] *sic.* in text.

[4] In June 1776 it was enacted that all persons suspected of unfriendliness to the United Colonies should take a test oath declaring their belief in the justice and necessity of resistance to Great Britain and undertaking not to aid the enemy but to support the cause of the United Colonies (Bates, op. cit., p. 65).

£2700 which he took with him to New York & he laid it out in a Privateer which was taken by a French Frigate.

Whilst at New York he rec^d an Allowance of £200 a Y^r from Sir Henry Clinton from the middle of the Y^r 1780. This was continued by Sir Guy Carlton to Jan^y last. He had likewise an House allow'd to him. He was appointed one of the Comm^rs for settling Debts by Sir Guy Carlton but had no Allowance for it. In June or July last he was appointed by Adm^l Digby Purveyor of the Hospital with a Salary of 10*s*. a Day which was paid up to January last.

Bounty £100 a Y^r.

M^r Wanton receives £100 a Y^r from the Treasury from the 5^th of April 1784. He wishes to have one Y^r in advance otherwise he cant get out. He is going out to S^t Johns New Brunswick in Nova Scotia as Collector of the Customs But does not know what the Salary is to be or when it will commence.

John Halyburton—sworn.

Resided at Newport about 17 Y^rs & practised Physic & Surgery. Knew M^r Wanton. His principles were that Great Britain had no right to tax America but the family were never for opposing G. B. by arms on the Contrary as soon as the Rebellion was open & avowed they took part with G. B. & this Gent^n took Arms ag^t the Rebels.

Determin'd the 7^th of Sept^r 1784.

## Memorial of Hannah Flucker widow of Tho^s Flucker [1] Esq.

Hannah Flucker—the Claimant—sworn. 2^d of Sept^r 1784.

Widow of a Zealous & meritorious Loyalist who render'd services to the British Gov^t.

She is the Widow of the late M^r Flucker Secretary of the Province of Mass. Bay. He was a Man of great Loyalty. He was settled at Boston in 1775. He was Secretary of the Province & one of the Mandamus Council. He came to Eng^d with Gen^l Gage in Oct^r 1775. She claims only as Executrix of her Husband & waves any Claim for her own property as she thinks she shall recover it. For Certificates of Loyalty &c Refers to the papers at Whitehall as she produces none. M^r Flucker made a Will & left her Sole Ex^t. Produces the Will which is dated 10^th Oct^r 1775. After a few Legacies he devises the whole of his Estate real & personal to his Wife.

Determin'd the 4^th of Sept^r 1784.

## Memorial of John Henry Carey

John Henry Carey—the Claimant—sworn. 2^d of Sept^r 1784.

Is a Native of Maryland. In the Year 1775 He was Master of a Vessel which traded to the West Indies And in consequence of refusing to bring a Cargo of Gunpowder from S^t Eustatia for the rebels he was dismiss'd & obliged to fly precipitately to Lord Dunmore. He remain'd with Lord Dunmore about 3 weeks & then went to Jamaica & from thence to Eng^d. Since that time he has served as Master in the British Navy but has not served long enough to receive half pay. He was wounded which was the Occasion of his being dismiss'd. He was blown up in the Pelican. He has left his family in America who are now upon

A Loyalist.

[1] *b.* 1719, *d.* 1783. He was a member of the Massachusetts Council from 1761 to 1768, and in 1770 succeeded Andrew Oliver as Secretary of the province. His death was very sudden (Stark, op. cit., pp. 402–3). Curwen, *Journal*, p. 368, writes: 'He is the forty-fifth of the refugees from Massachusetts within my knowledge that have died in England.'

his Estate. The Commissioners however have obliged her to give a Bond & Security which probably was to pay a rent or to acknowledge them as Owners of the Estate but M$^{r}$ Carey knows nothing more than he collects from a Letter which he has lately rec$^{d}$ from his Son & which is produced & read.

M$^{r}$ Carey has an Allowance from the Treasury of £50 a Y$^{r}$. He first rec$^{d}$ it in 1780. Before which time He only rec$^{d}$ £20 to fit him out for his Employment in the Navy. The Allowance of £50 a Y$^{r}$ was continued by M$^{r}$ Wilmot & M$^{r}$ Coke & he now continues to receive it.

Bounty £50 a Y$^{r}$.

## Further Witnesses to the Memorial of John Henry Carey

Will$^{m}$ Bacon—sworn. 4$^{th}$ of Sept$^{r}$ 1784.

Knew M$^{r}$ Carey in America before the troubles. He then lived in Maryland. He was Capt$^{n}$ of a trading Vessel & he knew he had some land but can't speak to the Quantity or Value. His Character was that of a very honest Man & a firm Loyalist. Has heard that he was mark'd out for their resentment by refusing to bring Gunpowder for them from the West Indies. He was driven off for this he could not remain at his own House & was obliged to fly to Lord Dunmore for protection.

George Fenner—sworn.

Lived on the Eastern Shore of Maryland. Knew M$^{r}$ Carey very well. But he left the Country in July 1774. Therefore he can't speak to the Conduct of M$^{r}$ Carey at the Commencement of the troubles. But he was as he knows a Man of very good Character & supposed to be a Man of Property. He lived within four Miles of him. Can't speak to his property but knows that he had a Plantation of his own. And says if M$^{r}$ Carey had wanted Goods in his Way he would have trusted him for £200. M$^{r}$ Carey did not keep a Store before he left America. Believes him to be a Loyalist.

## Memorial of John Vandyke [1] Major of the New Jersey Volunteers

Determin'd the 4$^{th}$ of Sept$^{r}$ 1784.

John Vandyke—the Claimant—sworn. 3$^{d}$ of Sept$^{r}$ 1784.

He is a Native of Somerset County in New Jersey. In 1774 He was a Magistrate & a Farmer & one of the Inferior Judges of the Court. Upon the Commencement of the Troubles He immediately took part with G. B. He was an Officer in the last War. The Rebels applied to him in the Y$^{r}$ 1776 & offer'd him a Reg$^{t}$ & he repeatedly refused. In 1776 He was cited by the Committee & was obliged to give Security to take no part. The British Troops came into Jersey in 1776. He immediately join'd the British Troops. He was taken Pris$^{r}$ in Dec$^{r}$ 1776 & carried to Philadelphia & kept closely confined for 4 Months When he was exchanged. Produces a Certificate of Exchange. He then join'd the British at Brunswick & afterw$^{ds}$ went to Philadelphia. He was then appointed by Sir W$^{m}$ Howe to raise a Corps. He accordingly rais'd 300 Men & rec$^{d}$ a Commission of Major Commandant thereof. Produces a letter

A Zealous Active & spirited Loyalist bore Arms & render'd Services.

[1] Sabine, op. cit., vol. ii, p. 378, writes: 'Vandyke ——. He belonged probably to New Jersey, but possibly to Pennsylvania. In 1777, or 1778, he was commissioned to raise a corps of loyalists.'

from the Adjut[t] Gen[l] by which it appears that he had such a Commission. He was at £300 in the Expence of raising the Men & was never repaid. He had 15*s*. a Day for the Pay of this Comm[n] to the 24[th] of Oct[r] 1778. Since which time he has had half Pay paid to the 24[th] of Oct[r] 1783 And he expects to receive it on.[1] He arrived in Eng[d] the 6[th] of June last. He came from Nova Scotia. Says he has been attainted by a Law of the State of New Jersey for his loyalty. Produces an American Newspaper by which it appears that his Name is mention'd & the Property is advertised for Sale.

Determin'd the 7[th] of Sept[r] 1784.

## Memorial of Richard Cochran

6[th] of Sept[r] 1784.

Richard Cochran—the Claimant—sworn.

A Zealous Loyalist. Did not bear Arms.

Is a Native of Edinburgh & went first to America about 35 Y[rs] ago but he has been in Eng[d] & the West Indies. He has been settled & constantly resident in New Jersey for 20 Y[rs] from this time. In 1774 He was settled on a Plantation of his own which he purchased in 1765. He kept no Store but occasionally imported some goods from the West Indies. Was frequently called upon by the Americans to take a part & he was frequently obliged to leave his own House & go into the Woods. He never took Arms for the Americans nor any Oath or enter'd into any engagement whatever. He was obnoxious to them frequently threaten'd & obliged to conceal himself. In this Way he remain'd till Sir W[m] Howe came into Jersey in 1776. Before which time he had two or three times endeavor'd to obtain Intelligence & sent it to the Army at his own Expence. He join'd Sir W[m] Howe on his Arrival at Princetown & before that he had repair'd a Bridge at his own Expence for the Convenience of the Army. He never bore Arms. He was in the line of a Commissary. In Dec[r] 1776 He had an order from Sir W[m] Erskine[2] to procure Waggons &c for the Army for which he had a Dollar a Day. His House was about a Mile from Princetown. He rec[d] that Dollar a Day till he left America. In a few Days after he acted as Deputy Commissary for which he had likewise a Dollar a Day which he rec[d] in the whole about 3 or 4 Months. He left America in Nov[r] 1777 & came to Eng[d]. He was likewise appointed to examine all persons who came in to examine them & make a report to the Commanding Officer. He had this Appointment from Gen[l] Leslie.

The Rev[d] D[r] Chandler.

Has been acquainted with M[r] Cochran many Y[rs] but not intimately. Knew him to have been a Man of loyal Principles. Proves the hand writing of M[r] Pintard & M[r] Boudinot. Witness left that Country too soon to know much of what he did in the rebellion but knows him to have been a Man of very good Character & he was reputed a Man of Substance. He knew the House he lived in. It appear'd a good House & was a good farm. Does not know his Houses at Princetown. He thinks from his Character that he would not exaggerate. Says he came home poor & that he lent him some Money.

[1] *sic* in text.

[2] In April 1776 Lieutenant-Colonel Sir W. Erskine was made Colonel and Brigadier-General in America of the Brigade of Highlanders (*Hist. MSS. Comm.*, *Am. MSS. in R. Inst.*, vol. i, p. 35). In 1779 he was made Major-General (ibid., p. 410), when he gave up the position of Quartermaster-General to the Forces (ibid., vol. ii, p. 285).

Gov$^{r}$ Franklyn—sworn.

Has known M$^{r}$ Cochran for some Years. Has not the least doubt of his Loyalty if he had not been loyal His Wife's family would have drawn him aside. He made him a Judge which was a proof of good Character. Looked upon him to have been a Man of property. Never heard anything ag$^{t}$ his Character. Did not know his property at Princetown. Has been in his House it was a very good one. It was well furnished but can't tell what it would cost to furnish such an House. Says he lived very comfortably as a Country Gentleman.

### Memorial of Mather Byles[1] D.D.

Determin'd the 7$^{th}$ of Sept$^{r}$ 1784.

7$^{th}$ of Sept$^{r}$ 1784.

The Rev$^{d}$ D$^{r}$ Byles—the Claimant—sworn.

Is a Native of Boston & at the Commencement of the troubles he had the Living of Christ Church at Boston. He was appointed to it in 1768. He preach'd uniformly submission to Gov$^{t}$. This made him unpopular. But he met with no danger nothing more than insults in the Street. He held the Living till the siege of Boston. His Income from his Parishioners was £100 a Y$^{r}$ & £50 from the Society for propagating the Gospel. This remains. When Boston was besieged he lost the Living because his Parishioners left the place. He staid at Boston till the Evacuation when he went to Halifax where he has remain'd during the whole War. He is Chaplain to the Garrison w$^{ch}$ was £110 a Y$^{r}$. This is not an Establishment & he is afraid of losing it. It is a military Appointment. The Gen$^{l}$ gave him leave of absence for six Months.

A Loyalist.
Did not bear Arms.
Living £100 a Y$^{r}$.

He charges the Income of the Living for nine Years £900 but admits that since that time he has rec$^{d}$ more than £100 a Y$^{r}$ as Chaplain of the Garrison but he says it is not permanent otherwise he should think this Loss made good. — rejected.

He was obliged to leave all his furniture at Boston excepting two feather beds & values it at £100 thinks it would have sold for near £200. — £100.

D$^{r}$ Byles applied to the Treasury for temporary Support. He has no pension but he rec$^{d}$ £30 from Gov$^{t}$ to carry him back again to Nova Scotia. — Bounty £30 in full.

Joseph Domet—sworn.

Knew D$^{r}$ Byles. Was one of his Parishioners. It was after some Dispute settled to be £100 a Y$^{r}$. Knows him to have been a very warm friend of Gov$^{t}$. Has frequently heard him preach Doctrines favorable to Gov$^{t}$ & his Parishioners disliked him for it. Has frequently been in his House. It was very decently furnished. Knows he had Money which he lent on Interest.

Rev$^{d}$ M$^{r}$ Peters—sworn.

Has known D$^{r}$ Byles from his Infancy. Believes him always to have been loyal. He was a Dissenting Minister till he had the living of Christ Church. It was £100 a Y$^{r}$. Knows but little of his property. His House was well furnished thinks it would have cost £300 to furnish such an House. Says his

[1] *b.* 1734, *d.* 1814. His father, also Dr. Mather Byles, was the only minister of the Congregational Churches who opposed the revolutionary party. He continued to live in Boston and died there in 1788. Stark (op. cit., pp. 276–8) gives several specimens of his readiness in humorous retort. The son was chaplain of the garrison at Halifax until he became Rector of Trinity Church, St. John, in 1788. His biography is in G. Herbert Lee, *History of the Church of England in the Province of New Brunswick.*

Charge of £100 is very reasonable. It would have sold for that Sum at an Auction. Does not know wher his property is confiscated or not. His name is in the Act of Attainder.

Determin'd the 9th of Septr 1784.

### Memorial of Jas Edwd Boisseau

8th of Septr 1784.

An active & Zealous Loyalist from the Yr 1780. But before that time he had taken the Oaths to the Rebels & served in their Militia.

James Edwd Boisseau—the Claimant—sworn.

Is a Native of America was born in So. Carolina about 40 Miles from Charlestown. He was settled in St Stephens Parish in the Yr 1775. Until he had an opportunity of joining the British he did Militia Duty with the Americans. He was too young to take any part when Genl Prevost came into that Province. He first join'd Sir Henry Clinton in 1780 after he had taken Charlestown. He is now 24 Yrs of Age. About the Yr 1775 or 1776 He took the State Oath. He was obliged to take it or quit the Province. In Septr 1780 He was taken prisr on an Expedition to Black Mingo [1] Post & confined him for 11 Months & 3 Months in a Dungeon. After this he escaped & join'd Major Craig at Wilmington. After this he went to Charlestown & recd a Cornet's Commn in the So. Carolina Royal Dragoons & was afterwds promoted to be Lieutt in the same Corps. He has been in that Corps to the end of the War. On the Evacuation the Corps was sent to St Augustine where he remain'd a Yr & then went to Halifax. He has now the Half Pay of Infantry in that Corps. His friends & relations tempted him to desert & offer'd him tempting offers & Govr Rutledge told him in person that if he wd return to them & be active All should be forgot. This was a Conversation when he was in prison. He refused the Offer & returned to his Confinement.

Bounty £30 a Yr.

Mr Boisseau applied to the Treasury and was heard about 3 Months ago. The result of that report was an Allowance of £30 a Yr from the 5th of July 1784.

John Gaillard Esq—sworn.

He was a Major in the British Ma & lived in Carolina. Mrs Gaillard is related to Mr Boisseau. He has known him from his Infancy. Thinks he always wished well to this Country. Did not know that he had taken the State Oath to the Americans. Since he came into the British Lines he has acted with great spirit. This was in the Yr 1780.

Knows his property very well. Did in Conjunction with two other Gentn make a Valuation upon Oath of it. Knew his Plantation. It was his. It was not good Land But there was a very good House upon it. The Buildings were worth as much as the Land & he thinks they would have cost £500. The Buildings were not new. Says if it had been to be sold he thinks it would have fetched 12 or £1400 before the troubles. He says they valued the whole moderately at his request.

Knows the 300 Acres of Swamp. This was very good Land tho' not the best of Swamp. This came by his father & did belong to his Grandfather. There was a part of it too low for Cultivation. It was not so valuable as the higher. Says it was not abandon'd by the father as unfit for Cultivation. Thinks the reason of his carrying his Negroes to work at the plantation of the father was

[1] See McCrady, *S. Carolina in the Rev., 1775–80*, pp. 749–50.

only because his father's lands had Buildings on them & were fit for immediate Cultivation. He says these Lands are worth at least 40*s*. per Acre. He thinks them worth more. He says in their Valuation they consider'd what they would have been worth before the troubles. Now they are worth five times as much. He thinks it a low Valuation before the troubles. He thinks he had about 20 Negroes. He thinks that M^r^ Boisseau will never get a farthing from his father in Law. The Witness saw him 3 Months ago & he said he had nothing belonging to M^r^ Boisseau. He had but a small Stock of Cattle 25 or 30 head.

### Memorial of John Murray

Determin'd the 15th of Sept^r^ 1784.

John Murray—the Claimant—sworn. 8th of Sept^r^ 1784.

Is a Native of Scotland & went first to America in 1769 & returned again & went back & settled in 1771 in North Carolina & remain'd in Carolina till June 1775 When he went to Georgia & resided there till May 1776. He left it in consequence of the rebellious Situation the province was then in. He came away with the Lieut^t^ Gov^r^ & others. They were obliged to come Previous to his Departure he took no part. They never tender'd any Oath or any paper to him & he never sign'd any test. He remain'd in Eng^d^ till May 1778 when he embarked for New York. He was taken by a Privateer & carried into New London. He was a Pris^r^ on Parole. He remain'd in that Situation about 3 Months & then he went to Charlestown. After staying a Week or ten Days he was permitted to go to Georgia. Soon after he left Georgia the first time they pass'd an Act of Attainder ag^t^ him. He then desired to be tried they refused to try him & a Mob carried him off & set him down on the Carolina side of the river where he remain'd till Gen^l^ Campbell came & he immediately joined him. He remain'd with the Army in the Province till it was evacuated. He never fill'd any Military Situation. He was taken Pris^r^ when Savannah was besieged. Says that his property has been confiscated & himself attainted in three Provinces. That in Georgia has been sold. He was settled in Georgia as a Planter when the troubles broke out. He says he had no property in So. Carolina notwithstanding he is attainted.

A Loyalist.

Did not bear Arms.

Confiscation proved.

He has never made any Application to Whitehall for temporary Support.

Lieut^t^ Gov^r^ Graham—sworn.

Has known M^r^ Murray a great many Years. He always did consider & does consider him as attached to this Country tho' he says there is a part of his Conduct which is exceptionable. Which is his requesting to be permitted to return & applying to the rebel Gov^r^ for that purpose. Says there were great doubts of his Loyalty. He thinks he is attached to this Country but thinks he would have sacrificed a little principle to save his property. He has an Estate in Scotland.

John Murray Esq—the Claimant—called in again.

Has lost the paper which contain'd his Petition to the Rebel Gov^r^. He made no Offer of any Sacrifice whatever. He said in his petition that he had done nothing ag^t^ them. But he meant nothing more than to state the fact & not to insinuate that he would be with them.

Will^m Telfer—sworn.

Knew M^r Murray from the Year 1769. He resided in Georgia in 1771 & 1772. He knows the farm which he had in Georgia he has frequently been there. It was his Bro^r David's property & he bought it at public Sale it was in 1772. He gave upwards of £300 S. for it. It was bought considerably under its Value. Does not know the state of this farm in 1775. He saw it before the Evacuation & then it was much improved. Says provided it was in as good a State in 1775 Thinks it was worth £1000. Knows nothing of his other property. Knows nothing of his Loyalty but by report prior to the Y^r 1778 because the Witness was in Eng^d from 1772 to 1778. But he never heard his Loyalty disputed after that time.

Thomas Tollemash—sworn.

Knew M^r Murray in Georgia before the troubles. Believes him to have been a true Loyalist. Remembers his making an Application to the Assembly at Savannah to take off the Attainder. He was not permitted to Stay in the province. Never heard that he made any Offer to be with them if they would take off the Attainder. He knows his Estate believes it was about 100 Acres. It was not very good Land but from its Situation it was reckon'd valuable. The Witness & a M^r Douglas valued the Land for M^r Murray after the Evacuation at £1000 & they put the value upon it which it was worth in the Y^r 1782. Says it was not so valuable in 1775. Does not know anything of M^r Murray's other property.

Determin'd 10^th of Sept^r 1783.

**Memorial of John Fenton**[1]

John Fenton—the Claimant—sworn. 10^th of Sept^r 1784.

An Active & Zealous Loyalist.

Did not bear Arms.[2]

Offices.
Judge of Probate £70 a Y^r.
Clerk of the In C^t £120 a Y^r.
Confiscation proved.

Is a Native of Ireland. He was an Officer in the last War & after the War he settled in America. He married in America in the course of the former War. He went to America upon the reduction of his Reg^t in 1763 or 1764 to settle & lived there in the Year 1775. He lived in New Hampshire & resided in Portsmouth. He was appointed to command a Fort in June 1775 & chosen to represent the town of Plymouth in the Gen^l Assembly. Upon the commencement of the troubles he took part with Gov^t. He was Col^l of the M^a for the County of Grafton Judge of Probate for D^o Clerk of the Inferior Court of D^o & Justice of the Peace throughout the Province. Judge of Probate about £80 a Y^r Clerk of the Inferior Court 120 per Ann. He had no pay as Col^l of M^a. The Emoluments of the two places arose from fees. He exerted himself upon every Occasion to support the Authority of Gov^t. He had many proposals from the Americans if he would join them. He was offer'd any Command but M^r Washington's but always refused. He had the same offer when Pris^r. The Gov^r of the Province fix'd upon this Gent^n to introduce Lord North's Conciliatory proposition. He made this Motion in the Assembly to read the Bill which was negatived And he was afterwards expell'd for the part which he had taken upon this & some other Occasions. And he was immediately taken Pris^r out of the Gov^r's House when

[1] See Sabine, op. cit., vol. i, p. 420. Howe for some reason or no reason doubted his loyalty, if he is the Mr. Fenton to whom he alluded when writing to Lord G. Germain on May 12, 1776 (*Hist. MSS. Comm.*, *Stopford-Sackville MSS.*, vol. ii, 'Papers relating to the Am. War', p. 32).

[2] *Sic* in text.

he went to communicate to the Gov[r] what pass'd in the Assembly. This was in June 1775. They carried him to prison & kept him confined till Dec[r] following. Many offers made to him there & he said he never would put his head upon a Pillar & die a Rascal. This put an End to any further Offers. He was releas'd on Parole in Dec[r]. Promises to send the Parole which was to take no part. They drew up the Conditions which were either to come to Eng[d] or Ireland. He came to Eng[d] immediately in the Pacquet & since that time he has not been in America. Gov[r] Tryon was the Gov[r] of New York at that time.

Produces the Commission of Gov[r] of the Fort sign'd by Lord George Germaine & sign'd by the King. There was a Warrant annex'd to it for the pay of 20*s*. a Day. Produces his Appointment to be Judge of Probates sign'd by Gov[r] Wentworth in 1773.

Stephen Holland Esq—sworn.

Late of New Hampshire. Knew M[r] Fenton for some time before the troubles. Always looked upon him to be an active & Zealous Loyalist. He was a Member of the Gen[l] Assembly & remembers M[r] Fenton making the Motion alluded to. It respected Lord North's conciliatory proposition. The Witness seconded the Motion & there was only a third person for it. It was not owing to his making this Motion that he was expell'd but it was owing to the Gov[r] having summon'd a representative for Plymouth which was never represented before. The Witness was in the House of Assembly when the Mob attacked the Gov[r's] House for M[r] Fenton. The Gov[r] sent for the two Houses to defend him. The Mob soon after carried M[r] Fenton away by the House. The Witness was very unpopular & quitted the Town that night. Believes the reason that the Mob took him away was some Advice that he had given to the Inha[ts] of .[1] In consequence of this the Congress sent for him but he refused to go & laughed at their Authority believes this was the reason of their seizing him.

Knows very little of M[r] Fenton's property. Has seen his House at Bunker's Hill but does not know the Value of it. It was a very good House. Has seen his farm in New Hampshire. Knows the Land & knows that he was building an House it was not finished in 1774 when he saw it. If it was finished in a Common Way thinks it might cost £200 La Mo.[2] Thinks the land might be worth 3 or £4 an Acre La Mo. independ[t] of the Buildings. Has been in M[r] Fenton's House at Portsmouth & it appear'd to be very well furnished.

Benning Wentworth Esq—sworn.

Was well acquainted with M[r] Fenton from 1771. After he came into New Hampshire He knows he was particularly active & frequently came to the Gov[r] to know if he could be of any use. This brought very much the resentment of the people upon him. He was present at the Gov[rs] House when the Mob came they were armed & took him away. Believes the Gov[rs] reason for summoning a Representative from the town of Plymouth was a wish to have M[r] Fenton in the Assembly & thinking that he would be elected. Believes the Gov[r] desired

[1] Blank in text.

[2] Can 'La Mo' stand for 'Proclamation money' (of Queen Anne in 1704)? According to this the official rating of the Spanish or American dollar in the North American provinces was six shillings.

him to make the Motion. Knows nothing of M^r Fenton's property but by repute. Has seen his property at Charlestown. His House at Portsmouth was very well furnish'd. Thinks it would cost more than £200.

### Further testimony to the Memorial of Capt^n Fenton

John Fisher Esq—sworn. 11^th of Sept^r 1784.

Has known M^r Fenton many Years. He was appointed by Gov^r Wentworth Gov^r of Fort Will^m & Mary. Remembers his being Col^l of M^a & Judge of Probate. He was one of the first persons imprison'd in the Dispute. He was very active & Zealous which was the Occasion of his being seiz'd. The Mob were afraid of his making head in the Assembly being a very sensible Man & therefore believes they seiz'd him. Can't speak precisely to any part of his property but knows his House at May place. He lived there & it was esteem'd to be his property. It was a very good House & an excellent Situation. Does not know the Value but it was very early & very good Land. Plymouth was a new Sett^t but it was very good Land. Does not know the value of the Office of Judge of Probate. It is generally looked upon to be a place for Life. Should consider it as a Loss of Office. Does not know that he was Clerk of the Inferior Court if he was says it was less permanent than the other. Remembers seeing all the buildings eras'd. Believes it was done by the Gen^l's order & remembers a Redoubt being built near to that Spot.

Determin'd the 27^th of Sept^r 1784.

### Memorial of Philip Goldthwaite [1]

Philip Goldthwaite—the Claimant—sworn. 11^th of Sept^r 1784.

A Loyalist But took an Oath to the Rebels.

Is a Native of Boston. At the Commencem^t of the troubles he resided at Woolwich in Kennebeck river & was then in his Majesty's Service. He had a Contract with Gov^t for Wood which made him unpopular. He then resign'd this Contract & got the Command of the Neptune Schooner under Gov^t. He was taken Pris^r frequently & ill treated & put in Irons & once he thought his Life in Danger. When he left the Neptune & went down into the Country He was carried before the Committee of Safety & swore to oppose all the Measures of G. B. When he took it he meant to break it & he did break it. After he got away from these people He has constantly been employ'd on board his Majesty's Ships. He came to Eng^d in 1779 by order of the Admiral. He looks upon those who gave him the Oath as having no right to administer it & therefore he paid no Attention to it.

Certificate produced & read to his Loyalty from Admiral Arbuthnot & Sir George Collier.

Has no Allowance from Gov^t. He applied about a Y^r ago to M^r Wilmot & M^r Coke & they held it to be no Case because he was then one of the Band of Pensioners. But he has since been obliged to sell that place.

[1] *b.* 1733. In 1775 Captain Philip Goldthwaite was brought before the New Hampshire Committee of Supplies on suspicion of being unfriendly to the liberties of America. Upon examination nothing appeared against him (Force, *Am. Arch.*, 4th ser., vol. iv, p. 5). He bought an annuity in the King's household and became one of the Gentlemen of the Bedchamber. He had died before October 1786 (Stark, op. cit., p. 359).

## Memorial of John Twine—a Black

Determin'd the 15th of Septr 1784.

John Twine—the Claimant—sworn. 13th of Septr 1784.

Was Christen'd about four Months ago & knows the Nature of an Oath. Does not know how old he is. When the troubles broke out he lived at Petersburgh in Virginia. He swears that he is free born [1] & that his free papers are left at the Treasury. They were given to him by Coll Balinghall. In 1775 He lived with Mr Bradley who kept a Tavern. Six Years ago he join'd the British at Trentown. Before that he was in the rebel Service. He drove a Waggon for the rebels. Since he join'd the British he has served with the Army & been a Servt to an Officer. He was wounded in the Thigh at Camden.

A Loyalist since he join'd the British.

Did not bear Arms.[2]

Property.

One Lot of Land containing one Acre & a Dwelling House. He got this from his father. It is in a small Island. One Peters lived in the House. He paid him 7*s*. per week Virginia Money. But he afterwds says that he lived with Peters & that he the Claimt was a Lodger. However he continues to swear that the House was his own. Says Coll Bannister who wanted to buy it said it was not worth more than £150 including some few Articles of furniture. Says that nobody knows this to be his property but one Mr Dudley who is gone to America. But if he returns soon he will bring him.

Disallowed for want of Evidence.

## Memorial of Samuel Burke—Black

Determin'd the 15th Septr 1784.

Samuel Burke—the Claimant—sworn. 13th of Septr 1784.

He is a Native of Charlestown & was Christen'd in Ireland. When the troubles broke he was Servt to Govr Brown [3] who was then on the Missisippi. He swears that he was born free. He had free papers but he has lost them. He took no Notice of them. He remain'd with Govr Brown whilst he was raising a Regt. He bore Arms. He has been twice wounded. He has remain'd ever since with the Army. He never recd pay. Swears that he killed at least ten Men at the Hanging rock.

A free negro.

A Loyalist.

Bore Arms as Servt to Govr Brown & was wounded.

Certificate produced from Govr Brown in which he speaks of his Loyalty & says that he was a free Man & has been twice wounded.

Property.

He married a Dutch Mulatto Woman at New York & he got about £40 with her & an House & Garden. His Wife got this from her former Husband This was in Dutch Street No 5. He left it to her & she had the papers & gave them to the Claimt. He has lost them. He says it was valued at £350 by the Genls Aid de Camp. Besides this He had furniture which he values at £7 9*s*. This was used as a Barrack House. He has no Witnesses here. He desired

Disallow'd for want of Evidence.

[1] See J. H. Russell, *The Free Negro in Virginia*, Johns Hopkins Univ. Studies in Hist., &c., ser. xxxi, No. 3.

[2] *Sic* in text.

[3] Thomas Brown, Lieutenant-Colonel of the King's Rangers, was appointed in 1779 Superintendent for the Creek and Cherokee Indians (*Hist. MSS. Comm.*, *Am. MSS. in R. Inst.*, vol. ii, p. 59). There is a glowing tribute to his merits in a letter of Governor Tonyn to General Howe, dated February 24, 1778 (ibid., vol. i, p. 198).

a person to attend who had seen him in his House but he does not attend & Gov^r Brown he is afraid will not live to attend. He has rec^d the Sum of £20 from the Treasury.

Bounty £20 in full.

## Memorial of Scipio Handley—a Black

Determin'd the 15^th of Sept^r 1784.

13^th of Sept^r 1784.

Scipio Handley—the Claimant—sworn.

A Free Negro.

He has been Christen'd here about a Year ago & knows the Nature of an Oath. He lived in Charlestown & was free born. He was carrying on trade for himself as a fisherman. He never carried Arms or took any Oath for the Americans. He was taken by the rebels when he was carrying things to Lord W^m Campbell on board. They took his Boat. He was put in Irons & confined for this six weeks. He left the province at that time & never returned. He came to Georgia with the British Troops.

A Loyalist.

Property.

He had no Land. He Lost some furniture & a few other Articles which are contain'd in the Schedule which he values at £97 9*s*. He kept his House with his Mother but says the furniture was his own. £28 Cash left in the House. Two Trunks valued at £15. He had 7 Hogs Valued at 8 Gās. He has rec^d £5 in full from the Treasury.

£20.

Bounty £5 in full.

Ellenor Listor—Widow—sworn.

Knew Scipio Handley at Charlestown. Knows his Mother to have been a free Woman. The Mother sold Gingerbread. Knows that he carried things to Lord W^m Campbell & the Americans confined him for it. She believes him to have been loyal. There was some furniture used both by the Mother & the Son but she does not know to whom it belonged She never saw any Mahogony furniture. She left Charlestown in Easter 1782 & she believes the Mother is in poss^n of the furniture.

## Memorial of William Haywood

Determin'd y^e 28^th of Sept^r 1784.

14^th of Sept^r 1784.

William Haywood—the Claimant—sworn.

He is a Native of New York. In 1775 He kept a Store in Orangebourg District & was settled on a plantation which he bought for his eldest Dau^r. He was called upon by the Americans to join them in July 1775 & paid Duties for not doing it from July to Dec^r. They fin'd him £15 for himself & £15 for his Servant for every fortnight from July to Dec^r. Thinks he paid in the whole £163 C. In Dec^r 1775 He was then drafted to serve ag^t the Loyalists but he refused to go & was fin'd £400 & they seiz'd for it. He never took any Oath or did anything for the Rebels. He join'd the Kings Army at Wilmington. He was once or twice Master of a Galley. In 1778 He was employ'd in the Quarter Mast^r Gen^l's department & had 5*s*. York C. per day. He continued this for a Month after & in March 1778 He was made Master of a Galley by Sir Andrew Snape Hammond. Since the Y^r 1780 he has been in no public employ.

A Loyalist.

Bore Arms.

Certificates produced & read from Col^l Balfour & many other Officers to Loyalty & in addition to that a Certificate from Gov^r Bull to his knowing all those who sign'd the Certificate. Likewise Certificates from M^r Phepoe & M^r Andrew Cumming to general Loyalty &c.

Has an Allowance of £50 a Y^r from the Treasury from Jan^y 1783.

Bounty £50 a Y^r.

### Memorial of the Rev^d Jacob Duché [1]

Determin'd the 28^th of Sept^r 1784.

The Rev^d Jacob Duché—the Claimant—sworn. 14^th of Sept^r 1784.

A Loyalist after his resignation of the Chaplainship to the Congress.

Did not bear Arms.

Is a Native of Philadelphia & was settled at Philadelphia in 1775. He was in the Y^r 1775 elected Minister of the united Churches of Christ Church & S^t Peters. He was for many Y^rs before Assistant Preacher of them. The Emolument in 1775 was about £600 a Y^r. The Salary was £300 a Y^r C. The Glebe £100 C. & the Surplice fees about £200 C. Says it was at least £300 a Y^r S. When first the People of America talked of associating & taking up Arms he gave his Sentiments ag^t it. In 1774 before any Associations had taken place he was appointed Chaplain to the first Congress. He preached in 1775 the only political Sermon he ever preached to a Reg^t of Militia in Philadelphia & it certainly was to encourage them in their Opposition to Taxation. This Sermon was printed & dedicated to M^r Washington. He never had any political Connection with the Congress. He only preached before them a few times. When they were prosecuting the idea of Independence He opposed it very warmly. Independence was declared the 6^th of July 1776. Soon after this He rec^d a Letter from M^r Hancock saying that the Congress had appointed him their Chaplain. Upon receiving this Letter He was in great Distress how to Act. He thought by his refusing to accept the Church might suffer & so he accepted. The Congress then sat in Philadelphia. He was at German Town when he rec^d this Letter. He never did anything but read prayers. He did not believe that they meant to persist in their Independence. Lord Howe wrote to the Congress & He was extremely happy to hear that Lord & Sir W^m Howe were appointed as he had great Expectations from the weight of Lord Howe & Sir W^m in America. But finding from a Member of the Congress that there was no hope of a reconciliation & that they insisted on their Independence He immediately the next Day wrote a Letter to resign his Appointment. He mention'd no reasons for his resignation in his Letter. He was never called upon to take the Oaths but not going to take them his persecution followed. He took no Oath when he was appointed Chaplain to the Congress. He staid

[1] *d.* 1798. The worthy clergyman seems somewhat to have minimized the change in his opinions. In the prayer which he offered up for Congress the words occur: 'Look down in mercy upon these our American States, who have fled to Thee from the rod of the oppressor and thrown themselves upon Thy gracious protection, desiring to be henceforth *dependent upon Thee*' (the prayer is given in full in Sabine, op. cit., vol. i, p. 389).

When Duché resigned the chaplaincy in October 1776, he resigned it on the ground of the state of his health and his parochial duties (*Journals of the Continental Congress*, vol. vi, p. 886). It was not till the following October that he addressed to Washington the memorable letter which threw the gauntlet to the Congress. In April 1783 he appealed to Washington to effect a repeal of the Act which kept him in banishment away from the arms of a dear aged father and the embraces of a numerous circle of friends. He returned to Philadelphia in 1790, and died there.

Curwen notes under April 8, 1781: 'Accompanied Colonel Browne to hear the famed pulpit orator, Mr. Duchée . . . who figures even in London. His performance in point of language and delivery greatly pleased us' (op. cit., p. 312).

after this at Philadelphia untill the British Army came there & he was permitted to keep the Church open & he read the Service but he did not pray for the King. When the Army came to Philadelphia He called on Lord Cornwallis but not finding him He preach'd & pray'd for the King after the Service was over. He was seized by a Major Madden & confined by Orders of Sir W$^{m}$ Howe. He was kept in prison for one Night & the next Day his Key was brought with a Message from Sir W$^{m}$ Howe that he was at liberty. He took no public part afterwards excepting the writing a Letter to M$^{r}$ Washington which has been since published. He shew'd the letter before he wrote it to Lord Cornwallis. Upon this Letter being made public He thought it not safe & he came to Eng$^{d}$ with the Consent of the Vestry & Sir W$^{m}$ Howe. He arrived in Eng$^{d}$ in July 1778.

Former Bounty £150 a Y$^{r}$. Present Bounty £100 a Y$^{r}$.

Receives £100 a Y$^{r}$ from the Treasury. Formerly receiv'd an Allowance of £150 a Y$^{r}$ which was reduced by M$^{r}$ Wilmot & M$^{r}$ Coke.

15$^{th}$ of Sept$^{r}$ 1784.

The Rev$^{d}$ Will$^{m}$ Andrews—sworn.

Rector of Portsmouth in Virginia. Has known M$^{r}$ Duché for many Years. When he first knew him He was a Man of very good Character. Did not know him at the time of the troubles as they were separated & lived at a great Distance. Knows that he was Rector of S$^{t}$ Peters & Christ Church. D$^{r}$ Peters resign'd in his favor in the Year 1775. The Witness was for six weeks in Philadelphia in 1769. M$^{r}$ Duché was then Assistant Minister. The Livings were always reckon'd £300 a Y$^{r}$. Knew the House in which M$^{r}$ Duché lived has frequently been in it. It was a good House & the Witness then asked him what the House would cost & he said that it would cost when finished £2000 S. Knows nothing of his Loyalty but from report & from his publications.

Sam$^{l}$ Shoemaker Esq—sworn.

Has known M$^{r}$ Duché from his Infancy. His Character as a Clergyman was perfectly unexceptionable. His Connections influenced him he believes in political Matters. His father he says had a Bias his father's Brother has disinherited this Gent$^{n}$ for it & his Wife's family were all rebels. This induced him to accept of being Chaplain to the Congress. After his resignation he believes him to have been sincere. He looks upon him to be a very honest Man. Being asked his Opinion as to what people thought of the fate of the War in 1776 He says all the Loyalists & most of the rebels thought that Great Britain would prevail. But he says he hopes that M$^{r}$ Duché acted from principle when he alter'd his Sentiments. Knows the House very well in which M$^{r}$ Duché lived. It was a good House. He can't speak to the Value. He says it was not finished when he came away. Thinks £2000 would be a very good Price for what was done. Thinks £1500 S. would pay for the Building & the Lot. He never heard of any Surprize in the town that the Congress had appointed M$^{r}$ Duché their Chaplain & that M$^{r}$ Duché was not well affected to the Congress. On the contrary he as a Loyalist thought that M$^{r}$ Duché was lost to the Cause Remembers Sir W$^{m}$ Howe confining M$^{r}$ Duché under an Idea that he was a Rebel. He held the Chaplainship only two Months. He says he has no doubt but that M$^{r}$ Duché was of opinion with the Americans up to a certain point & afterwards he is willing to suppose that he acted upon principle.

## Memorial of James Edw$^{d}$ Powell Esq.

Determin'd the 28$^{th}$ of Sept$^{r}$ 1784.

James Edw$^{d}$ Powell Esq—the Claimant—sworn. 16$^{th}$ of Sept$^{r}$ 1784.

Is a Native of Eng$^{d}$ & went to America in the Y$^{r}$ 1744 as a Super Cargo. He went to settle there in April 1746 in So. Carolina. When the troubles broke out he was settled in Georgia as a Merch$^{t}$. In 1755 & to the Y$^{r}$ 1776 He was a Member of the Council. In Jan$^{y}$ 1776 He with the other Members of the Council were taken Pris$^{rs}$ by an armed Mob & a Parole extorted from them. He never took any Oath to the Rebels. He was required to do it but he refused as an Officer of the Crown in consequence of which he was frequently insulted. He quitted the province & went in June 1777 to Charlestown to procure a passage for Europe. He staid there two Months & then quitted it in a Vessel for Nantz. He was taken & carried into S$^{t}$ John. He then came to Eng$^{d}$ in Nov$^{r}$ 1777 & staid in Eng$^{d}$ till 1781 When the King appointed him Lieut$^{t}$ Gov$^{r}$ of all the Bahama Islands & the Lords of the Admiralty appointed him Judge of the Admiralty there. He had only been there five Months when it was captured by the Spaniards. He came home in a Cartel with the Gov$^{r}$ & has remain'd in Eng$^{d}$ ever since. He never bore Arms in any military situation before the Troubles. Has an Allowance of £100 a Y$^{r}$ from the Treasury which he has rec$^{d}$ from the 1$^{st}$ of Jan$^{y}$ 1784.

A Loyalist.
Did not bear Arms.

Bounty £100 a Y$^{r}$.

He says he is still Lieut$^{t}$ Gov$^{r}$ but receives no Emolument from it.

## Further testimony to the Memorial of the Rev$^{d}$ M$^{r}$ Duché

The Rev$^{d}$ D$^{r}$ Chandler—sworn. 16$^{th}$ of Sept$^{r}$ 1784.

Was well acquainted with M$^{r}$ Duché before the troubles. Never saw him personally since the troubles. His Character was very amiable & very good & he was the most popular Preacher in America. Believes that for a time he swam with the Stream & encouraged rebellion to a certain point but thinks he afterwards saw his Error. Believes he changed his Conduct from principle. Says all the Clergy in Philadelphia were promoters of the rebellion. Does not think he has anything of merit in his Loyalty perhaps he may have an excuse. As a reason for thinking that he changed his Conduct upon principle he says he rec$^{d}$ a letter from D$^{r}$ Inglis in the Winter of 1777 in which speaking of M$^{r}$ Duché he said he was upon the Stool of repentance And the troops were not then come to Philadelphia.

He knew his House very well says it was an elegant House. Thinks the House in building would cost £3000 New York Cur. & the Lot about £500 C. Says the House actually sold for £7000 C. which is about £4000 S. Thinks if it had been put up to Sale in the Year 1775 it would have sold for £1500 S.

## Memorial of John M$^{c}$Leod

Determin'd the 28$^{th}$ of Sept$^{r}$ 1784.

John M$^{c}$Leod—the Claimant—sworn. 16$^{th}$ of Sept$^{r}$ 1784.

Is a Native of Scotland & went to America in 1771. In 1775 He was settled on a plantation of his own in N$^{o}$ Carolina where he remain'd till the Expedition

An Active & Zealous Loyalist. Bore Arms.

under Col[l] McDonald[1] in 1776 When he was appointed a Lieut[t] by Gov[r] Martin & taken Pris[r] at Moor's bridge. He was above ½ a Y[r] in close Confinement & two Y[rs] & ½ on Parole. He was exchanged & served with the Army under Lord Cornwallis until they came to Wilmington where he was taken sick but before he was sick he rais'd some Men about 27 in all. He has not as yet half Pay but he expects it. He has a Commission of Lieut[t] from Lord Cornwallis & Gov[r] Martin.

Bounty £20 a Y[r].

Has an Allowance of £20 a Y[r] which he has rec[d] from the 10[th] of Oct[r] last.

He never took part with the Americans nor ever took any Oath to them but always opposed them in all their Proceedings.

Alexander M[c]Leod—sworn.

Is no relation to the Claimant. He was an Officer in the same Corps with the Witness & conducted himself with Spirit. He knows that he was taken Pris[r]. Their Corps is to have half pay when the Par[t] meets again. Knows the place where he lived in Anson County. Believes he had in that place 100 Acres. The 200 Acres belonged to him & his Bro[r] jointly. It was good Land & a good House upon it which cost him a good deal but it was not finished. Values the 100 Acres & the House. Believes the two Bro[rs] were building the House together that was the general Opinion of the County. The Witness lived within 4 Miles of him. The Brother married in 1773 or 1774 & left him & left the plantation to him but believes the Bro[r] had not sold his Share believes about 50 Acres were clear'd. Has seen his Cattle but does not know the number remembers 3 Horses & an Horse taken from him at Camden. Says the other Land lay 5 or 6 Miles from these 100 Acres & that they were uncultivated. Has been in his House. Not very good furniture.

## Memorial of Henry Flower

Determin'd the 28[th] of Sept[r] 1784. A Native of America who has resided in G[t] B[n] since 1766.

Disallowed altogether for want of Evidence of property or Loss.

18[th] of Sept[r] 1784.

Henry Flower—the Claimant—sworn.

Is a Native of Philadelphia but has been in Eng[d] from the Y[r] 1766. He had taken an active part for Gov[t] in the Stamp Act & was obliged to come away. He did not return to America because being appointed to act as Agent to M[r] Bayard here he was obliged to stay in Eng[d] & M[r] Bayard acted for him in America. Has taken no part in the present dispute & therefore has no reason to imagine that he is particularly obnoxious to the Americans.

Produces a Letter from M[r] Bayard but nothing is said in it of property.

He says he has never rec[d] anything from his property since 1774.

## Memorial of James Munro

Determin'd the 28[th] of Sept[r] 1784. A Loyalist & bore Arms.

18[th] of Sept[r] 1784.

James Munro—the Claimant—sworn.

Is a Native of Scotland. Went first to America in 1757 & remain'd there in the same County (Cumberland) till the Year 1776. When the troubles first

[1] To judge from the number of Highland claimants, W. Purviance's statement in a letter dated February 24, 1775, would seem justified, that the insurgents, both officers and privates, at the time of the engagement at Creek Bridge, consisted principally of Highlanders whom he termed 'banditti' (*N. Car. Records*, vol. x).

broke out He took part with Great Britain. He lived near Cross Creek & as soon as the Reg[t] of Highlanders was compleat he was embodied in it & had a Lieut[ts] Comm[n] from Gov[r] Martin. He was taken Pris[r] the morning of the Action at Moors Bridge & was kept in Prison near 5 Y[rs]. He rec[d] Pay for all that time (half Pay). He was asked frequently to take an Oath to the Americans but constantly refused. When he was released he came to New York & served during the rem[r] of the War. He came to Eng[d] about a Y[r] ago.

He receives from the Treasury £20 a Y[r] & has rec[d] it from October last. Bounty £20 a Y[r].

### Memorial of David King—a Black

Determin'd the 28[th] of Sept[r] 1784.

David King—the Claimant—sworn. 18[th] of Sept[r] 1784.

Is a Native of America the province of New York. He lived in New York in 1774. He belonged to W[m] Kippen in 1774. His Master gave him liberty to do as he pleas'd during the rebellion. He worked at the forts & made Shoes for the Army. He came to Eng[d] 4 Y[rs] ago. He had put himself into danger by carrying letters on board a Man of War. He was not paid for it. In consequence of this a reward was offer'd for him by the Americans.

A Loyalist. Did not bear Arms.

He has lost nothing by the War & has gain'd his Liberty.

Produces Certificates from M[r] Matthews & Major Dauban. The one to his being employ'd in carrying Letters on board a Ship & the other to his being employ'd by the Engineers & M[r] Matthews says he was a trusty & serviceable person.

He rec[d] from the Treasury 5 in full. Admits that he has gain'd his Liberty & that he now gets 2*s.* a Day. Bounty £5 in full.

Property Lost.

He has Lost Leather & Shop Goods & other Effects at New York to the Amo[t] of £30 S. Says he could not carry the Leather away. He was worth 5 or 6 Dollars when the troubles broke out.

He got the paper Money by his Labor & with the paper Money he bought the Leather.

### Memorial of The Rev[d] D[r] Seabury [1]

Determin'd y[e] 28[th] of Sept[r] 1784.

The Rev[d] D[r] Seabury—the Claimant—sworn. 18[th] Sept[r] 1784.

Is a Native of Connecticut & lived at West Chester when the troubles broke

A Zealous & meritorious Loyalist.

[1] *b.* 1729, *d.* 1796. He wrote: *Free Thoughts on the Proceedings of the Continental Congress held at Philadelphia, September 4, 1774. The Congress canvassed, or an Examination into the Conduct of the Delegates at their Grand Convention held in Philadelphia, September 1774. A view of the Controversy between Great Britain and her Colonies. An Alarm to the Legislature of the Province of New York occasioned by the present Political Disturbance in North America, 1775.* The first three were written under the signature of 'A Westchester farmer' and had considerable influence. The official life of Seabury is mainly devoted to his religious side; but Mr. Herz has contributed an exhaustive article on him to the *English Hist. Review*, vol. xxvi, pp. 57–76.

On November 20, 1775, Seabury with three others was arrested by a party from Connecticut under Captain Sears and sent to Newhaven (Moore, op. cit., vol. i, p. 173). One of his companions, Jonathan Fowler, signed a recantation, but no recantation could be got from the sturdy clergyman. On September 11, 1776, the New York Committee of Safety reported that the Rev. Samuel Seabury had been confined to the farm of Colonel Brinkenhoff, 'being notoriously disaffected to the American cause' (*Am. Arch.*, 5th ser., vol. ii, p. 683). Tyler, op. cit., vol. i, pp. 334–49, gives an excellent account of his writings.

It was fitting that one who had written: 'I have no interest but in America. I have not a relation out of it that I know of' (*A View of the Controversy*, p. 23), should have returned to America as the first bishop of the Episcopal Church in the United States.

out He took the strongest part he could from the first in favor of $G^t$ $B^n$. He never conceal'd his Sentiments but chose to make them known & was concerned in many publications to support the Authority of G. B. This made him very obnoxious & in 1775 He was first molested. Swears to the truth of the whole Memorial.

*He appears to have render'd Services to $Gov^t$ by his publications.*

Property.

He had the Living of West Chester which was worth about £120 N. Y. C. to which he had the addition of 40 a $Y^r$ from the Society which he still has. His Living was £50 Glebe £50 from his Parishioners & 20 Surplice fees. He now receives £50 a $Y^r$ from the Society. He receives nothing from the Treasury.

*£67 a $Y^r$.*

He kept about 20 Young Men to instruct &c. By this he clear'd about £150 a $Y^r$ C. He left his Living in 1776 but he lost it in 1775 having never $rec^d$ the last Years Salary.

*Disallowed.*

The Living was for Life as it is here.

Besides this he lost 12 Cattle & Swine & Hay which with the Damages done to the Glebe he estimates at £50.

*Stock &c £50.*

The Living is lost to him but he believes it is not yet filled with another Clergyman.

John Wetherhead Esq—sworn.

Has known $D^r$ Seabury near 20 $Y^{rs}$. He lived near him within 25 Miles. He was a most Zealous Loyalist & a very active one. He wrote a Pamphlet called A. W. Farmer & several other papers. He thinks his writings had a considerable Effect in stopping the progress of the rebellion at least in his own Parish. They were very able Compositions & he thinks as able as any that he saw.

Knew that he had the Living of West Chester & that he had £50 C. from the Province & believes the Society here allowed him £40 or £50. Besides he profess'd Physic but thinks he got nothing by that. He had a School by which he thinks he got £200 a $Y^r$ & as he was much respected & well qualified he thinks the School would have increas'd. The part which he took made him extremely obnoxious & it being known that he was a Writer he was still more obnoxious. He was kept $Pris^r$ for some Months. His Living is finally lost to him.

## Memorial of Normand $M^c$Leod

*Determin'd $y^e$ $28^{th}$ of $Sept^r$ 1784.*

$20^{th}$ of $Sept^r$ 1784.

Normand $M^c$Leod—the Claimant—sworn.

Is a Native of Scotland. Went to America in 1771. When the troubles broke out He was settled in Anson Co. upon a farm of his own. The Americans applied to him to take the Oath but he refused this was in the latter end of 1775. He first took part with the British in 1776. He is the Brother of John $M^c$Leod[1] & his Case is exactly under the same Circumstances. They both were Officers in the Corps of Highlanders rais'd by $Gov^r$ Martin. The $Claim^t$ was a $Lieut^t$ & he was in the Engagement at Moors Bridge. He was taken $Pris^r$ upon that Occasion together with all the Officers of that Corps & was detain'd $Pris^r$ between 4 & 5 $Y^{rs}$. He was exchanged in 1780. He was then made $Lieut^t$

*A Zealous & active Loyalist. Bore Arms.*

[1] See p. 201.

in another Reg[t] rais'd by Gov[r] Martin at New York. He went to Charles Town & after the Evacuation he came to Eng[d] where he arrived in Sept[r] 1783. Since which time he has had an Allowance of £20 a Y[r] from the Treasury from the 10[th] of Oct[r] last. Bounty £20 a Y[r].

He receives no Half Pay but expects it.

### Memorial of George Sprowle [1] Esq.

Determin'd y[e] 28[th] of Sept[r] 1784.

George Sprowle Esq—the Claimant—sworn. 20[th] of Sept[r] 1784.

Having rec[d] a similar Appointment (Surveyor of Lands in New Brunswick with a Salary of £150 a Y[r]) He desires to withdraw the first Article in his Schedule which is £1500 for the Loss of a similar Office in New Hampshire. Waved.

Is a Native of Ireland And at the Commencement of the troubles he was settled in New Hampshire as Deputy to M[r] Holland & in April 1774 He was appointed Surveyor Gen[l] of the Lands in New Hampshire. It was an appointment by the Gov[r] confirmed at home. It was the intention of the Gov[r] to have given a Salary of £150 a Y[r] but the troubles prevented it because it was to have been paid out of the Quit rents. An Active & Zealous Loyalist. Bore Arms & render'd Services as an Engineer.

He went first out to America in 1765. He was in the Army & meant to have retired but the troubles coming on he continued in the service during the whole War.

M[r] Sprowle had an Allowance of £30 a Y[r] to continue only untill he had an appointment in Nova Scotia which he then expected. He has only rec[d] one Quarter's Allowance & apprehends it to be stopped. Bounty £30 a Y[r].

Produces an Act of their Assembly by which in general terms all his property is confiscated. And he bore Arms ag[t] them. Evidence of Confiscation proved.

Stephen Holland Esq—sworn.

Knew M[r] Sprowle in America. He was a Surveyor under Capt[n] Holland. He acted as an Engineer in the War. Has heard that he had a tract of Land in Wolfborough & that he bought it of W[m] Torry. Does not know the Value of it.

Thomas M[c]Donough—sworn.

Knew M[r] Sprowle in America before the troubles. Believes him to be a very loyal Subject. Knows that he had a tract of Land at Wolfborough but can't speak to the Value. Has seen the Deed. Confirms M[r] Sprowle as to the Capture of the Ship.

N.B. Col[l] Dundas speaks very highly from his own knowledge of M[r] Sprowle's Services.

### Memorial of Sam[l] Sewell [2] Esq.

Determin'd the 29[th] of Sept[r] 1784.

Rob[t] Achmuty Esq—sworn. 20[th] of Sept[r] 1784.

Knew M[r] Sewell in America. He was a very Loyal Subject. He acted as such at the Blockade of Boston. He was esteem'd a Man of considerable

[1] *b.* 1741, *d.* 1817. 'He was a most efficient official and estimable man' (Raymond, *Winslow Papers*, p. 250, note). Captain Sproule of the Engineer department is referred to in *Hist. MSS. Comm., Am. MSS. in R. Inst.*, vol. ii, p. 330.

[2] *b.* 1745, *d.* 1811 in London. He was the grandson of the Samuel of Sewall's *Diary*.

A Loyalist. Did not bear Arms.

fortune. He has seen some parts of his property. He has seen the farm at Pine Judith. It was esteem'd to be a very fine & valuable farm. It came to him from his father his two elder Brothers were dead without Issue & he believes this Gent$^{n}$ was sole Heir. Knows an House of his at Boston with a large piece of Ground. Thinks the House with the Ground worth £1500 or £1600. Knows there was a Wooden House adjoining but did not know it was M$^{r}$ Sewells. Should think it might be worth £150. Does not know his property at Brooklyme but says he lived there. Does not know anything about the Confiscation but says he apprehends that the part which lies in Mass. Bay will be confiscated. The Witness was Judge of the Admiralty at Boston. Says that M$^{r}$ Sewell was bred to the Law.

Samuel Sewell Esq—the Claimant—sworn.

Is a Native of America. He lived upon his own property at the Commencement of the troubles. He was in the profession of the Law. He never was actually ill treated but he was often threaten'd & came to Boston in 1775 just before the battle of Lexington. And he came to Eng$^{d}$ in July 1775. All his property has been seiz'd & confiscated. It was seized soon after he quitted his House. He says he was render'd unpopular by having sign'd an Address to Gov$^{r}$ Hutchinson in 1774. He had practised at the Bar about two Years before the rebellion. He made about £50 in the two Years by his profession.

Bounty £100 a Y$^{r}$.

Has an allowance of £100 a Y$^{r}$ from the Treasury which he has rec$^{d}$ from the Y$^{r}$ 1776 & now continues to receive it.

## Further testimony to the Memorial of Sam$^{l}$ Sewell Esq.

Will$^{m}$ Wanton Esq—sworn. 27$^{th}$ of Sept$^{r}$ 1784.

Is related to M$^{r}$ Sewell but never saw him till a fortnight ago. He says he is perfectly satisfied with the Loyalty of M$^{r}$ Sewell. Knows that the property of Point Judith belonged to his father because his family rec$^{d}$ the rents of the Estate. With respect to the Value & Quantity he says he thinks his father has told him that it was 1600 Acres. It was looked upon to be as valuable a farm as any in the Colony. Being asked to the rent he says he does not know but he believes that it let for £180 or £200 S. a Y$^{r}$. Thinks it would have sold for 30 Dollars an Acre. Believes The Tenant paid his rent entirely in the Wool. Knows nothing of any other Estate in Rhode Island. Knows that this property has been confiscated & been advertised for Sale in the American papers in Lots of 100 Acres. He does not know whether any part has been sold or not but he supposes that they have been sold. Says he thinks the Year in which he saw these Advertisements was the Year 1780 or 1781.

Determin'd the 29$^{th}$ of Sept$^{r}$ 1784.

## Memorial of W$^{m}$ Calderhead

Robert Gilmour Esq—sworn. 21$^{st}$ of Sept$^{r}$ 1784.

Knew M$^{r}$ Calderhead in America. He join'd Lord Dunmore & was under Arms with his Lordship in Nov$^{r}$ 1775. Thinks him as staunch a friend to Gov$^{t}$ as could be. He remain'd all the War in America & was finally taken Pris$^{r}$ at York Town. He was upon Duty at the Great Bridge.

Knows part of his property. He was Manager of the Distillery at Norfolk of which the Witness was a Partner & he had one Share & afterw$^{ds}$ upon a Settlement He bought another. There were 20 Shares. He has heard that he had a 3$^{d}$ Share but knows nothing of it. The Stock was £300 S. per share at the Settlem$^{t}$ when he bought his 2$^{d}$ Share. It was more valuable at the time it was destroyed. The Witness saw this Distillery destroy'd. It was destroy'd by the rebels it was about half a Mile from the Town. The House never applied for payment to Gov$^{t}$. Knew the Schooner it was his own. Remembers that he had a Quantity of Salt rather thinks it was his private property. Has seen his furniture & thinks the Charge which he has made was reasonable. Believes the ground on which the Distillery stood has been sold. He was consider'd as a Man of property. Remembers one riding Horse it was a good one. Says that in the Virginia Committee they never would permit any Man to claim for Paper Currency because they might have parted with it.

Will$^{m}$ Calderhead—the Claimant—sworn. 22$^{d}$ of Sept$^{r}$ 1784.

Is a Native of Scotland & went to Virginia in 1765 & in 1775. He was settled at Norfolk in the Distillery business. In the Y$^{r}$ 1775 He join'd Lord Dunmore soon after he came to Norfolk & as soon as Lord Dunmore called upon the people to join him. He was Lieut$^{t}$ of Volunteers & did Duty in the town of Norfolk. Never took an Oath to the Americans. He bore Arms with him in different parts of Virginia. He was a Volunteer at York Town. He was there as a Merch$^{t}$ when the Town was taken. He came to Eng$^{d}$ in Jan$^{y}$ 1783. When he applied to the Treasury about May or June & He rec$^{d}$ an Allowance from the Treasury of £50 a Y$^{r}$ from the 5$^{th}$ of Jan$^{y}$ 1783 And now continues to receive it.

A Loyalist.
Did not bear Arms.[1]

### Memorial of Will$^{m}$ Blaine

Determin'd the 28$^{th}$ of Sept$^{r}$ 1784.

Barbara Blaine—Widow of the Claimant—sworn. 22$^{d}$ of Sept$^{r}$ 1784.

She is the Widow of the Claimant. He died the 26$^{th}$ of July last. He made a Will & left the Widow Sole Executrix. Will produced & read by which he leaves everything to the Witness who is now the Claimant. The Will is dated the 10$^{th}$ of March 1784.

Her Husband a Loyalist.

Her Husband was a Native of Scotland & went to America in 1774. They went to Woodbridge in New Jersey. Her Husband bought a Plantation & lived upon it. He bought it before the battle of Lexington. He lived upon it till Jan$^{y}$ 1776. He left his Plantation because he would not take an Oath &c to the Americans. She was present when they offer'd him the Oath. She staid two Months after him & would have staid longer if she could but the Rebels drove her away & said they would burn the House if she did not go. She was not permitted to bring away anything but afterwards she brought away her own & her Husbands Cloathes. Her Husband bore Arms as a private Soldier at Amboy. He was in no Corps but a Volunteer. He served afterw$^{ds}$ in an Association at New York. He left it a short time before the Evacuation. Her Husband gave in a Memorial to the Treasury but died before it was heard. But upon recollection she says he did live to have his Case heard & died soon afterwards. He had

Claim$^{t}$ & her father entitled to the property of which the Husband & father were Joint tenants.

[1] *Sic* in text.

Former Bounty £36 a Yr. Present Do. £20 a Yr.

an Allowance of £36 a Yr & recd one Quarter before he died. Since he died her Case has been heard but it has not been reported upon. Now £20 a Yr.

James Aitken—sworn.

He was a Shoemaker & lived at New York. Knew Mr Blaine. He was a very loyal Subject. He knew him in Scotland & he has been upon his property in New Jersey. There was a tolerable good House upon it. It was almost all clear'd. He saw some Cattle but does not know how many. It was in Augt & Decr 1775 that he was upon it. He understood it belonged to the family but he does not know whether to the old Man. Was in the House. The furniture was tolerably good for a Country place. Does not know what the Land is worth. Imagines it has been confiscated because he knows the Rebels were violent agt him. Says that Mr Blain served as a Volunteer at New York.

Determin'd ye 2d of Octr 1784.

## Memorial of George Barry

George Barry—the Claimant—sworn. 22d of Septr 1784.

A Loyalist. Did not bear Arms.

Is a Native of Barbadoes & went to Georgia to settle in 1771. When the troubles broke out he was settled on Tyber Island. He was always uniformly on the British side. The Rebels frequently tender'd him an Oath which he refused to take. He was first molested in feby 1776. They frequently came to the Island & took his Stock & did him very material Injury in March 1776 by burning his Houses Lumber &c. The reason of this was he believes that he had supplied the British with provisions &c. He went in 1776 after this to St Augustine & staid two Years. He carried his Negroes with him. He did not lose them then but he sold them there for Bills upon Engd which were protested. He went from thence to ye Bahama Islands & staid there till they were taken by the Spaniards. He soon after came to Engd where he has been ever since.

Bounty £80 in full.

He says he applied to the Treasury in Novr last & recd £80 in lieu of an Allowance.

John Lightenstone—sworn.

Knew Mr Barry very well. He was perfectly well. He lived on the Islands of Tyber. Saw part of his property in flames it was burnt by the Rebels on acct of his principles & they carried him Prisr at the same time to Savannah. Is sure he must have sustain'd great Damage but does not know how. He had a great number of Sheep & Hogs. Heard that many of those were destroy'd by the rebels. He was a Man of considerable property when he came to that province. Has heard that the Rebels shot one of his Negroes.

Determin'd the 23d of Septr 1786.

## Memorial of Willm Ogilvy

Willm Ogilvy—the Claimant—sworn. 23d of Septr 1784.

Is a Native of Scotland. He first settled in America in 1764 And in 1765 He was appointed Secretary to Mr Stuart [1] Superintendt of Indian Affairs. In this Situation he remain'd till 1775. He was then obliged to return to Engd

[1] There is a biographical notice of John Stuart in *New York Col. Docs.*, vol. viii, p. 158.

on Acc^t of ill health He returned to Carolina in 1780 having gone in May 1776 to West Florida. He settled in Pensacola as a Merch^t & remain'd there till July 1780 when he went to Carolina & came to Eng^d in 1781. He was never called upon to take any Oath to the rebels. He never carried Arms but he acted as an Officer of Militia at Charlestown as a 2^d Lieut^t.

A Loyalist. Did not bear Arms.

**Memorial of Alexander M^cLeod**

Determin'd the 23^d of Sept^r 1784.

Alexander M^cLeod—the Claimant—sworn. 23^d of Sept^r 1784.

Is a Native of Scotland & first settled in America in 1772 & settled in Anson County where he was situated upon his own plantation at the Commencem^t of the troubles. He never took any Oath or made any engagement with the Americans. He join'd his Majesty's Forces about 10^th or 11^th of feb^y 1776 in a Corps of Highlanders rais'd by Gov^r Martin's authority. He had a Company of his own raising 44 Men rais'd by himself & Subalterns. He was at no Expence they were Volunteer Loyalists. He went with this Corps to Moors bridge where all the Officers were taken Pris^rs. He was 12 Months close Pris^r & had his parole for Y^r & ½ more. He was in no Service afterwards till he went to the South again. He was at the siege of Charlestown but he was not at that time doing duty. However he afterw^ds was with Lord Cornwallis in sev^l Engagements. He follow'd the Army as a Recruiting Officer. He had a Warrant from Lord Cornwallis to raise a Company but he never rais'd it there was not time. He rais'd only 8 Men. He rec^d 5*s*. a Day from his first Comm^n to the 24^th of Oct^r 1783. He came to Eng^d in Sept^r 1783. He has an Allowance of £20 a Y^r from the Treasury which he has rec^d from Oct^r last & now continues to receive. He does not receive half Pay but expects it.

An Active & Zealous Loyalist.

Bore Arms & suffer'd a very long Imprisonment.

Bounty £20 a Y^r.

**Memorial of Alexander Morrison**

Determin'd the 25^th of Sept^r 1784.

Alexander Morrison—the Claimant—sworn. 24^th of Sept^r 1784.

Is a Native of Scotland. He went in 1772 to America with 300 of his Neighbors & settled in Cumberland Co. North Carolina. He was settled there when the troubles broke out. He first join'd the Royal Cause in Feb^y 1776. The first meeting of the Loyalists was at his House. In that Month he rais'd 37 Men & served under Col^l M^cDonald. He was in the Action at Moors Bridge. About this time he disbursed £135 for the Troops which he has been since repaid. He was soon after taken Pris^r & was confined 7 Months in one Gaol & afterw^ds was on Parole for more than two Y^rs. He came to Eng^d in 1780. He applied to the Treasury & rec^d £100 a Y^r which was afterwards reduced by M^r Wilmot & M^r Coke to £50 a Y^r upon his receiving about that time the £135 above alluded to.

An Active & Zealous Loyalist.

Bore Arms.

Former Bounty £100 a Y^r. Present Bounty £50 a Yr.

Major M^cLeod—sworn.

Knows the Claim^t. Remembers him before he went to America & afterwards. He was under his Command in 1776. He never knew a more loyal Subject. He employ'd him to be his Agent with the Committees from the great Confidence he had in him. He rais'd near 40 Men. No Man ever conducted himself better & he suffer'd for it. He was a Capt$^{n}$ & rec$^{d}$ 5*s*. a Day until he came to Eng$^{d}$. Thinks he will not be entitled to half pay from his own Conduct by putting himself off the seconded List.

Connor Dowd—sworn.

Knew the Claimant at Cross Hill in 1776 & before. He knew the place but he was only once there after he lived there. There was no Cultivation upon it when he first saw it but when he saw it last there was a great deal of Cultivation. He saw it last in 1778. His Wife & family were then upon it but they were very much Distress'd. They had been often plunder'd. Has heard at the time of their being plunder'd of Corn &c. Has seen him ride different Horses. Knows his Son left an Horse & Saddle at Wilmington. It was not sold but believes it was confiscated in 1781.

### Memorial of Roderick M Kinnon

Determin'd y$^{e}$ 25$^{th}$ of Sept$^{r}$ 1784.

24$^{th}$ of Sept$^{r}$ 1784.

Roderick M$^{c}$Kinnon—the Claimant—sworn.

An Active & Zealous Loyalist.

Bore Arms.

Is a Native of Scotland & went out to America. He settled on Drowning Creek Anson Co. & was there when the rebellion broke. He first took up Arms in feb$^{y}$ 1776 under Col$^{l}$ M$^{c}$Donald. He had a Lieut$^{t's}$ Comm$^{n}$. He was in the skirmish at Moor's Creek. He rais'd 15 Men. He was 36 Weeks in close Confinem$^{t}$ & afterw$^{ds}$ more than 4 Y$^{rs}$ on parole. He was exchanged in Oct$^{r}$ 1780 & continued in the service till the Peace. Had half pay from the date of his Comm$^{n}$ till the 24$^{th}$ of Oct$^{r}$ last. He came to London in Feb$^{y}$ last & has an Allowance of £30 a Y$^{r}$ from the Treasury of which he has rec$^{d}$ one Quarter.

Bounty £30 a Y$^{r}$.

He admits that he was not rich when he went out. He says he never was rich. He was always richer in imagination than pocket—this not uncommon. He expects to receive Half Pay.

Colonel James Cotton—sworn.

Remembers the Claim$^{t}$ in Anson County. He was very loyal. He did survey a tract of Land for him but does not know what it contain'd. He paid the Office fees for the patent & Grant but does not recollect whether he brought the Patent & Grant home. This was in 1774. The fees would be about £4 10*s*. pro c. Can't speak of the Value. He has been at his House & has seen the 100 Acres between 10 & 20 Acres clear'd. Thinks that this 100 Acres improved as it was would fetch £60 S. He says the Man was a good Man but rather poor & adds that Gov$^{r}$ Martin gave him ½ Joe[1] & the Witness bought two Cows for him in 1774. He says this Man has done all in his power to serve this Country & that nobody has suffer'd more tho' he cannot express himself very well.

[1] A half-Joe, or Johannes, a Portuguese coin worth 4 dollars; at the time in common currency along the Atlantic seaboard. (R. H. Thornton, *American Glossary*. 1912.)

# ADDITIONAL NOTES

JAMES DE LANCEY (page 145).

He was the son of James de Lancey, Chief Justice and Lieutenant-Governor of New York. He was born in 1732, and educated at Eton and Cambridge. He was captain in the army, but retired in 1760. He represented the city of New York in the Assembly from 1768 to 1775. He was appointed to the Council 1769, but declined the honour without vouchsafing any reasons for his refusal (*New York Col. Docs.*, vol. viii, p. 148). For his political conduct during the first years of the dispute see Becker, op. cit., *passim.* There is a biographical notice in *New York Col. Docs.*, vol. vii, p. 402.

According to Flick (op. cit., p. 212) the total amount of James de Lancey's claim was $284,000, of which $166,000 were allowed. The same work contains an account of sales of loyalists' estates from which it appears that James de Lancey's property was bought by some two hundred and seventy-five purchasers (ibid., pp. 218–50). It is obvious of what importance such a transaction must have been in the movement toward social equality.

In January 1788 James de Lancey petitioned Parliament that the Commissioners of American Loyalists' Claims should be ordered to lay before Parliament the several rules and principles they had formed for their inquiry, and under which they had acted. In a further letter to Pitt he protested against deductions being made from the sums found due to the claimants and against any distinction being made between loyalists who had and who had not borne arms.

EARL OF DUNMORE (page 150).

John Murray, fourth Earl. Is in *Dict. of Nat. Biography*. 'Edmund Randolph,' Dr. C. R. Lingley, writes (*The Transition in Va. from Colony to Commonwealth*, Col. Univ. Studies in Hist., &c., xxxvi, 2, p. 61), 'described Governor Dunmore as a man who preferred crooked ways to the direct ways of winning the human heart, a pedant, a cynic, barbarous in manners and sentiment, lacking in genius, irreligious, coarse and depraved. Similar judgements by other contemporaries might be quoted.'

'Governor Dunmore's acts do indeed indicate that he had many characteristics which made him an unfortunate choice as the chief Executive of a colony in so grave a crisis. He was a tactless man, oversensitive to slights, and seemingly timid.'

Bancroft *more suo* expends on Dunmore the full force of his invective : 'No royal governor showed more rapacity in the use of official power. . . . He had reluctantly left New York, where, during his short career, he had acquired fifty thousand acres of land, and himself acting as Chancellor, was preparing to decide in his own court in his own favour a large and unfounded claim which he had preferred against the Lieutenant-Governor. Upon entering on the government of Virginia, his passion for land and fees outweighing the Proclamation of the King, and reiterated and most positive instructions from the Secretary of State, he advocated the claims of the colony to the west ; and was himself a partner in two immense purchases of lands from the Indians in Southern Illinois. . . . The area of the ancient Domain expanded with his cupidity' (*Hist. of the United States*, new ed. in 7 vols., vol. vi, pp. 95–6). The *Aspinwall Papers*, Mass. Hist. Soc. *Collections*, 4th ser., vols. ix and x, contain Dunmore's correspondence with the home Government in 1774 and 1775.

SAMUEL HAKE (page 155).

In *Rivington's Gazetteer*, November 1773, there is an advertisement of Samuel Hake's stores in Queen Street. He had imported from London, Bristol, and Liverpool a general assortment of European and East Indian goods suitable to the season. A petition of his to Carleton (dated June 8, 1782) states that as a merchant he had an opportunity of knowing the temper and disposition of the people ; that he had sought safety by flight to England ; that by the patronage of the ministry he was induced to return early in 1778 ; that he was captured on his passage and carried to Connecticut. He explains that he succeeded in obtaining passports by interesting Robert H. Livingston and his brother John in a scheme for bringing goods from New York. On his arrival he communicated his plan, and the Royal Commissioners, Governor Johnston and Mr. Eden, who were desirous of transmitting into the country the declaration held forth to the rebels, pressed him to return speedily and take some with him ; and he was supplied with a flag and goods. Unfortunately the flag was seized, the goods forfeited, and himself detained in jail or on parole for three years. During this time he endeavoured to disseminate principles of loyalty, and with others formed the accompanying propositions, together with two addresses signed on behalf of 2,300 loyalists. Though the Board of Associated Loyalists endeavoured to further the scheme, the delays proved fatal, and to avoid capture one of the agents was obliged to return to the garrison (New York) (*Hist. MSS. Com.*, *Am. MSS. in R. Inst.*, vol. ii, pp. 515–16). The enclosures show Hake to have stood high in the opinion of the Loyalists of Dutchess County. In 1785 we find Samuel Hake storekeeper at Fort Howe, when he was charged with embezzling provisions. Lieutenant H. M. Gordon wrote to E. Winslow on November 20, 1785 : 'General Arnold arrived yesterday (at Halifax) and I understand means to visit your province. Mr. Hake and he will be good company' (Raymond, op. cit., p. 321). See note on Dr. Calef's Case, p. 173.

The Case of Joshua Huddy (page 180).

The Board of Refugees Loyalists was established in 1780 at New York under the presidency of William Franklin, Governor of New Jersey. Joshua Huddy was put to death in 1782 by American loyalists in retaliation for murders alleged to have been committed by Whigs. The words were pinned upon his breast : 'Up goes Huddy for Philip White !' A Captain Lippincott was put upon his trial by court martial for the murder. The majority of the Board was of opinion that Lippincott's trial was illegal and unjustifiable (May 1782). In a previous statement they had complained of the murder of many loyal British subjects. They gave particulars of three instances where retaliation had had a good effect, and maintained that, in the circumstances, such retaliation was not surprising. While disapproving of it, they feared that if the loyalists were not better protected they would either leave the country or join the rebels (*Hist. MSS. Comm.*, *Am. MSS. in R. Inst.*, vol. ii, pp. 508, 469).

A full account of the Huddy-Lippincott story is given in Colonel J. J. Graham's *Memoir of Gen. Sam. Graham*, 1862. There is a letter of Washington, April 21, 1782, to Clinton, demanding Captain Lippincott or the officer who commanded at the execution of Captain Huddy ; or, if that officer was of inferior rank to him, so many of the perpetrators as would, according to the tariff of exchange, be an equivalent. Clinton replied (April 22) that as soon as he heard of Huddy's death (which was only four days before Washington's letter) he instantly ordered a strict inquiry into all the circumstances, and undertook to bring the perpetrator of it to an immediate trial. A British statement pointed out that after the capitulation of Lord Cornwallis many loyalists urged Sir H. Clinton to threaten vengeance for injuries inflicted on those who had joined the royal standard, but he declined issuing any proclamation, and was deterred, by the advice of the principal refugees, from establishing the civil government which would have permitted the trial of captive continentals as rebels. While he was engaged in projects of defence, and while commissioners, appointed by him and General Washington, were negotiating for an exchange of prisoners, one Joshua Huddy, a captain in the service of Congress, was taken by a party of loyalists, and . . . delivered to Captain Lippincott for the ostensible purpose of being exchanged ; but Huddy was strung on a tree with a label on his breast directing that his fate was a retaliation for that of one White, an associator. Sir H. Clinton, highly resenting this disgraceful outrage on humanity and insult to himself, as commander, arrested Lippincott and . . . ordered him to be tried for murder. But the Americans were not appeased by this act of justice, and the inhabitants of Monmouth County urgently entreated General Washington to bring a British officer of the same rank as Huddy to a similar end ! Unfortunately some excuse was given to Washington by the fact that Lippincott was acquitted, on the ground that he acted under the order of a Board which he was bound to obey. Washington insisted that an officer of equal rank from among those who had capitulated at York Town should be put to death. Thirteen cast lots ; and the lot fell on Captain Asgill, of the Guards. Whatever had been done in the way of partisan warfare, this young guardsman was as innocent of anything of the kind as Washington himself. Nevertheless Washington seemed of adamant, and his cold compassion strikes a jarring note, when the remedy lay with himself. The conclusion one draws is that it was only the powerful intervention of Vergennes, the French Minister, called into action by Lady Asgill's entreaties and the sympathies of the French King and Queen, that gave Asgill his reprieve. A resolution of Congress, November 5, 1782, finally accorded him his liberty ; but the whole story is not one on which admirers of Washington—which means humanity—can dwell with satisfaction. Granting that the Loyalists were the only offenders, about which much might be said, the execution of an innocent outsider, a prisoner of war under wholly different circumstances, was not thereby to be justified. Wrong begets wrong ; and, had Asgill been executed, his death, no less than that of Huddy, would have called to Heaven for vengeance.

# BOOK IV

## Memorial of Donald Shaw

Determin'd the 25$^{th}$ of Sept$^{r}$ 1784.

Donald Shaw—the Claimant—sworn. 24$^{th}$ of Sept$^{r}$ 1784.

Is a Native of Scotland & went to America in 1772. He first join'd the Loyalists in feb$^{y}$ 1776. He was at Moors Bridge & was taken Prisoner soon afterwards. They let him go home & several others & he staid at home till Oct$^{r}$ 1777. Then he was drafted to serve in the Rebel Army. He never served in the rebel Army or took any Oath to them. He remain'd in that County till March 1781. When Lord Cornwallis came into that Country He went to meet him & was taken Prisoner but he escaped & got to the British at Wilmington in June 1781. He was appointed Lieut$^{t}$ in Oct$^{r}$ 1781. He has rec$^{d}$ the half pay of a Lieut$^{t}$ from Dec$^{r}$ 1781 to Oct$^{r}$ 1783. He then went to Jamaica & came home in September last. He applied to the Treasury & obtain'd an Allowance of £20 a Y$^{r}$ which he has rec$^{d}$ from October last.

A Loyalist.
Bore Arms.
Bounty £20 a Y$^{r}$.

Being asked how he could escape taking the Oath between 1776 & 1781 He says he spent a great deal of his time in the Woods & Swamps & persists in swearing that he never took any Oath to the Rebels & he says there were 50 others in the same Situation with himself.

Connor Dowd—sworn.

Knew the Claim$^{t}$. He was always loyal. He remembers his coming to his House in the Y$^{r}$ 1780 with a Party of Loyalists who took Gov$^{r}$ Burke Prisoner. Knows nothing of his property.

## Memorial of Margaret M$^{c}$Nabb & Isabell M$^{c}$Leod—Sisters

Determin'd the 28$^{th}$ of Sept$^{r}$ 1784.

Margaret M$^{c}$Nabb—one of the Claimants—sworn. 25$^{th}$ of Sept$^{r}$ 1784.
Isabell M$^{c}$Leod—the other Claimant—sworn.

They went from Scotland to America in 1774. They are Natives of Scotland & were single when they went there. They both married in 1775. The Husband of one is Norman M$^{c}$Leod & the other Duncan M$^{c}$Nabb who are both Loyalists & receive Allowances.

Their Brother & Husbands Loyalists.

## Memorial of Lillias M$^{c}$Lean Widow

Determin'd the 27$^{th}$ of Sept$^{r}$ 1784.

Lillias M$^{c}$Lean—the Widow—sworn. 27$^{th}$ of Sept$^{r}$ 1784.

Her Husband was a Native of Scotland & went out to America in 1774. She went out with him. They first settled in Charlestown & kept a Store. She says afterwards they did not stay long at Charlestown but went & settled at Cross Creek. They purchased a farm in 1775. When the troubles broke out her Husband went out with the rest of his Countrymen & went to Moors bridge. She believes he was a Lieut$^{t}$. He was taken Pris$^{r}$ soon after the engagement & very ill used whilst he was Pris$^{r}$. He was kept Pris$^{r}$ 3 or 4 Months. When

Her Husband a Loyalist & bore Arms.

Lord Cornwallis came he join'd him. He went to Charlestown & afterwards to Jamaica where he died.

Bounty £14 a Yr.

She has made Application to the Treasury & receives an Allowance of £14 per Ann. from the 5th of April 1784.

Duncan McKa [1]—sworn.

Lived at Cross Creek. Knew the Claimant's Husband. His name was Donald McLean [2] & he knew her. He join'd the Loyalists at the first rising & went to Moors Creek. He does not know whether he had any Commission. He has no reason to believe that he was an Officer. He knows he was taken prisr. He believes he was a Loyalist.

Determin'd the 5th of Octr 1784.

## Memorial of Major Alexander McLeod [3]

29th of Septr 1784.

Alexander McLeod—the Claimant—sworn.

A Loyalist.

Bore Arms & render'd Services.

Is a Native of Scotland & went to settle in America in 1774. He went out with an Intention to settle in North Carolina. He found the Country at that time in great Disorder & he wish'd to come back. The Congress were then sitting at Philadelphia. He went into the Country & used his influence with his Countrymen to keep quiet for the present. After this he endeavor'd to keep them ready to be embodied at any time. They embodied in feby 1776 by orders from Govr Martin. The number of the battalion consisted of 450 Men. He had a Commn under Genl McDonald.[4] After the defeat at Moors Bridge He was obliged to conceal himself for six weeks in woods & swamps until he made his Escape. Since that time he was employ'd in America till the Yr 1778 When he came to Engd upon his private business. He has served since the Yr 1780 in the Army at New York. He served with Lord Cornwallis after that time but in no particular Situation. He only followed the Army. He staid with him till 1781. He left New York in Augt 1781 with the General's Dispatches. He never took part with the Americans. He recd Pay when he acted as Major. He recd full pay for a part of the time & half pay for the remainder of the time. From Jany 1776 to the end of that Yr he recd full pay & afterwards half pay untill Decr 1777. When he came home He recd neither pay nor Allowance till the 5th of July 1779 when he recd £200 a Yr which he continued to receive till the 5th of Octr 1782 when it was reduced to £100 a Yr which he now receives. Expects to receive the half pay of Major.

Former Bounty £200 a Yr. Present Do £100 a Yr.

Alexander Morrison—sworn.

Knew Major McLeod in America. He was a very active Loyalist & rather violent. He was there but a short time before the troubles. He only rented a place. He paid £15 C. for it. He knows he had 20 Milch Cows at least. They cost him 2 Gãs apiece. He had other Cattle but he does not know how

[1] *Sic.* ? McKay.

[2] Not to be confused with Donald McLean, apparently of New York, of whom there is mention in the *Hist. MSS. Comm., Am. MSS. in R. Inst., passim.*

[3] See Additional Notes, p. 278.

[4] Brigadier-General Macdonald, who was taken prisoner, was unwell that day and not in the battle (*N. Carolina Records*, vol. x, p. 482).

many. He had 2 Horses & working Horses besides. There was an House upon it but it was a Log House. Thinks his farming Utensils would not at the utmost be worth more than £20. He says the furniture was fit for a larger House & part of it unpacked. He saw plate in his House. Knows he had indented Serv$^{ts}$ he had six or seven. He thinks he was worth £1000 in the Isle of Sky.

Donald Shaw—sworn.

Knew Major M$^{c}$Leod in America. He was a very active Loyalist. The Witness was in the same Corps with him. He had a good deal of influence in raising them. He knew several Horses that he had upon his farm in 1774 1775 & 1776. He mentions five or six corrects himself to four or five. Says they were very good Horses. He lived within three or four Miles of him. He had between 15 & 20 grown Cattle besides their followers. His House was very well furnished but the whole of his furniture was not displayed. He had some in Chests. He saw no Library put up but he saw books scatter'd in the House. There were about 20 Acres clear'd on his farm. Knows he had several ploughs & a Cart. Does not know the Value but says he thinks it might amount to £20 S. Knows nothing more of Major M$^{c}$Leod's property.

### Memorial of Duncan M$^{c}$Nabb

*Determin'd the 11$^{th}$ of Oct$^{r}$ 1784.*

Duncan M$^{c}$Nabb—the Claimant—sworn. 30$^{th}$ of Sept$^{r}$ 1784.

*An Active & Zealous Loyalist. Bore Arms.*

Is a Native of Scotland & went to America in the Y$^{r}$ 1771 to North Carolina & in 1775 he was settled in Anson Co. on a plantation of his own. In feb$^{y}$ 1776 He join'd his Countrymen under Col$^{l}$ M$^{c}$Donald & went as Volunteer & was in the engagement at Moors Bridge. After that he escaped And he went from home again in April 1778 & join'd the troops in Philadelphia. He went with the Army again as a Volunteer. He has rec$^{d}$ Lieut$^{t's}$ half pay since he came here in consequence of a Warrant which he had from Gov$^{r}$ Martin & he now receives 2*s.* 4*d.* a Day for half pay. From 1778 he served till the end of the War. He came over to Eng$^{d}$ the 10$^{th}$ of feb$^{y}$ last. He applied to the Treasury in March & rec$^{d}$ £25 in full. He never took any Oath to the Rebels.

*Bounty £25 in full.*

### Memorial of Alexander M$^{c}$Kay [1]

*Determin'd the 11$^{th}$ of Oct$^{r}$ 1784.*

Alexander M$^{c}$Kay—the Claimant—sworn. 30$^{th}$ of Sept$^{r}$ 1784.

*A Zealous & active Loyalist. Bore Arms.*

Is a Native of Scotland & went to America in the Y$^{r}$ 1752 And he remain'd there till the troubles. He was then living on his own plantation. He took part with Great Britain from the first & when the Loyalists rose in 1776 He had a Commiss$^{n}$ of Capt$^{n}$ from Gov$^{r}$ Martin & was at the engagement of Moors Bridge & taken Prisoner afterwards. He was kept Pris$^{r}$ till Aug$^{t}$ 1778 during which time he had half pay 5*s.* a Day. After that he was taken Pris$^{r}$ in 1779 & exchanged the same Y$^{r}$. In the Y$^{r}$ 1780 He went to the siege of Charlestown

[1] In ibid., p. 595, is a Report of the Committee of Safety that 'Alexander M$^{c}$Kay, regardless of the said obligations, did actually take up arms and lead forth to war as Colonel of a Regiment a division for the avowed purpose of assisting the enemies of America; and that he is a freeholder and lived in Cumberland County'.

He is not to be confused with Alex. A. McKay, who acted as assistant surgeon at New York, who also had property in North Carolina (*Hist. MSS. Comm., Am. MSS. in R. Inst.*, vol. iv, pp. 140, 468).

as a Volunteer & he served till the Evacuation. He then went to Jamaica & from thence he came to Eng[d] on the 12[th] of Sept[r] 1783. He applied soon after to the Treasury & rec[d] an Allowance of £25 a Y[r] from the 10[th] of Oct[r] & now continues to receive it. He expects to receive half pay as his Name is returned to the War Office.

Bounty £25 a Y[r].

### Further testimony to the Memorial of Will[m] Haywood

1[st] of Oct[r] 1784.

Alexander Mill—sworn.

Late Master of a Vessel at Charlestown. Knew M[r] Haywood in 1772 first. He was then a Blockmaker in Charlestown. He was a Master Blockmaker & kept a Shop. Remembers him in Beaufort Gaol in 1776. He was put in for his Loyalty. The Witness was then in the fort. Does not know whether he had any plantation in 1772. Has heard him say since that he had a plantation but does not know it. There is no person here from that part of the Country in which he says his plantation [was]. It was the Year 1776 when he was taken Prisoner. He was very ill treated by the Americans when in prison. He says the Man is much alter'd since he came to England & he thinks that he is not in his right mind. Does not know whether the House in which he lived in Charlestown in 1772 was his own or not. He believes him to be a very loyal Man. Says that the more loyal people were they were more severely treated when in prison.

### Memorial of Connor Dowd

Determin'd the 11[th] of Oct[r] 1784.

1[st] of Oct[r] 1784.

Connor Dowd—the Claimant—sworn.

Took the Oath to the Rebels in 1777 But since that period a Loyalist.

No proof whatever of his property being confiscated.

Is a Native of Ireland & went to America in 1754. He worked at first as a Labourer. In the beginning of the troubles he was settled on a farm of his own on Deep River. He first exerted himself in 1776 & served the Troops rais'd by Gov[r] Martin with several Articles for which he has never been paid but £50. The Amount of it was £540 so that there is £494 due. That £50 was paid by order of Gen[l] Leslie. He was called upon by the Americans & made Pris[r] & put several times into confinement & at last he took the Oath to them. He took it in Aug[t] 1777. He staid at home till 1780 & 1781 when he was obliged to remain in the Swamps & Woods for fear the Americans should compel him to take Arms. His Son was killed in the service. He had not taken the Oaths to the rebels. He never carried Arms. He never had any turn for Arms. He never did any service but serving the Army with provisions. He join'd the British at Wilmington. He continued with the British from Sept[r] 1781 to July 1782. When he took the Oath to the Americans He consider'd it as an Oath by compulsion & he meant to break it.

2[d] of Oct[r] 1784.

Colonel John Hamilton [1]—sworn.

Knew M[r] Dowd in America. Says he was very active in supporting the

[1] John Hamilton was Lieutenant-Colonel of the North Carolina Volunteers raised in 1779. His name is among those embarking in 1783 for St. John's River in the Bay of Fundy, having served since his appointment in the southern colonies (*Hist. MSS. Comm., Am. MSS. in R. Inst.*, vol. iv, p. 480). Ibid., p. 75, is a letter from him to Brigadier-General McArthur (May 10, 1783), stating that the officers and soldiers of the North Carolina regiment under his command were resolved to embark for some British settlement, 'however soon they may be ordered either to Britain, Halifax, or the West Indies'.

Sabine (op. cit., vol. i, p. 511) quotes the remark of Stedman, that the British nation owed more, perhaps,

Loyalists in 1776. He supplied them with Provisions & Ammunition. Supposes he expected to be paid. It was at his own House. He says he stated the Acc[t] to him at Charlestown in 1782 & he submitted it to Gen[l] Leslie who paid him £50 in part. Being asked as to the nature of the Proclamations [1] issued at different times he says he thinks it was the Intention of all the Commanders who issued those Proc[ns] to consider Men who had been obliged to take the Oaths to the Rebels upon the footing of Loyalists. Knows the Claim[t] had a valuable Plantation on Deep River. Has not seen it so as to put any Value upon it. He was reputed to be a Man of considerable property & lived extremely well.

Alexander Morrison—sworn.

Knew M[r] Dowd in America. He took the part of Gov[t] at the Commencement of the troubles. He says he had no doubt of his Loyalty. He mentions his sending a Letter to Gov[r] Martin about some Gunpowder which if discover'd would have hanged him. He says that he rais'd about 30 Horse & his Son was killed about that time. He knows some of his property. He has been at his House & he has seen another of his plantations. He did not know that he had ever taken any Oath to the Americans. He thinks it was wrong to take that Oath but believes his Actions were loyal. Thinks that he could not get his property again. Knew his plantation on Deep river there was a great deal of Clearing upon it. But he can't value it. Being told the Circumstances of it He says he thinks it is worth 10*s*. an Acre without the Buildings. Says that 500 Acres would be worth 15*s*. an Acre & the rest 10*s*. He includes the Dwelling House when he says this but not the Mills Still House &c. Thinks Dowd's Mill as good as Cochrans & says he has heard that Connor's Mill cost £1000. Has pass'd by another of his plantations but does not know the name of it there was a great deal of clearing upon it. Knows nothing of his personal property but that he had a large Store & knows that he had a Tan Yard. He saw Negroes about the House. Has been several nights at the House. He had good furniture but he can't value it. Says he had plenty of everything.

Donald Shaw—sworn.

Knew M[r] Dowd in America but not much before the troubles. Always consider'd him to be a Loyalist & thinks so from the Circumstance of his serving Col[l] M[c]Donald's Corps with provisions &c. Never heard of his having taken the Oath. Has been upon his own place & four or five other places which he said were his. It was a very valuable plantation. Knows the M[c]Lendon plantation & thinks it must be worth at least £30. Has been upon Gov[rs] Creek. He

to Colonel Hamilton, of the North Carolina regiment, than to any other individual loyalist in the British service. At the same time he secured the cordial regard of the best men in the ranks of the enemy. After the peace he became British Consul for the State of Virginia, and lived at Norfolk. He died in England in 1817.

[1] A proclamation of Clinton, dated June 30, 1780, declared that all inhabitants of South Carolina, who were prisoners on parole, and were not in the military line, should, from and after the 20th of that month, be freed and exempted from all such paroles, and be restored to all their civic rights and duties. If they afterwards were guilty of acts of disloyalty, they should be treated as rebels (see McCrady, *S. Car. in the Rev., 1780–3*, pp. 553–4). Cornwallis expressed to General Patteson his strong disapproval of this proclamation, under which some of the most violent rebels were declared faithful subjects and promised protection (*Correspondence*, vol. i, p. 46).

bought 67 Bushels of Corn from him at this plantation in the Y^r^ 1774. Says there was a great deal of clearing on this plantation & Buildings. Thinks it must be worth 10s. an Acre. Has been on Haw Branch Plantation must be worth 12*s.* or 15*s.* Knows the Mills on his Plantation on Deep river but can't value them. Has heard & believes all these plantations to be his. Says he was a rich Man.

Lilias M^c^Lean—sworn.

Remembers him (M^r^ Dowd) in Gaol with her Husband. Understood that he was there on Acc^t^ of his Loyalty. He was severely used by the rebels. She knows he was a Man of great substance.

Determin'd the 26^th^ of Oct^r^ 1784.

### Memorial of Doct^r^ Sylvester Gardiner [1]

4^th^ of Oct^r^ 1784.

Doct^r^ Sylvester Gardiner—the Claimant—sworn.

A Loyalist.
Did not bear Arms.

A Native of Massachusets Bay. At the Commencement of the Troubles he was settled as a Physician at Boston & gave his Assistance to the King's Army after the battle of Bunkers Hill without fee or reward. Went with the Army to Halifax & from thence to New York where he remain'd till Oct^r^ 1778 when he embarked for Eng^d^ & on his arrival applied for Subsistence to Lord George Germaine at whose recommendation he had an Allowance of £150 per Ann. from the Treasury.

Bounty £150 a Y^r^.

Benj^n^ Hallowell Esq—sworn.

Knew the Claimant & believes that no Man could be more loyal. That he had a very considerable property speaks to the Mansion House & says that he believes it was worth £1500 S. It was well furnished & he had a good Library. Knows that he had other Houses but can't speak to the Value of them. Says that the Claimant was certainly under a Necessity of quitting Boston on acc^t^ of his Attachment to Great Britain.

Doctor Mich^l^ Morris—sworn.

Knew the Claimant at Boston. Believes that he was very loyal & looked upon by every person there as a Man of exceeding good Character. That he was the first in Boston in his Line of business & is sure that he had more than a thousand pounds Sterling worth of Medicines & Drugs. The Witness bought as much of him as cost from 3 to £400 S. just before the Troops left Boston.

Determin'd the 9^th^ of July 1785.

### Memorial of Angus Campbell [2]

5^th^ of Oct^r^ 1784.

Angus Campbell—the Claimant—sworn.

A Native of Scotland. Went to Cape Fear in Oct^r^ 1774 & arrived there

[1] *b.* 1707, *d.* 1793 (Sabine, op. cit., vol. i, pp. 459–62). In G. E. Ellis, *Memoir of Sir Benjamin Thompson, Count Rumford*, Boston, n.d., it is stated that D. S. Gardiner had acquired immense wealth and was known as a noble, public spirited, and popular man. As one of the partners of the so-called 'Plymouth Purchase' on the Kennebec River he owned one-twelfth of it, and had been assiduous in improving and settling it.

[2] A correspondent wrote to Governor Caswell (February 22, 1777): 'There is one Angus Campbell in Cumberland County, who was with the Tory army. He gave the Congress last spring security for his good behaviour and was ordered to reside in some other county; but the Council of Safety permitted

in Jan$^{y}$ 1775. In feb$^{y}$ 1776 He raised a Company of Men at Cross Creek about 60 Men they were put under his Command & he had a Warrant as a Capt$^{n}$ in the Corps of Provincials from Gov$^{r}$ Martin's Commissioners. Was taken Prisoner at the defeat of Moors Creek Bridge & detain'd from feb$^{y}$ 1776 to Aug$^{t}$ 1778.

A Loyalist.

Bore Arms.

In 1780 He was by a Warrant appointed Capt$^{n}$ of an Independ$^{t}$ Company of Highlanders. The warrant from Lord Cornwallis He rais'd only 10 Men. Was taken Pris$^{r}$ a second time in 1780 in South Carolina. Continued with the Kings Troops till the Evacuation of Charlestown. Arrived in England the 10$^{th}$ of Aug$^{t}$ last from Jamaica to which Island he went from Charlestown.

He rec$^{d}$ from the Y$^{r}$ 1781 till Aug$^{t}$ 1783 the half pay of Captain. He has no Allowance from the Treasury but has presented a Memorial lately to Whitehall.

Bounty £20 a Y$^{r}$.

He had also Half Pay as Captain from the time he was taken Prisoner till Aug$^{t}$ 1778.

## Memorial of James Torry

Determin'd the 5$^{th}$ of Oct$^{r}$ 1784.

James Torry—the Claimant—sworn. 5$^{th}$ of Oct$^{r}$ 1784.

Born in Scotland. Went to North Carolina in 1770. Was bred to the trade of a Cooper followed his trade for near a Year near Cross Creek. Settled afterwards at Beaver's Creek on a Plantation which he purchased. Took up Arms in 1776 with a great many other Loyalists under Gov$^{r}$ Martin. The Americans tender'd the Oaths to him & he refused to take them. Continued with the British Troops during the War. Went to East Florida after the Evacuation of Charlestown. Came to Eng$^{d}$ in May last. Followed his Trade whilst he was with the Army & was paid by the Kings Commissary when employ'd by him.

A Loyalist.

Bore Arms.

Has an Allowance of 15 a Y$^{r}$ from the Treasury which he has rec$^{d}$ from the 5$^{th}$ of July 1784.

Bounty £15 a Y$^{r}$.

Duncan M$^{c}$Nab—sworn.

Knew the Claimant in North Carolina at Cross Creek in 1771. Says that he took up Arms in 1776. Believes him to be a firm Loyalist. Knows the Plantation on Beaver Creek heard of there being 400 Acres—10 or 12 cleared. And that he had a Grant. There was an House. He was in it after the Claimant left his family there in 1776. To the best of his Judgment the 400 Acres were worth £50 S.

Knows the 100 Acres. Says that the Claimant bought them from Neil Clark in 1775 or 1776. Thinks that he paid £20 C. in all for the 100 Acres. The Tract was worth £40 Curr. The Man who sold it was very much in Debt & obliged to quit that part of the Country.

Saw some Cattle on the plantation at Beaver's Creek.

He heard in East Florida from some of the Loyalists that the Claimant's family had been obliged to quit their residence on Beaver's Creek.

The Claimant's Wife died in North Carolina.

him to go back to Cumberland County. I have been credibly informed that he has not been called upon to go with the other prisoners. . . . I think it my duty to mention these circumstances, as Mr. Campbell has great influence among his countrymen ; and if there is any omission, the blame may possibly be laid at your Excellency's door ' (*N. Car. Records*, vol. xi, p. 396).

## Memorial of Major James Munro [1]

Determin'd $y^e$ $23^d$ of $Oct^r$ 1784.

A Loyalist.

Bore Arms.

$6^{th}$ of $Oct^r$ 1784.

Major James Munro—the Claimant—sworn.

A Native of Scotland. Went to America in 1763 & settled in Hilsborough North Carolina in 1766 as a Merchant & Planter. In 1775 he $rec^d$ a Message from $Gov^r$ Martin informing him that some British Troops were expected in the fall of the Year & that he should use his Endeavours to engage as many of his friends in that part of the Country as he was able in order to cooperate with the Troops in suppressing the Rebellion at that time beginning to spread throughout the Southern Provinces. Towards the latter end of the same year $Gov^r$ Martin dispatched a Messenger with a general Commission directed to the Claimant & other persons in different parts of the province investing them with Authority to appoint Officers & grant Commissions to all Loyal Subjects. The Dispatch fell into the hands of a Rebel Committee soon after the $Gov^r$ had sent it by which Discovery the Claimant & several others mention'd in the Dispatch were privately seized upon & confined Prisoners till the Defeat of the Highlanders at Moors Bridge. They remain'd confined upwards of 3 Weeks. Says that he was brought to trial & dismissed in $Feb^y$ 1776. He remain'd quiet at home till $Aug^t$ 1777 when he was called upon to take the Oaths to the States & renounce all Allegiance to the King of Great Britain which he refused to comply with & was in Consequence thereof obliged to quit the Country in 60 Days. He waited at Newbern & Wilmington near four Months without any Opportunity offering for his getting to New York at last he $rec^d$ Letters from his friends at that place advising him to remain in Carolina if he could possibly do so for the purpose of keeping up the Spirits of the Loyalists in Consequence of which he applied to the Assembly then sitting at Newbern for leave to return home. It was granted after having been repeatedly press'd to take the Oaths which he as constantly refused. He returned home on giving his Parole that he would remain upon his own Estate & not interfere in the business that was going on unless the British Troops should come to the Province. This indulgence he attributed to the friendship of $Col^l$ Rochester $Col^l$ Hogan [2] & $M^r$ Macbeen.[3] The latter was Sheriff & the two former had been his Clerks. This indulgence granted to him was not publickly known people imagined he had been obliged to take the Oaths. He had a Certificate from the Sheriff that he had taken the Oath altho' in fact he had not. When he was order'd to quit the Country in $Aug^t$ 1777 he disposed of some part of his property the remainder made over to some of his friends but took possession again of it on his return.

On Lord Cornwallis's arrival with the Army at Hilsborough in $feb^y$ 1781 his Lordship spoke to him & observed that as he understood there were a great many Loyalists in that part of the Country he desired he would invite his friends to repair to the Standard agreeable to a Proclamation deliver'd by his Lordship to him. Says that he immediately put himself under the direction of Lord

[1] He is mentioned by Sabine, op. cit., vol. ii, 'Fragments,' p. 560. James Munro was evidently a man of considerable local influence.

[2] General James Hogan commanded the North Carolina contingent of the garrison which surrendered at the capitulation of Charlestown, May 11, 1780.

[3] ? Maclean.

Cornwallis & used his utmost efforts to forward the King's Service. Produces a Copy of the Proclamation. Remain'd with Lord Cornwallis's Army until the Surrender of the Army at York Town.

He was appointed by Warrant from Lord Cornwallis & Gov^r^ Martin Major to the North Carolina Highlanders in April 1781. He had during Lord Cornwallis's Stay at Hilsborough given in proposals for raising a Reg^t^ of his own but his Lordship quitting Hilsborough so suddenly he was prevented from so doing. He rec^d^ only half pay as Major from April 1781 to Dec^r^ 1782 with Bat [1] & Forage as Major. He rec^d^ only half pay from not having rais'd his Numbers of Men when he quitted Wilmington but the Number was afterwards made up to 61 altogether. He is in expectation of being established upon the Half pay List as Major.

Colonel John Hamilton—sworn. 7^th^ of Oct^r^ 1784.

Has known the Claimant many Years And says that he is able to speak to his Loyalty. Confirms the Acc^t^ given by Major Munro of his being seized & confined of his going to Newbern & Wilmington. And that he the Witness was one of the Persons at New York who advised him to remain in North Carolina if he could possibly do so in order to keep up the Spirits of the Loyalists. Witness was made Prisoner at the same time with Major Munro but got away to New York 2 or 3 Months before the Claimant went to Newbern. Witness heard of what Major Munro has stated concerning the Indulgence he experienced from the American Colonels Rochester & Hogan & M^r^ Maclean but never heard of any Certificate being given to him. He is confident that Major Munro never took an Oath to the Americans & that no Man could be more firmly attached to Great Britain. Thinks it probable he might be permitted to remain from the influence he had in his Neighborhood which might induce them to permit him to remain quiet & moreover the Witness was himself informed by M^r^ Jones who brought the Bill into the Assembly for obliging all persons to take the Oath that he was so much hurt at seeing his best friends driven out of the Country by the Operation of the Act that he repented that he had brought it in. Thinks it likely the Claimant might obtain a Certificate of his taking the Oath without taking it. The same thing was offer'd to himself.

Is asked whether it was not in his Opinion extraordinary that the Claimant should purchase Lands in 1778 & 1779. Says it was his own intention if he could not otherwise have got rid of the Paper Currency which he was obliged to receive for various Articles to have invested it in Lands as the safest method of disposing of it. Does not pretend to say what was the Claim^ts^ Motive for purchasing. The Loyalists passed the old Proclamation Money current among them the same as before the troubles.

Ely Branson—sworn.

Knew the Claimant long before the troubles. Was acquainted with him in 1776 & says that he was very loyal. Heard of the Claimant obtaining permission to remain in Carolina but does not know how he obtain'd it. Says that he was highly esteem'd by every person in that part of the Country does not believe that he ever took an Oath to the Americans & that it consists with his

[1] ? Battels.

knowledge that many people obtain'd Certificates from the Justices similar to that which Major Munro stated to have got.

Captⁿ Alexander McKay—sworn.

Knew the Claimant in 1775 or 1776. Always consider'd him as a Loyalist. Heard of his being taken up and tried by the Americans. In the Yr 1777 He was at the Claimant's House at Hilsborough was there an whole night had a great deal of Conversation with the Claimant & found him well attached to Great Britain. Never saw him again till 1781. Don't know how he managed to remain in the Country so long is satisfied that he never took an Oath to the Americans but recollects his hearing a Mr Wood say that Major Munro had managed Matters so as to be able to remain in the Province without taking the Oaths. Mr Wood was at that time attached to the American Interest. Is not able to speak to any part of the Claimant's property.

Captn Alexander McLeod—sworn.

Has known the Claimant since 1776. He was a very zealous Loyalist & one of the Commissioners under Governor Martin for assembling the Loyalists. Witness when a Prisoner was with many others at the Claimant's House who supplied them with Provisions & such as wanted Money he gave it to. Witness heard of the Claimant being at that time on his Parole. Says that his Interest was so great in the Country that he obtain'd the same for him & the other Loyalists that were with him. And tho' this appear'd extraordinary He was nevertheless well satisfied of Major Munro being a true Loyalist. Says again that the Claimant's Interest in the Country was very great. Knows nothing concerning the property. All the Loyalists consider'd Major Munro as very well attached to Great Britain.

Captn Duncan Fletcher—sworn.

Belonged to the Loyal American Regiment. His first knowledge of Major Munro was in November 1780 at a Plantation near Hilsborough which he understood was the property of the Claimant. Says that the Loyalists in that part of the Country looked upon Major Munro as their Head. The Witness was at Hilsborough two Months heard all the Loyalists say that the Claimant was sincerely attached to Great Britain.

Can only account for the Circumstance of Major Munro being permitted to remain in the Country but by the great Interest he had in the Country.

Bounty £100 a Yr. N.B. No allowance was given to Major Munro at the time his Case was heard But in our last Report an Allowance of £100 per Ann. is recommended to him.

### Memorial of the Revd Doctr Caner [1]

The Revd Doctr Caner—the Claimant—sworn. 8th of Octr 1784.

Is a Native of England. Went to America when he was a Child to Boston. He was settled at Boston in the Year 1775 & had a Living there called the Kings Chapel. He quitted Boston with Sir Willm Howe. He quitted it because he could not remain. He came to Halifax with the fleet & in about a Month

[1] See Additional Notes, p. 278.

afterwards to London. He recommended from the Pulpit obedience to Gov$^{t}$. Believes he is about 80 Years of Age.

He had an Allowance of £100 a Y$^{r}$ from the Treasury when he first came over & he now continues to receive it. Bounty £100 a Y$^{r}$.

Property.

House in Boston. He built it. He has no Deed. He bought the Ground & thinks he gave £50 for it. And his House cost him about £1100 S. He made the purchase & built the House he thinks in 1732. (Says his Memory is very bad from an Accident which happen'd to him about 2 Y$^{rs}$ ago & deprived him of his Memory.) Says it was as good in 1775 as when he built it.

Says he left Liquors in his House to a considerable Amount But can't say exactly what. He charges for it in his Schedule £53 16*s*. 0*d*. He charges £12 17*s*. for Kitchen furniture. He had a Chaise & Harness which he values at £25. He was possess'd of a Library. He gives a valuation of this & many other Articles in his Schedule which makes the personal property £805. He says he put down the Articles himself & that he did it when he was in a better state of Mind than he now is.

His Living was worth about £200 a Y$^{r}$. He was chosen by the People for their Rector. Before he quitted Boston they had appointed an Assistant to him. In the Y$^{r}$ 1775 the value of the Living to him was £200 a Y$^{r}$. He says he knows his Name is in the Act of Attainder & that his House has been sold to a Gent$^{n}$ of the profession of the Law.

Doct$^{r}$ Gardiner—sworn.

Knew D$^{r}$ Caner very well in Boston. He was a very steady Loyalist. He exerted himself very much both in public & private & frequently in the pulpit. He knew his House at Boston it was commonly reported to be his property. Knows he bought the Land. Says he built the House about 22 Y$^{rs}$ ago. It was a Wooden House all but the back part of it. It was a large House. Says a Wooden House is half worn out in 20 Y$^{rs}$ & therefore thinks if it was to be sold it would not fetch more than £600 S. In this He includes the Lot of Ground & says it would have been the full Value. Says the Situation was bad as it looked to the Burying Ground. The House was decently furnished. Knew the picture it belonged to the Church but being too large it was put up in D$^{r}$ Caner's House. He says he had a tolerable Library thinks it was worth £50. The Witness says he left many Pipes of Wine in his own Cellar but he made no Charge of them & thinks it wrong to do so. He had a Living in Boston the profit of which was £150 S. a Y$^{r}$. And he was obliged to pay out of that £37 S. a Year to a Curate as he was infirm & could not do the whole of his Duty.

Charles Paxton Esq—sworn.

Has known D$^{r}$ Caner for 40 Years. He conducted himself with great Loyalty. He says he built an House in the Churchyard & it was understood that it cost him £1200. The Parishioners he says often talked of giving him something towards it but believes he has never rec$^{d}$ a farthing. He was Rector of the Kings Chapel the Living worth about £120 a Y$^{r}$. Says that the Parish offer'd to give him an addition of £40 a Y$^{r}$ but he generously refused it until they were out of Debt. Recollects the Picture it was presented to the Doct$^{r}$ by M$^{r}$ Trecothick & was to have been presented by him to the Church but believes they were to have paid him the Value of it & believes that M$^{r}$ Trecothick meant that the Parish should pay him for it. Thinks the House was worth £1000. Thinks that D$^{r}$ Caner did not mean to give this House to go with the Living.

Determin'd y$^{e}$ 26$^{th}$ of Oct$^{r}$ 1784.

## Memorial of Peter Frye [1] Esq.

8$^{th}$ of Oct$^{r}$ 1784.

Peter Frye Esq—the Claimant—sworn.

A Zealous & meritorious Loyalist & render'd services in the Execution of his Duty as a Magistrate. Did not bear Arms.

Is a Native of Andover in New Eng$^{d}$. In 1774 he was settled at Salem. He has been an Officer under the Crown from his Youth. When the troubles broke out He took as active a part as it was in his power to do. In 1774 He issued a Warrant to take up some Committee Men the Consequence of which was that they privately threaten'd that they would ruin him but at that time he was protected by the Military. When the Military were withdrawn they were more open in their threats. He issued his Warrants as a Justice of the peace. When he was threaten'd He armed his Horse & was determin'd to resist. In the Y$^{r}$ 1774 in the Month of Oct$^{r}$ one Evening he was alarmed in the Night & discover'd his House to be in flames. He got up & escaped with great difficulty but not without being much hurt. His House was compleatly burnt & he says it must have been done by design As Combustibles were put into the Store. He never found out the person who did it nor does he suspect any person in particular. He soon after removed to Ipswich in hopes of being quiet there but he found it impossible & was obliged to confine himself a good deal in his own House. He remain'd at Ipswich for two Years. The Clergyman of the Parish recommended it to the Parishioners to assassinate M$^{r}$ Frye & all the Tories. Soon after this he made his Escape in Aug$^{t}$ 1777 & got on board a Ship. He came to Eng$^{d}$ in 1779. Before he got to this Country he rec$^{d}$ a Letter from Gen$^{l}$ Gage telling him that he had obtain'd for him an Allowance of £150 a Y$^{r}$ Which he has rec$^{d}$ from Jan$^{y}$ 1778 & he now continues to receive it.

Bounty £150 a Y$^{r}$.

He says he is banished but his property is not confiscated. And he says that notwithstanding his property is not confiscated by any known Law yet by Taxes & expences it is very much reduced. His Wife & family are still at Salem & she is in possession of the property which remains.

Doct$^{r}$ Gardiner—sworn.

Knew M$^{r}$ Frye in America for about 15 Y$^{rs}$. He was remarkably loyal. And mentions a Vote which he gave ag$^{t}$ the establishment of a Congress which he says cost him the Loss of all his Offices. Remembers the burning of his House. Has no doubt but it was done by design. It was an old House but he thinks it was worth £500 S. The situation was extremely good. Says that he had all the Offices which he has mention'd. Says the Office of the Register of Probate was given him by Gov$^{r}$ Hutchinson to make him amends for some of those Offices which the people had taken from him. Says it was worth £150 C. a Y$^{r}$. No one was a more active Loyalist or has suffer'd more. He says the reason of their permitting his Wife to remain is owing to her having no principles.

[1] *b.* 1723, *d.* 1820. He signed the Address to Governor Gage on his arrival at Salem, June 11, 1774.

Doct^r Caleff—sworn.

Knew M^r Frye both at Salem & at Ipswich. He was a very loyal Man. His House was burnt & he believes it was owing to the loyal part he took & he mentions the Circumstance of his granting the Warrant. Thinks he was appointed Register in 1771 or 1772 & that it was £150 a Y^r S. Justice of the Inferior C^t worth about £50 a Y^r. Knew his House it was a large House & he had a good deal of plate.

Benj^n Hallowell Esq—sworn.

Knew M^r Frye in America. He was a very loyal Man. Mentions some Acts of Loyalty. Says Gen^l Gage called upon him to act & he acted as a Magistrate when nobody else would act. Knows his House was burnt & believes it was done by Design. He was very obnoxious to the rebels. Says it was very surprizing that they should permit him to remain so long amongst them but does not believe that he ever made any sacrifice of his principles. Says he held the Office of Register &c.

John Chandler Esq—sworn.

Knew M^r Frye in America. He thinks he was a very Loyal Man. Knows no particular Acts of Loyalty as he lived 60 Miles from him. Has heard that he was Register. He had the fees of the same Office in the County of Worcester they were about £90 a Y^r Ster. And therefore he supposes that the fees for the County of Essex must have been £130 or £140 a Y^r.

Richard Saltonstall Esq—sworn.

Knew M^r Frye very well. He was a very loyal Subject. He recollects his acting as a Magistrate at Salem at the request of Gen^l Gage this was in Aug^t 1774 & the Witness knows it because he was the Sheriff of the County of Essex & he in part executed the Warrant. Thinks his issuing the Warrant was granted at a great risque. Has heard that his House was burnt. Says he was Register & that he was so before he granted that Warrant.

## Memorial of Niel Colbreath

Niel Colbreath—the Claimant—sworn. 9^th of Oct^r 1784.

Is a Native of Scotland & went to America in 1768 to North Carolina. When the troubles began he lived near Cross Creek upon his own plantation. He was frequently asked by the Americans to take the Oaths. They treated him frequently very ill. He was taken Pris^r at Moors Bridge & kept 3 Days & then they let him go home the next time he was taken he was kept Pris^r five Months. In 1779 He join'd the British in Georgia. He continued with the Army & was a Soldier afterwards till Lord Cornwallis went to York Town. He came to Eng^d about 7 Weeks ago. He has applied to the Treasury. And his Case is decided upon but not reported to the Treasury. An Allowance of £15 a Y^r will be recommended to him from the 5^th of July 1784.

When he was taken by the Americans They bit him & bit a piece out of his Lip & bit his Legs &c.

Kenneth Stewart—sworn.

Knew Niel Colbreath about the Y$^{r}$ 1775 or 1776. He first saw him at his own plantation & then he saw him at Cross Creek. He believes him to be a very loyal Subject. Says his Lip was not bit off when he first knew him & that he has heard that it happen'd in a quarrel between him & —— Little. Has been upon his plantation. He had a new House upon it & 10 Acres clear'd when he saw it. This was either in Dec$^{r}$ 1775 or Jan$^{y}$ 1776. Can't put a Value upon it. He saw some Cattle upon it.

James Torry—sworn.

Knew Niel Colbreath in N$^{o}$ Carolina first in 1771 or 1772. He knew him in 1776. He was a Loyalist & was at Moors Bridge. He says he has heard that his Lip was bit off when he was taken by the rebels. He has heard it from himself & others & believes it. Never heard of it being bit off in a drunken Quarrel. He has been upon his plantation & believes it to have been his own. Has heard him say so in America. There was an House upon it & a field clear'd but he can't say how much. He saw some Cattle upon his farm. He saw two Horses. It is currently said that it has been sold & that a rebel is in possession. Does not know the Value of the Plantation.

Donald M$^{c}$Doughal—sworn.

Knew Niel Colbreath in North Carolina. He knew him at Cross Creek. Knows that he join'd the Loyalists & that he continued with the British Army during the War. Has heard that his Lip was bit off in a Quarrel with another Man but does not know who was the Man. He was once at his plantation. Does not know how he became possess'd but knows he was possess'd of it & that he had Cattle & Horses. Does not know how many Acres.

The Claimant—called in again.

Says the Man's name who bit his Lip was Little & that he did it when he was taking him. Little was a Rebel. Swears positively to this fact & that it was no private Quarrel between him & Little.

## Memorial of Isabella MacDonald

Determin'd y$^{e}$ 26$^{th}$ of Oct$^{r}$ 1784.

9$^{th}$ of Oct$^{r}$ 1784.

Isabella MacDonald—the Claimant—sworn.

A Loyalist & her Husband an active & Zealous Loyalist.

She is the Widow of Capt$^{n}$ Ja$^{s}$ M$^{c}$Donald. Her Husband was born in Scotland & went to America in 1774. He went to N$^{o}$ Carolina & settled there. She went with him from Scotland. He refused to swear to the Americans. He was taken Pris$^{r}$ at Moors Bridge & he might have procured his Liberty if he had taken the State Oath. He was confined 2 Y$^{rs}$ & $\frac{1}{2}$. He died at Camden of a fever in 1780.

Certificate produced & read from Col$^{l}$ M$^{c}$Donald to her Husband's Loyalty & to her being robb'd & plunder'd by the rebels after his Death.

She has never applied to Gov$^{t}$ for an Allowance. She has only been in Eng$^{d}$ from S$^{t}$ Augustine about ten Days & means to make an Application.

## Memorial of Donald M^c^Kinnon

Determin'd the 11th of July 1785.

Donald McKinnon—the Claimant—sworn. 9th of Octr 1784.

Is a Native of Scotland. His Brother went to America in 1774. He claims for his Brother Lauchlin McKinnon who is dead. He has no papers to produce. His Bror died at Camden in 1780. He was then serving in the British Army. He is his only Brother there is one Sister but he does not know where she is. Produces a Certificate sign'd by the Minister of the Parish where they lived by which it appears that he & Lauchlin McKinnon were Brothers.

The Claimt Heir at Law & Representative of Lauchlan McKinnon who was a Loyalist & bore Arms. Personally £85.

Alexander Morrison—sworn.

Knows Donald McKinnon & believes him to be a Brother of Lauchlin. Knew Lauchlin in America. He was Lieutt with them. He died to the Southward about 1780 or 1781. Does not know the property further than that the Land was his. He bought the Land just after he went over. Does not know the Number of Acres but there was a large Clearing & a Grist Mill upon it. Can't speak to the Value. Says the Mill was but a small one. Was twice upon it. There were Cattle upon it but can't say how many. He says he might pay for it as he had Money. The Land was neither very good nor very bad.

## Memorial of Thomas Oliver [1] Esq. Lieut^t^ Gov^r^ of the Province of Mass. Bay

Determin'd ye 26th of Octr 1784.

Thomas Oliver Esq—the Claimant—sworn. 12th of Octr 1784.

Is a Native of Antigua & was carried to America when he was two Yrs old & lived there till the troubles. He was bred to the profession of the Law but he was prevented following it. In 1774 he was appointed Lieutt Govr of the province without any solicitation by himself. He says he foresaw the Storm & was sorry that the Situation of the Country made it necessary for him to accept the Appointmt tho' he did not hesitate to take it. And he thought he might be of service because he was a popular person with the people. His motives in taking it were to serve Govt. He was appointed Lieutt Govr in Augt 1774 upon the death of a former Lieutt Govr. The Commission is produced which is dated in May 1774. He thinks the troubles were began at that time. He had a Salary of 300 a Yr & in the absence of the Govr he had £750. He was first molested in 1774 by a large number of people surrounding his House & he was in their hands for 5 or 6 Hours & they threaten'd him with destruction if he did not resign the office of Prest of the Mandamus Council. This made him more unpopular than the office of Lieutt Govr. He could not hold the office without being President of the Mans Council. He had no Emolument as a Mans Counsellor. He maintain'd a determined resistance for sevl Hours & then he gave up that Situation & the resignation was convey'd to his Majesty's Ministers & he recd an Approbation of his Conduct from Lord Dartmouth. As soon as he got into Boston under the protection of the Kings Troops he reassumed his Office. He really thought that his Life was in danger if he had resisted. They never asked him to take an Oath to the Rebel State. He remain'd in the

A Zealous & meritorious Loyalist & Did his Duty as a servt of the Crown.

Did not bear Arms.

Loss of Office £300 a Yr.

[1] See Additional Notes, p. 278.

exercise of the Offices of Lieut Gov$^{r}$ &c till the Evacuation of Boston & then he went with the Troops to Halifax & from thence to Eng$^{d}$ in about a Month & he has never been in America since he came to Eng$^{d}$ in 1776.

Former Bounty in the Shape of Salary £300 a Y$^{r}$. Present Bounty £200 a Y$^{r}$.

The Salary of £300 a Y$^{r}$ was paid up to Oct$^{r}$ 1782 from which time he has rec$^{d}$ an Allowance of £200 a Y$^{r}$.

Produces no Certificates to Loyalty. During this Rebellion he has held no military Commission & has never borne Arms. He considers his Office as a Civil Appointment.

Rich$^{d}$ Lechmere Esq—sworn.

Knew M$^{r}$ Oliver very well. He was Lieut$^{t}$ Gov$^{r}$ & conducted himself with perfect Loyalty. Thinks he had merit in taking it & he was very popular & likely to be of service.

Knows M$^{r}$ Oliver's property. Knows the House he lived in & thinks he had 100 Acres. He says he thinks the House would cost £1700. He had improved it much. The Value of Land at Cambridge from £15 to £20—the meanest Land he thinks would be worth £10 per Acre. Thinks the House & the Land would have sold for £2500 in the Y$^{r}$ 1774. Knows the Salt Marsh that M$^{r}$ Oliver had some & thinks it worth 12 an Acre.

His House was well furnished says he knows & believes that he brought away his Linen & plate & thinks the rem$^{r}$ would be worth £300. Knows his Carriages & says they would be worth £80. Says that his Coach Horses were good & the price in general is about £20. He saw his House last in Aug$^{t}$ 1774 but cant speak to the Hay. Says the farming Utensils might cost about £30 & if sold would probably sell for £15.

John Vassall Esq—sworn.

Knew M$^{r}$ Oliver. Believes him to be attached to Great Britain. Remembers his House it was a very good House. It was a Mile & Q$^{r}$ from the Town. He has given £50 per Acre. Thinks as a farm it w$^{d}$ sell from 17 to £23 per Acre. Thinks the house & land before the troubles would have sold for £2500. Says that Salt Marsh Land is worth about £11 or £12 an Acre. He knows the small House in Boston. He was sole Ex$^{r}$ of his father & deliver'd him this House. Thinks it might be worth £60 or £70. He had a Pew in Trinity Church. He says the Value is £10. He had several Carriages & values them at £90. Thinks the 4 Horses to the Carriage worth about £50. The furniture was good thinks what was left would be worth £250. He had a good Stock of Hay. Had several Cattle. Says that the prices which he has mention'd are what he thinks each Article would have sold for.

### Memorial of Rich$^{d}$ Lechmere[1] Esq.

Determin'd the 13$^{th}$ of Oct$^{r}$ 1784.

Rich$^{d}$ Lechmere Esq—the Claimant—sworn. 13$^{th}$ of Oct$^{r}$ 1784.

A Zealous & meritorious Loyalist. Did not bear Arms.

Is a Native of America was born in Boston & was settled there when the troubles commenced. He was appointed one of the Mandamus Counsellors in 1774. He immediately accepted the Appointment. He was at that time appre-

[1] *b.* 1727, *d.* 1814. See Stark, op. cit., p. 413. He did not apparently take the oath of office (ibid., p. 136).

hensive that it would be attended with great difficulty. But he accepted it wishing to strengthen the hands of Gov$^{t}$ & thinking the Prerogative very weak in that Country. He acted in that Capacity to the time of the Evacuation. He says he was at one time in personal Danger of being attacked & carried to the Enemy's Camp but he always went armed & that being known he escaped. He was in no profession but he was Agent to Lane Son & Fraser who are Merch$^{ts}$ here. He quitted Boston with the Army & went to Halifax & from thence came to Eng$^{d}$ in 1776.

He has an Allowance of £200 a Y$^{r}$ which he has rec$^{d}$ ever since he came to Eng$^{d}$ & he now receives it. And he had likewise an Allowance of £100 a Y$^{r}$ given to him for his Son which he continued to receive until the last Year when by the Report of M$^{r}$ Wilmot & M$^{r}$ Coke it was struck off. Bounty £200 a Y$^{r}$.

John Vassall Esq—sworn.

Knows M$^{r}$ Lechmere. No doubt about his Loyalty. Knew his House in Boston thinks it must be worth 13 or £1400 S. Knew his farm at Cambridge but does not exactly know the extent of it. He sold part of it to M$^{r}$ Lechmere but does not know how much he sold it for per Acre. He says as to the Value he thinks the Estate might be worth £10 or £11 per Acre. Knows he had some Land at Muscongus but can't tell the Quantity. He had some part of this from the Witness. Thinks that the House in Boston would let for £55 or £60 S.

David Phipps Esq—sworn.

Knew M$^{r}$ Lechmere very well. Knew his House at Boston is a bad Judge of the Value of the House but thinks it might be worth £1800 or £2000 S. Knew the farm at Cambridge thinks it was about 140 Acres. It was in good Cultivation. Thinks from its Situation it would have sold for £12 or £13 per Acre. Knows that M$^{r}$ Lechmere had Land in the Muscongus Patent & believes he had 3000 Acres. Remembers a Share of 9000 Acres sold for 9*d*. S. per Acre & therefore he values the remainder at the same price.

John Chandler Esq—sworn.

Knew M$^{r}$ Lechmere very well. Did not know M$^{r}$ Lechmere's property at Bromfield & Sturbridge. But he knows this District & says that he thinks Lands in this Situation are worth about 15*s*. S. per Acre.

Will$^{m}$ Bowes—sworn.

Was concerned in a Distillery with M$^{r}$ Lechmere at Boston. The Witness had one fourth Share. He bought this Share in 1774 & he gave £500 C. for it. It cost him altogether about £400 S. He produces the Deed of Conveyance. The whole of this Confiscated & the Witness has given in a Claim for a Share. Some Money was laid out upon it after he bought it.

Peter Johannot—sworn.

Knew that M$^{r}$ Lechmere was a Partner in a great Distillery at Boston. The works were very extensive & he thinks if the business was skilfully managed they might clear £1000 S. a Year by it. Thinks the Value of the whole of it had been to be sold before the troubles would have sold at least for £1000. He understood that he had the half of the business & the half of the Premises.

## Memorial of David Phipps [1] Esq.

Determin'd $y^e$ $14^{th}$ of $Oct^r$ 1784.

$14^{th}$ of $Oct^r$ 1784.

David Phipps Esq—the Claimant—sworn.

An Active & Zealous Loyalist and acted in a very spirited Manner in the Office of Sheriff.

Bore Arms.

Is a Native of America born in the Town of Cambridge & settled there at the Commencement of the troubles on a property of his own. And he held the Office of High Sheriff of the County of Middlesex. The Execution of this Office made him very obnoxious. And in 1774 upon dispersing the Writs in his Office under a new Act of $Par^t$ a Mob attacked him & he thinks they meant to have destroy'd him. They extorted a promise from him that he would issue no more of these Writs. He apprehended that his Life was in danger after he had removed the Gunpowder to Boston. The powder & Cannon were lodged in a Magazine at Cambridge. There were 260 Casks & two Field Pieces. The Powder belonged to the Province. In Consequence of this treatment he removed himself to Boston & his family soon followed him. He staid at Boston till the Evacuation & went to Halifax with the Kings Troops. Whilst at Boston he acted as Marshal to the Admiralty which was to give him some little Support. He had no Salary but the fees amounted to about £150 or £200 whilst he held it which was only for a few Months. He was at this time a $Lieut^t$ in the Navy on Half Pay. In 1779 He was made Master & Commander at New York under Sir George Collyer And he commanded the Allegiance Sloop. He continued in her till he was taken in $Aug^t$ 1782 when he was taken & carried into Boston where he was exchanged & he came to $Eng^d$ the March following & he has been in $Eng^d$ ever since. Produces no Certificates.

Former Bounty £100 a $Y^r$ alter'd to £50 a $Y^r$ afterwards alter'd to £80 a $Y^r$.

He $rec^d$ from April 1777 an Allowance of £100 a $Y^r$ up to the time that $M^r$ Wilmot & $M^r$ Coke examined into the List. It was then reduced by them in the absence of $Capt^n$ Phipps to £50 a $Y^r$ & afterwards upon his remonstrating & proving the largeness of his family &c it was augmented again to £80 a $Y^r$ & it so stands at present.

$Rich^d$ Lechmere Esq—sworn.

Knew $M^r$ Phipps very well. He married $M^r$ Phipps's Sister. He confirms him in the $Acc^t$ he gave of the Gunpowder but says that he did it by the Order of $Gen^l$ Gage. He was taken by the Mob & ill treated & is perfectly satisfied that he could not be safe & that he was obliged to come to Boston.

## Memorial of John Vassall [2] Esq.

Determin'd the $30^{th}$ of $Oct^r$ 1784.

$15^{th}$ of $Oct^r$ 1784.

John Vassall Esq—the Claimant—sworn.

Is a Native of Cambridge in America. He was settled at Cambridge in

[1] *b.* 1724, *d.* 1811. His father was Lieutenant-Governor Spencer Phips. Spencer was the nephew of the wife of Governor William Phips; and the Governor and his wife being childless, Spencer was adopted as heir, and, accordingly, changed his name from Bennett to Phips (Stark, op. cit., pp. 419–21).

[2] *b.* 1738, *d.* 1796. The obituary notice of him in the *Gentleman's Magazine* said: 'He had a considerable property in America, where he lived in princely style. Some time after the disturbances took place, having taken a very active part and spared no expense to support the royal cause, he left his possessions there to the ravagers, and, having fortunately very large estates in Jamaica, he came with his family to England. He carried his loyalty so far as not to use the family motto, "Saepe pro rege, semper pro republica".' Hutchinson (op. cit., vol. i, p. 337) speaks of Vassall as 'naturally timid. He seems to despair of ever seeing peace restored in America'.

1774. He never took a very active part but he sign'd the Address to Gov[r] Hutchinson. He acted as a Magistrate & always resisted all popular Clamour. He was obliged to quit his House in 1774. He was afraid of the Mob who knew his principles & he went to Boston a Day or two after Gov[r] Oliver's House was attacked. When he came to Boston he was made one of the Mandamus Council but he was never sworn in owing to an Accident which made him lame. He never bore Arms & being unfit to live in a garrison'd town he got leave to go to Halifax in 1775. He staid there till 1776. He came then to Eng[d] & has been here ever since. He has two Sons in the Army and one in the Navy. He never rec[d] any Allowance from the Treasury & he subscribed in the Y[r] 1777 £100 towards carrying on the War.

A Loyalist.
Did not bear Arms.

to be stated that he gave £100 to carry on the War.

Property.

A large House in Boston with extensive Gardens & Stables. Produces a Deed dated in 1772 by which Mary Ann Jones in Cons[n] of £1800 conveys the above Premises to M[r] Vassal. He had laid out £1200 S. before the troubles. It was not quite finished at that time. He values it at £3156 3*s.* 5½*d.* which is the exact Sum that it cost him. He says however that it would not take so much Money if sold. But he says he was once offer'd £2600 for it. The House was sold last December. The Garden was at least an Acre. It was supposed to be the best House in the Town. All his Estates were unincumber'd. And he has a Certificate to shew it. He thinks it would at any time have sold for 2500 Gās.

£1800.

Lieut[t] Gov[r] Oliver—sworn.

Knows M[r] Vassall he is his Brother in Law. He states some facts to prove Loyalty being better than giving an Opinion. He has three Sons now in the Army & Navy. They were placed there since the troubles. He sent out one of his Horses which was a valuable one to assist Lord Percy in going to the battle of Lexington. After he came to Eng[d] he subscribed Money towards carrying on the War. And his Estate has been confiscated & sold.

## Memorial of John Barnard

Determin'd y[e] 16[th] of Oct[r] 1784.

John Barnard—the Claimant—sworn. 16[th] of Oct[r] 1784.

Is a Native of Germany & went to Boston from London in 1771 & he was settled at Boston in 1774 & 1775 as a Furrier. The Officers of the British employ'd him in making Caps &c & he came away with the Army. He was afraid to stay. He did not carry Arms but he was one of the Association & patrol'd the Streets. He went to Halifax & finding no Employment there he came to Eng[d].

A Loyalist.
Did not bear Arms.

Will[m] Jackson—sworn.

He knows John Barnard knew him at Boston. He was in the town during the Blockade from which Circumstance he thinks he was loyally disposed. He might have gone out if he had pleased. Knows nothing of the Man's Circumstances or his property. He used to work for the British Officers upon his Furs the Officers used to buy them & send them to this Man to work. He thinks it likely that he might have had some Furs as his own. He could not have any valuable Furs but supposes he might have some Common ones. At the same time he says he might not have any. In fact he knows nothing of it & he did not know till this morning that he should be called upon to attend as a Witness for this Man.

N.B. The Board are of Opinion that this Man has rec[d] a full Compensation for his Losses by the £10 which he rec[d] from the Treasury.

Determin'd the 23[d] of Oct[r] 1784.

**Memorial of Rob[t] Hallowell [1] Esq.**

18[th] of Oct[r] 1784.

Robert Hallowell—the Claimant—sworn.

A Loyalist & Did his Duty with spirit as an Officer of the Crown. Did not bear Arms.

Is a Native of Boston & at the Commencement of the troubles he was Comptroller of the Customs appointed by the Lords of the Treasury. He suffer'd considerable persecution in the Execution of his Office & continued in this disagreeable State till April 1775. He had been removed to Plymouth in the Y[r] 1774. The Boston Port Bill passed the 30[th] of March 1774. He continued at Plymouth in the Execution of his Duty till the battle of Lexington when he removed to Boston & staid till the Evacuation. He did Duty in the Association whilst he remain'd at Boston. He went with the Army to Halifax & from thence came to Eng[d] in 1776.

Office.

Salary £70 a Y[r]. Fees £300.

His Salary was £70 a Y[r]. The legal fees about £380 a Y[r]. Produces a Book of fees for the Y[r] 1773. Has no other Voucher. It appears by that Book that the fees amounted to that Sum for the Y[r] 1773. Extra fees He charges £50 a Y[r] tho' he says he is confident it was £100 a Y[r]. His Share of Seizures On an Average for three Years he puts at £100 a Y[r]. The Income of his Office of Receiver of the Dues for Seamen for the Royal Hospital at Greenwich. This he says amounts to about £50 a Y[r]. He had this appointment from M[r] Hulton who was Gen[l] Receiver all over America. He had this in Nov[r] 1771. Says that M[r] Hulton could have taken this away from him.

Disallowed.

Lieut[t] Gov[r] Oliver—sworn.

Knew M[r] Hallowell at Boston. He was uniformly loyal. Says that he was a very active & vigilant Officer & that he was in consequence of it very unpopular. He left Boston on the Evacuation. He was pitched upon in any hazardous situation to execute the Office. Knew his House the furniture was good. Thinks it would cost £600 & that it was worth £300. Says afterwards it might cost five Hundred. Knows nothing of the Coffee &c. Remembers he had a single Horse Chaise. Says he was entitled to a part of the Seizure to which Gov[r] Oliver laid Claim in his Memorial. The Seizures were left in the Harbour

[1] *b.* 1740, *d.* 1818 in Maine, U.S.A. He 'ordered Hancock's vessel the *Liberty*, seized for smuggling wine, to be removed from the wharf to a place covered by the guns of the *Romney* frigate; and in the affray which occurred received wounds and bruises that at the time seemed fatal'. Hallowell visited the United States in 1788 and again in 1790 as the executor first of his own, then of his wife's father. In 1792 he took up his abode at Boston in a house which had not been confiscated because of his mother's life interest. He was well received by the inhabitants (Stark, op. cit., p. 281). Robert's brother Benjamin, *b.* 1724, *d.* 1799, wrote to Edward Winslow (February 10, 1784): 'Your friend Bobby continues still at Bristol on account of the cheapness of living. His friends use every means in their power to be of service to him. With the little money which he has been able with great industry to pick up, added to the allowance of £100 a year from Government, he is able to rub along' (*Winslow Papers*, p. 166, quoted by W. H. Siebert, *The Colony of Massachusetts Loyalists at Bristol*, in Mass. Hist. Soc. *Proceedings*, vol. xlv, p. 412).

at Boston. Being asked as to the profits of his Office exclusive of the Seizures He says he has heard the Merch[ts] there say that it was worth £300 a Y[r].

**Memorial of John Webster**

Determin'd y[e] 26[th] of Oct[r] 1784.

John Webster—the Claimant—sworn. 18[th] of Oct[r] 1784.

Is a Native of Eng[d] & went to Philadelphia in 1773. He went to carry on the trade of a Whitesmith. He was there when the troubles commenced. They applied to him to take the Oaths & he refused. He came away when Gen[l] Howe was in possession of the City & came to Eng[d] in April 1778.

A Loyalist.
Did not bear Arms.

**Memorial of Jonathan Sewell [1] Esq.**

Determined the 30[th] of Oct[r] 1784.

Jonathan Sewell Esq—the Claimant—sworn. 18[th] of Oct[r] 1784.

Is a Native of America. Was born in Boston. At the Commencement of the troubles He was Attorney Gen[l] of the Province & in possession of his Estate at Cambridge. He removed from thence to Boston by order of Gen[l] Gage in 1774. He continued at Boston till Aug[t] 1775. All Civil Justice was then at an end & Martial Law prevail'd. Therefore he came away & resigned his Commission. He assisted Gen[l] Gage in everything & laments his not being in Town to speak to his Case. He arrived in Eng[d] in Sept[r] 1775. Has been in Eng[d] ever since. He acted for a time as private Secretary to Gen[l] Gage.

A Zealous Loyalist & render'd Services to Gov[t] by writing in favor of it.
Did not bear Arms.

Produces a Certificate from Lieut[t] Gov[r] Oliver to Loyalty & professional Eminence.

He has no Allowance on the Pension List. But he holds a Commission at Halifax. He is Judge of the Admiralty. He has leave of Absence & executes the office by Deputy. He has a Salary of £600 a Y[r] from Gov[t] & he pays £150 a Y[r] to a Deputy. M[r] Putnam was appointed Att[y] Gen[l] by Gen[l] Gage when he quitted Boston. This was about 6 or 7 Months before the Evacuation.

No Allowance.

Has an Office at Halifax of £600 a Y[r].

**Memorial of Harrison Gray [2] Esq. Jun[r]**

Determin'd the 19[th] of Oct[r] 1784.

Harrison Gray Jun[r]—the Claimant—sworn. 19[th] of Oct[r] 1784.

Is a Native of Boston & the eldest Son of Harrison Gray Esq one of the Mandamus Council. When the troubles broke out his father was Treasurer of

A Loyalist.

[1] *b.* 1728, *d.* 1796. Sewell, one gathers, was by far the most brilliant of the New England loyalists. There are numerous references to him in S. Curwen's *Journal and Letters*. There is a characteristic letter from him dated June 28, 1784 (p. 408): 'My design is to go out to Nova Scotia this autumn or early in the spring. Then, if you wish, you may see me; but while the unjust, illiberal, lying Act of 1779 remains unrepealed, never will I set foot in the territories of the thirteen united independent states.' No less characteristic are the letters set out in *Winslow Papers*, pp. 13, 36, 60, 76. Sewell had been an intimate friend of John Adams; and it was to him that the words were addressed: 'The die is now cast. I have now passed the Rubicon; sink or swim, live or die.' It is pleasant to find that when the two met again in 1788 in London they renewed their old friendship (Stark, op. cit., p. 455). In 1788 Sewell took up his abode at St. John's, New Brunswick, having been appointed Judge of Admiralty for Nova Scotia and New Brunswick. He had been as early as 1769 Judge of the Admiralty Court of Nova Scotia, but continued to live at Boston (*Winslow Papers*, p. 175, note). His son Jonathan, the Chief Justice of Lower Canada, played for many years a leading part in Canadian history.

[2] 'Until 1830 Harrison Gray, the younger, lived a grumbling existence in London, supported by a small pension from the Government and the little American property that his nephew (Harrison Gray Otis) had managed to save from the old Treasurer's estate' (S. E. Morison, *Harrison Gray Otis*, 1913, vol. i, p. 239).

Did not bear Arms. the Province & he was Deputy to his father. He took the same part with his father & was steadily attached to this Country. He had no Opportunity of distinguishing himself by his Exertions & he never bore Arms. He was never ill treated by the Mob. He left Boston in Aug$^{t}$ 1775 & came home to Eng$^{d}$ on acc$^{t}$ of his health with the leave of Gen$^{l}$ Gage & has been in Eng$^{d}$ ever since. He did not receive any allowance from the Treasury till he had been in Eng$^{d}$

Bounty £100 a Y$^{r}$. a Year & then he rec$^{d}$ £100 a Y$^{r}$ & now continues to receive it. He has two Children & a Wife.

Produces Certificates from M$^{r}$ Murray & the late M$^{r}$ Flucker but they only go to his Office & not to loyalty.

He swears that the only reason for his coming to Eng$^{d}$ when he did was on Acc$^{t}$ of his health & that he would have staid if his health had permitted.

Harrison Gray Esq Sen$^{r}$—sworn.

The Claim$^{t}$ is the Witness's eldest Son & he lived with him at the Commencement of the troubles. He was Deputy Treasurer for a number of Y$^{rs}$. It was an appointment by him & his Son had no Allowance from the Province. He could have removed his Son & he might have been removed himself. He gave his Son £100 a Y$^{r}$ S. Thinks he made between 2 & £300 a Y$^{r}$ besides. He married before the troubles.

John Chandler Esq—sworn.

Has known the claim$^{t}$ from his infancy. Believes him to have been a loyalist. The witness was at Boston during the blockade. Remembers his coming to England in Aug$^{t}$ 1775. Does not know that he was much out of order & believes that nothing ail$^{d}$ him. Says he believes that he came away from fear of being killed. He was first clerk in the office of his father. Never heard of a Deputy Treasurer in the Province. His father's office was annual & he was liable to be turned out every year. Does not know anything of the Claimant's losses.

Determin'd the 30$^{th}$ of Oct$^{r}$ 1784.

## Memorial of Benj$^{n}$ Faneuil [1] Esq.

19$^{th}$ of Oct$^{r}$ 1784.

Benj$^{n}$ Faneuil Esq—the Claimant—sworn.

A Zealous & meritorious Loyalist And as a Consignee of the Tea conducted himself with great firmness. Did not bear Arms.

Is a Native of Boston. Just before the rebellion The Claimant was appointed one of the Consignees of the Tea. Before this time he was a Merch$^{t}$. The Office was obtain'd for him by Mess$^{rs}$ Watson & Rashleigh. It would have been attended with a considerable profit & matters had been peaceable. And he wished much to have it. The moment it was known Town Meetings were held & the Consignees were immediately insulted & he & the other Consignees were driven to Castle William in Nov$^{r}$ 1773. They were frequently threaten'd if they did not resign & rec$^{d}$ incendiary Letters (produces one of them). Notwithstanding this he adhered to his Office & preserved his Attachment to this Country at great personal risque. He was at Castle William for 9 Months protected by the British Troops. He came to Boston before the blockade. He was obliged to quit the House to which he had retired about 7 Miles from Boston. He remain'd at Boston till the Evacuation When he went to Halifax & from thence to Engl$^{d}$

[1] See Additional Notes, p. 279.

in 1776 where he has been ever since. Upon his Arrival in Eng[d] he rec[d] an Allowance of £150 a Y[r] from the Treasury & he now continues to receive it. Bounty £150 a Y[r].

Produces a Letter signed by order of the Court of Directors of the E. India Company address'd to M[r] Fanueil & the three other Consignees in which they express themselves perfectly satisfied with the Conduct of the Consignees.

Robert Rashleigh Esq—sworn.

Has known M[r] Faneuil as a Correspondent for many Years & has known him personally ever since he came to Eng[d]. He believes him to have been very well attached to Great Britain. The Witness & M[r] Watson thinking him to be a Man of strict honor & loyalty got him appointed by the East India Company without his knowledge. They consider'd at that time that they were giving him a lucrative Office. He believes that he conducted himself very well in the Office. He has seen his Books & thinks he clear'd about £200 by his business.

Benj[n] Hallowell Esq—sworn.

Knew M[r] Fanueil in America. Knew that he was Consignee of the Tea & says he conducted himself with great spirit & Loyalty. Believes he was well attach'd to Great Britain. Has heard that great pains were taken to draw him aside from his Duty but to no purpose. He was in good business. His father is a Loyalist. He understands that the Consignees of the Tea are in as bad a Situation as the Mandamus Counsellors & that as the Law now stands he will not be able to recover. M[r] Hallowell knows nothing of his property.

### Memorial of Sam[l] Porter [1] Esq.

Determin'd the 21[st] of Oct[r] 1784.

Sam[l] Porter Esq—the Claimant—sworn. 20[th] of Oct[r] 1784.

Is a Native of New Eng[d]. In the Year 1775 He was settled at Salem & followed the Law. He took no part but followed the Advice of the Crown Officers in keeping as quiet as possible. He was however frequently insulted & lost part of his business by being esteem'd a Tory. He remain'd in Salem till the 24[th] of May 1775 & he arrived in Eng[d] in Aug[t] 1775. He has not been in America since that time. In feb[y] 1776 He applied to the Treasury & rec[d] £100 but not as an Allowance. And he had an Allowance of £100 a Y[r] from Jan[y] 1777 And now continues to receive it.

A Loyalist.
Did not bear Arms.
Bounty £100 a Y[r].

### Memorial of Jonathan Simpson [2] Esq.

Determin'd the 21[st] of Oct[r] 1784.

Jonathan Simpson Esq—the Claimant—sworn. 20[th] of Oct[r] 1784.

Is a Native of Boston. He was in trade there till the Year 1770. He took a decided part from the first. He refused to sign the Non-importation Agreement in consequence of which his House was attacked. He left Boston the 25[th] of April 1775 & went to Halifax. He arrived in Eng[d] in June 1776 & in Aug[t] or Sept[r] of that Y[r] He rec[d] £100 & afterw[ds] an Allowance of £100 a Y[r] which he continues to receive.

A meritorious Loyalist.
Did not bear Arms.
Bounty £100 a Y[r].

[1] Mentioned by Curwen, op. cit., as a member of the New England Club which held a weekly dinner at the Adelphi, Strand.

[2] Jonathan made his peace with the Americans and died at Boston in 1804 (Sabine, op. cit., vol. ii, p. 303).

Jonathan Sewell Esq—sworn.

He knew Mr Simpson but not intimately. He can speak to his Loyalty from his Conversation & general reputation. He believes him to be as loyal as anybody. Says he was appointed one of the Mandamus Council but he did not accept on account of his Age & Infirmities.

Robert Hallowell Esq—sworn.

Knew Mr Simpson very well. Believes him to have been loyal. He had a paralytic Stroke before the troubles & his life was thought to be in Danger. Does not know whether he was named one of the Mandamus Council but has heard so. He had made himself very obnoxious by his Loyalty & he gave protection to one of the Commissioners of the Customs when it was dangerous to do so. He cannot speak to his property.

Richd Lechmere Esq—sworn.

Knew Mr Simpson he married his Sister. His Conduct has been perfectly loyal. His reason for leaving Boston in 1775 was on acct of his health. He is 75 Yrs of Age. Knows that he protected Mr Hulton.[1] He was appointed one of the Mandamus Council & sat several times at the [2] but he was obliged to resign on acct of his Health. Values the Warehouse & the Land at £850 S. Speaks to the Circumstance of the furniture being taken. Says the furniture on board that Vessel was worth £300 & says what remain'd must be worth £200.

The Claimant—called in again.

Says that he forgot to mention the Circumstance of his being a Mandamus Counsellor.

### Memorial of Margt Simpson Spinster

Determin'd ye 21st of Octr 1784.

20th of Octr 1784.

A Loyalist As also her Representative.

Jonathan Simpson Esq—sworn.

He is the Uncle & was the Guardian of this Young Woman. She quitted Boston at the Evacuation & died in 1777. She was about 18 or 19 Yrs of Age. Believes her to have been well attached to this Country.

This Lady was possessed of a Sum of Money which he had in his hands & lent out for her in his own name.

Debts £1668 13*s.* 11*d.*

He says she has two Brothers & one Sister living. As this is wholly personal property they would take it in equal Shares. Both the Brothers & the Sister were Loyalists. He says that neither the Sister or Brothers have mention'd this in their Memorial.

### Memorial of Nicholas Lechmere [3]

Determin'd the 21st of Octr 1784.

21st of Octr 1784.

Nicholas Lechmere—the Claimant—sworn.

A Meritorious Loyalist and did

Is a Native of Boston & was settled at New London first as an Officer in the Customs. In 1775 He was Searcher & Land Waiter in the Customs at Newport Rhode Island appointed by the Lords of the Treasury. In the Month

1 Henry Hulton was one of the four Commissioners of the Customs.

2 *Sic* in Text. ? Insert 'Board'.

3 *b.* 1727, *d.* 1814 in England. See Stark, op. cit., p. 414.

of Dec[r] 1775 He was first molested. He was sent for by Gen[l] Lee [1] & made a prisoner & carried to providence & kept Pris[r] about a Week. Gen[l] Lee tender'd a paper which he believes was an Oath. He refused to sign it. They set him at liberty at the end of a Week. Gen[l] Lee told him that he had sent for him because he understood that he & his family were very inimical to American Liberty the Claimant answer'd that he did him & his family a great deal of Honor. Produces a Copy of the Oath tender'd to him. He was afterwards sent to Gloucester & kept 11 Weeks. Then he was permitted to go home & he remain'd at Rhode Island till the Evacuation. He left Rhode Island with the Troops & went to New York & he came to Eng[d] in feb[y] 1780. He had an Allowance of £40 a Y[r] from the Treasury before he arrived in addition to his Salary. This was procured for him by his Brother who presented a Memorial for him in his Absence. The Salary was £40 a Y[r] & was paid to him up to Oct[r] 1782 when it ceased & since that time he has rec[d] an Allowance of £60 a Y[r].

his Duty as an Officer of the Crown.
Did not bear Arms.

Former Bounty £40 a Y[r].
present bounty £60 a Y[r].

Office.

His Salary was 40 a Y[r]. Produces his Commission dated 1[st] of feb[y] 1761. The legal fees as nearly as he can judge were about £140 a Y[r] S.

Salary £40 a Y[r].
Legal fees £140 a Y[r].

Charles Dudley—sworn.

Knew M[r] Lechmere at Rhode Island. He was Searcher & Land Waiter there. He has not the smallest Doubt but he was an excellent Subject. Had many opportunities of knowing it as he was under the Witness. The Witness paid him the Salary which was £40 a Y[r]. There were many fees legally belonging to him & he says he thinks they must have amounted to £140 or £150 S.

General Arnold [2]—sworn.

Knew the House Water Lot & 3 Acres of Land. He rented the House for two Years & gave £40 C. for it. He had only the House & Garden. He had neither the Water Lot nor the 3 Acres. It was one of the best Houses at New-haven. Says he knows the Value tolerably well because he had it in contemplation to buy it before he built an House for himself. He says he would have given £1000 S. for it. Thinks it would have sold for that Money. Understood that he was very loyal.

Rev[d] M[r] Bisset—sworn.

Knew M[r] Lechmere very well has known him for 16 Years. He believes him to be strictly loyal. His friends & Enemies believed that. Says he was enthusiastically Loyal. Speaks of his being taken up in consequence of his refusing to sign the test which was put to him & says the form of the Test was to be true & bear Allegiance to the Rebel States.

[1] General Charles Lee, *b.* 1731, *d.* 1782, whose meditated treachery has only recently come to light. Is in Appleton, op. cit., vol. iii, pp. 657–61, and in *Dict. of Nat. Biography*.

[2] The famous or infamous Benedict Arnold of whom Sir George Trevelyan has written with such power (*George III and Charles Fox*, vol. i, ch. ix).

## Memorial of Peter Johonnot[1]

Determin'd the 21st of Octr 1784.

21st of Octr 1784.

Peter Johonnot—the Claimant—sworn.

A Zealous Loyalist.

Did not bear Arms.

Bounty £100 a Yr.

Is a Native of Boston in America. Was settled there at the Commencement of the troubles as a Distiller. He sign'd an Address to Govr Hutchinson which contain'd not only an Approbation of the Govrs Conduct but contain'd the political Creed of the Signers. This made those who signed it very obnoxious. He partook of all the Measures in opposition to the rebels. He was of the Association but did not bear Arms. He left Boston at the Evacuation & went to Halifax with the Army. He came to Engd from Halifax in 1776. He very soon afterwards recd an Allowance of £100 a Yr which was granted to him in 1776 & he still continues to receive it.

Richard Lechmere Esq—sworn.

Knows Mr Johonnot. He was always consider'd as a very staunch friend to Govt. He thinks he quitted Boston merely from principles of Loyalty. Knew his House at Boston. He was in very extensive business. He carried on one Distillery on his own private Acct & the other was jointly between him & his Bror in Law Mr Scaver. Thinks he might have made 5 or £600 a Yr by his own private Distillery the joint Concern he thinks might nearly produce 7 or £800 a Yr. Mr Lechmere says that notwithstanding all his family were Rebels He has not the least doubt of Mr Johonnot's Loyalty.

Harrison Gray Esq—sworn.

Knew Mr Johonnot before the troubles. He kept a Distillery. When the troubles broke out He took a very strong part in favor of Govt & particularly in the Tea business. Believes his father & Brother were Rebels but thinks him very firm in his Loyalty both in public & private.

Knew that he had a very large & good House it was well furnished. Does not know the Value of it. But says it is worth above £1000 S. Says he was in considerable business but does not know what he might gain by it. He was in partnership with one Scaver. He does not suspect that the two Partners took different sides from any Agreement between them tho' admits it might sometimes happen.

## Memorial of Henry Barnes[2]

Determin'd the 30th of Octr 1784.

22d of Octr 1784.

Henry Barnes—the Claimant—sworn.

A Zealous & meritorious[3] & acted as a Magistrate in a very spirited manner.

Is a Native of Boston & lived at Marlborough for many years before the troubles. He was in the mercantile Line. He took an active part from the Yr 1770 & says no other Magistrate but himself dared to act as he did. He issued out billeting orders for the Kings Troops in 1775 this made him very obnoxious & the Mob threaten'd to pull down his House. He thought himself in danger & went to Boston the 17th of April. His Wife staid in the Country

[1] *b.* 1729, *d.* 1809, of Huguenot stock. He married the granddaughter of Governor Joseph Dudley. See Stark, op. cit., p. 410.

[2] *b.* 1724, *d.* 1808. Stark (op. cit., pp. 400–2) gives a very graphic account of the manner in which Barnes enabled two British officers, sent out by Gage, to escape the hostility of the people of Marlborough (Mass.).

[3] ? Add loyalist.

till the Oct[r] following. He left Boston the 26[th] of Dec[r] 1775 & came to Eng[d] where he has been ever since. He never bore Arms in the Dispute. He left Boston with the consent of Gen[l] Gage. When he came to Eng[d] he sent a petition to the Treasury & he had an Allowance of £50 which he refused to accept & they then gave him £100 which was augmented thro' the Interest of M[r] Rigby[1] to £150 a Y[r]. This was reduced by the Commissioners to £100 a Y[r] which he now continues to receive.

Did not bear Arms.

Former Bounty £150 a Y[r]. Present Bounty £100 a Y[r].

Thomas Goldthwaite Esq—sworn.

Has known M[r] Barnes for 40 Years. Knows his principles. He is a good Loyalist. He was a Magistrate & has heard that he did his Duty very well. He has heard that he brought himself into trouble by billeting the British Soldiers.

### Memorial of Joseph Domett[2]

Determined the 30[th] of Oct[r] 1784.

Joseph Domett—the Claimant—sworn. 22[d] of Oct[r] 1784.

Is a Native of Boston. Was settled at Falmouth in Casco as a Custom House Officer in 1774. He was appointed Deputy Comptroller of the Customs at Falmouth in 1772. He was appointed by the Comptroller with the Approbation of the Commissioners. He as well as the other officers of the Crown were very obnoxious to the rebels. He had done no particular Act but was strenuous in supporting Gov[t] & he was obliged to go on board a Kings Ship in 1775. Between this time & the Evacuation at Boston (as he could not get into it during the Blockade) he was obliged to live very secretly. He then lived at Boston from 1776 to 1779. He swears that he never did make any sacrifice of his principles or pretended to do so in order to stay there. He was exiled in 1779 from a Discovery of some of his Letters. Says if he had left Boston he supposes he should have lost his property. He came in 1779 to this Country & applied to the Treasury. He obtained an Allowance of £80 a Y[r]. He did not state to the Treasury that he had taken the Oaths to the Rebels—the Allowance remains.

The Claim[t] was in the Employment of the Crown under the Comptroller of the Customs at Falmouth & after the Evacuation of Boston he *voluntarily* went into that Town when he must have known the Oaths would be tender'd to him. He accordingly did take those Oaths. The Board therefore do not deem him an Object of the Act of Par[t].

Office.

He had a small Salary £30 a Y[r]. But he accepted the Office in hopes of being appointed Comptroller upon the removal of M[r] Savage.

George Lyde—sworn.

Knew M[r] Domet 15 or 16 Y[rs]. He married his Sister. He believes him to be perfectly loyal notwithstanding he has taken that Oath. He had no means of Support which made him go to Boston & says his taking that Oath can be only justified upon Self preservation.

Arthur Savage—sworn.

Knew M[r] Domet very well in America. He was his Deputy & he gain'd near £50 by it. He could have turned him out any Day. He behaved very well in the Office. He has always understood him to be loyal. He had very little Acquaintance with him before 1772. He afterwards conducted himself so as to convince the Witness that he was a Loyalist. He & M[r] Savage were separated in 1775 & he has

[1] Richard Rigby, *b.* 1722, *d.* 1788, the notorious placeman and politician. Is in *Dict. of Nat. Biography*. For his character see Trevelyan, *George III and Charles Fox*, vol. ii, pp. 99–101.

[2] Sabine (op. cit., vol. i, p. 384) states that he became an episcopal minister.

known very little of him since. He never heard of his taking an Oath. He says that he should not have taken it himself. Does not know anything of his property.

## Memorial of Frederick Philips [1] Esq.

25th of Octr 1784.

Frederick Philips Esq—the Claimant—sworn.

Is a Native of America. Was born in New York. In 1775 He was settled at the Manor of Philipsborough near New York. He had been settled there many Years before. When the troubles commenced He immediately promoted an association with many loyal Subjects for ye support of Govt. This was in the Spring of 1776. An opposite Party was formed & the Loyalists were intimidated. And in Augt of that Yr he was taken Prisoner & carried into New England & kept six Months. He was then let out on his own parole & he kept his parole & went to New York where he remain'd the whole War. He came to Engd immediately before the Evacuation. He is banished & all his Estate confiscated. He had five Sons [2] in the British Service two of whom he has lost they enter'd into the service as soon as they were old enough. He purchased Commissions for two of his Sons & still owes the Money which he borrowed for that purpose. He has never made any Concessions at any time to the Rebel Govt. He was 25 Yrs a Member of ye Assembly & Chairman of the Committee. By his Interest a Motion to have the province govern'd by Congress was promoted & they unanimously rejected the Govt of Congress. He was many Yrs ago a Colonel of Militia.

Bounty £200 a Yr. He had an allowance of £200 a Yr at New York which has been continued by the Treasury since he came to Engd. And he now receives an Allowance of £200 a Year.

Colonel Beverly Robinson [3]—sworn.

Has known Mr Philips for many Years before the troubles & esteems him very loyal. He was possess'd of great property in the province of New York

[1] *b.* 1746, *d.* 1785. He was one of the two Tory leaders in the New York Assembly which met in January 1775. He went, indeed, some way with the popular party, and was an assenting member of the committee which reported on grievances; but he preferred the maintenance of the existing order of things to the redress of grievances, and so threw in his lot with the British.

'The county of Westchester contained six manors, which together covered more than half of the entire county . . . Scarsdale . . . Cortland Manor, and Philipsburgh covered approximately four hundred square miles of the choicest land in the province. In Dutchess County the Philipse family had a second estate larger than the manor, which made that family second only to the Van Rensselaers in landed possessions' (Becker, *The History of Political Parties in the Province of New York, 1760–76*, p. 9). In *Hist. MSS. Comm., Am. MSS. in R. Inst.*, vol. iii, p. 406, under date March 19, 1783, is a warrant to pay Frederic Philipse, senior, the sum of £200 allowance for his support, 'having been obliged to leave his estate and property on account of attachment to Government.' In June 1788 Mr. D. P. Coke spoke in Parliament of Colonel Philipse's case as peculiarly meritorious. He had a landed estate worth £40,000 when the war broke out and he had seven children. During the war he had rendered the most important services to the British cause (*Hans.*, vol. xxvii, p. 615).

[2] John Philipse entered the navy, was in thirteen engagements, and died a post-captain at the age of forty-seven. Charles Philipse was commissioned an ensign in 1783, a colonel in 1812, a major-general in 1814, and a lieutenant-general in 1830 (Sabine, op. cit., vol. ii, p. 187). Frederick, the eldest (see next page), escaped Sabine's researches.

[3] *b.* 1723, *d.* 1792.

Has a general knowledge of the Manor of Philipsbourgh. The Extent of it was about 24 Miles in length & 6 Miles in breadth. This was a very valuable property & all let to Tenants except what he had in his own hands which he fancies was about 2 or 3000 Acres. He always supposed his rents to amount to £2400 C. a Y^r exclusive of what he had in his own hands. Says that the land at Philipsbourgh would be worth 4 or 5 an Acre for the whole Manor. Says that when these people originally settled they agreed to pay such a rent & upon every improvement to give one sixth of the improvement to the Landlord. Does not know whether M^r Philips could turn these Tenants out or not. He says he let one Set of Mills for £200 a Y^r. Col^l Robinson is desired to value the whole property. He says if Col^l Philips could have sold the whole at one time he thinks it would have fetched £150000. He says he should value the whole supposing him to have the right of turning out the Tenants at 4 or £500000. But in its present Situation he thinks £150000 would be enough for it. He does not think that M^r Philips could get the Tenants out of possession. He says again that he should value it at £150000. He confines this Value to Philipsbourgh. Never knew of any Quit rents being sold. Looks upon Col^l Philips's Estate to be a much better one than Gen^l Delancey's. Col^l Robinson being asked whether he thinks the land occupied by the Tenants to be the property of Col^l Philips or not He says to some purposes he thinks it is to others he thinks it is not. He says he could not turn out the Tenants but he says he could raise them as much as he pleased which he considers as tantamount to it. The Rental is produced to him & he says he believes it is the true one. Being asked as to the value of the Mills House &c & the Demesne Land in the possession of M^r Philips Says he thinks it would rent for £350 or £400 a Y^r C. The Value is included when he speaks of the whole. Knows he had some Salt Meadow but can't say how much. As to the Value He meant to include this likewise in the general Valuation. Thinks it would let for 30*s*. an Acre. Thinks it would sell for £30 or £40 an Acre if sold in small Quantities. Knew his Houses in Dock Street thinks before the troubles they would be worth £1000 or £1200 C. Knew the Lot in Stone Street thinks it was worth without the Buildings £250 or £300 C. Another Lot in Stone Street where the House tumbled down He values at £300 C.

Knows he had 4 fine Oxen Sheep &c. Says the 4 before the War would sell for £100 a P^r. He averages Sheep at 8*s*. Thinks the farm Utensils might be worth the Money. Says a pipe of Madeira would cost from 60 to £100. Old Madeira would sell for £100 a Pipe. Says that Frederick Philips Jun^r is the eldest Son of the Claimant.

**Memorial of Frederick Philips Esq. Jun^r**

Col^l Robinson—sworn. 25^th of Oct^r 1784.

Says the Claimant is the eldest Son & Heir of Colonel Philips.

Frederick Philips Jun^r—the Claimant—sworn. 26^th of Oct^r 1784.

He is the eldest Son of M^r Frederick Philips Sen^r & is a Capt^n in the Loyal

Americans & now upon half pay. He has served as an Officer since the Year 1779 always in the provincial Troops. Does not produce his Commission.

He says he had no Personal Property & no Money due to him in America. Says his father is 64 or 65 Y[rs] of Age.

The whole of M[r] Philips's Claim is as Tenant in Tail under the family Settlement after the Death of the father. His father's life is valued at five Years & his Interest afterwards at 8 Years. Says that this was done by M[r] Galloway. He had not concurr'd with his father in doing any Act to cut off the Entail. It was their Intention to have done it but he (the Claimant) was not old enough before the troubles being now only 24 Years of Age. He thinks he has sustain'd a Loss of more than £20000. He thinks his Loss is greater than his father's. Says he values his Interest in the Manor of Philipsbourg at £14166 7*s*. 1*d*.

Values his Interest in the Mansion House Demesne Mills &c at £3009 7*s*. 0*d*. by Mistake it was put in the Schedule at £5350.

Values his Interest in the Salt Meadow at £501 11*s*. 3*d*.

Values his Interest in the House on Kings Bridge Island at £501 11*s*. 3*d*.

### Further testimony to the Memorial of Frederick Philips Esq.

13[th] of Dec[r] 1784.

The Rev[d] Sam[l] Peters—sworn.

Knows the Estate but he never had seen the Deeds. Says many of the Leases were for ever many for 99 Y[rs] and many for 3 Lives the first period for a nominal rent as a pepper Corn &c & then the rent to increase. Says the Tenants could sell their farms first obtaining the consent of their Landlord & he knows an instance of a Tenant of his selling her farm for £1200 & M[r] Philips took £400 for it. Says the land in general was not good excepting where M[r] Philips lived. M[r] Philips he says was so omnipotent that nobody would contest it with him. Has known M[r] Philips buy out a Tenant but does not know what proportion the Money which he gave bore to the Value of the fee simple. Says he believes that the increase of the annual Value of the Estate did not depend upon the Will & pleasure of M[r] Philips or any part of his family but upon certain periods named in the Leases. He believes a Lease may be procured. He has seen two or three.

### Further testimony to the Memorial of Frederick Philips Esq.

17[th] of Dec[r] 1784.

John Watts Esq—sworn.

Knows M[r] Philips's property by Report. Says it was very like what is called Copyhold property in this Country but there was no Copyhold Land in America. Believes the whole of the Land was not in this Tenure. Does not know whether there were any Leases. Says the Laws of Eng[d] prevail in America & that 60 Years possession gives an absolute title. Says that he does not think that it would be fair to raise the rents & that he could not do it with those Tenants who had sold but thinks he might with the others. By Degrees it became a Custom for the Tenants to sell paying one third to the Landlord. He thinks he might turn off the Tenants who had not sold but does not know any Instance of it being done. Says they had no right to dispose of the farms but with the Consent of the Landlord. Says he believes he was a very mild Landlord & never heard of his putting any of his Tenants into prison. Cant tell the Value of his Estate. Believes they have confiscated the whole of it for ever & that they will not mind the Entail.

John Pator Kempe Esq.

Has seen M^r^ Philips's Estate. Never understood that his Tenants had any leases but thinks they were originally Tenants at Will. Never heard of any Dispute between Col^l^ Philips & his Tenants. Believes the forefathers of M^r^ Philips permitted Settlers to come upon his Lands & that they became Tenants at small rents. Has heard that Col^l^ Philips when he came to the Estate rais'd the rents but that he promised not to do it any more but thinks the Son might have done it. Has heard of Sales being made & has heard that M^r^ Philips had a part of the purchase Money. Believes M^r^ Philips's Consent was necessary. Has always understood that the Son might raise the rents. He has consider'd that M^r^ Philips's Estate was verging fast towards a Copyhold but from the Infancy of the Colony that the Tenants had not been there long enough to acquire Copyhold rights. Thinks that when he had sold a Court of Equity would compel him to let that Man have the Land. Thinks the original Intruder stood upon different Grounds. But still He thinks that if he had attempted to turn out a Tenant who had never sold by course of Law there was a possibility if not a probability that he would have fail'd.

### Further testimony to the Memorial of Frederick Philips Esq.

James Delancey Esq—sworn. 4^th^ of Dec^r^ 1784.

The Witness's & his family have been long acquainted. Says he was uniformly loyal. He was in the Assembly of New York & he always voted for all Measures to support the Authority of G. B. Knew his Property. It was in the province of New York on Hudson's river. It was very considerable it extended 24 Miles. He says when his father died he believes he had 1000 a Y^r^ & understands that he doubled it. He never heard that he had said that Col^l^ Philips would never raise his Estates but says the Tenants understood from his Ancestors that they should never be raised. He does not consider it as an Estate in fee Simple if he did He would give £100000 for it. Says he could not turn out the Tenants but believes he could raise the Rents. Thinks he could not turn them out in a Court of Law.

### Memorial of Basil Cowper Esq.

Basil Cowper Esq—the Claimant—sworn. 27^th^ of Oct^r^ 1784.

Determin'd the 1^st^ of Nov^r^ 1784.

Is a Native of Eng^d^ & went to America in 1764. He went first as Attorney to his Uncle & at the Commencement of the troubles he was fixed at Savannah & settled for himself he enter'd into trade in 1766. He came to Eng^d^ in 1774 & went back in Dec^r^ 1774. Soon after which he was appointed a Member of Congress. He continued in it till they took the Gov^r^ & Council Prisoners. He then quitted them. He then says he went to the West Indies to get out of the troubles & returned to Georgia in 1777. He remained from 1777 to 1779 quiet

An Object of the Act of Par^t^ in Consequence of Proclamations. Did not bear Arms But bore Arms ag^t^ Great Britain.

on his plantation but he was obliged to quit the Province of Georgia & go to South Carolina. When Count D'Estaing arrived in 1779 He took an active part. He hired a person to serve as a Soldier for him & fancies he gave him about £50. He took the Oaths to the rebels in Georgia in 1778. He join'd Sir Henry Clintons Army when they came to the South. He says if he could have foreseen the Event of the War to be as it is He would have taken part with the British at the time that he did. He says that he has assigned over all his Effects & his Expectations under the Act of Par$^t$ to his Creditors in Eng$^d$ in May last & he is going to Jamaica & they have given him an Acquittance. He was in partnership with W$^m$ Telfer in an House in London during the whole time. He has no concern in this Assignment. But he has made a similar one. He went into partnership in 1774 for five Years. Says he looked upon himself in the Year 1774 to be worth £30000 S. Says that M$^r$ Telfer had very little property. Can't say what Capital he put into the trade. He allotted the whole of his property. M$^r$ Telfer's Brother is & always has been with the Americans. M$^r$ Telfer he says was likewise under a Necessity of living under the rebel Gov$^t$. There were no more Partners than he has mention'd. Admits that for near two Years all the Partners were Rebels. He was he says proscribed in 1778. He arrived in Eng$^d$ in Aug$^t$ 1783 from Jamaica. He never applied for any Allowance to Gov$^t$ & does not receive any. Being asked upon his Oath whether upon the whole he does not wish that he had taken the rebel part He says he does not. He says he is better satisfied that he has taken part with Great Britain & lost all his property than if he had taken the other side of the Question & kept his property.

Josiah Pattnall—sworn.

Is acquainted with M$^r$ Cowper knew him at the Commencement of the troubles. He always looked upon him as Loyal until he submitted to be a Member of the Congress. But he gave him reasons for going into it & he believes he was sincere tho' he confesses he would not have done it. Did not know that he took the Oaths but supposes that he must when he was a Member of the Assembly. Admits that it makes against him. Has been on his plantation. He was one of the Committee to sign the rebel Money. Says he was single in joining the Army when Gen$^l$ Prevost advised him not to do it. Can't speak particularly to M$^r$ Cowper's plantations but says that he had one or two very valuable ones.

Lieut$^t$ Gov$^r$ Graham—sworn.

Knew M$^r$ Cowper for many Years before the troubles. Thinks him a very Zealous Loyal Subject tho' he mentions some Circumstances which he says do not lessen his Opinion of his Loyalty. He was elected a Member of the Provincial Congress. But he told him at that time that he did it merely to keep the Port open & to prevent violence & he afterwards went to Jamaica. He afterw$^{ds}$ returned to his plantation & remain'd quiet. He never heard of his taking the Oaths. When Count D'Estaing came off the Coast M$^r$ Cowper came to the Lines & offer'd to take a part tho' upon parole. Gen$^l$ Prevost dissuaded him from it but he did it. After all the Circumstances of M$^r$ Cowper's says if he had known all that he now knows he should not have objected to his being put into a situation of Confidence. Knows his plantation N° in the Memorial was present when he bought it but does not know what he gave for it. Values it at 30*s*. per Acre. Believes he did not give more than £100 for it. Remembers his paying for the Land at S^t Paul thinks he paid about £100 or £150 for it. It was bought at public Sale before the rebellion. Never saw the Land. Confirms him in saying that in all the Sales which were made by the Provost Marshall he paid no Money but that if the Provost Marshall had sold them to others he would have paid the Money. Being asked his Opinion about these purchases He says he disapproves of them very highly. Says that he believes no Man who purchased Lands from 1774 forwards ever gave the full price for them but he will not say that they do not deserve some Compensation. However he thinks that they deserve no more compensation than the price they gave.

Sir James Wright Bar^t—sworn.

Has known M^r Cowper for 20 Years. He was a Merch^t & Planter. He always looked upon M^r Cowper to be a Loyalist tho' he confesses appearances are against him. Says he was a Member of the Congress which sat at Savannah. He is told that he went in from principles of Moderation & he is inclined to believe it. Never heard of his taking the Oaths. When told that he took the Oaths &c &c He says that he is stagger'd. Says that he would have bought Lands in 1781 but if he had he should not have claim'd. At least he should not more than what he gave. Says that in his Opinion Lands purchased in 1776 & in 1782 stand exactly upon the same foundation & that in no Case the purchaser of Lands since the troubles ought to claim for more than he actually gave because the Lands sold cheaper on account of the troubles.

Lewis Johnston Esq—sworn.

Knew M^r Cowper some Years before the troubles. Never had any doubt about his Loyalty. He was obliged to act a part & believes that he took the Oaths to the Rebel Gov^t. Believes he was a Member of the Rebel Congress & believes his Motives were to preserve his property. Believes he got a person to serve for him but believes many good & loyal Men have done as much. Knows nothing of any of his Lands or the value but has heard that he had made a purchase.

William Thomson—sworn.

Knew M^r Cowper very well for many Years. Always consider'd him to be as loyal a Subject as the King had tho' there are some extraordinary Circumstances. They don't alter his Opinion of him because he knew him so well. He blames his head but not his heart. He thinks it was a very foolish plan to go into their Assembly. He believes he sign'd the Paper Money has seen Paper Money sign'd by him. Does not know what he did after he quitted the Assembly. Did not know that he had taken the Oaths till today. He is one of his Creditors & the Acquittance has been sign'd by a person authorized to sign for him. Says he has so high an Opinion of him that he would have sign'd his Acquittance if he had known all the Circumstances. Knew he had a large plantation on the black Swamp but can't speak to its value.

James Butler—sworn.

Knows Mr Cowper knew him at the Commencement of the troubles & many Yrs before. Thinks him as loyal a Subject as any in the province & thought so when he was a Member of the Assembly. Says he went there with an intention to decline taking his Seat. The Witness's father was a Member of the same Assembly. Saw some paper Money sign'd by him. The Witness took the Oaths to the Americans & believes that he (Mr Cowper) did so likewise. Knew that he had purchased some Lands or his partner for him. Thinks he went into the Congress & took the Oaths to protect his property.

## Memorial of Lewis Johnston [1] Esq. Senr

Determin'd ye 1st of Novr 1784.

29th of Octr 1784.

Lewis Johnston Esq—the Claimant—sworn.

A Zealous & meritorious Loyalist.

Did not bear Arms.

Is a Native of Scotland & went first to America in 1752 & went from the West Indies to settle in 1753. He bought some land in 1752. He carried considerable property with him from the West Indies in Negroes &c. He was settled in the Year 1774 at Savannah He was then a Member of the Council having been a Member of the House of Commons from the time that he went there. When the troubles broke out he took an active part immediately & all his family. He has 4 Sons in the Army. He was one of the Council who were confined by the Rebels. Soon after this He went on board Captn Barclay's Ship with Sir Jas Wright where he remain'd six weeks. After this Govr Graham & he were permitted to return to Savannah upon an Exchange of Prisoners. He continued after this at Savannah till Coll Campbell came. The Rebels frequently offer'd him the Oaths but he constantly refused. He says he can't say that he met with any personal Insult. When Coll Campbell came he join'd him & was with the British till the Evacuation of Savannah. He never took the Oaths or made any Sacrifice of his principles to induce them to permit him to remain quiet. He says he consider'd himself all that time as a Prisoner. Upon the Evacuation of Savannah He went to settle at Augustine where he bought some property & meant to have remain'd if the Peace had not obliged him to quit. He did not choose to remain in Florida because he must have taken the Oaths to the King of Spain & changed his religion. He enter'd into an Association but never bore Arms in any other Way. He has been in Engd six Weeks & applied to the Treasury & has an Allowance of £180 a Yr from the Treasury.

Bounty £180 a Yr.

Office of Treasurer. He was appointed in 1775. The Appointment produced dated the 7th of Novr. Says the place had been promised to him many Years & had no connection with the troubles. He values it at £500 tho' he says he only made £400 a Yr & he made the £400 a Yr after the reestablishment of the King's Govt. Has heard that his Predecessor made 100 a Yr by it.

Disallowed.

Profits of his profession he states to be at least £800 a Yr for 3 Yrs before the troubles. He had a Partner. And states the Profit in the whole to be £1600 a Yr. Says he meant to have given up the profession of Physic if the office of Treasurer had turned out as well to him as his Predecessor.

Profession £700 a Yr.

[1] Sabine, op. cit., vol. i, p. 589, writes: 'Johnston, Lewis, Residence unknown.'

Lieut[t] Gov[r] Graham—sworn.

Says to the Question asked of him yesterday that he thinks all those Loyalists who have purchased since the troubles should be allowed to charge the Sum given & no more.

Knew M[r] Johnston has known him for 30 Years. He was for several Years a Member of each Assembly. He has been uniformly loyal & a very deserving Man. All his family were loyal. He had four Sons in the Army & one of them was killed in the field. No Man was more Zealous in support of the King's Gov[t] but he does not know that he ever did any particular services. He was made Treasurer of the province in 1775. Thinks it would have been given to him if there had been no troubles. He was Partner with M[r] Wylly. And they fail'd several Years before the troubles. Did not look upon him to be a very rich Man in 1774. He & Wylly made an Assignment to Greenwood & Higginson of all their Effects. Has seen M[r] Johnston's Memorial & says there is no property in that which was assigned to Greenwood & Higginson.

**Memorial of George Johnston**

Determin'd the 5[th] of Nov[r] 1784.

George Johnston—the Claimant—sworn. 2[d] of Nov[r] 1784.

Is a Native of Ireland & went to America when he was a Child. He went first to Philadelphia. But at the Commencement of the troubles He lived in Georgia. He join'd Gen[l] Campbell when he came into that Country in 1779. He took no part before. Says he never sign'd any Association or took any Oath. When he got Col[l] Campbells protection they took him prisoner. Says he was in the siege of Savannah. Says the Americans burnt his House because he was serving with the British. He was in the Militia. At the Evacuation of Savannah He went to S[t] Augustine from whence he is lately come to Eng[d]. He has applied to the Treasury lately & receives an Allowance of £20 a Y[r] from the Treasury from the 5[th] of July 1784. It was reported in the Alternative either £20 a Y[r] or £20 [1] in full & he chose the Allowance annually.

A Loyalist.
Did not bear Arms.
Bounty £20 a Y[r].

David Marrin—sworn.

The Witness was in Georgia during the War & before it. He knew George Johnston there before the rebellion. He lived at the Distance of 12 Miles. Says he heard a flying report that he had join'd with the Rebels at first. Does not know that he ever took an Oath. He heard that he had a Mill & a Still & two tracts of Land but he has seen one tract of his. Does not know the Value of the Mill but it was said to be a good Mill. He can't tell whether his property was taken from him or not.

Sam[l] Montgomery—sworn.

Knew George Johnston. Never heard of his taking any Oath. Has seen him in the Royal Army. He acted in the siege of Savannah with him. He understood him to be a Man of property. He says he never knew him till he join'd Col[l] Campbell. Has seen his Mill & his Still & has been in his House he lived well. He can't speak particularly to the Value of the Land or any part of his property. The Witness took an Oath to the Americans but never heard

[1] *Sic* in Text. ? £200.

that the Claimant did. When Col[l] Maitland[1] went to Georgia the Claimant join'd him. Has seen a good Waggon & Horses belonging to the Claimant.

Determin'd the 5[th] of Nov[r] 1784.

### Memorial of Will[m] Arter

Will[m] Arter—the Claimant—sworn. 2[d] of Nov[r] 1784.

A Loyalist.

Bore Arms.

Bounty £25 in full.

Is a Native of Ireland & went to America in 1773 to Charlestown. He carried no property with him. In 1775 He was settled near Ninety Six. He did not join the British till 1779. He says he never join'd the Americans for which reason he was banished. Says the Oath was frequently tender'd to him but he always refused & he was frequently fined. He join'd Col[l] Campbell in 1779 & staid afterwards constantly with the Army. He staid till the Evacuation of Charlestown & then came home. He applied to the Treasury some time ago & was reported to have the Sum of £25 in full. But he has never rec[d] it.

Determin'd y[e] 5[th] of Nov[r] 1784.

### Memorial of Tho[s] Hutchinson

Thomas Hutchinson—the Claimant—sworn. 2[d] of Nov[r] 1784.

A Loyalist.

Did not bear Arms.

Is a Native of Ireland & went to America in 1773. He carried some Cloaths tools &c & paid his own passage. In 1775 He was settled near Ninety Six. He join'd the Loyalists in that Year & was in Action ag[t] them at Ninety Six. He never pretended to be a friend to them. They tender'd an Oath to him but he never took it. He went to the Musters & promised to fight for them but never bore Arms for them in his Life. He was frequently ill used & imprison'd because he would not take up Arms. He served with the British Army till the Evacuation of Charlestown but he was not a military Man.

Will[m] Arter—sworn.

Knew Tho[s] Hutchinson in America. He was a Loyalist & bore that Character. He was a Carpenter & rode about the Country. He had 4 Horses to his positive knowledge at one time. He knew a place which he called his but he does not know whether it was his or not. He has heard it reported to be his & he had some writing for it. Knows of no more of his property. There was no clearance upon it & he knows nothing of the Value.

Col[l] Zacharias Gibbs—sworn. 3[d] of Nov[r] 1784.

Did not know Tho[s] Hutchinson till 1779. Knows nothing of his property. He was in two Engagements with the Witness & behaved well. Thinks him a very good & loyal Subject.

Determin'd the 5[th] of Nov[r] 1784.

### Memorial of Capt[n] John Mills

John Mills—the Claimant—sworn. 3[d] of Nov[r] 1784.

A Loyalist.

Is a Native of Scotland & went to America in 1766 & settled as a Timber Merch[t]. When the troubles commenced he resided in Savannah. The first Step he took in

[1] Major John Maitland of the Marines became lieutenant-colonel of the 71st Regiment at the end of 1778. He commanded at Stono Ferry in July 1779, and repulsed an attack made by the Americans. ('He acted very much like himself,' wrote Sir H. Clinton (*Hist. MSS. Comm., Am. MSS. in R. Inst.*, vol. i, pp. 172–3; vol. ii, p. 28). He died at Savannah in November 1779, 'much & justly regretted' (ibid., p. 59).

the rebellion was to sign a protest ag$^{t}$ one of the first measures this he thinks was in 1774. He was obliged to take refuge on board a Man of War in March 1776 from that time to the end of the War he continued in the Navy as a coasting Pilot. His pay was 5*s*. a Day. He has no Allowance from Gov$^{t}$. He arrived in Eng$^{d}$ the latter end of April last.

Bore Arms.

No proof of Confiscation.

## Memorial of James Butler [1]

Determin'd y$^{e}$ 22$^{d}$ of Nov$^{r}$ 1784.

James Butler—the Claimant—sworn. 3$^{d}$ of Nov$^{r}$ 1784.

must be consider'd A Loyalist.

Took the Oaths to the Rebels & served in the Assembly in 1778. Did not bear Arms.

Is a Native of America was born in South Carolina. At the Commencement of the troubles he resided in the province of Georgia as a Planter on Great Ogeeche river. On the commencement of the troubles he took part with Great Britain but was persuaded by his friends in 1776 to take the Oath to the Rebels. They imprison'd him in May 1776 but let him out in a Day or two upon parole. He then went home & his friends persuaded him to take the Oaths. He has since taken them before Col$^{l}$ Innes & when he took them to Col$^{l}$ Innes He was fully persuaded that Great Britain would succeed. After he took the Oaths the Rebels called upon him to bear Arms but he paid £100 fine sooner than do it. After he had taken the Oaths to Col$^{l}$ Innes He did all he could to serve Great Britain. Says he join'd Col$^{l}$ Campbell as soon as he had taken Savannah & admits that if Col$^{l}$ Campbell had been beat off he should not have join'd him. Says he did not come in Consequence of any proclamation. He came to Eng$^{d}$ in Aug$^{t}$ last. He has no Allowance from Gov$^{t}$. His Agents applied to the Treasury for the payment of Money for Rice destroy'd &c. And the Report was that that was not the Object of the Enquiry at Whitehall. When he went to take the Oaths for Col$^{l}$ Campbell Georgia was not quite reduced.

He was a Member of the Rebel Assembly in the Y$^{r}$ 1778.

Sir James Wright Bar$^{t}$—sworn.

Has known M$^{r}$ Butler for 20 Years. He was a very Substantial Man. He was a Man of very good Character & he consider'd him as a Man of very good Substance before the troubles. He knows nothing of what he did when he was absent from 1776 to 1779 but he has heard yesterday that he took the Oath to the Rebels. He says however that he believes him well attached to the British Gov$^{t}$ & he knows that the Rebels never consider'd him as of their Party. He has a general knowledge of the family & the property. Believes the elder Brother was not disinherited from any party Motives.

Lieut$^{t}$ Gov$^{r}$ Graham—sworn.

Has known James Butler for many Years before the troubles. He has heard that he was under the Necessity of taking the Oaths. He found him at Savannah when he went back. From the time of his Arrival to the Evacuation no Man could be more Zealous. He served in the Lines. He can't speak to his Loyalty before 1776. Rather supposes he must have temporized. Knows two plantations of his at Ogechie. Has not been upon them since 1774 or 1775. They were very fine plantations. He never saw better back Swamp. He says he & his father were both the best Planters in the Country. Does not know what Quantity was clear'd. He

[1] *b*. 1738, *d*. 1817.

was deem'd a very rich Man & owed nothing. Values the Rice Land at £5 or £6 S. per Acre. Can't say how much provision Land values it at 50*s*. or 55*s*. Unclear'd Swamp from £3 to £3 10*s*. per Acre. He had a considerable Number of Negroes but does not know how many. Knows nothing more of his Landed property. His farm appear'd to be well stocked. Remembers a Dispute between this Man & his elder Brother but believes it was determined in favour of this Man.

### Memorial of Patrick Reid

Determin'd the 5th of Novr 1784.

A British Subject.

And appears to have lost a property under the Prohibitory Act.

The Board are of Opinion he was acquainted with the Provisions of it & that he has been very fortunate in having been allowed the Sum he states by the Award of the Arbitrators.

5th of Novr 1784.

Patrick Reid—the Claimant—sworn.

Is a Native of Scotland & went to America in the fall of 1775 as a Mercht & part Owner of the Cargo of the Ship Crawford. He carried out goods of different sorts & went out on Speculation & for his own advantage. That Ship came safe to Boston where he staid till the Evacuation & went to Halifax. Since which time he has been a Mercht attending the Army during the whole War. In 1777 a Ship of his called Sir Wm Erskine was taken under the Prohibitory Act between Boston & New York. She sail'd from Clyde for New York but she was clear'd out for Halifax excepting Provisions for the Army which were clear'd out for New York. He was not on Board. He was at New York. He did know of the Prohibitory Act but had never read it or known the provisions of it. He admits that he knew & that his Agent knew that if these Goods were clear'd out for New York they would have been the Subjects of Capture. The Goods on board of this Ship were at first Cost £9378 17*s*. 8*d*. He had one fourth of this Vessel the Loss upon which including Interest upon the whole Ship is £5348 2*s*. & without Interest £4456 15*s*. Three other persons were jointly Owners with him therefore his share of the Loss is about £1200. Being asked whether in the Voyages which he made antecedent to this he did not clear as much he says he cannot answer that Question. The Vessel was taken by an American Privateer in Octr 1777 & was retaken by the Ambuscade. She was then carried into Halifax & libel'd & condemn'd excepting such Goods as were included in the Licence which made about one fifth of the burthen of the Ship. After she was condemned he appeal'd at Halifax & sentence was given agt him. He then came over to Engd to appeal here & finding a Difficulty & meeting with Captn Macartney it was referr'd to Arbitration & he got back one half. He never made any Claim agt Govt until the fall of 1783 when he applied to the Treasury & they referr'd the Application to this Board. He is a Mercht now & he looks upon himself to be a Loser by the whole of his Concerns during the American War. He has been in America before the troubles but never lived in it before 1775.

### Memorial of Patrick Reid on behalf of his Brother Thos Reid who is now disorder'd in his Mind

Determin'd the 5th of Novr 1784.

A Loyalist.

Did not bear Arms.

5th of Novr 1784.

Patrick Reid—Brother of the Claimant—sworn.

Says his Brother is now disorder'd in his Mind. He was in the Mercantile Line born in Scotland & lived the greatest part of his Life in America. When the troubles broke out he lived at Richmond in Virginia. He came home in Decr 1775. He always understood that he was well attached to Great Britain & believes him to have been loyal. When he quitted Virginia He left an Agent who collected part of his Debts in the best way he could & vested it for him in the legal paper Money of the province of Virginia. He (the Witness) has the Money in his own Custody & it amounts to £1782 0*s.* 3*d.* C. or in Ster^g £1425 12*s.* 2½*d.* His Brother never went back to America afterwards. He believes he must have owed some Debts in America & does not know whether they are paid or not. His agent was compell'd to take the Congress Paper & he thought it prudent to exchange it for this Money thinking it better because he thought Great Britain would prevail in the end. Certificate produced from two Surgeons at Musselburgh to his Brother's Lunacy.

Disallowed. The Money being taken voluntarily & he might have parted with it.

## Memorial of Isaac Du Bois

Isaac Du Bois—the Claimant—sworn. 5th of Nov^r 1784.

Determin'd the 5th of Nov^r 1784.

Is a Native of Wilmington in North Carolina. He iv ed there at the Commencement of the troubles & was not above 13 Y^rs of Age. He never in his Life took any part with the Americans but in the Y^r 1780 He was instrumental in releasing a Spy & went to Charlestown. He was requested by Col^l Balfour to leave Charlestown & go to a Detachment of the Kings Troops at Wilmington & in Nov^r 1781 He had a Commission of Ensign in the New York Volunteers in consequence of the recommendation of Col^l Craig. He served in South Carolina till the Evacuation then went to New York till Sept^r 1783 & then was sent to Nova Scotia where the Reg^t was disbanded in Oct^r 1783 & he is now on Half pay as a Lieut^t. He made an Application to the Treasury for temporary Support but receives no Allowance.

A Loyalist And bore Arms.

## Memorial of Benj^n Gridley [1] Esq.

Benj^n Gridley Esq—the Claimant—sworn. 6th of Nov^r 1784.

Determin'd the 8th of Nov^r 1784.

Is a Native of Boston & resided there at the Commencement of the troubles. He was a barrister. He was a Magistrate & was active & imprison'd a rebel Officer in 1774. Was courted by the Rebels but refused their Offers with disdain. He left Boston at the Evacuation & went to Halifax & from thence to Eng^d in 1776. He applied to the Treasury & in a short time obtain'd an Allowance of £150 a Y^r which is continued to him.

Produces a Commission as a Magistrate dated in 1774 & a Commission as a Judge of the Court of Common Pleas dated in 1775.

He made very little by his profession in 1772 & 1773.

He owes Money in America but he thinks not so much as is due to him.

Says he was a Volunteer at Boston & likewise afterwards a Volunteer of an American Corps in Eng^d under Sir W^m Pepperell.

He had no Salary as a Judge of the Court of Common Pleas.

A Zealous & active Loyalist & in the spirited execution of his Duty as a Magistrate render'd services to Gov^t. Bounty £150 a Y^r. Did not bear Arms.

No professional Loss.

Capt^n George Dymond—sworn.

He commanded a Custom House armed Vessel station'd at Boston in 1774.

[1] He signed the address of the merchants and others of Boston to Governor Hutchinson, May 30, 1774; the address of the barristers and attorneys of the same date, and the loyal address from the gentlemen and principal inhabitants of Boston to Governor Gage on his departure for England, October 6, 1775. Gridley went to Halifax with the British in March 1776. His name occurs in the Massachusetts Banishment Act of 1778.

He knew Mr Gridley then & for many Years before. His Conduct was always that of a loyal Subject. From the time of the Troops arriving there He was the only Magistrate who would act & he has known Instances of his having acted when others would not.

Says Mr Gridley was possess'd of his fathers Estate which was a large Brick House but he did not live in the House in 1774. Understands that it was mortgaged. There was a Rope Walk adjoining to the House & Negroes belonging to the Estate. He never looked upon him to be a rich Man. He lived in a small House in 1774 & believes the furniture was his own. He had a very good Library. Knows that Mr Gridley had made himself very obnoxious to the people by the active part he took.

Says he had lost his business in Consequence of the violence of the times & that he was getting nothing in his profession in 1774.

**Memorial of Robt Beard**

Determin'd the 8th of Novr 1784.

Not an Object of the Act of Part therefore the whole of his Claim disallowed.

6th of Novr 1784.

Robert Beard—the Claimant—sworn.

Is a Native of London & went to America in 1766 to Charlestown as a Tradesman. He carried Materials for his business but nothing else. In 1774 He was living at Charlestown in 1774 & lived there till Sir Henry Clinton came there. He took the Oaths of Allegiance to the Rebels because he could not settle his Affairs. He refused the Oath for three or four times & then took it. He was upon guard at different times in the Town but he went into the Country during the siege & when Sir Henry Clinton came to Charlestown he came & offer'd himself to the British. He had before paid a Substitute to fight against the British. He has taken no Oath since he took that to the United States. But he does not consider himself as a Subject of the united States of America. He applied to the Treasury & has recd an Allowance of £40 a Yr from the 1st of Jany 1784. It appears by one of the American Acts that he is restored to his Estate by name. He is asked now whether he means to insist upon his Claim.

Bounty £40 a Yr. ye 8th of Novr a Letter sent to ye Lords of the Treasury to discontinue his Allowance.

He now claims 12 per Cent Loss only upon the property.

Doctor Garden—sworn.

Says Robt Beard was known to him in America. He knew him in 1775 & 1776. He esteem'd him as a loyal Subject of America. He lived next Door to him for two Yrs before the Town was taken. He was an exceeding good Man & Workman. Says the Rebels would not let him go because he was essentially necessary. He has lost his property under the Confiscation Law. Does not know whether it will be restored or not. Says he never gave him Advice to claim for the whole of his Losses. Thinks no Claim should be made for property restored from Confiscation but where the property had been sold. He thinks otherwise because he says they charge 12½ per Cent upon it & then pay in certain papers called Indents which are not worth above £12 per Cent & says that all Expences being deducted instead of gaining he would be a Loser of 2 per Cent. The property if specifically restored is so much more valuable that it will extremely well bear a Deduction of 12 per Cent. Knows the House in which he lived next Door to him & thinks it wd have sold for £1000 or £1200 in 1774 or 1775.

Thomas Harper—sworn.

Knew M^r^ Beard since the Year 1767. The Witness quitted Charlestown sooner than take the Oath. He always consider'd him as a loyal Subject. Says he believes he was persuaded by his Wife who was an American. When he came away in 1778 He thinks he was not able to come away.

Says he looked upon the Claimant as a Loyalist. He applied to him to come away when he did but he could not get a Passage in the Ship. He certainly looks upon himself as a better Subject than the Claimant.

When he came away himself He believes the Claimant had not a Sufficiency to render himself any ways comfortable at home which is the reason he believes that he staid.

### Memorial of James Devereux

Determin'd the 8th of Nov^r^ 1784.

8th of Nov^r^ 1784.

James Devereux—the Claimant—sworn.

Is a Native of Ireland & went first to America in 1744 as Mate of a Vessel. He was afterwards Master of a Vessel. He was settled at New York at the Commencement of the rebellion. He has lived there since 1744. When the troubles broke out he had many Offers from them but he refused them. They never tender'd any Oaths to him & he never sign'd any Association with them in Consequence of his refusal they threaten'd him. He then went to the West Indies & in his return was taken & carried into Boston. When he returned to New York He took his turn of Duty. He was kept a prisoner 8 Months. He came from America about 4 Years ago & having some Money of his own he never applied to the Treasury for any temporary support & receives no Allowance from Gov^t^.

A Loyalist. Did not bear Arms.

Rev^d^ D^r^ Inglis—sworn.

Knew M^r^ Devereux at New York before & after the troubles. Believes him to have been perfectly loyal. Understood that the Americans made great offers to him & that he refused them. He was comfortably settled there & was esteem'd to be a Man of property. He understood that before the troubles he had considerable Sums at Interest & believes he had left off going to Sea before the troubles. He was the first Man who gave notice to the Witness that New York was set on fire by the Rebels & he proved it to him.

Rev^d^ John Vardill—sworn.

Knew him at New York & says he left it in 1774 & therefore can only speak to his Loyalty by reputation. Mentions a transaction to shew his Loyalty which proves him to be a Scoundrel.

### Memorial of Will^m^ Snow

Determin'd the 8th of Nov^r^ 1784.

8th of Nov^r^ 1784.

Will^m^ Snow—the Claimant—sworn.

The Claimant is a Mulatto & a Protestant. Born in Charlestown. Lived there at the Commencement of the troubles. He was a Taylor & lived in an House of M^r^ Simpson's. They tender'd the Oaths to him but he refused to take them. Admits that he sign'd the Association. He was summon'd to turn out & he refused to muster. They sent a file of Men for him. He ran away & lived in the Country till Charlestown was taken. Says he lived in the Country many Years & that his

A Loyalist. Did not bear Arms.

property was obliged to pay for a Substitute. Admits that he made 500 Suits of Clothes for the rebels. He took the Oaths to us after the Capture of Charlestown. When he join'd the British he thought that Great Britain would succeed. Says that Lord Cornwallis advised him to apply to Whitehall & he did accordingly & obtain'd an Allowance of £10 a Y[r] from the 5[th] of Oct[r] 1782.

Bounty £10 a Y[r].

Property.

Disallowed for want of Evidence.

He charges a Loss of £280 for Cattle &c but admits that he had none of them when he first ran away. Says he got the Money from the rebels with which he bought the Cattle.

James Simpson Esq—sworn.

He knows the Claimant. His Wife was a Serv[t] in the Claimant's family. Knows nothing of his property & says that in the beginning of the Dispute the Americans would not have employed any person of his Complexion. Says he was a Taylor & an industrious Man. Does not know the reason of his leaving Charlestown. Says he believes he had some little Money & knows that he brought some over with him As he had some trouble to obtain Money for a Bill which he brought over with him drawn upon Harley & Drummond. This Bill was for more than £60. M[r] Simpson being asked whether the Circumstance of his being employ'd by the Rebels as a Taylor is not a proof of his being in their Cause He says that will depend upon his working by Compulsion or otherwise.

Determin'd the 9[th] of Nov[r] 1784.

## Memorial of the Rev[d] John Vardell[1]

9[th] of Nov[r] 1784.

The Rev[d] John Vardell—the Claimant—sworn.

A Zealous Loyalist & render'd Services to the British Gov[t] by his publications. Did not bear Arms.

Is a Native of New York. At the time the rebellion broke out he was settled at New York. He came to Eng[d] for Orders in 1774. He was then Professor of Natural Philosophy & had a promise of being made Regius Professor of Divinity after he returned. They destroy'd the Tea before he left America. It had not arrived at New York but it was expected & there was great Opposition to it upon which he wrote a series of Letters under the signature of Publicola. Produces some of these papers. He was known to be the Author. He wrote many other papers in support of Gov[t] & several Songs which had a great Effect. When he came to Eng[d] in 1774

[1] Letters under the signature of 'Poplicola', presumably the ones referred to, appeared in *Rivington's Gazetteer* of November 18, 1773, and subsequent dates. 'While we are watchful,' the author wrote, 'against external attacks on our freedom, let us be on our guard lest we become enslaved by dangerous tyrants within.' Again: 'To draw a line with precision between our liberty and dependency is almost impossible. The nature of civil society requires that there shall be somewhere in every state a governing and uncontrollable authority. While our local circumstances prevent our being completely represented in the Grand Council of the nation . . . a lasting union can only be obtained by preserving our common interest in view, and by a generous and liberal confidence in each other. Jealousy in the one will beget jealousy in the other.' Once more: 'Examine the conduct of the men who would revive our fatal dissensions. . . . Their positions have already proved subversive of liberty, their measures introductive of the most injurious tyranny.' Trumbull, the American satiric poet, wrote in *McFingal* (Philadelphia, 1775):

'In Vardell that poetic zealot
I view a lawn-bedizened prelate.'

Tyler, op. cit., has little about Vardell. Indeed he writes (vol. ii, p. 80): 'It is chiefly by the bitter allusions made by the revolutionist writers . . . that we now know of the existence in those days of such masters of political sarcasm as . . . Vardell.'

He never returned. He was elected in 1775 Assistant Minister at New York with a prospect of succeeding to D$^{r}$ Inglis. He staid in this Country at the request of Lord North & Lord Dartmouth & furnished information in the American War & wrote many papers. Admits that he was rewarded for it. Says that he was appointed Regius Professor & has the Warrant to produce tho' it was never made out. It was intended to be established as a reward for the Loyalty of the persons of the College. Says he performed all the Services stated in the Memorial.

He applied to the Treasury & has rec$^{d}$ from the Year 1774 an Allowance of £200 a Y$^{r}$ which he now continues to receive.

Bounty £200 a Y$^{r}$.

Produces a testimonial from the College of New York for Ordination & a Certificate from Gov$^{r}$ Tryon to his general Loyalty & to his writing in favor of Gov$^{t}$ & one from Col$^{l}$ Fanning & from D$^{r}$ Chandler (D$^{r}$ Chandler being to attend as a Witness it is not read) & likewise from D$^{r}$ Cooper. Produces a Letter from M$^{r}$ Eden speaking of his Loyalty & services & a very confidential Letter from M$^{r}$ Jenkinson & proof that he was the Author of Coriolanus.[1] The Warrant of Professorship produced.

Losses.

Professorship of Moral Philosophy refers to the Testimonial & the Witnesses. He acted gratuitously as Professor for four or five Years. This he states as a Loss of 100 a Y$^{r}$ because he says he should have had that Salary. The next Loss is Assistant Preacher & Lecturer. Two other persons were appointed with him the Vestry elected him but they permitted him to stay here & indeed there was no Necessity for his attending as Trinity Church was burnt down. He says he never rec$^{d}$ any Money from this. States next the Loss of the Regius Professorship & produces his Warrant of Appointment sign'd by the King & countersign'd by Lord George Germaine.

£100 a Y$^{r}$.

£200 a Y$^{r}$.

Disallowed.

He now receives £200 a Y$^{r}$. But he says he formerly rec$^{d}$ £400 & that he rec$^{d}$ £500 on the 15$^{th}$ of Nov$^{r}$ 1780 for the Arrears of his Salary as Professor of Divinity.

Former Bounty £400 a Y$^{r}$.
Present Bounty £200 a Y$^{r}$.

He makes no Claim for any property. He has no Debts due to him. And he owes nothing in America.

Rev$^{d}$ D$^{r}$ Inglis—sworn.

Knew M$^{r}$ Vardell when the troubles broke out. He took a very decided part on the side of Gov$^{t}$. He believes he thereby render'd Services to Gov$^{t}$ & thinks his publications were of use to Gov$^{t}$. Mentions the paper Publicola & several other papers. Knows likewise that he wrote papers in this Country because he transmitted them to him. For some time he was Professor of Moral Philosophy & Nat$^{l}$ Law. They fully intended to give him a Salary when he came back. D$^{r}$ Inglis was one of the Gov$^{rs}$ of the College. In Nov$^{r}$ or Dec$^{r}$ 1774 He was chosen Assistant Minister with a Salary of 400 a Y$^{r}$ Currency. They had drawn up a new Charter which was never confirmed. It was intended to establish such a Professorship under the new Charter. But no such Office in fact ever existed. M$^{r}$ Vardell's father is alive & was a Loyalist & is a Man of some property in that Country. The Claim$^{t}$ was uniformly & steadily loyal.

[1] The pamphlet *Coriolanus*, published in 1782, is ascribed in the British Museum Catalogue to Joseph Cawthorn.

Dr Chandler—sworn.

Knew Mr Vardell very well at New York in 1773 & 1774. When the Disputes broke out He was a very active Man on the side of Govt. He was the Author of many papers in support of Govt. He was Professor of Moral Philosophy & Natl Law but as he was not of the College He can't speak very particularly to it. He was chosen Assistant Minister in 1774. He says he wrote the paper Coriolanus after he came to this Country.

John Wetherhead—sworn.

Late of New York where he knew Mr Vardell. He was uniformly loyal. He says he can only adduce as instances of Loyalty certain little pieces which he published. And believes they were of service to Govt.

James Devereux Junr—sworn.

He was acquainted with Mr Vardill at New York. He was Professor & Tutor. The Witness was a Pupil of his. Mentions several publications that he published at New York which made him very obnoxious.

John Clarke—sworn.

Knew Mr Vardell only in Engd. The Witness lives in Chancery Lane & was then Secretary to the Maritime School at Chelsea. Says that Vardill at that time made many publications as he believes & produces a Pamphlet which he published for the benefit of the Maritime School. He recd it from Mr Vardill in Manuscript. He is acquainted with some of the Examiners & went with them to Mr Christie. Mr Vardill meant at that time to publish the prevailing Opinions of the times in the Morning Post for which purpose he wished to have a Share in the paper. The tendency of the Pamphlet which the Witness produced was to check the Spirit of Rebellion & the title of it is Unity & Public Spirit recommended in an Address to the Inhabitants of London & Westminster to which were added Two Odes—viz—the Miseries of Dissention & Civil War & the true Patriot.

Determin'd ye 23d of Novr 1784.

## Memorial of John Taylor

John Taylor—the Claimant—sworn. 10th of Novr 1784.

A Loyalist.

Did not bear Arms.

Is a Native of Yorkshire & went first to America in 1768. When the troubles commenced he was settled at Branford in Connecticut in the Mercantile Line. He carried out about £1000. He uniformly took the part of Great Britain. He was a Master of a Vessel in the Yr 1780 & order'd by Admiral Graves to make Observation in the Yr 1780 or 1781. In 1778 or 1779 He went on board the Isis as a Volunteer. The first thing he did was bearing Arms in the three rivers as a Volunteer where he had a skirmish. In 1775 early before the battle of Lexington He went to Canada in order to go to the West Indies. He staid in Canada a Yr & ½ & in 1776 He was in this Engagement at the Three Rivers with Canadian rebels (He appears very inconsistent in his Acct). He went to the West Indies in 1776 & staid till 1778. He came from the West Indies to New York in 1777 & staid there till 1778 when he went on board the Isis then He went on board the Monmouth for two Months then he bought a Vessel & went to the West Indies as a Trader. He was taken in his own Ship in 1779 & lost it. He was put into Gaol at Philadelphia. He then bought another

Vessel & was taken again by the Iphigine & carried into Martinique. He then came back & staid at New York till he was sent out upon this Observation by Adm^l Graves.[1] He then came back after 8 Weeks to New York & staid there until he went with Col^l Philips to Virginia. He had another Vessel of his own & Cargo. He afterwards went to York Town & served as a Volunteer at York Town & from that he came to Eng^d. He had a Store at York Town. He says he never rec^d a farthing from the Isis. He speculated & went a privateering during the whole war. His Wife came to Philadelphia in 1777. Says that part of his property is confiscated but does not know whether the whole is confiscated. He applied to the Treasury & obtain'd an Allowance of £50 a Y^r which was given to him from April 1783 & he now continues to receive it. Bounty £50 a Y^r.

He never took any Oath to the Rebels or sign'd any Association.

### Memorial of John Cumming [2]

Determin'd the 23^d of Nov^r 1784.

John Cumming—the Claimant—sworn. 10^th of Nov^r 1784.

Is a Native of Scotland & went first to America in May 1774. He settled at Katskill in the County of Albany. He carried over above 200 persons with him. He carried out in Money & goods about £4000. He bought Land immediately. He advised all those who went with him to take part with Gov^t. He never did anything to support the Rebel Cause. He never bore Arms. He came from New York in 1780. He was taken up & imprison'd at Æsopus about six Months & then he escaped. He was imprison'd again at Albany. When he came to Eng^d in 1780 He applied to the Treasury & he rec^d no Answer for two Years but M^r Wilmot & M^r Coke reported an Allowance of £60 a Y^r from the beginning of the Y^r 1783. And he now continues to receive it.

A Loyalist.
Did not bear Arms.
Bounty £60 a Y^r.

Lachlin M^cIntosh—sworn.

Knew M^r Cumming first in 1777. He saw him at Albany. He was remarkably loyal. He saw him afterwards in Gaol at Æsopus where he was imprison'd for his Loyalty. Knows nothing of his property but he was reputed to be a Man of property. He adhered to his Loyalty amidst his Sufferings.

Alexander Cumming—sworn.

He is Brother to M^r John Cumming remembers his going to America in 1774. He was then in business with the Witness. He did not go out by the Advice of the Witness. He did not consider America as being in rebellion at that time. He believes he carried out with him about £4000. Upwards of £2000 was the property of the Claimant & he lent him the remainder of the Money. He says that he began to draw upon him very soon after he went. He has at different times drawn upon him for about £1800. He does not know whether his Land was cultivated or not. He says that great part of the Money which he carried with him was spent in supporting the people who went out with him & that the Money paid for the Land was the smallest part of the Expence.

[1] Samuel Graves, *b.* 1713, *d.* 1787. Is in *Dict. of Nat. Biography.*
[2] See Additional Notes, p. 279.

## Memorial of D^r Nath^l Perkins [1]

Determin'd the 11^th of Nov^r 1784.

11^th of Nov^r 1784.

Doct^r Nath^l Perkins—the Claimant—sworn.

Is a Native of Boston & lived there as a Physician from the Y^r 1740 to 1776. When the troubles broke out he took a decided part with the British. He quitted Boston with the Troops in 1776. He thought it was necessary to do so because he applied to the select Men & they would not permit him to stay. He went to Halifax & came to London in Aug^t 1776. He applied to Gov^t & rec^d an Allowance of £150 a Y^r from the 5^th of Jan^y 1777 & he continues to receive it. The Treasury besides gave him £100 which he understood to be to defray the Expences of his Passage.

A Loyalist.

Did not bear Arms.

Produces no Certificates.

Loss of Profession £600 a Y^r.

Claims for the Loss of his Profession only. He chooses to rate his practice low & he states the profits of his profession at 600 a Y^r in the Town of Boston. He had likewise other practice in the Neighboring places & puts it at 100 a Y^r.

He owed no Money in America.

Debts £200.

Says a great deal of Money is due to him in America at least £2000 C. But his Books being lost he cannot be particular.

Says that his furniture & Plate were saved by the intervention of friends & therefore he makes no Claim for them.

He is not banished that he knows of & believes that his Name is not in any Act of Attainder.

Sir Will^m Pepperell Bar^t—sworn.

Knew D^r Perkins for many Y^rs. He always understood him to be perfectly loyal. He was the most eminent Physician in the province but does not know what he gain'd by his practice.

Doct^r Jeffries—sworn.

Knew D^r Perkins. He practis'd as a Physician only. He looked upon him to be the first Physician of the place. And he always thought that he made 6 or £700 a Y^r. The Witness practis'd Physic himself & the fee for a Visit to a Patient was 3*s*. & if another was called in then the fee was 6*s*. & He says that D^r Perkins had a great deal of that sort of business. He says that D^r Perkins did not practise Surgery but that he sold Medicines.

## Memorial of Tho^s Stringer

11^th of Nov^r 1784.

Tho^s Stringer—the Claimant—sworn.

Is a Native of Ireland & went to America in 1772. He was in the mercantile Line. But he bore arms for Great Britain at Savannah. He never sign'd any Association or took any Oaths to the Rebel Gov^t. He left Savannah in feb^y 1776 went to Halifax then to the West Indies & then to Eng^d. He has been principally concern'd in privateering since & since the peace he has been in Eng^d. He had a Partner in trade but he is dead.

[1] The Massachusetts Banishment Act, which speaks of William Lee Perkins, physician, and Nathaniel Perkins, Esq., would seem to have described the latter incorrectly.

## Further testimony of the Memorial of Tho$^{s}$ Stringer

Governor Tryon—sworn. 3$^{d}$ of March 1785.

He was Gov$^{r}$ of North Carolina from 1764 to 1771. And during that time he built the House for the Gov$^{r}$ in the Town of Newbern. He did it under an Act of Assembly pass'd in 1766 which he produces. And the Assembly voted £5000 C. to build it. And the Assembly gave £10000 more in 1768 which compleated it. The two Acts read by which power was given to him to buy & fix upon any Lots in any part of the Town of Newbern which he chose. This pass'd in 1766 & then an Act passed to vest these Lots in the Governor. The second Act states that the title to some of these Lots was in persons absent Infants &c & therefore directs a Jury to be appointed to value such Lots & assess the Sums to be paid to the persons to whom such Lots did belong. The Money was accordingly lodged with the Treasurer to pay to all those who are entitled. Does not know whether the whole has been paid. Has heard the name of Stringer & has heard of D$^{r}$ Stringer. Can't speak with certainty whether the Stringer family ever made any claim for these Lots nor does he recollect any of the Claims by whom they were made.

The Board upon hearing these Witnesses were clearly of Opinion that M$^{r}$ Stringer ought to be reported to the Treasury as falling within the Clause of a fraudulent Claim & that he be also reported as guilty of wilful & corrupt Perjury.

Lewis De Rosset Esq—sworn.

Remembers the Stringer family & particularly D$^{r}$ Stringer. Believes he died in 1751 or 1752. Does not know whether he had any of the Lots in the Town of Newbern. He left two Daughters. Does not know whether he made any Will. Remembers the Act of Assembly pass'd in 1766 to build a Gov$^{t}$ House & remembers a second Act pass'd to quiet the province in the possession of these Lots. Never heard of M$^{r}$ Stringers putting in any Claim & he the Witness staid in the province till 1779. Never heard of any Action brought ag$^{t}$ Gov$^{t}$ Martin. He says he is sure that he died in 1751 or 1752 because he succeeded him in his Reg$^{t}$ in 1753 or 1754.

Rob$^{t}$ Palmer—sworn.

He went to North Carolina in 1753 when D$^{r}$ Stringer was dead & he saw the Widow in 1754. Does not know that he made a Will there was one Daughter. Knows the Ground on which the Gov$^{t}$ House was built. Remembers Mackil Vane who married a Daughter of D$^{r}$ Stringer & that he had a Lot or two contiguous. Knows nothing of Tho$^{s}$ Stringer.

## Memorial of Rob$^{t}$ Ferguson

Determin'd the 12$^{th}$ of Nov$^{r}$ 1784.

Robert Ferguson—the Claimant—sworn. 12$^{th}$ of Nov$^{r}$ 1784.

A Zealous Loyalist. Did not bear Arms.

Is a Native of Scotland & went first to America in 1750 as Master of a Vessel to Rhode Island where he settled about the Year 1770 & kept a kind of Store. He was settled there in Newport at the Commencement of the troubles. He absconded when they were pressing their test upon people & they never tender'd the Oaths to him but he receiv'd many insults & incendiary Letters. When Gen$^{l}$ Clinton came to Rhode Island he tender'd his Services & render'd him every assistance in his power. He quitted Rhode Island when the troops evacuated it & went to New York & came to Eng$^{d}$ in the latter end of the Year 1779. He had £100 a Y$^{r}$ from

former Bounty £100 a Y$^{r}$.

present Bounty £80 a Y$^{r}$.

the beginning of the Year 1780 from the Treasury but it has been since reduced to £80 a Y$^{r}$ which is his present Allowance & he has rec$^{d}$ it from Jan$^{y}$ 1783.

Sir James Wallace—sworn.

He remembers him very well at Rhode Island. He was a very honest Man & he lived upon the little which he had saved out of the Guinea Trade. He found him very loyal & has rec$^{d}$ material Intelligence from him. He believes he quitted the Island on principles of Loyalty. Thinks he remembers one of his Negroes on board his Ship & that he died on board. Says he lived comfortably.

Rev$^{d}$ George Bisset—sworn.

Has known M$^{r}$ Ferguson for 16 Y$^{rs}$. When he first knew him He was in the Guinea Trade but he had retired before the troubles & lived upon his Savings & by keeping a Store. He is perfectly sure of his Loyalty. He lived very comfortably. He has seen two or three Horses & he understood that he had some in the Country which he never saw. He has seen one Negro but thinks he had three. He had a Sloop which was taken by the Rebels at New London. Believes it was used in carrying wood & says that he understands that to be a lucrative trade because it was attended with great risque.

Determin'd the 12$^{th}$ of Nov$^{r}$ 1784.

## Memorial of Robert Nelson

12$^{th}$ of Nov$^{r}$ 1784.

Robert Nelson—the Claimant—sworn.

A Loyalist.
Did not bear Arms.

The Claim is for a Vessel & Cargo stated to have been taken under the Prohibitory Act But it appear'd to the Board that she was American property at the time she was captured & therefore fair Subject of Prize—therefore the Claim is disallowed altogether.

Is a Native of England & went over in 1774 & went to Halifax in North Carolina. He went to collect some Debts which were then due to him from a Partnership Acc$^{t}$. He had resided at Halifax many Years & had left it in 1771 to come to Eng$^{d}$. He went first to America in 1754. He recover'd many of his Debts & bought of M$^{r}$ Mountforts Executors a Brig & purchased the Cargo. Her Cargo consisted of Pipe Staves & Bees Wax. He sail'd the 1$^{st}$ of Sept$^{r}$ 1776 for Lisbon. He had no Clearance only a permit. He was taken by an American Privateer on the 19$^{th}$ & carried into Rhode Island. Which was restored he says because they could not prove him to be a Tory. He sail'd from Warren with an American Register describing him to be a Subject of the United States. On the 7$^{th}$ of Dec$^{r}$ Sir Peter Parker came in & seized the Vessel & the Claimant deliver'd all the papers. He made a prize of her. In consequence of which he persuaded Gov$^{r}$ Martin to apply to Sir Peter Parker for the restoration of the Ship. The letter is produced & read in which he presses it very strongly. But the Ship was condemn'd. When he first went out of the American Port He gave Security in the Penalty of £5000 that he would return to the United States with Salt Arms &c. He says he never meant to do this but he should have resign'd her to the British Consul & got her attached to pay a Debt in Eng$^{d}$ which w$^{d}$ have released his Security. He came to Eng$^{d}$ in 1777 & applied to the Treasury for a Satisfaction for the Capture of his Ship they did not do that but they gave him an Allowance of £100 a Y$^{r}$ which he rec$^{d}$ untill it was reduced by M$^{r}$ Wilmot & M$^{r}$ Coke to 40 a Y$^{r}$ which is the Allowance that he now receives.

He values the Ship & Cargo at £2000 S. He lost a Negro who was on board & taken at the same time. He lost likewise an Indented Apprentice at Sea. Values the Negro at about £50.

Certificate produced & read from Gov$^{r}$ Martin in which he speaks well of M$^{r}$ Nelson's Loyalty. Several other Certificates read to Loyalty.

No other Loss is stated in the Memorial. He says between 1774 & 1776 He did take opportunities of shewing his Attachment to G$^{t}$ B$^{n}$. Being asked whether he lost this Vessel on acc$^{t}$ of his Loyalty He does not go so far as that. But says he lost it in Consequence of the War.

When carried into Warren he saved his Ship by saying that he was a Subject of the United States of America & when taken by the British he endeavours to save his Ship by saying that he was a Loyalist. When they were proceeding to condemn his Ship at Warren He shew'd them his American Pass & said if they condemn'd his Ship He should complain to the Rebel Congress. And upon this they released the Ship.

No Debts due to him in America.

Says the Partnership owed about £700 in this Country.

### Memorial of James Cumming

Determin'd y$^{e}$ 12$^{th}$ of Nov$^{r}$ 1784.

12$^{th}$ of Nov$^{r}$ 1784.

James Cumming—the Claimant—sworn.

He claims 1000 Pipe Staves & 100 & ½ of Bees & desires it may make a part of M$^{r}$ Nelson's Claim & be paid to him. The whole of this is not quite £5 S.

Speaks again to M$^{r}$ Nelson's Case.

Says when they came from Halifax they ran a risque of being taken by an English Vessel. The Witness receives no Allowance from Gov$^{t}$.

The Part of the Cargo claim'd by James Cumming being under the same Circumstance with M$^{r}$ Nelson's the Claim therefore disallowed.

### Memorial of John Wormington

Determin'd the 13$^{th}$ of Nov$^{r}$ 1784.

13$^{th}$ of Nov$^{r}$ 1784.

John Wormington—the Claimant—sworn.

Is a Native of Ireland & went first to America in 1769 to settle. He was settled in 1775 in Philadelphia. He was Tide Waiter & Surveyor appointed by the Comm$^{rs}$ in America in 1772. In 1774 He was interrupted in his Duty but they never extorted any Promise from him. He was cruelly beat & had four ribs broke for doing his Duty in seizing a Vessel. They asked him to join them but he refused it. In 1777 He could do his Duty no longer & he join'd the British Troops at Staten Island in June & in order to get to them he was 19 Nights in the Woods. He was with the Army afterwards to the End of the War & left America in Ap$^{l}$ 1783. He has been much injured in his feet by the Cold. His feet were frostbitten & he is Occasionally lamed with it. He arrived in Eng$^{d}$ in June 1783 & he obtain'd an Allowance of £30 a Y$^{r}$ from the Treasury which he has rec$^{d}$ from the 5$^{th}$ of Jan$^{y}$ 1783 & he now continues to receive it.

A Loyalist & Did his Duty as an Officer of the Crown.
Did not bear Arms.

Bounty £30 a Y$^{r}$.

Zachariah Hood—sworn.

He was Comptroller of the Customs at Philadelphia at the beginning of the troubles. M$^{r}$ Wormington was an Officer under him & he knew him as such. He was the best Tidesman in the Port by which he means the most attached to His Majesty. In consequence of this He was very obnoxious & beaten several times. He never swerved from his Duty. His standing Salary was £30 a Y$^{r}$ & whenever he was put on board a Vessel he had 1*s.* 6*d.* a Day extra. This Man was more employ'd in the extra work than any other because he could be trusted. Knows nothing of his property.

John Smith—sworn.

The Witness was the principal Land Waiter at Philadelphia &c. Knew Mr Wormington very well. He was an Officer in the Customs & employ'd under his Eye. He conducted himself very well in the Office & he looked upon him as the most trusty of Men. He was a determin'd Loyalist & much persecuted for it. He has heard that he has been beat several times. He had a Salary of £30 a Year. He had besides 1*s*. 6*d*. for extra Work so that he believes in the whole the Office was about £50 a Yr. He put him upon this extra work as often as he could because he knew he could trust him.

Determin'd the 13th of Novr 1784.

**Memorial of Luke Kendall**

13th of Novr 1784.

Luke Kendall—the Claimant—sworn.

A British Subject.

Did not bear Arms.

Is a Native of Engd & went to America first in the latter end of the Year 1779. He went to recover part of his property which he was possess'd of before the troubles. He sail'd the latter end of Novr 1779 & says he then knew of the Expedition agt Charlestown. When he went to Charlestown after the Capture He had only Debts. He receives no Allowance from Govt.

Determin'd the 3d of Decr 1784.

**Memorial of George Rome [1] Esq.**

15th of Novr 1784.

George Rome Esq—the Claimant—sworn.

An Active Zealous & meritorious Loyalist.

Did not bear Arms.

Was born on the Borders of Scotland & went to America in 1761. When the rebellion broke out he was settled at Newport. He was both Mercht & Planter & his Commerce was very extensive. In 1774 & 1775 He took a very active part for Govt which made him very unpopular & he was frequently mobb'd. In 1774 & 1775 when the Agents of Govt refused to send provisions to the Army He supplied Sir James Wallace with provisions. He was to be paid for them. When the American Troops invested Boston He sent a Messenger to Govr Tryon to apprize him of a design to take him prisoner. For his Loyalty he was frequently attacked by Day & by night. Christoper Champlin was the Agent who refused to supply the King's Ships. When Genl Gage wrote to Sir Jas Wallace to send some fresh provisions for the Garrison at Boston He exerted himself much to assist Sir James Wallace which made him very obnoxious & he was in consequence obliged to go on board the Rose Man of War. Being asked whether he meant to make a profit of the Articles which he laid in for the Army He evades giving an Answer. He never did at any period when he laid in Stores apprehend that the Govt of this Country was in Danger. He did not lose any to any considerable Amount & he never charged those which he lost. In April 1776 He went to Halifax & from thence to Engd. Says since he came to Engd he has frequently given material Information to the Administration & particularly in Decr 1777. He gave his sentiments in writing to Mr Wm Eden.[2] He ran a risque of his Life by supplying the Kings Ships.

[1] See Additional Notes, p. 280.

[2] *b*. 1744, *d*. 1814. First Baron Auckland. Is in *Dict. of Nat. Biography*.

Certificates read to Zeal & loyalty by Sir James Wallace Gen[l] Gage Gen[l] Clinton & Lord Percy.

He has rec[d] no temporary Support from Gov[t]. When the Refugees appointed Agents here He was chosen Agent for the Colony of Rhode Island.

Charles Dudley—sworn.

Late Collector of the Customs for Rhode Island. Has known the Claimant M[r] Rome 15 or 16 Y[rs]. The Witness was in Rhode Island at the Commencement of the Rebellion. He was a Loyalist from principle. Remembers his purchasing some Articles of provision which he thought would be necessary for the Army at Boston. There was an Embargo laid by the rebel Assembly that no Ships [1] Notwithstanding which M[r] Rome applied to him & he did do it & says it was attended with risque. Afterwards he says that he never did send any but that he express'd a wish to do so & consulted the Witness upon it. Says that M[r] Rome did everything in his power to promote the Cause of Gov[t]. He is acquainted with his Landed Estates & can speak very particularly to some of them.

Recollects his clearing out a Ship in 1775. She went to the West Indies with a Cargo. She was a Mts Vessel. Thinks he hasten'd the Departure of the Vessel on Acc[t] of the troubles. Heard that the Ship was taken by an American Privateer. Remembers M[r] Rome on board Sir James Wallace & that he was useful to Sir James Wallace in getting fresh provisions for the Army at Boston. Knew the Agent for Gov[t] & says that he refused to provide the Quantity for the King's Troops when called upon by Sir James Wallace & that M[r] Rome did it at great risque & says he had no doubt but he had a Merchants Profit. Upon the whole he thinks that M[r] Rome did real service to the Cause of Gov[t] whilst he remain'd in the Island & that he was always ready to do more. Says that he thinks that he might be worth £10000. He says he has heard that he made £1500 a Y[r] by the Spermaceti but thinks it the best part of his trade. Thinks he had merit in serving the Kings Ship. Says he was always understood to be a Man of large fortune & that he had large Concerns in business.

Sir James Wallace Bar[t]—sworn. 18[th] of Nov[r] 1784.

Knew M[r] Rome before the rebellion began. He was a Merch[t] at Rhode Island & He did a piece of Service when the Contractors refused to serve the Kings Army. He employ'd M[r] Rome to do it & he did it at some risque. Sir James says that he does not know that no other person in the Island would have done it but M[r] Rome. He applied to M[r] Rome as the most likely person in the Island. He says he was one of the foremost to serve the Cause of G[t] Bri[n] & lost his property by so doing. He offended the people & they rose to pull down his Stores. Sir James cannot go so far as to say that he was the only Man on the Island that would have done this for the Cause of Gov[t] because he applied to no others & to say that would be to say that there was but one loyal Man in the Island. He says he was thought one of the most considerable Mercht[s] there & believes he was a Man of Substance. Supposes as a Merch[t] that he would have made a profit by it. He was present with him one Evening when he was very near being tarr'd & feather'd. Says he was an eminent Merch[t] at Rhode Island that he stepp'd forward to serve the Cause of Gov[t] &

[1] *Sic* in Text. ? Add 'should export merchandise'.

did it with great zeal. Remembers the Brig he fitted her out for him & gave her a passport to the West Indies. Conceives the object was to remove as much of his property as he could & he did get safe to the West Indies. He sent a great number of Spermaceti Candles. Has heard that she was taken.

### Memorial of Thos Goldthwaite [1] Esq.

Determin'd the 10th of Decr 1784.

Thos Goldthwaite Esq—the Claimant—sworn. 18th of Novr 1784.

A Zealous & active Loyalist & did his Duty as Govr of Fort Pownall.

Bore Arms.

Is a Native of Boston. He was settled long before the troubles at Penobscot as Captn of Fort Pownal & Colonel of the District. It is 250 Miles from Boston. His papers were all destroy'd & therefore he does not produce his Commission. It was sign'd by Sir Fras Bernard & dated in 1763. This was a Military Command & he consider'd it as for life if he behaved well. When the troubles commenced He lived with his family at fort Pownal & he dates the Commencement of the troubles from the Lexington Battle. He immediately took an active part for Govt. He looked upon himself as an Officer of the Crown & he had in Pay & Perquisites above £530 a Yr. The Assembly took away the Office of Truckmaster in 1774 on Acct of his Loyalty. In 1775 Genl Gage dismantled the fort & he remain'd there afterwards. He was then frequently insulted by the Mob & he apprehends that his Life was frequently in real Danger. He remain'd in that Country till 1779 & submitted to every Insult. He never did in those four Years do anything to induce them to think that he was with them. He had considerable Offers from them. He came to Engd in 1780. Between 1779 & 1780 He was at New York in the hopes of raising a Corps. He arrived in Engd in feby 1780. And he applied to the Treasury & recd an Allowance of £100 a Yr which is now continued to him.

Bounty £100 a Yr.

Offices.

The Office of Commandant of Fort Pownal to which he was appointed in 1764 & he says he understands it to be so far a place for Life that he never knew an instance of a person being dismiss'd but for bad Conduct. His own Pay was £3 S. per Month. He was allowed £9 per Month for six Servants. He values the Loss of the whole Office at £530 a Yr. He had rations for all his Servts. By employing the Soldiers in the farm he gain'd £200 a Yr. An annual present of Rum & Sugar which he estimates at £30 a Yr. He was appointed by the Province Truck Master the Election was annual. They did turn him out in 1769. He values this Office at £230 a Yr.

Loss of office £36 a Yr.

Truck Master. Disallowed.

[1] *b.* 1717, *d.* 1799 in England. Fort Pownall was an important frontier post commanding the entrance to the Penobscot River and offered the advantage also of a rich trade with Indians. Goldthwaite's explanation of his conduct in delivering the fort with its arms to a British officer was: 'I went into the fort and got the Governor's letter to me, and it was read to them. I then informed them that this was the king's fort and built at his expense; that the Governor was commander-in-chief of it and that I could not refuse to obey his orders' (Stark, op. cit., p. 357). In 1775, however, Goldthwaite had appealed to the Massachusetts Assembly for arrears of pay (Force, *Am. Archives*, 4th series, vol. iii, p. 1476). There is frequent mention of Goldthwaite in Hutchinson's and Curwen's journals.

'Colonel Goldthwaite deserves a word of more extended notice on account of the important part he took in settling and developing the Penobscot Valley. While in command of Fort Pownall, he was appointed agent for a vast tract of land belonging to the Waldo heirs in that region. Later, in conjunction with Sir Francis Bernard . . . he purchased a part of the Waldo patent from General Jebediah Preble, and appears to have been chiefly instrumental in settling the Penobscot country with a population which he estimated at more than 2,400 able men' (Siebert, *The Exodus of the Loyalists from Penobscot to Passamaquoddy*, Columbus, Ohio, 1914, p. 7).

He was Collector of the Customs at Penobscot in the Y$^{r}$ 1769. He was appointed by the Comm$^{rs}$ of the Customs at Boston & he was in that Office when the rebellion commenced. He had no Salary with it but he was allowed all the fees. They amounted to about £80 a Y$^{r}$. He was appointed by a Commission in writing. Fees £50 a Y$^{r}$.

Capt$^{n}$ Mowatt—sworn.

He was the Commander by Sea at the siege of Penobscot.[1] Knew Col$^{l}$ Goldthwaite. He has been on that Coast for ten Years. He has always heard him spoken of as a very loyal Man & a very good Gov$^{r}$. He saw all his Buildings burnt in 1779 by the rebels in their retreat. Has no doubt but they did it on Acc$^{t}$ of his Loyalty. Does not know the Value of the Houses burnt. His Dwelling House was a decent House. He thinks the House must cost more than £120. Supposes from the decency of the family that the charge is moderate. Can't speak to the Clothes of the family but says they were well dress'd. Has seen Boards &c on the shore & has heard that they belonged to him. Has seen several Horses but they were small & not very valuable. He does not know how much the Office.

Tho$^{s}$ Bernard Esq—sworn.

Knew M$^{r}$ Goldthwaite & was with his father when he & M$^{r}$ Goldthwaite purchased some Land at Penobscot. They purchased 2700 Acres of Brig$^{r}$ Prebble. They gave £360 S. Does not recollect anything of any Agreement between him & his father but says about a Y$^{r}$ ago the Witness agreed with him that he should have 100 Acres more of the Cultivated Land for his trouble of cultivating. He has often heard his father speak of him as a good Serv$^{t}$ of the Crown. The Witness knows no more of M$^{r}$ Goldthwaite or his fathers title to the great tract than what he has been able to extract from his father's Books. Produces a Book by which it appears that in 1767 £418 had been laid out in the improvements of the 2700 Acres. Knows nothing of the Estate at Chelsea. Explains the Agreement between them by which it appears that Col$^{l}$ Goldthwaite's share was exactly 1200 Acres.

Thomas Goldthwaite Esq—Jun$^{r}$—sworn.

Knew the Estate which his father had in common with Sir Fra$^{s}$ Bernard. Says 5 or 600 Acres of it were in some Degree of Cultivation. There were more than 20 Houses entirely built by his father. Thinks the Buildings must have cost his father 4 or £500 S. or upwards. Says they originally paid 6*s.* per Acre. And says that in his Opinion in 1775 with all the improvements it would have sold (the 800 Acres) for between £2 & £3 an Acre thinks the 400 Acres would be worth 25*s.*

Knows the 5000 Acres which his father had adjoining to this. His father had a Conveyance upon condition that he settled so many families but he paid no Money. This was in 1765. His father proceeded to settle this Country as far as he could. He improved the Meadow Land (thinks above 100 Acres) in Frankfort. He did it himself & at his own expence. Thinks it would cost him more than 2 or £300 S.

Knew his fathers Saw Mills. One cost £300 S. He had three Saw Mills. The best produced £100 S. a Y$^{r}$. These Mills were 18 Miles up the River. This Mill was standing when he came away. Knew the Grist Mills they were not so valuable as the Saw Mills he had only one. He thinks this would cost him £130. Remembers the Rebels breaking open his father's Stores & quartering Men upon

[1] The siege of Penobscot was in 1779. See note under Dr. John Calef at p. 173.

him. They were under M^r Cargill thinks they did him at that time Damage to the Amo^t of £200. His father's House at Fort Point was burnt it was not compleat when he left the Country but he thinks the House must then have cost him £75 this was in the Y^r 1775. Values the farm of Fort Point at £4 an Acre. There were about 200 Acres. Knew the Estate at Point Shirley it was owned by 8 Gent^n & he thinks there might be 40 or 50 Acres belonging to them all. There were 5 or 6 Houses. He lived in one which was a very good one. He values this at £500. He values the other at £300. These Houses were mostly destroy'd before he came away. Says upon the whole with all its Advantages the Offices which his father held were altogether were worth between 7 & £800 a Y^r S. These Offices made him very obnoxious to the rebels & he executed them with great zeal thinks his Life was often in danger before he left the Country. He was a Justice of the Inferior Court of the Eastern part of the province. Thinks it was £30 or £40 a Y^r to him & it w^d have been better.

Determin'd y^e 10^th of Dec^r 1784.

## Memorial of John Rose [1] Esq.

John Rose Esq—the Claimant—sworn. 20^th of Nov^r 1784.

A Loyalist. Never bore Arms.

Is a Native of Scotland & went to South Carolina in 1750 as a Ship Builder. He had no Appointment from Gov^t but he did their business there. He had retired from business for 14 Y^rs before the troubles. He generally lived in Charlestown but when the troubles began he went to his House in the Country. He never took any part with them. He retired into the Country in May 1775 before they tender'd any of their Oaths &c. He came to Charlestown in the fall of 1775 for a short time but afterwards resided principally at his plantation till 1780. He confesses that he sign'd a paper w^ch he supposes was tantamount to a full approbation of their Measures. They threaten'd to send him away if he did not sign it. When Sir H. Clinton came he join'd him. The British Army had provisions from his plantation. He remain'd within the Lines till the Evacuation of Charlestown. Says after he had sign'd that paper they did not molest him.

Sign'd a paper which he understood to be an Oath to the Rebels.

Certificates produced to his Loyalty & Character from Lord Cornwallis & Colonel Balfour.

Bounty £180 a Y^r.

He receives an Allowance of £180 a Y^r which was given to him from the 5^th of April 1784.

Proof of Confiscation & Sale.

Produces a Copy from the Records of the States of America by which it appears that the whole of his real property has been sold to the amount of £65749 S. This includes some personal property.

No Mortgage or Incumbrance on any part of his property.

Colonel Alexander Innes—sworn.

Knew M^r Rose very well in 1775. He always thought him a very sincere friend of Gov^t. His Conduct was uniformly so. The Witness was Secretary to Lord Will^m Campbell & says he was very useful. Does not recollect to have heard that he sign'd a paper to the rebels. Says M^r Rose was reckon'd a Man of very great property. He has been at one of his plantations Richfield. It was a very fine Plantation & valuable & he was reckon'd a Rich Man.

[1] *b.* 1722, *d.* 1805. Sabine (op. cit., vol. ii, p. 238) does not seem quite accurate in his account.

Gideon Dupont—sworn.

Knew M^r Rose many Years. He says he was uniformly looked upon as a Loyalist from the Commencement of the troubles & he was particularly obnoxious. Does not know that he ever took part with the Americans. Knows his Lands in S^t Helena Parish. Does not know the Extent. Says it was very valuable property & that he render'd it much more so. Supposing it to be 7000 Acres thinks the Land when he bought it must have been worth £3 C. per Acre. Says he saw it in 1775 & thinks that then it must be worth full £3 C. per Acre. Being desired to reconsider the Matter he says it would have sold in 1775 for £10 per Acre C. Knows Mitchell's Island but can't speak to the Value.

Knows that M^r Rose had lands in Granville County but they were uncultivated. Did not know his Land at Hobceau. Has rode thro' his plantation at Richfield but can't value it. Knows the 3 Story Brick House in the Bay & that it was M^r Rose's property. Can't speak to the Value but supposes it to be worth £2000 S. Can't speak to the Value of the Pew. Knew the two 3 Story Tenem^ts in one of which he lived. Can't value them. Understood himself to be called particularly to speak to the value of the Lands at S^t Helena. Knew the Wooden House but can't value it. Can't speak particularly to anything else.

### Memorial of Moses Hart

Determin'd the 23^d of Nov^r 1784.

Moses Hart—the Claimant—a Jew—sworn. 23^d of Nov^r 1784.

Is a Native of America. Born in Connecticut. Was settled in the Y^r 1774 at Rhode Island. He kept a Shop of Goods there. The Americans never tender'd any Oath to him & he never sign'd any paper. He says he gave information thro' his Mother & Sister to Sir Ja^s Wallace they gave it to M^r Rome. They were by this means obnoxious & quitted the Island with the British Troops & went to New York where he remain'd till the 15^th of Sept^r 1783. He was enrolled in the Militia at New York. His father had an Allowance of 40 a Y^r. He died about 3 Weeks ago & his Mother has now a Memorial at Whitehall. The Claim^t asked for a subsistence but it was not granted as it was esteem'd to be one Case & the whole was given to the father. His Uncle was murther'd in Oct^r 1780 for his Loyalty. His father had no Memorial in Lincolns Innfields.

A Loyalist.
Did not bear Arms.

Bounty to his father £40 a Y^r.

George Rome Esq—sworn.

Knew Moses Hart at Newport. He always consider'd the family to be good Subjects. He rec^d much Information from the Ladies. Says the Men acted with great Caution. Knows there was some real Estate. He saw the Deeds. The Estate belonged to his Uncle before. He was very well acquainted with it. He did upon the Evacuation of Rhode Island put a Value of £2000 upon it but he thinks it would have sold for about £1800. He understood that there were Mortgages upon it. He says the father's House was worth about £300 S. Says part of the family were much distress'd. He consider'd the family altogether as a loyal family. The father was a quiet Man but he believes he was loyal. He got his Information from the Ladies.

Determin'd the 25$^{th}$ of Nov$^{r}$ 1784.

## Memorial of Eliz$^{th}$ Fielde Widow

24$^{th}$ of Nov$^{r}$ 1784.

Eliz$^{th}$ Fielde—the Claimant—sworn.

Her Husband a Loyalist.

Did not bear Arms.

Her Husband died in 1781. Her Husband went to America in the Y$^{r}$ 1770 & she follow'd him soon after. He was a Native of Eng$^{d}$. He went to America by the persuasion of his friends. He had a promise of preferment. In 1771 He was made Rector of the Parish of Kingston in the County of Gloucester [1] they lived there in 1774 & 1775 & till 1777. Her Husband wished to have been quiet but he would not take their Oaths & they then told him that he must give up his Parish. He staid for six Months in order to get a permission which he obtain'd from Patrick Henry [2] the then Gov$^{r}$ of Virginia. They came to New York in 1778 where they staid till the latter end of the Year 1781 when her Husband & then she & her two Children came to Eng$^{d}$. Her Husband supported himself at New York by a Chaplaincy. When she came to Eng$^{d}$ She applied to the Treasury & obtain'd an Allowance of £50 a Y$^{r}$ from the beginning of the Year 1782 which was confirmed to her by M$^{r}$ Wilmot & M$^{r}$ Coke & she now continues to receive it.

Bounty £50 a Y$^{r}$.

Loss of Living.

Living £180 a Y$^{r}$.

Lost for 4 Y$^{rs}$ which is £682 as in the Schedule.

Died in the course of Nature in Feb$^{y}$ 1781.

The Tobacco which was usually given to him amounted to 1600 llb W$^{t}$ & was worth £160 C. per Ann. The Perquisites were worth 40 C. Besides which he had between 5 & 600 Acres of Glebe Land which she values at £60 a Y$^{r}$ Amounting in the Y$^{r}$ to £198 S. He never rec$^{d}$ anything from this Living since 1777 & dying in Feb$^{y}$ 1781 She has charged a Loss of 3 Y$^{rs}$ & ½ upon the Living which amounts to £682 10*s*.

He rec$^{d}$ as Chaplain to a Reg$^{t}$ for 3 Y$^{rs}$ £350.

Her Son an Allowance of 50 a Y$^{r}$ for 4 Y$^{rs}$ £200.

She herself £50 a Y$^{r}$ for 3 Y$^{rs}$ & now receives it £150.

Therefore they have rec$^{d}$ more than they have lost On which Acct The Claim disallowed altogether.

As soon as her Husband went to New York Sir Henry Clinton gave him a Chaplainship which commenced in Oct$^{r}$ 1778 which is £110 a Y$^{r}$ & which he rec$^{d}$ till Feb$^{y}$ 1781. She receives no pension from any military Funds. She has rec$^{d}$ the Allowance of £50 a Y$^{r}$ from the Treasury for two Years & ½.

She says they lost nothing but the Living because they were permitted to sell everything before they went.

Lieut$^{t}$ W$^{m}$ Henry Fielde—sworn.

A Lieut$^{t}$ in the 17$^{th}$ Reg$^{t}$. He lived with his father in Virginia in 1775. Remembers the Rebels tendering the Oaths to him in 1777. He refused them & was obliged in consequence to quit his Living in Virginia which he imagines was worth £200 a Y$^{r}$ S. He left his father before he went to New York & came to Eng$^{d}$ in 1778 where he had a pension of £50 a Y$^{r}$ till the Y$^{r}$ 1780 when it was taken off in Consequence of his having an Ensign's Comm$^{n}$ in y$^{e}$ 60$^{th}$ Reg$^{t}$. He rec$^{d}$ £200 in y$^{e}$ whole from Gov$^{t}$. This Comm$^{n}$ was given to him in cons$^{n}$ of the Loyalty of his family.

[1] Virginia.

[2] *b.* 1736, *d.* 1799. He was elected Governor in June 1776, and re-elected in the following year. He continued in office till June 1778. Besides the three volumes of the official life, there is a short life of him by M. C. Tyler in the 'American Statesmen' series.

## Memorial of Cavalier Jouet [1]

Determin'd $y^e$ $14^{th}$ of $Dec^r$ 1784.

Cavalier Jouet—the Claimant—sworn. $24^{th}$ of $Nov^r$ 1784.

A Loyalist.

Never bore Arms.

Is a Native of Jamaica & went to America above 30 $Y^{rs}$ ago & has lived there from that time to the time of the troubles. In the $Y^r$ 1774 He lived at $Eliz^{th}$ Town where he was married & settled. The troubles first broke out about 1774 or 1775. Before Sir $W^m$ Howe came his principles were generally known to be in favor of $Gov^t$. He refused signing the Association paper. At length he was so far persecuted that they brought the paper again to him & he sign'd it & he told them that he sign'd it by compulsion & says he scratch'd his name out again & he meant by so doing to insult them. He was in consequence of this & many other proceedings—a file of Musqueteers took him about the Month of $feb^y$ 1776 & tried him & imprison'd him for that & many other Charges. He was five days in close Confinement & afterwards at Basking ridge for about 7 Months. When Sir $Will^m$ Howe came He join'd him at $Eliz^{th}$ Town. He had no military $Comm^n$. But he has been instrumental in being a Guide. After the Affair at Trenton He resided at Staten Island & New York where he staid till the $13^{th}$ of $Dec^r$ last. He did no business at New York. He had about a short time after he came to New York an Allowance of £200 a $Y^r$ which he $rec^d$ up to the time of the Evacuation. It was given by Sir $W^m$ Howe. He came to $Eng^d$ last Spring & applied to the Treasury since which time he has $rec^d$ an Allowance of 180 a $Y^r$ from the $5^{th}$ of $Jan^y$ 1784.

Bounty £180 a $Y^r$.

$Will^m$ Luce—sworn.

Knew $M^r$ Cavalier Jouet for many $Y^{rs}$ & in the $Y^r$ 1774. He was then settled in $Eliz^{th}$ Town upon his property & was esteem'd a Man of considerable property. He always appear'd very loyal. He wished to be as quiet as possible. He frequently avowed his Sentiments which were uniformly loyal. He remembers an Association Paper carried about at the time of Bunker's Hill. Does not know whether he sign'd it or not. Has heard he was frequently brought before their Committees. The Witness went to the West Indies in $Jan^y$ 1776 & when he return'd in $Oct^r$ He found him in the British Lines & heard that he had been confined by them. He looks upon him always to have been attached to Great Britain.

He has heard he had a good deal of Money at Interest. And he had some Land about 50 or 60 Acres. He knows the Land. Knows that he had sold his House & part of the Land. He knows the small House & thinks the whole was worth £1500. Thinks the Wood Land worth 40 an Acre—viz—£810. Supposes the Meadow Land worth £30 an Acre £720. In this value he means to throw in the House. He thinks that Wood Land is more valuable than open land.

[1] There is an application from Cavalier Jouet under date November 15, 1783, New York: 'Illness for nine weeks past. Is advised to go to England to solicit compensation. His family has been supported of late entirely by what was paid by the Navy Department for the Hospital and Brewery on Long Island which terminates with this quarter' (*Hist. MSS. Comm.*, *Am. MSS. in R. Inst.*, vol. iv, p. 459). For striking description of Jouet's treatment in New Jersey after the Peace, see Introduction, p. xxix.

## Further testimony to the Memorial of Cavalier Jouet

27th of Novr 1784.

Alexander Wallace Esq—sworn.

Mr Wallace having said that he could say something material in this Case was desired to attend. He attends accordingly & speaks principally to a debt which Mr Jouet claims as due from Philip Livingston. Mr Wallace says he might have had his Debt some time ago if he would have waved his Interest Money. The principal Money was £6000 & he might have recd it in 1782. He knows nothing of his Loyalty but he has frequently heard that during the war he occasionally went backwards & forwards to the Rebels. Says he was permitted to receive his Interest from the Estate within the British Lines. He says this was not Common & he believes it was the only Instance where a Mortgagee was permitted to receive the profits of the Estate. Says that if Mr Jouet had taken the Bills which were offer'd to him He knows they would have been paid. He knows nothing more relative to Mr Jouet than what he has said.

## Memorial of John Clarke & David Millegan Esqres

Determin'd ye 14th of Decr 1784.

25th of Novr 1784.

David Millegan Esq—sworn.

Disallowed as not within the Meaning of the Act.

Mr Clarke & he are Partners & he appears to claim for a Ship (Inverness) burnt in the river of Savannah in 1776. He comes here as a British Mercht & not as a Loyalist. The name of the Ship was Inverness John McKenzie Master. He & Mr Clarke owned a Quarter of this Ship Lauchlin McGilliwry another Quarter & John McGilliwry an half. Governor Graham had some rice on board. The Ship was loaded with Rice & Deer Skins & lay at Savannah. Some of the Kings Ships went up the back River to get rice out of this & other Ships for the sake of the Army at Boston & the Rebels finding out this burnt her to prevent her being of any use to the British & some records belonging to the Custom House being sent on board was an additional reason for the rebels to burn it. The papers were public papers. If Captn Barclay [1] had not been there he thinks they would not have burnt her on acct of the records being on board of her. This was the 3d of March 1776. He says he believes there was no Embargo on these Ships. Captn Fletcher's & sevl other Ships were destroyed at the same time. But he believes they were all the Ships of Loyalists. His share of the Cargo was not in proportion to his share of the Ship for they had the greatest share of the Cargo. He values the Ship at £2000 The Cargo was all lost but she was in part insured. £1200 was insured on the Ship—the Loss on the Ship only £800. The Cargo was insured for £8594 15*s.* 6*d.* & this insurance was recover'd they paid 5 Gās per Cent. The Cargo consisted of Rice & Deerskins. The two McGilliwrys owned no part of the Cargo they had only a share in the Ship. £9900 S. of the Cargo belonged to him & his partner this is the first Cost—& he says he speaks of £3 10*s.* as the original price that the Rice cost them. He claims for the Insurers—but if it should be thought that the Insurers ought not to have any compensation then the Difference will be £1306. Part of the Cargo belongs to Grayham Johnson & Co to the amot £306. Does not

[1] Presumably Captain Andrew Barkley of the Royal Navy, of whom there is frequent mention in *Hist. MSS. Comm., Am. MSS. in R. Inst.*, vols. i and ii.

know what has been insured on this. John Nutt £763 Greenwood & Higginson £120. The Amo^t^ of the freight is £618 15*s.* 6*d.* Being asked as to the original price of Rice whether he really gave £3 10*s.* a barrel for Rice He hesitates & says that Rice would take that price in Eng^d^ but won't be positive to that being the prime Cost. Being asked whether by the insurance of £8594 He meant to cover his whole Loss & he says he does not know. But he is desired to attend tomorrow & to bring the Invoice & the Policy of Insurance.

**Memorial of David Millegan & others**

26th of Nov^r^ 1784.

David Millegan Esq—sworn.

Produces an Invoice of the Deer Skins but has no Invoice of Rice. And says he never rec^d^ an Invoice of the Rice. But he says the price of the Rice is express'd in the Policy of Insurance which is produced. Says the Rice belonged to Gov^r^ Graham. Says the £3 10*s.* is above the prime Cost but not so much as it would sell for in Eng^d^. He swears that the Invoice of the Deer Skins is the original one. He says that he has not the original Invoice of the Rice but he is directed to produce it.

Lieut^t^ Governor Graham—sworn.

Was at Savannah in the beginning of the Year 1776. Saw the Ship Inverness burnt by the rebels. Believes the reason was to prevent this & other Ships falling into the hands of Capt^n^ Barclay for the use of the British Troops. There was no Embargo at Savannah at that time the Rebels had not possession of the Gov^t^ at that time. Thinks if the Troops had not come in Jan^y^ 1776 that the rebels would not have prevented this Ship & others sailing. There were Skins & Rice on board. Did not at that time know who were the Owners of the Ship. He had 360 barrels. He has not the Invoice but says M^r^ Millegan has it. Says the price of rice per barrel was at that time from 40*s.* to 50*s.* He often used to send rice without sending an Invoice of it. Says that Merch^ts^ very often in London make insurance of Articles at the price that it would have sold for in London. Never thought that this Claim would have come before this Board. He says he thinks the Under Writers have a claim upon Gov^t^. Believes that the Insurers must have known the Circumstances before they paid the Money. Says that the Treasury have in many instances paid for Rice thrown overboard 20*s.* per Hn^d^ which is £5 10*s.* per Barrel. He says he thinks that if he had not insured his Rice he should have had the best Claim in the world upon Gov^t^. Governor Graham thinks from what M^r^ Milleghan said that he must have sent this Rice without any Invoice. Says he has frequently put the Invoice price on the back of the Bill of lading. But upon looking at the Bill of Lading Nothing appears because it is said *as per Invoice* on which Gov^r^ Graham says there must have been an Invoice but he says if there was an Invoice it certainly could not have been invoiced at more than 50*s.* a Barrel. Gov^r^ Graham says that Clarke & Millegan are Men of as good Character as any in the City.

Tho^s^ Stringer—sworn.

Remembers the burning of the Ship & says it was to prevent her falling into the hands of the Enemy. Says the Price was about 43*s.* or 44*s.*

Determin'd the 14th of Decr 1784.

## Memorial of Sir Edmund Head Bart [1]

Sir Edmund Head Bart—sworn. 26th of Novr 1784.

Zealous. A Loyalist. Did not bear Arms.

Is a Native of Engd & went to Charlestown in 1764. He resided during the whole time at Charlestown. He was a Mercht. He constantly refused taking any part with them. They chose him in 1775 to sit in the provincial Congress & he refused & produces a letter from Mr Laurens [2] to him which shews that Sir Edmd has written to him to ask his Opinion as to the mode of declining to serve in the Congress. He afterwards refused & proves from a printed paper that a new Election was had in his room. He was frequently summon'd to muster & constantly refused. He told his Sentiments to Mr Laurence. He was never fined & was never publickly insulted. He chose rather to quit the province than to take the Oaths. He quitted the Province the 12th of May 1778. He was obliged to give Security in £200000 that he would not go to any British Port. So he clear'd out for Rotterdam. She was run aground upon Charlestown Bar & was afterwards with difficulty got into Port again. When the Vessel was unloaded they got her into a Carpenter's Yard & after some time she was ready for Sea again. But she was detain'd by an Embargo laid by the Provincial Congress. They were obliged to unload again as they could not take provisions & sell their Rice for one half. They were allowed to take Naval Stores. They got on weigh the 14th of July (their Outlawry taking place the 15th of July) & lay in rebellion road. The Pilot disappointed them for some time & at last he gave him £100 to carry them out to Sea which he did. They then proceeded to Rotterdam. But between Dover & Calais He was taken first by a Privateer who had no right to take him having only a French Commission but he was the same Day taken by a Sloop & a Kings Cutter & carried into Portsmouth by Captn Mainwaring & Captn Inglis. The Ship & Cargo were libel'd in the Commons. The Ship was given up to the former Owners on acct of her having been British property before. The Cargo was deliver'd to the Owners.

Ship Disallowed. Loss on Rice £240. Indigo Disallowed.

He claims for the Loss which he was obliged to sustain by leaving that Country. And first he claims the Loss of the Ship. He had a 3d share of it & a 3d of the Cargo. And for a Loss upon the Rice which they were obliged to sell at Charlestown. And he likewise charges a Loss upon the Indigo sold in London. The ten Casks of Indigo were his own & he had a third of the Rice which was sold at Charlestown.

Determin'd the 18th of Decr 1784.

## Memorial of Isabella McLawrin

Isabella McLawrin—the Claimant—sworn. 27th of Novr 1784.

Her Husband an active zealous

She is a Native of Scotland & Widow of Evan McLawrin [3] late Lieutt Coll of the So. Carolina Royalists. She was married in 1768 & went in 1774. Her Husband

[1] He was the grandfather of Sir Edmund Head, who was Governor-General of Canada from 1854 to 1861.

[2] Henry Laurens, *b.* 1724, *d.* 1792, was a leading South Carolina statesman. In 1776 he became Vice-President of South Carolina and was elected a delegate to the Continental Congress, of which he was President from November 1777 to December 1778. Appointed Minister to Holland in 1779, he was captured by the British. At the end of 1781 he was exchanged for Lord Cornwallis, and was one of the negotiators of the treaty of November 1782 (Appleton, op. cit., vol. iii, p. 630).

[3] Evan McLaurin was a party to the treaty of November 1775, between Major Williamson and the Loyalist assailants of Ninety-Six (McCrady, *S. Carolina in the Rev., 1775–80*, p. 92).

had been there for 3 Years. She went to Charlestown & found him in the District of Ninety Six. America was not in open Rebellion. As soon as the Rebellion broke out Her Husband refused to sign the first Association & immediately took part with the British. He was one of the most leading Men for Gov$^{t}$ & he was in the first Engagement at Ninety Six. Knows that he brought into the field 500 Men. He made his Escape in 1777 to Florida. She remain'd upon the plantation more than a Y$^{r}$ & then she was obliged to leave it being persecuted for her Husbands Loyalty. In 1778 He had a Major's Comm$^{n}$ from Sir Henry Clinton. And in 1779 He was made Lieut$^{t}$ Col$^{l}$ by Gen$^{l}$ Prevost. He died in June 1782 at Charlestown worn out by fatigue. He was not killed. He spent all he had in the King's Service. She is left with two Children. She came from America at the Evacuation of Charlestown & as soon as She came to Eng$^{d}$ She applied to the Treasury & has rec$^{d}$ an Allowance of £40 a Y$^{r}$ from the 5$^{th}$ of Jan$^{y}$ 1783 & she now continues to receive it.

& meritorious Loyalist & bore Arms as a Lieut$^{t}$ Col$^{l}$.

Bounty £40 a Y$^{r}$.

Copies of several Certificates read (the Originals being at Whitehall) to the Loyalty Character & situation of Col$^{l}$ M$^{c}$Lawrin from Gen$^{l}$ Prevost [and] Col$^{l}$ Balfour.

When her Husband went over in 1771 He did not carry over much Money & at that time he had no American property.

They had a Negro Man which he brought with him from East Florida. He was a Waiting Serv$^{t}$ & she values him at £50. She knows that he lost him when he was taken Prisoner on his March with Gen$^{l}$ Paterson from Savannah to Charlestown in 1780.

£50.

She says it cost him £500 to raise a Corps under Lord Cornwallis. He had not compleated this Corps. Being asked whether he had his Commission in consequence of it She says he was a Lieut$^{t}$ Col$^{l}$ before Lord Cornwallis's.[1] Warrant read dated in Nov$^{r}$ 1780. She says that she has heard him say so. Says that Col$^{l}$ Innes knows this. And she refers entirely to Colonel Innes for this As she knows very little of the Matter.

Disallowed.

**Further Testimony to the Memorial of M$^{rs}$ M$^{c}$Lawrin Widow**

7$^{th}$ of Dec$^{r}$ 1784.

Colonel Innes—sworn.

Knew Col$^{l}$ M$^{c}$Lawrin. He was a Major to the Reg$^{t}$ which Col$^{l}$ Innes commanded. He join'd the British very early in 1775. He did not raise that Corps. But he afterwards got a Warrant from Lord Cornwallis to raise a Corps & got the Comm$^{n}$ of Lieut$^{t}$ Col$^{l}$. Does not know what progress he made in it or whether he expended much Money in it or not. Says if Col$^{l}$ M$^{c}$Lawrin had rais'd a Corps he would have been entitled to Levy Money. Believes the Man went upon a Scheme which he could not execute & that he embarass'd himself very much. Says he was one of the most Zealous Men he ever knew. Says there is a provision for the Widows of Provincial Officers but this Woman is not upon it. Says he rather apprehends that he employed improper people to get Men for him & very soon after he obtain'd his Warrant the Affairs of the British in Carolina got into great Confusion which render'd it difficult to obtain Men which never can be reimbursed to him. He speaks more from his Judgm$^{t}$ than from knowledge.

[1] *Sic* in Text. The meaning is he was already a lieutenant-colonel before his efforts to raise a corps under Lord Cornwallis.

## Memorial of Daniel Coxe[1] Esq.

Determin'd the 16th of Decr 1784.

29th of Novr 1784.

Daniel Coxe Esq—the Claimant—sworn.

An Active Zealous & meritorious Loyalist.

Did not bear Arms.

Swears that the whole of the Memorial is true. He is a Native of America. And when the Rebellion broke out He was exercising the profession of the Law at Trenton. He says he was of the highest Degree which he says was the Degree of a Serjt. He was likewise one of the King's Mandamus Counsellors. He dates the Commencement of Hostilities from the battle of Lexington. He took an invariable Opposition to the measures of the Rebels & never in any one Instance gave them reason to think that he was wavering. They tender'd him an Association paper which he refused but they never tender'd him any Oath because they knew his principles. Says he has no particular Services to state. The Army came into New Jersey first in 1776 & then the Rebels wishing to seize all the Loyalists He retired into Pensylvania where he staid till Sir Wm Howe took Philadelphia & then he join'd the Army. He never held any military situation during the troubles. In the Winter of 1777 & Spring of 1778 He raised a Corps of West Jersey Volunteers principally by his Influence but it cost him no Money. He staid at Philadelphia till the Evacuation (Produces a Certificate to his raising the Corps from Gabriel de Webber) & framing the Articles of Association. He acted as a Magistrate of Police whilst he was at Philadelphia (produces the Commn sign'd by Sir Wm Howe). This was attended with a great deal of trouble but no emolument. Produces a Letter from Sir Wm Howe wherein he expresses his Approbation of his Conduct in that office. He went with the Army from Philadelphia to New York. He remain'd at New York for some time without Employment. And then in June 1781 He was appointed Assistant Secretary to the Commissioners. He was afterwards the Principal (Commission produced) & became so by the Absence of Mr Simpson. He recd 10*s*. a Day as Assistant & when he was the Principal He recd 20*s*. a Day. He continued in that Situation till the Evacuation of New York when he came to Engd. He acted likewise as a Member of the Board of Directors for controuling the Affairs of the Loyalists. He was appointed by Lord George Germaine in 1780 to this Office. This was attended with no Emolument. Besides his pay as Secretary He had an Allowance of £200 a Yr which he recd till he came to Engd for the two last Years He recd £565 a Yr. When he came to Engd he applied to the Treasury & has recd from the 5th of Jany 1784 an Allowance of £200 a Yr which is to be £300 a Yr when his family come to Engd. He did refuse many Offers from the Rebels but at that time He thought that Great Britain would succeed.

Bounty £200 a Yr. When his Wife comes to Engd £300 a Yr.

Proprietory Rights.

The Council of Proprietory granted to the Claimt the first Order in Feby. The Order signed by the Surveyor Genl dated in Apl produced. He had not located but says that £12 per 100 Acres is a Common price. He values them at that—£293 C.

1st of Decr 1784.

Danl Coxe Esq—sworn.

Says that he has reason to believe that his property in this Province will not be confiscated but as he does not know it Officially he makes his Claim conditionally.

[1] See Additional Notes, p. 280.

12637 Acres being ¼ of 47000 Acres granted to himself his Uncle his Aunt & his Sister granted in 1769. Produces a Mandamus from hence to the Gov^r of New York to grant 100000 Acres in Lots of 20000 each in consequence of his Cession of his title to the province of Carolana. Patent produced for the 47000 Acres upon Condition that they shall plant one family upon every 1000 Acres & cultivate 3 Acres out of every hundred. The patent was dated in May 1770 & these Conditions had not been complied with. The Patent fees & other Expenses were very large. It cost he thinks £25 for every 1000 Acres & the whole Expences of the 47000 Acres were about £700 C. & the Surveying about £300. Partition Deed produced by w^ch it appears that he has ¼. He values this Tract at 10s. C. per Acre. He goes principally upon the Opinion of the Surveyor Col^l Guy Johnson [1] &c. Disallowed.

Professional Loss. Says he gain'd at least as a Lawyer 400 a Y^r which for 8 Y^rs makes £3200 C. Means to prove this by Witnesses. An Aff^t by Colin Campbell read to prove this.

He carries on this Loss forward which he has estimated upon the common Calculation of the Chances of Life as an Annuity at £4320 C. But he thinks he made £200 a Y^r in addition to this as Counsel but he did not put it down in his Schedule because he could give no positive proof of it. However he thinks he ought to charge.

General Skynner—sworn.

Knew M^r Cox very well in America before & after the troubles. He was uniformly loyal. Knew Moore Furman Isaac Pearson & Isaac D'Cow the valuers of his Estate. They were Men of good Character but Furman was a violent Man a Rebel but he was a sensible Man & one of the Judges of the Court of Common Pleas. Knew M^r Abraham Hunt of Trenton. Says that the names of Furman & D'Cow are in their handwriting. M^r Hunt is a Man of Character & a Loyalist. Knew Nathaniel Petit. He was a Judge of the County of Sussex. Believes he was a very good Judge of the value of Land. Knew M^r Dan^l Ellis of Burlington. He was a Man of good Character & a good Judge of the Value of Land. M^r Coxe was esteem'd a Man of great property & he was a Proprietor of East & West Jersey. He followed the profession of a Lawyer. He was not of the foremost but thinks he might get as an Attorney £400 a Y^r in this he does not estimate his business as a Counsel. He knows the farm call'd Vandyke's farm. Has heard that the Land was worth £5 an Acre. Knows it was his property because he was concern'd in the Suit in which M^r Coxe recover'd it. Recollects the Corps of West Jersey Volunteers but does not know who raised them. Says that M^r Coxe was instrumental in raising the Corps but that Major Vandyke was principally concerned in raising the Men. Knows M^r Coxe's House at Trenton it was an old House but a very convenient House & very good Garden. Cant set a Value upon it but says the ferry was very valuable. Knows his farm at Belmont. It is a good Grass Farm but he can't value. Says that he had a right to a Ferry. Says that M^r Coxe some Years ago came over to Eng^d & says he made that Claim & he understood that it ended in his receiving a Grant

[1] *b.* 1740, *d.* 1788, succeeded his uncle, Sir William Johnson, as superintendent of Indian affairs. He was superseded by his cousin, Sir John Johnson (J. N. McIlwraith, *Sir F. Haldimand* in 'Makers of Canada' series, p. 156).

of 100000 Acres of Land in another part. Says it was mention'd that he had a right to it but he does not know much about it. Says that a Share of propriety is a saleable Article but does not know the Value of it. Never remembers any Decision about the forfeiture in Grants. But says that he apprehends that if such a thing had come into Court he thinks it would have been decided that it was forfeited. And he says as a professional Man he should think that any person who claims here or anywhere else for an Estate granted where he has not complied with the Conditions has no title whatever in strictness to the Land. Knows Rebecca Coxe & says that this Gent^n^ is her Heir at Law & would inherit. But he says the Laws of the province are such that he would not be permitted to inherit. He has heard that her Estate was worth £20000. Remembers his House at the Ferry being burnt. Has heard that his House was used as a Barrack. When he was absent from Trenton He says he thinks it was on Acc^t^ of his Principles. He saw his Mother in 1777 & she told him that M^r^ Coxe was with his Wife in the Country to avoid Abuse &c. Upon the whole he says he has no Doubt but that he was from the beginning to the End of the War (he was) uniformly & invariably loyal.

6^th^ of Dec^r^ 1784.

Brig^r^ Gen^l^ Skynner—sworn.

M^r^ Coxe's Law Library was a very good one thinks it was worth at least £400 C. He had many other Books besides Law Books.

**Further testimony to the Memorial of Daniel Coxe Esq.**

2^d^ of Dec^r^ 1784.

Barnardus Lagrange—sworn.

Knew M^r^ Coxe in America very well before the troubles. Believes him to have been perfectly loyal. Knows Moore Furman & Isaac D'Cow they are Men of good Character tho' of opposite principles. Thinks they understand the Value of Land. Knows Abraham Hunt believes him to be a Man of good Character. Says he was a farmer & Supposes he understands the Value of Land. Knows Nathaniel Petit. Says he is a Man of very good Character & knows the value of Land. Knows Dan^l^ Ellis believes him to be a Man of good Character but cant tell whether he is a Judge of Land. M^r^ Coxe was in the profession of the Law. He was not one of the most eminent. Says his practice as an Attorney must have been £400 a Y^r^. Knows none of his property but that which lay at Trenton. Knew the House in which he lived but he cant value. The House was well furnish'd but cant value the furniture. He was esteem'd to be a Man of great landed Estate.

Daniel Cozens—sworn.

Has known him personally since the Army took Philadelphia. He conducted himself with great Loyalty from that time & believes he was always a Loyalist. When some of the Witnesses Countrymen came into Philadelphia he went to M^r^ Coxe to mention it to him that if any encouragement was given 500 Men would come in. M^r^ Coxe made proper applications to Head Quarters but none of the Men enlisted in consequence of the influence of M^r^ Coxe or their Attachment to him. Knows Lands in the County of Salem & says the Lands about Alloway's Creek are very rich but he does not know which are M^r^ Coxe's Lands. Values Marsh Meadow Lands at 50*s*. per Acre. Knows the fork of Prince Maurice's River.

Knows Cohansey's Bridge. Has sold Ground in that Neighborhood. Thinks Lands in that situation would sell for 40*s*. an Acre. He has had Meadow Land for which he could have got £65 an Acre. Knows no other part of M^r^ Coxe's property but says he was reckon'd a Man of great property. Says M^r^ Coxe has been attainted of High Treason. And believes his Lands have been sold as well as confiscated.

Major Vandyke—sworn.

Has known M^r^ Coxe long before the troubles. He opposed all the Measures of the Rebels. He was uniform in his Loyalty. He never bore Arms. M^r^ Coxe recommended & encouraged the raising [of] the West Jersey Volunteers but never took any part in raising any Men. The Witness says that he himself rais'd that Corps. Knows part of M^r^ Coxe's Lands. Knows the farm at Rock Hill very well it was called Vandyke farm. It consisted of 207 Acres it was very well cultivated & a good House upon it & good fruit. Says it wo^d^ have sold for £7 an Acre C. in the Y^r^ 1775. Does not know any of the other property of M^r^ Coxe's so as to put a Value upon it. M^r^ Coxe was always esteem'd a Man of great property. He has often heard him called a Man worth £15000 C. from 1772 to the time of the troubles. He does not think there was one Man in the province worth more than 15000 Proclamation money. When he explains himself he says he means to confine himself to his property in New Jersey. Thinks that many people are apt to overvalue their uncultivated Lands in America. He understands & believes that many persons have valued these Lands shamefully. Says the value of uncultivated Lands in Jersey would be about 10*s*. an Acre after the Expence of locating & surveying &c.

Knows the Land about Philipsbourgh at the forks of the Delaware. Knows that M^r^ Coxe had some Land there. Says the Town Lots used to sell from £5 to £10 per Lot & the Land round it He should suppose to be worth from £5 to £6 per Acre. Knows no other part of M^r^ Coxe's property. Says they used to think a Man of £10000 or £15000 a Man of great property. Never knew a large Estate sold in that Country when the whole Money was paid down. And says if an Estate was sold for ready Money in his opinion it would sell much cheaper thinks it would make the Difference of at least one fourth.

Governor Franklyn—sworn.

Knew M^r^ Coxe in America before the troubles. He was one of the Council & was likewise esteem'd one of the first property in the Country. He always consider'd him as a Loyalist & well inclined but not active. They were very well disposed but were cautious. Believes he never took any Oaths to the rebels but when he was in the Country he made Interest with some of the rebels to let him remain quiet. He was a considerable proprietor in West Jersey. He has been at fort Stanwix & says that M^r^ Coxe's Lands were in the prime part of the Country & thinks they would have sold well on acc^t^ of an Idea that there would be a Settlement at Fort Stanwix.[1] Says it was frequently matter of Speculation for persons to buy Lands in America in hopes that Settlements would be made in the Neighborhood.

[1] 'Fort Stanwix was erected by Brigadier Stanwix in 1758 at the Carrying Place between the Mohawk River and Wood Creek, an important link in the communications between Albany and Oswego' (A. G. Doughty, Knox's *Hist. Journal of Campaigns in N. Am., 1757, 1758, 1759, and 1760*, vol. i, note at p. 480. Champlain So. Publics., No. viii).

# ADDITIONAL NOTES

## Major Alexander Macleod (page 214).

In July 1775 Governor Martin wrote to Major Alexander Macleod: 'It is impossible for me to express my respect for the gentlemen who have cultivated the good dispositions that are manifested by the Highlanders throughout the Province in this time of unnatural revolt. . . . I perfectly agree in your sentiments of the propriety of the good and faithful Highlanders forbearing any open declarations until there is a necessity to call them into action and they are provided to take the field with dignity and effect. . . . I concur in your opinion of your services being more useful here than anywhere else, and I have concerted a plan with Mr. McDonald . . . of making use of your influence here' (*Hist. MSS. Comm., Am. MSS. in R. Inst.*, vol. i, pp. 4, 5). There is a letter of Governor Martin to General Howe (November 4, 1776) recommending Major A. Macleod for honourable provision (ibid., p. 68). Ibid., vol. ii, p. 7, is a memorial from Alexander Macleod to Lord North. Settled in North Carolina in 1774. Had already served twenty-two years, at Quebec, Pondicherry, and Manilla. Was appointed Captain in 1775, one of the companies of Highlanders of Major Macdonald of the Royal Highland Emigrants, and in services expended £278. After reverses, and living six weeks in woods and swamps, escaped to Sir Henry Clinton. Rewards were offered for him, his wife, children, and servants scattered, and his property destroyed and carried off to the amount of £1,500.

In 1780 the sum of £278 16*s*. 4½*d*. was paid to him (ibid., p. 195). R. Caswell, writing on February 29, 1776, was under the impression that Captain Macleod, 'who seemed to be the principal leader', was among the slain (*N. Carolina Records*, vol. x, p. 482).

## Rev. Doctor Caner (page 222).

*b*. 1700, *d*. 1792. A graduate of Yale, he became a convert to the Church of England. He became Rector of King's Chapel, Boston, in 1747, and it was mainly owing to him that the old wooden structure was replaced by a stone building (J. S. M. Anderson, *The History of the Church of England in the Colonies of the British Empire*, vol. iii, pp. 551–2). Dr. Caner took an active part in the controversy regarding an American bishopric (Cross, *The Anglican Episcopate and the American Colonies*, pp. 150, 317–18). He was a devoted loyalist, and Stark, op. cit., p. 347, notes that he made the following entry in the Record Book of his chapel when about to start for Halifax: 'An unnatural rebellion . . . obliged the loyal part of his subjects to evacuate their dwellings and take refuge in Halifax, London, and elsewhere; by which means the public worship at King's Chapel became suspended, and it is likely to remain so until it shall please God to change the hearts of the rebels or to give success to his Majesty's arms for suppressing the rebellion.' Dr. Caner wrote from Halifax, May 10, 1776: 'I continued to officiate to the small remains of my parishioners, though without support, till the 10th of March, when I suddenly and unexpectedly received notice that the king's troops would evacuate the town. It is not easy to paint the distress and confusion of the inhabitants on the occasion. I had but six or seven hours to prepare for this measure, being obliged to embark the same day for Halifax, where we arrived the 1st of April. This sudden movement prevented me from saving my books, furniture, or any part of my interest, except bedding, wearing apparel, and a little provision for my small family during the passage' (ibid., p. 348).

Hutchinson, *Diary and Letters*, vol. ii, p. 72, notes under June 22, 1776: 'Dr. Caner, passenger in the *Adamant* from Halifax, came to town to-day, and I called on him at his lodgings in the Haymarket. The soldiers, set to guard his house, plundered it of his books, furniture, &c.' Hutchinson had already in July 1774 (ibid., vol. i, p. 169) informed the King that 'Dr. Caner, a very worthy man, frequently inculcated upon his hearers due subjection to government and condemned the riotous, violent opposition to it.'

## Thomas Oliver (page 227).

*b*. 1734, *d*. 1815 in England. He succeeded Andrew Oliver as Lieutenant-Governor of Massachusetts in 1774. The two Olivers were not related.

A very graphic account, given by himself, of the manner in which he was coerced by the mob into resigning his seat as a Mandamus Councillor, is quoted by Stark, op. cit., pp. 185–7. Hutchinson wrote to Thomas Oliver on November 24, 1774: 'I should not treat you as a friend if I represented the manner in which people express themselves upon the subject of your resignation different from the whole truth. In general it is said a man is excusable who, when he is in the hands of four thousand people and threatened with death, submits to the terms imposed upon him. Some have got it here, I know not how, that before you went to the Governor more had been said to you by the mob (for I call them mob though freeholders) than you communicated; and that, if the Governor had known the whole, he would have laid you under arrest. Others say that unless our mobs differ from those of England, no man is in danger of his life in open day. It is impossible for people here to know all the circumstances of the case. A succession of other great and important events, some come and some coming, will probably put an end to further speculation' (op. cit., vol. i, p. 321).

Again, under July 20, 1776: 'Lieutenant-Governor Oliver called to acquaint me with his intention to apply to Lord North for his salary. It seems, as I had it from Mr. Knox, that when General Gage was superseded in the command of the army he was promised that the whole of his salary as Governor should continue; otherwise I should have thought that the Lieutenant-Governor might have stood a chance for half; but now he can have no more than his £300 as Lieutenant-Governor (ibid., vol. ii, p. 83).

BENJAMIN FANEUIL (page 234).

He was the nephew of Peter Faneuil, the generous citizen, of Huguenot extraction, who founded Faneuil Hall, that 'cradle of liberty, in which the Revolution was rocked'. Stark (op. cit., pp. 231–2) quotes from *Tea Leaves* the following letter addressed to B. Faneuil:

Gentlemen,

It is currently reported that you are in the extremest anxiety respecting your standing with the good people of this town and province, as commissioners of the sale of the monopolised and dutied tea. We do not wonder in the least that your apprehensions are terrible, when the most enlightened, humane and conscientious community in the earth view you in the light of tigers or mad dogs, whom the public safety obliges them to destroy. Long have this people been irreconcileable to the idea of spilling human blood on almost any occasion whatever; but they have lately seen a penitential thief suffer death for pilfering a few pounds from scattering individuals; you boldly avow a resolution to bear a principal part in the robbery of every inhabitant of this country in the present and future ages of everything dear and interesting to them. Are there no laws in the book of God and Nature that enjoin such miscreants to be cut off from among the people, as troublers of the whole congregation? Yea, verily, there are laws and officers to put them into execution, which you can neither corrupt, intimidate, nor escape, and whose resolution to bring you to condign punishment you can only avoid by a speedy imitation of your brethren in Philadelphia. This people are still averse to precipitate your fate, but in case of much longer delay in complying with their indispensable demands, you will not fail to meet the just rewards of your avarice and insolence. Remember, Gentlemen, this is the last warning you are ever to expect from the insulted, abused and most indignant vindicators of violated liberty in the town of Boston.

O. C. Secy. per order.

Thursday Evening, 9 o'clock,
November 4, 1773.
To Messrs. the Tea Commissioners.
Directed to B—— F——, Esq.

JOHN CUMMING (page 257).

There are several entries relating to John Cumming in *Minutes of the Commissioners for Detecting and Defeating Conspiracies in the State of New York, Albany County Sessions, 1778–81*, ed. by H. Paltsits, New York, 1909.

August 4, 1778. John Cumming was also cited to appear before the Board; and appearing he was tendered the oath which he refused to take. Ordered that the said J. Cumming appear at the City Hall of the city of Albany on Friday the 14th day of August, it being the time appointed for their being removed within the enemies lines with fourteen days provision for themselves and such of their family as they chuse should accompany them (Persons able to bear arms excepted). They are also permitted to take with them all their clothing and household furniture (vol. i, pp. 192–3).

August 8. Ordered that a certificate be sent down to John Morris Scott Esq., Sec. of State of New York, certifying that . . . John Cumming . . . were in pursuance of the Act of the Legislature duly passed respecting neutral and equivocal characters cited to appear before us; and, on their appearance, we having tendered them the oath in the above mentioned Act set forth and prescribed, they refused to take the same (ibid., p. 198).

December 7. John Cumming, who refused to take the oath . . . and was in consequence thereof to be removed within the enemies' lines but was detained by his Excellency the Governor for exchange, made application to the Board to be permitted to go and reside at Kats Kill with his family; and, there being no prospect of an exchange taking place as yet, . . . therefore ordered that the said John Cumming enter into a parole to remain within the limits and bounds of the district of Grote Imboght and abide by such restrictions as are in the said parole specified (ibid., p. 295).

November 13, 1779. Ordered that a letter be wrote to John Cumming informing him that it is the determination of the Governor not to exchange him until the enemy shall consent to exchange Henry van Schaack (ibid., p. 280).

February 8, 1783. List of the names of persons who have refused to take the oath . . . and who have, in consequence, been removed within the enemy's lines or detained by his Excellency the Governor for exchange . . . John Cumming (ibid., vol. iii, pp. 834–5).

### George Rome (page 262).

'A letter of his to Dr. Moffat, in which he indulged in some remarks upon the political heresies of the time, and especially upon the manner of administering justice in the Colonies, found its way to England, and was thence transmitted by Franklin to Massachusetts with several letters of Hutchinson, Oliver, and others. The House of Representatives of Massachusetts censured Rome, by resolutions; the Assembly of Rhode Island, however, required him to acknowledge himself the writer . . . and, upon his refusal, committed him to prison, but finally permitted him to go at large' (Sabine, op. cit., vol. ii).

In *Hist. MSS. Comm., Am. MSS. in R. Inst.*, vol. i, p. 447, is a letter: '1779, 6th month, 16, Newport, Respected Friend, George Rome,

'We have endeavoured to get rent for thy wharf and stores, which has been employed by the Commissary ever since the arrival of the army, but without effect.'

Rome wrote from John Street, Adelphi, to the Treasury on October 1, 1779, requesting that the Commissary-General might be instructed to co-operate with his own agent at Rhode Island in the choice of proper persons to adjust the amounts of rents, wharfage, &c., to be paid. When their lordships are informed that it is a custom to pay rents of stores and wharves so employed at New York he is sure that he may expect speedy relief; for it would be unjust if the Deputy Commissary at Rhode Island should enjoy emoluments of the remains of his (Rome's) estate saved from the rebellion, when these emoluments are insufficient to support himself (ibid., vol. ii, pp. 44–5).

Rome was in October 1780, along with Governor Franklin, J. Martin, Ruggles, Coxe, Ludlow, Lutwyche, and Leonard, appointed a member of the Board of Associated Loyalists (ibid., vol. ii, p. 198).

### Daniel Coxe (page 274).

D. Coxe became a member of the Council in 1771. He was the fifth member of his family who took a prominent part in New Jersey. Dr. Fisher, *New Jersey as a Royal Province, 1738–76*, p. 71, describes him as 'an ardent and active Tory'; but he quotes Governor Franklin as writing on January 5, 1776, that 'three of the leading members of the Council are strongly inclined to favour the measures of the Congress, and the most who were present have a leaning the same way, except two or three at most; and even these think it necessary to their safety to observe a kind of trimming conduct'.

As corroboration to this view of Coxe's character we may note a letter written by him to Skinner in which he expresses the hope that Gage will be cautious in assuming the offensive, for fear of retaliations in the south. 'They are not even allowed to preserve a neutrality, and passiveness becomes a crime' (*New Jersey Archives*, 1st series, vol. x, p. 645).

Sabine (op. cit., vol. i, p. 339) quotes from a letter of Christopher Sower to the effect that Coxe was made chairman of the Board of Refugees to deprive him of the opportunity of speaking, as he had the gift of saying very little with many words.

It was claimed that Sir R. Heath conveyed his rights under the grant of 1630 to the Earl of Arundel, and that these rights became eventually vested in Dr. Coxe. A memorial to this effect was addressed to William III; and the goodness of his case is asserted by his son, Daniel Coxe, in his book *Carolana*. The Heath Grant, however, was formally annulled August 12, 1663 (Winsor, *Narrative and Critical Hist. of Am.*, vol. v, p. 335). Nevertheless, like the importunate widow, Coxe, by his assiduity, succeeded in impressing the authorities.

*Carolana* was published in 1722.

# BOOK V

## Memorial of Eliz^th Smith—Widow

Eliz^th Smith—the Claimant—sworn. 3^d of Dec^r 1784.

Determin'd the 3^d of Dec^r 1784.

Is a Native of Eng^d & her Husband likewise. He went out in 1772 & in 1773. He was appointed Naval Officer at Beaufort.[1] Commission produced signed by Gov^r Ball [2] in 1773. He held this till he was displaced by the Rebel Gov^r in 1776. He always took a loyal part. He died a few days after he was Displaced in 1776. She left America in 1777 & came to Eng^d in 1778. She applied to the Treasury & they allowed her £100 a Y^r & in nine Months they order'd her to go out again but she could not go. She likewise rec^d £100 from Lord North & 20 from Lord Shelburne & since her Case was heard by M^r Wilmot & M^r Coke She has rec^d from Oct^r 1783 an Allowance of £60 a Y^r & now continues to receive it.

Her Husband a Loyalist but died in consequence of an Accident in 1776.

Former Bounty £100 a Y^r.
Present Bounty £60 a Y^r.

Doct^r Fraser—sworn.

Knew M^r Mich^l Smith. He was then Sheriff of Beaufort. He was loyal. He died by running a Splinter into his hand which produced a locked Jaw. He attended him. Believes that M^rs Smith quitted that Country to get to her own friends. Was at Beaufort at that time. Recollects her going & promoted a subscription to carry her away. Her Husband left her in very distress'd Circumstances & he died in Debt. Says the troubles would not have prevented her selling her property. Says he should not have promoted a subscription if he had thought she had anything to sell. Being shewn the schedule he says she might be possess'd of the Articles but knows they were incumber'd. Says the property after she went was sold by the Sheriff he bought a Negro of the Sheriff himself. Thinks after the Man's death at Beaufort they were not worth so much as the Widow has rec^d from Gov^t (£250) since that time.

## Memorial of Frances Dongan [3]—Widow

Frances Dongan—the Claimant—sworn. 6^th of Dec^r 1784.

Determin'd y^e 18^th of Dec^r 1784.

Is a Native of America. Was Born at Brunswick.[4] Her Husband resided at Rahaway. She was married in 1773. When the rebellion began he followed the profession of an Attorney which he had followed five or six Y^rs. The Rebels knew he was a Loyalist & therefore treated him very ill. They took him out of his Bed. Believes he refused to take the Oaths or sign any Association paper &c. He join'd the King's Army when Sir W^m Howe came into the Jerseys. Col^l Dongan's Commission not produced. He was then made Lieut^t of the 3^d Batt^n of New Jersey Volunteers. He died in 1777 & was killed in Action [5] the Claimant's father will

Her Husband a Loyalist & kill'd in Action fighting ag^t the Americans.

[1] South Carolina.
[2] ? Bull.
[3] Mrs. Dongan was the daughter of Barnardus Lagrange (*Hist. MSS. Comm., Am. MSS. in R. Inst.*, vol. iv, p. 107).
[4] New Brunswick, New Jersey.
[5] In a skirmish on Staten Island in August (Sabine, op. cit., vol. i, p. 385).

produce the Will. He made the Will the 23^d^ of Aug^t^ the Day on which he died. She had only one Child who died the same Day that M^r^ Dongan died. She receives an Allowance of £40 a Y^r^ whch she has rec^d^ from the 5^th^ of Jan^y^ 1784.

Bounty £40 a Y^r^.

Brig^r^ Gen^l^ Skynner—sworn.

Knew M^r^ Dongan he was an Attorney at the Commencement of the rebellion. He behaved extremely well. Believes he was taken prisoner in Aug^t^ 1776. In Dec^r^ 1776 He gave him a Warrant at Eliz^th^ Town to raise a Corps which he afterwards did & he was killed at the head of that Corps in Aug^t^ following. He was a very Zealous Man & knows that he was killed in Action. He was present with him after he was wounded. He thinks he might get £200 a Y^r^ as an Attorney. Says there is no provision made for the Widows of Officers in his Corps. His pay as a Col^l^ was better than his profession in the Law. Believes M^rs^ Dongan had some Allowance at New York. Knows nothing of M^r^ Dongan's property.

## Memorial of Barnardus Lagrange [1]

Determin'd the 17^th^ of Dec^r^ 1784.

7^th^ of Dec^r^ 1784.

Barnardus Lagrange—the Claimant—sworn.

Is a Native of America & when the troubles broke out He lived at Brunswick [2] & practised as an Attorney. He took an early opportunity of shewing his Sentiments & was insulted & beset early in 1775 this was for refusing to sign their Associations. They never offer'd the Oath to him. He was obliged to leave his home the 1^st^ of July 1776 & join'd Sir W^m^ Howe the 14^th^. He continued with the Army till Dec^r^ 1776 when he came again to his own House & the Army marched to Brunswick. Gen^l^ Skynner appointed him to administer the Oaths to such persons as were disposed to take them. He continued at his own House till the 20^th^ of June 1777. He then went to New York where he staid till Aug^t^ 1783. He had sometimes 17 Hessian Officers at his House at Brunswick. States no Services.

A Zealous Loyalist.

Did not bear Arms.

He has an Allowance of 80 a Y^r^ which he has rec^d^ from the 5^th^ of July 1783 & still continues to receive it.

Bounty £80 a Y^r^.

8^th^ of Dec^r^ 1784.

Daniel Coxe Esq—sworn.

Knows the Claim^t^ & has known him many Years. He join'd the British Troops as soon as they came into Jersey. He believes him to have been uniformly loyal & has heard that he rec^d^ many Insults. Did not know his farm near Fox Hill. Knows that M^r^ Lagrange had Lands on Schooley's Mountain because he has frequently heard that M^r^ Lagrange had lands there & once was shewn a Tract which he was told belonged to M^r^ Lagrange. Thinks he can put a general Value upon Lands in this Situation & says upon a Supposition that they had the necessary Quantity of Meadow they would be worth £3 or £4 an Acre. Never heard it to be the best tract on the Mountain. Says that M^r^ Lagrange was in exceeding good business as an Attorney. Thinks M^r^ Lagrange's practice might produce to him between 5 & £600 a Y^r^. Says he has stated his own practice very modestly in putting it at £400 a Year.

1 In a memorial dated May 27, 1783, New York, B. Lagrange asked for a passage to England for himself, son, and daughter (see note 2 on previous page).

2 New Brunswick, New Jersey.

General Skynner—sworn.

Knew Mr Lagrange very well many Years before the rebellion. He took a very early & a very decided part from the beginning in opposing their Committees. He made himself very obnoxious. Believes him to have been uniformly loyal. Knew a good deal of his property.

John Antill—sworn.

Knew Mr Lagrange's farm on the Rariton. He saw it last in 1775. Does not know the Number of Acres. It was then in good Condition. Supposes it to be worth £9 or £10 an Acre. Knew several Lots which he had in New Brunswick but can't tell the selling price of Lands there. Values Meadow Land at £50 an Acre. Thinks the 5 Acres worth £30 an Acre. Knows the roundabouts. Says the Land is good for nothing but the Wood. Supposes it might be purchased for 20*s*. an Acre. Knew his House at New Brunswick. Should have thought it worth £700 in 1775. It was one of the best Houses in the Town.

### Memorial of Saml Shoemaker [1] Esq.

Saml Shoemaker Esq—the Claimant—upon his Affirmation. 9th of Decr 1784.

Determin'd the 15th of Decr 1784.

Is a Native of Philadelphia & was settled there when the troubles began. He had been a Magistrate & an Alderman many Years before. When the troubles began he uniformly opposed all their meetings & Associations. Nothing very material happened till 1776 when he was taken up & was order'd to give a parole that he wd not quit his House or hold any Correspondence with Sir Wm Howe. They confined him for two Days & then set him at liberty. He says it is one of the principles of his religion not to bear Arms. He kept himself from this time very much within doors till Sir Wm Howe came to Philadelphia which was in Septr 1777. Says Mr Galloway gave him an Acct of all the Loyalists & the Claimt was sent to very early to know whether he would accept of being a Magistrate of Police. He consented to it & the trouble of it was immense & he had an Allowance of £300 a Yr as long as Sir Wm Howe remain'd there. When the British evacuated Philadelphia He went with them. When Sir Wm Howe left Philadelphia Sir Henry Clinton only gave him £200 a Yr. In March 1778 whilst they sat at Lancaster the Congress passed a Law attainting him by name & confiscating all his property. He was particularly obnoxious on acct of his principles. When the Army quitted Philadelphia he went round by Water to New York. He had no Office or place of trust till Sir Guy Carleton when he was appointed one of the Board to manage the Affairs of the Loyalists. The £200 a Yr was continued to him at New York & Sir Guy Carlton gave him at two different times £100 & Sir Henry Clinton at another time gave him £100 for procuring Intelligence which with the £200 a Yr is all that he ever recd before he left America. He came to Engd upon the Evacuation of New York & arrived at Spithead the 28th of Decr 1783. He has recd an Allowance of £180 a Yr from the Treasury which commenced from the 5th of April 1784. And he now continues to receive it.

A Zealous & meritorious Loyalist.
And by his early & uniform conduct &c render'd services to Govt.
Did not bear Arms.

Proof of Confiscation.

Bounty £180 a Yr.

[1] The volumes of the *Hist. MSS. Comm., Am. MSS. in R. Inst.*, show S. Shoemaker to have been a very active member of the Board of Refugees Loyalists. His name is in a list of persons to be apprehended by order of the Council of Pennsylvania (T. Gilpin, *Exiles in Virginia*, p. 72).

Loss of Office.

He was Treasurer to the Corporation of Philadelphia which was usually held for Life. He held it as long as the Corporation existed & never knew an Instance of any person being removed. He says the Value of it was from £70 to £100 a Y$^{r}$.

Phineas Bond Esq—sworn.

Has known M$^{r}$ Shoemaker for many Years. He was always a very respectable Man both in public & private. He always consider'd him to be uniformly attached to the royal Cause. He was always active in Elections to keep out disaffected persons & he was very active as a Magistrate of Police & he has heard that he was engaged in obtaining Intelligence. He was particularly obnoxious & thinks if he had staid behind the Army he would have suffer'd. He was consider'd as a Man of great property but he thinks he is unable to value it. He knows all the Valuers & says they are Men of unexceptionable Character. He knows the new House which he built & all the premises. Thinks it would have sold in quiet times for £3400 C. or £2000 S.

Knows the Dwelling House with the Wharf & Warehouses. It was a comfortable House. He thinks it was worth 14 or 1500 S. Knows the Store Stables & Coach House but can't value it. Thinks the Acre of Land at Kensington worth £15 or £20. This is about the same distance from Philadelphia as Kensington from Hyde Park Corner. Has frequently been in M$^{r}$ Shoemaker's House. It was plain but neat. Can't tell the Value. Knows M$^{rs}$ Shoemaker's House in the Country. Doubts whether if it was let it would let for £50 a Y$^{r}$ S. Should have guess'd £40 a Year. Corrects himself to £50 a Y$^{r}$. Has heard that M$^{rs}$ Shoemaker is very ill treated by the Americans & that she is not permitted to enjoy any part of it. Believes M$^{r}$ Shoemaker has finally lost all his property & has heard that part of it has been sold.

Joseph Galloway Esq—sworn.

Knew M$^{r}$ Shoemaker. He was a very respectable Man in private life. Before the troubles He was a Magistrate & one of the Corporation. Knows his public principles as they relate to this Dispute. When the other Magistrates were less active ag$^{t}$ the Measures of the rebels He was particularly active ag$^{t}$ them. Believes him to be a Man of uniform & decided Loyalty. Thinks notwithstanding he is a Quaker if it had been necessary He would not have scrupled to take up Arms. When Sir W$^{m}$ Howe came to Philadelphia he was by M$^{r}$ Galloway's recommendation made a Magistrate of Police. He recommended him from a Conviction of his zeal & principles. He thinks he has render'd essential Service to this Country by his Advice & his Conduct.

## Memorial of James Rogers

Determin'd the 10$^{th}$ of Dec$^{r}$ 1784.

10$^{th}$ of Dec$^{r}$ 1784.

James Rogers—the Claimant—sworn.

A Loyalist Did not bear Arms.[1]

Is a Native of Ireland & went to America in the Year 1770 & was settled in Georgia when the rebellion broke out. He took an early part in the War. He never took the Oaths to the rebels. He says he never was in the Militia with the Americans. He join'd the British under Col$^{l}$ Maitland. He never enlisted but he rec$^{d}$ Pay for one Month & an half. After he join'd the British he served as a Militia Man during

[1] *Sic* in Text.

the whole War. He came from Savannah at the Evacuation & came to Charlestown. He applied to the Treasury & rec^d^ the Sum of £10 in full. Bounty £10 in full.

George Johnson—sworn.

Knew James Rogers in America. He lived 6 or 7 Miles from him. He was a Loyalist. He had some land in that Country but he can't tell how much. He has been by his plantation there was some clearance on it. He had Horses & Cattle. He used to bring Corn to his Mill sometimes with an Horse & sometimes with a Cart. Says he bore Arms with the British.

Sam^l^ Montgomery—sworn.

Knew James Rogers in Georgia. Has often seen him at the Stations of the British Army. He was a sickly Man at the beginning of the War. Believes him to have been a loyal Man & a very peaceable honest Man. Knows him because he was a Magistrate & when he used to summon persons upon Juries he summoned this Man because he knew him to be a freeholder.

### Memorial of John Hennesey

Determin'd y^e^ 10^th^ of Dec^r^ 1784.

11^th^ of Dec^r^ 1784.

John Hennesey—the Claimant—sworn.

Is a Native of Ireland & has been in America more than 20 Y^rs^. Went out as an indented Serv^t^ for 4 Y^rs^. When the War began he lived in Charlestown & followed Carting & kept Horses sometimes two & sometimes three. He was obliged to quit the province sooner than take the Abjuration Oath. He quitted Charlestown in 1778 & went to France. He came thro' Germany to Eng^d^. When he heard that Charlestown was taken he went to New York & he was at the taking of Charlestown. He was Conductor of Waggons. He came to this Country at the Evacuation of Charlestown. He has an Allowance of £20 a Y^r^ which he had rec^d^ from the 5^th^ of Jan^y^ 1783.

A Loyalist. Did not bear Arms. Bounty £20 a Y^r^.

Luke Keaton—sworn.

Knew John Hennesley in Charlestown before the rebellion. He followed the trade of buying & selling at public Auctions. He had likewise Carts & Drays. He came away because he would not take the Oath. Knew an House that he had. He bought it at public Auction. He bought it in 1775 & paid £3000 C. for it. After the siege the House was pulled down.

### Memorial of Luke Keating

Determin'd the 11^th^ of Dec^r^ 1784.

11^th^ of Dec^r^ 1784.

Luke Keating—the Claimant—sworn.

Is a Native of Eng^d^ & went to America 18 or 19 Y^rs^ ago. He followed the Sea & went on board a Merch^t^ Ship. He lived in Charlestown in 1774. He followed the Carting business & his Wife kept a small Shop. When the troubles began the Oaths were tender'd to him but he refused to take them & went into the Country 160 Miles from Charlestown. He staid there till the Town was taken. He lived in Ninety Six District. He was employ'd as a Waggon Driver by the British & had half a Crown a Day. He staid at Charlestown till the Evacuation when he came to Eng^d^. He receives an Allowance of £20 a Y^r^ which he has rec^d^ about two Y^rs^ from the 5^th^ of Jan^y^ 1783 & now receives it.

A Loyalist. Did not bear Arms. Bounty £20 a Y^r^.

## Memorial of Major Poynton

Determin'd the 13th of Decr 1784.

Brereton Poynton—sworn. 13th of Decr 1784.

Husband a British Officer & the Wife a Loyalist.

Is a Native of Engd & was in 1774 on Duty as an Officer in Jamaica. He returned to Trenton in 1774 where he had resided before that time. He married Mrs Poynton in 1772. He staid a Month at his House at Trenton & then returned to Jamaica & then returned to Engd. He left Mrs Poynton who was born in Trenton there in 1774. Her Parents were loyalists but says they were dead before the troubles. He went out in 1777 to bring her away & he brought her to Engd. All her friends were loyal. Mrs Poynton had no Allowance till 1782 from which time she has had an Allowance of £50 a Year. He never recd any Letter from her for 23 Months.

Bounty £50 a Yr.

Danl Coxe Esq—sworn.

Knew Mrs Poynton very well. She used to speak her Mind about the Rebellion & was very loyal. Knew the Tavern thinks if it had been let to a Stranger it would have taken £50 a Yr independent of the two Houses which were let separately. Including the two Houses He values the premises at more than £1000. Says that Mrs Poynton asked him his Opinion before she made her Schedule & therefore his Valuation will probably be much the same as hers. And being asked in general terms He says he approves her Schedule. Being asked as to the words of the Will where her father leaves certain property in these words *If I have a Child* then I leave to that Child he thinks under these words the Sisters would be equally entitled as Coheiresses.

## Memorial of Garrett McGragh

Determin'd the 28th of Jany 1785.

Garrett McGragh—the Claimant—sworn. 24th of Decr 1784.

A Loyalist & bore Arms.

Is a Native of Ireland & first went to America in 1762. In 1774 He was settled in Middletown in Connecticut. He was in trade. He says he bore Arms as a Volunteer in the Prince of Wales's American Volunteers. In 1775 He was called upon by the Americans to go into their Service. But he refused & join'd the British in New York in 1776. He never had pay. He continued with the British till 1779 when he came home & recd from the Treasury £20 & afterwards in Jany 1781 He recd £17 10*s*. And from that time He has recd an Allowance of 50 a Year which was confirmed by Mr Wilmot & Mr Coke.

Bounty £50 a Yr & two Sums of £20 & £17 10*s*.

## Memorial of Mrs Anne Reak

Determin'd the 24th of Decr 1784.

Anne Reak—Widow—the Claimant—sworn. 24th of Decr 1784.

Her Husband a Loyalist.

Is a Native of Engd & went to America about 18 or 19 Yrs ago. In the Yr 1774 She lived at Newport & her Husband carried on the trade of a Stationer. Her Husband died in the Yr 1780. He was a Loyalist & had never taken part with the Rebels. Upon his Death she carried on the business a little time. Her Husband was made Conductor of Stores & continued for 4 Yrs. The Appointment was worth £100 a Yr. Says that he got more than that by his business. She clear'd 20 or £30 a Yr by her business whilst she carried it on.

She has been in Engd three Yrs. She applied to the Treasury about two Yrs ago but her Case was postpon'd for want of a Certificate. A Certificate afterwards being brought in Her Case was heard & She recd £15 in full.

Bounty £15 in full This being given Conditionally that she should relinquish all further claims. Therefore the Claim disallow'd altogether.

N.B. This sum was given to her upon Condition that she relinquished all further Claims upon this Country.

Besides the £15 appears to the Board to be a full Compensation for her Losses.

She swears that she did not understand it to be in that light but she did not read the Rec^t which she sign'd at Whitehall.

## Memorial of Alexander Wallace Esq [1]

Determin'd the 14^th of May 1785.

Alexander Wallace—the Claimant—sworn. 24^th of Jan^y 1785.

Is a Native of Ireland & went to America in 1757 to New York to settle as a Merch^t & was there in that Capacity when the troubles broke out. He frequently assisted Gov^r Tryon when on board a Ship with Money &c. And from the first uniformly supported the Cause of Gov^t. He was Partner with his Brother & the firm of the House was Hugh [3] & Alexander. He always refused to sign any Association. He supplied Sir Henry Clinton with Money when he went to the Southward. He suffer'd much for this & that was given as the Cause of his being taken up by the Congress. He remain'd in Confinement on parole for five Months. He had no Commission upon the Money only the Exchange. He supplied above £4000. He was sorry to do it. But he says no other House could have supplied the Money. He says the House never did nor did he personally & he says it on his Oath. He says neither he nor his Brother advanced a farthing to the Congress to fit out Gen^l Arnold's expedition ag^t Quebec. He says that such a report prevail'd & that it was mention'd at Gen^l Tryon's table but Gen^l Tryon winked at it & said it was better not to contradict it because it would be better that it should not be known that the Money was (as it really was) advanced to the British Army. Promises to call upon Gen^l Tryon to desire him to attend. Lord Howe offer'd him to be put upon the List for £200 a Year if he pleas'd but he refused it this was in 1776. He had the command of a Company in 1777 & he rais'd 76 Men. He was active upon many Occasions but states no particular Services. He never rec^d a Shilling from Gov^t at New York but he has rec^d 2 Quarters of an annual Allowance of 120 a Y^r which was granted to him from Midsummer last.

A Loyalist.

Did not bear Arms.[2]

Bounty £120 a Y^r.

Alexander Wallace—sworn.

Says he never did upon any Occasion advance a Shilling to the Congress. Produces his Book to shew that he supplied Gov^r Tryon with Money at great risque. He never rec^d any Advantage from this Money on the contrary he lost a Years Interest upon it.

Lawful Money of the Province of New York Jersey & Congress Paper which in 1776 He was obliged to take for a Debt of £1590 by which he lost £1299 13*s*. 4*d*. All this was lawful Money which he now has in his possession. He never had it in his power to pass a Shilling of it. He says he lent a great deal of Money to Loyalists & has receiv'd very little back again.

Disallowed.

[1] There is a signed letter from Carleton to Lord North, dated November 22, 1783, in favour of Mr. Wallace, a merchant at New York (*Hist. MSS. Comm.*, *Am. MSS. in R. Inst.*, vol. iv, p. 469). A. Wallace was a member of the Committee of Fifty-one, appointed in May 1774 (Becker, op. cit., p. 114). A letter dated August 17, 1776, states that Messrs. Hugh and Alexander Wallace were committed to jail, having refused to take the oath of allegiance to Congress (Moore, op. cit., vol. i, p. 289).

[2] *Sic* in Text.

[3] Hugh was appointed a member of the New York Council in June 1769 (*New York Col. Docs.*, vol. viii, p. 148). The fact of his imprisonment was reported by Governor Tryon on August 22, 1776 (ibid., p. 685).

Willm Bayard Esq—sworn.

Has known Mr Wallace for more than 20 Years intimately. He thinks that he was perfectly loyal. He never associated or took any part with the Rebel Govt. Does not know anything of his supplying Sr Henry Clinton with Money. Admits that he has heard a flying report that the House had advanced Money to the Congress. Believes that it was not true with respect to Alexander Wallace. The other Brother was not so zealous. And the report was confined to Hugh Wallace. Says that Alexr Wallace was a firmer Man than Hugh but believes that Hugh wished well to Great Britain. Says the report was generally believed & not contradicted. He is not much acquainted with Alexr Wallace's property. He was in the first Situation as a Mercht. His Storehouses were advantageously situated. Does not know the Lot of Land in New York. It being explain'd he says he does know it & that the Value put upon it in the Schedule is a fair one.

Determin'd the 25th of Jany 1785.

## Memorial of Louis Deblois [1]

25th of Jany 1785.

Louis Deblois—the Claimant—sworn.

A Loyalist.

Did not bear Arms.

Is a Native of New York but had lived at Boston 40 Years before the troubles where he was fix'd as a Mercht in a very extensive line. He was uniformly loyal from the beginning & sign'd Addresses to Genl Gage & Genl Hutchinson. He was a Cadet but in no military Situation. He left Boston at the Evacuation & he came to Halifax & from thence to Engd in 1776 where he has been ever since. He was obliged to leave many of his Goods. He first recd an allowance when he had been near a Year here but it went back so that he has recd it from the Month of July 1776 & he now continues to receive it.

Bounty £100 a Yr.

Harrison Gray Esq—sworn.

Knew Louis Deblois very well. He was a Shopkeeper of great reputation & carried on a great trade. He was always looked upon as a friend to Govt. He was esteem'd a Man of Substance. He has frequently been in his Shop but he can't judge of the Value of the Stock it was well stocked & was one of the principal Houses in the Town. Thinks it very probable that he might be obliged to leave a great part of his Stock as everybody was obliged to leave more or less. He knows that he was a Fireward. Upon the whole he thinks him a very good Loyalist & a Man of good Character.

Gilbert Harrison Esq—sworn.

Is a Mercht in London but has been in America was there in 1770. Knew him for many Years. He carried on business with great reputation. He dealt with the Witness & he found him always a punctual & good Man. Believes he imported about £6000 a Yr & thinks he must have made a profit of 20 per Cent upon it. Thinks he must at least have made £1000 by it. He knows his principles so well that he is able to say that he is no new Loyalist.

[1] There is a mistake or misprint in Stark (op. cit., p. 446). He says that Louis Deblois died very suddenly in England in 1779; but he was very much alive on January 25, 1785. It is true that mention is made of a Louis Deblois, Jr., who died in 1802, but, as this Louis was born in 1762, he was not the above claimant.

## Memorial of Theodore Maurice

Theodore Maurice—the Claimant—sworn. 26th of Jany 1785.

Is a Native of Engd & went to America in 1754 to Govr Morris [1] Govr of Pensylvania. He continued in America till the Commencement of the troubles. He was then Prothonotary of the County of Newcastle. No Salary but the Profits arising from fees about £500 a Yr C. likewise Register of the Probate of Wills. No Salary but the Profits about £150 a Yr C. Likewise Comptroller of the Customs under the Crown with a Salary of £50 S. a Yr fees about £30 C. He never sign'd any Association or took any part with them tho' much solicited to acknowledge their Govt. He came away from America in 1778 determin'd not to remain there after the King's Govt was overthrown.

He recd the £50 the Salary of Comptroller up to Octr 1782 at that time he recd an Allowance of £25 a Yr. When the Salary ceas'd to be paid it was recommended by Mr Wilmot & Mr Coke to add £25 a Yr more & he now receives an Allowance of £50 a Yr.

Produces his Appointment as Prothonotary dated by Mr Penn in May 1766. It was not an Office for Life but during pleasure. He likewise produces his Appointment as Register of the same Date. This Office likewise for pleasure but it was not usual to remove persons except for ill Conduct. Produces his Appointment from the Commrs of the Customs at Boston dated in 1770 of Comptroller. This an Office for pleasure but seldom removed.

Debts amounting to £720 S. They were all arrears of Fees.

His Offices required a good deal of Attendance or Superintendance for he did great part of his business by Clerks.

He still acts under Mr Jenkinson in the Muster Office the emolument of which is £50 a Year. He was recommended to it by Mr Charles Jenkinson.[2]

Joseph Galloway Esq—sworn.

Has known Mr Maurice long before & since the Rebellion. He believes he was always averse to the measures of the Rebels. He thinks he might be permitted to have remain'd in that Govt which was one of the most moderate Govts still longer without sacrificing his principles. He knows the Prothonotary's Office & thinks it must be worth more than 400 a Yr C. clear of the Expence of Clerks. Knows likewise that he had the Office of Register & thinks that it might be worth more than £100 a Yr. He was likewise Comptroller of the Customs with a Salary of £50 a Yr but does not know the fees. Says in the Prothonotarys Office there must necessarily be many fees owing.

[1] Robert Hunter Morris, *b.* 1700 ?, *d.* 1764. He had been Chief Justice of New Jersey and was Governor of Pennsylvania from 1754 to 1756 (Appleton, op. cit., vol. iv, p. 414). His position was one of extreme difficulty between the Quaker and German colonists, who refused to recognize imperial obligations and the Proprietary which was unwilling that its lands should contribute to the public taxes. That Morris's own opinions were not very liberal is shown by his statement that the Albany plan of union 'was formed upon such republican principles . . . as it seemed calculated to unite the colonys in such a manner as to give the Crown little or no influence in their Councils' (*Pennsylvania Archives*, 1st ser., vol. ii, p. 499).

[2] *b.* 1727, *d.* 1808. Created Baron Hawkesbury in 1786 and Earl of Liverpool in 1796. He became Secretary at War in 1778.

## Memorial of Gov^r Martin[1]

26^th of Jan^y 1785.

Josiah Martin Esq—the Claimant—sworn.

Is a Native of Ireland & went to America in 1770 & was appointed Gov^r of North Carolina in 1771. He dates the Commencement of the troubles from the Year 1774. He gave the earliest information of the Commotions to the Ministers here & did everything in his power to suppress them by employing Agents &c. He took no actual Measures for raising the Country till 1776 because Hostilities were not commenced before that time. He quitted the Shore in May 1775 & went on board a Ship but he never acted as Gov^r afterwards. He was with the Army at Wilmington & attended Lord Cornwallis in his march thro' that Country. Gov^r Martin receives an Allowance of £500 a Y^r which he rec^d from the Y^r 1775. At the same time he rec^d his Salary of 1000 a Y^r from the Treasury up to the time that M^r Wilmot & M^r Coke enquired into the Case & their Report was that if M^r Martin continued to receive his Salary he should have no Allowance but that if the Salary was stopp'd then he sh^d receive £500 a Y^r. The Salary was continued up to Oct^r 1783 when it stopp'd.

He had several Grants of Land which he granted to his Children but as he had an unlimited right of granting Lands he thinks it would be very illiberal & unhandsome in him to make a Demand. He says he probably had granted more than 10000 Acres. Being asked his Opinion as to others making a Claim for uncultivated Lands He does not choose to give his Opinion but says his own Example is the best Comment. Being asked as to his Opinion about the Clauses of forfeiture in Grants for want of Cultivation He says it is clear & does not admit of a Doubt that they are forfeited. Says great part of these Lands are *Moonshine*.

## Memorial of Will^m Lloyd

Determin'd the 27^th of Jan^y 1785.

27^th of Jan^y 1785.

Will^m Lloyd—the Claimant—sworn.

A Loyalist.

Did not bear Arms.

Bounty £20 a Y^r.

Is a Native of Ireland & went to America in 1771. Took out £600 S. with him & settled in Baltimore. Before the troubles broke out he affected to be with them but told them that they were not strong enough in order to dissuade them from their purpose but swears that these were not his real Sentiments. He staid in the Country till 1776. He was taken in going to New York by a Rebel Privateer & carried to Philadelphia where he staid till 1777. They let him go home & said he might stay at home if he would have taken an active part. He told them that perhaps he might. He remain'd about three weeks after which time he was obliged to hide himself otherwise he must have associated. He join'd the British fleet in 1777. He came home to Eng^d in 1778. He enlisted in the 85^th Reg^t in 1782. He was discharged in 1783. And he applied to Gov^t. And he has an Allowance of 20 a Y^r which he has rec^d from the 5^th of April 1783.

D^r Henry Stevenson—sworn.

Knew W^m Lloyd in America at the Commencement of the rebellion he was strictly loyal to his knowledge. Thinks he went to join the British Army. He

[1] See Additional Notes, p. 332.

afterwards returned & afterwards join'd Sir W^m^ Howe in the Chesapeak. He knew that the Man had a piece of Land near to the Witness in Coales Addition. He has reason to think that it was his own. He thinks he had upwards of 60 Acres. Says it was worth 25 Gās an Acre & he would have given that for it in 1775. He offer'd to buy it for M^r^ Delancy & another Gent^n^. Believes he built the House on this tract & thinks it might cost £100 S. Knew that he had an House in Market Street. Values it at £100 S. Did not know his Lands at Palapseco. Remembers his giving a Deed of Trust as stated & D^r^ Stevenson was a Witness to it.

### Memorial of Will^m^ Shepard

Determin'd the 27^th^ of Jan^y^ 1785.

Will^m^ Shepard—the Claimant—sworn. 27^th^ of Jan^y^ 1785.

Is a Native of Eng^d^ & went to America in 1768. He went out as a Farmer & carried out some Money about 80 Gās besides farming Utensils & some household furniture. In 1775 he was settled in Philadelphia he had a farm out of Town & kept a livery Stable in Town. His farm was 4 Miles from the Town. He never was under the Necessity of taking part with the Americans. He kept as quiet as possible & frequently assisted the British Prisoners. The first open Act he did was to endeavor to procure Pilots for Lord Howe. He did this at the request of M^r^ Galloway this was in the Spring of 1777. He procured one & sent him to New York his name was John Keyton & he piloted on board Lord Howe's Ship. Another person who was employed as he was was hanged for it. After this happen'd the Claim^t^ was apprehensive & fled to the British Army. He rec^d^ £50 at New York which paid what he had given to Molesworth. He rec^d^ no other Reward. He had no Appointment in the Army until he went to Philadelphia when he was appointed to collect & issue forage for the Army. He had a Dollar a Day & he served in this Capacity till near the Evacuation of New York. He came home after the Evacuation with the Army & applied to the Treasury for an Allowance & has rec^d^ £30 a Y^r^ from the 5^th^ of July 1784.

A Loyalist & render'd Services to Gov^t^ at the risque of his Life. Did not bear Arms.

Bounty £30 a Y^r^.

### Memorial of James Brooks

James Brooks—the Claimant—sworn. 29^th^ of Jan^y^ 1785.

Is a Native of Eng^d^ & went to America in 1763 to Anapolis.[1] He went to live with his Uncle. He was settled at Anapolis at the Commencement of the troubles. He held the Office of Clerk of the Council Clerk of the Upper House of Assembly Clerk of the Court of Appeals & Clerk of the Loan Office. He had these Appointments from the Governor. He produces an Appointment dated 1^st^ of Jan^y^ 1774 as Clerk of the Council by Sir Rob^t^ Eden in consequence of which he was Clerk of the Upper House. He looks upon all these Offices as places for life because they were during good behaviour. He was appointed Clerk of Appeals by Gov^r^ Sharp [2] in 1768. Produces his Comm^n^. He held the Clerk of the Loan Office from the Comm^rs^ but the real Appointment was from the Gov^r^.

[1] Maryland.

[2] Horatio Sharpe. His correspondence has been edited for the Maryland Hist. Soc. by W. H. Browne (*Archives of Maryland*, 6, 9, 14), and Lady Edgar has written a life of him, *A Colonial Governor in Maryland, H. Sharpe and his Times, 1753–73*, 1912.

He was appointed in 1769 & he produces his Appointment dated in 1773. He refused to sign all Association & paid a fine of £10 to avoid taking the Oaths. He was once insulted & hurt. He quitted Anapolis in Oct$^{r}$ 1781. They applied to him to take up Arms in 1775. He gives as a reason for his staying so long that he had the Care of a person's Estate. He went to Alexandria in Virginia from whence he embarked for S$^{t}$ Crux. He arriv'd in Eng$^{d}$ the 27$^{th}$ of Jan$^{y}$ 1782.

He has no landed Property. He had some Land 2000 Acres but he sold them in 1779 for a Dollar an Acre. He was obliged to sell them for his Support & he got Congress paper for them. He charges for the Loss of a Negro Boy £10 & he charges £52 10*s*. for the Loss of the Sale of the Land. He sustain'd a Loss of £100 by depreciated Paper Currency. He admits that he repeatedly went into Company where success was drank to Gen$^{l}$ Washington & that he drank his Glass but never repeated the Toast. He charges for the Expence of his Voyage from Maryland to S$^{t}$ Croix £70.

As Clerk of the Upper House he had a Salary of £60 Fees about £50. He had no Salary as Clerk of the Privy Council but fees about £150. As Clerk of the Court of Appeals no Salaries but fees to 37 10*s*. He had a Salary of £116 5*s*. as Clerk of the Loan Office. Eight Years loss on all but the Clerk of the Loan & upon that only a Loss of 7 Y$^{rs}$ Income. He says he had repeated Offers if he would stay to have all his old Offices but he refused. Says he left the Records in the hands of Scott who is a rebel & admits it to be wrong but says he was forced to do it but cannot tell how. Swears again that he never made any Sacrifices whatever to induce them to permit him to stay. He receives an Allowance of 40 a Y$^{r}$ & has rec$^{d}$ it from the 5$^{th}$ of Jan$^{y}$ 1783. He never muster'd or paid for a Substitute.

Rev$^{d}$ John Boucher—sworn.

Knew M$^{r}$ James Brooks in Anapolis. He was Rector of Anapolis. He was in the Neighborhood of Anapolis at the Commencement. Thinks him perfectly loyal. Thinks he was permitted to remain because he was a quiet Man. But thinks if he disposed of any property so late as 1779 he must have done it privately. He left it in 1775 & therefore he can only speak his Opinion. Rec$^{d}$ some Letters after he came away from M$^{r}$ Brooks which lead him to think that after he came away he still held sentiments of Loyalty.

Horatio Sharp Esq—sworn.

Was formerly Gov$^{r}$ of Maryland. He left his Gov$^{t}$ & came to Eng$^{d}$ in 1773. He was acquainted with M$^{r}$ Brooks 6 or 7 Years. He remembers D$^{r}$ Scott shewing him a Letter which he rec$^{d}$ from M$^{r}$ Brooks in which Brooks appear'd to be anxious to come away. He held two or three Offices at Anapolis. He enumerates them. He had £60 Salary as Clerk of the Upper Assembly can't tell the fees or the fees of the Clerk of the Council. Can't tell the Emoluments of the other Offices which he held. Thinks he might have enjoy'd all his Offices now if his Attachment to Great Britain had not prevented it. The Office of Clerk of the Council & of Appeals was attended with a great deal of personal Attendance.

### Further testimony to the Memorial of James Brooks

George Chalmers Esq—sworn.

Was acquainted with M^r^ Brooks at Anapolis in 1774. Always consider'd M^r^ Brooks as a very good Loyalist. He gave an early proof of it when resolutions were enter'd into not to pay British Debts in Maryland a Protest was enter'd into by the Inha^ts^ ag^t^ it & M^r^ Brooks signed it. Thinks he was permitted to stay because he did not take an active part. Thinks that he could not avoid delivering up the records. Believes that several persons have remain'd in Maryland without taking part with the Rebels & without making any Sacrifices but that of being quiet. Thinks that every Officer of the Crown ought to have left the Country the moment that Independence was declared. Thinks that Loyalists in general might have sold their property till the Year 1780. Believes M^r^ Brooks was always consider'd to be a Tory. He thinks that M^r^ Brooks has during the whole of the War adher'd to the Cause of Great Britain. Admits that he was not an active Loyalist. Thinks the papers which M^r^ Brooks had in Custody were not of much Use to the new Gov^t^.

### Further testimony to the Memorial of James Brooks

Rev^d^ John Montgomery—sworn. 8^th^ of Feb^y^ 1785.

He had lived on great terms of friendship with him. And he mentions an Instance of his riding 40 Miles to tell him that the Gov^r^ was about to issue a Warrant ag^t^ him & thinks that he ran great risque in giving him this Information. He likewise drew up the leading Characters of the Rebels for Sir Guy Carleton in 1782 which he apprehends was of considerable Use. He saw these Characters & they were well done. He says he suffer'd great inconvenience by writing a loyal Letter which fell into the hands of a Man who struck him. The Witness says it was a dangerous Wound & he saw him in his bed. Does not think it right that he should have gone into Company when Gen^l^ Washington's Health was drank & thinks he would not have gone voluntarily into such Company.

### Further testimony to the Memorial of James Brooks

Will^m^ Molleson Esq—sworn. 24^th^ of Feb^y^ 1785.

Knew James Brooks since he came to England but did not know him in Maryland but knew there was such a person. Says he was looked upon as a neutral Character. Being asked whether M^r^ Molleson thinks that he could have staid so long in that Country as he did without making some sacrifices says he thinks a very quiet Man might. Thinks it possible that a real Loyalist might continue in that Country during the whole War & preserve his Loyalty. Knows some Instances of it. M^r^ Molleson never heard of M^r^ Brooks being consider'd as an avowed Loyalist. Says in his Opinion he might have lived in that Country. Says he might be fairly said to have lost his Offices by his Loyalty provided they were offer'd to him by the Rebel Gov^t^ & that it will depend upon that fact. The Evidence Book being referr'd to it does not appear that any of the Offices ever were actually offer'd to Mr Brooks but his words are if he had done so & so he might have held the Offices.

## Further testimony to the Memorial of James Brooks

14th of April 1785.

Uriah Forest—sworn.

Knew Mr Brooks first in 1777. He was at Anapolis as an idle Man. He held certain Offices & lost those Offices by his principles & the Witness says he believes he might have held those Offices or better if he would have changed his Principles. Says that any person might have remain'd there quiet without taking any Oath. Thinks he never made a sacrifice of his principles. He admits that he has been in Company with him when he has either drank Genl Washington's health or assented to it. Believes he never held any Office under any Assembly except under the authority of Great Britain.

Daniel Wolston—sworn.

Is a Subject of Great Britain. Knew Mr Brooks in Anapolis. He knew him in 1775. He has always look'd upon him to be a good Subject. Says he was a very quiet & peaceable Man but does not believe he ever took any part with the Rebels.

Philip Bardon Key—sworn.

Is a Captn in the Maryland Loyalists. Knows Mr Brooks. He is a distant relation of his. Says he has heard Gentn frequently say in America that if he would have taken the Oaths he might have held Offices under their Govt. Says there are many instances of persons remaining in the Country who remain'd quiet. He does not believe that he ever took the Oaths or muster'd but supposes he paid the treble Taxes. Says he thinks he would have left the Country sooner if he had not had Ties which obliged him to stay. Thinks he held the Clerkship of the Loan Office for two or three Months after the Rebel Assembly was established but it was merely to wind up his Accts & he thinks he never recd any Salary from them. He says he could not have left the Province sooner & have join'd the British Troops because there was an Act making it treason to leave the province & go to any of the British Settlements—he says he could not have gone away without taking an Oath.

## Memorial of Thos Welbank

28th of Jany 1785.

Thos Welbank—the Claimant—sworn.

This Man appears to have been heard the 14th of Septr 1783 at Whitehall by Mr Wilmot & Mr Coke who recommended the Sum of £35 to be paid to him *in full of all his Losses* he admits to have received the Money tho' he for some time hesitated thereon. He now attends with his Claim under the Act of Part amounting to £553 3*s*. 9*d*. S. £200 of which is for two Horses & £250 for 5 Years Loss of business as Stable Keeper & Horse Dealer. He is told that having recd the £35 in full for his Losses the Board cannot take any cognizance of his Claim. He is therefore dismiss'd & his Claim not enter'd into.

## Memorial of James Brisbane

Determin'd ye 5th of March 1785.

James Brisbane—the Claimant—sworn. 31st of Jany 1785.

Is a Native of South Carolina & was settled at Charlestown in 1774 & 1775 living upon the Income of his plantations. He has been a marked Man from the time of the Stamp Act. He avowed in all public places in 1775 that the province of South Carolina was subject to British Acts of Part. Admits that he took the Oaths but says he was obliged to do it. An Association was offer'd to him in 1775. He sign'd it & it was to associate agt all Enemies of that State. He did it on compulsion for he must have quitted the Country. He did not mean to act accordingly on the Contrary he laugh'd at all their Oaths. Mr Lawrence[1] sent to him to say that he heard he had sign'd by Compulsion & if that was the Case he might take his name out. In Octr 1775 He was called before the Congress. He was then asked whether he would fight agt British Troops having said no He was told he might scratch his name out. He asked if by so doing he should forfeit the protection of the State they all said no. And he scratch'd it out. In 8 Days a sentence of Banishment came out. He went to Georgia & there he was again hunted. He came to his plantation in Carolina where his Wife died which prevented his being persecuted so soon & he was permitted to remain quiet till 1776. When he was sent for by the Congress in feby to answer the Charge agt him. He retired to Johns Island by the advice of Mr Lawrence.[1] When Sir Peter Parker came he was called upon to go out & refusing a Negro of his was sold to pay the fine & he sold for £400 C. In June 1776 He was taken up & put into close Confinement at Charlestown. He was kept about four Months in prison when he took an Oath. He refused the first Oath. But he took the second which was framed by Mr Routledge.[2] There was no part of it abjuring Great Britain. He did not mean to keep it no otherwise than necessity obliged him. He remain'd quiet after the Oath till the Yr 1779. And he took the Oaths to this Govt in May 1779. There was no Compulsion by the British to take the Oaths. He took them from Inclination. In 1779 a party of Americans broke into his House & took him prisoner & confined him some weeks on board a prison Ship & then carried him to prison where he remain'd six weeks & then he was discharged. He staid on his plantation till Jany 1780 by the advice of Govr Routledge. He then went to join the British. He knew the Numbers of the British & thought they were sure to succeed. He swears if he had thought the British would have been beat he still would have join'd them as he did. He went to Charlestown & continued till the Evacuation. Says he was of material use to Coll Moncrief in shewing him a place where a battery was built. He was appointed Sheriff which produced him £700 a Yr S.

[1] ? H. Laurens.

[2] John Rutledge, *b.* 1739, *d.* 1800, was a delegate to the Continental Congress. He became President under the new Constitution in South Carolina in March 1776; and in January 1779, although he had 'in March before vetoed the Constitution and resigned the office of Chief Magistrate rather than take part in closing the door to an accommodation with England', he 'was now recalled to be the head of the State; and being elected Governor and Commander-in-chief under the Constitution he had refused to approve, he was proclaimed amidst the acclamation of the people' (McCrady, *S. Car. in the Rev. 1775–80*, p. 281). He was afterwards one of the framers of the American Constitution.

Bounty £120 a Y^r^. He had this from Col^l^ Balfour. He has an Allowance of 120 a Y^r^ from the Treasury which he has rec^d^ from the 1^st^ of Jan^y^ 1783 & he now continues to receive it.

Rob^t^ Rowand—sworn.

The Witness staid in that Country till July 1778. He has always consider'd him as a Loyalist & he was consider'd as such by the other Party. Believes that he took an Oath. The Witness took the Test Oath. He refused to take the Oath which M^r^ Brisbane took. Knows that M^r^ Brisbane had property but can't tell how much. Says that if any Man without compulsion took the Oath of Abjuration he ought not to be consider'd as a Loyalist.

James Simpson Esq—sworn.

Has known him 25 Years. Remembers his signing the Association as it was reported & understood from common report that M^r^ Brisbane meant in so doing only to sign an Association to resist the Attempts of the Negroes. Heard a Member of the Congress say that he was called before the Congress & was told that if he had sign'd inadvertently he might take his name out. He did do so accordingly & it made him obnoxious to the Congress. Whilst the Witness staid in the Country he never took any part with them. The Witness staid till 1777. Supposes he must have taken an Oath. Does not know the form of the Oath. There was an Abjuration Oath. Thinks he must have taken it. Thinks he has suffer'd from his Attachment to this Country. He was consider'd a Man of respectable Character that is he never heard to the Contrary. Thinks that signing the Association was more improper than taking the Oaths because it was voluntary. Knows that M^r^ Brisbane was Sheriff of Charlestown. Says that would be a Bar to his return because he would be liable to Actions. Knows his House at Charlestown it was built in direct Contradiction to a Law of the Province & he meant to have prosecuted him for it. It was within the range of the Batteries.

Rev^d^ D^r^ Hewatt—sworn.

Has known M^r^ Brisbane from the Year 1763 & he knew him in 1777 when he left the Country. He was then consider'd generally to be a Loyalist. He was active in declaring his Sentiments. He thinks many people sign'd that Association who wished well to Great Britain. Has heard that he took an Oath. He the Witness refused. Does not think any Loyalist should have taken that Oath & does not think that any person who took it unless upon Compulsion ought to be called a Loyalist. Being told that M^r^ Brisbane did all this He says he does not consider him as a Loyalist.

James Brisbane—the Claimant—sworn.

He took the first Oath after he rec^d^ a Letter from M^r^ Lawrence which is left at the Office. He took two or three Oaths & says he would have taken twenty if they had pleased because they had hooked him for one Oath. He says he took the Oath for self preservation. Says M^r^ Hewatt was called to speak to his Loyalty. He was from his intimacy with him perfectly conversant with his principles & as well able as anybody to judge of his Loyalty. He was never upon any terms with M^r^ Lawrence after he rec^d^ that Letter or had any Intercourse with him. Being asked why he did not produce Witnesses to his Landed property He says that his property lay in such a Corner of the Country that he does not know any person who can speak to it. He does not know a single person here who knows anything of his property but Sir James Wright who has some Land adjoining. He says that tho' his House at Charlestown stood in opposition to a general Law yet he had permission from one of the Commissioners of fortifications to erect it. He has been informed that it would be of use to him to prove this fact & that an Aff^t^ will be rec^d^ as the person who knows the fact is in America. M^r^ Brisbane says he has one Child in Scotland but is a single Man here.

### Memorial of Hugh Ferguson [1]

Determin'd the 19^th^ of Feb^y^ 1785.

Hugh Ferguson—the Claimant—sworn. 2^d^ of Feb^y^ 1785.

Is a Native of Scotland & went to America in 1769 or 1770. He was settled at Graham Park in Pensylvania about 19 Miles from Philadelphia when the troubles broke out. He was living upon his own Estate. He came to Eng^d^ in Sept^r^ 1775 & he came away because there was no Opportunity of shewing his Attachment to G. B. He remain'd till the Spring of 1777 when he went out with Sir W^m^ Howe as a Volunteer. He left M^rs^ Ferguson in America when he landed at the head of Elk he could not go to M^rs^ Ferguson as it was without the British Lines. In Nov^r^ 1777 He was appointed Commissary of Pris^rs^ for which he had 10*s*. a Day & rations. He did not bear Arms. He rec^d^ this until the Evacuation of Philadelphia. He went with the Army to New York. He had no Office or Emolument. He staid there till Jan^y^ 1779. And then he came to Eng^d^ where he has been ever since. He saw his Wife at Philadelphia & Elizabeth Town. M^rs^ Ferguson is now in America & upon Graham Park. She is in possession of a part of it. She is a Native of America. Her friends were divided but principally with the rebels.

A Loyalist.

Did not bear Arms.

He first rec^d^ an Allowance in June 1779 of 100 a Y^r^ with half a Year in advance which M^r^ Wilmot & M^r^ Coke confirmed.

Bounty £100 a Y^r^.

Property.

He got the whole of his property in America by his Wife admits that she is in possession of the whole excepting such part as she has sold without his Consent for which she has rec^d^ £2640. She had sold it before she met him at Philadelphia. She has appropriated it to the payment of a Debt & Legacy of her father. He claims this Sum from this Country.

He wrote to her to send him an Acc^t^. Admits—Being asked whether he thinks it fair to charge Gov^t^ with the Schedule which he produces He thinks himself entitled to what was sold in 1778 but not to any other part. He meant to have claim'd the whole. He does not know what part was sold in 1778. He thinks the annual Value of his Estate was 3 or £400 a Y^r^ C.

The Estate is not confiscated on the Contrary the Americans have given it to M^rs^ Ferguson under an Idea that the fee belonged to M^rs^ Ferguson & believes they knew nothing of the Sett^t^. A Copy of the Law produced by which the State give the Estate to M^rs^ Ferguson & they state that all the right title &c which he acquired by Marriage is forfeited & he personally attainted.

[1] There are letters to him in *Hist. MSS. Comm., Am. MSS. in R. Inst.*, vol. i, pp. 177, 181.

She complain'd of her Distress at that time (April 1782) & her having a Difference with her Husband. Has great reason to think that the difference arose from a Difference in political opinions. Thinks it highly improbable that they sh$^{d}$ ever live together again if the laws were less severe.

Daniel Coxe Esq—sworn.

Has known M$^{r}$ Ferguson some Years before the rebellion. He believes him to be uniformly loyal. His Wife was of a different Opinion. Knows the Estate at Græme Park it came by his Wife. He has heard his father in law say that he knew that M$^{r}$ Græme had refused £10000 for it. It was better cultivated than farms in general. M$^{r}$ Ferguson complain'd to him in 1777 that she had sold Lands without his consent. He asked his opinion whether he could not stop her. He told him that he might by revoking the power of Att$^{y}$. He understood that the Estate was vested in D$^{r}$ Redman for M$^{r}$ Ferguson. Knows that there is a great difference between them & that it originated from political differences. Does not believe that they could now ever live together. Has understood from his Wife's family that the Rebels seized upon the personal property & sold it but does not know what they sold. In 1777 He saw the farm & it appear'd to be well attested. By the Laws of Pensylvania He would take the Estate for Life. Thinks the Estate if settled need not be register'd in that province. Says the Assembly have vested the Estate in her. Thinks the Americans knew nothing of the Sett$^{t}$. Thinks there was no Collusion intended between the Parties. Thinks that the Sett$^{t}$ was not revocable & that the Destruction of the Deed makes no Difference. Being asked whether M$^{r}$ Ferguson ought to make any Claim or what sort of Claim he should make Thinks that the possession of the Estate in the Wife is not in his poss$^{n}$. He thinks that in M$^{r}$ Ferguson's Case he should have only claim'd for a life Estate. Thinks there should be no Charge of those Articles which M$^{rs}$ Ferguson used & consumed between the Y$^{rs}$ 1775 & 1778. Says that furniture under those Sales sold very cheap.

Phineas Bond Esq—sworn.

Knew M$^{r}$ Ferguson in 1773. He married Miss Græme in 1772. He left America upon political Sentiments. Believes him to be very loyal She a violent Rebel. There was a difference between them in politics which had subsisted some time before he came to Eng$^{d}$. It was an excellent Estate. The old Man valued it at £10000. His Interest in the Estate would have been for her Life. M$^{rs}$ Ferguson often consulted him as a Lawyer. There was a Deed of Trust which he understood to be that if he survived her he was to have it & if she survived she was to have it. M$^{r}$ Boudineau wrote to him (M$^{r}$ Bond) to procure a release from M$^{r}$ Ferguson. Does not know the Date of the Sett$^{t}$. Being asked what sort of Estate M$^{r}$ Ferguson should claim he says a Life Estate at least. Says he has frequently talked with M$^{r}$ F. about the imprudence of giving such large powers in the Letter of Att$^{y}$. Thinks it might be worth £200 or £250. Thinks he has no chance of returning to his Estate both for public & private reasons.

James Parker Esq—sworn.

Speaks to Loyalty only.

## Memorial of P. Rob[t] Howarth [1]

Determin'd the 19[th] of Feb[y] 1785.

P. Rob[t] Howarth—the Claimant—sworn. 4[th] of Feb[y] 1785.

Is a Native of Eng[d] & first went to America in 1738 & remain'd there till 1749 & returned to Carolina in 1750 & staid there till the troubles began. In 1774 He commanded Fort Johnston near Charlestown. Commission produced dated in 1760 & likewise the King's Warrant for the payment of a Salary of £200 a Y[r]. He had likewise fees upon all Vessels coming into the Harbor. He had always £50 a Y[r] from the Province. The fees from the Vessels were about £250 a Y[r]. The Emoluments of his Situation altogether were about £500 a Y[r]. He was at Fort Johnson when the troubles broke out. They called upon him to take the Oaths to them but he refused. This was in 1777. He had refused to sign the Association in 1775. He was obliged to depart the province within 60 Days after the Oath was tender'd to him & he did do so. They suffer'd him to remain quiet till 1777 but they dispossess'd him of his Gov[t] in Oct[r] 1775. They took the fort in the night. On the 4[th] of June 1776 He dined with several other King's Officers & they were afterw[ds] imprison'd. The Fort was in no State of defence & it was not expected from him. He had only ten Men. He has never had approbation or censure from the Commander. He says it was not possible for him to come away till 1777. He rec[d] the 50 a Y[r] from the Province till the beginning of 1777. He would have left the Province sooner if he could but they would not permit him to go anywhere but to France or Holland. When he came away he divested himself of all his property & gave it to his Daughter who is now in possession of it. She is married to M[r] Graham of the 64[th] Reg[t]. He has rec[d] his Salary here till 1782 of £200 a Year or rather an Allowance in lieu of it. And since the 5[th] of April 1783 he has rec[d] an Allowance of £100 a Y[r] from the Treasury & he now receives it. The Fort has been demolished. He has done no Duty as Gov[r] of this Fort since 1775 and has rec[d] £200 a Y[r] for 7 years.

A Loyalist.

Bounty £100 a Y[r].

He gave up his property to his Daughter to prevent its being confiscated. He has no Half Pay. He did no Duty when he returned to Charlestown only as Intend[t] of the board of police for which he had 20*s.* a Day whilst it continued which was about six Months.

Loss of Office.

The Office was for Life. He gave up his rank in the Army for it. He does not apprehend that he could have been removed from his Situation without a Court Martial.

Salary £250 a Y[r].
Fees £200 a Y[r].

He had no Debts due to him in America & he owed nothing.

James Simpson Esq—sworn.

Knew M[r] Howarth very well since the Year 1760. Says he behaved uniformly loyal. He was Gov[r] of Fort Johnston. He had an annual Allowance from the province of 50 a Y[r]. His friends blamed him for taking it because it was generally understood that as the £200 a Y[r] was uncertain in its nature

[1] Colonel Probart Howarth commanded at Fort Johnson. McCrady (*S. Carolina in the Rev., 1780–3*, p. 585) comments on the fact that his name does not appear on the list in the Confiscation Act which purports to contain the names of the known subjects of his Britannic Majesty. Howarth had accompanied Governor Lyttelton in 1759 in an expedition against the Cherokees.

it would be a bad bargain as he parted with his rank in the Army. The Fort was dismantled by us in 1775 but he thinks if we had kept America that he would have been continued in the Situation of Gov$^{r}$. Says that many fees were given larger than the parties were obliged to give & thinks if he had only rec$^{d}$ the fees which were necessarily paid it would have lessen'd the value of his Office about £75 a Y$^{r}$.

Tho$^{s}$ Irvin—sworn.

Was well acquainted with M$^{r}$ Howarth before the troubles. Considers him as a Loyalist. Knew his Situation as Gov$^{r}$ of the Fort. He as Rec$^{r}$ Gen$^{l}$ paid him £200 a Y$^{r}$. He had £50 a Y$^{r}$ from the Province & several Fees all which together he thinks made the Office worth 500 a Y$^{r}$ S. He consider'd the Office nearly as a sinecure for Col$^{l}$ Howarth lived in Charlestown & the fees were collected by the Gunner.

## Memorial of Philip Kearney

4$^{th}$ of Feb$^{y}$ 1785.

Philip Kearney—the Claimant—sworn.

Is a Native of America & was settled at Perth Amboy as a Wine Merch$^{t}$. He never took any active part with the Americans. He was called upon early in 1776 to sign an Association. He refused at first to sign it but he at last sign'd one drawn up by Gen$^{l}$ Skynner. He was called upon by them to take an Oath but he refused it this was in 1776. The Association was to act with the Americans as long as they acted upon Constitutional principles. He was obliged to give Security in £1000 that he would not act with the British. On the 4$^{th}$ of July 1776 He was first taken prisoner as a Loyalist & in the Sept$^{r}$ following he was brought before the Gov$^{r}$ & Council. He forfeited his Security & join'd the British Troops in Nov$^{r}$ 1776. He has remain'd with the Kings Troops ever since. He has no Services to state. He has an Allowance of £70 a Y$^{r}$ from the 10$^{th}$ of Oct$^{r}$ 1784.

Brig$^{r}$ Gen$^{l}$ Skynner—sworn.

Has long known M$^{r}$ Kearney. He was always loyal. Admits that he approved of their signing a paper that they were friends to Liberty & the Constitution this was in 1775. And says he gave this advice to them as Attorney Gen$^{l}$. He is acquainted with his property in the Town of Amboy. Knows the Acre Lot which was given to him by his father. Thinks that Lot in 1774 was worth £200 or £250 C. Knows the 15 Acres. Says it belonged to the Claim$^{t}$ & believes he had it by his father's Will but he had it in his possession before. He values it at £20 per Acre. Knows the 22 Acres & that they are the property of the Claimant.

## Memorial of the Rev$^{d}$ Gilbert Buchanan

7$^{th}$ of Feb$^{y}$ 1785.

Gilbert Buchanan—the Claimant—sworn.

Is a Native of this Country & is now Rector of Woodmanston in Surry. He is the only Son of John Buchanan of Maryland. He went first to America in 1773 for the purpose of settling the Affairs of the Partnership his father & he having just fail'd at that time. He was settled there in 1774 & 1775. In May 1774 there was a Meeting convened to consider of this proposition not to pay British Debts. He divided ag$^{t}$ it & conceiv'd it was ag$^{t}$ his Interest to do so. He refused to enter into any Association or to take the Oaths to them. He offer'd his Services to Sir Rob$^{t}$ Eden. He quitted the Country in Aug$^{t}$ 1775 & arrived in Eng$^{d}$ in Sept$^{r}$ 1775. He had no Assistance from Gov$^{t}$ till 1783 since which time he has had £80 a Y$^{r}$. He applied to the Treasury in 1779 but his Memorial was never consider'd his Allowance commenced in Jan$^{y}$ 1783. He had not the Living when his Case was heard. He had it thro' his Wife it is 150 a Y$^{r}$. He has no family but his Wife is with Child. His father & he were settled in London as Merch$^{ts}$ trading to America for many years before 1773. He was sent by the Trustees to America. He was to receive so much per Cent upon the Money which he remitted thinks 3 per Cent. The Trustees allow'd his father 500 a Y$^{r}$ for five Y$^{rs}$. That expired in 1778. He is the only Son of his father but he has three Sisters married.

Richard Holland—sworn.

Speaks to the Loyalty of M$^{r}$ Buchanan. He went in the same Ship with him to America in 1773 & lived in the same Town with him in America & was intimate with him. He took the side of Great Britain & declared his Sentiments to Sir Rob$^{t}$ Eden & he was consider'd to be a Loyalist & he believes him to be attached to this Country. He was obliged to take shelter at Marlborough from the Circumstance of being consider'd as a Loyalist. He refused to muster. Believes he fought a Duel in America from political motives. Believes he could not have remain'd there unless he had retired into the back Country. Upon the whole believes him perfectly attached to this Country.

## Memorial of Abel Evans

Determin'd y$^{e}$ 26$^{th}$ of Feb$^{y}$ 1785.

Abel Evans—the Claimant—sworn. 7$^{th}$ of Feb$^{y}$ 1785.

Is a Native of America. In 1774 He was settled in Philadelphia following the Law. He was Clerk of the Assembly & remain'd so till Sept$^{r}$ 1776. In 1775 He sign'd an Association to learn the use of Arms & he did learn the Use of Arms. He consider'd himself in some Degree as a Serv$^{t}$ of the Crown & an Officer under the British Gov$^{t}$. There were many resolves made in that Assembly inconsistent with their Duty to this Country. He continued to hold that Situation in the hope that Peace might be restored. Those resolves extended to rebellion ag$^{t}$ this Country. He was appointed Clerk of the Assembly in 1776. He succeeded D$^{r}$ Moore but does not know why he quitted it. He had acted as an Assistant Clerk for 3 Years before. He was not a Candidate to be continued as Clerk after 1776. It was not offer'd to him. The Clerk was to undergo an election annually but yet he says it is so far consider'd a place for life that there was no instance of such an Officer being removed. Says his Predecessor quitted the Office in his lifetime but he does not know his reasons for so doing. He was rather in Years. The Salary was 10*s*. a Day for the Days that he attended. The whole Office worth from 2 to £300 a Y$^{r}$ C. They generally sat 3 Months in the Year. He went into the Country when the New

A Loyalist with this Observation that he was Clerk to the Assembly after the Declaration of Independence.

Loss of Office disallowed.

Assembly appointed another Clerk. They sent to him for the Books but he did not wish to be continued because he could not continue without taking the Oaths. He remain'd in the Country till Sir W$^{m}$ Howe came to Philadelphia. He took the Oaths in Philadelphia. He was soon after appointed Clerk to the Superintend$^{t}$ of the Police under M$^{r}$ Galloway. He had 10*s.* a Day for this.

Bounty £40 a Y$^{r}$.

He came to Eng$^{d}$ in 1780 or 1781. He has an Allowance of £40 a Y$^{r}$ from the Treasury which he has rec$^{d}$ from Jan$^{y}$ 1783 & he continues to receive it.

No Certificates produced.

Profession £60 a Y$^{r}$.

He followed the profession & gain'd about £150 a Y$^{r}$. He had practised about 4 Years before the Year 1776. He claims as a person of uniform Loyalty & not as coming in under Proclamations. Admits it to be wrong to have been Clerk to an Assembly which M$^{r}$ Galloway had quitted. Says the Majority of the Assembly knew his Sentiments in favor of G$^{t}$ Britain corrects himself & says many of them knew it but cannot say that if a Majority had known it he should have been elected. The Assembly of which he was the Clerk was elected in the usual way but had different Sentiments. His father is alive now but being an old Man believes he has taken no part.

Joseph Galloway Esq—sworn.

Knew the Claimant in America for many Years. He believes he has been uniformly loyal from the beginning. He served his time with M$^{r}$ Galloway. D$^{r}$ Moore declined because he did not like the proceedings & saw the troubles coming on. Says it was the Constitutional Assembly till Sept$^{r}$ 1776. Thinks if he had been with them in Opinion he might have been continued. Thinks the principal Clerk was at least worth £200 a Y$^{r}$ C. He followed the profession of the Law & thinks he must have made more than £100 a Y$^{r}$ C. He is attainted & can't return. His father was a very reputable Man & had a large family. Believes the whole family were loyal.

James Rankin Esq—sworn.

Knew M$^{r}$ Evans in America not particularly till 1776. At that time he looked upon him to be a Loyalist & well attach'd to this Country. And says he was consider'd by a Majority of that Assembly to be a friend to Gov$^{t}$. The Witness was a Member of the Assembly in May 1776 & then he says the Majority of that Assembly were friends to this Country. He has no Doubt of his being a very good Loyalist & speaks very strongly of his Attachment to the Cause of Great Britain.

Determin'd the 26$^{th}$ of Feb$^{y}$ 1785.

## Further testimony to the Memorial of Abel Evans

12$^{th}$ of Feb$^{y}$ 1785.

Joseph Galloway Esq—sworn.

Says that he is perfectly satisfied that M$^{r}$ Evans was loyal & he attends at the request of the Claim$^{t}$ to explain the Circumstances of his having sign'd the Association in 1775 to learn the Use of Arms. Says that he knew of the Circumstance at the time. Saw the Association paper & declares that M$^{r}$ Evans explain'd to him that it only went to learn the use of Arms for the purpose of protecting the Civil Magistrate from Insults. M$^{r}$ Galloway rather disapproved of the Association thinking it would neither be of use nor look well. Soon after which Mr Evans quitted the Association. In the Spring of 1776 the Americans suspected Mr Evans to be carrying on a secret Correspondence with Mr Galloway & a Warrant was issued by the Committee of Safety for apprehending Mr Evans. He was in fact apprehended on his return to Philadelphia from a Visit he had made to Mr Galloway & search'd in hopes of finding some papers about him. Mr Galloway is firmly of Opinion that the Claimant was always strictly loyal.

### Memorial of Thos Skynner

Determin'd the 4th of March 1785.

8th of Feby 1785.

Thos Skynner—the Claimant—sworn.

Born at Amboy. Resided in Perth Amboy in 1774 & 1775. Was a Baker. He was applied to to join the Rebels but he refused. He was confin'd with some others for a Month. He then took the Oath to them which he believes was an Oath of Allegiance. Upon the Arrival of the British Troops he remain'd in his House & baked for them. When the British Troops evacuated Amboy he went with them. He liked the Oath best which he took willingly. He took the Oath to the British willingly. Went to New York with the Army where he staid till June last. He has an Allowance of £40 a Yr from the Treasury from the 5th of July 1784.

A Loyalist but took an Oath to the Rebels. Did not bear Arms.

John Smyth Esq—sworn.

Has known Mr Skynner many Years. He is as loyal a Subject as ever the King had. He knows he took the Oath. He never knew a Man less attached to the rebels. He had two Sons who took part with the Rebels & he remembers the father refusing to speak to them unless they produced their Discharge & he threaten'd to disinherit them & one of them obtain'd his Discharge in consequence of it. Knows he had an House & Lot of Ground in Amboy he purchased it & he thinks he made some Addition to it. Values it at £750 or £800. Knows the Store House &c in High Street it was a late purchase. Values it at £500 or £550. The Lot adjoining to the House Lot he values at £80. The two Acres of Meadow he says were very valuable & thinks they are worth £60 an Acre. Knows the Lot of 12 Acres. Thinks they are worth £20 an Acre & that they would have sold for it. Knows he had two Horses. Thinks he might have lost furniture to the Amount of £80 or £100. Believes the whole has been confiscated & that there was no Mortgage &c.

### Memorial of Willm Friend

Determin'd the 2d of March 1785.

8th of Feby 1785.

Willm Friend—the Claimant—sworn.

Is a Native of Engd & went to America with the Army in the last War. He was settled at Ticonderoga. He commanded a Vessel in the service of Govt. He was appointed to it by the Commander in Chief. The Army under Ethan Allen [1] in 1775 plunder'd him of all his property. He was at Montreal at the time. About the same time he lost property on board of a Sloop taken by Coll

A Loyalist.

[1] The notorious free lance, who distinguished himself at the beginning of the war by the capture of Ticonderoga, and whose treatment as prisoner by the British authorities bulks large in the *American Archives*. There is little doubt that his own particularist interests counted for much more with him than those of America as a whole.

Bore Arms.

Arnold. About 12 or 13 Days after He was appointed by Sir Guy Carleton to command a Schooner. He lost her too. Soon after this he was made a Prisoner & sent to Albany for 22 Months. He never took any oath to them. He refused a Command with them. When he was releas'd at Albany He went to Canada. He came to Eng$^{d}$ in 1781 on Acc$^{t}$ of his Health. He never rec$^{d}$ any Allowance from Gen$^{l}$ Carlton or Gen$^{l}$ Haldimond for his Losses. He has an Allowance of 18 a Y$^{r}$ from the Treasury from the 10$^{th}$ of Oct$^{r}$ 1784.

Bounty £18 a Y$^{r}$.

Robert Hoakesly—sworn.

Knew the Claim$^{t}$ at Albany. He then commanded a Vessel upon Lake George. Was in his House two or three Years before the War. Says he was very loyal & that he had an opportunity of knowing it. He heard that he lost his Household furniture & that he had a Quantity of Liquors. He heard it from several people. Was intimate with him when he was a Prisoner. Has heard him mention when in Prison that he had considerable offers from the Americans to join them.

Lachlan M$^{c}$Intosh—sworn.

Knew M$^{r}$ Friend for many Years & knew him in 1774. He was at Ticonderoga. Knows that he was plunder'd but can't speak to the exact sum but supposes between 3 & £400. Thinks it probable. Thinks it was taken from him because he was a Loyalist & that it would not have been taken if he had been on the other side. He saw the Sloop in Gen$^{l}$ Arnold's possession & heard him say that he was obliged to break open the trunks of Capt$^{n}$ Friend because he could not find the Keys & he heard the Gen$^{l}$ say that it was more than £200 but he said he should return it to him.

Determin'd y$^{e}$ 5$^{th}$ of March 1785.

## Memorial of Samuel Carne

Samuel Carne—the Claimant—sworn. 9$^{th}$ of Feb$^{y}$ 1785.

A Loyalist & a British Merch$^{t}$.

Is a Native of Eng$^{d}$ & after having spent many years in the younger part of his Life in America he returned to Eng$^{d}$ in 1764 to carry on the business of a Merch$^{t}$ here without any intention of returning to America. Considers himself as a British Merch$^{t}$ here when the troubles broke out. He went out to America in 1775 merely to collect his Debts. He went to Charlestown. He staid above a Year & ½ at Charlestown. He refused to sign any Association viz. it was never offer'd to him. He left that Country in 1777 & was coming home by way of France & was taken & carried into Liverpool by an English Privateer. He has put that property into his Schedule but it was legally condemn'd in the Court of Admiralty. He had likewise a concern for another person which would have neated[1] him 7 or 800. Besides which he carried out some Articles of trade. He could not have gone on in this Country any longer without remittances from America & he call'd his Creditors together. He heard of the Independence before it happen'd & might have come away before but he remain'd more than a Year in America after Rebel Gov$^{t}$ prevail'd. He went to the West Indies

[1] *Sic* in text. ? 'netted' him, i.e. by which he would have made a profit of. The *Oxford English Dictionary* gives examples of this use of the word earlier than the date of this Commission.

in 1779 & early in 1780 He went to Mr Rose's [1] plantation & staid there whilst the Town was besieg'd. He went to Charlestown in 1780 & the Govr said You are come to join us the Claimt said no he never would & the Govr said he must go to prison or the Hospital. However he went to the Govr & got his permission to go. He knew Mr Routledge in 1775 & 1776 but he did not know his principles. He carried out no goods with him to the West Indies. After the taking of Charlestown he join'd the British. He assisted their Surgeons for one Day & this he did to avoid going to prison. He staid till the Evacuation at Charlestown & he took the Oaths to the British Govt. He never applied to Whitehall & has no Allowance. He never applied to the Treasury for any relief when he came home in 1777.

### Memorial of George Richd Walker

George Richd Walker—the Claimant—sworn. 9th of Feby 1785.

Is a Native of Engd & went first to America in 1769 & acted under his father who was Gunner in fort Johnson. He was Coxswain of a Pinnace. He was in the fort in 1774 & 1775 & was Coxswain of the Pinnace under Govt. He had £10 a Yr for it besides provisions. In 1775 He went on board the Tamur & carried the powder out of the fort to prevent its being of use to the Rebels on which acct he was ill used. When the fort was taken in Septr 1775 He recd a blow on the Arm when the Men came which lamed him & they did this because he had spiked the Guns. He came home to Engd the latter end of 1776 & staid in Engd till Carolina was taken & had no Allowance from the treasury but £20 to carry him out. He went back with Govr Bull & was made Master & Pilot of the Cornwallis Galley & it was £3 10*s.* per Month. He remain'd near 12 Months & then was made Commr of a Galley. He was sent by Captn Cochran [2] afterwards with 45 Men to protect the Watering of the transports when he was taken Prisoner & severely wounded. When he was exchanged he returned to Charlestown but was order'd to Engd on Acct of his Health. He has an Allowance of £25 a Yr from the Treasury which he has recd from July 1783. Bounty £25 a Yr.

### Memorial of John Ewing [3]

John Ewing—the Claimant—sworn. 10th of Feby 1785.

Is a Native of Boston & was settled there as a Mercht 20 Yrs before the troubles. He was a Mandamus Counsellor always attended his Duty & did all in his power to promote the King's Service. He never bore Arms. Upon the Evacuation he went to Halifax from whence he came to Engd in 1776 where he has resided ever since. He has an Allowance from the Treasury which he has recd from April 1776—viz—£200 a Yr. And he recd 100 Gās from Sir Wm Howe at Halifax. When he came to Engd he recd one Year's Salary in advance.

[1] A Hugh Rose was amongst the signers of an Address to Clinton on June 5, 1780, declaring their readiness to return to their allegiance to the Crown (McCrady, *S. Carolina in the Rev., 1775–80*, p. 536).

[2] *b.* 1758, *d.* 1832. Became Sir Alexander Cochrane.

[3] John Ewing, *b.* 1727, *d.* 1816. He married a daughter of Governor Shirley. In 1760, along with his brother George, 'he signed the Boston memorial, and was thus one of the fifty-eight who were the first men in America to array themselves against the officers of the Crown' (Stark, op. cit., p. 298).

Harrison Gray Esq—sworn.

Was well acquainted with M^r Ewing at Boston. Knows that he was a considerable Merch^t at Boston. Accepted the Office of Mandamus Counsellor without hesitation & it was a dangerous Situation. He was very loyal. Knows his Store Houses they were newly built. Values them at 7 or £800 C. Has frequently been in his House it was very genteelly furnish'd. Says he could not have carried away his furniture. He was in good business but he can't estimate his profits.

### Memorial of George Ewing[1] Esq.

11^th of Feb^y 1785.

George Ewing Esq—the Claimant—sworn.

Is a Native of Boston & when the War broke out he was settled there as a Merch^t. He was very active in protecting M^r Clarke who was one of the Consignees of the Tea. In 1774 He was made a Mandamus Counsellor & acted as such until the Evacuation of Boston. He did not sign the Association but he did Duty for the defence of the Town. He came to Halifax with the Army & came to Eng^d in June 1776. He applied to the Treasury & immediately rec^d £200 & upon a Second Application He rec^d an annual Allowance from the 1^st of Jan^y 1777 which he now receives.

Bounty £200 a Y^r.

Harrison Gray Esq—sworn.

Knew M^r Ewing's family but was not intimate with him until he was a Counsellor. He always spoke his Sentiments. He was in great business as a Merch^t & he married a Lady with a great fortune. Never was in his Store at Boston. Looks upon Trade being at an end after the Boston Port Bill. Thinks he might have made 6 or 800 a Y^r. M^r Ewing has three Sons. Mentions a Circumstance to prove M^r Ewing's attachment to Gov^t that he gave up his House to the Commander in Chief & took another.

### Memorial of John M^cAlpin

Determin'd the 12^th of Feb^y 1785.

11^th of Feb^y 1785.

John M^cAlpin—the Claimant—sworn.

Is a Native of Scotland & went to America in 1773 to buy lands & settle. He carried out about 30 Gās & 30 Gās in Goods. He was settled near Crown Point. He & his Serv^ts were dragged out & ill treated by Elhan Allen's people in 1775. They frequently killed his Cattle & treated him ill because they thought him a Tory. He remain'd at home. He join'd the British in Nov^r 1776. He went as a Guide with Sir Guy Carleton. He mentions many instances of Exertion &c. He conducted the Horses belonging to the Army in Gen^l Burgoyne's Expedition with great zeal & it was a service of great Danger. Colonel Kingston confirms this. He never rec^d Pay but for one Month. He has been to settle at Port Shelburne & was one of the first Settlers. He has a Town Lot a Water Lot & a 50 Acres Lot in Shelburn & he has 500 Acres at Liverpool. He receives nothing from the Treasury.

The Board are of Opinion that this is a fraudulent Claim & that it ought to be so reported to the Lords of the Treasury.

[1] *b.* 1736, *d.* 1806. He stood high in the opinion of Governor Hutchinson (see letter to Gage of July 4, 1774, *Diary and Letters*, vol. i, pp. 177–8).

## Continuation of Mr McAlpin's Case & his Evidence

Determin'd ye 12th of Feby 1785.

Joshua Chandler—sworn. 12th of Feby 1785.

Was a perfect Stranger to Mr McAlpin till July 1779 when he found him with the British Troops at Lloyd's Neck. Understood that he had a Negro & was told that he was taken from him by the rebels & he bought another Negro from his Son which he believes was likewise taken.

N.B. Upon considering the whole of this Case The Board were of Opinion that Mr McAlpin had made a very improper Demand & that he fell within that Clause of the Act of Part which excludes him from any Compensation—Directions were accordingly given to make out the proper Report.

## Memorial of John Watson [1]

John Watson—the Claimant—sworn. 14th of Feby 1785.

Is a Native of Engd & went to America in 1752. At the Commencement of the rebellion he was settled at Rhode Island & kept a Store & took the part of Govt. He traded to New York & in 1774 He carried some Dispatches to Captn Vandeput from Sir James Wallace & he was taken upon Suspicion & releas'd the next Day after they had broke open the Letters with which he was charged. Upon his return to Rhode Island in Octr 1774 A Mob attacked his House forced him out of his House & threaten'd to pull him to pieces if he did not damn the King & Lord North which he was compell'd to do. He was repeatedly ill treated on Acct of his Loyalty obliged to go on board a Vessel to avoid ill Usage. In July 1776 He was sent for by the Court & obliged to sign the Test. He refused three times & a Cart was brought to the Door to tar & feather him & he sign'd an Engagement not to take any part against the Americans nor give any Intelligence to the King's Troops or any Enemies of the State. Says it was notworded *I swear* but *I promise*. After this he returned to his House but was not suffer'd to live quietly. He was frequently molested but he remain'd till Sir Henry Clinton took the Island & went with the British Troops at the Evacuation. He never took any Oath. He was called upon in 1776 to take an Oath Genl Lee being then at Rhode Island but he avoided it by keeping out of the Way. At New York he was appointed Captain of a Prison ship (by Captn Drake [2] who commanded at New York). He had frequently from 200 to 300 Rebel Prisoners under his Care on board this Ship. His Allowance for this was three Shillings a Day & Rations for three Months. Afterwards Sir Henry Clinton allowed him a Dollar a Day & two Rations as a Loyalist. When Sir Guy Carleton came he allowed him £90 Sterg but no Rations. This he receiv'd till August 1783 when he came to England. He came home with 120 Loyalists under his Care produces a List of their names with a Direction to take care of these people for Coll Willard.

[1] The Board of Refugees Loyalists recommended him for £40 New York currency per quarter in 1783 (*Hist. MSS. Comm., Am. MSS. in R. Inst.*, vol. iv, p. 483).

[2] Commodore Drake is mentioned by General Robertson as proceeding to sea from New York in May 1780 (*New York Col. Docs.*, vol. viii, p. 791).

Certificates to Loyalty &c from Col[l] Willard & George Leonard.

Bounty £30 a Y[r].

He has an Allowance of £30 a Y[r] from the Treasury which he has rec[d] from y[e] 29[th] of Sept[r] 1783 & he now continues to receive it.

George Rome Esq—sworn.

Knew M[r] Watson very well at the Commencement of the troubles. He kept a Shop there. He believes him to be a very loyal Subject few people in his Station of life distinguished themselves more than he did. Knows that he was mobb'd several times & has heard that he was obliged to sign a paper. Thinks it was an Oath & supposes Watson was obliged to swear to it. Understood that he left Rhode Island at the Evacuation. Knew his Dwelling House & Store. Has been in it but can't speak exactly to the Value of it but thinks about 4 or £500 S. for the House independent of the Store. Says he was consider'd always as a monied Man. Can't speak to the Value of his furniture. Can't speak to his Negroes but makes no doubt but he had some. Says that when he calls him a monied Man he means that he was a Man in easy Circumstances.

John Watson—the Claimant—called in again.

Left no Debts of any sort in America. Says that he only sign'd a paper but that he took no Oath. However he admits that if an Oath had been tender'd to him when Gen[l] Lee was at Rhode Island that he thinks he should have taken it. He was so much afraid.

Determin'd y[e] 5[th] of March 1785.

## Memorial of Capt[n] Tho[s] W[m] Moore [1]

15[th] of Feb[y] 1785.

Tho[s] Will[m] Moore—the Claimant—sworn.

A Loyalist.

Bore Arms.

Is a Native of Pensylvania & was settled as a Merch[t] at New York when the troubles broke out. He immediately shew'd his Attachment to Great Britain. He never conformed to the American Measures but he did apply to the Congress & saved his father from persecution but did not sacrifice his principles but he pretended to be a friend to the Americans in order to obtain his father's liberty. The Congress offer'd to make him a Major & Gov[r] Tryon advised him to take it this was in the Spring of 1776. He kept the Deception on till the Spring of 1776 & until that time he appear'd to be with them to save himself from persecution. After he refused the Comm[n] they summon'd him & upon his refusing to sign the Association & to take the Oaths to them they order'd him to be confined. He was in consequence confined a close Prisoner for six Weeks. When he went to the Congress He confess'd his Attachment to Great Britain but said he wished to be Neuter. He was asked if Independence was declared he would be Neuter. He said no He sh[d] risque his Life for G[t] B[n]

[1] There is in *Hist. MSS. Comm., Am. MSS. in R. Inst.*, vol. iii, p. 264, an order dated December 14, 1782, to pay to Thomas William Moore, late Barrack-Master at Savannah, Georgia, the sum of £980 3*s.* 7*d.*, being amount of expenses attending the barracks at Savannah from May 5 to June 30. In July 1775 a Captain Thomas William Moore had the command of the guard appointed to preserve the peace of New York and interfered to protect His Majesty's stores (*New York Col. Docs.*, vol. viii, pp. 599, 600); and Thomas William Moore, a captain in de Lancey's second battalion, enlisted an English bluecoat-boy for a drummer (*Winslow Papers*, p. 23).

& then they committed him. He on the 29th of June join'd the British on Staten Island. He served as a Volunteer from the Landing on Long Island till Sept[r] 1776. He then had a Commiss[n] as Capt[n] in Gen[l] Delancey's Brigade on the 6th of Dec[r] 1776. He continued in America till the Evacuation of Georgia. And he has been in Eng[d] ever since. He is now a Capt[n] on half pay. He receives no Allowance from the Treasury & never made any Application.

Produces his Capt[n's] Commission.

He is desired to summon Gov[r] Tryon to attend to explain the Advice which he is said to have given to the Claimant.

Phineas Bond Esq—sworn.

The Claimant is a very near Relation to the Witness. The first Acc[t] he heard of the Claimant's political Conduct was his coming to Philadelphia in an American Uniform to gain intelligence by the advice of Gen[l] Tryon. Consider'd him then in a dangerous Situation but believ'd him well attached. He pass'd at that time for a Well Wisher to America & was very boisterous. The first Acc[t] that he had of him afterwards was that he was confined by the Congress & he was alarmed for him. Thinks he was uniform in his Loyalty from principle.

Says he was a Vendue Master & got a good deal of Money by business. His House was very well furnished. Can't say whether the furniture sent to Brunswick was worth £700. He knows that he had plate & is confident that M[r] Moore would not rate it at more than it was really worth.

John Chevalier Rome—sworn.

Does not know much of M[r] Moore previous to May 1776. He was in the same Gaol with him. Says that Capt[n] Moore got out by signing the Association. Knows that he sign'd it because he was liberated. The Witness was remanded to prison because he would not sign it. Thinks him unequivocally loyal notwithstanding he sign'd that paper because at that time he told the Witness that he did it in order to get out of prison & that he meant to join the British.

The Claimant—called in again.

Repeats the Security which he gave upon coming out of prison & says that he only sign'd a paper to be forthcoming when called upon. Repeats that he never made any sacrifices to get out of prison. Swears that he never sign'd any Association paper to the Congress to induce them to let him out of prison.

John Chevalier Rome—called in again.

Produces a Copy of that Association which he refused to sign & which he is clear that M[r] Moore must have sign'd.

The Claimant being again asked says he does not think that he sign'd any such Paper.

**Memorial of Phineas Bond [1] Esq.**

15th of Feb[y] 1785.

Determin'd the 5th of March 1785.

Phineas Bond—the Claimant—sworn.

Desires a Witness who is an Invalid to be examin'd.

Moses Franks—sworn.

Has known M[r] Bond for many Y[rs] before the troubles. Says that when

[1] See Additional Notes, p. 333.

the troubles broke out he had very flattering prospects in his profession. He believes his principles were as strictly loyal from the beginning as it was possible to be. Says he has reason to think so from certain Letters which he rec$^{d}$ at diff$^{t}$ times from M$^{r}$ Bond & which he produces. The Letters are written at diff$^{t}$ periods & his language was always the same. He & his family have frequently employed M$^{r}$ Bond & have entrusted matters of great moment to his Care. Has employ'd M$^{r}$ Bond to recover considerable Debts for him. Should have been glad to have employ'd him still if he had not left America. He has several times shewn M$^{r}$ Bond's Letters to the Administration to Lord North & different Ministers. Says he apprehends they must have been of great Use but he cannot point out any particular Advantage derived from it. He can't speak with certainty to his professional Gains but says he got a great deal. Can't speak to any Acts of Service done by him.

Phineas Bond Esq—the Claimant—sworn. 16$^{th}$ of Feb$^{y}$ 1785.

A Loyalist.

But he sign'd an Association & muster'd in their M$^{a}$ in 1775. Did not bear Arms.

Was born at Philadelphia. His Grandfather was one of the first Settlers of that Country. He came over in 1770 to follow the Bar & went back to America in 1773. Dates the Commencement of the troubles from the Y$^{r}$ 1774 when he practis'd in Philadelphia. The first Step he took was opposing the proceedings of the people at Boston. About the Y$^{r}$ 1776 the Cloven foot began to appear. He was one of a Committee who opposed the constituting a provincial Congress. He never appear'd to favor the Cause of the Americans & always declared ag$^{t}$ violent measures & reprobated Independence as ruinous to both Countries. Tho' he well knew the right which the English Par$^{t}$ had to tax America yet he always thought it highly inexpedient & publickly declared this. In April 1776 His name amongst others was published & held out as a Tory. In 1777 Upon a resolve of Congress to seize all suspected persons they seiz'd him & confined him for ten Days & then sentenced him to banishment. During this time they frequently tender'd the Oaths to him & the rest but he always refused. He escaped & confined himself until the King's Army came to Philadelphia & then he went to meet them. Whilst the King's Army staid at Philadelphia he remain'd there but he never was in any military or civil Employment. He removed with the Army to New York where he remain'd a short time & then came to Eng$^{d}$ in 1778. He wrote several papers during the Dispute reprobating their Measures & was known to be the Author of them by which means he was made very obnoxious to the Americans. He has been here ever since 1778. He applied to the Treasury in July 1779. In July 1780 a Proclamation came out ordering him to appear within a certain Day & not doing it he was attainted of High Treason. He never held any military Situation under the rebels. It was proposed to many persons early in the Dispute to go into the Militia but he refused it. However he & some friends agreed that it would be better to appear to favor their Cause & so just before the Election he went out two or three times with the Militia & then finding that his friends hung back He quitted it. In consequence of this they prevail'd upon many of the persons in their Companies to vote for Tories in that Election upon which so much depended. Upon his disobeying the Proclamation if they could have discover'd that he had any real property it would have been confiscated. He sign'd the

Association Paper which pledged him to support the Cause of America. He was a private in the Militia & admits that he might have avoided it. It was in the Summer of 1775 that he join'd the Association. He applied in the Summer 1779 & has rec^d^ an Allowance of £200 a Y^r^ from Jan^y^ 1780. Bounty £200 a Y^r^.

Loss of Profession. He gain'd about £900 a Y^r^ Cur. by his practice. He states that in 1776 He gain'd £556 *16s. 6d.* in the Court & about £400 a Y^r^ by Agency for two Houses in Great Britain. This Acc^t^ is for the Year 1776. He thinks he got above £300 a Y^r^ in Court in the Year 1774. Says his business would have increas'd.

### Further testimony to the Memorial of Phineas Bond Esq.

Sam^l^ Shoemaker—upon his Affirmation. 21^st^ of Feb^y^ 1785.

Being asked about M^r^ Bond's Loyalty Says he has no Doubt about it. He always looked upon M^r^ Bond to be a Loyalist because he was one of those whom they intended to send to Virginia. Says that if M^r^ Bond learn't the Use of Arms he was inexcusable because he must have seen the Drift of it. M^r^ Shoemaker admits that measure to have been extremely wrong that he has frequently talked with his friends upon the Subject & told them that they ought not to do evil that good may come of it. M^r^ Shoemaker says being told of these Circumstances that M^r^ Bond had associated & learnt the Exercise of Arms. He says he is very sorry for it & that he could not in such a Case give a Certificate that the person who acted in such a manner had been uniformly loyal.

### Memorial of Sarah Winslow [1]

Determin'd the 26^th^ of Feb^y^ 1785.

Sarah Winslow—the Claimant—sworn. 17^th^ of Feb^y^ 1785.

The Memorial of the father [1] first read. Then the Memorial of the present Claimant who has Authority (as she states) from the Mother & Sister to make Claim on the part of the whole family. Letter of Att^y^ produced dated the 9^th^ of Nov^r^ 1784 Executed at Halifax. Has not taken out Letters of Administration and no part of her family have administer'd. She has one Brother & one Sister but she produces a Release from her Brother of all his Interest & an Authority from the Brother to her to take out Adm^n^. Her father died the 9^th^ of June 1784 at Halifax. Her father made no Will. Her father was Collector of the Customs in the Town of Plymouth & Register of the Court of Probate & Clerk to the Common Pleas & Justice of the peace. He was loyal from the first & her Brother was in the Battle of Lexington. Her father was too old to take a part being 63 Years of Age. Says he was much persecuted after his Son took an active part. The Mob in 1775 took him out of his House & carried him to take the Oaths which he refused & they confined him to the Town for two Years & to his House for one Year. He staid at Plymouth till 1781 & then went to New York. Her Brother went with the British Army at the Evacuation of Boston & has been with them ever since. Her father had leave to go to New York for six Weeks & not returning they turned out the family & took possession of all the family furniture goods &c. Her Mother was never able to get back

A Loyalist & her father & family very loyal.

[1] See Additional Notes, p. 333.

a single Bed. Does not know whether the Property has been confiscated or not but they seiz'd the Estates cut down the Wood &c. Thinks that these Sufferings accelerated her father's death. Her father had £200 a Y^r at New York which he continued to receive till the Evacuation & afterwards upon the Application of M^r Brook Watson an Allowance was given to him from the 25^th of March 1784 And he did not live to receive a single Quarter as he died in June.

Determin'd the 26^th of Feb^y 1785.

### Memorial of Rob^t Lewis Fowles [1]

Robert Lewis Fowles—the Claimant—sworn. 17^th of Feb^y 1785.

A Loyalist but printed under the Rebel Gov^t.

Is a Native of Boston & was settled at Portsmouth in 1774. Was in good business as a Printer. He has been loyal from the beginning & all his Connections were loyal. He sign'd an Association at Portsmouth to protect the Gov^r this was before the battle of Lexington & he sign'd it at Plymouth. He never at any time took any part with them. He never sign'd any Association took any Oath or muster'd. Admits that he printed on both sides everything that was brought to him tho' he says he has sometimes refused to print for the rebels. He left Exeter in July 1777 because he should have been obliged to join them. He should not have conceiv'd it possible that Great Britain could fail. He was taken up by the rebels in 1777. He join'd Gen^l Burgoyne in 1777. He rec^d an Allowance of 3*s.* 8*d.* a Day from Sir Guy Carleton as a Supernumerary Officer in Sir John Johnson's Corps.[1] He rec^d it about 6 Months. At New York he join'd Wentworth's Volunteers & had ½ a Dollar a Day & rations. He rec^d this at New York till Dec^r 1781 when he came to Eng^d where he has been ever since. He has an Allowance of £50 a Y^r from the Treasury which he has rec^d from the 10^th of Oct^r 1782. He is going over to Nova Scotia to endeavor to get into the printing business.

Bore Arms in Wentworth's Volunteers.

Bounty £50 a Y^r.

Determin'd y^e 26^th of Feb^y 1785.

### Further testimony to the Memorial of Rob^t Lewis Fowle

Samuel Hale Esq—sworn. 18^th of Feb^y 1785.

Has known M^r Fowle since the Y^r 1766 the Claimant & the Witness lived at Portsmouth. He thinks tho' not a Man who was likely to take an active part yet his Inclinations were always loyal but he had not resolution enough to refuse to print any seditious paper. His Brother & he were the only Printers in the Province thinks they might have made £300 a Y^r by their business. Knows they had Lands at Brenton Woods but thinks them worth little or nothing. Does not know what they might get by their Stationers. Understood that the Claimant had half of the business. Does not know that he ever resisted to effect putting in any seditious paper for he believes that the Committee were always sent to compel him. And he mentions an instance where M^r Fowle was very anxious to print a paper calling the rebels together to pull down a Loyalist's House & the Witness took it upon himself to destroy the paper. He has quarrel'd with the Uncle several times because he refused to put in papers in favor of

[1] In an entry 1777, October 25 / 1778, June 24 Robert L. Fowles is amongst the loyalists, specified as gentlemen, receiving subsistence from Carleton (*Hist. MSS. Comm., Am. MSS. in R. Inst.*, vol. i, p. 268).

Gov$^{t}$. Cannot give any Answer to this Question whether the Claimant & his Uncle were Loyal Printers Because it was a Matter of Opinion. Admitted that the publications which he printed did great Mischief. Says that Gov$^{t}$ never offer'd to pay this Man for his printing press if he destroy'd it. Thinks that he cannot live there because he would be insulted. Says that their Indignation in America ag$^{t}$ him he believes arises upon this Idea that he was concern'd in emitting forged Money.

George Meserve—sworn.

Was well acquainted with M$^{r}$ Fowles & has known him 20 Years. Believes they published on both sides in their Capacity as Printers but thinks that if they ever publish'd anything ag$^{t}$ Gov$^{t}$ it must have been by compulsion. Says that if they had refused to publish anything he thinks their property & even their Lives would have been in danger. Knows no particular Act of Loyalty in M$^{r}$ Fowle. Can't speak to any part of his property but has always understood that they had property. Does not know that he was ever insulted by the Mob. But yet he says he is sure that he could not have conducted himself otherwise.

### Memorial of Will$^{m}$ Luce [1]

Determin'd the 18$^{th}$ of Feb$^{y}$ 1785.

Will$^{m}$ Luce—the Claimant—sworn. 18$^{th}$ of Feb$^{y}$ 1785.

A Zealous Loyalist.

Is a Native of Boston & lived at Elizabeth Town in New Jersey in 1775 as a Merch$^{t}$. He declared his Sentiments from the beginning in favor of Great Britain. He has been ask'd to sign their Associations but he never did. The Oaths were never tender'd to him But he was asked to muster but he refused. They had erected a Gallows for him in 1775. He went in Jan$^{y}$ 1776 to Jamaica where he remain'd till Aug$^{t}$ when he was returning to America & he was taken & carried into New Hampshire. He was allowed to go to New Jersey & to see his family. At this time the British Troops came into the Province And he went to them. He has remain'd with the Army ever since. He rais'd for his Majesty 100 Sea faring Men but he was paid for it. And he had the pay of 10*s.* a Day for 15 Months & commanded the Company. Warrant to raise the Men produced sign'd by Sir Henry Clinton. From the time that he join'd the British Army he was constantly employ'd in procuring Intelligence & declares that he neither was paid for his Exertions or ever made any Demand.

Bore Arms & render'd Services.

Produces the Adjutant Gen$^{ls}$ orders for raising the Batteau Men.

A very full Certificate to his Loyalty from General Skynner.

In 1779 he plann'd & assisted in the Execution of an Attempt to surprize the New Jersey Brigade.

This attempt did not succeed But it was not his fault. This is very fully attested by Governor Franklyn.

He has an Allowance of 40 a Y$^{r}$ from the Treasury which he has rec$^{d}$ from the 5$^{th}$ of July 1784 & he now continues to receive it.

Bounty £40 a Y$^{r}$.

It was in Feb$^{y}$ 1779 that M$^{r}$ Luce proposed his plan to Sir Henry Clinton

[1] 'Armed Boats Company. A/c of subsistence for Capt. William Luce's Company of armed boatmen for ninety-two days, £967 16*s.* 8*d.*' (*Hist. MSS. Comm., Am. MSS. in R. Inst.*, vol. ii, p. 534). Other notices of these armed boatmen will be found in ibid., vol. iii.

for seizing the New Jersey Brigade & General Stirling [1] was the person who was employ'd to carry it into Execution.

Major Van Cortland in speaking of this Scheme says it was a very meritorious plan & very much approved of notwithstanding the execution of the Measure was defeated.

Philip Cortland—sworn.

Knew Mr Luce in America. Always consider'd him as a loyal Man. Knew his House in Elizth Town has been in it. Can't value it. Believes he plann'd a Scheme for taking the New Jersey Brigade & that it was solely his doing. The Plan was thought so good an one that it was attempted but it fail'd. Says that Captn Luce had great merit in collecting the Batteau Men. Believes that he has lost all his property. He was understood to be a Man of very good Circumstances before the troubles. Says that Mr Luce was station'd at the advanced Post for the purpose of obtaining Intelligence & that he did furnish very material & useful Intelligence & this he knows as the Witness's Regt was station'd upon the advanced Post.

### Memorial of Matthias Aspden [2]

Determin'd the 21st of Feby 1785.

21st of Feby 1785.

Matthias Aspden—the Claimant—sworn.

The Board are of Opinion that this Man has not sufficiently proved his Loyalty so as to render himself an object of the Act of Part.

Is a Native of Pensylvania & resided there at the Commencement of the troubles as a Mercht at Philadelphia. He was applied to by the Inhabitants in May or June 1775 to arm but he refused. But finding every Man's Eye upon his Neighbour he thought it right to swim with the Stream at that time & learnt the Exercise of Arms & went out with them for about 2 Months. He did not sign the Association paper. He says he was consider'd as a Tory. He left the Country in Septr 1776. He took part with them in no other Instance. He came to Engd in 1776 in Septr where he has been ever since. He has never applied for temporary support. He remain'd quiet for 12 Months before he came. He came away because he disapproved of their Measures. He went to New York in March 1776 with a view to come to Engd. He got a Letter of recommendation to Govr Tryon who said he might go in the Pacquet if he would permit his papers & letters to be seal'd up & sent to Lord George Germaine. He refused to take an Oath to reveal everything in his power to the Secretary which Govr Tryon insisted upon or he should not go. And he went back to Philadelphia. He offer'd to take the Oath of Allegiance. He says he refused the Oath for two reasons because he had no confidence in Govr Tryon & because he thought the Oath unnecessary. Says he knew nothing of the rebellion which would have been of use to the Secretary of State. He afterwards came to Spain in a Schooner. He was not obliged to quit America but he found his Situation so disagreeable that he did not choose to stay. When he came to Engd he was called upon to go to Lord George Germaine by Mr John Nutt. Should not

[1] Presumably Colonel Thomas Stirling, who was Brigadier-General.

[2] Sabine (op. cit., vol. i, pp. 186–90) gives a long and curious account of this claimant. 'Like the bat in the fable, he sought to find gain from both parties, and obtained it from neither.' 'His will gave rise to the most extraordinary suit that ever occurred under the Confiscation Acts of the Revolution.' The decision was in favour of the American heirs, who thus received more than $500,000.

have gone to Lord George Germaine if Mr Nutt had not asked him to do it. When he was there He gave the fullest Information to Lord George.

Saml Shoemaker—on his Affirmation.

Has known the Claimant from his Infancy. He resided at Philadelphia at the commencement of the troubles. He was a quiet Man but he believes he wish'd well to Gt Bn. Says he went away soon after Independence was declared. Says if he was concerned in learning the Use of Arms no good reason can be given for it. Considers it as a very bad measure. Thinks Mr Aspden did very wrong in refusing to take that Oath thinks it makes very much agt him. Knew the House which his father left him it was in King Street. Values it at £1200 S. Thinks the Congress would not now restore his property but says he might have had it in 1782. Does not know the Plantation.

### Memorial of Willm Orange

Determin'd the 12th of Apl 1785.

Willm Orange—the Claimant—sworn. 22d of Feby 1785.

Is a Native of Engd & went first to America in the Year 1743. He lived there till 1771 when he returned to Engd & has been here ever since. He was obliged to quit it from the part he had taken in the Stamp Act. He has taken no part in this Dispute. He applied to the Lords of the Treasury after the burning of Norfolk & they gave him £100 a Yr. He never intended to go back to America but admitted that he recd a Letter from Lord Dunmore but he was then ill of the Rheumatism or he says as he was order'd he should have gone. He now receives an Allowance of £150 a Yr which was augmented in April 1778 to £150 a Yr which he now receives. Says his Lands have been confiscated as an Absentee. When he left America there was a great Dispute in the Town of Norfolk about Inoculation & Party ran very high but he took no part & that was not the Occasion of his coming to Engd. Says they confiscated his Lands as he understands because one Captn Murphy had informed the Americans that he was concerned in fitting out Privateers agt them. But he had no concern in Privateers at all. And he sent out to give that information to the Americans. He has taken no part at all during this War but has lived in Engd as a British Subject. Considers himself as a British Subject & not as an American.

A British Subject. Did not bear Arms.

Bounty £150 a Yr.

### Memorial of Willm Burton Esq.

Determin'd the 26th of Feby 1785.

William Burton—the Claimant—sworn. 23d of Feby 1785.

Is a Native of Engd & went to America in 1772. He was settled at New Brunswick & came to Engd in 1775. He was in America at the time of the Lexington business & came away about a Month afterwards. His reason for coming away was on Acct of the rebellion. He returned to New York in 1776 where he staid till 1779. In the Interval he went over to his own property but it was always occupied by the British Officers. He did not dare to go at any other time. He got into a Difficulty in a Coffee house in a Quarrel by striking the Son of a Congress Man for bad Language. The person's name

A Loyalist.

was Livingston.[1] There was an Association set on foot at that time. He did sign but when he found the Drift of it he erased his name & was allowed to do it by a Delegate of the Congress. He was understood to be what they called a Tory & they have treated him as such by confiscating his property. He had no Allowance from the Treasury until he came to Eng$^{d}$ in 1779. He had from that period £200 a Y$^{r}$ which has been reduced to 100 a Year by M$^{r}$ Wilmot & M$^{r}$ Coke. The 200 a Y$^{r}$ was given by Lord North upon the recommendation of his Uncle who was a Commissioner of Excise. He never bore Arms at New York.

former Bounty £200 a Y$^{r}$.
present Bounty £100 a Y$^{r}$.

When he was at New York he was made a Naval Commissary by Admiral Gambier[2] with a Salary of 10*s*. a Day which he rec$^{d}$ for nine Months. Says that in the Year 1778 he had a paper put into his hands which was an Advertisement for the Sale of his Estate & he has heard that it was sold to one Bergem. Has no doubt of the Sale of it & has a Witness who will prove it.

### Memorial of Thomas Cutter

Determin'd the 26$^{th}$ of Feb$^{y}$ 1785.

Thomas Cutter—the Claimant—sworn. 24$^{th}$ of Feb$^{y}$ 1785.

A Loyalist.

Did not bear Arms.

Is a Native of Eng$^{d}$ & went first to America in 1755 & settled in Rhode Island. He worked with a Tobacconist for some time & then enter'd into business for himself. He never bore Arms but he assisted in procuring Intelligence for the British. He never took any Oath or gave any Assistance to the Rebels. He join'd the British in 1778. About three Weeks after he had join'd the British they seized all his property & sold it. After the British left Rhode Island they put him in Gaol & kept him five weeks. They let him out of prison on Security given by two Securities. He did not come away at the Evacuation because his Wife & Child were ill. He left Rhode Island in June 1783. And he lived more than three Years under rebel Gov$^{t}$.

George Wightman—sworn.

Has known Tho$^{s}$ Cutter for 12 Years. He took no part at first but says that he afterwards took part with Gov$^{t}$. Considers him as a Loyalist. Knows that he remain'd behind when the Island was evacuated. Believes it was owing to the Sickness of his family. Says it was dangerous. Does not know how he made his peace. Thinks after they had stripp'd him that there was no Occasion to persecute him. Knows nothing of the Confiscation & Sale of his property but by hearsay. He is a Man of good Character & of truth. Says he had a con-

[1] The Livingstons were a leading family for generations in New York. Such was their importance that the Presbyterian or popular party was also known as the Livingston party. It was opposed to the Episcopalian or de Lancey party. Two members of the family, Philip and Robert R., were delegates to the Continental Congress of 1775 (*Journals of Cont. Congress*, vol. ii, p. 15). Philip had been a delegate in the previous year (ibid., vol. i, p. 19). He 'took an active part in the Revolution and was a signer of the Declaration of Independence. His whole career makes it plain that he was by no means inclined to submit to British restrictive measures. On the other hand, he was connected with the colonial aristocracy and was known to be opposed to the growing influences of the unfranchised classes' (Becker, op. cit., note at p. 122). Becker quotes John Adams (*Works*, vol. ii, p. 351): 'He seems to dread New England, the levelling spirit, &c.'

[2] James Gambier, *b*. 1723, *d*. 1789. Is in *Dict. of Nat. Biography*.

siderable Stock of Snuff. Says if he had £100 worth of Snuff it was a great deal. Admits that property sold much cheaper in 1777 on Acct of the troubles. Knows the Dwelling House &c but does not know whether it is his or not thinks it worth 150 the small Lot in Kingston he values at £30. Knows the Signature of some of the people who have signed the paper.

Doctr Halyburton—sworn. 25th of Feby 1785.

Knew the Character of Thos Cutter very well. Believes he has always been uniform in his Loyalty. Was at Rhode Island when he came over. Says the Rebels often put Arms into his hands & he refused to use them. Has often heard that his property was seized by the Rebels. Is not at all acquainted with his property but thinks he must have been worth Money. Knew his business. He had a considerable Share of business. Says the Virginia Tobacco always sold much higher during the War than before. Thinks 8 or 900 Dollars would be a great deal for him to have whereas he claims £8000 Dollars. Says that Genl Prescot advised the Loyalists to stay behind at the Evacuation. Says his Wife was unable to move at the time. Thinks he might have continued there after the Peace but without any prospect of recovering his property. Thinks it a very improper Demand.

### Memorial of Wm Taylor Esq.

Determin'd ye 26th of Feby 1785.

25th of Feby 1785.

Willm Taylor Esq—the Claimant—sworn.

Is a Native of America & was settled as a Lawyer in New Jersey in 1775. He ceas'd to practise in July 1776 when the new Govt was established & then he refused to practise & was accordingly sent for into Court & the Oaths of Allegiance were tender'd to him which he refused. He never was obliged to make any Concessions to the Americans the Number of Loyalists was so great that they never attempted to take anybody up in that County. He join'd the British Army in 1776 at Brunswick. Prior to his joining them he was never under any Necessity of taking any Oaths. He has remain'd with the British Army ever since as a private Character. He left them in Novr 1783 & landed at Portsmouth in Decr. He has an Allowance from the Treasury of £40 a Yr since Christmas 1783. He had likewise during the latter part of his time at New York recd a Dollar a day for no situation but that of a Loyal Refugee. He remonstrated agt the provincial Congress for not [*sic* in text].

A Loyalist.

Did not bear Arms.

Bounty £40 a Yr.

Certificate from Govr Franklyn produced. He charges the Loss of Surrogate's Office at 40 a Yr & the practice at £300 a Yr. He had the promise of another Office but he never got it.

Profession £300 a Yr.

Major John Antill—sworn.

Has known the Man before & during the rebellion. Believes him uniformly loyal. Does not remember the Grenadier Co. Says he was in considerable business in the profession of the Law. Believes he must have got 400 a Yr.

Willm Taylor—the Claimant—called in again.

Admits that he belonged to the Grenadier Company & that they were a Company of American Militia but they signed no Association.

Determin'd the 1st of March 1785.

## Memorial of Josiah Tatnall [1] Esq.

Josiah Tatnall—the Claimant—sworn. 28th of Feby 1785.

A Zealous & meritorious Loyalist.

Is a Native of Charlestown. He was settled in Georgia at the Commencement of the troubles. He has a Planter & Sawyer. He was a Col^l of a Reg^t of Militia & one of the Council by Mandamus. Dates the Commencement of the troubles in Georgia from 1776. He was frequently call'd upon by the Gov^r to protect the town & the Gov^rs House & he gave assistance to Sir James Wright in withdrawing himself. In consequence of this being known he was taken Prisoner & kept six Weeks. He was then releas'd on Parole by Exchange. He then went back to his plantation where he remain'd till Dec^r 1777 when he left the province. They frequently tender'd the Association & Oaths but he refused both. Produces the Oath which they tender'd to him. He was summon'd before the Committee & he told them that he despis'd them & their Oath. He was then order'd to quit the province within 60 Days. He was permitted to stay a few Days longer by asking leave & produces some of the Permits. He quitted the Province in Dec^r 1777. They were clear'd out for Cape Francois but the Witness & some others bought the Ship for £500 & they stood for the Bahama Islands where they arrived & were taken by an English Privateer but they were releas'd by the Court of Admiralty. Produces the form of a second Oath which was tender'd to him & others it is much stronger than the other. He embarked for Eng^d in June 1778 & was taken by Count D'Estaing's fleet & carried into Philadelphia & kept 7 Weeks. When he went to New York & came to Eng^d immediately & landed in Eng^d in Dec^r 1778. He remain'd in Eng^d 11 Months & went out again to Georgia in Nov^r 1779. He had an Appointment from Lord George Germaine of Receiver Gen^l of the Quit rents &c & also reappointed a Member of the Council. He had a Salary of £100 a Y^r as Rec^r. He arrived at Savannah in March 1780 when he was put into possession of that Office. He was also Judge Surrogate of the Admiralty under Lieut^t Gov^r Powell. He was Country Comptroller & Deputy Auditor. He continued there until the Evacuation. He has at present an Appointment of Surveyor Gen^l of Lands at the Bahama Islands [2] with a Salary of £100 a Y^r. He has applied for an Augmentation to the Salary but does not know the fate of it. He now receives the Salary & has rec^d it for one Year. When he first came to Eng^d in 1778 He rec^d £200 after he had been 3 Months in Eng^d & he afterwards rec^d £200 more besides Passage Money. Since he returned last he has rec^d no Allowance from the Treasury except the Salary.

Did not bear Arms.

Bounty £400.

Lieut^t Gov^r Graham—sworn. 1st of March 1785.

Has known M^r Tatnall for many Years long before the troubles. He says

[1] Lieutenant-Colonel Archibald McArthur wrote to Lieutenant-General Leslie on October 30, 1782: 'I have formed a Committee of four of the principal refugees, Colonels Ball and Cassells for Carolina, and Colonels Tatnall and Douglas for Georgia, to ascertain by oath the number of refugees and blacks and superintend the delivery of provisions (*Hist. MSS. Comm.*, *Am. MSS. in R. Inst.*, vol. iii, p. 192). He signed a dissent from the Resolutions of August 10, 1774 (White, *Hist. Collections of Georgia*, p. 49).

[2] Professor Siebert might have added his name to the list of loyalists holding offices of some importance in the Bahama Islands (*The Legacy of the Am. Rev. to the British West Indies and the Bahamas*, p. 49).

he has been uniformly loyal from the first. Says he remain'd in Georgia some time longer than the Witness but he understood that he refused the Oaths & therefore was obliged to go away. He exerted himself always for the Service & was very useful. He was Col$^{l}$ of Militia & a Member of the Council. Says he was Rec$^{r}$ Gen$^{l}$ &c &c. Knows the 105 Acres where he lived. Says it was valuable from its vicinity to the Town. The land was not valuable. Thinks in the State it was in exclusive of the Buildings it was worth £500. Knows he had a share in a Tan Yard & understood that he had a 3$^{d}$ Share but he is no Judge of the Value. Knows the land which he bought of M$^{r}$ Box. When he bought it the Cultivation was very trifling. Thinks it well worth £800.

Knows the tract of the 796 Acres. Says it was a valuable Tract of Land but thinks that he gave the full Value for it. Can't say whether he clear'd any part of it afterwards. He admits that he sold a tract of Land to M$^{r}$ Tatnall at Zamacho. Does not recollect the price but believes it was 50 Gãs. Knows his Lands on Tybec Island but does not know the particulars. The land was worth nothing in itself but valuable from situation to make little buildings upon it. He gave him £50 for a small piece of it. Knows little more of his property.

Rev$^{d}$ M$^{r}$ Renny—sworn.

Knew M$^{r}$ Tatnall very well in America before the troubles. He appear'd to be very firmly attached to this Country. He knows that he refused to sign their Associations or to take any Oaths. He has frequently been in his House. When the Armed Men came down to search his House &c he always was very firm & rather than take the Oaths he quitted the Province. He supplied the Town of Savannah with many Articles which made it necessary for him to rear many Horses &c. He says that M$^{r}$ Tatnall was a Man of very handsome fortune & that he lived extremely well in that Country.

**Memorial of Jane Constable Widow**

Determin'd the 2$^{d}$ of March 1785.

2$^{d}$ of March 1785.

Jane Constable—the Claimant—sworn.

A Loyalist & the Representative of a Loyalist.

Is a Native of Eng$^{d}$ & went first to America in 1776. She is the Widow of Capt$^{n}$ Constable. He had been in America before the troubles. He went first about a Year before the troubles. Says her Husband was in the Engagement at Bunkers Hill. She went with her Husband from Boston to New York from thence he was sent to Georgia & they were taken in their passage. Her Husband died in Oct$^{r}$ 1780. He was wounded in an Engagement with Gen$^{l}$ Leslie in the Jerseys. Says that he died in Consequence of his Confinement. She left Charlestown in Nov$^{r}$ 1780. After repeated Applications She obtain'd nothing from the Treasury but she now has an Allowance of £20 a Y$^{r}$ which commenced from y$^{e}$ 5$^{th}$ July 1783 & she now continues to receive it.

Bounty £20 a Y$^{r}$.

Produces a Charlestown Gazette of the 30$^{th}$ of June 1780. Certificate from the Dep$^{y}$ Inspector Gen$^{l}$ of the forces to Capt$^{n}$ Constable's Situation in the Army to his Imprisonment &c. Certificate of her Marriage produced. Certificate from Gen$^{l}$ Leslie to Capt$^{n}$ Constable's zeal & saying that he believed it shorten'd his Life.

The whole of the Claim disallowed the Ship being lost by Accident.

The whole Loss consists of certain Articles which she was bringing home in 1780. Her Husband had no other property. Certificate from Col[l] Balfour to his raising a Corps. He carried no Money out with him. The Articles which she was bringing home were Indigo Tobacco & Bees Wax. Her Husband had bought these things from his Savings. The Ship went to the bottom & She & the passengers were taken up by the Hydra. She asks whether if she receives the half pay of an Officers Widow it will preclude her from receiving her Allowance at the Treasury. She is told not but is desired to consider the Nature of the Oath which she must take if she receives that pension.

Produces an Affidavit of Capt[n] stating the Loss of the Vessel & the Articles contain'd.

M[rs] Constable speaks of a Witness whom she means to call but it not being to a material point it is of no importance whether he attends or not.

Determin'd the 2[d] of March 1785.

## Memorial of Samuel Smith

Samuel Smith—the Claimant—sworn. 2[d] of March 1785.

A Loyalist.

Did not bear Arms.

Is a Native of Eng[d] & went to America in 1768. When the rebellion broke out he was settled in New Jersey at Spotswood & had the Direction of the Iron Works there. He never took an Active part with them but he sign'd their Muster roll & appear'd on the Ground. He went round with them & carried a Stick. He was appointed Lieut[t] in their M[a] but he says he did not accept because he had so much business to take care of. His real reason was that he did not like their Measures. This was about a Month before Independence was declared but he admits that it was generally expected. He continued unmolested till Dec[r] 1776. He says he was obliged to get a Man to go out in his room. He never took the Oaths but he did sign an Association early in the business. Says that when a Paper was brought about to take the Sentiments of the Province whether they were for Independence or not & he sign'd ag[t] it & 50 of his Workmen did the same. He was in consequence of this summon'd before the Committee & they meant to imprison him but they did not do it. He join'd the British Troops when they came. He escaped from his House & after being two nights in the woods he join'd the British at Brunswick. He wished to have returned home if possible but he could not. When the Country was in the possession of the British he came again to his own House. He left his House again the 1[st] of Jan[y] 1777 & went to Amboy for a few Days & from thence to New York where he staid three Years. He came from thence in Dec[r] 1779 & landed in Eng[d] in Jan[y] 1780. He never applied to the Treasury & has no Allowance. The only Act he ever did to serve Great Britain was to assist a British Commissary.

## Memorial of Dan[l] Dulany [1] Esq. Jun[r]

Daniel Dulany—the Claimant—sworn. 3[d] of March 1785.

Is a Native of America & lived at Anapolis with his father when the troubles

[1] Daniel Dulany must not be confused with his more distinguished father of the same name (see Johns Hopkins Univ. Studies in Hist., &c., xxi, 6 and 7, *The Political Services of Daniel Dulany the elder*,

commenced. He then resided with his father who is now alive in Maryland. In 1774 He protested ag[t] the resolve not to pay British Debts. He refused to sign all their Associations. And in 1775 he met several other persons armed at Sir Rob[t] Eden's House to oppose all those persons who meant to attack the Tories. He remain'd in Maryland till July 1775 & he came to Eng[d] in Sept[r] 1775 since which time he has been in Eng[d]. In 1778 He applied to the Treasury & rec[d] £400 in advance & £200 a Year from that time to this.

Bounty £200 a Y[r].

Certificate read to Loyalty & to his Exertions on the Occasion abovemention'd from M[r] Will[m] Eddis.

His father has been treble tax'd for his Attachment to Great Britain. Has been uniformly loyal. His Estate has not been confiscated.

John Swan—sworn.

Knew M[r] Dulany in 1772 or 1773. He was then just returned to America from Eng[d]. He understood that he was disaffected to the Cause of America that he refused to muster &c in consequence of which he was obliged to leave the Country. He had a great & extensive property which he had convey'd from his father. Believes that the father convey'd all his landed property to this & his other Son excepting a very small part indeed. He left America in June last. He believes he has lost the whole of his property & that it has been sold. He cannot put a value on any of his property in Frederic County. Knows that he had property at Anapolis but not the Value. Cannot value any part of his property. Speaks to the names & Characters of M[r] Fairbrother & Bullin they are Men of fair Character the same of M[r] Murdock & M[r] Marshall the same of Betty & Deakins.

Thomas Eden—sworn.

Has known M[r] Dulany before the troubles. He was constantly with him & he believes he was constantly loyal. Knows that he had very great property & that he had a concern in some Iron Works because the Iron was consign'd to the Witness for a Y[r] or two. Believes he had great property but can't speak to the value of any part of it.

James Brooks—sworn.

Has known M[r] Dulany many Years. Remembers him in Maryland in 1774. He took a decided part in favor of this Country. It render'd him obnoxious & has cost him his Estate in the End. Knows great part of his property but can't speak to the Value. Remembers his Grand Mother M[rs] Tasker & that she left him residuary Legatee & some Land in Anapolis but can't value it. Knows that he had a tenth share of the Iron works but can't value it. Understood that M[r] Tasker by his Will left a Legacy to M[r] Dulany.

Richard Holland—sworn.

Has known M[r] Dulany since the Year 1773. He lived with him a great deal & knew his Opinions very well. He was very decidedly in favor of Gov[t]

by St. G. L. Sioussat). We find Daniel Dulany, jun., offering on January 26, 1787, to be one of Haldimand's esquires at his installation as Knight of the Bath (Brymner, *Can. Archives*, 1886, Haldimand Coll., vol. i, p. 572).

& he has been informed that he sign'd the Protest ag^t the proposition for not paying British Debts. Thinks the Confiscation of his Estate a proof of his Loyalty.

Determin'd y^e 5^th of March 1785.

### Memorial of David Propert

5^th of March 1785.

David Propert—the Claimant—sworn.

A Loyalist.

Is a Native of Wales & went to America in 1770. He was Organist at Boston. Admits that he sign'd a paper in Aug^t 1785 [1] & swore to it he believes it was merely to swear that he would not buy provisions &c for the British. They took from him the provisions that he had bought. He was then at Rhode Island. He got on board the Swan Sloop of War & went in that to Boston. He left Boston in Nov^r 1775 & went to Halifax & from thence to Eng^d. He never carried Arms or served in the Militia. His reason for leaving Boston was that he could get no provisions. Says a Proclamation was issued. Says he receives nothing from the Treasury & never has done. But upon looking into the Cases for temporary support it appears that he has an Allowance of £20 a Y^r from the 5^th of Jan^y 1783.

Did not bear Arms.

Bounty £20 a Y^r.

Says he got £300 a Y^r at Boston by teaching Music & he had £40 a Y^r as Organist. Says he carried out about £100. Says that he has four Spinnets which he left in America but he makes no Claim for them. He left them with four or five friends. He thinks he makes £50 or more by teaching Musick & he receives £16 a Y^r from Mess^rs Lane & Fraser.

N.B. To write to the Treasury to desire that the Arrears of this Man's Salary may be paid to him up to Jan^y 1785 & that as he does not appear to want it it should be discontinued in future.

Determin'd on the 24^th & 25^th of March 1785.

### Memorial of Will^m Bayard [2] Esq.

7^th of March 1785.

Will^m Bayard—the Claimant—sworn.

A Loyalist & has render'd Services to the British Gov^t.

Is a Native of New York. His family were some of the Original Settlers there. In 1774 he was an Inhabitant of New York. In every part of the rebellion & in every instance he opposed the rebellion in every stage of it dates the Commencement of the rebellion from 1775. He had been in a very extensive line of business but he was then quitting his business. In 1774 he was appointed one of a Committee of 51 [3] persons to oppose the Measures of the rebels. He remain'd at New York until the Rebels brought in some of the Connecticut Troops. He quitted his House then to avoid being insulted & went to his Estate at Wehounck & afterwards to his Estate in Orange County & he remain'd afterwards conceald until he join'd the British Troops. He join'd them the Day

[1] *sic.* ? 1775.

[2] William Bayard was delegate from New York to the Continental Congress of 1765. 'On Manhattan Island the most valuable estates were those of Stuyvesant, Bayard, Heathcote, de Lancey, and de Peyster' (Becker, op. cit., p. 9). The Bayards thus belonged to the class of large landed proprietors. These men 'at heart and by habit were true aristocrats and denunciators of the democratic movement. They were loyal to the Crown because of received and anticipated favours. Their material interests were connected with the established order of things and their conviction tended to loyalism' (Flick, op. cit., p. 33).

[3] See Becker, op. cit., pp. 114–66, for an account of this committee of fifty-one.

after they took the Town & gave them all the Intelligence in his power. He brought his family to New York in two Days. After the fire He gave every information in his power to Lord North & sent him Evidence to prove that it was set on fire by Design. He took the Management of the Police at New York at the request of Gov$^{r}$ Tryon. He offer'd himself to every Commander in chief to be useful to the utmost of his power. He procured Spies Guides &c on many Occasions. A Reg$^{t}$ was rais'd by his means in 1776. It was to consist of 550 Men they were call'd the Orange Rangers his Eldest Son was appointed Lieut$^{t}$ Col$^{l}$ & the next Brother Major. He says his eldest Son is in the East Indies & that these two were his Second & third Sons. They now both receive half pay. He had a Warrant to raise a Brigade but he only raised one Reg$^{t}$. He acted in the Refugee department without any Emolument. He had an Allowance of £200 a Y$^{r}$ w$^{ch}$ was given to him here in Jan$^{y}$ 1779 & it has been continued ever since. He had no other Allowance but he had an appointment of Vendue Master likewise in 1779. He had no emolument from it. He wished to have been Sole Vendue Master but Lord George Germaine did not choose to give him such an Appointment. Upon his return in 1779 He was appointed Agent for Prizes by several Captains. He was Sole Agent for particular Captains. He had 5 per Cent for this. Says he did not get £10000 C. by it. He acted as Agent for the Contractors of Provisions M$^{r}$ Devayner &c. He never got in the whole by this more than £200 or £250. He was employ'd in this Situation for near two Y$^{rs}$. He was not concern'd in any Contracts with the Quarter Mast$^{r}$ Gen$^{l's}$ Department. He had two Waggons which he was paid for at the Common price & a Pettyaugre. The Profit of these was more than £1000 a Y$^{r}$ but it was his Support. In the latter part of the time he had two Boats. This Contract continued for about three Years. He was allowed an House but his House at Greenwich was occupied by the King's Troops. The House was allotted to him by Sir Henry Clinton but he had two small Houses in the Town which he rented at £150 a Y$^{r}$ & afterwards for the three last Years at £300 a Y$^{r}$. These Houses were too small for him & his family. He had another House (a rebel House) which he rented for 38 a Y$^{r}$. He had this about 3 Years. Being asked whether he ever sign'd an Association He says he never sign'd any to the best of his knowledge. The Committee of 51 were Men of principles unfavorable to G$^{t}$ Britain & he was put amongst them as being friendly to the King's Gov$^{t}$. Says this Committee never sign'd any papers or came to any public Declaration of principles. Admits that this Committee was appointed to correspond with the other Provinces & to aid & assist the Rebellion but he always opposed them. Can't recollect when he quitted that Committee. He had an Allowance at New York. He arrived in Eng$^{d}$ in 1783. He never concurr'd in any Measure of that Committee which had the least tendency to hurt Great Britain. He never sign'd one of the resolves or proclamations of this Committee. When he quitted that Committee cannot be positive that he declared his reasons but says they were very well known. Says that no person in New York gave so great Opposition to the Measures of the Rebels.

Bounty £200 a Y$^{r}$.

He applied to Sir Henry Clinton for the Loss sustain'd at that time. He produces a Copy of the Mem$^{l}$ reciting the Loss by the Post at Casteal.

He desires to have leave till tomorrow to consider whether he should claim this *here* or not.

N° 4. The large House & Improvements at Greenwich on N. York Island.

Rev[d] Charles Inglis—sworn.

Was well acquainted with the Claim[t] before & after the Rebellion. He always consider'd him as uniformly attached to the British Gov[t]. There was a Committee of 51 at New York in the Year 1774 & 1775. Many persons of the first Loyalty & Character were of it for the purpose of checking the Measures then in Agitation. Does not recollect for what purpose the Committee was first established.

In 1776 the Claimant was obliged to hide himself in an Hovel in New Jersey for fear of being seized by the Americans on acc[t] of his Loyalty. Witness saw him in this Situation & says that he suffer'd greatly by being so long obliged to live in a miserable Garret. Does not think there could be a more firm Loyalist than M[r] Bayard who he frequently thought was too violent at the Commencement of the troubles against the Americans. Always understood that M[r] Bayard had a very considerable property in America but he is not able to speak to any particular parts thereof.

Will[m] Cunningham—sworn.

Knew M[r] Bayard in 1774 & 1775. He consider'd him as a Loyalist. Mentions many Acts of Loyalty. M[r] Bayard attempted to prevent his being put in Gaol. And he was used ill in Consequence. Thinks M[r] Bayard's private Character protected him at that time. Says that when the Alarm of fire was given in 1776 He went to the Top of the Gaol when he saw the town on fire in five different places at considerable Distance from each other. One Mariner a Noted Rebel who has been three times in his Gaol told him they would burn the Town if they could. From these Circumstances he thinks the fire was by Design.

Governor Tryon—sworn.

Speaks fully as to the Claim[ts] Loyalty. By his Interest & Influence the Orange Rangers [1] were rais'd. He took charge of the Police of New York at Gov[r] Tryon's request. Thinks M[r] Bayard render'd material Service to Gov[t]. He was supposed to be a Man of very good property.

Sir Henry Clinton—sworn.

Says that from all he knew of the Claim[t] he was perfectly loyal. Speaks to the Claim[t] having thro' his influence been the Cause of the raising of the Orange Rangers. That the Claim[t] often gave him material Intelligence & accompanied him in an Expedition up the North River. Being asked whether on the whole of M[r] Bayard's Conduct he thinks that he render'd Services Says that he did.

[1] In 1779 the King's Orange Rangers, quartered at Halifax, under Lieutenant-Colonel Goreham, were recommended by Sir H. Clinton for the work of establishing a post on Penobscot River (*Hist. MSS. Comm., Am. MSS. in R. Inst.*, vol. i, p. 415). It was proposed in October 1782 to form the three Provincial Corps, the Fencibles, the Orange Rangers, and the King's Rangers, into one regiment (ibid., vol. iii, p. 183).

Henry White—sworn.

Knew the Claimant. It was generally understood that He had a Concern in the Vendue business at New York. The Firm was Taylor & Bayard. Taylor had an half Share. The profits were very considerable. Says that Taylor had been a Clerk of his & on the Evacuation the Witness brought home for him £8000 S. He also bought an House from Alexander Wallace for which he paid £3000. Thinks that Mr Bayard must have made full £10000 Currency by his Agency for prizes during the War.

Being asked what was the general Opinion at New York concerning Mr Bayard's profits during the War He says that he does not think he made so much as his Brother Robert (£20000 S.).

Has heard that Mr Bayard has £10000 or £15000 in this Country but does not know how far his Information ought to be relied on.

Is asked as to the Valuation of the Lot fronting little Dock Street (No 6). Says that £2800 exceeds anything he could have formed an Idea of.

Says he has heard that Mr Bayard's Claim amounts to £130000 Cur. but that he the Witness had no Idea of his property being more than half that Sum. Mr Bayard was not consider'd among the Number of the very rich Men in the Province.

Thomas Coffin—sworn.

He was employ'd in Mr Weir's Office at New York & afterwards with Mr Watson as a Chief Clerk. Imagines that Mr Bayard's profits by his Waggons & Boats might be worth to him £15000 New York Currency per Annum. He promises to furnish us with some particulars relative thereto.

Thomas Coffin—sworn again. 22d of March 1785.

Produces an Account to shew what had been paid to the Claimant at New York by the Commissary General between the Years 1777 & 1781 by which it appears that on an Average it was £1700 per Annum. Says that from November 1781 to May following Mr Paumier[1] acted as Commissary General but the Witness not having his Books is not able to say what was paid to Mr Bayard during that time. The Claimant's Waggons & Boats were not continued by Mr Watson as Mr Coffin believes.

Note.

It appears that Mr Bayard must have made during the War 24000 Currency at least—which is £13500 Sterg.

## Memorial of Major Robt Bayard

Determin'd ye 28th of March 1785.

Robert Bayard—the Claimant—sworn. 17th of March 1785.

A Native of America. Born in New York & on the Commencement of

[1] According to his own account Peter Paumier's position was no bed of roses. In May 1782 we find a memorial from him for £30,000 for forage and expenses. A few days later he writes that the people who have demands against the department begin to be very pressing for payment. In June he describes himself as the victim of unjust suspicions during the short time he was in charge of the Commissary-General's department, and asks that his disagreeable position may be represented (*Hist. MSS. Comm., Am. MSS. in R. Inst.*, vol. ii, pp. 492, 505, 512, 513).

A Zealous Loyalist.

the troubles resided on his Estate at Bloomendale 6 Miles from New York. At this time he held no Office under Gov$^{t}$ but 2 or 3 Y$^{rs}$ before he was Collector of the Customs at Philadelphia. He had served before that time in the King's Army & sold out before he was appointed Collector.

Gain'd during the War by his Office £16000 St$^{g}$ as appears by his own Evidence. White thinks full £20000 Sterling.

In June 1776 He was applied to by Gen$^{l}$ Montgomery[1] & a M$^{r}$ Morris[2] who told him that if he chose to join them he might have the Command of the Canada Army. His Answer was that he had been a Crown Officer all his Life & should never think of changing his Sentiments. Soon after this his House was frequently beset by Mobs but did him no hurt but finding that he still continued in his House he was summon'd on the 19$^{th}$ of June 1776 to appear at the City Hall in New York the 21$^{st}$ following. In Consequence of this Summons he made his Escape on board the Dutchess of Gordon where Gov$^{r}$ Tryon was. Continued with him till the British Troops put him in possession again of his House which was in Sept$^{r}$ following. No other Damage done than what was lost of the furniture which his Wife removed to the Country & which they never got any Acc$^{t}$ of has heard that the Americans got possession.

After the Landing of the Troops at New York he was appointed by Gov$^{r}$ Tryon Judge of the Vice Admiralty Court. No Salary annex'd thereto. He had one half & the Register & Marshal the other half of the fees. Says that during the War he made by his Office between 15 & £16000 St$^{g}$ but his Expences of Living were considerable. He held no other Office but the one mention'd. He came to Eng$^{d}$ just before the Evacuation but with the consent of the Commander in Chief He left a Deputy. Never made any Application for temporary support. Certificate to his Loyalty from Gov$^{r}$ Tryon.

Henry White—sworn. 18$^{th}$ of March 1785.

Knew the Claimant. Says that he heard M$^{r}$ Abthorpe the Claimant's Wife's Brother say that her first Husband Ja$^{s}$ M$^{c}$Evors had left her an Annuity of £700 per Ann. Does not think any part was rec$^{d}$ during the War.

Knows the place at Bloomingdale thinks it would have let before the War for £200 Currency per Ann.

Major Bayard lived there during the War & he thinks that the whole produce of it during that time might have been £900 per Annum.

Says he was Judge of the Vice Admiralty Court at New York during the War & thinks he must have made £20000 Sterling. He lived in a very genteel & handsome manner.

Determin'd y$^{e}$ 19$^{th}$ of March 1785.

## Memorial of David Thomson

David Thomson—the Claimant—sworn. 18$^{th}$ of March 1785.

A Zealous Loyalist & render'd Services to the B. Gov$^{t}$.

A Native of Dundee. Went to America in 1752. In 1775 He was settled at Philadelphia. Always refused to sign the Associations. He was a Ship Builder & the only one of Sixteen who join'd the British. On Sir W$^{m}$ Howe's going

[1] Richard Montgomery, *b.* 1736, had been a Captain (1762) in the 17th British foot regiment and retired in 1771. He commanded the expedition against Canada, and was killed at the abortive storming of Quebec on December 31, 1775.

[2] ? Lewis Morris, *b.* 1726, *d.* 1798. He was a delegate to the Continental Congress, and one of the signers of the Declaration of Independence.

to Philadelphia he join'd him. He gave Assistance to raise the Vessels near Mud Island & in opening the Passage of the Delaware in 1777. And he was also of service to Lord Cornwallis.

Says that he sent to Eng$^{d}$ by the hands of a M$^{r}$ Barcklay before the Troops went to Philadelphia a Plan of the Chevaux de Frize. He sent it by M$^{r}$ Barclay who was a Tea Commissioner. He contrived the Bridge over the Schuykill for which he had Sir W$^{m}$ Howe's thanks. Laid down all the Platforms of the Redoubts round the Town but says he was paid for his trouble. Went to New York with the Troops. Had no pay from Gov$^{t}$ after he quitted Philadelphia. Staid at New York about 2 Years & then went to Port Shelburne in Nova Scotia.

He rec$^{d}$ 4 Dollars per Day for part of the time & two Dollars for the other part. Lord Cornwallis got him 40 per Ann. S. for two Years after he came to New York. Carried on business at New York & made £800 per Ann. He was appointed at Philadelphia (by Lord Howe) a Master Carpenter.

Has no temporary support from Gov$^{t}$.

Capt$^{n}$ Shadd—of the Navy—sworn.

Knew the Claimant at Philadelphia on the Troops going to Philadelphia. Understood that he was well attached to the British Gov$^{t}$ & had reason to think so himself. Understood that he had the constructing of the Bridge over the Schuykill & erected the Platforms. Believes that the Claimant was principally concern'd in the constructing of the Bridge. Remembers his being very usefull in raising a Ship that was loaded with Provisions for the Navy & had struck on a Chevaux de Frize. He built a Galley for Gov$^{t}$ & kept the flat bottom Boats in the best Order. Had the sunken Vessel not been rais'd the Men of War could not have been got down the Delaware. Capt$^{n}$ Shadd thinks he was of material Service to Government in raising the Ship & that he had no other Idea in exerting himself but to render a Service to Gov$^{t}$.

## Memorial of Mary Loring Widow

Determin'd y$^{e}$ 4$^{th}$ of April 1785.

Mary Loring Widow—the Claimant—sworn. 21$^{st}$ of March 1785.

The Representatives loyal & Ex$^{rs}$ also.

Her Husband [1] was an Half pay Captain in the Navy. At the Commencement of the troubles he resided on Jamaica Plain 5 Miles from Boston. Join'd Gen$^{l}$ Gage at Boston in Aug$^{t}$ 1774. Produces a Certificate from him to her Husband's Loyalty & Sufferings.

Her Husband had an Allowance of £200 per Ann. from Gov$^{t}$ from 1776. He died the 5$^{th}$ of Oct$^{r}$ 1781 since when she has been allowed £100 per Ann. She claims here under her Husband's Will and is entitled to a Life Interest in all her late Husband's property.

He had £100 in Boston from Gen$^{l}$ Gage.

[1] Commodore Joshua Loring, *b.* 1716, *d.* 1781. He was commissioned a Captain in the British navy in December 1757, and was Commodore of the naval forces on Lakes Champlain and Ontario. He took part in the campaigns of 1759 and 1760. On the morning of the battle of Lexington he rode post haste into Boston. 'I have always eaten the King's bread,' he told a friend, 'and I always intend to' (Stark, op. cit., p. 424).

Determin'd the 19th of March 1785.

## Memorial of Joshua Wingate Weeks

Joshua Wingate Weeks—the Claimant—sworn. 19th of March 1785.

A Native of America. Born at Portsmouth. Was Rector of St. Michaels Church Massachusets Bay. He had been Rector 16 Years.

A Loyalist.

In 1774 General Gage appointed him Deputy Chaplain to the 59th Regt. He constantly opposed the Measures of the Americans as far as lay in his power.

Has Half Pay as Chaplain.

He had been frequently summoned before Committees to turn out with Arms after the Battle of Lexington but always refused. He concealed himself for about a twelve Month at a little place he had on Kennebeck River. In October 1777 He was tried before a Special Jury at Salem for attempting to oppose their Measures by keeping the Church open which he did for a twelvemonth after the Independence was declared. Their Verdict was that he was a Tory but not so inimical as his person was unsafe.

He was called upon in April 1778 to take the Oath of Abjuration with 30 others. He refused as did a Captn Coombes the others took the Oath. He was taken into Custody & confined for a Day & a night. Applied for Liberty to remove himself & family got to Rhode Island from whence he went to New York. Came to England in 1778. Has no Allowance from Govt.

## Testimony to the Memorial of Mary Loring Widow

Joshua Loring—sworn. 21st of March 1785.

Says that his father (He is the Son of the Claimant) had an Estate near Roxbury with 60 Acres of Land. Thinks it would have sold for £2500. It was in high Cultivation. Thinks the House cost £2000 Currency.

18 Acres of Meadow & Dwelling House near the former. His father repaired it. The House was worth £225. The Land £270. Thinks it would have sold for as much.

23 Acres of Woodland. Thinks it was worth £10 S. per Ann.—7 Miles from Boston. It would have sold for that Sum.

Knows that his father had an House at Boston. Thinks it was worth £450 S. it would have sold for as much.

Knew the Negro. Says he was worth £50. He chose to remain in America. His father was a Mandamus Counsellor.

Major Bayard—sworn. 17th of March 1785.

Says that her late Husband was possess'd of a large well built House & 60 Acres on Jamaica Plain 5 Miles from Boston left to her by her Husband's Will as he understood. Thinks the whole would have sold for £2600 S. in 1774. The 60 Acres He thinks were worth £18 S. per Acre. Witness gave as much for Lands in the same Situation & not so good. He gave £25 Lawful Money for what he purchased which were 21 Acres Payable at the Death of a Life thereon Interest at 6 per Cent.

A Dwelling House large Barn &c with 18 Acres of Meadow Land adjoining near the former. She became possess'd as he has heard by the Will of her

Husband. Thinks that they would have sold for about £500 Sterg. The House was an indifferent one. The Land was in his opinion full as good as the other.

Sir Willm Pepperell Bart—sworn. 21st of March 1785.

Knew the late Mr Loring. He was a very loyal Subject. And he was one of the 29 notorious Conspirators.[1] Cannot speak to Property. Knows nothing of it. He was one of the Mandamus Counsellors.

John Joy—sworn.

He was a Master Builder at Boston. Says the Claimant's Husband's House at Roxbury would cost £1400 & might have sold for that Sum.

Dwelling House adjoining Major Bayard lived in it. Thinks it was worth £200. A Barn adjoining worth £100.

House in Boston with Stable & Garden worth 4 or £500 not less than £400.

Joshua Loring—again sworn. 22d of March 1785.

Produces the Probate of his father's Will dated in 1774 by which he devises his House & Lands at Roxbury to his Wife during her Widowhood. Specifies Legacies to his Children & appointing 3 Executors Mrs Loring Mr Joshua Loring & Mr Royal Loring.

The Children are himself Joseph Royal of the Navy a Lieutt John Loring also a Lieutt in the Navy Benjamin Loring a Surgeon in the Army & the late Mrs Winslow the Sister of the Witness. None of whom have claim'd under this Will.

### Memorial of Thos Boone[2] Esq.

Determin'd the 29th of March 1785.

It appears that the Claimant has not been in America since the Year 1764 & that he resided in England during the whole of the War. He is one of the Commissioners of his Majesty's Customs appointed in 1769.

22d of March 1785.

Thos Boone Esq—the Claimant—sworn.

A Native of Engd. Went first to America in 1752 to take possn of an Estate left to him by a Relation. Came to England & returned to America in 1758. Was appointed in 1759 to the Govt of New Jersey in which Situation he remain'd till 1762 when he went to South Carolina & return'd to Engd in 1764 from 1762 to 1764 he was Govr of South Carolina. His Agent there took upon himself to sign the Nonimportation Agreement for him which the Claimant on being informed thereof shew'd his Displeasure & directed him to erase his Name.

Mr Boone is one of the Commissioners of the Customs. He was appointed in 1769.

[1] i. e. Loyalists mentioned by name in the Confiscation Act of April 30, 1779.

[2] McCrady writes (*S. Car. under the Royal Gov., 1719–76*, p. 353): 'Little is really known of his history besides the episode of his gubernatorial career. The time and place of his birth and even of his death are matters of doubt; but it is believed that both of these events took place in England.' Thomas Boone wrote on November 23, 1763, that eleven years' acquaintance with nearly every province of America had convinced him of the necessity of the steps taken to prevent illegal trading (G. L. Beer, *British Colonial Policy, 1754–63*, note at p. 238). Boone wrote on October 9, 1762, that he had enjoined 'a magistrate to use every lawful means to protect the properties and persons of colonists settled under the sanction of this Government' (*Acts of the Privy Council, Unbound Papers*, p. 340).

29th of March 1785.

The Board upon Consideration determined upon his Case as follows

| | £ |
|---|---|
| Pon Pon Estate | 7500 |
| Mopshoo D° | 1700 |
| 162 Negroes on Pon Pon at £45 | 7290 |
| 36 Negroes on the Mopshoo Estate the other 41 We disallow as their Loss was occasion'd by an incident of the War & should have been insured by the Claimant when he sent them from Charlestown to St Augustine | 1620 |
| To allow 4 Negroes more which were born after 1780 | 180 |
| 24 Working Oxen at £4 | 96 |
| 60 Head of Cattle at 30s. | 90 |
| A Stallion | 25 |
| 35 Head of Horses | 70 |
| Hogs Carts & Plantation Tools | 100 |
| 3 Wind Fans | 20 |
| A Boat Pon Pon | 30 |
| A D° Mopshoo | 80 |
| 300 Barrels of Rice in barn taken by the American Genl Lincoln | 600 |
| Rice Machine furniture & Stock on the Mopshoo Plantation | 180 |
| Sum Total | £19581 |

Determin'd the 14th of May 1785.

A Loyalist.

Observation

Amount of the Legacy to be paid out of the Mopshoo Estate . . . . £1000

50 per Ann. to be paid during the Life of the Claimt estimated at 10 Yrs purchase . . . . £500

## Memorial of Hugh Wallace [1]

Hugh Wallace—the Claimant—sworn. 30th of March 1785.

Is a Native of Ireland. Went first to America in 1752 & settled at New York as a Mercht where he resided at the Commencement of the troubles & continued until the Evacuation. In 1769 He was appointed one of his Majesty's Council for the Province of New York. Never bore Arms for or agt Great Britain. Says that in 1776 he supplied Sir Henry Clinton with a Sum of £4000 S. & that nobody but himself & his Partner could have procured it at that time. He had Bills on Govt & says that the premium was 10 per Cent. The Exchange at Boston at that time was 17 per Cent. He had no other view in supplying the Money but rendering a Service to Govt. Thinks that Sir Henry tried to get the Money elsewhere but could not. Some Months after Information was recd in America from Engd of his having supplied Money to Sir Henry & he was made a Prisoner & sent to Connecticut where he was confined 5 Months. Says that he was applied to in 1775 by a Mr Ransom for a Sum of Money for the Use of Congress to send to St Eustatia but he refused advancing any tho' he had some by him at the time. This was before he was applied to by Sir Henry Clinton. He was

[1] See note 2 on p. 287.

also applied to by a M^r^ Wanschaack & others for the Loan of Money for the Use of the American Army then going into Canada he refused supplying any. Being asked if he had been at any time plunder'd of Money by the Americans says not but that when they were about taking possession of New York in 1776 he sent his Plate into the Jerseys for Security where it remain'd until Gen^l^ Howe took possession of New York when M^rs^ Wallace thought proper to order it back into the City & on the Way it was seiz'd by a Party of Americans.

Swears that neither directly nor indirectly did he at any period of the War supply the Congress with a farthing.

He had been applied to to be a Committee Man but refused. Never rec'd any Allowance from Gov^t^ at New York.

In May 1782 Sir Guy Carlton appointed him one of the Board of Acc^ts^ in which he continued to act till the Evacuation in Nov^r^ 1783. No Allowance for this. In 1775 Gen^l^ Gates told him that if he would take part with them Gen^l^ Washington would give him any employment he liked.

He has no Allowance from the Treasury.

General Robertson—sworn.

Knew the Claimant to be a very respectable Man in New York. He was one of the King's Council & Gen^l^ Robertson says he rec^d^ great Assistance from him owing to the Knowledge he had of Persons & things.

The General thought he should do him a pleasure by furnishing him with an Occasion to serve Gov^t^ wherefore he wrote to him by Sir Henry Clinton when he left Boston desiring he would furnish him with what Money he might want for his Expedition as no adequate Supply could then be furnished from the Military Chests at Boston. M^r^ Wallace did furnish him with Money & did it with Caution & Secrecy but some Rebels in Eng^d^ gained Intelligence thereof & sent out Information to the Americans. M^r^ Wallace was taken up upon this & confined some Months in Connecticut. Is of Opinion that this was the Cause of his being taken up & of his property having been confiscated as many others who continued within the Lines had not their property confiscated. He was uniformly loyal throughout the War & at the time he furnished the Money to Sir Henry Clinton the Servants of the Crown declined serving him with Money from fear of exposing themselves to the resentment of the people. Knows he lost his Plate which was said to be worth 6 or £700 S. He had a large landed Estate. He knows nothing of his furnishing Money to the Americans.

Sir John Johnston [1] Bart^t^—sworn.

Knows the Claimant. Thinks that the 2000 Acres on the North side of the Mohawk River from what he has heard of them & the general Character they bore were worth 8*s*. Currency per Acre. His father had 28000 Acres to the Northward of the 14000 Acres which are claim'd by M^r^ Wallace on the Susquehannah. The Consideration was £600 New York Currency upwards of 30 Years ago. His father sold 1500 Acres in 1770 for 8*s*. Currency per Acre & was led to dispose of them at so moderate a rate in order to encourage people to settle in the Neighbourhood. Believes his father took Mortgages for the

[1] Johnson.

payment. His father bought Lands of the Secondago Patent in June 1770 & paid 8*s.* & 9*s.* Currency per Acre about 750 Acres. They were totally uncultivated & unimproved. They were within a few Miles of a Settlement.

Colonel Guy Johnston [1]—sworn.

Speaks to the 5000 Acres at Whitesborough. He never was upon them but from general Reputation he has heard that it was very good Land. They lay a great way from the Mohawk River. Thinks they might be worth 10*s.* an Acre New York Currency if put up in Lots of 100 to 200 Acres.

Says that Sir Willm Johnston [1] sold Lands on the Susquehannah in 1769 or 1770 at a Dollar an Acre. Believes he was paid in Cash Bonds & Mortgages.

The 2000 Acres on the North side of the Mohawk River given to the Claimt by Sir Wm Johnston.[1] He values them at 2 Dollars per Acre supposing they had been put up in Lots of 200 Acres. Says again 10*s.* an Acre York Money.

The Lands in the Secondago Patent he knows he had some there himself. Sir Willm Johnston [1] paid as he has heard 8*s.* to 10*s.* an Acre Currency for some in 1768 or 1770. He values them at 20*s.* an Acre Currency. The Patent was 28000 Acres. A part of it about 3000 Acres called the Tameris Swamp He does not value at more than a Dollar an Acre. The Agent managed the Affair for him & got them back for him. Lands have been sold without the knowledge of the proprietors for the payment of the Quit rents. 14000 Acres of Lord Southampton's were advertised to be sold about 1770 to pay the Quit Rents due for a great many Years. He heard that Mr Delancy was the Agent who managed the Affair for him.

Governor Skene—sworn. 6th of Apl 1785.

Speaks of the Lands East of Wood Creek Charlotte County. He had thoughts of purchasing them himself. He understood they were so much within the York Line as to keep them out of any Dispute with the Vermontese. He thinks they would have sold for a Dollar an Acre.

Grand Isle Lake Champlain He considers without the New York Line. He is satisfied a Loyalist would be received in Vermont. New Hampshire Grants in his Opinion were far preferable to the New York ones. Always looked upon Mr Wallace as a Loyalist but as a selfish Merchant.

[1] Johnson.

## ADDITIONAL NOTES

### Governor Martin (page 290).

Josiah Martin, *b.* 1737, *d.* 1786, who retired from the army as Lieutenant-Colonel in 1769, became Governor of North Carolina in 1771. He was one of the ablest British officials in America at the time of the Revolution. He wrote in November 1774 : ' My short sojourn in this province has led me to conclude that the spirit of loyalty was higher than in any other colony of the Continent, and there are in it more friends to government on principle, if not enough to control the domineering spirit of licentiousness, provided that they had sufficient confidence in each other to come to a fair explanation of their minds ; but for want of assurance of their own principles and mutual support . . . their good dispositions discover themselves only in murmurs of dissatisfaction. . . . Another cause of their backwardness, I apprehend, is their uncertainty of the mob, and of their influence over it. The people of consideration find too late their ill policy in having made it so consequential and omnipotent at the time of the disturbance occasioned by the Stamp Act. . . . They now see a monster of their own creation become formidable to themselves' (*N. Car. Records*, vol. ix, p. 1084). Martin wrote to Gage on March 16, 1775: 'With the aid of a considerable body of Highlanders in the Middle Counties . . . if your Excellency will assist me with two or three stands of arms and a good store of ammunition, of which last we are totally destitute, I will be answerable to maintain the sovereignty of this country to his Majesty' (ibid., p. 1167). Lord Cornwallis wrote to Lord G. Germain on August 20, 1780, that he was greatly assisted by Governor Martin, from whose abilities and zeal for the public service he had, on many occasions, derived great advantages (*Correspondence*, ed. by C. Ross, 1859, vol. i, p. 489). Again, describing to Lord George the battle of Camden, Cornwallis wrote (August 21): 'Governor Martin became again a military man and behaved with the spirit of a young volunteer' (*Hist. MSS. Comm.*, *Stopford-Sackville MSS.*, vol. ii: 'Papers relating to the Am. War, 1775–82,' p. 181).

Lastly, in his report on the battle of Guilford, Cornwallis wrote: 'I have constantly received the most zealous assistance from Governor Martin, during my command of the southern district. Hoping that his presence would tend to excite the loyal subjects to take an active part with us, he has cheerfully submitted to the fatigues and dangers of our campaign; but his delicate constitution has suffered by his public spirit, for, by the advice of the physicians, he is now obliged to return to England for the recovery of his health' (quoted by Moore, op. cit., vol. ii, p. 408, from *London Gazette* of June 5, 1781).

### Phineas Bond (page 309).

*b.* 1749, *d.* 1815. He was the son and nephew of eminent physicians. He went to London in 1770 with a letter of introduction to B. Franklin from Mrs. Franklin, and was called to the Bar in 1779. He then returned to Philadelphia, where he practised the law. In the statement of the Friends exiled to Virginia we find that on September 3, 1777, No. 8 or Phineas Bond was brought into the room as a prisoner. He informed us that he had been induced to accept of the parole, when offered to him, but for reasons which he gave us he had surrendered it and voluntarily accepted a place of confinement with us (Gilpin, *Exiles in Virginia*, p. 69). For some reason or other he was not exiled to Virginia. He resided in London until 1786. In April 1785 Bond was commissioned as British Consul for the States of New York, Pennsylvania, Delaware, and Maryland, and as Commissary for Commercial Affairs throughout the United States. He arrived at Philadelphia in November 1786. He was never able to secure recognition of his commission as Commissary for Commercial Affairs; and, even with regard to his commission as Consul, the Continental Congress showed itself dilatory. He remained in Philadelphia as British Consul for many years and enjoyed a great reputation there. In February 1793 he was appointed Consul-General for the Southern States, and from August 1795 till March 1796 acted as Chargé d'affaires. He remained Consul-General for the Middle and Southern States till 1812 or 1813, when he returned to England (J. Franklin Jameson, Introduction to Letters of Phineas Bond, 1787, 1788, 1789, in *Report of Hist. MSS. Comm., of the Am. Hist. Assoc.*, 1897). ('These letters make a not unimportant contribution to our knowledge of the relations between the United States and Great Britain during an interesting period, and especially of the causes of friction which still remained after the conclusion of peace, to our understanding of the economic status of this country, and in a less degree to our information on the facts of our political history': ibid., p. 516.)

### Sarah Winslow (page 311).

The father was Edward Winslow, *b.* 1714, *d.* 1784, the brother of General John Winslow, one of the most distinguished soldiers that New England produced, whose unpleasant task it was to carry out the expulsion of the Acadians. Edward was from 1757 to 1762 one of a board of select men, and in 1760 was Treasurer of the colony. There is a memorial dated March 23, 1783, from E. Winslow, sen., to Carleton. Is 70 years of age. On his arrival at this garrison (New York) in December 1781, with one daughter and a servant, he was not only allowed a pension from Government, but one ration and a half of provisions, fuel for his fires, and candles. Has not received these since last September. His family being enlarged by the arrival of another daughter and a negro boy, and he himself having had a severe fit of sickness, begs orders for the payment of the fuel and rations as heretofore and such additional allowance as may be just (*Hist. MSS. Comm.*, *Am. MSS. in R. Inst.*, vol. iii, p. 411). The inscription on his tomb recorded that 'Although his fortunes suffered shipwreck in the storm of civil war, and he forsook his country from an attachment to his sovereign, neither his cheerful manners nor the calm reward of conscious rectitude forsook him in old age. He died as he lived, beloved by his friends and respected by his enemies '.

Edward Winslow, jun., having been sent by Carleton to Nova Scotia to make arrangements for the disbanding and settlement of the Loyalist regiments, was appointed Military Secretary for the Commander-in-chief of the forces in Nova Scotia. He was largely instrumental in promoting the division of Nova Scotia. He became a member of the Council in New Brunswick and in 1807 was appointed a Judge of the Supreme Court. He died in 1815 (O. V. Raymond, Introduction to *Winslow Papers*, pp. 7–9).

In a letter to Joshua Loring, December 2, 1788, Edward Winslow recapitulated his services. 'The Tory company at Plymouth was not only formed by me, but also supported at my expense and by my means the town of Plymouth was kept in quiet long after all the towns in the neighbourhood were in extreme confusion. . . . I think, on proper application, Lord Percy would condescend to honour me with a certificate of my services at Lexington . . . his Lordship was pleased to declare that my services on that day did me great honour and that the army was greatly indebted to me. . . . Colonel Innes will certainly give a testimony of my industry in the execution of the duties of my Muster-Master's office if it is necessary. . . . Colonel Balfour will also do me the justice to acknowledge that I undertook with cheerfulness many enterprises out of the line of my duty. . . . During the command of Sir H. Clinton you know how I was embarrassed. It is known to General Vaughan and others now in England that the party of refugees at Rhode Island would have gone to the devil if I had not taken charge of them. . . . The duty pointed out for me to execute in Nova Scotia was of all that I ever performed the most tedious and unpleasant. How it was executed—how far my representations contributed to the establishment of the new province of New Brunswick, and how far I have been instrumental since in arranging the affairs of the government, I leave to be explained by Colonel Fox. . . . While I was in constant expectation of an office of equal emolument and importance to those which I had sacrificed, it surely would have been improper to solicit for other recompence. The assurance to me was from good authority, Colonel Fox and Mr. Watson. They in the most emphatical language said, " that the arrangement was made, and that Sir Guy Carleton had acceded to it that I was certainly to be Secretary of New Brunswick " ' (*Winslow Papers*, pp. 363–6).

E. Winslow addressed in 1803 a memorial to the Lords of the Treasury :

That previous to the rebellion . . . he resided at Plymouth in the province of Massachusetts, which was the residence of his ancestors from the first settlement of the country. That his father and himself held various public offices—among which the Custom House appointments at the port. That when the persecutions commenced your memorialist joined the British army and was a volunteer at the battle of Lexington. That when the port of Boston was opened he was appointed Collector . . . and continued to execute the duties of that office till the evacuation of that place. That he served during the whole American War in the capacity of Muster-Master-General of the British American forces and at the close of the war was appointed by General Carleton, now Lord Dorchester, to explore and lay out a tract of land for the disbanded Provincial regiments, which duty he performed and settled them in that part of Nova Scotia which is now the province of New Brunswick. That he afterwards served as Military Secretary to Generals Fox and Campbell, successive commanders at Halifax, until New Brunswick was made a separate government. That he was then appointed a member of his Majesty's Council for that province to which he removed, when the Council was called and that he has remained here ever since and has executed many arduous services without salary or emolument. That representations have recently been made to the Lieutenant-Governors of this and the neighbouring province stating the illicit practices and trade carried on at the frontier between New Brunswick and the American States from which great injury results to our commerce. To remedy these evils it has been proposed that a Custom House shall be established at St. Andrews, or Campo Bello, . . . and that some active and experienced person shall be appointed Collector of Customs there. Your memorialist therefore humbly hopes that the recommendation of the Governors of Nova Scotia and New Brunswick and the Superintendent of Trade and others, added to his long and faithful services in war and peace, will induce your Lordships to bestow the appointment upon him (*Winslow Papers*, pp. 503–4).

Nothing, however, appears to have been done in the matter.

# BOOK VI

## Memorial of John Chandler[1] Esq.

John Chandler Esq—the Claimant—sworn. 31$^{st}$ of March 1785.

A Native of New England. When the Troubles began he lived in the Town of Worcester (1774). He was Judge of Probates for the County Colonel of the first Reg$^{t}$ of Militia & had a Comm$^{n}$ as Justice of the Peace throughout the Province but never acted as such. He followed business as a Merchant.

A Zealous & meritorious Loyalist & render'd services to Gov$^{t}$.

In June 1774 He was the first Person who sign'd an open protest against the popular proceedings—52 persons signed it. It was drawn up by M$^{r}$ Ja$^{s}$ Putnam. He constantly opposed them in their Town Meetings & did everything in his power for the Support of the Kings Gov$^{t}$ whereby he made himself very obnoxious. In Sept$^{r}$ 1774 a great Mob assembled. He with other Loyalists were taken up & carried about the Streets they forced him at different times to declare himself attached to their Cause it was for fear of losing his Life. They did not tender any Oath to him if they had he would he says sooner have lost his Life than take it. In less than 2 Months he was able to get to the British Troops at Boston where he did Duty with the Patrole. Quitted it at the Evacuation. Went to Halifax & came to Eng$^{d}$ in July 1776. In Feb$^{y}$ following He had an Allowance of £100 per Ann. from the Treasury but it was increas'd to £150 at the recommendation of M$^{r}$ Wilmot & M$^{r}$ Coke. On his Arrival in Eng$^{d}$ the Treasury gave him £100 towards his Expences.

Former Bounty £100 a Y$^{r}$.
Present Bounty £150 a Y$^{r}$.

Captain John Walker—sworn.

Never made any other Submission to the Americans but what he has stated & which he should not have done had he not consider'd that his Life was in Danger.

Knew the Farm near the Court House which had been his father's. He built a stately fine House upon it the finest House in the County. The Buildings he says were very valuable. Thinks he could have sold it any Day for £2000 Sterling. Has heard that a M$^{r}$ Green of Boston once offer'd the Claimant £2000 for it. Does not know the Extent of it.

The Claimant—again sworn.

He is desired to produce some satisfactory proofs concerning that part of his property in possession of his Children. He does produce some Certificates (tho' not under the Seal of the Province) dated in Nov$^{r}$ 1783 signed by John Kirkland & Benj$^{n}$ Bonney Commissioners for the Sale of confiscated Estates in the County of New Hampshire whereby it appears that all his Property has been confiscated for the Use of the State except what was reserved for his Wife who is now Dead & that it has been sold under the Confiscation Act.

[1] See Additional Notes, p. 393.

He is desired to inform us when he is able upon what footing his Children are permitted to reside in His House in Worcester.

The Claimant said in the former part of his Evidence when he was speaking to his own Conduct at the Commencement of the troubles That he was the first person who signed the Protest in 1774. This render'd him extremely obnoxious to the people. And when the people assembled & put a Stop to the Courts of Justice they carried the Claimant through their Body & forced him to retract his Protest & to promise to join in their Proceedings. Says he was intimidated into this Conduct as he conceived his Life to be in Danger had he refused & although he had in this manner renounced the Protest his House was nevertheless fired into & he thought it necessary to withdraw himself from home & put himself under the Protection of the Kings Troops.

The Claimant says he never made any other Submission to the Americans than what he has mention'd nor would he have done that but through fear of his Life.

He makes no Claim for any part of his Estate but what appears to be confiscated. Has no Doubt but he shall be able to recover such Parts of it as are not confiscated.

Determin'd the 4th of April 1785.

A Loyalist.

**Memorial of Eliz$^{th}$ Brinley—Widow**

2$^{d}$ of April 1785.

Eliz$^{th}$ Brinley—the Claimant—sworn.

She is the Widow of Tho$^{s}$ Brinley [1] who was a Native of Massachusets Bay. On the Commencement of the troubles he was settled at Boston as a Distiller. Says that he sign'd every Paper that was drawn out in favor of Gov$^{t}$ by which means he made himself very obnoxious & lost a great many of his Customers. Her Husband had an Allowance of £200 per Ann. from 1776 to Oct$^{r}$ 1784. He quitted Boston on the Evacuation on Acc$^{t}$ of his principles & went to Halifax from whence they came to Eng$^{d}$. They arrived in 1776. He died the 7$^{th}$ of Oct$^{r}$ last. A Memorial was presented by her the 25$^{th}$ of Nov$^{r}$ last praying for a Continuance of the Allowance but which was negatived on Acc$^{t}$ of her having £2000 in this Country. She is a Sister of M$^{r}$ Achmuly's Wife.

Peter Johonnot—sworn.

Knew the Claimant's husband very well. He was a Distiller & in good business. Says he was very loyal & sign'd all the addresses in favor of Gov$^{t}$. He thinks that the House & Garden Distill House Store Lot of Land & Wharf would have sold for 13 or £1400 S. before the troubles. Believes he had a Pew in King's Chapel. He has heard that the Salt was landed some time before the troubles. Believes the Deceas'd might have had 1400 Bushels of Salt. He also heard that it was destroy'd by orders of the Commander in Chief lest it should fall into the hands of the rebels.

[1] Thomas Brinley was a Mandamus Councillor and signed the Addresses to Hutchinson and Gage. In 1778 he was proscribed and banished. His widow died in 1793 (Stark, op. cit., p. 396).

## Memorial of Mary Swords[1]—Widow

Determin'd the 6$^{th}$ of April 1785.

Mary Swords—the Claimant—sworn. 6$^{th}$ of April 1785.

Her Husband was a Lieut$^{t}$ in the 55$^{th}$ Reg$^{t}$. Sold out in 1771. She was a Native of Ireland. Settled at Saratoga when the troubles broke out—he settled in America in 1776 as a Farmer. He never sign'd any Association or took any part in favor of the Americans but he sign'd a Parole in 1776 to remain quiet at Home. Yet they took him Prisoner & confined him at Albany from whence they removed him into Connecticut. He afterwards was sent to New York where he died.

A Loyalist & her Husband likewise.

She says that in the beginning of 1777 She had an Opportunity of supplying Gen$^{l}$ Burgoyne's Army with provisions. Sir Guy Carlton allowed her £75 per Ann. In the fall of 1777 she was sent to New York. She remain'd there till the Year 1783 when she came to Eng$^{d}$ And she has an Allowance of £40 per Ann. from the Treasury.

She claims in behalf of herself & her Children. She has a Copy of her Husband's Will.

Rev$^{d}$ Henry Munro—sworn.

He was Minister at Albany. Knew M$^{r}$ & M$^{rs}$ Swords. Was frequently at their House where he saw a Number of persons who were well attached to G. Britain. Believes that M$^{r}$ Swords was always well disposed to G. Britain. Says that he had a very good House & thinks it might have cost about £400 C. There was some Land he says adjoining to it 10 or 12 Acres of very good Meadow & about 8 Acres in another Spot. There was a good deal of other Land which was not so good. He thinks about a 3$^{d}$ of 150 Acres might be clear'd possibly one half. Says it was very usual in that Country to take Leases for ever paying so much annual rent. Says he never knew an Acre of Land well clear'd in that part for less than £3 10*s*. C. per Acre. He has heard M$^{r}$ Swords say that the clearing of his farm cost him a great deal of Money.

## Memorial of Samuel Dashwood

Determin'd the 6$^{th}$ of Ap. 1785.

Samuel Dashwood—the Claimant—sworn. 6$^{th}$ of April 1785.

He came from Boston in Dec$^{r}$ last. He is a Subject *now* of the American States. Lived at Boston 30 Years. He was formerly before the Mast with Sir Peter Warren.[2] Never took the Oaths to the American States. He never took part either for or against G. Bri$^{n}$. Says that Mess$^{rs}$ Lane Son & Fraser before the War sent him Goods by his Directions. He understood that this Board took Cognizance of such Matters. He does not consider himself as a Loyalist.

Not an Object of the Act of Par$^{t}$.

The Goods were he says taken by Orders of Sir W$^{m}$ Howe in the Year 1776

[1] In *Hist. MSS. Comm., Am. MSS. in R. Inst.*, vol. iv, p. 262, there is a memorial from Mary Swords, widow of Lieut. Swords of the 55th Regiment, dated August 4, 1783. It states that she is returning to England, and asks pay in advance or other assistance to provide herself and her children with necessaries.

[2] *b.* 1703, *d.* 1752. He was naval commander at the taking of Louisbourg in 1745. He is in the *Dict. of Nat. Biography*.

& that they were worth £2578 10*s*. S. That he had a promise of protection from Gen[l] Gage & the like Assurances afterwards from Sir W[m] Howe.

Determination.

The Claimant appears to have been & is a Subject of the American States therefore cannot be consider'd as coming within the Description of those who have suffer'd in consequence of Loyalty to his Majesty & attachment to the British Government.

Determin'd the 11[th] of April 1785.

**Memorial of Peter Van Shaack [1] Esq.**

7[th] of April 1785.

Peter Van Shaack—the Claimant—sworn.

A Loyalist.

Is a Native of America. Was a Practitioner of the Law in New York from 1769 to the Commencement of the troubles. In 1776 He was summon'd before the Committee of Albany the Oaths were tender'd to him which he refused to take & was banished to Boston from whence he was removed to the County of Worcester by an Order of the Council of that State. In 1777 He was put under Parole to remain within the District of Kinderhook & not to say or do anything prejudicial to the Cause of America. Produces a Copy of the Parole. And in July 1778 he was called upon by the Commissioners for detecting & defeating Conspiracies in Consequence of an Act of the State of New York prescribing an Oath of Allegiance & Abjuration upon his refusal he was sentenced to perpetual banishment & was removed within the British Lines. By the same Act he was made subject to the Penalties of Misprision of Treason in Case of his return to the said State. His Estate was made subject to Double Taxation.

Bounty £60 a Y[r].

Has an Allowance of 60 a Y[r] from the Treasury which he now continues to receive. He was one of the 51 of the Committee establish'd at New York in 1775 called a Committee of Correspondence. He says that he opposed all their violent Measures.

After he came within the British Lines He declares that he never did anything in favor of the American Cause.

Property.

He waves his Claim for Loss of Property as it is only confiscated conditionally.

Profession.

£150 a Y[r].

He claims his Loss of Profession on an Average at £300 per Ann. New York Currency. Says it would have been worth to him this Sum the Year that the troubles commenced. The preceding one it amounted only to £200 per Ann. The probability is that he will not be allowed to reassume his Profession at New York.

Thinks he shall be well rec[d] by the Principal people. He never made himself obnoxious to them.

Will[m] Smith Esq—sworn.

Says the Claimant was a Writer in his Office from 1767 to 1769. He always consider'd him attached to Great Britain. He was a rising young Man in his

[1] See Additional Notes, p. 394.

profession & thinks that the Claimant has stated his profits very moderately at £300 Currency per Ann.

Mr Vanshaack solicited as Mr Smith understood leave from the States to come to Engd in order to be cured of a Complaint in his Eyes.

### Memorial of Robert Nics Achmuty [1]

Robert Nics Achmuty—the Claimant—sworn. 7th of April 1785.

Is a Native of America. At the Commencement of the troubles he had just finished his Clerkship at New York. As a Loyalist he could not remain there went to Long Island in 1776 & remain'd there till the Arrival of the British Troops. He had been called upon at New York to take part with the Americans but got a Certificate from a Doctr Jones of his being in a bad State of health by which means & hiding himself he was able to avoid joining them. He join'd the British Troops on the 27th of Augt 1776 & remain'd within the Lines till the Evacuation of New York. He acted as a Volunteer in the Militia at New York in which he afterwards rais'd a Company which was meant as a Compliment to him. General Robertson gave him the Commission & he produces it.

Claims the Loss of his Situation as Public Notary & Attorney at New York. Produces his Appointment dated in May 1780.

He has an Allowance of 50 a Yr from the Treasury which he has recd from the [2] & he now continues to receive it. Bounty £50 a Yr.

He made by his profession of Attorney & public Notary 1300 C.

In the Year 1781 he was appointed Clerk to the Church at New York which was worth to him £200 C. per Ann. The Salary was only £6 per Ann.

George Folliott—sworn.

Knew the Claimant. Says he was always consider'd as a Loyalist & believes he was very Zealously attached to Great Britain. Also that he was under the Necessity of hiding himself in order to avoid taking part with the Americans.

Speaks of his being bred to the Law & that he had just finished his Clerkship when the Rebellion broke out.

### Memorial of John Henderson

John Henderson—the Claimant—sworn. 8th of April 1785.

Is a Native of Scotland. Went to America in 1765 & settled in Georgia at the Commencement of the troubles. Resided in the Parish of St Paul 112 Miles from Savannah. In June 1777 He gave a Bond for £15000 that he would take no active part agt the Americans. Never took any part in their favor. Join'd Genl Campbell in 1779 raised a Company of Militia & served as a Volunteer during the siege of Savannah where he remain'd till the Evacuation & came to Engd on the Evacuation of Charlestown. A Loyalist but took an Oath to the Americans.

He took an Oath to the Americans in 1778 in Consequence of a Summons dated 7th of March. Prior thereto he took the Oath of Fidelity to the States

[1] This Robert Achmuty is not to be confused with the Massachusetts barrister who signed the Address to Governor Hutchinson, May 30, 1774.

[2] Thus in original.

it was the Oath of Abjuration. Says if he had not taken the Oath he would have been forced away but admits that he might have avoided taking it had it not been for the fear of losing his property. He took the first Opportunity afterwards of joining the British Troops he did join them in 1779. He consider'd the taking of the Oath as a Matter of much less Consequence than taking part with them. He did not consider the Oath as a lawful one as it was tender'd to him by people who were in rebellion. He produced at Whitehall Certificates to his Loyalty & property from Sir James Wright M^r^ Jameson & M^r^ Simon Munro.

He has been allowed £60 per Ann. from the Treasury from the 5^th^ of January 1783.

Will^m^ Goodgeon—sworn.

Knew the Claimant before the War. He resided near him in the Country. He was generally deem'd a Loyalist before General Campbell arrived. He never heard of the Claimant having taken an Oath. He was obliged to take the Oath himself. All those who were deem'd Loyalists were obliged to take the Oaths. He thinks that Oaths were only administer'd to those who were suspected of being attached to this Country. Knew his Saw Mills in the Parish of S^t^ Pauls is not able to say what they were worth. The Claimant had a great deal of Timber which was taken by the Americans. There was as much as would have built a Barrack for 200 Men.

John Simpson—sworn.

Knew the Claimant before the War. He always consider'd him as a Loyalist. Knows nothing of the Oath does not recollect to have heard of his doing so. Although he did M^r^ Simpson considers him as a Loyalist as he must believe if he did so that it was by compulsion.

## Memorial of Tho^s^ Tollemash

Determin'd the 16^th^ of Ap^l^ 1785.

11^th^ of April 1785.

Tho^s^ Tollemash—the Claimant—sworn.

A Loyalist But took the Oaths to the Rebels.

Is a Native of England & went to America in 1771. He went to Savannah. He went out as Clerk to a Merch^t^. He resided at Savannah at the Commencement of the troubles. He took the part of Gov^t^ at first. He went out to assist Sir Ja^s^ Wright. He staid after Sir Ja^s^ Wright went on board a Ship. He bore Arms & produces some Commissions in the Militia. He was afterwards order'd away by the Americans & he went to Jamaica & was taken by the Rebels. He was carried into S^t^ Augustine & returned to Savannah in Dec^r^ 1776. He remain'd there for some Months before the Oaths were tender'd. And afterwards He was obliged to take an Oath at the end of a Bayonet. Afterwards it was publickly known that the Oaths of Allegiance would be tender'd but Gen^l^ Campbell came in the meantime. He says he had made no preparations for quitting the Province. He remain'd in Georgia till the Evacuation. He has no Allowance from the Treasury.

Will^m^ Telfer—sworn.

Knew M^r^ Tollemash first in 1778 just before Savannah was taken. He consider'd M^r^ Tollemash as a Loyalist. Does not know that he took an Oath to the Americans but has heard it. And he believes it was to remain quiet in the Country. Knows that he lost some furniture because he could not bring it away at the Evacuation. The Witness belonged to the Georgia Militia. He never was paid. His House appear'd very well furnished.

Josiah Tatnall Esq—sworn. 12th of March 1785.

Knew Mr Tollemash before the troubles. He was Clerk in a Store. He was well disposed at first but he staid behind. Remembers his going to Jamaica in 1776 but he knows that he returned whilst the Govt was in the hands of the Rebels. Thinks he returned voluntarily does not know that he was brought Prisoner into Savannah. Says he was thought a Loyalist before he left the Country but has since heard that he has taken the Oaths & blames such Conduct extremely. Being asked whether he thinks such a Man under all the Circumstances a Loyalist He says he should not think so in his own Opinion independent of Proclamations &c.

## Memorial of John Jamieson

Determin'd the 18th of May 1785.

John Jamieson—the Claimant—sworn. 12th of April 1785.

Is a Native of Scotland & went first to America in 1755 where he resided till the troubles. He was a Mercht. He dates the troubles from 1774 tho' Georgia was the last province that sent Delegates to Congress. He was uniformly loyal from the beginning. Produces a Georgia Newspaper in the Yr 1774 by which it appears that the Claimant very early dissented & opposed the measures of the Rebels. He was a Member of the Assembly of Georgia & continu'd to be so until the Govt was overturned. He remain'd in the Country till the Yr 1778 but he remain'd with great difficulty. He was at last taken in June 1776 & was obliged to take an Oath otherwise he should have been obliged to go on board a Ship & have left the Province. He says it was an Oath of Neutrality. And he did it to save his property & his Life being in bad health. He lived for two Years a Subject of the Rebel State. In the Year 1778 they tender'd him an Oath of Allegiance & Abjuration & on this Acct he quitted the Province. He thought at this time that the Arms of Engd would prevail. If he had thought otherwise he would have acted in the same way. In 1778 He went to South Carolina & remain'd there till the Province of Georgia was restored to the King's peace. South Carolina was at that time under Rebel Govt & he knew it. There he took another Oath with a Proviso that the Obligation should bind him only as long as he staid in the Country. And this he did in order to be enabled to collect his Debts & to leave the Province. Gives as a reason for going to South Carolina instead of going to the Northward because he could not go into any other Province & he was in a bad state of health. If he had not applied to take away his Negroes he might have avoided taking the Oath. He bore Arms in the Militia but had no Commission. He came to Engd in March 1780. He recd £100 from the Treasury early in the Yr 1781. And he recd no more until [his case] was heard in 1783 when an Allowance of £80 a Yr was given to him which he has recd from January 1783 & he now continues to receive it.

A Loyalist But took an Oath to the Rebels.

Did not bear Arms.

Bounty £80 a Yr.

Doctor Garden—sworn.

Knew Mr Jameson many Years before the troubles. He always consider'd him as a very loyal Man. He knew nothing of his taking the Oaths in Georgia but believes he had heard of his taking them in Carolina. He never to his knowledge did anything to assist the Rebels. Being asked as to what he gave for the Land which was convey'd to him He says he knows nothing of the purchase or what he gave for it. But admits it was convey'd to him & he understood it to be for the benefit of his Creditors Mr Ogilvie & others. Mr Jamieson had been in business & he had ceas'd to be a Mercht. Does not say that he had fail'd but the House fail'd of which he was a Partner but he believes he had left it before the troubles. He then consider'd him to be worth nothing. Being asked whether he thinks it reasonable to ask Govt for a Compensation for lands bought under Rebel Govt He declines giving his Opinion but says he would not have bought it. Says he was in a bad State of health in 1778 & says if he had been confined in prison it would have killed him.

Charles Ogilvie Esq—sworn.

Is a Mercht in London. Knew Mr Jamieson very well. He was a Correspondent of his. The Partners owed him a great deal of Money in 1773 more than £10000. And he agreed with them that upon assigning all their Securities he would abate a third part of their Debt. He says he does not think they would have been able to have paid him the whole £10000 but after he had abated one third They put the papers into his hands in 1773. He says they are in his hands still. Being asked whether he was a Man of property in 1773 He says he was not worth much in 1775.

John Henderson—sworn. 14th of April 1785.

Has known Mr Jamieson many Years before the rebellion. When it broke out he took no part but he believes he was a staunch friend to Govt. His Opinion is not alter'd of his Loyalty by knowing that he took an Oath to the Rebels. The Witness took the same Oath. He was looked upon as a Man of property. Admits that he has heard of the Assignment to Ogilvie. But says he still looks upon him as a Man of Property.

Determin'd the 9th of May 1785.

**Memorial of Revd Thos Gwatkin [1]**

Revd Thos Gwatkin—the Claimant—sworn. 15th of April 1785.

A Zealous Loyalist.

Is a Native of Engd & went to America in 1770. He was at the Commencement of the troubles Professor of Languages [2] at Williamsburgh. The Salary was £200 a Yr Sterling & the Perquisites £100 a Yr S. An Application was made to him in 1775 by Mr Ley & others to draw up Memorials in favor of the Proceedings of Congress. He refused this & he was afterwds insulted & consider'd as dissaffected from that time & frequently put in danger of his Life. He was never confined or had any Oath tender'd to him. His Health was much affected by this & he was obliged in the Month of July 1775 to go on board Lord Dun-

[1] In 1771 he took an active part against the proposal to institute an American bishop and was the author of *A Letter to the Clergy of New York and New Jersey*, 1772 (Cross, op. cit., pp. 232–3, 238–40).

[2] Cross describes him as professor of mathematics.

more's Ship. He came to Eng[d] in Aug[t] 1775 with Lord Fincastle. When he was desired to draw up Memorials he was told that he should have everything which that Country could afford &c.

Loss.

His Loss is the Loss of the Professorship. He was recommended by the B[p] of London & appointed by the Visitors. It was consider'd as a place for Life. It was £200 a Y[r] & £100 in Perquisites.

Office £200 a Y[r]. Perquisites £100 a Y[r].

He has no Allowance from the Treasury. He has a small Living in Berkshire which Lord Gower[1] obtain'd for him from the Chancellor. He was presented to it 3 Years ago & the Value of it is £80 a Year.

No allowance from Gov[t]. But has a Living of 80 a Y[r] from the Crown.

The Earl of Dunmore—sworn. 14[th] of April 1785.

Knew the Claim[t]. Says his Salary was £200 a Y[r] other Advantages about £100 more S. He was Professor of Humanity & Languages. It was a Situation for Life & Lord Dunmore says the Claimant would certainly have had the Rectorship which would have been £200 a Y[r] more. Says that M[r] Gwatkin was a very loyal Subject & that he was strongly solicited by the Americans to take part with them which he refused & was in consequence thereof frequently ill treated. He had no Property but Household Furniture & Books.

## Memorial of Hamilton Usher S[t] George

Determin'd the 30[th] of April 1785.

Hamilton Usher S[t] George—the Claimant—sworn. 15[th] of April 1785.

He is a Native of Ireland & went to America in 1763 or 1764. He was settled in Virginia from the Year 1766 & was there at the Commencement of the troubles. In 1775 He made a tender of his Services to Lord Dunmore & Lord Dunmore advised him to remain at his plantation for the purpose of gaining Intelligence for him &c. He promised him a Commission but he never had it. However he bore arms at Yorktown during the siege. He supplied Lord Cornwallis with great Quantity of Provisions for which he has been paid but he has never been paid for what he supplied to Lord Dunmore. His House was attacked in Sept[r] 1781 it was near York Town. In 1775 His House was burnt & he was arraign'd at the Bar for holding Correspondence with Lord Dunmore & supplying him with provisions. He was acquitted but was confined to his County. He was frequently carried before their Committees but he never made any Submission to them. They offer'd him the Command of a Reg[t] of Horse but he refused it. He was obliged to keep his principles secret otherwise he could have been of no Use. Supposes that all his Property is confiscated. His Wife has been turned out of his House.

A Zealous Active & meritorious Loyalist & render'd Services to the British Gov[t]. Bore Arms.

Certificates read from Lord Dunmore to his zeal &c likewise from Lord Cornwallis & a letter from Lord Dunmore to the Lords of Treasury certifying that he had been of great Use to the Army & recommending payment of his Acc[t] but they are not yet settled. Col[l] Dundas likewise certifies to M[r] S[t] George's being of use to him at York Town. Two Certificates from Lord Cornwallis.

He has an Allowance from the Treasury of £100 a Y[r] which he has rec[d] from the 10[th] of Oct[r] 1782 & he now continues to receive it.

Bounty £100 a Y[r].

[1] Granville Leveson-Gower, *b.* 1721, *d.* 1803, first Marquis of Stafford.

Says that Lord Cornwallis in 1782 gave him £460 for the support of his Wife & family & he entrusted the Money to the Care of M$^{r}$ Coleborne Barrell who kept the Money & only gave to M$^{rs}$ S$^{t}$ George 60 Dollars.

Charles Steadman [1]—sworn.

Has been at the House of M$^{r}$ S$^{t}$ George. The Witness was Commissary to Lord Cornwallis's Army. He was there in Sept$^{r}$ 1781. He can speak to the Stock then upon it. Lord Cornwallis desired the Witness to go & drive all the Stock from the Coast. On the 4$^{th}$ of Sept$^{r}$ 1781 he rec$^{d}$ 23 full grown Head of Cattle. On the 24$^{th}$ He rec$^{d}$ 59 Sheep & 15 Cows some Steers &c & some Sheep—59. These were not valued. They gave for Steers £5 for Cows £3 10*s.* for three Years old £2 5*s.* two Years old £1 15*s.* Yearlings £1 5*s.* for Sheep 16*s.* Lambs 8*s.* The Witness thinks he had double the Quantity of Stock left behind. He can't speak to the other Stock. Saw some Horses. The Witness dined at his House two or three times he was consider'd to be a Man of property. Says that from his Situation the Witness knew those who were active Loyalists & he thinks M$^{r}$ S$^{t}$ George was one of the most active. He knew but one who was superior to him.

Major Grymes—sworn.

Was well acquainted with M$^{r}$ S$^{t}$ George says he was perfectly loyal. Knows none of his property but Hogg Island. Does not know the Extent of it but says it was a very fine Estate. Says it was known that he had a very beneficial Lease from his Brother in Law. He says he understood always & it was generally understood to be a good & valid Lease. Says he knows that there is a Law in Virginia empowering Tenants in tail to make Leases for 3 Lives & he himself has had such a Lease granted to him by a person who was Tenant in Tail. Says these were the Common Leases in Virginia. Says there is no similitude between Leases in that Country & this. Says it was a very valuable Lease but can't speak to the Value. Thinks upon the presumption that the Lease was a good one that it is worth from £1500 to £2000. Says he would have given that for it himself if he had wanted it. Says he was the best Planter & farmer in that Country & a very industrious Man. Does not know his Land on the Main. Knows nothing more of his property but says it was generally understood that he had a lease from M$^{r}$ Wythe & that he was to have half of the profits. Believes it to have been very beneficial. Has understood the Agreement to have been for S$^{t}$ George's life & understood it from M$^{r}$ Randolph who was his Lawyer & drew all his Writings Deeds &c.

The Earl of Dunmore—sworn. 14$^{th}$ of April 1785.

Knew the Claimant in Virginia at the Commencement of the troubles. Says he was very loyal & useful in procuring Provisions. That in consequence of his Loyalty he was treated in a very cruel manner that they set fire to his Habitation in which his Wife & Children were lying in their Beds & would all have been burnt had it not been for the very great Assistance they received from a Frenchman who was on a Visit at their House at the time. Lord Dunmore

[1] C. Stedman, author of *The Hist. of the Origin, Progress, and Termination of the Am. War*, 2 vols., 1794, which is the best contemporary account from the British side.

says that Mr St George was looked upon as an opulent Man in the Country & in a very thriving way. He had two farms with large Stocks of Cattle upon them. Mentions the Claimant having loaded a Vessel with Oats for Sir Wm Howe's Army. Says that he frequently supplied the Witness & the Loyalists with provisions.

### Memorial of Donald McInnes

Determin'd ye 20th of Apl 1785.

20th of April 1785.

Donald McInnes—the Claimant—sworn.

Is a Native of Scotland. Went to America in 1773 on the Commencement of the troubles. He join'd Govr Martin's Corps. Was in the Battle of Moors Bridge. Afterward he joind Genl McCarter & did Duty as an Ensign. He was taken Prisoner in 1781 & imprison'd at Cross Creek. He had then no Commission. On his release he join'd Coll Craig & continued with the British Troops till the Peace. He was appointed a Captn by Coll Craig. After the Evacuation of Wilmington he marched with the Army to Charlestown where he acted as Captn of a Galley lying off the Town. He was allowed 7*s.* a Day.

A Loyalist. And bore Arms.

Has no Allowance from the Treasury nor has he half Pay.

Coll Donald McDonald—sworn.

Knew the Claimant in 1775 is not able to say whether he had then any property. Says he was very loyal. His father had property but it was seized on his Death to discharge his Debts.

### Memorial of Captn Allen McDonald[1]

Determin'd the 20th of Apl 1785.

20th of April 1785.

Captn Allen McDonald—the Claimant—sworn.

Is a Native of Scotland. Went to North Carolina in 1773 with the Intention of settling there. He carried about £700 in Specie out with him. At the time that he arrived Committees were forming. Soon after Govr Martin issued his Proclamations & the Claimant exerted himself in collecting People who were well affected to Govt. He commanded the Anson Battalion & was at the Battle of Moors Bridge Creek when he was made Prisoner & kept in different Gaols 3 Months. He was 10 Months on Parole. On his release he join'd the Army under Sir Henry Clinton. At this time he was a Captn in the 84th Regt. Has his Commn. Continued to serve with the Regt till it was reduced after the Peace in Nova Scotia Octr 1784. He has half pay as Captn. He has no Allowance from Govt as an American Sufferer. His Commn as Captn is dated in June 1775.

An Active Zealous Loyalist. Bore Arms & render'd Services.

Colonel McDonald—sworn.

Knew the Claimt very well. Says he raised a Number of very good Men full 50. He was very instrumental in collecting a Number of Loyalists & looks upon him as a very gallant & zealous Man. Witness recollects his being an Officer in our Army before the battle of Culloden. Heard of his purchasing Lands in Chick Creek Anson Co. He had two Plantations which he saw in ye harvest time. They were in good Order but don't recollect the Extent. Remembers the Mill. Believes that the Claimt carried to America with him

1 'Ensign McDonald of the 84th Regiment is the only officer willing to purchase.' Brigadier-General McLean to Sir H. Clinton, September 16, 1780 (*Hist. MSS. Comm., Am. MSS. in R. Inst.*, vol. ii, p. 183).

a good deal of furniture he has been in his House in America & says it was well furnished. He saw some Articles of Plate. There was a good deal of Stock on the Plantation.

Daniel Bethan—sworn.

Knew the Claim^t from his Arrival in America to the time he was taken Prisoner. Says that he carried out a good deal of furniture. Remembers the Claim^t buying Lands from one Zouchton but does not know to what extent. There were several fields & Orchards. Thinks he saw 40 Acres of Corn Land. There was a Mill. Has seen several Articles of Plate at the Claim^t's house. He had a Silver Punch Bowl Ladle & Tankard.

### Memorial of Abraham Bates [1]

Determin'd the 9^th of May 1785.

Abraham Bates—the Claimant—sworn. 20^th of April 1785.

Is a Native of America. When the troubles commenced in 1775 He remain'd quiet. On the report of Independence being declared he determin'd to take part with Great Britain in preference to joining with the Americans. They did not force him to disclose his Sentiments. About the end of 1775 He was chosen one of the Committee of Safety he attended twice. Left them in 1776. Was frequently insulted on Acc^t of his doing so. He was desired by some of his friends who were Loyalists to be of the Committee thinking that he might be able to keep matters quiet. Never took an Oath. Says that in Jan^y 1777 being apprehensive of losing his Life he got away in a Vessel of his own accompanied by 7 or 8 Loyalists & went to Long Island. He took also another Vessel with him which was his property. They were both loaded with Provisions & Flax Seed. Says there were others concerned with him in the Vessels & their Cargoes. His Share of both produced him from 300 to £400 S.

A Loyalist.

Did not bear Arms.

Bounty £30 a Y^r.

Remain'd at New York during the War & came to England in Nov^r 1783. He has an Allowance of £30 a Y^r from the 5^th of Jan^y 1784.

Bounty £30 a Y^r.

Abraham Bates—the Claimant—sworn. 21^st of April 1785.

Admits that his Brother had an equal Moiety in the Lands. But says he is not in possession of any part of the Estate. He knows that Circumstance from the persons who survey'd the Estate.

William Jervis—sworn.

Knew M^r Bates before he join'd the British. His general Conduct was that of a good Subject. But he was of the Committee. He did not consider him when he went into the Committee as an Enemy to Great Britain & says he was then consider'd by the Loyalists as well attached to G^t B^n & he believes he went to the Committee by their Desire. Does not know whether he resign'd before the Declaration of Independence but rather believes that he was a Committee Man when he left the Country which was in Aug^t 1776 but is not sure. Says he was a Man of fair Character.

[1] The name of Abraham Bates does not occur among the eleven constituting the Committee of Safety in 1775 (Becker, op. cit., p. 211). Is he the same as Abram Brasher ?

## Memorial of W^m Houghton

Determin'd the 5th of May 1785.

21st of April 1785.

Will^m Houghton—the Claimant—sworn.

A British Officer.

He was in America in a former War as an Officer in the Artillery Lieut^t & got a Grant of 2000 Acres for his Services. He resided there for six Years during the Peace from the Y^r 1768. Came to Eng^d in 1774. Is a Native of this Country. He went out again with Gen^l Burgoyne in 1776. Produces a Grant dated the 3^d of July 1770. Before this he had a Warrant of Survey. He got some Tenants to put upon it. Says there are more than 600 Acres clear'd by M^r Harpur who first settled it but could not pay the fees & relinquish'd it & it appears by the Grant to be relinquish'd. The Tenants were to pay 1*s*. per Acre C. per Ann. He let only 400 Acres & he had 4 Tenants. They never paid him a farthing. He made no Demand upon them before he left America. Says he found one upon the Ground & the others were sent to him by the Surveyor. He laid out more than £50. He was bid a Dollar an Acre for them & he values them at that price. Does not know that they are confiscated but thinks they are. Has never applied to know that fact. He is at present a Capt^n in the Artillery.

## Memorial of James Tait

Determin'd the 30th of Ap^l 1785.

21st of April 1785.

James Tait—the Claimant—sworn.

A Loyalist & render'd services to Gov^t.

Is a Native of Scotland & went to America in 1774. He went recommended to Lord Dunmore to assist in matters of navigation. He carried little or no property with him. No appearance of troubles in Virginia for a Year & ½ after he arrived which was in March 1774. He join'd the British Army under Gen^l Arnold in 1781 & continued with the Army till he was made Prisoner at the Surrender of York Town. Says during his Continuance in the Country he render'd every Assistance in his power to British Prisoners. He was employ'd in Lord Cornwallis's Army as an Assistant in the Qu^r Mast^r Gen^l's Department from the time he join'd the Army till its Surrender.

Col^l Dundas informs the Board that when the Claim^t join'd the Army he address'd him & express'd his uneasiness at remaining in the Country & a wish to join the British Troops. Upon Col^l Dundas mentioning this his inclination to Gen^l Arnold the Gen^l express'd a wish that he should remain in the Country & make Drawings of the different roads Passes &c which M^r Tait agreed to do expressing a Desire to be of every service in his power to the British Troops. He accordingly did remain in the Country & Col^l Dundas says that he particularly conformed to the Instructions which were given to him.

Produces a Paper containing a particular Acc^t of all his Exertions &c. Col^l Dundas says that the Paper which he produces contains as far as falls within his knowledge a very fair Acc^t of his Conduct. He came to Eng^d in 1783 & applied to the Treasury where he got an Allowance of £20 a Year which he has rec^d from Jan^y 1783 & now continues to receive it. Says that Lord Dunmore advised him to stay in the Country & to conform to their Gov^t to a certain Degree. He says he was sent for by a Magistrate in 1776 & 1777 to take an Oath but he did not do it. However he obtain'd a Certificate that he did. And he says he was

Bounty £20 a Y^r.

obliged to declare in all public Companies that he had taken the Oath. From the time that Lord Dunmore left him being asked whether he could have join'd the British Troops sooner He says he could have left the Province sooner or at any time. He never sign'd any Association paper. Says if he had been obliged to take the Oath or leave the Country he thinks he should have left the Country. Does not think that any Man could have staid in the Province at that time without taking an Oath or getting such a Certificate as he did.

Colonel Jacob Ellegood—sworn.

Was not personally acquainted with the Claim$^{t}$ till 1778 or 1779. Always consider'd him as a friend to Gov$^{t}$. He frequently called upon M$^{r}$ Ellegood whilst a Prisoner on Parole & communi$^{d}$ what was going on.

James Ingram—sworn.

Knew the Claim$^{t}$ in Virginia. Believes him to have been well attached to Great Bri$^{n}$. When the Witness was a Prisoner Claim$^{t}$ told him of his having obtain'd a Certificate of his taking the Oath but that he had not in fact taken the Oath & believes he said true. Knew another instance of the same kind. Says M$^{r}$ Tait assisted him to make his Escape & was of use to many other Loyalists.

The Earl of Dunmore—sworn.

Knew James Tait perfectly well in Virginia. He came out as an Engineer in the hopes of being employ'd at a Salary of £100 a Y$^{r}$. Thinks it must have been in 1772. He came to Lord Dunmore immediately. He afterwards became a Surveyor & rec$^{d}$ £600 from the Assembly to make Salt. He offer'd to join Lord Dunmore at the beginning of the War but he advised him to remain there. Thinks he was of more use by staying as he did. Was very active in protecting Prisoners &c.

Determin'd the 7$^{th}$ of July 1785.

Upon considering the whole of this Case The Board were of Opinion that Col$^{l}$ Boyd's Claim was a fraudulent Claim & ought to be so reported under the Act of Par$^{t}$.

## Memorial of Colonel Boyd[1]

George Boyd Esq—the Claimant—sworn. 22$^{d}$ of April 1785.

Is a Native of New Hampshire in America. In 1774 he came to Eng$^{d}$ but previous to that time he was settled at Portsmouth as a Merch$^{t}$. When he left America the province was quiet. He was at Boston the night that the Tea was destroy'd. He was a Col$^{l}$ of the Light Horse rais'd to escort the Gov$^{r}$ & paid by the Province. Never sign'd any Association. He returned in May 1775 & was appointed one of the Council. He acted in that Situation for about a fortnight. Nobody acted after he ceas'd to act. A File of Musqueteers took him out of his House. He was releas'd the next Day & got a Passport to New York. He rejected many offers from the Rebels never took any Oath to them. He arrived in Eng$^{d}$ in January 1776. Since which time he has never been in America but all his family are in America.

George Boyd—the Claimant—sworn.

Produces a Letter from his Att$^{y}$ M$^{r}$ Clap who has inclosed him the Acc$^{t}$

[1] Sabine (op. cit., vol. i, p. 247) writes: 'While abroad he acquired wealth. In 1787 he adjusted his affairs and embarked for his native land full of hope. Riding was among his enjoyments, and he procured a handsome coach and an English coachman. He died at sea, two days before the ship arrived at Portsmouth and his remains were interred from his elegant mansion.'

of his Losses by which it appears that Clap does not think the Claimants Estates to be lost. Produces an Estimate of his property made in 1775 by the Claim[ts] Clerk M[r] John Forster.

An Act of the 19[th] of Nov[r] 1778 read by which it appears that M[r] Boyd is banished by name.

An Act of the 28[th] Nov[r] 1778 whereby the Estates of many persons are confiscated by name but M[r] Boyd's name is not in that Act but he says the general words reach him.

Another Act read pass'd in 1781 to prevent persons residing here &c from purchasing Lands in America.

Another Act pass'd in 1782 read for confiscating the Estates of certain persons who being Inha[ts] of America have adher'd to the Cause of Great Britain. He was never called upon under any of these Acts. Cannot give a positive Answer to this Question whether he can safely swear upon the whole that he believes his Estate to be confiscated.

Stephen Holland Esq—sworn.

Knew M[r] Boyd for many Years in New Hampshire. He understood that when he returned from Eng[d] in 1775 he took an active part in favor of Gov[t]. He lay at his House the Evening that he quitted Portsmouth & went to New York. Never heard anything to impeach his Loyalty. He was a Man of very considerable property. He told the Witness that he went away sooner than take a part with the Americans for if he had staid he must have fitted out Privateers &c. Knew M[r] Clap. Does not believe that he was a Partner believes him to have been his Clerk. Does not think there was any private Agreement between M[r] Boyd & M[r] Clap to take different parts out of policy. Supposes the property will not be lost. Can't speak accurately to the property. Knows that M[rs] Boyd is in poss[n] of it. Does not consider the Estate to be confiscated as no Proceedings have been had under any of the Acts & says the Law is so in every province as well as Hampshire. Being asked as to the Character of Col[l] Boyd he says he has heard people speak well & ill of him but he has had transactions with him & he always found him a very honest Man. Considers him as a very illiterate & weak Man.

Tho[s] M[c]Donnough—sworn.

Knew Col[l] Boyd in N. Hampshire before the troubles. He was admitted in 1775 one of the Council by Mandamus & he believes he attended. Has heard that he was threaten'd & insulted. Considers him as a firm Loyalist. Has heard some imputations upon his Loyalty but he does not think them well grounded. Does not know anything of his property or Ships. Does not consider Col[l] Boyd's property to be lost to him. Conceives however the general Act of Confiscation to extend to his Case. Thinks M[r] Boyd a Man of tolerable good Understanding & that he knows the difference between Sterling & Currency. He was consider'd as an interested Man but in general he was consider'd as an honest Man.

John Lane—sworn.

Has known Col[l] Boyd since the Year 1764 when the Witness was in America. Knew him here afterwards in 1774. He always looked upon him as a loyal Man.

He has some little knowledge of his real Estate. He knows the place which he purchased of Mr Livius[1] tho' he did not buy it till after he left America. He has had Dealings with Col[l] Boyd as a Merch[t]. He sent many Ships to Eng[d] more than anybody. Says he dealt in a particular manner he had always more Money than most people in Eng[d] & therefore he was a very good Customer to Mr Lane & he never objected to his Accounts. Says he is a clever Man in business but admits that he is a very illiterate Man he has had no Education. Says he understands very well the difference between Sterling & Currency in all the provinces. Being shewn the Acc[t] which had been presented by Mr Boyd & the mistakes which had happen'd between Sterling & lawful Money He says he is of Opinion that such an Opinion could not happen from Stupidity.

## Further testimony to the Memorial of Colonel Boyd

25th of April 1785.

John Meserve—sworn.

Knows a person who calls himself Col[l] Boyd but thinks he has no right to be called so. Has known him for 40 Years. He has not a spark of Loyalty. Has heard him say during the War that he was of a Club of Citizens who used to meet frequently & the first Toast given was Gen[l] Washington & Success to him. Knows he sent a Letter to Mr Clap which was publickly read in America in which he desired him to distribute Money to the Widows &c of those who were killed in the War & he express'd a Wish in that Letter that his Children would take the part of the rebels & that he would disinherit them if they did not. He has not a Doubt in his own mind from these Circumstances that during the War he has frequently sent intelligence to America to the prejudice of the Country. He did not bear the Character of an honest Man in the Country. On the Contrary it was supposed that he would take all Advantages. His own Certificate is read to him & being asked why he gave it Says he does not think his Certificate imports Loyalty. He only states facts he says. Admits that he has had Quarrels with Col[l] Boyd. He owed Money to Col[l] Boyd at that time. And it was since that time that he quarrel'd with him. Thinks if he had not owed him Money he should have given him that Certificate. Thought he wanted the Certificate to shew to the Commissioners. Can't say whether he thought the Certificate would be of service to him or not. Admits that he was intimate with him at that time. Doubts whether he should have written that Letter to Mr Forster if he had not quarrel'd with Col[l] Boyd. Says that Mr Boyd's Character is very well known to Mr Hale Mr Little & Mr Terry. He was confined in the same place with the Witness for $\frac{1}{2}$ an Hour but at that time he did not

[1] Livius was appointed by Lord G. Germain Chief Justice of Canada in 1775. He was described by Carleton as 'greedy of power, more greedy of gain; imperious and impetuous in his temper, but learned in the ways of eloquence of the New England provinces, valuing himself particularly on his knowledge of how to manage Governors' (A. G. Bradley, *Lord Dorchester*, p. 185). (Livius had already quarrelled in New Hampshire with the Governor Wentworth.) It should be noted that Livius was the cause of the important decision by the Privy Council that the Governor had no right to consult an inner circle of his Council, and thus in effect to introduce the Cabinet system (Munro, *Acts of the Privy Council, Col. Series*, vol. v, pp. 467–71).

think him a Loyalist. Says he was taken up by a Man who had had a Quarrel with him. Has heard of his having a Passport from the Committee to go to New York & says the Committee would not have given such a Passport to a Loyalist. Does not know that M^r^ Hale has had any Quarrel with M^r^ Boyd. Never heard that there was any Agreement between M^r^ Boyd & M^r^ Clap to take different sides.

Sam^l^ Hale Esq—sworn.

Knows M^r^ Meserve to be a Man of Character & Delicacy & that he would not say a wrong thing if he knew it. Has known Col^l^ Boyd from the Y^r^ 1766. He lived in Portsmouth himself. And he knew him when he returned from Eng^d^ in 1775. America was then in a flame. He return'd as a Merch^t^ & some time after he returned he was appointed a Mandamus Counsellor under the Idea that he was a Loyalist. But he was never esteem'd there so far a Loyalist as to run risque. He was never consider'd as a Loyalist & the Witness did not look upon him as such. Knew M^r^ Clap he was a violent rebel he lived with Col^l^ Boyd in his House. Thinks there was no intrigue between Col^l^ Boyd & that party. Says they would never trust him. Thinks it probable that M^r^ Boyd may lose his property. The Province is so distress'd that they cannot pay their Quota to Congress. During the War he always appear'd to be a friend to America he has often conversed with him upon the Subject. Says that M^r^ Boyd is a cunning Man & apprehends that he knows the Difference between Sterling Money & Currency.[1]

## Further testimony to the Memorial of Colonel Boyd

13^th^ of May 1785.

Stephen Little—sworn.

He was settled in the Town of Portsmouth. Knew M^r^ Boyd many Years before the troubles. He never thought him attached to Great Britain. When he was made a Member of the Council He thinks he was a very improper Man on Acc^t^ of want of Education & likewise on Acc^t^ of his political Principles. His political principles were known to everybody. Says he was sworn into the Council. But he consider'd from his Conversation that he espous'd their Cause. Remembers his being made Prisoner. He was taken up as a Tory but when his name was mention'd to the Committee they releas'd him immediately. Many others who were taken were kept two Days & obliged to give Bonds but he was releas'd without. Never heard of his taking any Oath. Knew M^r^ Clap he was a Rebel. He has often heard him speak in favor of the Americans & say they would succeed. Speaks of the Letter to M^r^ Clap in which he desires his Children to take part with them. Does not recollect his keeping a Store. He had two Ships. Has heard him say that he meant to go back to America. Says he has strong abilities in trade but he is a Man of low Education. Thinks he would know the Value of Money. Says nobody will say that he was a loyal Subject.

1 'At the outbreak of the Revolution the New England Governments . . . had issued Paper Money for immediate use. . . . By 1778 the whole system of currency had broken down hopelessly. . . . By 1780 . . . Continental money was forty to one. . . . Bancroft gives the value of the dollar "buoyed up by the French alliance" in 1778 at 20 cents. It fell to 12½ c. in January, 1779; to 5 c. in April; to 2½ c. in December' (W. B. Weeden, *Economic and Social History of New England*, vol. ii, pp. 797–8). It is thus apparent that Boyd's mistake was a very material one.

## Further Testimony to the Memorial of George Boyd

Bamber Gascoigne [1] Esq—sworn. 27th of May 1785.

Says when he was in the Board of Trade & Plantations Col^l^ Boyd came over here in 1774 or 1775 & was recommended to him as a person of considerable fortune & trade in the Province of New Hampshire & well attached to his Majesty's Gov^t^. And who from the Extent of his trade had a great influence in the Country. Says he gave very material Intelligence to the Board of trade & also gave him a clear Acc^t^ of the State of the Country & he asserted at the time that if he had known the Intentions of this Country before he came over here he had that Influence that he could turn the minds of the people there & he had reason to think from the Enquiry he made that he had considerable Influence. He was appointed one of the Council at the recommendation of M^r^ Gascoigne. He rec^d^ two Letters from M^r^ Boyd after his return to America & believes he continued firm in his Loyalty. He has reason to think from the Information he has rec^d^ of his Conduct that he might have been of more service to Gov^t^ if he had not been too open in his Conduct.

## Further testimony to the Memorial of Col^l^ Boyd

Peter Livius Esq—sworn. 7th of July 1785.

Knew Col^l^ Boyd at the beginning of the troubles & before. Knew him in Eng^d^ in 1775 & he heard M^r^ Gascoigne say that he was to be sent out under an Idea that he would be of service to Gov^t^. And he says he thinks if he had been well paid for it & had contracted to do anything for Gov^t^ he would have kept his word. Does not know anything to impeach his Loyalty. Has heard such Reports. Says he had considerable property. Has had some transactions in Money Matters with him & has a bad Opinion of him from some things which he has seen in the Courts where he was Judge. Thinks he knows the difference between Currency & Sterling. Has not a good Opinion of his moral Character. Says if he has made a Charge in Sterling when he ought to have made it in Currency that he must have done it wittingly because he must have known better. Says from what he saw of him in the Court where he presided if the other Judges had been of the same Opinion with him he should have directed a prosecution for Perjury. Thinks that M^r^ Boyd's natural wishes & Bias were in favor of that Country & that he wished well to America. But at the same time he says that he thinks he would have kept his word with Gov^t^ if he thought that Gov^t^ would succeed. And he says he believes that it must have been his Opinion at the time that he went to New Hampshire that this Country would succeed. Being desired by the Commissioners to give his private Opinion whether from all that he knows of M^r^ Boyd he considers him to be a Loyalist He says No. He does not consider him entitled to make any Claim under this Act of Par^t^ as a Loyalist.

[1] Bamber Gascoigne became a member of the Board of Trade in 1763. After the abolition of that Board he was appointed Receiver-General of the Customs (*Annual Register*, 1763 and 1791).

## Memorial of Joseph Adams

Determin'd the 25th of Apl 1785.

25th of April 1785.

Joseph Adams—the Claimant—sworn.

Is a Native of Cornwall. He went first to America in 1756. He had an House & Wife at Boston & resided there occasionally but was principally at Sea. He was not in America during the Yrs 1774 & 1775 his Wife & family were then dead. He had then no property in America. He went to New York in 1776. We were then in possn of New York. His Loss was as a Trader at Sea. He remain'd at New York till 1777 when he sail'd from New York in his own Vessel to Philadelphia. He was employ'd to supply the Army the Ship was called the Lord Drummond. She was blown off the Coast & then went to Antigua & was condemn'd there. First charges £156 for a Loss sustain'd in 1769—Waved.

A British Subject.

He bought the new Ship Lord Drummond in Antigua in 1778 & fitted her out to go to Philadelphia & she was taken. He values the Ship & Cargo at £1210.

He bought the Rosamond soon after at Antigua & fitted her out for New York. She was worth with the Cargo £505. She was taken by the French fleet off Sandy Hook going into New York. He bought the Ships for his own Use & used them in the Way of trade & he meant to get Money by it. He knew of the American & French War & knew that they would take him if they could.

Claims these Ships to be compensated because he lost them for his Loyalty. He was advised by several persons to put in a Claim under the Act of Part. He has mention'd the whole of his Case & says his Witnesses are to prove his Situation at New York in the Years 1777 & 1778.

N.B. The Board upon considering the Case of Mr Adams were clearly of Opinion that it was not a Case at all fit to have come under the Consideration of the Board & therefore refused to hear any Witnesses & were unanimous in thinking that it ought be dismissed & to be reported upon as not the Case of an American Sufferer entitled to relief under this Act of Part.

## Memorial of Edward Oxnard [1]

Determin'd ye 25th of Apl 1785.

25th of April 1785.

Is a Native of America & was settled at Falmouth in Massachusets as a Trader & at the Commencement of the troubles adher'd to the British Govt. After the battle of Lexington he was called upon by the Rebels to join them which he refused. In May 1775 he went on board Captn Mowatt to avoid being confin'd. He came on Shore again in a few Hours & remain'd 6 Weeks without being molested. In June 1775 he came to Engd. They insisted on his taking up Arms if he had staid.

A Loyalist. Did not bear Arms.

He was a Storekeeper & had been settled in business about eight Years before the Rebellion. His reason for coming to Engd was that he apprehended he could not stay with Safety. The Town of Falmouth was burnt in 1775 after he came to Engd. He was insulted & ill treated before he came to Engd which was in Augt 1775. When he came to Engd he applied to the Treasury & after he had

[1] E. Oxnard was a member of the New England Club of American Loyalists in London (see Curwen, op. cit.).

Bounty £100 a Y^r^. been here a Y^r^ & ½ He rec^d^ £100 a Y^r^ & ½ a Y^r^ in advance & he now continues to receive it.

Tho^s^ Cummings—sworn.

Has known M^r^ Oxnard since the Y^r^ 1769. In 1774 He was keeping a Store in partnership with Kent. They were in very good business & he consider'd them as Men of Substance. Says that M^r^ Oxnard was always esteemed a Loyalist & he thinks him one. Kent he thinks was as much a Loyalist as Oxnard. He helped him to rescue Capt^n^ Mowatt when he was attacked by the Mob. Saw the Shop of Oxnard & Kent six Days before the fire it was middlingly stocked. He look'd upon him to be worth more than £500. He was in credit. Does not know that the Partners ever had any Quarrel about Politics but he has heard Kent check his Partner for being so open. Does not know whether M^rs^ Oxnard was a Loyalist or not.

N.B. Capt^n^ Mowatt was to have attended as a Witness but being obliged to go before he was called in he said he should return. However the Board were of Opinion that it was not necessary to examine him at any future time & that there was sufficient Evidence before us to enable us to decide upon the Case of M^r^ Oxnard.

Determin'd the 30^th^ of Ap^l^ 1785.

## Memorial of Will^m^ Smith

26^th^ of April 1785.

Will^m^ Smith—the Claimant—sworn.

Is a Native of Eng^d^ & went to America in 1769 to settle as a Merch^t^ & was

A Loyalist. in that Situation at the Commencement of the troubles. He never bore Arms but he attended the first Meeting & upon all Occasions conducted himself as a Loyalist & was on that Acc^t^ treated with Contempt & threaten'd & was drove from the Town of Baltimore in Dec^r^ 1776. Produces an anonimous paper to shew that he was in danger. He quitted the Town of Baltimore upon this but he returned in Six Weeks. He join'd Sir W^m^ Howe at the head of Elk when he removed he was pelted out of the Town for his Loyalty. They called upon him to take an Oath but he never took any Oath. Went to Philadelphia & came

Bounty £100 a Y^r^. to Eng^d^ on acc^t^ of his health in 1778. He has an Allowance of £100 a Y^r^ which he rec^d^ from the 25^th^ of March 1778 & he now continues to receive it.

George Chalmers Esq—sworn.

Knew M^r^ Smith very well. He was very loyal & universally so consider'd. Remembers his Rope Walk near Baltimore Town. There was a Dwelling House Sheds &c. Can't speak to the Value. He was a Man of very fair Character. The Witness says it is probable that persons may recover their Debts.

N.B. A Strong Certificate from Sir Rob^t^ Eden had been left with his papers at Whitehall.

Uriah Forest—sworn.

Knew nothing of Smith till lately. Recollects the Rope Walk which he held with buildings &c & says it was confiscated & sold. Can't speak to the Value of it before the troubles. It appears to have been sold for £1541 in 1781 in Specie or Continental Money. Continental Money was at that time 3 or 5 for one. Says the Premises were not in very good repair. Thinks the Money given for it was not worth more than £500.

### Memorial of Archibald M$^{c}$Kay [1]

Determin'd the 5$^{th}$ of May 1785.

Archibald M$^{c}$Kay—the Claimant—sworn. 28$^{th}$ of April 1785.

Is a Native of America was born in Carolina remain'd at home till 1781 & until that time took no part on either side. He join'd Lord Cornwallis at Cross Creek. He stood his Draughts at different times & never was drawn but once & then he got a Man to serve for him. He never took the Oaths but was treble tax'd. He never served with the rebels. He says he forged a Certificate to get an House can't recollect but he believes the Man's name whom he forged was Smith. He served in the Militia after he join'd Lord Cornwallis. When Wilmington was evacuated he was a prisoner & afterwards made his Escape into Charlestown where he remain'd till the Evacuation & went to East Florida & when he knew the Spaniards were to have East Florida he went to Halifax. He came to Eng$^{d}$ in Nov$^{r}$ last. He obtain'd an Allowance of 30 a Y$^{r}$ from the 10$^{th}$ of Oct$^{r}$ 1784 & he now continues to receive it. Says he was only 18 Y$^{rs}$ of Age when his father was banished in 1777 for not taking the Oaths of Allegiance.

A Loyalist.
Bore Arms.

Certificate from Gov$^{r}$ Martin to the Loyalty of the Claim$^{t}$ & his family.

His Brother took part with the Rebels. Admits that he & his Brother both took the same part up to the Y$^{r}$ 1781 with this difference that his Brother took the Oaths & he did not.

### Memorial of M$^{rs}$ Kearsley

Determin'd y$^{e}$ 30$^{th}$ of Ap$^{l}$ 1785.

Mary Kearsley—the Claimant—sworn. 28$^{th}$ of April 1785.

Is the Widow of the late D$^{r}$ John Kearsley [2] of Philadelphia. He was an Englishman She a Native of America. Believes that he went to America about 40 Y$^{rs}$ ago. When the troubles began he was a practising Physician at Philadelphia is sure he was well disposed to G. B. Says she has heard the Memorial read & knows the Contents as far as a Woman can know she believes the Contents to be true. She came to Eng$^{d}$ in 1778 & has since rec$^{d}$ an Allowance of £100 a Y$^{r}$ from Gov$^{t}$. Says her Son in Law Capt$^{n}$ Douglas is better acquainted with the particulars of her property than herself & she refers to him for an Acc$^{t}$ thereof. Says when D$^{r}$ Kearsley was first apprehended in 1775 the Mob destroy'd great part of their furniture. The Valuation of £94 S. is stated from the joint recollection of herself & her family. She believes it was rather more than less. In Oct$^{r}$ in the same Y$^{r}$ when he was again taken up further Destruction was done by the Mob in D$^{r}$ Kearsley's Library Surgery &c to the Amount of £300 S.

She & her Husband Loyalists.

Bounty £100 a Y$^{r}$.

Capt$^{n}$ Rob$^{t}$ Douglas—sworn. 29$^{th}$ of April 1785.

Is Son in Law to the Claim$^{t}$. Says D$^{r}$ Kearsley's Estate is not confiscated

[1] Archibald McKay was presumably the son of the Alexander McKay who 'did actually take up arms and lead forth to war as colonel of a regiment of a division of men for the avowed purpose of assisting the enemies of America', and who 'was a freeholder and lived in Cumberland County' (*N. Car. Records*, vol. x, p. 595).

[2] See note at p. 143.

as Mrs Kearsley supposed when she deliver'd in the Memorial & Mr Baker her Attorney is now in possn thereof. Part of Dr Kearsley's Estate was sold under Execution after the Evacuation of Philadelphia. A Loss sustain'd by this of £1100 S. Believes from what he has heard & knows of Dr Kearsley's practice that he lost between the Years 1775 & 1777 £2000 S. Says the Wine Store was in truth a Vinegar factory. Dr Kearsley made & sold Vinegar. All that he can say about the Destruction of it is that he saw it standing in 1774 & it was not standing in 1777. Dr Kearsley said before his Death that the Damage was £500 S.

Saml Shoemaker—on his Affirmation.

Knew Dr Kearsley 40 Yrs ago. He was a very respectable Man in his profession. Says he was a violent Loyalist one of the most zealous that he ever knew believes it hasten'd his end. He was one of the first Physicians in Philadelphia. Had been in greater business some time before the troubles than he was at that time. He was violent in his politics & lessen'd his practice. Can't tell how much he got. Says no Confiscation took place until after his Death. Remembers his having a Vinegar Distillery he often advised him agt it. Thinks it probable that it was destroy'd but does not know it because it was a wooden Building. He was a Dealer in Horses & had several Horses. Knows nothing of the Destruction of the property at Strawbery Hall.

## Further testimony to the Memorial of Mrs Kearsley

29th of April 1785.

Charles Steadman—sworn.

Was in Philadelphia in the Yr 1775 & was not present when the Mob pulled down the Surgery &c of Dr Kearsley but he understood that it was so. He has been in the Surgery before it was destroyed but never saw it afterwards. Can't tell & has never heard what Loss he sustain'd but says the Shop was full of Medicines. The report was that it was done on Acct of his Loyalty. Was at Philadelphia when Strawbery Hill was destroy'd & has understood it was by the British. He knew Mr Kearsley. He was a very distinguished Loyalist. The Witness was in prison with him in 1776 & Says that Dr Kearsley was a very firm Loyalist in that Situation. Being asked whether Dr Kearsley could have got satisfaction for his Losses if he had applied to the Commander in Chief He says he does not know. He was not then a Commissary of Captures.

Determin'd the 29th of April 1785.

## Memorial of John Harrison

29th of April 1785.

John Harrison—the Claimant—sworn.

A Loyalist.

Did not bear Arms.

Is a Native of Great Britain & went to America in 1765 to Charlestown. He went as a Surgeon & Physician. He was settled in Charlestown at the Commencement of the troubles. They first handed about an Association & were very severe with those who refused to sign it. He was obliged to sign it & did so. He was quiet for near a Yr afterwds. Then he was taken up by Coll Hale for not doing Duty as a Soldier. Afterwds they excused him from that & said he should do Duty by attending the sick. He made no reply which they took to be an Assent & they releas'd him. It was 10 Months afterw$^{ds}$ before any Oath was tender'd to him & four Months afterw$^{ds}$ when the Abjuration Oath was tender'd. He refused all the Oaths. He was in consequence insulted & threaten'd by two or three people. He had 60 Days time allowed to quit the province but he quitted it in 30 Days & went to Nantz. He has not been in America since. He went to the Treasury soon after he came home & he rec$^{d}$ £340. He had been in Eng$^{d}$ a Year before he received it. Says he did not understand it to be in full for all his Losses. He has besides an Allowance of £40 a Year which was given to him from the 5$^{th}$ of Jan$^{y}$ 1783. And he now continues to receive that Allowance.

Bounty £300 & £130.

It appears by recurring to the Whitehall Book that he rec$^{d}$ at two different times £430.

He got £500 a Year by his profession once got 1500 a Y$^{r}$ but can speak to £500 a Y$^{r}$ S.

£500 a Y$^{r}$.

### Memorial of Sam$^{l}$ Cooke Clerk

Determin'd the 2$^{d}$ of May 1785.

2$^{d}$ of May 1785.

The Rev$^{d}$ Sam$^{l}$ Cooke—the Claimant—sworn.

Is a Native of Eng$^{d}$ & went first to America as a Missionary in 1751. He was settled in Monmouth Co New Jersey in 1774 & 1775. He had two Churches in Monmouth Co One where he lived. He came to Eng$^{d}$ in May 1775. He says the troubles were then began. He came upon private business. He prevented any Committee being chosen in Shrewsbury where he lived by his influence. He rec$^{d}$ several threats before he came away this hasten'd his departure & he left New Jersey & came to New York & he arrived in Eng$^{d}$ on the 1$^{st}$ of July. He returned in May 1776 as Chaplain to a Brigade of Guards. And he staid with them till 1782. He had *6s. 8d.* a Day during the time that he staid in America. He expects half Pay from the Day of his reduction to the Day of his Appointment of Chaplain to the Garrison at New Brunswick. This was on the 25$^{th}$ of Aug$^{t}$ 1784. He had an Allowance of £40 a Y$^{r}$ from the 1$^{st}$ of Jan$^{y}$ 1784—which he now continues to receive.

A Loyalist.

Bounty £40 a Y$^{r}$.

Loss of the rent of Glebe for 3 Y$^{rs}$ £67 10*s.*

He had the Church of Christ Church of Shrewsbury & another at Middleton. It used to produce him by subscription 30 a Y$^{r}$ S. besides the Glebe which let annually for £22 10*s.*

Living £50 a Y$^{r}$.

Says he did not mean to have charged the Livings as he considers the Chaplainship more than a Satisfaction for the Livings.

### Memorial of Edw$^{d}$ Mumford

Determin'd the 2$^{d}$ of May 1785.

2$^{d}$ of May 1785.

Edward Mumford—the Claimant—sworn.

Is a Native of Newport in Rhode Island. He lived there in 1774 & 1775 as a Merch$^{t}$. No Offer was made to him to sign any association because they knew his principles. However in 1775 they tender'd a Test to him which he refused to sign. However at the request of all his friends he sign'd it sooner than be banished. Upon this they suffer'd him to remain quiet until the Kings troops came to the Island. Says the Test was trifling. When the Kings Troops

A Loyalist but sign'd a Test.

Did not bear Arms.

came to the Island they gave him an Oath & he took it. He continued with the British afterwards till 1783. He remain'd inactive at New York for 15 Months. Never rec^d any pay. Then went with a Venture to Virginia in the Spring of 1781. He was afterw^ds taken with Lord Cornwallis at York Town. He was in no military Capacity.

Claims for the Loss of business which he estimates upon an Average at a profit of £200 a Year. And he claims it for 5 Years from the beginning of the troubles to the present time £1000. He deducts for those Years in which he was permitted to carry on the Business.

Determin'd the 6th of May 1785.

## Memorial of David Stewart

David Stewart—the Claimant—sworn. 6th of May 1785.

A Loyalist.

Did not bear Arms.

Is the Son of George Stewart [1] one of the Council & Judges of the Land Office of Maryland. In Sept^r 1774 he was appointed Register of the Land Office at Anapolis by the Judges. From 1774 to 1779 he took no part. In 1776 the Records were moved from Anapolis to Marlborough he went with them & continued to do the Duty of the Office till 1777. In June that Year this Office was taken from him by the new Gov^t. This by an Order of the Gov^r & Council. He had been called upon to associate & muster & to take the Oaths of Allegiance which he had refused. Has reason to believe that if he had consented to take the Oaths he would have been continued in the Office. This was an Office during good behaviour but was generally looked upon to be for life. The profits of this Office were £150 a Y^r in Salary & fees. In 1775 he was called upon to muster which he refused was threaten'd by them but did not receive any personal ill Usage. Then he was required to associate which he refused & in 1776 He was called upon to take the Oaths which he refused & in 1777 the Office was taken away from him. He attempted to get away in 1778 but could not & he procured leave to return to Great Britain by way of Spain. He was taken on the passage & carried into New York from thence he came to Eng^d in 1779.

Loss of office. £60 a Y^r fees. £90 a Y^r.

Present Bounty £60 a Y^r. former Bounty £100 a Y^r.

M^r Stewart had an Allowance of £100 per Ann. which was reduced to £60 a Y^r by M^r Wilmot & M^r Coke. He found it inconvenient to remain in Maryland but thinks he might have remain'd without taking an Oath subject to the treble taxes. He made over his property to his Brother before he left the Country. His private Affairs required his presence in Europe at the time he came home & thinks he would have come home at any rate. He lost his Office from the part he had taken. His father came to Eng^d in 1775. He would have come home at the same time but for the business of this Office. His Brother was of a very different way of thinking & had muster'd early in the War.

He Claims the Loss of his father's Office his property was saved by being made over to his Brothers Charles & Will^m. His father is dead. He is the 3^d Son his eldest Brother is in Scotland & has not been in America since he was ten Years old. This was 26 Years ago.

[1] See on George Stewart's conduct as one of the judges of the Land Office, B. C. Steiner, *Life and Administration of Sir Robert Eden* (Johns Hopkins Univ. Studies in Hist. and Polit. Science, vol. xvi, nos. 7, 8, 9, p. 87).

He is asked if he should have found it impossible to remain in Maryland without taking the Oaths. He says he should have found it inconvenient but not impossible. He should have been subject to treble Taxes.

Being asked whether it was on Acc$^{t}$ of his Loyalty that he came away or on private business Says it was both. His Situation was unpleasant & he had business to settle with his father.

Being asked whether he should have come away if he had not had private business Says expecting nothing under the American Gov$^{t}$ he thinks he should. He can't positively say that he should.

His Brother Will$^{m}$ came likewise to Eng$^{d}$ with his father but he returned to America & is favorable to them.

Says his Brother George is a Native of America but he left it 25 Years ago when he was a Child.

Says in the fall of 1778 he attempted to get to New York thro' the Jerseys but without Success. He returned back & applied for & obtain'd leave to go to Great Britain by way of Spain but refused Permission for him to go by way of Spain. He came away in Feb$^{y}$ 1779 & was taken immediately on his coming out of the Chesapeak & carried into New York from whence he came to Eng$^{d}$ in June.

His father was one of the Judges of the Land Office in Maryland which he was in possession of for 20 Y$^{rs}$. Says he left America in Sept$^{r}$ 1775 upon the Death of a Brother who left him an Estate in Scotland. He did intend to return. Before he left America He declared his Inclination to support Great Britain to Governor Eden. The Place of Judge of the Land Office was worth £400 Ster$^{g}$. It consisted entirely of fees. During the troubles it was an Office of little profit only sufficient to pay the Clerks it was taken from him on Acc$^{t}$ of his Loyalty. Until 3 Months before he died he could have returned. He had no Allowance from Gov$^{t}$. He died in June 1784. The Claim is made for the intermediate Profits. His father previous to his coming away absolutely refused to sign any Association.

James Brooks—sworn.

Says the Claimant is a firm Loyalist. Believes he never took an Oath or associated. Does not recollect any open Act of Loyalty. He was Register of the Land Office. It was a public Office appointed by the Judges during pleasure. It was not customary to remove persons from this Office. His Salary was £60 S. per Ann. the fees were worth £120 more.

Has heard it said before the troubles that the Register has sometimes made 400 a Y$^{r}$ by fees. Believes that M$^{r}$ Stewart must have made £100 a Y$^{r}$ by fees. He was dismiss'd by the new Gov$^{t}$ & conceives it was because he was a Non Conformist & believes if he had conformed he would have been continued. The father was one of the Judges of the Land Office it was worth £400 a Y$^{r}$.

George Chalmers Esq—sworn.

Knew M$^{r}$ David Stewart at Anapolis. Always looked upon him as a Loyalist but he never took an active part corrects himself & says he thinks he did take an active part Because he sign'd the protest ag$^{t}$ [not] paying British Debts & went about the Town with it which was in some measure dangerous. Admits that several Persons who sign'd that protest did afterwards become Rebels. Says the Brothers of the Claimant took the other part. Believes he never took any part with the Rebels. Knew the Office that he held Register of the Land Office. Thinks it was worth from £150 to £200 S. Imagines that he lost it on acc$^{t}$ of his Loyalty but had quitted the Country before he lost the Office. The Claim$^{ts}$ father was Judge of the Land Office & in general all Offices in Maryland were consider'd to be Offices for Life but still Lord Baltimore might have turned him out if he had pleased. Thinks the office was worth from 4 to £500 a Year. The father had very considerable property in Maryland which was saved by being made over to one of the Sons.

Determin'd the 11$^{th}$ of May 1785.

### Memorial of Will$^{m}$ Telfair [1]

Will$^{m}$ Telfair—the Claimant—sworn. 10$^{th}$ of May 1785.

A Loyalist. Bore Arms both for & ag$^{t}$ the British Gov$^{t}$ but the latter by Necessity.

Is a Native of Great Britain & went to Georgia in 1759. In 1762 he commenced Merch$^{t}$ in Savannah. In 1772 he returned to Eng$^{d}$ & commenced business in London without any intention of returning to America. The firm of the House in London was Cowper & Telfair. In 1776 the House stopp'd payment from the want of remittances from America.

In 1778 his Creditors had a Meeting & he then determin'd to go to New York. He went to secure his property & meant to go into that part of the Country which was the Seat of War. He went from New York to Savannah & was there 9 Weeks before Gen$^{l}$ Campbell arrived. He had taken no Oath but he was obliged to bear Arms ag$^{t}$ the British when Gen$^{l}$ Campbell came. He apprehends they would have put him to death if he had not join'd them. He would have gone to prison sooner than bear Arms. Knew that Savannah was under Rebel Gov$^{t}$ & he meant to submit to their Gov$^{t}$ for a time. He had a Brother who was a Member of Congress. Thought that the British would succeed when he join'd them. He remain'd with them till the Evacuation of Savannah. Would have quitted the Province sooner than take an Oath. Never sign'd any Association. He was appointed a Comm$^{r}$ of Claims for sequester'd Rebel Estates & Col$^{l}$ Campbell appointed him one of the Council. He served in the Assembly under Sir James Wright & served in the Militia.

John Hodgson—sworn. 11$^{th}$ of May 1785.

Is a Merch$^{t}$ in London. Knew M$^{r}$ Telfair before & after the troubles. Has frequently heard him express his Sentiments in the Year 1776 favorably to this Country. He lived with him as Clerk. He fail'd in 1776. In 1780 the Witness made out a State of their effects & the House then had more than £7000 C. due to them in America. Never was in America.

Lieut$^{t}$ Gov$^{r}$ Graham—sworn.

Has known W$^{m}$ Telfair many Years. Has understood that he submitted to the Rebel Gov$^{t}$ for some time. Does not know whether he was to blame

[1] William Telfair was among the signers of a memorial, dated from Jamaica, April 8, 1783, requesting a further allowance of provisions till they could find lands or employment especially for their negroes (*Hist. MSS. Comm., Am. MSS. in R. Inst.*, vol. iv, p. 19).

for it or not under the Circumstances. Says his Brother was a Rebel. Believes him to be a most worthy Man & thinks him a very zealous Loyalist upon the whole. Believes he was connected in business with his Brother. Thinks that he might have staid in Georgia after the Evacuation. Knows that he is in the Act of Confiscation. Says that Sir James Wright could not continue him of the Council & that the old Members took their Seats again.

The Claimant—called in again but not sworn.

He says he is going to leave the Country & is in distress'd Circumstances & wishes to have some Allowance for temporary support & says he has a paper before the Treasury. But being told that we have once decided upon it & that there is no Memorial before us. And therefore no Steps can be taken.

### Memorial of Thomas Macknight [1] Esq.

Determin'd y^e^ 18^th^ of May 1785.

Tho^s^ Macknight Esq—the Claimant—sworn. 11^th^ of May 1785.

A Zealous & meritorious Loyalist bore Arms & render'd services to the British Gov^t^.

Swears in general to the truth of his Memorial it being very long. He is a Native of Scotland & went to America in 1755. At the Commencement of the troubles He resided in North Carolina at Belville as a Merch^t^ & as a Planter & Farmer. He had very early an Opportunity of shewing his Attachment to this Country in his Character as a Member of the Assembly. He mentions an early instance of his attachment to this Country by an opposition to the Regulators.[2] In 1775 He was particularly called upon by Gov^r^ Martin to oppose their Measures which he did & in the latter end of 1775 He was obliged to leave his House not thinking himself perfectly safe. Became a Member of the 2^d^ Convention at the request of many friends this was in the Spring of 1775 before they knew of the Lexington business. After some time he & 8 Members retired from the Convention & protested ag^t^ all their proceedings. Did not know that the Second Convention was illegal. He was instructed by his Constituents to oppose all violent Measures. He did not go into the Convention until he was requested by all his Neighbours. There was an attempt in that Assembly to move to pay the Expences of Delegates to the General Congress & M^r^ M^c^Knight opposed it. He refused to sign any Association in the Convention. In April 1775 he was proscribed. He did not go to Norfolk till the latter end of that Year. In the meantime he was offer'd great things to seduce him to command the Army or to be sent a Delegate to the Congress. Upon his Arrival in Virginia he waited upon Lord Dunmore. During the time he was with Lord Dunmore He bore Arms as a Volunteer & says he ran a risque of his Life at Kemp's landing. He & M^r^ Hunter persuaded 80 Men to take Arms. He afterwards built a Rampart round about the town of Norfolk & produces a Warrant for it from Lord Dunmore he was never paid for it. Produces likewise a Commission from Lord Dunmore making him Engineer & Captain. He can't speak with certainty of

[1] There is a letter from Governor Martin to Lord G. Germain, July 6, 1776, speaking very warmly of Thomas McKnight's services. He had abandoned a property valued at £30,000 sterling (*N. Car. Records*, vol. x, p. 655). The claim of Messrs. McKnight, Parker, and McCormick was the subject of a special debate in the House of Commons on July 7, 1785 (*Morning Chronicle*, July 8, 1785). It was decided to leave the claim to the decision of the Commissioners.

[2] See for an account of the 'Regulation' troubles C. L. Raper, *N. Carolina*, pp. 61–2, 238.

the Expence that he was at in building the Wall at Norfolk. He says the Gov[r] did not desire him to become a Member of that Convention. But he publish'd papers declaring that Assembly to be illegal.

Tho[s] Macknight Esq—the Claimant—sworn. 12[th] of May 1785.

In the Year 1774 after the Congress had published the Vote of Approbation for the Resolutions of the County of Suffolk he consider'd it as a Measure declaratory of Independence & tends in the most direct manner to produce a Revolt of the Colonies & indeed a Dec[n] of War from that time he opposed their Measures & endeavour'd to the utmost of his power to propagate similar sentiments in the Counties where he lived for this purpose he not only called a Meeting to bring them over to the same way of thinking but induced his friends to procure the same Measures & in doing so he was at a very considerable Expence.

Lord Dunmore having heard that a Body of Men had assembled at the Great Bridge in Arms & thinking it proper to attack them consulted him upon the properest way to get round them & embarked with part of the 14[th] Reg[t] & a Party of Volunteers sail'd up the Southern Branch in the Night of which he furnish'd Lord Dunmore with a Draught to shew the practicability of the measure. His Lordship succeeded in getting round them & they fled to Kemps Landing where they join'd a great Body of the Inhabitants of that County then under Arms. His Lordship march'd in pursuit of them & was attacked. Was applied to by his Lordship on several other Occasions & particularly to take Anthony Lawson on his return from Williamsburgh & refers to Lord Dunmore for further particulars. Held a Correspondence with the people of Carolina & engaged a considerable number of Men to come round to Lord Dunmore's assistance. When they were ready to come Lord Dunmore was obliged to quit. He had hired a Vessel to bring them round by Sea as the passage by Land was stopp'd.

In 1776 in the Spring he join'd Gov[r] Martin at Cape Fear & at whose request he accompanied the Expedition to Charlestown. Remain'd with him from March till the Expedition failed. On the Troops being directed to the Northern Colonies & his not thinking he could be of further Service he determin'd to come to Eng[d] & arrived in the fall of the Year 1776. On his arrival the Sum of £100 was order'd to be paid to him by the Treasury & an allowance of £200 per Ann. both which he refused & remonstrated ag[t] the smallness of the Sum towards the end of the Year the Treasury order'd £500 in addition to the £100 to be given to him & £200 a Y[r] Allowance which he admitted. The Allowance commenced in 1777. In 1782 M[r] Wilmot & M[r] Coke recommended an increase of £100 to his annual Allowance. Mentions his having rec[d] £250 more which was order'd to be paid to him by the Treasury on his going out to Virginia but as he did not go it was for a time stopp'd. M[r] Pitt afterwards order'd the Money to be paid as M[r] M[c]Knight was consider'd to have been at some Expence in preparing to go out.

Bounty a Sum of £600 and an Allowance of £200 a Y[r]. Afterwards augmented. Present Bounty £300 a Y[r].

Says he procured the Instructions from his Constituents for doing what he did in the Convention.

A printed Copy of a Letter dated 6[th] of July 1776 from Gov[r] Martin to Lord

George Germaine is read which speaks fully to M$^{r}$ M$^{c}$Knight's Loyalty & essential Services. M$^{r}$ M$^{c}$Knight declares that it is a true Copy. Produces a printed Copy of the Journals whereby it appears by resolves therein that the Negroes were order'd to be taken off M$^{r}$ M$^{c}$Knight's Estates before the Declaration of Independence.

Governor Martin—sworn.

M$^{r}$ M$^{c}$Knight was very well known to him for many Years. Believes him to be a firm Loyalist. Can't say that he render'd services to this Country. He used his best Endeavors to do so but the services of the best people in that Country were render'd abortive. He has the highest sense of M$^{r}$ Macknight's Services. The Depositions formerly made by Gov$^{r}$ Martin & printed in M$^{r}$ Macknight's memorial are read to Gov$^{r}$ Martin & he says they are the truth.

Says being asked about the Grant of Lord Carteret that it was incompleat but says that seven Years possession gave an indisputable title. Does not know whether M$^{r}$ Macknight had been 7 Years in possession. Says this tract was in dismal Swamp & that it was an uninhabited & impassable Forest. Can't say whether the cutting a road merely can be consider'd as possession.

Has been upon the Estate at Belville. It was a very fine Country charming Pasturage. He was there in the Y$^{r}$ 1773. He was consider'd as one of the most wealthy Men in the province. Looks upon him as a Merch$^{t}$ when he says this. Considers a Man who has £10000 in North Carolina as a very rich Man. But thinks he was worth more. Can't speak to the Value of this Estate.

Knows that he had the Clerkship of Pasquotank but he can't speak to the Value of it now. Says he knew it when he was Governor.

Will$^{m}$ M$^{c}$Cormick—sworn.

Knows the Dismal Swamp. He has been in parts of it. Does not know M$^{r}$ M$^{c}$Knight's title to it. But knows he made an Entry in 1763. Believes he never got the Grant. Says any person might have taken Land to any amount. Says M$^{r}$ M$^{c}$Knight meant to take 40000 in one District. He has valued it at *6s. 8d.* per Acre. Says some Acres were worth *20s.* per Acre. The Swamp is about 30 Miles long & 15 Miles wide. Says M$^{r}$ M$^{c}$Knight & M$^{r}$ Parker went with their Negroes & they were a fortnight in penetrating 7 Miles & made a Squirrel Road & this was all the poss$^{n}$ they ever took. Can't speak to the right under poss$^{n}$. Says they must have been at some Expence for fees 100 or £200 C. Does not know that they ever cut Shingles from 1763 or derived any Advantage before the troubles. Says he believes they never had. Being asked whether under all the Circumstances they could be consider'd as having poss$^{n}$ He says he thinks it might but not ag$^{t}$ the proprietors. Believes they never paid a farthing Quit Rent. Knows he lost several Articles of Crop & says the Valuation is a moderate one. Believes $\frac{1}{3}^{d}$ belonged to M$^{r}$ Macknight. Says he had one half before 1772 & the Partnership was afterw$^{ds}$ divided into three Shares.

James Parker—sworn.

Tho' his Deposition seems to imply that the whole of his Land was worth *40s.* per Acre he does not think it was & he meant to except the Marsh Land. Thinks the high & arable Land was worth *40s.* an Acre & that the high Land consisted of about 8000 Acres. Mr Macknight's low Land was very bad Land. Says about 1759 or 1760 He wanted to purchase 100 Acres adjoining to Mr Macknight's & he was asked £3 an Acre for it but he did not buy it. He values the low Land at 5*s*. per Acre S. Does not know whether he gave Money or goods for Land & does not know what he gave for it. Thinks he should have given 45*s*. per Acre for the 100 Acres for which they asked him £3 an Acre. When Mr Macknight first went into that Country there was little or no Sea trade. The increase of Commerce rais'd the Value of Lands. Speaking of Lands in general in this Country He says between the Year 1759 & the time of the troubles that Lands in general were doubled in their Value & that Mr Macknight's rose in the same proportion with other Lands & no more. Thinks that in 1759 Mr Macknight's Land the 5000 Acres were worth about 30*s*. an Acre Proc. And in 1774 He thinks they were worth 40*s*. S. per Acre. Yet he thinks they would not have sold for so much. Would not have sold for near so much at publick Vendue. Mr Macknight he says made little or no annual profit by these Lands.

Robt Nelson—sworn.

Never has been at Belville. Has valued the Estate without ever having seen it. But says it is near Lancaster where the Lands are very good & he says he has valued the Land upon a supposition that it is as good as the Land at Lancaster. Has known Lands sell at Lancaster for £5 Proc.[1] per Acre. Never was in Dismal Swamp but has been on the sides of it. Says it was valuable for the Shingles which were sent to the W. Indies. Can't value it. Mr Macknight desired him to come to give his testimony. He was not a Surveyor in America.

Colonel Ellegood—sworn. 18th of May 1785.

His Deposition read. Confirms the truth of it. Was last upon this Estate in 1773. Has been frequently at it. Has had many Conversations with Mr Macknight & differs much with Mr Macknight as to the Value. Does not know the Quantity. There was some Land worth nothing. Mr Macknight had two Law Suits & prevail'd in both. Admits that the rise of Lands in this Neighborhood was immense from the Year 1763 &[2] 1774. In a Conversation with Mr Macknight he told him that tho' he could not value it he was sure it was not worth near so much. Is clear that property more than doubled itself between the Years 1759 & 1774. Says it would not have fetched £8000 S. even if sold in Lots & at a 12 Month's Credit. This he says he is positive of & can speak with Certainty. Says he would by no means have given £7000 for it. He would not have lived there upon any Acct. He is asked if he had been referr'd to to name a price between two Parties. He mentions the Sum of £5000. And this with a Year's Credit. The Interest of Money there was 5 or 6 per Cent. Says the Buildings were rather to be built. He had Materials & meant to have built a very good House. Thinks the Estate might have sold for the £5000. Knows the Dismal Swamp & that he had a concern in it. Has heard so from Mr Acheson. Coll Ellegood looks upon the Entry as valid as a Deed that the Parties making the Entry ought within a limited time to take out a Patent but

[1] Proclamation money (of Queen Anne, 1704) under which a Spanish or American dollar equalled six shillings.

[2] *Sic* in original. ? 1763 to 1774.

that Lord Granville [1] frequently shut up the Office for Years & people could not take out their Patents. Does not know when the Quit rents become due in Carolina wher upon the Entry or the Patent but says that in Virginia he believes they became due upon the Entry made. Says Entries have been sold. Does nor know when Lord Granville died. Believes that the reason that Mr Macknight did not take out the Patent was that the Office was shut. Thinks if they had agreed to sell the whole together it would have sold for very little.

### Memorial of Nathaniel Wilson

Determin'd the 19th of May 1785.

Nathl Wilson—the Claimant—sworn. 19th of May 1785.

Is a Native of Ireland & went first to America in 1766. He was settled in South Carolina when the troubles broke out. He first took part with the British after they took Charlestown. He had no Opportunity of doing it sooner. He was obliged to take the Oath to the Americans. He believes it was in 1778. He was obliged to carry Arms for the Americans agt the Indians in 1778. He served in their Militia before the Year 1780.

A Loyalist.

But took the Oath & serv'd in the American Ma join'd ye British in 1780.

Certificates to Loyalty & his being wounded at the siege of Ninety Six by Coll Allen & some other Officers.

He join'd Coll Balfour in 1780 & was at the siege of Ninety Six in 1781. He recd six Months' pay. He was wounded there. He staid with the British till the Evacuation & then he went to Halifax. Came from thence about 3 weeks ago. He means to go back to Nova Scotia & not to Ireland.

Says that he could not help taking the Oath but he took it to save his property until he could. He had one Brother killed in the British Army. He was settled on Sawny's Creek.

Isaac Stewart knows that many Loyalists took the Oath to the rebels. Knows that he did join the British as soon as he could. Has been upon his property often. He does not know the Quantity. Thinks there were about 50 Acres clear'd where his father lived & about 15 or 20 Acres clear'd where he lived himself. It appear'd to be in good Order. He values the clear'd Land. Thinks 400 Acres & 50 clear'd would be worth about £120 S. or 130—this is exclusive of the Houses thinks the House &c would cost £50. Knew his father but does not know to whom he left his property but knows the father to be dead. Knew the younger Brother & that he is dead. Supposes if the 15 clear'd Acres had 200 Acres belonging to it that it might be worth £60 S. with the Buildings.

Does not know what Stock there was but says they had the reputation of having a great Stock. Saw a great Stock himself. Remembers the Horse he was a very fine Horse thinks he would have sold for £40. Says the House was comfortably furnished. Has reason to believe that the Rebels took everything away but can't prove it. He says he thinks his Estate will be confiscated & that he cannot return. Does not know whether he is the oldest Son but believes he is. Says his Brother lost his life from his Attachmt to G. B. He fled to the Indians & being caught before he could join the British he was killed.

[1] John Carteret, first Earl Granville, *b.* 1690, *d.* 1763. By an Act of Parliament of 1729 seven-eighths of the original Carolina grant were surrendered to the Crown ; Lord Carteret, afterwards Earl Granville, retaining one-eighth. For an account of the land system see Raper, op. cit., p. 112.

Alexander Chavus—sworn.

He is a Loyalist himself. Knew Nath[l] Wilson about 8 Years ago—before the troubles. When the troubles commenced He & the Claim[t] both took up Arms with the Americans. Says they were obliged to do it. Says that it was not in the Claim[ts] power to join the British before he did. He join'd them at the same time. And he admits that he thought at that time that the British would succeed.

Determin'd the 11[th] of July 1785.

**Memorial of Tho[s] Macknight Esq. on behalf of himself & his Partners William Atcheson & James Parker**

Tho[s] Macknight Esq—one of the Partners—sworn. 19[th] of May 1785.

Claimants all Loyalists.

The Witness was in Partnership with these two Gent[n] when the troubles commenced. He reads a Narrative containing an Acc[t] of the Partnership the time when it was enter'd into the proportions & shares of the different Partners. He was a Partner in one third of the Belville Co in 1774 under the firm of M[r] Macknight & Co & the Memorial now in Consideration relates to that partnership. His two Partners were very firmly attached to Great Brit[n]. States the property so lost by the Partners to have been lost by their Loyalty. The Sum lost by the Partnership he states to be £13526 17*s*. 0*d*. S. or £23672 0*s*. C. This Acc[t] was made up in 1772 & was the Amount of their property at that time when this Partnership began. He has no later Acc[t] his Books being lost. Says it was increas'd in 1775 more than the £6000 which had been taken out of it to make another partnership. The Capital left then was 17000 which he says had at least increased to make it the £23672 C. which is all that he claims. That property consisted of Lands Slaves Vessels &c besides Debts.

Cannot enumerate any part of the Lands. He is told that he must give in a particular Acc[t] & Schedule of the Lands Slaves &c. He promises to do it ag[t] tomorrow.

James Parker Esq—sworn.

The Witness was a Partner in the House of Mess[rs] Macknight & Acheson. They were in partnership in 1775. He has seen the Acc[t] which M[r] Macknight produces & says if he had staid in the Country (M[r] Macknight) to have disposed of the property he would have made the Sum that he has charged which is £23350. Thinks it was saleable for that Money at that time. Says it was a thriving business when the troubles commenced. Can't tell how much they clear'd annually by it. Admits that they had never drawn anything out of it but three Negroes apiece.

Colonel Ellegood—sworn. 21[st] of May 1785.

Says that M[r] Macknight M[r] Atcheson & M[r] Parker were Partners in 1775. They were in considerable business. Does not know anything of the Lands belonging to the Co. But he knew their Negroes very well. They had the most valuable proportion of Negroes of any Man in America there were a great number of Tradesmen & they were able to build a Ship amongst themselves without any assistance but of a Master Builder. Thinks them under the Circumstances worth per Head £100 proc. Does not know the Store at Belville or what was in it. Says they imported a great Quantity of Wine in the Y^r^ 1773 or 1774. Can't speak to the other Articles in the Schedule as Salt Iron &c.

Col^l^ Ellegood's Deposition read to him & he confirms it. He says the reason that he was able to speak so particularly to the Partnership Acc^ts^ was that M^r^ Atcheson was his Guardian & M^r^ Parker likewise married his Sister. And the Witness wished to get M^r^ Atcheson & M^r^ Parker out of that Concern. They shew'd him the Acc^t^ in 1772 as a friend. And he was agreeably disappointed & satisfied that they were really worth that Money but did not know what they owed. Thinks they were worth much more in 1775 than they were in 1772. Knows they clear'd about £2000 Pro. by a Voyage in 1773. Has reason to believe that £6000 was taken out afterwards to establish another partnership. Can't say that the Partnership gain'd so much as to make up that Deficiency between 1772 & 1775 but can safely say they gain'd a great deal.

Col^l^ Ellegood—called in again—& sworn.

When he saw Belville there were no Warehouses by the Water Side therefore in his Valuation he could not include things which did not exist. He understands that these Warehouses were built by the Negroes belonging to the Partnership & that as they were built upon his (M^r^ Macknight's) private property he was to make an allowance to the Partners for the labor of the Negroes. Does not know whether he ever did make that Allowance or not.

Thomas Macknight Esq—sworn.

Since yesterday he has recollected three more Negroes. He names them & they are added to the List. One in the former List by a wrong name. So that two only are to be added. Says that in consequence of the Warehouses being built upon his Ground He was to pay & acc^t^ to the partnership for the labor of the Negroes. He has not paid it but says he is to account for it. Cannot say what the Warehouses cost. Has valued the Estate altogether. Produces some papers to shew that he had extensive Dealings in Rum Wine &c.

## Memorial of Tho^s^ Macknight on behalf of himself & his Partners W^m^ Aitcheson James Parker & W^m^ M^c^Cormick

Determin'd the 25^th^ of May 1785.

23^d^ of May 1785.

Tho^s^ Macknight Esq—one of the Claimants—sworn.

This Memorial is presented for the Loss of two Ships by himself & Partners. The Ship Belville was a Vessel belonging to W^m^ M^c^Cormick & Co. And these Gent^n^ here named had all Shares in different proportions. M^r^ M^c^Knight had 2/5^ths^. In 1775 She saild from Wingfield in North Carolina with a Load of Lumber for Cadiz & Bees Wax. The restraining Act not extending to North Carolina This Ship was regularly clear'd in 1775 & legally because it was done at the King's Custom House. She was taken by an American Vessel at the Bar before she got out to Sea but she had proceeded 150 Miles on her Voyage. The Americans threw the Cargo overboard & carried the Vessel up to Newbern. M^r^ M^c^Cormick who then resided at Wingfield applied to the Congress & upon giving Bond & Security to them to be answerable to the State for the Shares of his Partners they permitted him to reload the Vessel. He did so & sent her

The Claimant & his Partners Loyalists.

Cargo £300.

Ship Belville £1500. Cargo £600. Negro £80.

to Sea. She sail'd again under the old Clearance in the beginning of 1776 after the Prohibitory Act had taken place in America. But believes it was before Mr McCormick knew of it. When she was within a Day's Sail of Cadiz she was taken by an English Man of War & carried into Gibraltar & condemn'd under the Prohibitory Act.

Thos Macknight—sworn. 24th of May 1785.

Admits that he recd £800 from the Treasury since the Act of Part has pass'd but says it was given to him for the hire of a Sloop which Lord Dunmore hired of him & which was lost at Cape Fear.

James Parker Esq—sworn.

The Witness had one fifth concern in this Partnership. Says he was concern'd that his Partner staid so long in the Country not because he was afraid that he would change his principles but he really thought his Life in Danger on acct of his principles.

Determin'd the 11th of June 1785.

## Memorial of Willm McCormick

William McCormick—the Claimant—sworn. 24th of May 1785.

A Loyalist. Did not bear Arms.

Swears in general to the truth of the Memorial which is printed. Is a Native of Scotland & went to North Carolina in 1761. He was in the service of Mr McKnight & Co. when he went out & during the whole time only he did some business for himself. He quitted America in 1777. He never subscribed to any Association or took any Oath to the Rebel State. Genl Howe [1] the Rebel Genl wanted him to subscribe a Test but he refused. He had no Communication with his Partners before they fled & they did not desire him to stay. He came away when he did because he heard he was to be summon'd to take the Oaths & that they would treat him ill if he did not take them. Says the reason of his flying was publickly known. He went to New York But when they went out they pretended to be bound to Spain. He was made a Prize of by a British Man of War the Vessel belonged to the Company. The Ship was detain'd three Weeks & then she was restored this was done by the Interference of Govr Martin who bore testimony to his Character &c. He staid about a Yr at New York & came home in 1778 & has been here ever since. Never bore Arms. He has an Allowance of 100 a Yr from the Treasury which commenced from the 1st Day of Jany 1779 & he now continues to receive it.

Bounty £100 a Yr.

Determin'd ye 2d of July 1785.

## Memorial of Maurice Nowlan

Maurice Nowlan—the Claimant—sworn. 26th of May 1785.

A Loyalist. Bore Arms.

Is a Native of Ireland & went to America in 1770 to New York. He was settled in 1774 at Cross Creek & followed a Mercantile Line & carried out 200 Gãs. He took part with Govt at first & rais'd a Company in 1776 & join'd Coll Macdonald at Cross Creek. Produces a Warrant for the rank of Captn with the

[1] 'Robert Howe of North Carolina, Colonel 2nd North Carolina Continental Regiment, September 1, 1775; Brigadier-General, Continental Army, March 1, 1776; Major-General October 20, 1777. Served to close of war (McCrady, *S. Car. in the Rev., 1775–80*, note 4 on p. 137).

Pay as such. He was four Years & ten Months in Captivity. He broke Gaol at Reading in Oct^r 1780 & got to New York from whence he went in 1781 to Charlestown. He got a Warrant from Col^l Stuart to raise a Company in North Carolina but being obliged to evacuate Wilmington suddenly he was not able to raise the Company. Warrant produced dated 30^th of Oct^r 1781. At the Evacuation of Charlestown he came to Eng^d. He never sign'd any Association or took any Oath. When he was in confinement he was offer'd his whole property if he would join them. He rec^d the pay of Capt^n up to this time & now receives half pay. He has an Allowance of £50 a Y^r from the Treasury which he has had from the 1^st of Jan^y 1783 & he now continues to receive it.

To be stated as one of those who intercepted an Express from Governor Martin.

Bounty £50 a Y^r.

Neil M^cArthur—sworn.

Knew M^r Nowland in 1774. He was a very loyal Subject. He was a Storekeeper. He raised a Company in 1776. He was a long time confined. He married a Dau^r of one W^m White he married in Ireland. W^m White was an Irishman. He is not acquainted with any of his Lands. He knows he had an House at Cross Creek can't tell what he gave for it. Does not know what it was worth but believes £500 S. Would have given £500 for it.

### Further testimony to the Memorial of Maurice Nowlan

Maurice Nowlan—sworn. 2^d of June 1785.

Admits that he was one of the Party who went by the desire of the Rebel Committee to intercept a letter written by Gov^r Martin which they effected. Says however that he did not go by choice. Says he went by Compulsion & that he was taken out of his Bed. Says however that he should have been in no personal Danger if he had avoided going. Says there were two Companies in Arms in America at that time for the purpose of learning their Exercise. One Co was attach'd to America & the other to G. B. He was in that which was attached to America. He was an Assist^t Lieut^t. Being asked why he did not tell this Story when he spoke of his own Case he says he was confused & that he was not asked. Thinks notwithstanding this that a Man may be said to have been uniformly loyal. He chose his Co. from attachment to his friend. He join'd the British because he always meant to do it. Admits that he always thought that the British would succeed.

Alexander M^cKay—sworn.

Did not know that M^r Nowlan was one of the Party to take Capt^n Cunningham till this Day. Says in the Case of Vardy this affected his Opinion because he knew his Sentiments but it does not alter his opinion of Nowlan's Loyalty.

### Memorial of Capt^n John Martin

Determin'd the 9^th of June 1785.

John Martin—the Claimant—sworn. 26^th of May 1785.

Is a Native of Scotland & went to America in 1771. He carried out £100 in Money & Goods to £60. In 1774 He lived in Cumberland County [1] on a Plantation. He join'd the Loyalists in 1776. He was then a Lieut^t. He

A Loyalist & bore Arms.

[1] North Carolina.

was afterwards made a Capt[n] in 1776. He was made a Prisoner at the same time & let out on Parole. He had a Warrant from Col[l] Hamilton in 1779 to raise a Co. He came to Eng[d] the 10[th] of Oct[r] last. He has half Pay as Capt[n] now. His Reg[t] is now in Nova Scotia. He has 4 Children. He applied to the Treasury for an Allowance but he was refused.

Determin'd the 2[d] of June 1785.

### Memorial of Malcolm Love

27[th] of May 1785.

Malcolm Love—the Claimant—sworn.

A Loyalist & Bore Arms.

Is a Native of Scotland. Went to America in 1769. In 1774 & 1775 He was settled at Cross Creek as a Miller & a Blacksmith. In July 1775 he muster'd with the King's friends & constantly went out with the Men. Was at the battle of Moor's Bridge with 35 Men that he had raised for his Lieut[cy]. The Rebels offer'd him a Commission but he refused. He was wounded in four different places & taken Prisoner. The latter end of 1777 he was press'd to take the State Oath & left the Country to avoid taking it. He never took any Oath to them & was obliged to leave the Country in 60 Days. He went to Cape Francois & from thence to Jamaica in 1779 & came to Eng[d] in Oct[r] 1783. He has an Allowance of £30 a Y[r] since the Month of April 1784.

Bounty £30 a Y[r].

Neil M[c]Arthur—sworn.

Knew M[r] Love in Carolina in 1775 & 1776. He always conducted himself as a steady Loyalist & never waver'd. He kept a Blacksmith's Shop in Cross Creek & had a plantation in the Country. He was in a very thriving way. Thinks he might get £200 C. per Ann. by his business.

Heard that he bought Land on Stewarts Creek but does not know it And can't speak to the Value of it.

He knows he bought the Grist Mill of one Munro. He lived there. This was a valuable piece of Land. About 10 or 12 Acres clear'd when Munro lived there.

Says he would have given £200 S. for the 150 Acres & the Mill. He thinks the furniture worth £30 & knows that he was plunder'd of it.

Determin'd y[e] 28[th] of March 1785.

### Memorial of James M[c]Collough

28[th] of May 1785.

James M[c]Collough—the Claimant—sworn.

A Zealous Loyalist.

Is a Native of Ireland & went first to America in 1757 as a private Soldier in the 17[th] Reg[t]. He produces a discharge in 1764. He married in 1766 & settled in New Jersey. He came to Ireland in 1769 & returned to America in 1771 or thereabouts from which time he settled at Hakkensac. He kept a Store there & followed the business of a Weaver. He ever adhered to the Gov[t] of G. Britain. They asked him to associate but he refused they never tender'd an Oath to him. He join'd the British in 1776. He was made Lieut[t] in the Militia at New York. He remain'd at New York till the Evacuation. He traded at New York. He came to Eng[d] in Dec[r] 1783. He applied to the Treasury for an Allowance but obtain'd none. However he rec[d] £20 which he understood to be in lieu of any Subsistence. But it appears that it was in full for all his Losses by the Decision Book. He rec[d] the £20 from the Treasury in the Spring

Bounty £20 in full.

1784. And it appears by the Evidence taken down that the Money was given in lieu of an Allowance.

### Memorial of Sam[l] McCollough

Determin'd the 28th of May 1785.

Sam[l] McCollough—the Claimant—sworn. 28th of May 1785.

Is a Native of Ireland & went to America with his father about the Yr 1773 the last Claimt was his Uncle & was settled there before. He was a Loyalist & obliged to fly from his House & that he did rather than take up Arms. His father died in 1777. He lived afterwards with his Mother. His father kept a Stall in New York. He applied for an Allowance to the Treasury but it was negatived.

A Loyalist.

### Memorial of Neil McArthur [1]

Determin'd the 2d of June 1785.

Neil McArthur—the Claimant—sworn. 28th of May 1785.

Is a Native of Scotland & went to America in 1764 & he lived there till 1776. He lived in Cross Creek & kept a Store. He took part with Col[l] Martin's Loyalists in 1776. He join'd Col[l] MacDonald. Has a Captn's Commission. He continued with the British Troops during the War except when he was Prisoner which he was for more than 2 Yrs. He came to Engd in April 1784. He rais'd a Company in 1781. He got his Warrant from Lord Cornwallis. He had pay for it & has half pay now. He receives 90 a Yr. He has an Allowance of 30 a Yr from the Treasury. Has had it from July last & now continues to receive it.

A Zealous Loyalist. And bore Arms.

Bounty £30 a Yr.

Robert Nelson—sworn. 30th of May 1785.

Knew the Claimant first in the Yr 1771. He came to Cross Creek where he lived. Says he certainly was a Loyalist because he has a Commn & he saw him in Gaol at Halifax in 1776. When he came in 1771 He brought a Cargo of Goods with him & kept a Store. In 1773 Says he was doing a good deal of business & building of Houses. He was building two Houses one at Cross Creek & one at Campbeltown. Says he was very industrious & a Man of Substance.

Maurice Nowlan—sworn.

Has known Mr Neil McArthur ever since he went to Carolina. In 1774 & 1775 He took an active part with Great Britain. He knows his House in Cross Street. He built it & bought the Lot. He values it at £500 C. He would give that for it. It was as good as his own. Knows his House at Campbeltown. He used to let it for 80 a Yr. Thinks it would have sold for £500. He speaks of the whole with the Store &c. when he says £500. Knows a plantation he had near Campbeltown of 640 Acres. It was good Land. More than 50 Acres cleared. He was esteem'd a rich Man at Cross Creek & was in a thriving way. Says he had 6 or 7 Horses. They were valuable Horses. Says some of his Horses were worth 50 apiece. He had 3 or 4 Negroes but can't tell exactly.

Believes he was one of the Commissioners under Govr Martin. Has seen

[1] In *Hist. MSS. Comm.*, *Am. MSS. in R. Inst.*, vol. ii, p. 415, there is an account, dated March 8, 1782, from Neill Macarthur, captain in North Carolina Highlanders, for sundries furnished the loyalists in January 1776. The total for arms and provisions was, in North Carolina currency, £848 4*s.* 6*d.*, or £484 14*s.* in sterling money; exchange being at 175 per cent.

the Commission. He had Boats but they are not charged. He believes that his property has been confiscated & the Negroes sold.

Malcolm Love—sworn.

Knows Mr Neil McArthur since the Year 1769. He was a Mercht in Cross Creek in 1775. He was one of the richest Merchants there. He carried on a better stroke of business than Mr Nowlan. He took part with G. B. & was uniformly loyal. Knows a good deal of his property. Knows his House at Cross Creek. Thinks it was worth near £500 S. in 1775. He knows his House at Campbeltown. It was not so good as the other. Values it at 280 S.

Cannot say whether he was one of the Commrs under Govr Martin. Knows a tract of Land at Beaver Creek 100 Acres. It was Wood Land. He had 2 tracts there one 200 Acres & the other 100. They are woodland principally. Values the 200 Acres at £20 & he values the 100 Acres at £25 S. Knows the 640 Acres at Campbeltown. He would have given £120 for the 200 Acres. The 640 Acres were good land 100 Acres clear'd. Says he was offer'd for it 1500 proc. Says if he *wanted* a plantation & had the cash he would give £750 for it. Knows the two Lots near his House at Cross Creek with a Store &c. Values ye two at £200 S.

Knows the plantation he bought of Stevens thinks 290 Acres. He gave £500 for it. Thinks with his improvements it was worth £500 S.

Knows the piece of Land in the Swamps. It was very good Land 50 Acres. Values it at £42 S.

Knows the Land in Hammonds Creek. Values it at £90 S. Knows the Lot in Elizth Town. Has seen it & values it at £40 Cur.

## Memorial of George Glen

Determin'd ye 31st of May 1785.

George Glen—the Claimant—sworn. 31st of May 1785.

Is a Native of Scotland & went first to America in 1772 & went to settle there in 1774. He meant to purchase a farm & settle there. Carried with him £700 in Cash & £200 in Goods. He settled in Wolfsborough in Novr 1774. He remain'd as quiet as he could on his Estate till 1778. Says they put the test twice to him but he refused to take it. Never sign'd any Association or bore Arms with them but they fin'd him for not serving. They injured his Cattle & did him other Damage because he would not join them & finding he could not be quiet He obtain'd liberty to go away in 1778. He obtain'd a Pass to go to New Providence they did not allow him to take anything with him. They would permit him to sell but he could get nothing but paper Money. He did however sell Goods for 78 hard Dollars which were worth £180. He had two paper Dollars with them. He has recd an Allowance of £20 a Yr from Octr 1783 & now continues to receive it.

A Loyalist & bore Arms.

Bounty £20 a Yr.

Dr Stephen Little—sworn.

Has known George Glen since 1772. He was consider'd by everybody as a thorough Loyalist. He came with property & purchased the farm of Ringe & settled upon it & made considerable Improvements. Had many people at Work upon it. He was a Man of good Character. Knows nothing of the value of the property but knows that he did a great deal to it.

Stephen Holland—sworn.

Knew Glen at Rhode Island but not before the rebellion. Always heard that he was a Loyalist. Remembers his coming to Rhode Island in 1778. He behaved well & zealously at Rhode Island. Knows nothing of his property. He kept a little Store as a Grocer at Rhode Island.

George Meserve—sworn.

First knew Mr Glen in 1774. He was then removed from Portsmouth to Wolfsborough. Always consider'd him as a Loyalist. Knew he bought a right of Land of a friend of his at Wolfsborough & knows that he gave 100 Half Joes in hard Gold for it. It was not then improved but he understood that he laid out a good deal of Money upon it about £700. The Witness had Land adjoining but he had not seen it for many Years. Knows no more of the property.

## Memorial of Donald McDougald

Determin'd the 31st of May 1785.

31st of May 1785.

Donald McDougald—the Claimant—sworn.

Is a Native of Scotland & went to America about 14 Years ago. He settled in Cross Creek. He followed the business of a Taylor. He took about £60 with him. He never join'd the Rebels. They put him in prison because he would not join them. He went to Moors Bridge & was in the Engagement there. He was Prisoner about four Months. They took his House from him & made a Rebel Barrack of it. He went to Charlestown & put himself under the protection of the British Troops & remain'd there till the Evacuation & then he went to Jamaica where he staid near a Year. He has an Allowance of £20 a Yr from the Treasury which he has receiv'd about a Year & an half & he now continues to receive it.

A Loyalist & bore Arms.

Bounty £20 a Yr.

## Memorial of Aaron Vardy

Determin'd the 4th of July 1785.

1st of June 1785.

Aaron Vardy—the Claimant—sworn.

Is a Native of Engd & went out to America in 1770 & settled in North Carolina. In 1776 He join'd the Loyalists. He had a Captn's Commn & acted as Waggon Master. He rais'd the Men for his Commn. He never sign'd any Association or took any part with the rebels or took any Oath. In Novr 1775 He was compell'd by the Rebel Committee to go on an Expedition to intercept a Letter from Govr Martin to his Commrs. He did it thro' fear of being ill used. He was taken Prisoner at Moors Bridge & confined 3 Years & made his Escape into Philadelphia. Since 1778 He has been in public Employment during the whole of the War. He has an Allowance of £25 a Year which he has recd from the 5th of July 1784 & now continues to receive it.

A Loyalist & bore Arms.

Bounty £25 a Yr.

Certificate produced from Lord Cornwallis Lord Rawdon & Govr Martin to Loyalty. Govr Martins goes to his early exertions the others to his doing his Duty in his military situation. Likewise one from Coll McDonald to his raising the Company &c.

Says that Mr Maurice Nowlan was with him on the rebel Expedition.

Robert Nelson—sworn.

Knew the Claimt first in 1774. Says he was a Loyalist & he saw him in Gaol for his Loyalty. Knows nothing of his Property. He kept a Tavern & was a very industrious Man & well attached to Gov[t].

Neil M[c]Arthur—sworn.

Knew M[r] Vardy before 1776. Looked upon him as a Loyalist after he join'd the British. But says he was blamed for joining those people at Cross Creek who went on the Rebel Expedition. Thinks he did wrong in doing it & believes he was attached to the other Party before he join'd them. He kept the principal Tavern there & it was frequented by the Rebels. Admitted before he join'd the British that he was with them & that it was necessary to take their part. When he join'd them he behaved well but before he had no Confidence in him.

Maurice Nowlan—sworn.

Knew M[r] Vardy in America before the Action at Moors Creek. Thinks the Claim[t] was loyal before 1776. But he was concern'd in going with a rebel party to intercept a Letter from Gov[r] Martin. Says it was no injury to the British Cause. Says it was no Secret. There was none loyal but M[r] Vardy & himself. They were not armed. Says he might have avoided it & says M[r] Vardy did not shew any reluctance in going upon this Expedition. Admits that there were two Companies rais'd & that they were of different Sentiments one favorable to G. B. & the other to America. M[r] Vardy was in that favorable to America. M[r] Vardy left this C[o] & join'd the British Army in 1776 & since that time he has behaved with great attachment to Great Britain. He told the Witness that he join'd the Loyalists from an Attachment.

He rented an House in Cross Creek it was well furnished. Can't tell the Value thinks it was worth £100 S. Can't tell what became of it but thinks it was taken by the Enemy. Remembers the Waggon & Horses taken from him valued at £100 C.

Alexander M[c]Ray—sworn.

Knew Aaron Vardy prior to the embodying of the Loyalists in 1776. Before that time He was rather favorable to the then Measures of the Americans. Knew the Company commanded by Roan. Heard that M[r] Vardy was of the Party who took Capt[n] Cunningham they took him at the Witness's House. Look'd upon this Conduct as adverse to G. B. Supposes he went with his inclination. Did not at that time consider him as a good Loyalist. He join'd the British in 1776 & has since acted with uniform loyalty. Did not know his plantation but knew his furniture but can't value it.

Governor Martin—sworn. 24[th] of June 1785.

The Circumstances of this Man & M[r] Nowlan intercepting an Express of Gov[r] Martin he says have recently come to the knowledge of the Witness. Understood that this Man was among the first who took part with this Country. Since he & Nowlan came out upon the Half Pay List Says it has been said that they first took part with the rebels but he does not know it. Does not know that two Companies were establish'd at Cross Creek upon different principles. Says all that he says of Vardy applies to Nowlan.

## Memorial of Isaac Stuart

Determin'd the 9th of June 1785.

1st of June 1785.

Isaac Stewart—the Claimant—sworn.

Was born in Scotland. Went to America 30 Years ago. He never sign'd any Association or took any Oath to the rebels. He was settled at Ninety Six in 1775 When he went to St Augustine to avoid taking the Oath. He has been with the British ever since. He served in the Ma till 1780 & went into the Dragoons in 1781 where he rais'd a troop of Horse. He rais'd 46 Men. He served with this Company till the Evacuation of Charlestown. Has been wounded several times slightly in the Service. Has an Allowance of £40 a Yr from the Treasury which he has recd from the 5th of April 1784 & he now continues to receive it. He has applied for Half pay & hopes to receive it.

A Loyalist. Bore Arms & render'd services to the British Govt.

Bounty £40 a Yr.

## Further testimony to the Memorial of Isaac Stuart

3d of June 1785.

Colonel Cruger—sworn.

Knew Captn Stuart in the Yr 1780. He then found him a Militia Officer. He was then active in the King's Service. Lord Cornwallis desired the Witness to raise a Regt & to name his Officers & he named Mr Stuart for one thinking that he could not find a person more fit. Captn Stuart rais'd his Quota of Men. He was immediately under the Command of Colonel Cruger & he behaved extremely well he found him uniformly loyal. Thinks he might be said to have render'd service. Says he means only that he did his Duty gallantly but does not Doubt that many other officers behaved equally well. He recd the full pay of a Captn of a Troop of Horse. And says he is upon half pay now. Says from his Situation he was able to render Services which others might not have an opportunity of doing. Does not know a Man of the Country who had a Command in any of the Provincial Corps who conducted himself with more credit to himself than Captn Stuart did.

## Memorial of Mrs Mary Price

Determin'd the 8th of June 1785.

2d of June 1785.

Mary Price—the Claimant—sworn.

Is the Widow of Joseph Price who was a Native of Engd & went to America in 1772. He went there as Surgeon to a Regt. He returned to St. Vincents & died there in Jany 1775. He made a Will. But she has it not it was burnt. She was married at New Brunswick in 1772 where she was settled as the Widow of Richd Evans. Her first Husband left her some Money. After Mr Price's Death she remain'd at New Brunswick until 1778. She could not remain in the Jerseys. She brought part of her furniture. Says she could not bring the whole away.

A Loyalist.

She has an Allowance of £30 a Yr from the Treasury which she has recd for about 3 Years & now Continues to receive it. She has besides a Pension of £16 a Year as the Widow of a Surgeon. Certificates produced to Character & the truth of her Memorial by Genl Skinner Govr Franklyn Dr Chandler &c.

Bounty £30 a Yr.

Mrs Price is a Native of America.

Determin'd y[e] 3[d] of June 1785.

## Memorial of Lieut[t] Col[l] Cruger [1]

Lieut[t] Col[l] Cruger—the Claimant—sworn. 3[d] of June 1785.

A zealous & meritorious Loyalist.

Bore Arms & render'd services (most material services) to the British Gov[t].

Is a Native of Jamaica & went to New York an Infant. His father & family were Natives of America & he from his Infancy to the Commencement of the troubles was settled at New York. He was Member of the Council & Chamberlain of the City of New York & was in business as a Merch[t] when the troubles began & always exerted himself in support of Gov[t]. In the Winter of 1774 & 1775 He was after called upon by the Americans to take part with them which he constantly refused. He remain'd at New York after Gov[r] Tryon had quitted the City with a view to stem the Torrent & if possible to restore good order & reestablish Loyalty but in June 1776 He was obliged to fly to Long Island & take refuge in the Woods & Swamps till the arrival of the Kings Troops in Aug[t] when he immediately made a tender of his Services to Gen[l] Howe & in Sept[r] following was appointed Lieut[t] Col[l] of Gen[l] Delanceys Brigade & was on constant Duty till 1778 when he sail'd for Georgia & went with his Batt[n] into the town of Savannah & during the siege [2] he held an important Post in the Line. He commanded the Post at Ninety Six [3] in 1781. He had about 450 [4] Men there. They summon'd him to surrender & he refused the Siege lasted near a Month. He was second in Command at the Engagement of the Eutaw Spring.[5] Thinks he was of material use in saving that Army but wishes to decline the Explanation & leave it to his Witnesses. In 1782 his Health being infirm he had Sir Henry Clinton's permission to come to New York & then by Sir Guy Carleton's leave he came to Eng[d] in the Summer of 1783. He has at present an Allowance from the Treasury of £150 a Y[r] in addition to his Half pay. The Allowance commenced from the time that he was reduced to half pay & he now continues to receive it.

Bounty £150 a Y[r].

Copies of two Letters from Lord Cornwallis to the Claimant read which operate strongly as Certificates the Originals were afterwards produced. D[o] from Sir Guy Carlton to Lord North.

William Waddell—sworn.

Knew Col[l] Cruger at New York. Knew his House it was a Brick House. It was his House & was a good one & in good repair 4 rooms on a floor & two Stories high. Can't tell the Value of it. He was Chamberlain of the Corporation their Estates were £6000 a Y[r] & he had 5 per Cent for receiving the Money. Thinks the House must be worth at least £1200 Currency. Does not know his Land in Charlotte County. He was in good business in the Commission way.

[1] See Additional Notes, p. 394.

[2] There is a Diary of the siege (September 3 to October 20, 1779) in F. Moore, *Correspondence of H. Laurens*, 'Materials for History', pp. 161–73.

[3] *Strictures on Lieutenant-Colonel Tarleton's History*, by R. MacKenzie, contains an interesting account of the defence of Ninety-Six written by Lieutenant Hatton, who was one of the garrison. G. Damer wrote to Lord G. Germain (July 29, 1781), 'Ninety-Six under Cruger made a glorious defence' (*Hist. MSS. Comm.*, *Stopford-Sackville MSS.*, vol. ii, *Papers Relating to the Am. War*, p. 211).

[4] According to Hatton 350 Regulars and 200 Militia.

[5] September 8, 1781.

Lord Cornwallis—sworn. 6th of June 1785.

Did not know Col^l Cruger till the Y^r 1780. He was Lieut^t Col^l under his Command. In consequence of the very good Character which he had heard of him He gave him a very important Post at Ninety Six. He behaved both in his Military & Civil Situation so as to merit the approbation of the whole Country. He saved the Post of Augusta in 1780. In June 1781 He had particular merit in defending the Post of 96 & thinks the Safety of that place owing to him. Behaved well at the Eutaws. And he thinks he may be said to have render'd very essential Services to this Country.

### Memorial of Abel Willard

Determin'd the 4th of June 1785.

Abel Willard—the Claimant—sworn. 4th of June 1785.

The Claimant claims a Compensation for the Loss of his Uncle's Estate who died in 1781. The Claim^t is a Native of America & always took part with G. B. His Uncle [1] was a Loyalist. He lived at Lancaster in Mass. His Uncle took part with G. B. from the first in consequence of which the Americans have confiscated & sold his Estate. He made no Will. He was a married Man & left a Widow (Eliz^th) now living. Nobody has administer'd to him. He left three Brothers his the Claimants father was the Youngest Naon was the eldest Brother is now living took no part & lives in the Country & has Children. Abijah is the second Brother who has been heard here he is living & has Children. The next Brother Levi is dead but has left Children he took no part. The Claim^t's father Joshua remains in the Country & took no part. The Claim^t is the eldest. Abel who is dead & to whom this Gent^n claims was the Youngest & was loyal. Naon & his father conducted themselves exactly in the same Way. Thinks Naon has no right to come here. His father has no right in his Opinion to come here from the same reason. The Widow lives at Boston & the whole Estate is confiscated & sold. She lived in London till 1781. She had no Allowance. Abel Willard had an Allowance of £100 a Year. The Claimant was a Commissary in the Army. He says that Abijah Willard had releas'd his right to him & therefore he thinks he has a right to claim because his Uncle Abijah was the only Man who could claim here.

A Loyalist. But not the Representative of the Deceas'd.

Determination of the Board.

M^r Abel Willard cannot be consider'd in any Degree as the Representative of the Deceas'd because if there had been no Civil War He would not have been entitled to a farthing from the real or personal property His father being alive & of course entitled before the Son. And if the father had been dead this Gent^ns Claim to property coming thro' him could not have been rec^d because it appears to the Board that his father was no Loyalist.

### Memorial of Isaac Tomlinson on behalf of himself & Brother

Determin'd the 4th of June 1785.

Isaac Tomlinson—the Claimant—sworn. 4th of June 1785.

Is a Native of America & his Brother likewise. When the War broke out

[1] Abel Willard, sen.

The two Brothers Loyal.

Both bore Arms.

they were both settled at Woodbury in Connecticut as Merchants. He was uniformly loyal from the first & his Brother. He was in prison in 1775. He never sign'd any Association or took any Oath to the Rebels. He was obliged to quit his property in 1777 in Jan^y. He was then in Confinement & made his Escape. In 1775 His father & themselves were very cruelly treated for their Loyalty. In 1777 He fled to the British on Long Island. He took arms as a Volunteer & afterwards had a Comm^n in the Kings American Dragoons (produces it it is a Lieut^t's Comm^n dated in Feb^y 1781). He remain'd with the Army as a Volunteer till 1781. He rec^d no pay as Volunteer only for a short time he rec^d ½ a Dollar a Day. He rec^d pay to the End of the War 9*s*. a Day. He now receives half Pay which is 3*s*. Came to Eng^d last Dec^r. Never applied for any temporary Support either here or at New York.

Joshua Chandler—sworn.

Knew both these Gent^n in America & the father they were all Loyalists they were ill treated in Consequence of their Loyalty. Says it was supposed that the Sons had left a considerable property in the hands of the father but does not know it. Never heard to what amount. The young Men were in considerable business. They kept a dry goods Store. Thinks they might easily be worth £2300. Says the father gave them more than that. Says it was the general reputation that they had left 10 or £12000 C. Thinks they might have left 2 or £3000. Knows that the Rebels made a considerable Demand upon him & it was in Contemplation to bring Suit ag^t him but he left the Country before he could know it. Says he thinks that in 1781 the father could not have paid the Money in paper. Says when he left the Country in 1779 Congress paper was 30 for one. Thinks that Currency was stopp'd in the Year 1780. Says he has known many instances where judgment was recover'd ag^t a Tory they would not take their own paper. Thinks it probable that in this case they would insist upon old Tomlinson paying them in Money. If a Tory was able to pay they always made him pay. Speaks to the services of these Gent^n. Says this Brother was very active in raising a Corps. Does not think the two Brothers equally meritorious. Isaac has the most merit as having been longest in the Service.

Determined the 7^th of June 1785.

## Memorial of Jonathan Clawson

6^th of June 1785.

Jonathan Clawson—the Claimant—sworn.

A Steady Loyalist.

Did not bear Arms.

Is a Native of America of New Jersey. Was settled at Woodbridge in 1774 & 1775. Was a Farmer. Never took part with the Rebels but join'd the British first in Dec^r 1776 they came by his House. He was obliged to quit his own House the Feb^y following & from that time he remain'd with the British. He never sign'd any Association or took any Oath. The Rebels molested him so much on acc^t of his supplying the British Troops &c. that he could not stay at his own House. He moved his whole family at the same time. He never bore Arms & cannot plead any particular Service to this Country. His Son was taken by the rebels & put to Death.

Certificates produced to Loyalty from Gov^r Franklin Gen^l Skinner & M^r Kempe.

He applied for temporary Support & Has £40 reported to him in full to carry him to Nova Scotia. He had £50 given to him at New York by the Commr in Chief in 1781. Bounty £40 in full.

Thomas Crowell—sworn.

Is an American & lived near Mr Clawson. Has known Mr Clawson since he was 8 or 9 Years old. He was always a Loyalist. Knows the farm on which he lived but does not know the Extent. Knows it was his. It was a very good farm. He was industrious & as fast as he rais'd Money he bought land. Can't value it exactly but thinks it must be worth £7 or £8 C. per Acre before the troubles.

Knows he had a large Stock but can't tell the Number. He had several Horses & very good ones supposes 7 or 8. Should imagine about 30 Cattle. He had a Son who served under the Witness who afterwards was taken up as a Spy & executed. He had left Amboy before Mr Clawson left therefore does not know anything of their seizing his Cattle &c.

**Memorial of Robert Buchanan**

Determin'd the 6th of June 1785.

6th of June 1785.

Robert Buchanan—the Claimant—sworn.

Is a Native of Scotland & went to America in 1760 to serve an Apprenticeship in a Store there. In 1774 & 1775 He was in business for himself & had been so near ten Years. He lived at Anapolis. When the troubles broke out he took an active part against the Americans. He never join'd with them in a single measure. He was frequently insulted but never took any Oath or sign'd any Association. Produces a Parole which he enter'd into in 1776. It was not to give any intelligence &c but he reserved to himself a right to go to Engd or the West Indies. Says the Committee understood that he meant to join Lord Dunmore. About March 1776 He saild from Philadelphia for Lisbon. The property he left behind him was chiefly Debts & some few Goods.

Decision—The Claimant is a Loyalist But the Board are of Opinion that he has sustain'd no Loss as such.

Produces a Letter from Govr Eden to Govr Tryon recommending him for a passage dated 10th of April 1776. Produces a Newspaper of Maryland containing a Protest with the Claimants name to it protesting against the Non importation Agreement & the resolution not to pay Debts. Says the Assembly talked of Seizing his papers & therefore he sign'd the parole. Three Members of the Assembly called upon him to sign it & he sign'd it. He was in partnership with a Brother & Mr John Bristol.[1] Mr Bristowe[1] came over to Engd before him but went back in 1779 & has been there ever since. James Buchanan resided in Engd & Scotland during the whole War. Bristowe[1] took the Oaths to them as he believes. Knew that he was going to be a Subject of the States. Says there was a Settlement made at that time & produces a paper which appears to be an Authority given to Mr Bristowe[1] to settle the affairs & to be accountable. Says that Mr Bristowe[1] has lost as much by the trade as himself. Thinks the Goods left behind which belonged to the Company were worth about £700 S. Their Debts outstanding were about £6300. This the neat balance after paying all the Debts due by the Store & the partnership. Of this his proportion was

[1] ? Briscoe.

one third besides the Stores which he thinks ought not to be charged because the Stores have not been confiscated. He claims only for his 3$^{d}$. These goods were sold by a Factor on Acc$^{t}$ of the Partnership. This factor or Clerk was appointed by M$^{r}$ Briscowe with his Approbation. And he was appointed to collect the Debts likewise. He is dead & M$^{r}$ Briscoe is in poss$^{n}$ of his Effects & will bring him to Acc$^{t}$. Does not say that they have lost anything by this Clerk. He expects further Remittances from M$^{r}$ Briscowe & says he will acc$^{t}$ to him for what he receives. He lost no other property of his own.

Besides this He lost his Commercial Situation in the House by which he made £200 a Year & charges it as a Loss for 5 Years. Says there was no Agreement between the Partners to take different sides. Admits that he has been in business at Glasgow for these last 4 or 5 Y$^{rs}$ ago as an Underwriter. Says that he is going to Nova Scotia & probably will go from thence to Maryland.

George Chalmers Esq—sworn.

Knew the Claimant in America. He was always understood to be a Loyalist. He was active about the Protest in 1774.

James Brooks—sworn.

Knew the Claim$^{t}$ in Anapolis. He always esteem'd him a Loyalist. But he went away very early.

### Memorial of Christopher Sower [1] Jun$^{r}$

Determin'd the 9$^{th}$ of June 1785.

Christopher Sower—the Claimant—sworn. 7$^{th}$ of June 1785.

A Loyalist & render'd services to the British Gov$^{t}$. Did not bear Arms.

Is a Native of Germantown. At the breaking out of the troubles He was settled there as a Printer. He took part from the first with Gov$^{t}$. He published a paper called the Germantown Gazette. He published papers favorable to Gov$^{t}$ but frequently refused papers ag$^{t}$ the Interests of this Country. He never sign'd any Association or paid a Substitute but his property was seiz'd to pay the fine & he refused to take the Overplus. He was a Member of a religious Society who excommunicated all those who took part ag$^{t}$ G. B. He join'd Sir W$^{m}$ Howe in 1777. He has collected Intelligence & served as a Guide for the Army. He was taken Prisoner & one of the American Soldiers lamed him by striking him with a Musket on the Arm. He remain'd with the Army to the End of the War. He has an Allowance of £40 a Year from the Treasury which he has rec$^{d}$ from the 5$^{th}$ of April 1784 & now continues to receive it.

Bounty £40 a Y$^{r}$.

Colonel Beverly Robinson—sworn.

He knew the Claimant after he came with the British Army to New York. Says he was employ'd by the Witness in a confidential manner. And he always found his Acc$^{ts}$ to be true. He was employed to get intelligence from Pensylvania. He always found him very zealous & ready to do everything in his power to forward the Service.

[1] The Sowers were German Baptists. The elder, Christopher, died in 1784. The younger (*b.* 1756, *d.* 1799) settled at St. John, New Brunswick, and published there the colonial *Royal Gazette*. In 1792 he was Deputy Paymaster-General of the colony (Sabine, op. cit., vol. ii, p. 323). According to W. Chipman, writing in 1795, Sower was and had always been 'the most seditious firebrand in the province' (*Winslow Papers*, p. 419).

General Hyde [1]—sworn.

The Claimant acted upon one Occasion as a Guide to some troops under the Witness's Command. He executed that business extremely well. He was in no Danger from it & it was not a matter of much Consequence. He believes that he was consider'd as a Man who might be depended upon. Has often heard Major André speak of him to that Effect.

Sam^l Shoemaker—on his Affirmation.

Has known the Claimant from his Infancy. He always esteem'd him a good honest Man. Always looked upon him to be uniformly loyal in every Instance. Has understood from several Officers that he was very useful & very active. He says his father was esteem'd a Man of pretty large property. Recollects his House & Printing Office. Believes there might be 3½ Acres. Can't value it but being told that he values it at £600 S. Says with the Improvements it can't be much overdone. Says he knows that the father's property has been confiscated & that it is a very hard Case. He was of a particular religious Sect & wore a Beard & they singed his Beard & insulted him. Has heard from Philadelphia that the father is dead. Says the Sect to which M^r Sowers belonged were all loyal.

Will^m Rankin—sworn.

Carried on a Correspondence with Christopher Sowers when the Witness was without the Lines. He was not then in the Service of America. It was matter of considerable Consequence that they corresponded about. Saw the Claim^t when he was a Prisoner & understood that he had been illtreated. Sowers was much respected. Knows nothing of his property. Knew that he carried Arms in Virginia.

The Rev^d M^r Battwell—sworn.

Did not know the Claim^t till he saw him at New York But has heard of him & knows that he was a Man of some influence with his Countrymen & has heard that he exerted to keep the Germans steady to Great Britain. Mentions a piece of service that he did in 1778 by sending a person into the heart of York County Pensylvania to encourage the Loyalists to stand forth & the Messenger returned with an offer of their Services to the Comm^r in Chief. Is sure that M^r Sowers was of great use in this business & has frequently heard Major André say so. He kept a Store at New York & gave it up to be of more use at Head Quarters. Believes he serv'd Gov^t at his own Expence in order to appear more independent & be of more Use. Has heard Major André say that if he chose it He would get a Capt^n's Comm^n for the Claimant at any time. Can't speak to his Losses.

William Barrett—sworn.

Was a Serj^t in the Army & was taken Prisoner & confined at German Town in 1777. The Claimant then lived in that Town & was publickly known to be a Loyalist. He was as much as he dared friendly to the British Prisoners.

[1] Colonel West Hyde acted, along with André, as Commissioner to exchange prisoners in November 1778 (*Hist. MSS. Comm., Am. MSS. in R. Inst.*, vol. i, p. 342). He became Lieutenant-General in 1793 (*Annual Register*, 1793).

Joseph Fox—sworn.

Says Christopher Sower borrowed 12 Guineas of him for which he has his Note of hand—for the purpose of assisting him in getting his Passage to England in 1781 as he understood upon some business of the Loyalists. He was always loyal.

The Claimant—called in again.

He produces a little Pamphlet written in German which he says he published & that it was calculated to serve the Cause of Great Britain.

Determin'd the 9th of June 1785.

**Memorial of Christopher Sower Sen**

Christopher Sower Jun^r—sworn. 7th of June 1785.

A Loyalist & all the family Loyal. The Son entitled as Representative of the father for the family to what follows.

His father died in 1784. He is the eldest Son & Child. There was a Will found in his House but not signed or seal'd Written by himself. In the first place He leaves something to one of his Sisters. He left 7 Children. He names them himself—Daniel—Peter—David—Samuel—Catherine & Hester. He first leaves to Catharine something for keeping House. He next leaves the Money in the House & some Books to five of the Children. But he says he has a Copy of the Will & promises to produce it to-morrow—therefore his testimony is postponed to to-morrow.

Samuel Shoemaker—affirms.

House &c in German Town £400.

Knew the old Man in America for many Years. He was a Man well attached to this Country believes no Man more so. Very much ill used & distress'd by the Rebels. He is the only instance that he ever knew of Confiscation where the person resided in the Country all the time. Says the father is dead & this Son is the eldest. Some of them he believes were Minors. One Bro^r who went to the Bahama Islands was a Loyalist but does not know the Loyalty of all the family but believes they were in general Loyal. Has before spoke to the Printing Office. Does not know an Acre & ½ which he had in the middle of Germantown. Knows the Lots which were called his in Bowmans Lane. The Land was not valuable in that Situation. But says such Land might be worth £20 an Acre C. The Quantity Claim'd 9 Acres. Remembers the Saw Mill & Paper Mill. Says it was a valuable property with ½ an Acre adjoining. The Buildings were considerable & thinks they would have sold for £700 C. at any time. Does not recollect an House & 2 Acres which he had near it. Recollects that he had a tract of Woodland in Roxburgh. Woodland was valuable in that Quarter. Recollects he had a piece of Land on Reyser's Lane that was valuable for it was Meadow Ground. The Quantity Claim'd is 6½ Acres. Does not know the Quantity but thinks it must be worth £25 an Acre C. Believes he had a great number of German Bibles. Knows part of these were destroy'd by the Rebels. He kept a Drug Shop. He can't value the Drugs.

Determin'd y^e 9th of June 1785.

**Memorial of Isaac Lawton**

Isaac Lawton—the Claimant—sworn. 8th of June 1785.

A Loyalist.

Is a Native of America born in Portsmouth in Rhode Island. In 1774 & 1775 He lived at Newport & kept a Vessel for trade. He took part with the

Kings Troops as soon as they came & was insulted in Oct^r^ 1775 for his loyalty & publickly carted. He indicted them for this but they producing Evidence ag^t^ him he was obliged to desist from it. About two or three Months before the Kings Troops arrived he sign'd a paper with M^r^ Wanton being told that he should have been sent 100 Miles into the Country. Does not know what the paper was. Never took any Oath to them & never took up Arms for them. He join'd the troops when they came. He served in Col^l^ Joseph Wanton's Corps & bore Arms as a private Man. And when they evacuated Rhode Island He went with them to New York Where he staid till Oct^r^ 1783 & then he came to Eng^d^. He came to Eng^d^ in April last. He is settled at New Brunswick & came over to have his Claim heard. He has applied to the Treasury & has a Sum of £40 given to him to carry him back to Nova Scotia.

Did not bear Arms.

Bounty £40 in full.

### Memorial of John Brailsford

Determin'd y^e^ 22^d^ of June 1785.

10^th^ of June 1785.

John Brailsford—the Claimant—sworn.

Is a Native of England & went first to America with his father to Charlestown in Nov^r^ 1775. His father Rob^t^ Brailsford died in Eng^d^ in 1779. He return'd to Eng^d^ in 1778. The Rebellion was began when they went there. He went to live on an Estate which he had bought in 1772. About 6 Months after they arrived it became necessary to declare his Sentiments & he declared for G. B. There was nothing tender'd to him until the Oath of Abjuration—the Claim^t^ was between 16 & 17 Y^rs^ of Age when he went there. His father refused the Oath for himself & Son. In June 1778 he was accused of High Treason & imprison'd for 17 Days. He was releas'd on condition that he would come to Eng^d^ which he did do with the Claim^t^. Between Nov^r^ 1775 & June 1778 He did nothing for himself but followed the directions of his father. Knew of his father refusing the Oath for him & says it was with his Consent. After he heard that Charlestown was taken He returned with his Mother & Sisters & he did Duty in the Garrison as a Volunteer without pay. He staid there till the Evacuation & then went to Jamaica with his Mother & Sisters. He came to Eng^d^ in March 1784. He applied to the Treasury for relief but obtain'd no Allowance.

His father & he both Loyalists.

Did not bear Arms.

Robert Dee—sworn.

Knew Rob^t^ Brailsford. The Witness has a Claim here for a share of these Lands. Rob^t^ Brailsford was the father of the Claimant. He & W^m^ Sands & Jos^h^ Hogge (Agent for M^r^ Weyman) bought M^r^ Boss's Share. They bought it in April 1774. He gave him £500 S. for his own share besides supporting his family & giving him Money to recover the title. He the Witness went over & the title was then in Dispute. It was disputed by the Settlers. He is an Englishman. He stood trial with one M^rs^ Sturt a Settler & cast her in 1777. It was determin'd under the rebel Gov^t^ by Rebel Judges who were Lawyers. He served others with Ejectment & was obliged to come away in 1778 himself. Three other persons who had 500 tracts gave up. The Witness was a Loyalist. Knows of the general Survey made by James Peart. Rebecca Sturt quitted the poss^n^. She lived on the river May. He gave 100 Gās for his Share of it. Thinks it might cost more to M^r^ Brailsford. He sold 50 Acres to M^r^ Peart that is gave it to him. He values the Lands one with another at £1 per Acre. Recollects that some of the Settlers had Grants from the province but says Mrs Sturt had not. Looks upon his title as better than their Grants. He brought Ejectments agt those who had no Grants that Question was never tried. Govr Bull knew the business he came upon & says that he said his title was good.

The Claimant—called in again.

Produces an Agreement between his father & the Surveyors to survey the May Barony—read—& it appears that James Peart agrees for £100 5*s.* or for Lands equal in value to 100 Gās to resurvey the whole Patent & to make all necessary Plans & Drawings. Says his father afterwards had Separate Drawings made of many of the tracts which cost him a considerable Sum of Money.

Produces an Affidavit from John Rivers & James Peart to Mr Brailsford taking possession of some of the Lands in the May patent sworn at Charlestown in the Year 1777. Rivers was the Settler who bought some of the Land of Mr Brailsford afterwards. The Afft relates to his taking possn of 5888 Acres. Knew Mr Dee in America but does not recollect his going to Law with any of the Settlers.

Lieutt Govr Bull—sworn. 11th of June 1785.

Knew Mr Brailsford. He was a Loyalist as he believes. Thinks by the Limitation Laws of the Province his Grants would be good agt the old Grants of the Proprietors upon the Idea that 7 Yrs possession gives a colourable title. Has understood that Mr Brailsford had got some people to compound but is positive that it was not determin'd in a Court of Law. If he had known of Mr Hodgsons patent in the May Barony He should not have thought it proper to have granted in this Spot but if the Lands were not located He should not have scrupled to locate it. Does not know that the right was lost by not being exercised & put into Location. When the Crown purchased in 1728 of the proprietors all rights were extinguish'd not put into Location excepting some few reserved Baronies. Does not know whether the Barony of May was one of those Baronies. Thinks that where he had granted & the Settlers had been in possession 7 Years his Grant would be agt Hodgson's right. Says he should not have interfer'd if they had located & if there was a Survey there must have been a Location. Thinks there could have been no such tract of Land as the Barony of May without Survey & Location. If there had been a Survey it must have been found in the Office of Survey. If there had been a Survey & nothing done for 40 Years He should have not granted because if he did he should have thought it would produce litigation. Says if there had been an antient Survey it may be found in the Office unless the Deeds had been destroy'd by fire & He adds that no fire of Deeds has happen'd since the Year 1783. Says that he knows a similar Instance of a Mr Colleton who had a Barony upon Pon Pon river of which he believes there had been an antient Survey but not being able to find out where the Lands were Govr Bull considers it to be extinguish'd & he knows Mr Colleton consider'd it to be so.

James Simpson—sworn.

Knew very little of Robt Brailsford. He must have produced an original

Grant of the Land besides the right to take out a Barony if he did not he ought not to recover. Says that in all those Settlers who had possession by grants under Gov$^{r}$ Bull &c they had an absolute title by possession. Says he has been defective. Remembers M$^{r}$ Brailsford coming into the Country after the Courts of Justice were shut up. Does not know that there was not any regular Administration of Justice after the Rebel Government prevailed.

Says that in order to found a title to any Land it would be necessary for M$^{r}$ Brailsford to produce an original Grant of the particular Land claimed. The Grant of the Honour of Landgrave alone gives no right to particular Land. But even if he had an original Grant & could deduce his title clearly under it yet a subsequent Grant with 7 Y$^{rs}$ possession under it would by the Limitation Act of the Province be a good title ag$^{t}$ the former Grantee especially after so great a lapse of time.

He is of opinion that the Claim$^{t}$ merely producing the Grant of the Honor of Landgrave without a subsequent Grant of the Land in question has fail'd in America of proving his title.[1]

### Memorial of Colin Clark

Determin'd the 13$^{th}$ of June 1785.

Colin Clark—the Claimant—sworn. 13$^{th}$ of June 1785.

Is a Native of Great Britain & went to America to settle in 1771 & settled in North Carolina. He was settled at Windsor at the Commencement of the troubles in N$^{o}$ C$^{a}$. He was then in trade for himself. He was always a Loyalist. Is not certain whether he took an Oath to them or not prevaricates a great deal about it & admits that he did take an Oath but says it was about delivering up his Arms. Afterwards says he does not know what was in the Oath. This was in the Year 1775. He left Windsor in March 1778. He never took any other Oath. He had shut up his Store for six Months before he came away. He went to New York in April 1778. He quitted the province because he would not take the Oath of Allegiance & Abjuration. He took Arms with the British at Savannah in 1779. He came to Eng$^{d}$ in 1778 & went out again to Bermuda in 1779 & from thence to Savannah where he took Arms as a M$^{a}$ Man & did Duty as such during the siege. He left Savannah in April 1780 & went to Providence & returned in the latter end of the Year to Charlestown & staid with the British till he came to Eng$^{d}$ in 1784. Has no Allowance from the Treasury. He carried out £400 in goods in 1771. In 1778 when he was banished he admits that he might have disposed of his property. He brought away 14 Hogsheads of Tobacco. Says that a Hogshead of Tobacco was worth about £40 S. When he left Windsor He did not sell his Lands because he left his family behind. In 1777 they told him they would allow him to take away his property if he pleased but if he left it they would confiscate it. And he sign'd a paper of Confiscation.

A Loyalist.

The Board are of opinion that M$^{r}$ Clark has sustain'd no Loss which can be placed to his acc$^{t}$ because his Flag of Truce was contrary to all Rules & his family appear to be in possession of his property at Windsor. The Goods lost at Wilmington were matter of Speculation. And his Schooner which was lost in the Service of Gov$^{t}$ was lost at Sea & he must stand the risque.

### Memorial of Humphrey Roberts

Determin'd the 22$^{d}$ of June 1785.

Humphrey Roberts—the Claimant—sworn. 13$^{th}$ of June 1785.

Is a Native of Eng$^{d}$ & went to America in 1755 & settled at Norfolk in

[1] See on the South Carolina land system section 1 of W. Roy Smith, *S. Car. as a Royal Province, 1719–76*.

A Loyalist.
Did not bear Arms.

Virginia. He was settled at Portsmouth at the Commencement of the troubles as a Merch[t] & kept a Store there. In Nov[r] 1775 He had taken a decided part in favor of G. B. & he was alarmed for his Safety & was obliged to sleep on board his own Ship. He removed his Effects on board in Dec[r] 1775. He join'd Lord Dunmore in this Month & continued under his Direction till July or August 1776. He went then to Augustine with his property & arrived there in Sept[r] 1776. He staid there 12 Months & then went to New York. He arrived in Eng[d] in March 1779 & has been here ever since. He had £500 about 4 Years ago given to him but he never rec[d] an annual Allowance. M[r] Roberts's Son receives an Allowance of £100 a Y[r] from the Treasury. His Wife is an American & lives at Portsmouth. His property has not been confiscated but is all in the poss[n] of the family. He had an Order to go out again with Lord Dunmore when he rec[d] the £500. But not being on the List of American Sufferers He could not get his Passage Money & that was the reason of his not going out.

Bounty £500 in full.

Determin'd y[e] 22[d] of June 1785.

## Memorial of James Graham

20[th] of June 1785.

James Graham—the Claimant—sworn.

A Loyalist.

Is a Native of Scotland & went to America first in 1755. Settled there as a Merch[t] & left America in 1771 & came to London & settled here as a Merch[t]. In 1778 He went to America partly on business & partly to amuse himself. He went to South Carolina where he was called upon to take an Oath to the States which he refused & he was order'd to quit the Country. He went to S[t] Augustine & afterw[ds] came to Savannah during the siege & remain'd there till we took Charlestown & then came to Eng[d] where he has resided ever since. He is now in trade here the firm of the House Graham & Simpson. He bore Arms at the siege of Savannah but in no Corps in common with many others.

John Jamieson—sworn.

Knew M[r] Graham's property on Hutchinson's Island. Says it was valuable & worth £12 per Acre without the Buildings which were considerable. Never remembers Land in his Life sold upon the Island for £12 per Acre. If it had been sold for £12 or any other Sum per Acre probably the Money would have been paid by instalments in two or three Years.

Can't speak to the 90 Acres or the uncultivated Tracts.

Knew the Land on the Island but does not know what Stock M[r] Graham had. Can't tell what it would cost to put it into a State of Cultivation. Knows that some people have talked of 8 or 10 per Acre but cannot tell. Says it must have cost a great deal speaks positively with certainty to its costing more than £1000 but won't go farther & when asked whether it would cost £1500 he pauses about giving an Answer to it.

Determin'd the 20[th] of June 1785.

## Memorial of Rev[d] Will[m] Andrews

20[th] of June 1785.

William Andrews—the Claimant—sworn.

Is a Native of Ireland & went to America in 1770 as a Missionary under the Society for propagating the Gospel. In 1773 He obtain'd a Living from Lord

Dunmore in Southampton County. He obtain'd the Living which he has lost in 1779 the Living of Portsmouth. They required of him to conform in 1779 but he refused it & would not pray for the Congress. In 1776 He was Rector of Suffolk & he was threaten'd in the Reading Desk if he pray'd for the King by a Rebel Col[l]. However he did pray for him. In 1780 He was knocked down because he was an Enemy to Independence. He left Suffolk & went to Portsmouth in order to get out of the Country. When he changed Livings He was obliged to desist from praying for the King. His Wife was a great Rebel & her friends were the Occasion of his having preferment. She is now dead. Upon Gen[l] Arnold coming to Portsmouth he join'd him & he continued with the Army till York Town was taken & was Chaplain to the Garrison of Portsmouth & York Town. He was tried for his Life in 1781 & banished from that Country. He has an Allowance of £80 a Y[r] from the Treasury which he has rec[d] from the 10[th] of Oct[r] 1782 & he now continues to receive it.

A Loyalist.

Bounty £80 a Y[r].

Says the Living of Suffolk was about £10 a Y[r] less than that of Portsmouth. Thinks the Living of Portsmouth was worth £235 a Y[r]. Colonel Dundas being called upon recollects that he had the living of Portsmouth & that the Glebe was said to be valuable.

Living £150 a Y[r].

Says that there is a Rebel Clergyman appointed to his Living.

Being asked whether he has any Witnesses to produce who may be material to his Case—He states what he meant them to prove & upon reconsidering the Matter & being told that what the Witnesses would speak to is not very material He says he does not propose to call any Witnesses.

## Memorial of Philip Barton Key

21[st] of June 1785.

Determin'd the 22[d] of June 1785.

Philip Barton Key—the Claimant—sworn.

Is a Native of Maryland. Lived in Anapolis when the rebellion broke out. He was studying the Law & was under Age. In 1775 He refused to sign the Association. In 1777 when the British fleet went by he was called upon by the Rebel Gov[r] to arm & he refused. Sir Rob[t] Eden quitted in 1776 & the British fleet pass'd by in Aug[t] 1777. He was frequently called upon to serve in their M[a] & always refused & never in any one instance conformed to their Gov[t]. When he refused in Aug[t] 1777 They insisted upon his not coming within 7 Miles of Navigable Water. In consequence of which he left the province in Dec[r] 1777 & join'd the Army in Philadelphia. Sir W[m] Howe gave him permission to raise a C[o] & he rais'd 40 Men & had a Comm[n] of Capt[n] dated in March 1778 which Comm[n] he produces. He served in that Corps of Maryland Loyalists till Dec[r] 1782 when he came home on Acc[t] of his health & has been here & in France ever since. He applied to the Treasury for an Allowance but he receives none. He has the Half pay of a Capt[n]. He had Pay in that Country. He was indicted & attainted of High Treason in 1777 (produces a Copy of it). That Attainder has never been taken off & his Lands have been confiscated in Consequence of it.

A Loyalist.

Bore Arms & receives Half Pay of a Capt[n].

His Brother was a firm Rebel. It was not recommended to the two Brothers to take different sides.

James Brooks—sworn.

Knew the Claimant & his father in America. Says that he muster'd with the Americans for a very short time for the latter end of 1775 & the beginning of 1776. Does not know or to have heard that he refused to sign the Association. The elder Brother took the other side. He recollects his refusing to take up Arms for the Americans when the British fleet was there. His father had a considerable landed Estate & died in 1770. And left a Will not executed by which the personalty would pass. Recollects a Deed drawn in 1775 by which the elder Brother gave sev$^{l}$ tracts of Land to the Younger. The Witness wrote the Deed. Recollects the names of all the Estates in the Deed. But can't value them. Says when persons take Grants from the Proprietors of Maryland they generally pay 1*s*. an Acre besides the fees. Thinks the fees upon such Grants would not amount to more than £5 or £6 per Grant. Says it was not the Custom for the proprietors to bind them to cultivate. There was a great extent of uncultivated Lands in the province of Maryland & still remains a great Quantity of ungranted Lands. This Deed was executed in the Month of Sept$^{r}$ 1775.

**Memorial of Susannah Marshall**

Determin'd the 22$^{d}$ of June 1785.

Susannah Marshall—the Claimant—sworn. 21$^{st}$ of June 1785.

She & her Husband Loyalists.

Is a Native of Wales & went to America in 1774. Her Husband was an Irishman. They went to Baltimore & they carried out about £500 S. They kept a Lodging House. Her Husband left her in 1775. He refused to go with the rebels to demand the Arms of Sir Rob$^{t}$ Eden.[1] Her Husband soon after went to Providence & the West Indies & he died. He refused to take any part & therefore he could not stay in the province. They obliged her to keep several rebel soldiers till 1776. When Lord Dunmore issued a proclamation She refused & was obliged to quit her House otherwise she would have been tarr'd & feather'd. When she refused to take these Soldiers the Rebels seized a great many of her goods to the amo$^{t}$ of £50 S. They put a Stop to her Debts to the amount of £100 more. She sold the remaining effects afterwards for Money with which she afterwards bought Flour Hams &c. She sold all sorts of spirituous Liquors. When she sold her effects she put her Hams &c on board & took three Frenchmen on board. She was taken by James Wallace[2] & her Cargo was condemn'd & sold. In 1777 She had about £800 C. in paper Money with which she bought the Hams &c. She came to Eng$^{d}$ in Oct$^{r}$ 1777. In June 1783 She had an Allowance of £20 a Y$^{r}$ which she continues to receive. She never had an Allowance before.

£40.

Bounty £20 a Y$^{r}$.

Will$^{m}$ Lloyd—sworn.

Knew M$^{rs}$ Marshall & her Husband at Baltimore. They were both loyal. They kept a Lodging House & sold Liquors. The Witness was at Baltimore after she quitted it. Has heard that her House was Damaged but never heard what Damage. Remembers her selling her furniture & going to the Head of Elk. Remembers that she had several American Soldiers & Sailors & believes they quarter'd more upon her than if she was Inclined to them. They were looked

[1] April 28, 1775. See Steiner, op. cit., p. 90.
[2] *b.* 1731, *d.* 1803. He became Captain in 1771 and was knighted in 1777.

upon to be people of Property has heard that they were supposed to be worth £800 C. Says he knew their House & it was tolerably well furnished.

### Memorial of William Hest

Determin'd y[e] 22[d] of June 1785.

William Hest—the Claimant—sworn. 22[d] of June 1785.

Is a Native of Eng[d] & went to settle in America in 1763 & settled at Charlestown. When the troubles broke out He was always loyal. He left the Country because he would not take the Oath of Abjuration. Never sign'd any association. He refused the Oath in 1778 & was order'd to leave the Country. He never bore Arms for us. But he was obliged to turn out in their M[a] when Sir Peter Parker was off the town. Says he took a Gun which would not go off to prevent his being insulted. Never served afterwards. He quitted Charlestown in 1778 in July with Sir Edm[d] Head. Was permitted to sell his property & he converted it into Rice & embarked it on board the Hope. He came to Eng[d] in 1778. He applied to the Treasury for temporary Support but his Application was negatived.

A Loyalist but served in the American M[a] till he came away.

Claims for a Loss of business which for some Years previous to the troubles was at least £500 a Y[r] S.

Tho[s] Corbett—sworn.

Has known the Claimant from 1767. He avoided entering into the Dispute at all & was neutral. Says the Laws of the Country compell'd him to take up Arms ag[t] G. B. the Witness took up Arms himself. He never saw M[r] Hest in Arms. Believes him to be loyal & that he quitted that Country because he would not take the Oath. Knows that he was Part Owner of the Ship Hope with Sir Edm[d] Head & M[r] Kincaid &c.

### Memorial of James Parker [1] Esq.

Determin'd the 4[th] of July 1785.

James Parker—the Claimant—sworn. 23[d] of June 1785.

Swears in general to the truth of the facts set forth in his Memorial. He says he was attach'd to this Country from the beginning. Never conformed in a single Instance to their Gov[t]. Has borne Arms frequently ag[t] the Rebels first at Kemps Landing. Believes that he was detain'd longer a Prisoner by the French at the request of the Congress because he would be of great service to G. B. if exchanged. This is confirmed by Certificates from Sir Henry Clinton & the Duc de Harcourt annex'd to his Memorial.

Produces an Extract from an Act of North Carolina by which it appears that his Name is in that Act. Likewise produces an Extract from another Act in Carolina pass'd in Jan[y] 1785 by which all Confiscated Property then unsold was directed to be sold & Commissioners appointed. He has no doubt but the whole of his property in Carolina has been confiscated & sold.

He had the Office of Postmaster for some Years & in the Y[r] 1774 it produced £30 a Y[r] but he gave it to one of his Clerks. Admits that he might have been removed.

To state simply that he was Postmaster of Virginia & a considerable Merchant.

[1] In *Hist. MSS. Comm., Am. MSS. in R. Inst.*, vol. ii, p. 38, there is an order (September 22, 1779) to issue rations to Messrs. Parker, Crammel, and Blair and their families, being refugees from Virginia.

Says that in all his Concerns He thinks he might clear per Ann. £1200 a Year S.

Bounty £150 a Yr.

Has long had an Allowance of £150 a Yr from the Treasury & now receives it.

Governor Martin—sworn. 24th of June 1785.

Knew Mr Parker in Carolina but for a short time. Says he opposed all the Measures of the Rebellion from the beginning. Understood that he was a very considerable Mercht at Norfolk & was very useful to Lord Dunmore. He was well acquainted with him afterwards at New York. Says he attended the Army as a Volunteer from the time that he came to New York. Says he recommended him to Genl Matthews & Genl Matthews told the Witness that Mr Parker had been of material Use to him. Thinks upon the whole that he has been of considerable Service to Govt.

Captn Stair Agnew—sworn.

He was Prisoner with Mr Parker in France. He has always heard when in France that the reason for detaining him was that if they restored him he might be of great use in America. This was in common with four other Gentn. Produces a Letter from the Duc de Harcourt to Mr Parker. Has always understood Mr Parker to be a Man of Property.

Determin'd the 25th of June 1785.

**Memorial of Willm Aitcheson**

Lieutt Coll Ellegood—sworn. 25th of June 1785.

The Deceased a Loyalist & render'd Services.

The Memorial is presented in the name of Lieutt Coll Ellegood on behalf of the Widow & Children of Mr Aitcheson deceased. The Widow is Sister to the Witness.

Certificate which is annex'd to the Memorial sign'd by Lord Dunmore.

Did not bear Arms.

The Widow is Sister to the Witness & is in America. The Husband died in 1776. The Witness was in Prison with him both on Acct of their Loyalty. He was uniformly loyal to the Hour of his Death. He was formerly a Mercht in considerable business & had then a Concern in the business but the Younger Partners attended. The Ferm of the House was Aitcheson & Parker in Norfolk & Wm Ronald & Co in Virginia. He has left a Widow & 4 Children names them. He left a Will by which he left this House to his Sister—promises to send a Copy of the Will.

The eldest Child was killed in the service of G. B. & the other Boy has lately left England.

Thomas Macknight—sworn.

Mr Aitcheson was a very intimate friend of his for many Years. He was a very good & a very loyal Man. When Lord Dunmore was on board a Ship Mr Aitcheson join'd with the people of the town in inviting Lord Dunmore to come on Shore. He had great influence & his Example he thinks had great weight with the people. He order'd the Doors of the Court House to be broken open that the Meeting might be held. He was an Alderman of the City. He was imprison'd for his Loyalty.

He was Partner with Mr Parker in one Concern & with Mr Ronald in another.

James Parker Esq—sworn.

Knew Mr Aitcheson very well. He was one of his Partners. He was very loyal & more active than could be supposed as he was an infirm Man. Thinks he render'd Services by his Example & weight upon many Occasions. He is dead & was a Prisr when he died. He has left a Wife & 4 Children & lost his eldest Son fighting for this Country. He was likewise concern'd with Ronald & Co.

James Ingram—sworn.

Knew Mr Aitcheson very well. He was loyal he believes to the time of his Death & believes that his Sufferings hasten'd his Death. Knew his House in Norfolk it was a very elegant House but he can't value it nor the Coach House. His House was very well furnish'd believes he lost considerably but can't tell how much. Remembers one of his Negroes dying in the fleet. Believes he was concern'd in the Rope Walk Concern.

**To the Memorial of James Simpson [1] Esq—Attorney Genl of South Carolina which Case has not been heard**

6th of June 1785.

Earl Cornwallis—sworn.

First knew Mr Simpson at New York in 1779. Thinks him perfectly loyal. He was employ'd by the Witness in the most confidential Manner at Charlestown whilst he was in South Carolina Sir Henry Clinton had appointed him to be Secretary to the Commission but Lord Cornwallis found him so useful that he begg'd that he might stay longer with him. He found him a Man of perfect Integrity & tho' he had a very great property in that Country He never found him attentive to that. Being asked whether he thinks that Mr Simpson was of great use to this Country He says he thinks he may be said to have render'd very essential Services to this Country.

**Memorial of Henry Eustace McCulloch [2]**

Determin'd the 7th of July 1785.

28th of June 1785.

Henry Eustace McCulloch—the Claimant—sworn.

Reads an History of his Conduct during the War which is in writing & he swears it to be true.

Certificates presented to prove the Claimant's Loyalty & read. One from

[1] James Simpson was appointed Surveyor-General of Lands in 1772. He became Attorney-General in 1774.

[2] He was the son of Henry McCulloch, His Majesty's Surveyor, Inspector, and Controller of the revenue and grants of land. This McCulloch speculated largely in Crown lands, with the object of paying for them from the profit derived from importing settlers. Some three or four hundred such settlers were, it is alleged, introduced by him. He further impaired his large fortune by furnishing these immigrants with means. The son, however, profited by his work, as he succeeded in making good his claim to over 64,000 acres (N. M. Tiffany, *Letters of James Murray, Loyalist*, at p. 28). Dr. C. L. Raper would therefore seem to be wrong in asserting (*N. Carolina*, 1904, p. 118) that 'the grants to Henry McCulloch were made for speculative purposes, not for settlement, at least to any great extent'.

It is interesting to note that Henry McCulloch was the author of a tract, *Miscellaneous Representations relative to our Concerns in America*, submitted in 1761 to Lord Bute, which contained the scheme of the Stamp Act, as adopted by George Grenville. The tract has been reprinted with an introduction by W. A. Shaw, containing a sketch of some aspects of McCulloch's career.

Gov$^{r}$ Tryon D$^{o}$ a Letter to M$^{r}$ Eden from him & M$^{r}$ Eden's Answer. Likewise a Certificate from M$^{r}$ Eden. Certificate from M$^{r}$ Brummell. A Letter from M$^{r}$ Brook Watson.

Swears to the truth of his Memorial.

A Zealous Loyalist.

Did not bear Arms.

Former Bounty £200 a Y$^{r}$.
Present Bounty £300 a Y$^{r}$.

Is a Native of London & went first to America in 1740. Lived in America from 1761 to 1767. He was in Eng$^{d}$ till 1772 but was a Member of Council. He went back in 1772 & returned the next Year. His father died in 1779. He went to New York in July 1778. He went to serve this Country at all hazards. Says he did everything in his power to prevent the rupture between the two Countries. He returned to Eng$^{d}$ in 1779 with the Commissioners & had an Allowance of £200 a Y$^{r}$ from the Treasury. This was augmented by M$^{r}$ Wilmot & M$^{r}$ Coke to £300 a Year which he now receives.

In the Month of Sept$^{r}$ 1777 He had the first Notice of Proceedings being had ag$^{t}$ him. Never bore Arms in America.

Henry Eustace M$^{c}$Culloch—sworn. 29$^{th}$ of June 1785.

Says to the Question which was asked of him yesterday how much he had sold at different times from his Estate He now says he thinks he has sold about 8000 Acres. Leaves a paper explaining some things which pass'd in his Evidence yesterday. Produces a paper which shews the Original Order of Council made in May 1736 giving an Authority to the Gov$^{r}$ to grant 120000 Acres 80000 of which were to be granted to his father. Says that great part of the Expence was paid immediately & Interest charged upon it immediately.

Admits that Gov$^{r}$ Martin intercepted some Letters written by him in 1776 which being perfectly innocent were returned to him open. Says the Letters were of a private Nature & could not be otherwise.

William Brimage—sworn.

Was acquainted with M$^{r}$ M$^{c}$Culloch before the rebellion in 1772 & 1773 & he afterwards knew him at New York in 1778. He told the Witness that he was ready to serve Gov$^{t}$. Believes him to be a firm Loyalist from everything which pass'd. Says he was consider'd as a Man of very large landed property. Has heard that he had more than 200000 Acres of Land. Never heard what was the value of his property & cannot speak to particulars.

Colonel John Hamilton—sworn.

Knew M$^{r}$ M$^{c}$Culloch before the War. After the rebellion commenced He did not see him till 1778 at New York when he saw a great deal of him & his principles appear'd very much devoted to his Majesty & Gov$^{t}$. He had Opportunities of shewing his zeal for the Service & he believes him to have been a firm Loyalist.

He was possess'd of a very extensive Property in Carolina has seen many parts of it. Many plantations were settled & he thinks they were rented. Says those which he knew were acknowledged to be his property. Has pass'd thro' the Lands in N$^{o}$ 1 but can't speak to the Quantity or Value. They were looked upon as valuable. Has known lands sell in these parts from 2*s*. 6*d*. to 30*s*. without little or any improvement. Thinks that a large tract would sell for more in proportion than a small one. He cannot speak with precision to any one tract.

The Land on flat River he says was particularly valuable. Has known Land in that Situation sell for £4 per Acre.

Robert Palmer—sworn. 2^d^ of July 1785.

Has known the Claimant upwards of 20 Years. His father was a Loyalist & the Son he believes to be so. Knows that the father was a Man of great property the father is dead & the Claim^t^ is the only Child. He has understood they were the best Lands in the Country but he can't speak to the Value or give any Estimation of it. Thinks a Plantation in part clear'd more valuable than one in an uncultivated State. The Witness was Surveyor of Lands in N^o^ Carolina & he had a Deputy in each County. Says that he has known such Lots as these sell if divided into small Lots for a pistole per Acre & if sold in large Quantities for a Dollar. Supposes that if a Man's property of 100000 Acres was to be sold at once & in one Lot without adverting to the troubles [1] the best Lands in the province would not sell for more than 2*s.* 6*d.* per Acre & moderate Lands for 1*s.* 6*d.* per Acre. When he says this He means to say that the Money would be meant to be paid by instalments within 2 or 3 Years & probably without Interest. Says if divided into smaller Lots of 5000 Acres they would have fetched a Dollar an Acre. Never recollects a very large Quantity of Land sold at one time.

Governor Martin—sworn. 5^th^ of July 1785.

Had very little Acquaintance with M^r^ M^c^Culloch. Saw him in 1773. But cannot form any Opinion of him. Knows of no Circumstance but a Letter which was taken at Cape Fear in April or May 1776. All Letters were directed to be overlooked by Gov^r^ Martin that no improper Letters might get into the Country. Amongst these was one Letter from M^r^ M^c^Culloch to Cornelius Harnet who was a violent rebel. It seem'd to be intended to conciliate the Good Will of M^r^ Harnet & his friends. Refers us to M^r^ Macknight who he says knows a great deal more of it. At that moment it (the Letter) convey'd to the Governor's mind & to his friends that M^r^ M^c^Culloch's Sentiments were not quite orthodox. Believes that M^r^ Macknight at that time thought of the Letter as he did. But he says that his Jealousy was never confirmed by any subsequent Conduct & knows nothing to impeach his Loyalty. This was before the Declaration of Independence. Says he was consider'd to be possess'd of very valuable tracts of Land but can't speak to Quantity or Situation. Says M^r^ Elmsley who spoke to this property is he believes a Man of very good Character.

[1] i.e. without taking into consideration the question of the Revolution.

## ADDITIONAL NOTES

### John Chandler (page 335).

The case of John Chandler has been exhaustively dealt with by Mr. A. McFarland Davis in *The Confiscation of John Chandler's Estate*, Boston, 1903. Chandler was Selectman, Town Treasurer, Town Clerk, County Treasurer, Sheriff, Judge of Probate, and Representative of the General Court. He was also a Colonel of the Worcester Regiment and saw active duty in 1757. He was known in Worcester as 'Tory John', and in England as 'the modest refugee' because of the modesty of his claims. In a petition to the Treasury (February 17, 1779) he stated that he left behind him sixteen children. 'After suffering the most cruel insults, being deprived of his liberty and threatened in the most alarming manner, unless he would sacrifice his loyalty to the King, renounce the Worcester Protest, which he had promoted and signed, and adopt in its stead a very treasonable league and covenant . . . he was obliged, in order to save himself from an ignominious death, to fly from his home.'

The Worcester Protest was very outspoken. 'Committees of Correspondence, being creatures of modern invention, and constituted as they be, are a public grievance, having no legal foundation, contrived by a Junto to serve particular designs and purposes of their own; and, as they have been and are managed in this town, are a public nuisance. . . . These and all such enormities we detest and abhor, and the authors of them we esteem enemies of our King and Country; violators of all law and civil liberty; subverters of the established constitution and enemies of mankind.'

The *Gentleman's Magazine*, in an obituary notice of John Chandler in October 1800, stated that he died at eighty 'an honest man, a good member of society, and a pious Christian'.

### Peter van Shaack (page 338).

*The Life of Peter van Schaack*, by H. C. van Schaack, New York, 1842, shows him to have been one of those moderate men whose lot is especially hard in times of revolution. There will be found in it at p. 113 a powerful protest against the Banishing Act of 1778.

'Had you at the beginning of the war permitted every one differing in temper from you to take the other side, or, at least, to have removed out of the State with their property, as they unquestionably had a right to do, it would have been conduct magnanimous and just. But now, after restraining those persons from removing; punishing them if in the attempt they were apprehended; selling their estates if they escaped; compelling them to the duties of subjects under heavy penalties; desiring aid from them in the prosecution of the war, in many cases while those persons were actually deprived of the privilege of subjects; at such a time when no immediate danger is apprehended. . . . now to compel them to take an oath which the very Act supposes to be incompatible with their principles under the severe penalty of confiscation of property is an act of such complicated severity that it is impossible it should stand the examination of a dispassionate hour.'

Peter van Schaack's citation before the Albany Board and his refusal of the oath of allegiance are in *Minutes of Albany Board, 1778–9*, vol. i, pp. 171, 174.

'On August 11, Peter van Schaack appeared before the Board on behalf of a number of persons who are to be removed to the enemies' lines next Friday and requested of the Board to consider whether they were comprehended within the meaning of the Act, as they had taken an oath before the Committee of this place not to aid or assist the enemy, and that, if the Board should be of opinion that they do, that then they might be indulged with some longer time, which request was denied' (ibid., pp. 200–1).

### John Harris Cruger (page 376).

John Harris Cruger, one of the ablest loyalist leaders whom the war brought forth, had been at first opposed to the Stamp Act, and as late as 1769 was a member of the Committee of Inspection. But like other men of property in New York he was not prepared to go to extremities (Becker, op. cit., pp. 75, 87). His arrest was ordered in 1776. McCrady (*S. Car. in the Rev., 1775–80*, p. 834) speaks of his 'wise conduct, his gentle, yet firm, course', in the management of the Ninety-six district. The best tribute is the note, almost certainly written by Carleton, in *Hist. MSS. Comm., MSS. in R. Inst.*, vol. iv, p. 479. 'Has served during the whole war, and in all the campaigns in the southern colonies; where his singular good conduct and gallantry in the most critical situation have distinguished him too much to require a particular detail of his services.'

Cruger was the son-in-law of Brigadier-General Oliver de Lancey. He wrote to Winslow on March 28, 1784: 'The very ill treatment of the worthy loyalists hitherto has given me much concern. . . . This huge, unwieldy town (London) swarms with Americans grumbling and discontented; in two or three years, it is said, we may know what Government will, or will not, allow us for the loss of property, for services, &c., &c.' (*Winslow Papers*, p. 174). Mr. Onslow, in the debate in the House of Commons on the subject of half-pay for Provincial officers (June 27, 1783), spoke in the strongest language of the services performed by Cruger. Sir George Howard seems erroneously to have given the chief credit for the defence of Ninety-six to a Major Green (*Hans.*, vol. xxiii, p. 1055).

# INDEX